Lorca After Life

Lorca After Life

Noël Valis

Yale
UNIVERSITY PRESS
NEW HAVEN AND LONDON

Published with assistance from the foundation established in memory of Henry Weldon Barnes
of the Class of 1882, Yale College, and from the Frank M. Turner Publication Fund.

Yale University Press books may be purchased in quantity for educational, business, or promotional use. For
information, please email sales.press@yale.edu (U.S. office) or sales@yaleup.co.uk (U.K. office).

Set in Fournier MT type by Integrated Publishing Solutions, Grand Rapids, Michigan.
Printed in the United States of America.

Library of Congress Control Number: 2021945450
ISBN 978-0-300-25786-1 (hardcover : alk. paper)

A catalogue record for this book is available from the British Library.

This paper meets the requirements of ANSI/NISO Z39.48-1992 (Permanence of Paper).

10 9 8 7 6 5 4 3 2 1

In memory of my sisters Judi and Kathleen, faithful to family

And the curious thing about the legend of a personality is
that it may reach the highest fervor without being formulated.
It is something by itself that stands behind anecdotes,
death-notices, elegies.

—John Dos Passos, *Rosinante to the Road Again* (1922)

Poetry can't be all that bad, when living politicians and
the ruling class, with all the might of the State on their side,
still have to contend with dead poets.

—José María Pemán, "García Lorca" (1948)

I am as one disembodied, triumphant, dead.

—Walt Whitman, "So Long!" *Leaves of Grass* (1860 ed.)

Contents

Acknowledgments

It is impossible to thank enough all the people who have helped and supported me over the many years I was thinking about, preparing, and finally writing this book. First, I owe boundless debts of gratitude to all the wonderful Lorca scholars, devoted enthusiasts of the poet. Then there are the many Yale students, undergraduate and graduate alike, who have patiently listened to me rehearse these arguments and tested me at the same time, who have shared with me the joy and torment of Federico García Lorca's poetry and plays. I have learned as well from the lively discussions with colleagues, who heard me give parts of the book, at the University of Northern Colorado, the University of California–Los Angeles, Yale University, Brigham Young University, Princeton University, Brown University, Louisiana State University, Swarthmore College, Temple University, West Virginia University, Dartmouth College, the University of North Carolina–Chapel Hill, the University of Georgia, the Universidad de León, and the Universidad de Córdoba. The list of colleagues, friends, and family to thank is doubtless incomplete: my daughter Maura Valis, my brother Greg and sisters Judi, Tina, and Kathleen, Wayne Valis, Ame Cividanes, Laurie Lomask, Wan Sonya Tang, Daniel García-Donoso, Eduardo Castro, Manuel Antonio Estévez, Joseph Pearce, Derek Gagen†, Kevin Foster, Felipe Valencia, Adam Shellhorse, Evelyn Scaramella, Tanya Romero-González, Nicole Mombell, Diego del Río Arrillaga, José Antonio Simonet, José Ramón Sabín Lestayo, Luis Bautista Boned, Veronica Mayer, Sarah Glenski, Pura Fernández, Francisco Vázquez García, Elizabeth Horan, James Whiston†, Howard Bloch, Marilyn Wilkes, Dassie Weiner, Víctor Fernández Puertas, Betsy Wright, Stacey Dolgin Casado, Ángel Loureiro, Antonio Fernández Insuela, Jim Mandrell, Curt Wasson, Maite Zubiaurre, Edgar Neville Guille, Jaime Manrique, James Valender, Juan A. Ríos Carratalá, Christopher Maurer, Susanne Zepp-Zwirner, George Esenwein, Jeff Zamostny, José Carlos García Rodríguez, Rosa Illán, and Laura García-Lorca de los Ríos. I have benefited tremendously from the assistance given by the Interlibrary Loan staff of Yale University Library, the Beinecke Rare Book and Manuscript Library, the Biblioteca Nacional de España, the Archivo Histórico Nacional, the Biblioteca de Andalucía, the Centro Federico García Lorca (Granada), and the Fundación Federico García Lorca (Madrid).

Deeply missed are all the treasured conversations I had with my friend of over fifty years, Carol Maier, always thoughtful and subtle, who left us in 2020. Her comments more than once made me rethink this project. Dear to me also are Carolyn Richmond de Ayala and Rolena Adorno, whose steadfast support has never wavered. I especially want to thank my friend and colleague Roberto González Echevarría, who in a moment of comic exasperation told me I should go write a book on Lorca, after we argued over who counted in the canon of great writers and who didn't, and whether we should pay attention to noncanonical ones. I didn't take him up on the suggestion right away, and I certainly didn't know at first what kind of a book I would end up writing. Over the years, I have worked on both kinds of writers, and this book is no exception, giving a role to a minor player, Álvaro Retana, who, like his contemporary, the poet from Granada, was also a celebrity in his day. I would never have discovered Retana without Lorca, but I would never have written a book on fame and celebrity without Roberto's challenge. Above all, it's the force of nature, Lorca himself, who has driven this book forward. And now that it's finished, I still can't let go of Federico. Readers of this book, I hope, won't either.

Early versions of parts of *Lorca After Life* first appeared as "Lorca's 'Agonía republicana' and Its Aftermath," in *Spain's "Agonía republicana" and Its Aftermath: Memories and Studies of the History, Culture, and Literature of the Spanish Civil War*, edited, with an introduction, by Susana Bayó Belenguer, *Bulletin of Spanish Studies* (ISSN 1475-3820) 91.1–2 (2014): 267–94; "Lorca's Grave," *Yale Review* 104.3 (2016): 40–56; "Celebrity, Sex, and Mass Readership: The Case of Álvaro Retana," *Kiosk Literature of Silver Age Spain: Modernity and Mass Culture*, edited by Jeffrey Zamostny and Susan Larson (Bristol/Chicago: Intellect Books, 2017), 127–51; "Homosexuality on Display in 1920s Spain: The Hermaphrodite, Eccentricity, and Álvaro Retana," *Freakish Encounters: Constructions of the Freak in Hispanic Cultures*, edited by Sara Muñoz-Muriana and Analola Santana, *Hispanic Issues On Line* 20 (2018): 190–216; and "An Ordinary Life," *First Things* 301 (Mar. 2020): 29–34.

I am grateful to the following people and presses for permission to quote from these texts: Edgar Neville Guille, for Edgar Neville Romrée's "Su último paisaje"; Paloma Altolaguirre, for Manuel Altolaguirre's "A Saturnino Ruiz, obrero impresor"; Helena Ruiz Fernández and José Luis Romero Moragas, for Joaquín Romero-Murube's "Romance del crimen"; Javier Castroviejo and the Castroviejo family, for José María Castroviejo's "Paso firme" and "El último hermano"; "The Crime Was in Granada," ANTONIO MACHADO: SELECTED POEMS, translated by Alan S. Trueblood, Cambridge, MA: Harvard University Press, Copyright © 1982 by the President and Fellows of Harvard College; "Second New York Poem" and "A Postface to *The Lorca Variations*," by Jerome Rothenberg, from THE LORCA VARIATIONS, copyright © 1993 by Jerome Rothenberg. Reprinted by permission of New Directions Publishing Corp.; from *Eminent Maricones* by Jaime Manrique © 1999 by the Board of Regents of the University of Wisconsin System. Reprinted by permission of the University of Wisconsin Press; from "A Supermarket in California," in *Collected Poems 1947–1997*, by Allen Ginsberg Copyright © 2006 by the Allen Ginsberg Trust. Used by permission of HarperCollins Publishers and Copyright © Allen Ginsberg, 1956, 1961, used by permission of The Wylie Agency (UK) Limited; "The Search for Lorca's Shadow," from THE MERCY: POEMS, by Philip Levine, copyright © 1999 by Philip Levine. Used by permission of Alfred A. Knopf, an imprint of the Knopf Doubleday Publishing Group, a division of Penguin Random House LLC. All rights reserved.

Finally, my warm thanks go to Heather Gold, Eva Skewes, and Ann-Marie Imbornoni at Yale University Press for their expert guidance and to Andrew Frisardi for his skill and finesse in copyediting this book. *Lorca After Life* could not have been in more capable hands.

Lorca After Life

Introduction

In 1957 the San Francisco poet Jack Spicer published a book called *After Lorca*, which at first blush appears to be a series of translations based on Lorca poems and interspersed with letters to the Spanish writer Federico García Lorca himself. It begins with a pointedly funny introduction from Lorca, written "Outside Granada, October 1957." Some of the poems, he says, are clearly not his, but

> the reader is given no indication which of the poems belong to which category, and I have further complicated the problem (with malice aforethought I must admit) by sending Mr. Spicer several poems written after my death which he has also translated and included here. Even the most faithful student of my work will be hard put to decide what is and what is not García Lorca as, indeed, he would if he were to look into my present resting place. The analogy is impolite, but I fear the impoliteness is deserved.[1]

Spicer has cleverly alluded to the different meanings the word *after* possesses. The first meaning is chronological. Spicer the poet postdates Lorca, a fact the fictional Lorca rubs in by sending him new poems written *after* his death. Spicer's poems are also presumably written in the manner of Lorca (in itself debatable), that is after Lorca, and this too the fictional Lorca makes a peevish point of: "Even the most faithful student of my work will be hard put to decide what is and what is not García Lorca." There is an additional sense here, for the American poet has gone after Lorca, seeking him out and even courting him, the way younger writers sometimes do with older, more established ones. "When Mr. Spicer began sending [letters] to me a few months ago," says Lorca, "I recognized immediately the 'program[m]atic letter'—the letter one poet writes to another not in any effort to communicate with him, but rather as a young man whispers his secrets to a scarecrow, knowing that his young lady is in the distance listening."

Finally, the comic voice that Spicer gives the Granadine poet unites literary posterity in its different forms with something far more fateful: Lorca's death by execution squad somewhere in a lonely spot between two villages, Víznar and Alfacar (hence the allusion to his "present resting place"). Then as now there was no need to spell out the horrific circumstances of that death, even though we will never have a full accounting of his murder. This is the real "after": Lorca "after life." This is dead Lorca. Although it is also much more.

Spicer appears at first to trivialize his death, alluding in the most banal and euphemistic terms to his "present resting place" as though Lorca's death had been a peaceful one. A kind of morbid whistling in the dark infuses the phrase, however, when he says that it would be hard "to decide what is and what is not García Lorca." What, after all, divides the gray earth from Lorca's bones? The poet Philip Levine envisioned the ground as "a metallic gray covered here and there / by a loamy dust which may or may not shift in the breeze." But the earth really was gray ; it wasn't simply poetry.[2]

The gray clinging to the poet's resting place that is yet to be found is also another name for irony: the lack of a grave, the missing bones, have paradoxically given rise to a multiplicity of Lorcas, to hypotheses and counterhypotheses to explain his violent death at the start of the Spanish Civil War in 1936, to a revolving door of identities and counteridentities to explain his life and work and make them meaningful to other people. Gay Lorca? Andalusian Lorca? The poet-king of the gypsies? The scapegoat of persecution? The people's poet? The symbol of the Second Republic? The elusive spirit of *duende,* of "everything that has black sounds in it"? The hope of reconciliation for post–civil war Spain? Some of these myths started while he was alive, but much of what we think about Lorca merely covers up what we do not know: each one of the various identities and explanations becomes a kind of filler to flesh out the bare bones of a poet who was sharply aware of how incomplete he was, how mystifying to himself. He wrote,

> When the pure forms sank
> beneath the *cri-cri* of daisies,
> I saw they had killed me.
> They searched the cafés, cemeteries and churches.

They opened the casks and closets.
They destroyed three skeletons just to yank their gold teeth.
They no longer found me.
They didn't find me?
No. They did not find me.

These lines have often been cited as an eery premonition of his death, but I see them as a metaphor for a kind of death-in-life, for his inability to find himself (or for anyone else's, if truth be told). Small wonder we have yet to decide what is and what is not García Lorca. Neither could Lorca.[3]

In other words, what Lorca has never been is a corpse. One day perhaps, he'll be a handful of bones, the answer to the easiest mystery of all: locating the whereabouts of his remains. Meanwhile, think on this dismal thought: no one, to my knowledge, has ever described to us Lorca in death. At least no one convincing. A freemason claimed to have seen his face, serene and unbloodied, but other witnesses have questioned his statement, as Ian Gibson in *La fosa de Lorca* (Lorca's Grave) has pointed out. One moment he was there, the next he had disappeared. A mercy, no doubt, that we do not know, but one that points to the deepest mystery of all: who was Federico García Lorca? Lorca will forever be missing, even if someone manages to find what persists of his corporeal existence.[4]

In life and after life, Lorca is curiously disembodied, despite all the attempts to capture his enormous vitality and charisma. The sense of him as being illuminated, as his sister Isabel said. Most of the photographs taken of him are flat and pasty, documenting where he had been, who he was with, but also signaling how he had already moved on. His friends and family remarked that sometimes Federico seemed to forget where he was, a long vacant stare taking his place. He appeared to be in another world. Even his sister found it difficult, indeed impossible, to explain what he was like and, most poignantly, could no longer remember his voice.

Everything I have said about Lorca the man can be extended to his work. It is a common complaint in Lorca criticism that no one has ever fully grasped his poetry, especially the densely intuitive work of *Poeta en Nueva York* (Poet in New York). This elusiveness has been variously explained. He died too soon, his promise cut short. Some of the work was never finished. He was a vanguardist, so difficulty comes with the territory, as does the vision of incompleteness projected onto the vertiginous, fragmented image of modernity that avant-garde literature and art embody. The slipperiness of his work is intrinsic to his method and his vision, which helps explain—linguistic difficulties aside—why so many translations fail to come even close to the original or to move readers.

I would suggest a larger reason: incompleteness is built into Lorca and his work. There is something fundamentally unfinished about Lorca, not simply because his life abruptly ended but because an air of incompleteness characterizes the man and his work. Better to perpetually recreate the Parthenon, he wrote, in an unending state of becoming. The unfinished quality of his writing, I would also suggest, is something he himself sensed. He was often reluctant to publish, and he tinkered repeatedly with his work. Once in print, a poem was in effect "dead" to Lorca. He said: "When I begin to correct proofs, I experience the inevitable sensation of death; that the poem no longer lives, that for it to live it ought to possess a different architecture, more spine, greater clarity, a total simplicity and integrity."[5]

While it can be legitimately argued he valued oral performance over writing, his ambivalence toward publication can also be viewed as an admission of inner anxiety. Was the piece really finished, truly ready? Or had the "pure forms" already sunk, buried beneath "the *cri-cri* of daisies"? I don't know if Lorca can be considered a perfectionist, but at heart the perfectionist puts off life, its deficiencies and flaws, by refusing to credit imperfection as an option. Reluctance to publish is akin to the Young Man's unwillingness to live in Lorca's brilliant experimental play *Así que pasen cinco años* (Once Five Years Pass). Far better then, says the Old Man in the opening scene, "to remember before" (*recordar antes*), that is, before you even experience life, which can also signify that it is better to invent memories, thus improving on the past. Alternatively, he observes, one should remember "toward tomorrow" (*hacia mañana*). But what kind of memories are those? What kind of life? Memory becomes a fiction, as does, by extension, life itself. Imagined memories of this kind appear as a device to thwart the passage of time, to abolish time itself and hence death, in the play.[6] The Young Man's fear of death is really a fear of life. There is an enormous irony here, if one considers how fully Lorca the man seems to have lived his life.

These invented memories are somewhat like the myths and stories that have grown up around Lorca. Only instead of appearing before, they have largely come after, and may or may not bear resemblance to Lorca's life and writing, so they have a complicated relation with the past. In that sense, such accounts remember "toward tomorrow" insofar as they are projections of the poet's past, or of what we think is his past. Many of the efforts to interpret his poetry and plays—even to continue his work "in the manner of "—or to understand the man himself are quest narratives. Levine's poem, for example, is called "The Search for Lorca's Shadow." And biographer Ian Gibson has made a career obsessing over Lorca's disappearance. In *La luz prodigiosa* (The Prodigious Light), the novelist Fernando Marías created a traumatized Lorca who survived his own execution but not the memory of himself, so that the desire to identify an amnesiac vagrant as the poet turns into the pursuit of a ghost; the film version does the same. As did Spicer (to whom I will return in the last chapter), they have gone after the poet as though he were the holy grail, to this transcendent, if generally unstated, end: to raise up Lorca from the dead, to fulfill him, as it were, making him symbolically complete. For some this means starting with the most literal of reenactments, in a new vision of the prophet Ezekiel: finding the valley of his dry bones.

Lorca After Life is about how the poet has been remembered and imagined and, in this manner, brought back to life in a strange kind of afterglow. It is thus also about his fame, just as his posthumous life serves as a springboard to consider the larger question of why certain dead poets matter and why we obsess over them. Unique works of art possess a special aura, Walter Benjamin liked to point out, but so too, it seems, do some poets in life possess such an aura, as was true of Lorca, or at the very least in their afterlives. An afterlife is to a life as a translation is to its original. "Just as the manifestations of life," wrote Benjamin in another essay, "are intimately connected with the phenomenon of life without being of importance to it, a translation issues from the original—not so much from its life as from its afterlife. . . . [S]ince the important works of world literature never find their chosen translators at the time of their origin, their translation marks their stage of continued life."[7]

Arguably, however, the manifestations of life are indeed of consequence to us, if not to the phenomenon of life. Benjamin's subsequent remarks appear to acknowledge what I have said, when he wrote, "In the final analysis, the range of life must be determined by history rather than by nature." He was interested "in comprehending all of natural life through the more encompassing life of history." And that's because history matters; it is of consequence to us. Ultimately, with great works of art and literature, "their potentially eternal afterlife in succeeding generations" leads us to considerations of the work's fame. What distinguishes Lorca from most other writers and places him in the company of a select few, such as Whitman and Hemingway, is the manner in which his readers and admirers find it difficult, if not impossible, to separate the two, to parse the difference between the fame of his life and that of his work.[8]

Much of the joining of biography and writing comes from the specific historic circumstances of his life and death. Above all, the specter of his violent death continues to haunt everything connected to Lorca, no matter how many times his critics throw up their hands in exasperation, fed up with what many of them see as hopeless confusion over what literature is or how it should be read. Rather than dismiss the fascination with Lorca's persona, I am struck by its enduring appeal and the degree to which his celebrity, his iconicity, creates a hunger to fill in the gaps, the holes in the poet's life and work. Fame feeds on what we don't know and want to know about such a person. Leo Braudy observed, "the famous person is thus not so much a person as a story about a person."[9]

Lorca's afterlives are some of those stories, alternative versions of the man and his work. Jonathan Mayhew's book on "apocryphal Lorca," his presence in the writings of American poets like Spicer, Robert Creeley, Frank O'Hara, and Langston Hughes, is germane here. It is an insightful analysis demonstrating an Americanized Lorca's impact on U.S. poetic culture of the postwar and beyond, joining excellent studies such as Sultana Wahnón's research into the poet's reception in postwar Spain, Laura Dolfi's into his influence in Italy, and Emily Robins Sharpe's work into how Lorca's death and queerness helped explain Canadian identity for some writers. These, too, are manifestations of Lorca's afterlives, as are the meditations on his death and the role of memory like those of Antonio Monegal, Christian de Paepe, Melissa Dinverno, and Andrés Soria Olmedo. The same is true of his paper existence in the many translations of his work, as Mayhew, Christopher Maurer, Andrew Samuel Walsh, and others have shown. Indeed, Lorca's afterlives have been a steady subject of inquiry for scholars over the past twenty years, especially since his centenary in 1998, as Paul Julian Smith, Stefan Schreckenberg, María Delgado, and others have observed. I have found much to admire and to draw from in all these studies.

This book goes in another direction. What does it mean to be "Lorca" as a persistent memory and posthumous presence, but above all as a celebrity, whose iconic exceptionalism is writ large not only in those stories but in some of his own work and in the poet's own fashioning of self? Lorca is intimately tied to both an individual and collective identity, whether as the people's poet, a gay icon, or the fabled member of a dead poets society. His fame is a conduit throughout the book that allows us to explore the multiple associations connecting his death, his work and times, and his homosexuality (without forgetting that it is above all his work that counts). Emphasis on the various meanings and repercussions of the poet's death in the first three chapters (part I) leads into the last three (part II) centered on Lorca's homosexuality and what it meant to be gay in his time and a gay symbol in ours, beginning with a hinge chapter on celebrity murder among gay writers. There is a deep undercurrent running between his death and his homosexuality that is not simply biographical but cultural, literary, and political in nature. His murder was not only horrific but transformative, setting in motion many of the poet's afterlives, which includes those related to his sexuality and gender identity, and changing our perception of what fame means, how it rewrites our understanding of the poet and his work, and how both have also shaped the world. That fame lends itself as well to broader considerations of celebrity as a renewed expression of the marvelous in the modern world, one of whose manifestations is homosexuality itself. The aura surrounding Lorca and his posthumous existence is at once personal and supremely modern.

Like the relation of translations to their translators, the poet's afterlives also have a great deal to say about the people who write such accounts (including the author of this book). Indeed, for some, there exists a profoundly personal stake in their relation to Lorca. One thinks immediately of Gibson, who has spent much of his adult life researching the poet. It is easy to imagine the crushing disappointment he must have felt when the first forensic archaeological dig for Lorca's remains in December 2009 found nothing at the site where so many were convinced the poet met his end. "I feel ill. I think of this all day," he said. "I fear for my mental health. It's been forty-five years of my life." Gibson is not alone in his passion for Lorca. Some of that passion is inevitably political, given the poet's support for the Second Republic and his death at the hands of the extreme right during the civil war. The Republicans claimed him for their own cause, but surprisingly, as we shall see, a few on the right made similar title to Lorca.[10]

These afterlives, then, have their own histories. You could also call them "variations," in the spirit of Jerome Rothenberg's book of poems *The Lorca Variations*. Rothenberg was fifteen, when, in reading Lorca's poetry, "the words & what they seemed to fuse in combination hit me like electric charges." Many years later, he found himself translating his *Suites*. "I felt a frustration," he wrote, "in not being able to publish my own translations independently, thus diluting whatever sense I had of doing a Lorca homage, etc. With that in mind, I began to compose a series of poems of my own ('variations') that draw on vocabulary, especially nouns & adjectives, from my translations of the Suites (later from *Poet in New York* as well) but rearrange them in a variety of ways. . . . I mention it to explain the way in which these poems both are & aren't mine, both are & aren't Lorca." This last comment of Rothenberg recalls Spicer's. As Jonathan Mayhew has remarked, both Americans "create a hybrid voice and test the limits between translation and pastiche." Moreover, he questions "whether it is legitimate to graft one's own poetic project onto that of a dead poet," but it is more accurate to say that all poets are in bed with their dead peers. Ask T. S. Eliot. And while these are rewritings of the Spanish poet's work, they are also, in some cases, rewritings of Lorca himself, versions of the poet that are not strictly speaking biographical but literary imaginings of a life relived in someone else's poetry. That's because Lorca mattered to Rothenberg. Remembering Lorca was remembering his work as well.[11]

Thus, in the concluding part of "Second New York Poem," Rothenberg riffs on Lorca's "Danza de la muerte" (Dance of Death) from *Poet in New York*, taking the phrase "El mascarón. Mirad el mascarón" ("The mask. Look at the Mask") as his leitmotif. The mask becomes Lorca himself in much of this section:

> it's Lorca perched atop
> his pyramid, it's Lorca
> smuggling rifles through the forest,
> Lorca in the mask of anguish,
> trapped in vines,
> or Lorca in the stock exchange,
> the floor collapsing under him.

He ends with,

> it's Lorca's mask
> we wear together now,
> el mascarón,
> he cries to us,
> the mask! the mask!

In the last poem of the collection, "Coda: The Final Lorca Variation," Rothenberg writes, "the end for Lorca comes / only when we let it," recognizing that *"no homage can repay what we have lost."*[12] Rothenberg's homage in these poems not only refuses to let go of Lorca, despite the loss, but even goes so far as to assume the poet's persona, recalling persona's original meaning in Latin as a theatrical mask. But the mask also belongs to Lorca because those are his words, his imagery. You could say that the Spanish poet has lent his persona to Rothenberg's poem; he's given him the working parts of the story. In that respect, I am reminded of what Boris Tomaševskij had to say about biography. "The biography that is useful to the literary historian," he wrote, "is not the author's curriculum vitae or the investigator's account of his life. What the literary historian really needs is the biographical legend created by the author himself. Only such a legend is a *literary fact.*" The artist as hero became a feature of Renaissance biography. By the Romantic period, Lord Byron was turning life into poetry and poetry into life, making his own set of literary facts. As Svetlana Boym has observed, the line between documented fact and literary fact has become blurred. A poet's mere words—"they no longer found me"—can be taken as an indice of biographical truth, if not the truth itself, for some readers, so who is to say that Lorca, intentionally or not, hasn't already shaped his own life story for posterity? Where does the life stop, and the myth begin?[13]

Byron was also one of the first modern celebrities, his life equal parts charm and scandal. It is impossible to understand Lorca's national and international impact without considering his fame (or his own contribution to it). As with Lord Byron, his fame and celebrity were synonymous. These terms are now nearly indistinguishable, the dividing line between fame as above all attached to deeds, especially of valor, and celebrity mostly to fleeting notoriety having pretty much disappeared. Celebrity is the modern form of fame, an infinitely malleable image-maker in a media-driven era and so unnervingly diverse as to contain Stephen Hawking and the latest YouTuber in the same swath. Imagine Alexander the Great in our time, swinging the cudgel of mass media or tweeting conquest memes at four o'clock in the morning.

Lorca's fame has certainly not gone unnoticed. The impact of his personality, the influence of his writing, the obsession with his death, and the manipulation of his image as symbolic-cultural capital are all markers of his standing in Spanish and world literature. Along with Miguel de Cervantes, Jorge Luis Borges, and Gabriel García Márquez, he is the one name in Hispanic literature that people almost universally recognize. But we've also grown perhaps too familiar with Lorca. His ubiquity as a cultural-political presence has trivialized the poet, seemingly rubbing the shine off the sense of the marvelous that his person and work once evoked. The wondrous is another way of acknowledging the legend, the part invented, the part mysterious, that serves less to explain the poet than to expose the need for figures like Lorca in our lives. All of this is to say we've forgotten how much we really don't know about Lorca.[14]

The plethora of poems, films, commemorations, and exhibits devoted to him, however well intentioned and praiseworthy, has ended up domesticating him through overexposure and dulled our sensibilities with a surfeit of Lorca here, Lorca there, Lorca everywhere. When Rafael Alberti recited a poem in his honor in 1986, you could hear a continuous, chattering buzz over his words coming from the crowd in the poet's birthplace, Fuente Vaqueros. It was well known that Alberti never made it to Granada while Lorca was alive, so here he was reminding people of that fact with a mournful ballad. Watching the clip of Alberti in the documentary *The Spirit of Lorca* I wondered how many people were really listening, fifty years after the death of the poet. The town had held these commemorations nearly every year since 1976 (and continues to hold them), so maybe some in the audience were distracted, or uninterested in hearing Alberti talk about himself. Commemorations tell us more about the people participating in them than anything else.[15]

This isn't to say the fascination with all things Federico has disappeared. A website, *Universo Lorca* (The Lorca Universe), already receives more than twelve thousand monthly visits only four months after its launch in March 2019. Most of the traffic (80 percent) is from Spain, but the remaining 20 percent is not, with the United States the next most frequent user. Popular sections are the places and people associated with the poet. Interest is above all biographical, which the site, at present only in Spanish and an initiative of Granada's municipal government, along with other local and national entities and cultural institutions, has packaged in the form of itineraries, images, and events that promote tourism in Granada.[16]

You can follow in the poet's footsteps from Fuente Vaqueros and Valderrubio to Alfacar and Víznar, because he's been mapped out as something attainable, located in time and space as a poetic geography, with lines tracing his life from birth to death. Lorca is good business and has been for some time. The *Universo Lorca* is only the latest of tourist websites, guidebooks, and the like centered on the poet. Biographer Ian Gibson's *Lorca's Granada: A Practical Guide*, which appeared in 1992 (with a Spanish version in 1989), is a case in point. Purists may despise such exploitation, but it comes with the territory of modern celebrity, whether the person is dead or alive.

Oscar Wilde's visage appeared on trade cards advertising ice cream, corsets, and sewing machines in the United States, though without his permission. Walt Whitman endorsed a cigar in his name. In the early twentieth century, the dancer Tórtola Valencia lent her image to the popular soap and perfume Myrurgia, and Álvaro Retana, a wildly successful writer of kiosk fiction from the same period, was happy to shill a cognac label. Celebrities are as much objects of consumption as personalities. More pointedly, personalities themselves are consumable things, and they come in all shapes. These figures, as it turns out, happened to be gay, but what distinguished all of them— and Lorca—was a charismatic persona. Most of the commercialization of Lorca has taken place posthumously, the culture industry of Granada being a prime illustration.[17]

Lorca himself continues to be as elusive as that damned aristocrat, the Scarlet Pimpernel, who evaded the French revolutionaries through multiple disguises and role-playing. The poet's words take on an added meaning in this context:

> They no longer found me.
> They didn't find me?
> No. They did not find me.

No heritage trail exists for that. John Dos Passos put it this way: "And the curious thing about the legend of a personality is that it may reach the highest fervor without being formulated. It is something by itself that stands behind anecdotes, death-notices, elegies." Dos Passos went on to talk about the funeral of the popular novelist Benito Pérez Galdós in 1920. As the young American stood watching the massive turnout of people from all walks of life, he observed "a large-mouthed youth with a flattened toadlike face, who was balancing a great white-metal jar of milk on his shoulder." He was happy because Galdós's burial gave him "an excuse for being late for the milk," but then he slipped into the crowd, saying, "'How many books he must have written. . . . It makes a fellow sorry when a gentleman like that dies.'" Dos Passos used this story to illustrate what he called "the procession of the legend of Don Benito." This was what people were following in the streets of Madrid, the legend, not the person.[18]

In another context, he included himself among the crowd, when he said, "Like the milk boy I found myself joining the procession of the legend of Giner de los Ríos." Dos Passos hadn't in fact witnessed Francisco Giner de los Ríos' funeral in 1915, but rather was acknowledging his centrality as an important intellectual figure and reformer of the period. Significantly, his admiration of Giner's work placed him in a personal, albeit vicarious, relationship with Don Francisco. He sat under an evergreen oak tree near El Pardo, reading about the man's life and opinions, noting that "from Madrid to El Pardo was one of Don Francisco's favorite walks." It was the perfect setting, as Giner inspired Spaniards to rediscover the stunning natural beauty of their country.[19]

But then Dos Passos tossed aside the books because they "were dimming the legend in my mind, taking the brilliance out of the indirect but extraordinarily personal impact of the man himself." The American never met Giner, but he felt a connection with him, or rather, with the legend in his mind that was Giner. Leaving aside for the moment the Spaniard's achievement and influence, I cannot think of a more fitting image to express the dynamics of celebrity. The two men were, in effect, "intimate strangers," to use Richard Schickel's phrase. Schickel argued that modern celebrity sets up the illusion of intimacy for fans and admirers of famous people. The appeal of a celebrity resides partly in the capacity to evoke all kinds of feelings in others, especially unformulated longing. Dos Passos's experience points to that uncanny ability of the famous to lodge inside another person, to occupy, if you will, his soul. Yet it is the legend that prevails here, recalling its original meaning as a narrative, especially of saints' lives, read at matins and in refectories and later applied to the wondrous. Above all, to the mysterious and unarticulated, toward which stories can only gesture.[20]

The phenomenon Dos Passos spoke about is closely linked to the aura surrounding charismatic figures like García Lorca. The procession of Lorca's myth is as real as Galdós's or Giner's once was. Dos Passos's use of the word *procession* also points to a much larger context than one individual's perception. The thousands of people at Galdós's funeral was a mass phenomenon. The legend wasn't just in Dos Passos's mind. Lorca never had a funeral, but his afterlives have created virtual throngs of admirers eager to occupy the wake of his fame. The scope of that fame, already palpable during his life-time, has only grown in the past few decades, turning Lorca into a world unto himself. If *Universo Lorca* aims to bring visitors closer to his terrestrial biographical traces, another project, undertaken in 1998 to celebrate the centennial of the poet's birth, connects him to the cosmos itself. *El Universo de Lorca* is a multimedia program in which the poet's words, drawings, and images are spread across the starry screen of the planetarium at Granada's Science Park. Years before, in a poem written soon after Lorca's death, Emilio Prados almost looks as if he had anticipated the project, in the way he imagined the moon "looking for him, / slowly circling in the sky."[21]

Bette Davis was content to have the stars, in the classic movie *Now, Voyager*. Lorca's got the stars *and* the moon, as is only proper, considering how important the moon is in his work. The cosmic setting situates Lorca as a figure who at once embodies and transcends poetry. He draws the very universe to his side in all its multitudinous forms. He is a star, literally and figuratively. This over-the-top vision of Lorca also provides an analogue to something more earthbound: the diverse, sometimes contentious ways in which the poet's fame has placed him in relationship to different groups or constellations, as it were, to different communities across and in time. What has Lorca's celebrity created? To what extent did his personal charisma become a product and sign of the modern world? How did a poet strongly identified with high culture end up a mass phenomenon? Why did a man who was never out become a gay icon? In this respect, too, how has his image been used to promote causes and groups claiming ownership over the poet in disputes shot through with the fractured lines of Spain's history?

All these questions are really about the role of the poet in the world. Poets are generally seen as private figures today, irrelevant to the noisy workings of other people's lives and the public forum. Yet in earlier periods this was not always the case. The public personas and poetry of Victor Hugo and Walt Whitman shaped the national consciousness in France and the United States. For all that Lorca kept his personal life fiercely guarded and refused to be coopted by any specific political party, we now see him as a force of nature, a force in time who occupied the stage of life in consequential ways that only truly came to prominence after his death, haunting the present.

A poet his ideological contrary, José María Pemán, remarked in 1948, "Poetry can't be all that bad, when living politicians and the ruling class, with all the might of the State on their side, still have to contend with dead poets."

Inconveniently for the Franco regime, Lorca was a murdered poet. Pemán's observation indirectly reminds us that Lorca's afterlives are deeply rooted in his past. Those roots have now pushed their way to the surface, ignoring the carpet of moss that Lorca saw as covered in death. You could say that his death has been unending, a kind of public disturbance in the national psyche, while Pemán merely remains six feet under.[22]

Something that Whitman once wrote is apt here, "I am as one disembodied, triumphant, dead," which I take as an expression of the poetic afterlife. It is the last line of "So Long!" a poem that begins with a paradox: "To conclude, I announce what comes after me." Whitman's words are not just about the future status of the lyrical stand-in for the poet, but make poetry the vehicle for fame itself, shaping the very progression of the lines. Even his pronouncements on the indissoluble nature of the United States come from a sense of personal stake in, and identification with, the country that inevitably make you think of *his* indissoluble nature. The American poet's enduring fixation on his own posterity, on not concluding, left a mark on *Leaves of Grass,* as this and other poems suggest.[23]

He is not alone in his poetic exhibitionism. A good number of Lorca works, including the "Oda a Walt Whitman" (Ode to Walt Whitman), *El público* (The Public) (or, The Audience), and some of the poems in *Romancero gitano* (Gypsy Ballads), are shot through with a similar flamboyance, a performance of the self that is more often than not masked, pointing to the influence of iconic exceptionalism as a significant, formative element in his writing (though not the only one). It isn't simply the poet's death dictating his posthumous life but some of his own work that speaks to the charismatic presentation of self we associate with modern celebrity, the kind of literary fact that Tomaševskij found so compelling. It is also a curious thing that this same exhibitionism was observed in a very different sphere of behavior, that of bullfighters and *señoritos,* idle young men of the privileged classes.

In 1916 Eugenio Noel meant to excoriate by these remarks what he deemed the cultural and social excesses of Andalusianism, and linked the phenomenon to the obsession with making a name for oneself. "They want to be men in the public eye," he wrote, "to master the slipperiness of fame." The son of an affluent landowner, who relied on his father's financing for much of his career, Lorca was a señorito, though he certainly worked hard at his craft. He also joked about how his growing fame put him in the same basket as bullfighters. With no claims to reducing the poet's entire work to a single frame of reference (impossible at any rate), do we really know how much Lorca's imprinted persona has created his own legend in the minds of many?[24]

To see Lorca in his afterlives, I have also reached back, in fact all the way back to the nineteenth century (and even earlier), and forward into posterity to locate the poet in a place that simultaneously looks in both temporal directions. This approach focuses on Lorca, but also on a lot more than the poet himself, because a writer of his stature cannot be properly understood without a collective past that is redefined through its connection to the poet. I have worked to situate him in as broad a setting as possible, including a comparatist one, without neglecting the historical particularities of the poet. Lorca's fame is global, yet he remains stubbornly (and exquisitely) Spanish, not to mention Andalusian. Above all, someone as iconic as Lorca is and as superlative a demonstration of the cult of the individual as one could ever hope to find, must also be viewed through communal or group identities to grasp the impact of his fame. Celebrity does not exist in a vacuum, and no person is famous who hears only the sound of his own clapping.

For this reason, I have focused on his relation to four of them, recognizing that no doubt there are more, but that neither space nor time allows me to explore with the depth they require. Had I wanted to write a more conventional, predictable book, I would have provided the kind of overview that also included individual chapters, for example, on topics such as Lorca's Andalusianism, or his image as a "gypsy poet," or his stage presence, but such all-encompassing coverage can easily become unwieldy and tedious. Moreover, some of this work has already been done. Paul Julian Smith in *The Theatre of García Lorca* and María Delgado in *Federico García Lorca* have both explored this last-named subject in relation to the poet's status as a cultural icon. Smith, Jesús Torrecilla, Jorge Marí, and others have examined the poet's connection to Andalusian culture (often equated with gypsy culture, among Lorca readers and fans).

Instead, the communities I deal with are literary-cultural (the dead), social (the people), political (the right/left divide), and sexual (gays) in nature, and more than once overlap, as I return at different points under another angle to one or more of them. Moreover, some of the identities projected onto Lorca, such as that of national poet or gay icon, respond to the needs and desires of one community that are incompatible with those of another. His life and death were catalysts for contradictory reimaginings of a Lorca whose persona was already shape-shifting and elusive. One or more of my choices, I expect, may raise an eyebrow or two, or maybe not, but it seems to me perfectly appropriate to question them. What does the right have to do with Lorca, other than be complicit in his death? Why are the dead buried under a literary-cultural tombstone? How are the people, or *pueblo*, only social in character, or gays only sexual? The simple answer is all of them can be considered interrelated, but that it makes sense to distinguish among them in some fashion for purposes of clarity. Lorca's death is also a political matter, just as "the people" is a notion fraught with political significance. The right made symbolic-ideological use of the poet's death and work, though far less than the left in the immediate aftermath of his assassination. And being gay turned out to be politically fatal for Lorca. In a word, every one of these groupings can be construed as political in one way or another, but every one of them is also much more than political in character and effect. Politics alone didn't create Lorca's afterlives.

The first of these communities are the dead. Lorca is most commonly linked to the masses of victims from the civil war of 1936–39, but there is another group to which Lorca also belongs—that of the poets. His membership in the dead poets society cannot be seen separate from his larger one in the many anonymous dumping grounds and common graves, pockmarked earth on the subterranean map of an invisible Spain that lies beneath the one we know. The poet's dual membership is both literary and civic. There is always an entire literary and cultural tradition contained in a figure such as Lorca, in the sense that T. S. Eliot meant when he wrote that poets must be set "for contrast and comparison, among the dead." That notion took another turn when the Spanish Civil War revived the idea of poetry as civic engagement, using Lorca's death as a form of resistance to the Francoist forces. Antonio Machado's "El crimen fue en Granada" (The Crime Was in Granada) proved especially influential in promoting Lorca's afterlife. A literary cenotaph, the poem merges art and politics by symbolically placing Lorca in both communities of the dead.[25]

As a cenotaph "The Crime Was in Granada" also reminds us that not all dead poets rest easy, or indeed, rest anywhere that we can in fact locate in a tourist guidebook or in a plot of earth. The bodies of some poets, such as Garcilaso de la Vega and Quevedo, have been moved from time to time. Others have simply disappeared. Death is already an unsettling thing, but are you dead if you can't be found? Such disappearing acts—Lorca's above all—are paradoxical because instead of burying them in oblivion if not in reality, we are unable to forget them. They live, more-or-less rent free, in the legend in our minds, Dos Passos might say, creating tiny pantheons of remembrance.

Lorca, with a prime membership in the dead poets society, was once regarded as "the Poet" in Spain, a status he shares with two nineteenth-century writers, Gustavo Adolfo Bécquer and José Zorrilla. The fame of both these men took on a national hue, moving beyond the local in Bécquer's case, in an era when the unifying impulses of identity-driven nationalisms everywhere empowered people to promote and even create their own collective past. One nationalist idea especially, a Panteón Nacional de Hombres Ilustres (National Pantheon of Illustrious Men), inaugurated in 1869, tells, however, another story, one of competing political interests, rivalry, and neglect, leading ultimately to the abandonment of the project. Like other civic-minded enterprises, it was grounded on the revival of the past, which is another way of saying on the dead themselves, many of them writers. And like the family pantheon in Zorrilla's classic play, *Don Juan Tenorio,* this one arose from irreconcilable antagonisms. Situated in this broader historical and cultural context, in a longer look backward, the Republican civic apotheosis of Lorca that occurred immediately after his death becomes part of something larger, centered on the meaning of the relation between poet and community and what that community once was and is.

The pantheon is, ideally, a space of community that begins as a legend in the mind, but it comes from the uniquely intrinsic sociability that poets, living and dead, transmit in their work and personas, from the places of the mind that they invent and that we as readers inhabit. The merging of private and public poetic registers in Lorca's poetry and plays shows him fully immersed not simply in self but in the world. In the broadest sense of the word, works like the *Gypsy Ballads* and *Poet in New York* possess a civic quality, expressed in both traditional and experimental forms, by illuminating through art the plight of the marginalized or the alienated vulnerabilities of city dwellers.

This quality, I would suggest, predisposed him to be viewed as the people's poet in his lifetime and for years after, especially in the response to poems like the oft-recited "Romance de la guardia civil española" (Ballad of the Spanish Civil Guard). After Lorca read this poem in 1935 before a huge working-class crowd in Barcelona, they shouted out, "Long live the poet of the people!" Certainly his use of the popular oral tradition in poetry and his natural sympathies toward the pueblo contributed to such a perception, but what stamped this image in stone was his murder, because now he was a martyr attached to the Republican cause, to the Republican claims of representing the people, however ill-defined this constituency was. Since Franco's dictatorship, Lorca has stood for democracy itself in Spain, a reworking of the older people's poet model. From this idea it was a small step to a journalist proclaiming that "we are all Lorca," a statement that assumes consensus where there is none and ignores the civil conflict—the *lack* of community—from which the ashes of Lorca as the people's poet arose.[26]

It is ironic that the son of a landowner should have occupied such a position, but he was not the only señorito to have been hailed the people's poet. So was the founder of the Spanish fascist party Falange, José Antonio Primo de Rivera. He, too, had been executed during the civil war (though unlike Lorca, he was eventually buried with great ceremony). Historically, however, the relationship between señorito and pueblo was filled with class tensions. The class origins of both men were downplayed, especially in the case of the aristocratic Primo de Rivera. Lorca's social status was displaced onto his murderers, whom the Republicans characterized as señoritos. *Señoritismo* was rejected by Republicans and Falangists alike, though for different ideological reasons. Falangists associated the pueblo with the spirit of great enterprise in the name of empire, while Republicans saw the pueblo as a symbol of democratic ideals. The extremes on both sides of the conflict despised the capitalist bourgeoisie, predictably for oppressing the pueblo. Most significantly, the idolization of both men worked in tandem with the cult-like status of the pueblo itself, which had been enshrined aesthetically and politically since the nineteenth century.

Linking two such disparate figures as Lorca and Primo de Rivera, archetypes of the cult of the individual, additionally helps explain why some on the right, such as Luis Hurtado and Francisco Villena, initially attempted to bring the dead Granadine poet into the Falangist fold. They imagined him as a martyr for imperial Spain, part of the aspirational ideology of heroism that spoke at once to individual valor and comradely solidarity. Lorca as a fascist symbol is a fabrication, preposterous to most and offensive to others, but the propagandistic use of famous figures is not unheard of. Mozart, for example, was turned into an "honorary Nazi," a representative of "Aryan cultural supremacy" during the Third Reich. Goebbels called him "a people's artist" and wrote that his music was "part of what our soldiers are defending against the wild assault of eastern barbarism." The Nazis turned a blind eye to the composer's inconvenient freemasonry or his collaboration with Lorenzo Da Ponte, an opera librettist of Jewish origins. On the other side of the ideological fence, the French Communist Party made political hay of the death of twenty-six-year-old photographer Gerda Taro, crushed and ripped apart by a tank at the Spanish front near Brunete in 1937. She wasn't a party member, but no matter, there was an immense crowd for her funeral in Paris, and she was hailed as "a Joan of Arc of the left."[27]

The exalted rhetoric that some rightists used to claim Lorca as one of their own came in part from Primo de Rivera's speeches. Primo was also viewed as a poet, though strictly speaking he wasn't, but as the source of poetry for fellow Falangists he was enveloped in an aura that only intensified after his execution. "The Absent One," as he was called, was even more present in death. The emotional pitch into which Falangists like Hurtado and Villena threw themselves in praise of Lorca is more about Primo than the Granadine poet. Others on the right, such as Edgar Neville, who also saw Lorca as a martyr, wanted to remember a close friend, but war and politics made it impossible to remain neutral, and ambivalence ran deep. Perhaps the most conflicted of all these writers was Roy Campbell, one of the few in the English-speaking world to openly support the Francoist rebellion against the Second Republic. Campbell lit into Lorca in his long poem *Flowering Rifle*, in lines colored with homophobic innuendo turned defamatory when he added a splenetic footnote to the revised edition. For the South African, Lorca died a cowardly queer, not a martyr, especially in contrast with the heroically imagined Primo de Rivera in *Flowering Rifle*. Yet most surprising, Campbell also translated much of Lorca's poetry and wrote a beautiful book-length essay, filled with insight and a capacious understanding of the poet's work.

If it is difficult to reconcile some of these views—people's poet, fascist symbol, martyr, wimp—it is equally challenging to deal with Lorca as a gay icon, even to know exactly what is meant by that term. Lorca as a latter-day symbol of Andalusian identity, of postdictatorship democracy, or of national victimhood is an updated narrative of the poet found in his past, without the benefit of historical reckoning. The same is largely true of gay Lorca. The aura that envelops this specific image of the poet is a virtual transplant from Lorca's own age, flowing as much from the period and his death as from some of his own work. Just as his death has been politicized, so has his homosexuality, above all, by virtue of his death.

In his own time, the poet was never publicly "out," but even more significantly, the very notion of homosexuality was in flux. If there is one thing that the perceived ambiguities and oddness of being queer signified in the 1920s and early 1930s, it was the strangeness and fluidity of modernity itself. The current view of Lorca's conflicted, yet queer sexuality has been there all along, as works like the "Ode to Walt Whitman" and *The Public* that were already queer as texts told us well before the age of theory. Writers of the period, such as Rafael Cansinos-Asséns, Álvaro Retana, and Alberto Nin Frías, foregrounded an aesthetics of oddness that pointed to homosexuality as an especially modern and, one might say, even eccentric expression of the marvelous. It is no wonder that such exceptionalism lent itself not only to being celebrated but to creating a form of celebrity of which Oscar Wilde was the forerunner. Wilde's public performance of self played on an unstated gayness, while manipulating the exhibitionist nature of celebrity.

I note, too, that Lorca's death also placed him in a very select group of people, that of murdered gay poets, a transhistorical and transcultural community of my own making that emphasizes the line connecting his execution with his status as a gay icon. For this, I enlarge the scope by setting him alongside three other writers: Pier Paolo Pasolini, Christopher Marlowe, and the Conde de Villamediana, all of whom exemplify the politics of celebrity murder. Their violent deaths threw more veils of puzzlement over their sexuality, the role it may have played in their deaths, and the meaning of their lives and work. These were all contested deaths, generating more questions than answers, that were mostly played out in public. Significantly, we might very well not be talking about their sexuality, much disputed in the cases of Marlowe and Villamediana in any event, were it not for the political circumstances of their murders. All of them were heavily implicated in the politics of their day, with prominent public personas. It could be said that in each instance politics gave homosexuality a framework in which to recognize it in the first place and then to interpret.

Villamediana's life and death had repercussions in Lorca's time, after Narciso Alonso Cortés published a book on the Baroque poet in 1928. Alonso Cortés saw him as "the seventeenth-century's Oscar Wilde," reading him as a modern. The critic's ultimately muddled view of his sexuality, calling him bisexual at one point, then "a degenerate of vice," reflected the uncertainty and confusion of his own era over what homosexuality meant. Four decades later, Lorca's close friend the poet Luis Rosales published an impassioned account of Villamediana's death, rejecting the earlier thesis that he was homosexual or that homosexuality had anything to do with his murder. Nonsense, he said, this is a falsification of history and, worse, calumny. Why the Baroque poet's reputation should have mattered to him this much is somewhat baffling, until one remembers that Rosales's family protected Lorca in their home during the early days of the war. In the end, he was taken away and shot, and Rosales was accused of having betrayed the poet to the Nationalists, or Francoists. Over the years, the Nationalists in turn tried to deflect attention away from their responsibility for the murder and onto others, including Lorca himself. The calumny that so incensed Rosales was a doubly inflicted wound against both men. Lorca is never mentioned in the book, but as a silent subtext is never far from the surface of Rosales's roiled outrage. In 1961, another poet, Gerardo Diego, also spoke of similar parallels between Villamediana and Lorca, but Franco-era censorship prevented him from openly naming the Granadine writer.[28]

Rosales was determined to set the truth straight, as he saw it, but the motives for Villamediana's murder remain unclear, while the biographical legend by and large prevails. Celebrity invites calumny and scandal, for figures in the public eye. And, at the very least, made-up stories. César González-Ruano quipped that he surely had attained celebrity because "out of every ten anecdotes told about me, six or seven were absolutely apocryphal." All these poets—Marlowe, Villamediana, Pasolini, and ultimately Lorca too—were larger-than-life public personas. Small wonder that their deaths as well often appear as stagings, the theatrical dénouement to their lives, as though life itself needed to be written out, in both senses of the phrase. Machado's "The Crime Was in Granada" is pitch perfect, in dramatizing the scene of his death, as the opening line suggests:

> He was seen, surrounded by rifles,
> moving down a long street
> and out to the country
> in the chill before dawn, with the stars still out.

Lorca's death especially has been imagined repeatedly as literature (and as film, painting, music, and dance), blurring the border between life and art and reinforcing the poet's status as cultural myth.[29]

In Lorca's time, modern celebrity was already recognizable as the media-driven, mass phenomenon it is today. The first gay celebrity in Spain wasn't Lorca, however, but Álvaro Retana, a writer of popular fictions, set and costume designer, and lyricist, who redefined sex as a form of celebrity culture. He made a career of confusing the line between life and literature, portraying himself as a character in his fiction and performing like a character in his own life. Above all, he made such a fetish of his own ambiguous sexuality (and that of his fictional creations) that his work took on, and fused with, the sexualized aura of Retana in the minds of his adoring fans. He was especially adept at fostering the illusion of intimacy with admirers, some of whom wrote him letters in hopes of making that intimacy real. (In a few instances they did.) In other words, he played at being a celebrity so well he ended up becoming one.

He also played at being gay. Retana's sexual identity in life and in literature was always a performance. This is not to say he wasn't gay (or at the very least bisexual), but that in the 1920s he found a way to come out without coming out. If you performed gay, were you in fact gay? Álvaro Retana was, on this point, the Liberace of his era. Just as Liberace was Mr. Showmanship, so was Retana's heightened performance of the self a strong contender for entertainer of the year. His popularity had as much to do with the inexpensive, sensationalized kiosk literature he wrote as with his own persona. If Retana celebrated mass culture as something intrinsically modern, he did the same for his homosexuality, putting it on display in his work and life, for his fan base to admire as a new version of the age-old marvelous, refigured as the monster of sex itself.

Retana is a good test case against which to measure—and to decenter—Lorca as the premier gay icon, but also to situate the Granadine poet within the growing culture of celebrity in his day. Expressed another way, Lorca in our time (and his) belongs as much to mass culture as he does to high culture. As Antonio Monegal has remarked, scholars and critics have overall, at least until recently, tended to ignore the "popular dimension [of Lorca], as a myth or cultural icon." The broader public, however, is still enthralled with the poet's life and death. They "see" him on the internet, with over ten million googled results, and television news and documentaries, in music such as flamenco artist Camarón de la Isla's adaptations of his work and in films imagining the poet's fate such as *The Prodigious Light* (2003) and *The Disappearance of García Lorca* (also known as *Death in Granada*) (1997), this last with Andy García in the title role. Monegal makes my point, "If for Andy García, [Lorca] is the author of 'Son de negros en Cuba,' for others he's Andy García." The film, which takes considerable liberties with facts, makes a better case for the disappearance of history than of the poet himself. Twelve years later, the mainstream press, online venues, and television obsessively covered the controversial effort and subsequent failure to find Lorca's body, this now largely symbolic and tenuous corpse forever married to the devastation of civil war and the national consciousness. Were it to appear, would the poet's fabled procession in the minds of so many, fade?[30]

The popular side of Lorca's fame comes not simply from the many, but also from the few. Writers like Machado, Rafael Alberti, Arturo Barea, Langston Hughes, and Emilio Prados were among the first to promote him posthumously as the "people's poet." But even in life, Lorca connected with ordinary people and, as his fame grew, with crowds. Celebrity requires multitudes, whether real or virtual, as a form of mutual validation. If the legend is in the mind of others, the crowd is never far from that of the famous person. During Lorca's triumphant Latin American tour in 1933–34, he was thronged nearly everywhere, besieged by admirers, autograph seekers, and photographers. One of the poet's earliest experiences with crowds, however, was of a very different sort, the shock waves he felt thrust into the jam-packed streets of New York City and the beaches of Coney Island in 1929. His reaction to the mobs of people can be seen in "Paisaje de la multitud que vomita (Anochecer de Coney Island)" (Landscape of a Vomiting Multitude [Dusk at Coney Island]), which is, among other things, a poem about mass culture and the place of the poet in that culture. In that vein, he turns the figure of the "poet without arms" into as much a sideshow exhibit as the fat lady's performance in the poem.

Lorca was both fearful and astonished at the spectacle of modern life in New York. *Poet in New York*, to which this poem belongs, is filled with multitudes of people, things, and a vast variety of all manner of creatures, evoking the teeming cosmos of Walt Whitman's *Leaves of Grass* and the incessant tumult of Dos Passos' *Manhattan Transfer*, which had just been translated into Spanish in 1929. According to his friend Ángel del Río, Lorca was familiar with the Dos Passos novel, and he had certainly been introduced to some of Whitman's poetry in translation, though it is doubtful he had deep knowledge of his work. A central text of the collection, his painfully conflicted "Ode to Walt Whitman" also incorporates crowd culture, connecting it to a vision of Whitman as a gay poet occupying the heart of modern life. Significantly, Lorca's own image as a gay icon is closely identified with the poem, precisely because it is filtered through that of the biggest gay icon of all, Walt Whitman himself.[31]

If the "Ode" is part of the basis for Lorca's later fame as a gay icon, the poem itself is already founded on fame, that of Whitman. There is, however, a profound contradiction running through the work. The American poet was all-inclusive, regarding himself as the democratic poet of multitudes, but the "Ode" is structured through exclusion, specifically, the rejection of the *maricas,* or queers. The maricas function as a libidinized crowd in the poem, an enclave whose identity comes from a litany of negative name calling. The "Ode" is far more complex than I have indicated here, because Lorca doesn't simply single out the maricas as a kind of freak show. He also frames Whitman himself in an aesthetics of oddness, essentially imagining him as one of those fabulous creatures that appear in some of Lorca's pen-and-ink self-portraits. In this sense, the poem is unable to keep Whitman apart from the community of maricas, who jump all over the poet's beard. Whitman embraced the high and the low, the pure and the impure, the popular and the aesthetic, all elements that are also part of the "Ode." The challenge for Lorca was how to reconcile them. That the poem never manages to do so makes it fiercely, ambivalently modern. No matter how you approach it, the poem will not settle down, its perpetual unease and ambivalence signs of Lorca's (and modernity's) fundamental strangeness.

The iconic exceptionalism that is built into the poem speaks to a vision of the modern as belonging to the realm of the marvelous. That this image should also surface within a growing culture of celebrity *and* mass culture is, I believe, no accident. Neither is its coinciding with the late nineteenth to early twentieth-century interpretation of homosexuality as an expression of modernity's oddness and therefore as something difficult to define. Modern celebrity is invariably a mass phenomenon, paradoxically courting the cult of the individual in a period when even modernism, in the broadest sense of the word, was focused on the same intense fetishization of the self. Whitman himself obsessed over his reputation till the very end, reflecting a similar cultural and mass phenomenon that was already occurring in mid-nineteenth-century America. That he was sometimes ambivalent about fame is not surprising. So was Lorca. Ironically, the fame attributed to Whitman in the "Ode" was not reflected in his declining reputation found among American poets and critics during this period.[32]

The crowd of maricas in the "Ode" boost, by comparison and by contact, the figure of Whitman as someone celebrated, parodying, as though they were out-of-control fans, the illusion of intimacy with the famous that the lyric voice already suggests is desirable. There is a veritable "frenzy of renown" that runs through the poem. One of the most fascinating things to observe in some of the responses to this poem but, above all, to Lorca himself, is how the poet takes on the role of a phantom celebrity lover. In 1935, Nin Frías already anticipated this aspect of Lorca's after life, when he attached the writer, along with two far lesser lights, Juan Francisco Muñoz Pabón and Pedro Badanelli, to a homoerotic Arab-Andalusian tradition, creating an imaginary gay community founded on an aesthetic he called the "Andalusian spirit."[33]

Posthumously, Lorca has also drawn other gay writers and artists such as Jack Spicer, Jaime Manrique, Edouard Roditi, Manuel Ramos Otero, and the *copla* singer-dancer Miguel de Molina, into the illuminated circle of his poetry and persona, though not all have felt seduced, notably Ramos Otero. In his memoirs, Molina evoked Lorca as an "impossible love," while Roditi, who claimed to have had a one-night stand with the poet, ends up making love to a ghost-lover's spirit in another man's poetry, Manrique's "My Night with Federico García Lorca." Like Nin Frías and Spicer, Manrique himself, in his essay *Eminent Maricones*, also accentuates the dual individual and communal nature of Lorca's iconic exceptionalism.

All these communities that the poet's celebrity and of course his writings have created—the dead, the people, the right (and the left), and gays—have, in turn, enhanced Lorca's fame, posthumously filling in the sense of a life and work cut short. These are some of the worlds to which Lorca is connected, spin-offs coming both before and after the poet himself. While the poet's relation to these communities has sometimes slipped into mythic realms, controversy situates them in contested territory. Fractious or adoring, they operate in some ways like a crowd, whether real or virtual. The politically motivated multitude in Barcelona that listened with rapture to Lorca reading his "Ballad of the Spanish Civil Guard" could also be confused with a crowd of fans, given the electric atmosphere coursing through the theater. And what to make of a crowdfunding effort in 2017 to put together a new edition of the *Gypsy Ballads,* illustrated by more than 250 artists? A crowd today, in this example, of supporters and artists, can exist solely on the internet, but be no less real in its effect than the throngs of admirers who couldn't get enough of Lorca in Buenos Aires and Montevideo.[34]

All these instances bring home the public role of a writer whose private poetic universe seems at first glance far removed from the world at large. Yet an exploration of Lorca's afterlives reveals the very opposite, and a book on this subject inevitably must weave multiple strands together as best it can, in suggesting the cultural-literary richness of a writer who belongs to the class of world-poets, poets who are a world unto themselves and who represent the world in all its astonishing, terrifying complexity. In saying what *Lorca After Life* is, I am hard pressed to categorize it, as the book incorporates biography, history, literary criticism, gender studies, comparative literature, popular culture, celebrity studies, crowds, and the architecture of fame but is none of these things singly. The catch-all is cultural studies, an utterly undefinable entity, but a placeholder for everything we are still figuring out, for the mystery we call Federico García Lorca.

PART ONE

1. Why Dead Poets Matter

Poets die in all sorts of ways. Some die in their beds; more, it seems, die young, though I do not know if the statistics bear out such claims. Some have died in battle; some have died battling demons. Few are murdered, like Federico García Lorca, though twentieth-century politics have produced their share of assassinated and disappeared writers. One has only to think of such Latin and Central American names as Luis de Lión, Víctor Jara, Roque Dalton, Rodolfo Walsh, Pirí Lugones, Jesús Galíndez, and Julio Daniel Chaparro. All eventually joined a select community, which comprises a dead poets society. This name I have freely borrowed from the 1989 film with that title, a classic rite of passage story, which I strongly suspect has also served in a similar virtual capacity for many moviegoers. The camera illuminates a mural of young male students and then focuses on opening day ceremonies, lit with candles, at an elite private academy in 1959. With this ritual frame as the setup, the film introduces us to the theme of "the light of knowledge," embodied in tradition and discipline, as the headmaster emphasizes. What the students learn, however, is something apparently very different from their new English teacher, John Keating (Robin Williams), who tells them they should "seize the day" and "gather ye rosebuds while ye may," following Herrick's advice. *Carpe diem*, he teaches: "Make your lives extraordinary," as the clock ticks audibly in the background. For that, he says, we need poetry because poetry makes us alive.

Poetry also breeds nonconformism, in an era often characterized as asphyxiating and conventional. Yet Keating's message is less radical than it

appears. For one thing, the motif of *carpe diem* is part of a long literary tradition that was already well established in Herrick's day. For another, there
is something trite, if true, in flogging, however engaging Robin Williams's
persona, the revelatory powers of poetry. A more cynical view might ask
whether poetry can reveal anything, as the floundering writer-protagonist
of Ben Lerner's *Leaving the Atocha Station* (2011) wonders. Listening to a
cliché-ridden poetry reading, he sees the audience faces all wearing the look
of appreciation, as though they were "having a profound experience of art."
Feeling like a fraud himself, he questions whether "people were in fact
moved," whether they were seeing in the poem something that wasn't there
or simply felt the social pressure to demonstrate sensitivity. "I told myself,"
he observes, "that no matter what I did, no matter what any poet did, the
poems would constitute screens on which readers could project their own desperate belief in the possibility of poetic experience, whatever that might be, or
afford them the opportunity to mourn its impossibility." Evoking Auden, he
says, "Poetry makes nothing happen."[1]

Lerner's protagonist is, however, an unreliable narrator. A would-be
translator, he wreaks havoc on Lorca's poetry, translating words arbitrarily,
according to sound or whim. When he visits the city that is most associated
with the poet, Granada, he never mentions his name or tries to see his house.
Finally, asked which poets have influenced him, he lies and says, "Lorca." All
this is a far cry from the Romantics' exalted station of the poet as a visionary
or exceptional being, whose works are transformative in nature, full of life
while reminding us that everything must die. Hence, the irony of the Dead
Poets Society as a vehicle for the living. Echoing Kierkegaard, Robert Pogue
Harrison observed that to write constitutes "a gift of the dead to the future,"
because of "the intrinsically posthumous character of the literary voice."[2]

Another way of seeing this writerly predicament is to consider poets as
the living dead, as the philosopher María Zambrano viewed the tormented
submerged selves of Kierkegaard, Nietzsche, and Baudelaire. This existen-
tial dilemma cannot be divorced from a key aesthetic question that T. S. Eliot
envisioned in these terms: "No poet, no artist of any art, has his complete
meaning alone. His significance, his appreciation is the appreciation of his
relation to the dead poets and artists. You cannot value him alone; you must
set him, for contrast and comparison, among the dead." Peter Weir's film
Dead Poets Society is full of that living tradition, what Eliot called "the present moment of the past." The poet, Eliot writes, must be "conscious, not of

what is dead, but of what is already living." For this reason, in these pages I have placed Lorca in that longer trajectory, a collective past to which he belongs, dwelling on the significance of two nineteenth-century writers especially, Gustavo Adolfo Bécquer and José Zorrilla, as part of a national dead poets society, or pantheon, relevant to the Granadine poet. No matter how much we think we understand Lorca in his time (or in our own), our scope of things must necessarily also include a broader connection to the past. In this, there is no one more illuminating than Jorge Luis Borges, who observed that "every writer *creates* his precursors. His work modifies our conception of the past, even as it modifies the future." But critics do as well. Reading Bécquer and Zorrilla as though they belonged to a line of succession in their passage to death resituates Lorca within a larger culture and larger questions about why dead poets matter. What seems not to be about Lorca really *is* about Lorca, if we see him as the culmination of the quest for a national Poet, a quest that began in the nineteenth century with Bécquer and Zorrilla. We just haven't thought about it in quite these terms until now.[3]

All writers are to be found, existentially and literarily, "among the dead," though, as you can imagine, not always willingly. In a work aptly called *The Monument*, Mark Strand observed, "If I were to die now, I would change my name so it might appear that the author of my works were still alive. No I wouldn't. If I were to die now, it would be only a joke, a cruel joke played on fortune. If I were to die now, your greatest work would remain forever undone. My last words would be, 'Don't finish it.'" Clearly, the poet's death is part of the work itself, because the work is a monument to the poet. But like Scheherazade who lives to tell another story, Strand (who died in 2014) lives to write another poem, leaving the work unfinished and thereby postponing death. The poet also wants to be remembered. Strand's comments recall Wordsworth's view of the epitaph as "an epitomised biography," that "presupposes a Monument," both of which are predicated on the belief in immortality. The American poet wanted it both ways: to write his own epitaph, while erasing its fatal implications.[4]

Dead poets, then, have much to tell us, if only to insist that they prefer the land of the living. So Walt Whitman writes:

O to disengage myself from those corpses of me, which I turn and look at where I cast them,
To pass on, (O living! always living!) and leave the corpses behind,

lines that Strand chose to conclude *The Monument*. In other cases, as with Lorca, the death of a poet sometimes temporarily overshadows the poetry itself, becoming the symbol of a cause or an idea that appears to encapsulate an era, a movement or collective identity. In an earlier period, poets, often high-born, also bore arms and fell in battle, a literary, if not class, tradition that lasted into the twentieth century. The great lyric poet Garcilaso de la Vega died of war wounds in 1536, age thirty-five. He personified "the era of poetry and combat," joining action to thought.[5]

The role of poetry in the world was far more public than it is today, and poets were public figures. The Cuban writer José Martí was also a patriot. Tennyson exalted misspent heroism in "The Charge of the Light Brigade," but the trenches and modern weaponry of World War I shifted perception to the more private realm of suffering and loss. Apollinaire, who fought in this war, parodied the figure of the great poet in *The Poet Assassinated* in 1916, but nonetheless retained the myth. Standing before a crowd, in his public role of poet, Croniamantal, who claims to have "come face to face with God," is stabbed to death, in a mass persecution of poets. Afterward, a commemorative sculpture is proposed: "a profound statue out of nothing, like poetry and glory." In the end, a pit is prepared, such that "the void was shaped like Croniamantal, [and] the hole was filled with his phantom." Poetry is as nothing here, yet its specter persists. I am reminded of the Baroque gesture with which Cervantes ended his satirical sonnet on Philip II's ephemeral funeral monument, saying, "and there was nothing."[6]

The Spanish Civil War (1936—39) briefly brought back public poetry in the form of political engagement. As in the Great War, this conflict too had its share of dead poets, notably John Cornford, Charles Donnelly, and Julian Bell, who joined the International Brigades in support of the Second Republic and earned their membership in the Dead Poets Society, along with Rupert Brook, Wilfred Owen, Alan Seeger, and Julian Grenfell from the previous war. One of the greatest Spanish poets of the twentieth century, Miguel Hernández, died in a Francoist prison; and another, the extraordinarily gifted Antonio Machado, in exile, only a short time after crossing the border into France, as General Franco's forces wiped out the last ragged remnants of the Republican resistance. Undoubtedly the most celebrated and remembered of such poet-martyrs is García Lorca, executed by a right-wing firing squad in August of 1936 in the early days of the war.

My interest in these figures, and most especially Lorca, is in their meaning as dead poets. If the sharp intensity of their poetry calls us powerfully to life, their deaths also hold significance. Literary critics tend to downplay the value of biography and, even more so, the iconic status of dead poets like Lorca, as irrelevant or even frivolous, but not only is it impossible to separate a writer's life from his work or his impact, literary or popular; to do so distorts the very nature of the writing life. Dead poets have an afterlife that sometimes surpasses the work itself. How societies treat their dead poets also tells us much about the life and politics of culture, the life of nations. García Lorca was no warrior-poet, nor is his poetry political in the most self-evident ideological or public sense. Claims, however, that he was completely apolitical are no longer taken seriously. Lorca was a strong supporter of the Second Republic and was known to have signed left-leaning manifestos and made political statements, particularly in the last few years of his life.[7]

He became a public figure in his own lifetime, fêted and admired in Spain, Latin America, and elsewhere. Lorca's poetry belongs to both the private and public realms. If on the one hand, the *Gypsy Ballads,* which transformed him into a national celebrity in 1928, contains exquisite examples of the private mysteries of avant-garde poetry (and a rewriting of the traditional ballad, or *romance*), his exploration of a socially marginalized and persecuted group like the gypsies makes him a unique kind of civic poet. *Poet in New York* displays the same schizophrenic qualities as the earlier collection, though in a radically different register: the enigmatic secret universe of language burrowing deep into the dehumanized, emotionally and socially impoverished urban reality that Lorca evoked with such complete desperation creates an intricate play of private and public, signaling not simply the poet (private) in New York (public), but the underground city of language and psyche that *is* the poet. In this sense, he created a new form of civic language and awareness that poets like Allen Ginsburg, Jack Spicer, Jerome Rothenberg, Philip Levine, and others effectively exploited in their own poetry. For Levine, it was the discovery that "the poet could live in the tiny eye at the center of chaos and write."[8]

In "Nueva York (Oficina y denuncia)" (New York [Office and Denunciation]), from *Poet in New York,* for example, Lorca structures the poem around the multiplication, division, and addition of numbers—the signs of commerce and consumption—but not in order to make a neutral mathematical statement. Instead, the numbers accumulate in a kind of chaotic overdrive and pure exaggeration, in a frenzy of slaughter so that four million ducks, five million hogs, a million cows, two thousand pigeons, one million lambs, and two million roosters are killed in a daily ritual of sacrifice. All this consumable death, however, is on the surface of the city. Underneath the multiplication, division, and addition runs a river of blood:

> The ducks and the pigeons,
> and the hogs and the lambs
> deposit their drops of blood
> beneath the multiplications.

And in the dawn, come

> the interminable milk trains,
> the interminable trains of blood
> and the trains of roses, shackled
> by the merchants of perfume.[9]

Despite the relentless movement toward death and consumption, what dominates in these verses (and other poems of the collection) is the poetic awareness of the spiraling out-of-control, denaturalized character of the modern world. The proliferating numbers undermine the rational order they represent. The poetic voice ironically asks:

> What do I do now? Arrange the landscapes?
> Arrange the loves that turn into photographs,
> that turn into scraps of wood and mouths full of blood?

The world is "rust, fermentation, trembling earth." Nature cannot be set aright, when blood "hurls machines over waterfalls." Love does not respond to the rational, and when submitted to order, is stilled and loses its natural condition. Speaking to an unidentified you (but most likely the figure of the poet in the text), the voice says: "You yourself are earth swimming in office numbers." His reaction to this unsettling state is an unequivocal j'accuse, perhaps the clearest civic gesture in the poem: "I denounce everyone / who ignores the other half." And this:

> I denounce the plots
> of these deserted offices
> that blaze no agony,
> that erase the forest's design.[10]

Here is the public voice of the poet, the same poet who once hid himself in the elusive moon, green wind, and boughs of the earlier *Gypsy Ballads*, but who now offers himself up "to be devoured by the press of mangled cows" in this poem. Yet the poetic persona who opens himself to being dispersed in "New York (Office and Denunciation)" is not so radically different from the lyrical self that is dissolved in the verbal field of the ballads, akin to Rimbaud's disseminated identity. Despite the accusatory "I," he also drifts, the blood he sees is "clouded," and he is indistinguishable from the earth that rusts, ferments, and quakes, in a "world of shattered rivers and distances that flee," as "the Hudson gets plastered on oil." Where the gypsy nun's fantasy glimpses "rivers on their feet" in the *Gypsy Ballads*, these rivers are splintered and subterranean, underneath the multiplications, divisions, and additions of the poem. All of this is the city, all of this is the poet: this personal, yet civic, language that flows, gets blocked, then thrusts its way through the oily river, trains of blood, and deserted offices, that refuses to say which part is private, which is public.[11]

Lorca is rarely, if ever, thought of as a civic poet, though his concern with social issues is noted, partly perhaps because the idea of a public poetic figure is usually conceived as a leftover of the nineteenth century, in the prophetic tradition of a Victor Hugo speaking "for a mass of people who share his outlook and his interests." In 1948, for example, the Francoist poet José María Pemán was adamant that Lorca was never "a poet of ideas, of civic and social pronouncements," unlike what he saw as Hugo's hard, clear way of saying things. Yet there is an even more ancient history connecting poetry to civic discourse. During the fifth and fourth centuries B.C.E., Homeric epic and tragedy played almost as powerful a symbolic role as laws in Athenian democracy. Copies of poetic texts such as the tragedies of Aeschylus, Sophocles, and Euripedes were placed under guard in the Metroon, a temple dedicated to the goddess Cybele that also served as a state archive. Poetry was a civic possession of the demos, under state regulation.[12]

In the vein of Victor Hugo, if not with the same rhetoric and meaning, the language of *Poet in New York* is full of the apocalyptic and the divinatory, as in the last lines from "Ode to Walt Whitman":

I want the powerful air from the depths of night
to peel away flowers and letters from the arch where you [Whitman] sleep,

and a black child to tell the whites with their gold
that the kingdom of grain has arrived.

Or these lines from "El rey de Harlem" (The King of Harlem): "There will
be blood and it will flow / on rooftops and terraces, everywhere." These
verses speak implicitly to multitudes, the vast, abject crowds that are made
explicitly visible and experienced with intense ambivalence on Lorca's part
in such poems as "Landscape of a Vomiting Multitude (Dusk at Coney Island)" and "Paisaje de la multitud que orina (Nocturno de Battery Place)"
(Landscape of a Pissing Multitude [Battery Place Nocturne]). In the first one,
the poetic I is lost and mutilated amid the masses of people, while in the second, everything is a watchful witness, surrounded by "a world of death" ("un
mundo de la muerte"). By Lorca's time, the more personal note prevailed in
dealing with public themes, but what is public and what is private in a poet's
work? Isn't the knotted texture of public and private also part of a dead poets
society, the individual threads forming a whole that connects poet to poet,
poet to world?[13]

The relation of *Poet in New York* to world is no less intimate yet also
public than the admittedly different way that Dickens or Tennyson, Hugo,
Walt Whitman, or José Zorrilla, were perceived as binding their private selves
to something greater than the individual. In the nineteenth century poets and
their work occupied a far more central place in national cultures, no doubt
responding to a collective awareness of diminished transcendence in an age
of increasing secularization and materialism. Such prominence was extended
to their deaths as well, as witnessed in the emotional participation of immense
crowds at the funerals of Hugo, Zorrilla, Whitman, and Tennyson. In 1809,
William Godwin's *Essay on Sepulchres* anticipated the growing interest in the
exceptional nature of poets, in their passage through life, by suggesting that
the "affectionate recollection and admiration of the dead will act gently upon
our spirits." The then neglected tombs at Westminster Abbey provoked him,
above all, to recommend the creation and cataloging of plain white wooden
crosses that would dot the English landscape, mapping the physical resting
places of the illustrious dead.[14]

These visible markings "would be a precious relic to the man of sentiment," a far more valuable traveler's guide than the "catalogue of gentlemen's
seats." Speaking of all those "whose writings or deeds have ever interested"
him, he said, "I regard the place of his burial as one part of his biography."

In this way, Godwin reasserted both the public and intimate meanings of writers, conceiving them as sacred transmitters of moral significance to individuals and the social body. As Paul Westover remarked of literary biography in this period, his project "wants both to bring the dead close and to preserve them as icons. Indeed, it suggests that one cannot bring them close except as icons." This paradoxical relationship of ordinary persons with the illustrious dead has much in common with the later illusion of intimacy with celebrity that those less favored by fate or talent hope to attain.[15]

Lorca's achievement as a playwright placed him squarely in the public arena, a vantage point he explored in one of his most challenging plays, appropriately titled *The Public*, but what really turned him into a public figure was his death. Though arguably, he was already positioned to *become* Lorca before his assassination. In killing him, the Nationalists provided a potent civic symbol of resistance for the supporters of the Second Republic, a symbol implicated and prefigured in his life and in his work, in this reading, as though Lorca were a precursor to himself. In the introduction to *Poems for Spain* (1939), Stephen Spender and John Lehmann wrote that Spanish poets "defend their own lives whose fate under Fascism is foretold in the murder of García Lorca." The last section of their anthology is simply called "Lorca." Significantly, they noted, some writers "first awakened to poetry by Spain, died," in "a struggle for the conditions without which the writing and reading of poetry are almost impossible in modern society." Revisioning the joining of action to thought, the tradition of arms and letters, they maintained that "action itself may seem to be a kind of poetry to those who take part in it." For Spender and Lehmann, "the richness of a tomorrow *with* poetry" was linked inextricably to "the struggle for liberty itself." "There is," they said, "actually an identity of the ideas of public policy and poetry. This is the sense in which poetry is political." Arturo Serrano Plaja said something similar at the Second International Congress of Writers for the Defense of Culture in 1937. Whether public policy and poetry can be the same seems at the least questionable, but ultimately, they advocated merging "the life of literature in the life of action," or as Antonio Aparicio expressed it, in an updating of the epic tradition: "I say simply that there are no other gods but the hero and the poet who sings of him, and the poem is one with the deed itself."[16]

Lorca's older contemporary Antonio Machado wrote one of the first (and more memorable) of hundreds of poems on his death that would appear in multiple languages over the decades, a poem that speaks to that merging of "the life of literature in the life of action." In line with Spender and Lehmann's thinking, Machado considered the wartime intellectual as a kind of militiaman "with a cultural mission." Poetry, in this context, was a symbolic form of action. As James Whiston has observed, Machado's "The Crime Was in Granada" (1936) "is a concentrated commentary on the testimonial role of art." The poem "witnesses" a crime committed against art, in the figure of Lorca, and against the people, with whom the poet was closely identified in life and in death. This is, essentially, a civic poem, its allegorical impulse illustrative of a widespread Republican reaction, in poetry and prose, to the poet's murder. Unsurprisingly, the words *crime* and *criminals* were applied as a favored indictment to both sides of the conflict, but few literary works from this period have attained the resonance of Machado's poem, rising above insult.[17]

The witnessing, I would suggest, is on at least three levels. First, the lyric poet's voice re-creates and imaginatively dramatizes a scene he could not possibly have seen himself. Second, he places anonymous witnesses within the poem, Lorca's executioners and Death herself in the shape of a gypsy, among them. And finally, Lorca is transparently a poet-martyr, that is, he himself bears witness, as the original meaning of the word *martyr* attests. In witnessing, Machado makes you "see" Lorca's death, as the memorable refrain, "he was seen" ("se le vio"), stresses in the first line of all three parts. The poem begins with theatrical flair, as I have noted before:

> He was seen, surrounded by rifles,
> moving down a long street
> and out to the country
> in the chill before dawn, with the stars still out.

By contrast, the assassins close their eyes, because they cannot bring themselves to look at the poet, which of course makes the reader's seeing that more vivid.[18]

This seeing is a kind of knowledge that Machado expresses with the plural command form of *saber:* "sabed," "know this," that Alan Trueblood translates as "think of it," but the meaning is clear. (It is worth noting that the word is a later addition to the poem.) First, there is a public to whom the poet addresses his verses, when he says, "know this." Even more important for that public (and readers): to witness is to acknowledge a crime, in all its ethical and juridical implications, to which no one can shut his eyes. "Seeing" turns Lorca into a public figure (and theme), even as Machado himself embodies the same figure. In appealing to the moral imagination, the poem is doubly civic, for the doubly civic role that both poets play.[19]

The third and last part goes like this:

> He was seen walking . . .
> Friends, carve a monument
> out of dream stone
> for the poet in the Alhambra,
> over a fountain where the grieving water
> shall say forever:
> The crime was in Granada, his Granada.

Although a modest plaque commemorating Lorca was eventually placed on the walls outside the Alhambra in 1998, there is no fountain anywhere near it and, of course, Lorca's body has never been found. The true memorial is the poem itself, the dream stone that remembers the poet. The last part, while more intimate than the first two, as the lyric voice speaks to his friends, is no less civic-minded, indeed, perhaps even more so, given the metaphorical injunction to construct a public monument—*de piedra y sueño* / of stone and dream—meant to convey both grief and rage over Lorca's murder.[20]

Significantly, Machado's poem promoted and shaped Lorca's afterlife in ways that the poet most likely never anticipated, because lines and images from his poem began to show up in the work of other writers, a visible indication of the impact "The Crime Was in Granada" would have in Spain and well beyond. The key phrase, "the crime was in Granada," served as part of the title of perhaps the single most disseminated (and erroneous) newspaper account of Lorca's execution, in which the heroic image of the poet appears like a partial reworking of Machado's poem. Lorca walks "with magnificent serenity," fearlessly addressing his killers in defense of liberty and the people. In the poem, he faces death personified, unafraid, in the form of an intimate struggle. The report, which is more overwrought fiction than fact, ends with this line: "There they left the poet, unburied, outside Granada, *his* Granada." Machado's poem now serves as an historical reckoning of sorts.[21]

Indeed, as Juan Gil-Albert argued in 1938, what convinced people that Lorca had really been murdered *was* Machado's poem. Somehow, those initial lines of the poet walking toward his death, spoken with what Gil-Albert called "a serene, intimate voice," invested the scene of the crime with a sense of history. The murder was now "'historical fact,'" though also literary. "Machado's understated verses," he said, "made evident that what 'seemed untrue' was certain." Gil-Albert's opinion is, of course, unprovable, but nonetheless, it is remarkable that a poem, which could only imagine a scene Machado never witnessed, should be perceived as having such an effect on historical events, as making history. Machado himself later downplayed the significance of his poem. He found its "aesthetic expression insufficiently developed [in relation to] the actual thinking [informing it]." An underlying bitterness, he said, "implie[d] an accusation against Granada." Nonetheless, his poem prompted Gil-Albert to examine in the midst of war the meanings of history wrapped up in Lorca's life and death, pointing to the "intense precipitateness of a common destiny" for both the poet and the people, even if events seemed to occur "in precise, slow motion." He went on to say that there was a curious kind of "delicacy and penetration and a species of delirium of sensibility that precede historical upheavals and the most violent disturbances of a people," announcing the future is upon us.[22]

It is worth noting that these remarks were part of a commentary on one of the earliest collections published to honor the memory of Lorca, *Homenaje a Federico García Lorca, contra su muerte* (1937). Moving beyond shock and disbelief over the poet's death, beyond a stance "against his death" ("contra su muerte"), Gil-Albert was grappling not just with the out-of-sync quality, the dissonance felt between experiencing history and understanding it, but with the gap between the anticipated yet uncertain arrival of history and its brutal passing. Lorca's assassination crystalized something of this complex experience; or perhaps better said, his walking toward death was a walk into history. In Machado's poem, he is always at once walking and always dead, registering the "precise, slow motion" of forever seeing what was, in truth, an act of instant savagery. History is thus recorded by being remembered over and over, the way Machado repeated "he was seen" ("se le vio") in "The Crime Was in Granada," reenacting Lorca's final moments.[23]

As I point out more fully elsewhere in this book, and as a further indication of Machado's impact, one of the first to allude to his poem was a Falangist, Luis Hurtado Álvarez, who made use of the title in his article, "A la España imperial le han asesinado su mejor poeta" (Imperial Spain's Best Poet Assassinated). This too was a historical reckoning, though deeply divergent from Gil-Albert's. Republicans Antonio Sánchez Barbudo and Rafael

Alberti took issue with that borrowing. Clearly, Machado's poem had infiltrated the Nationalist zones of Spain. Years later, in 1966, another Nationalist and once-Falangist, Edgar Neville, also cited verbatim lines from the text, including the first four and the iconic refrain, in his poem "Su último paisaje" (His Last Landscape). But it was more common to see Machado's poem reflected in pro-Republican poetry and prose.[24]

In a prose piece called "¿Su muerte?" (His Death?) (1937), José Bergamín wrote, "And *the crime was in Granada, his Granada.* The voice of another poet, a master poet, was able, for the first time, to pinpoint for us the feeling, the awful truth; the reality denied, rejected." Bergamín's italicizing of the phrase, without naming its author, suggests how well known Machado's poem already was, how the poem drove home the fact of Lorca's murder, as Gil-Albert argued. Bergamín imputed the murder to ignorance, "in the same way they kill the people. Out of ignorance. . . . But that guilty ignorance is the worst crime." By referring to a crime, he connected his own text to Machado's, and like Machado, viewed Lorca's death as a form of political martyrdom symbolically linked to the Republican cause, here, the people. Later, he too tried to imagine how Lorca died. Bergamín also included the full text of Machado's poem in the posthumous edition of *Poet in New York,* published by the press he created in Mexico (Séneca, 1940).[25]

These two phrases—"the crime was in Granada" and "his Granada"—showed up in other writings. Pedro Garfias's poem "A Federico García Lorca" (1937), which appeared in the same wartime homage volume as did Bergamín's, expressed a similar thought: "The crime was in Granada, / the master Antonio said," later calling Lorca the "people's poet" ("poeta del pueblo"). (I have not been able to tell which of these poems came first.) Likewise, in an essay (1938; 1943), Guillermo de Torre referred to "his Granada," in quotation marks, though, oddly, he seems to suggest Machado merely repeated the phrase rather than having originated it. He cited as well the entire first stanza of "The Crime Was in Granada," while Juan Rejano repeated the iconic line and verses from the last stanza in 1940. He also reprinted the entire poem as a preface to the book he wrote in exile (1944). Serrano Plaja's prose piece on Lorca's death (1937) alluded to the last things on earth the poet might have seen in "*his Granada.*" The italicized phrase plainly needed no more elaboration to readers at that point. My suspicion is, Machado's compelling verses at once responded to commonly held sentiments that needed an emotional outlet, while no doubt quickly turning into a shorthand method to telegraph

one's politics and outrage. Lorca, meanwhile, was turning into his own ef-
figy, as impenetrable as the stone images he used to re-create the death of his
friend, the bullfighter Sánchez Mejías, in his *Llanto por Ignacio Sánchez Mejías*
(Lament for Ignacio Sánchez Mejías).[26]

Non-Spaniards also relied on Machado's poem for Lorca's afterlife.
D. Trevor included an English translation of it in an article for the *Left Re-
view* (1937), saying: "It may seem inhuman to put Machado's poem against
Lorca's death, but is the reward indeed so poor when that elegy lives in the
mouths of men? Is the word, the idea, 'hero,' indeed so suspect?" The Por-
tuguese poet Joaquim Namorado re-created his death "beneath the sky of *his*
Granada," in "Romance de Federico" (Ballad of Federico) (1941), while the
Uruguayan Juana de Ibarbourou simply repeated twice, "the crime was in
Granada," as she recalled her time with Lorca in Montevideo. In 1947, Louis
Parrot reprinted, using all capital letters, the entire Machado poem, in the
Jean Cassou translation. Gerald Brenan essentially paraphrased the point of
the poem by saying in *The Face of Spain* (1951): "This was a city that had
killed its poet." And Claude Couffon used the poem title as a reference to his
investigation into the poet's death.[27]

By 1998, the muted irony of Philip Levine's "The Search for Lorca's
Shadow" had achieved the kind of eloquence that only historical irrelevance
brings:

> Someone
> wrote, "The crime was in Granada,"
> though actually it was here among ants,
> stones, dust, olive trees, fallen fruit, the boots
> of armed men, the cries of women and men
> where now there is only silence and no
> darkness we can say is his, Federico's.

Machado has become anonymous, the city (and province) of Granada incon-
sequential, and Lorca dispossessed. Only the ants, stones, dust, olive trees, and
fallen fruit persist; only nature. The boots and cries? Not really. And then
there is that word, "his." A word that is in denial. Letting the emphasis fall
lightly on "his" while also negating it, Levine pushes back, as much against
Machado's "his Granada" as Federico's "my death" and "my Granada" in
the second stanza of Machado's poem, as if to ask what these things have to
say to us today.[28]

Where Lorca once was, is a vacuum, not even the dark of his shadow. The use of the poet's first name—a rhetorical device found in Lorca's own work and in many poems dedicated to him—to some extent mitigates that vacuum with an intimate touch and thus reasserts the poet's former material personhood. The loss of the poet is no less profound in Levine's poem than in other elegies, but absent here is the urgent sense of history and immediacy that filled many earlier homages. The American poet says that "this is a poem about historic death," but focuses more on the indifference of the natural world to human death (to all death), putting into question not only the possibility of recapturing history, in particular, an individual's history, but what history is for Levine. The darkness that envelops Lorca also swallows up history. If Machado ultimately aimed to give life to Lorca in his poem, as Bruce Wardropper argued, the same cannot be said for Levine, who proclaims Lorca's definitive disappearance into the earth, amid what he calls his "useless search."[29]

Incorporating bits and pieces of Machado's poem, these texts are paper shrines to Lorca, fragments of word-effigies, but they are not the only use made of "The Crime Was in Granada." In the northwest corner of Uruguay lies the provincial city of Salto. It was here, in December 1953, that the Uruguayan writer Enrique Amorim commemorated his friend Lorca's life and death with a simple tombstone-like wall, beneath which a fountain flowed. Engraved on the wall were the last six lines of Machado's poem, in which the poet urged his friends to "carve a monument out of dream stone," over a fountain of "grieving water." Buried behind the wall was a white box, large enough for bones. The mystery of this box has never been solved. Amorim hinted they might be the remains of Lorca himself, though this possibility seems very unlikely. As Santiago Roncagliolo writes, the ceremony passed almost unobserved, and the only celebrity of note to attend was the exiled actress Margarita Xirgu, Lorca's good friend. Amorim, who had hyped the wall as the first monument to Lorca ever raised, had his hopes dashed when neither Pablo Neruda nor Louis Aragon bothered to show up.[30]

The monument, which may have served more to shore up Amorim's own ego than anything else, continues to be a tourist attraction, though the fountain no longer works. Xirgu herself, who died in 1969, joined the cast of characters of Golijov's opera *Ainadamar* in 2003, resuscitated, alongside Lorca, in a work whose title in Arabic means "Fountain of Tears." Like the poet's own body, the fountain is both real and unreal, a metaphor of a material absence that includes even the dysfunctional fountain in Salto. Moreover, it isn't clear whose fountain we are talking about. The historic one, near which Lorca was executed? Machado's imagined one in the Alhambra, which weeps and repeats the words, "the crime was in Granada, his Granada"?

Or the same image reproduced in other poems, like Dámaso Alonso's "La Fuente Grande o de las Lágrimas (Entre Alfacar y Víznar)" (The Big Fountain, the One of Tears [between Alfacar and Víznar]), which in turn relies on Lorca's own words in an epigraph: "My heart sleeps beside the cold fountain?" Is the image any more real because this poem from 1940 (published in 1944), like Neville's later one, was rooted in an actual journey Alonso made to Granada to see where Lorca died? Machado's fountain speaks because Lorca can't. But even this fountain is as dysfunctional as the one in Salto because it can only point to a missing body, the way Amorim offered teasing hints about the poet's remains, prompting the novelist Santiago Roncagliolo to declare that Amorim "was the first who understood the importance of Lorca's body." The body that isn't there, while the "literary fact," or its artistic equivalent, lies in a white box.[31]

Machado's poem reminds us that many monuments, such as cenotaphs, are empty tombs, like Apollinaire's pit filled with the phantom of the dead poet. Funerary architecture is only one way of commemorating the dead. Writers and artists have elegized the famous and not-so-famous for centuries, with verbal and painterly portraits, sculpture, funeral orations, éloges, or encomiums. In 1853–54, Wenceslao Ayguals de Izco, for example, published El Panteón universal (The Universal Pantheon), a four-volume historical dictionary of famous men and women, which was something of a hodgepodge as it also included biblical, mythical, and fictional figures. For over four decades, the American abstract expressionist Robert Motherwell labored obsessively over a large body of paintings he called Elegy to the Spanish Republic, inspired in part by the memory of Lorca and his work. As he described the project, "Making an Elegy is like building a temple, an altar, a ritual place. . . . Unlike the rest of my work, the Elegies are, for the most part, public statements." Motherwell's black monoliths may seem far removed from an actual monument; yet they bear some resemblance to Machado's dream stone, as imaginary graves. Machado's poem is also as much a public statement as Motherwell's paintings.[32]

They are not, however, tombeaux, literally poetic (or musical) tombs, at least not as Jean-Luc Nancy characterizes the Renaissance genre, which he says is meant to celebrate, not to grieve. "The *tombeau* guards the dead person," he remarked, "takes him away from his death, presents him to the living." The genre enjoyed a revival of sorts at the end of the nineteenth century, notably with Stéphane Mallarmé's *tombeaux* to Edgar Allan Poe, Baudelaire, and Verlaine, in the form of the sonnet. Arguably, elegies, too, present the dead person to the living, but Machado and Motherwell are talking about absence, not presence. Because Lorca is not there. This not knowing where his body lies is not unique to Lorca. Not only have famous dead people disappeared—Velázquez, Lope de Vega, Cervantes (now relocated, it seems)—their remains have sometimes even moved from place to place.[33]

Writing in 1870, the late Romantic Gustavo Adolfo Bécquer, for example, once found himself in the mysterious, contemplative space of a Toledan church and vaguely remembered that the Renaissance poet Garcilaso de la Vega was buried in one of the city's churches. Was it this one? he asked himself. There was no sign, no inscription, and yet he was sure it was. But then doubts assailed him. "Had I really seen Garcilaso's tomb? Or was it all a story forged in my head on the theme of some tomb or other?" He considered consulting a guidebook, thought better of it, and finally did. His intuition was confirmed: the poet and his father were both buried in a chapel of the San Pedro Mártir Convent. Or so he thought. The guidebook, however, was out of date, as Bécquer himself recognized, when he added one more paragraph noting that Garcilaso's remains had recently been transferred in solemn procession to San Francisco el Grande Basilica in Madrid, which had been designated the site of a new National Pantheon of Illustrious Men in 1869.[34]

But this is not the whole story. Garcilaso was first buried in Nice in 1536, then removed and reburied in San Pedro Mártir Convent and Church two years later. His remains went to the National Pantheon in 1869, but returned to Toledo after six years, where they languished in the Casa Consistorial for a quarter of a century until 1900, when once again they were placed in the same church as before. Bécquer himself, who died less than a year after writing the piece, was buried in Madrid. In 1913—forty-three years after his death—he and his brother Valeriano, a noted painter of regional customs, were brought back to their hometown of Seville, first to the Chapel of the University and, since 1972, to the Panteón de Sevillanos Ilustres (Pantheon of Illustrious Sevillanos).[35]

In these strange funereal migrations resides another story about the meaning of dead poets, of neglect and rivalry, of politics and competing interests, both local and national, that is relevant to García Lorca's after-life as well, specifically to the contested excavation of his body in the twenty-first century (to which I return in the next chapter). Both stories—Bécquer's and that of the National Pantheon (with several other illustrious figures besides Garcilaso)—were as political and public as Lorca's, placing the Granadine poet in a larger context and longer trajectory than is usually recognized. The poignancy of Lorca's fate, not to mention its brutality, is even more striking by contrast. "Among the dead," to recall Eliot's phrase, situates such figures not only in the literary, but the political, historical, and cultural past, in the presence of a living past.

Bécquer's fame and his importance to the development of Spanish poetry are beyond dispute today, but this was not always the case. His work was posthumous in both the figurative *and* literal sense, as most of his poetry remained unpublished until 1871. With the second edition of his works in 1877, the emotional impact of his brother's idealized portrait of Gustavo (as well as Bartolomé Maura's, based on Valeriano's), and additional publicity in the form of a special issue of *La Ilustración Artística* in 1886, Bécquer's image as the misunderstood genius and the romantic dreamer started to take off. Dying young didn't hurt, and women especially loved his poetry, but serious critical attention was yet to come.[36]

If the edition of his works can be considered the first successful civic monument to the poet, as Rubio Jiménez argues, the next commemorative act—a portrait hung in the prestigious, historically important Biblioteca Capitular-Colombina, or Columbus-Cathedral Library, in 1879—backfired, as the painting was removed after only a short while. The astonishing reason: ultra-Catholics considered Bécquer to be lukewarm in his faith at best, heterodox at worst. They came to this conclusion based on a few lines of verse taken out of context, moments when the poet appeared to have expressed religious doubts. This, in turn, provoked heated discussion between conservatives and liberals in Seville. His most enthusiastic booster (and collector of Bécquer memorabilia), José Gestoso y Pérez, tried for decades to get commemorative projects off the ground and to bring back his remains to Seville.[37]

No doubt poor municipal finances played a role, but so too did cultural indifference on the part of the political class. Lack of support and even hostility toward the poet also reflected the endemic polarization of Spanish po-

Figure 1. Monument to Gustavo Adolfo Bécquer, 1911, Parque de María Luisa, Seville. Courtesy of Álvaro Cantos Encina.

litical life, split between right and left, which eventually led to civil war in the 1930s. Ironically, the constant squabbling in the press over whether to memorialize Bécquer kept him in the public's sights, his own enemies helping to create his myth, as Marta Palenque argues. It was only in 1910, when the enormously popular Andalusian playwrights the Álvarez Quintero brothers, also Bécquer enthusiasts and collectors, began a private funding drive to finance a monument for the new Parque de María Luisa (María Luisa Park) in Seville, that the project took off within months. The Quinteros ceded their authors' rights to the Bécquer-based play *La rima eterna* and started a national subscription. The monument, designed by the distinguished sculptor Lorenzo Coullaut Valera, has been a tourist mainstay for over a century (fig. 1). In 1910–11, the Bécquer craze spread from Seville to the rest of Spain. Two years later, the Bécquer brothers' remains were transferred from Madrid to Seville. Large, enthusiastic crowds of people across the social spectrum attended the ceremonies for the monument and the inhumation.[38]

There were, no doubt, other contributing factors: the monuments mania that affected all of Europe and the Americas and the growing regionalist movements that needed cultural symbols and artifacts to prop up what was in some cases an invented past. The Quinteros were particularly clever in promoting Bécquer not simply as an ethereal dreamer but as a popular, Andalusian poet. They were not the first to do so, and there is a strong case to be made for this latter characterization based on the poet's own work, his admiration for traditional song, and the inspiration he drew from centuries-old folk practice.

One of his most exquisite and celebrated lines—"There may be no more poets, but there will always be poetry" (Rima IV)—has been read as a metapoetic statement. But there is a parallel notion expressed in the pseudo-archaic language of Agustín Durán's verse adaptation of an oral tale, *Leyenda de las tres toronjas del vergel de amor* (Legend of the Three Grapefruits in the Garden of Love) (1856): "And without there being a poet / their poetry came from everyone." In a note, Durán, who became known for promoting the rich, popular tradition of the *Romancero,* explained that oral literature was impersonal, anonymous, and belonged to everybody. As sophisticated as Bécquer is in his *Rimas,* this notion of the popular, while mediated by a scholar-promoter, is deeply embedded in his poetry. This is also true of García Lorca, who was familiar with the *romance,* or ballad, tradition in part through Durán.[39]

Several years before the Álvarez Quintero brothers, an anonymous correspondent in 1901 described Bécquer as "the poet of Seville" and the embodiment of Andalusia, of southern Spain. "Bécquer is our people," he wrote, "the artist, and therefore, both happy and unfortunate. . . . He is the poet. No one captured like he did the delicate chiaroscuro of feeling, of language. No one expressed like he did those small things, *immensely* small things of the soul." This emphasis on smallness recalls Lorca's affection for the diminutive as part of a Granadine aesthetic: "The genuinely Granadine aesthetic is the aesthetic of the diminutive, the aesthetic of diminutive things." The Granadine diminutive is "like a startled bird, that opens secret chambers of feeling and reveals the richest nuances of the city. The diminutive's sole mission is to de-limit . . . to bring inside and place in our hand objects or ideas of large perspective." Regionalist fervor informs all these observations. Bécquer's afterlife has merged with the pueblo, here the Andalusian, not the Spanish, people.[40]

By the early twentieth century, regionalism was also part of the regenerationist movement in Spain. Swayed by the critiques of Spanish decadence, especially by writers like Ángel Ganivet, Miguel de Unamuno, Joaquín Costa, and Macías Picavea, critics tend to see this period as one of *national* regeneration, but renewal and reform were also the focus of attention in the provinces. Writers like Gregorio Martínez Sierra linked commemoration of Bécquer to the *patria chica*, that is to local identity, not to the *patria grande*, or Spain; he had little faith in the efficacy of the central government in such matters. By 1942 another *sevillano*, Luis Cernuda, whose own poetry revealed a persistent and subtle romantic influence, recalled, through Albanio his projected self, the mysterious effect of reading Bécquer's work as a child and the vague memory of his interment in the university chapel. He called this piece "El Poeta" (The Poet). Visiting the chapel numerous times, the message he encountered was one of universal "indifference and forgetting" ("indiferencia y olvido"), the local link now diffused within the general feeling of abandonment of the living and the dead. By contrast, thousands of people have left little notes expressing wishes, promises, and poetry as offerings before the pantheon of the Bécquer brothers.[41]

The identification of poet and pueblo was also made with the Granadine poet, especially by Spanish Republicans in wartime and in exile, as I further explore elsewhere in *Lorca After Life*. The title of Arturo Barea's book, *Lorca: The Poet and His People*, published in 1944, was representative. Similarly, Juan Rejano saw the poet and the people as one voice, in a publication, also from 1944, with a similar if elongated title, *El poeta y su pueblo: Un símbolo andaluz; Federico García Lorca* (The Poet and His People: An Andalusian Symbol; Federico García Lorca). The pueblo here is both Spanish and Andalusian, as is the poet. Lorca himself promoted his Andalusian identity, speaking of truth as "Andalusian and universal" ("andaluza y universal").[42]

But it is important to remember the precedent of Bécquer, if only to understand the broader and extended context for Lorca's afterlife, in local and national terms. The differences are equally significant: disease killed Bécquer, not a bullet, and his reputation, which assumed a national and even pan-Hispanic status beyond Spain, never went global, as Lorca's has. The initial link between the two poets is the Andalusian regionalist movement, in which the young Granadine participated. Both poets fomented local culture, privileging the note of authenticity over European influence. Bécquer complained in the late 1860s of modern sameness ruining the unique charms of Seville, while Lorca joined the composer Manuel de Falla to promote the purist forms of flamenco at the Cante Jondo Festival in 1922. In turn, both poets became symbols of that same local culture.[43]

Like Bécquer, Robert Burns in Scotland, and Victor Hugo in France, Lorca also became known as "the Poet," an expression of the growth of nationalism and national literatures since the late eighteenth century. Dead poets, once nationalized, were also signs of a search for national roots, of a national past, in a period when the past was becoming at once increasingly detached from the present and its history more deeply questioned. Celebrations of dead poets often brought out underlying conflicts and differing notions over what constituted national identity, what the past meant. Lorca is forever attached to the ultimate national crisis, civil war, a war that refuses to die in Spain. The noisy failure to find his remains in 2009 took place amid bitter accusations of partisan behavior and unseemly exploitation, so that unearthing Lorca was really like unearthing the war. Whether this was a good thing depended on which side you were on. And as I pointed out earlier, well before these events Pemán, a supporter of the Franco regime, attempted to depoliticize Lorca's influence, but ended up revealing what a problem that dead poets could be for politicians and ruling class alike.[44]

As national symbols and poetry incarnate, Bécquer and Lorca shared the stage with one other poet of note, José Zorrilla. His funeral in 1893 turned into the kind of spectacle that the author of the quintessential Spanish Romantic play, *Don Juan Tenorio,* had never wanted. Ironically, he first drew national attention at the funeral of another writer, Mariano José de Larra, who committed suicide at the age of twenty-seven. Zorrilla's public reading in February 1837 was electrifying, and only the first of many such occasions. Zorrilla popularized the practice of public readings and recitations, starting in the 1850s when he went on periodic tours, earning as much as thirty-six thousand *reales* for one of them. This initial performance, in effect merging a singular identity with a collective one, can be said to have transformed poetry emotionally, calling forth a national response. His most iconic work, a repertoire of loosely historical plays and legends, reinvented the Spanish past, relying on a conservative bedrock of traditional values, while seeming to rise above politics.[45]

By the time of his death, Zorrilla's image as the national poet was commonplace. One commentator wrote, "Zorrilla is more than a poet: he is the poet . . . the soul of Spain." Another observed that during the funeral, "the soul of the People trembled, and the spirit of the Poet triumphed!" The massive outpouring of popular sentiment spoke volumes. His own protestations aside, Zorrilla, who fancied himself a modern-day *cantor*, or troubadour, and sought the approval of the multitudes all his life, would have been pleased. The only thing he ever wanted, he said, was for the people to hear his song. At the viewing, held in a salon of the Royal Spanish Academy, somewhere between thirty thousand and fifty thousand people came to pay their respects. Included in this broad swath representing the entire spectrum of social classes were women of modest means, elegant señoritas, small children, students, aristocrats, and workers of all stripes. The multitudes were so vast no one could recall ever having seen so many at what amounted to a state funeral (fig. 2). As the burial commenced, the crowds surged, trampling over graves and vegetation, the guards unable to maintain order. Unruly, even violent at times, they grew silent when the casket was lowered into the ground.[46]

On a humorous note, an unhinged, if well-dressed, elderly man, claiming to be a doctor sent from heaven, showed up at the door of the Royal Spanish Academy so he could bring Zorrilla back to life. Even less seemly were the numerous peddlers of newspapers bearing the poet's semblance, who were spotted during the funeral. It could have been worse. Inside Westminster Abbey, where Tennyson lay in state, mourners could hear the "jarring cries" of vendors calling out, "'Crossing the Bar'-sixpence a copy'" and "Here's the latest photograph of Lord Tennyson." Tennyson himself was besieged by the crowd at Dickens's funeral, such was his popularity.[47]

There was much criticism of the pomp and circumstance with which Zorrilla's funeral was conducted. First, his death coincided with a municipal scandal of mounting corruption and incompetence deliberately hyped by rival political factions amid a looming national crisis. Beset by strikes and other disturbances, an attempted anarchist insurrection in Jerez, and fiscal, colonial, and regional tensions, Cánovas's conservative government fell at the end of 1892. Some observers felt that Madrid's beleaguered city hall exploited the occasion of Zorrilla's funeral to distract the populace. The official homage of the government and the Academy came off as inauthentic and shabby, failing to match the enthusiasm and emotion of the masses. Why didn't the body lie in state in the magnificent rotunda of the San Francisco el Grande Basilica? asked one journalist.[48]

Other accounts, such as that of the Carlist paper *El Correo Español*, were full of praise. This same publication claimed Zorrilla as one of their

PASO DE LA FUNEBRE COMITIVA POR LA CALLE DE LA MONTERA.

(Del natural, por el Sr. Comba.)

Figure 2. Zorrilla funeral procession. *Ilustración Española y Americana,*
30 Jan. 1893.

own, that is, a traditionalist, but observed that those who mourned the poet's passing were all Spaniards, even the liberals. A conservative, Zorrilla, nonetheless, appealed to a wide array of his fellow countrymen. The working-class Centro Instructivo del Obrero, for example, hung a black banner in honor of the poet. As in Bécquer's later commemoration or Lorca's exhumation, politics and political attitudes, though rather more muted here, crept into the proceedings.[49]

Second, Zorrilla's wishes were ignored, and that, too, was criticized. His last will and testament unequivocally stated that he wanted a simple interment with a wooden casket, in his hometown, Valladolid. Ironically, like the corpses of other notable personages, his was found to be eminently moveable only a few years later. A new Panteón de Vallisoletanos Ilustres (Pantheon of Illustrious Persons of Valladolid) was established, and he was the first resident. On the grave were inscribed the words he indicated in his testament, "The Poet José Zorrilla, Son of Valladolid." But not even his home-town respected his refusal to be turned into "vulgar allegory" as a designer corpse decorating a pantheon.[50]

There is added irony to Zorrilla's final (and very public) resting place. The second part of his celebrated work *Don Juan Tenorio* (1844) contains perhaps the most memorable scenes in Spanish theater ever situated in a pantheon. Only a few short years before, an actual national pantheon had been proposed in 1837, under a liberal government and in the middle of civil war but failed to prosper. Interest in funerary art and architecture was not new, but now it had spread to theaters and gardens. Eighteenth-century "sepulchral farces" with skeletons and tombs were popular entertainments on the Parisian stage, influenced by Piranesi's imaginary prison etchings, the *Carceri d'invenzione*. In Martínez de la Rosa's *La conjuración de Venecia* (The Venetian Conspiracy) (1830), which debuted in Paris and later played in Madrid (1834), act 2 is set in a family pantheon mixing death and desire, amid romantic omens. The third act of the anonymously authored *La estrella de oro* (The Golden Star), a magic play from 1838, takes place in a ducal pantheon populated with similar motifs, including the specters of the dead, though the deaths of the protagonists are only apparent. The setting was considered especially impressive, a print of the pantheon appearing in the journal *El Panorama*.[51]

Zorrilla's stage set is also a family pantheon, though of a peculiar sort, since some of its occupants are victims of Don Juan Tenorio, whose father has disinherited him and turned the space that once held a palace into a pantheon. While the play takes place in the sixteenth century, this is very much a nineteenth-century, Romantic cemetery in the form of a garden, replete with weeping willows, cypress trees, and flowers. In the foreground are three funerary statues representing characters, two kneeling and the third standing, this last reflecting a late eighteenth-century sculptural practice. Aristocrats in the sixteenth century would have been buried inside a church, not in an open-air space constructed outside the traditionally demarcated limits of the sacred. While the pantheon in *Don Juan Tenorio* is still attached to the spiritual realm, secularized elements of Zorrilla's stage set were later duplicated in the gardens of the Duke of Montpensier's Palacio de San Telmo in Seville, which included statues of Don Juan and the Comendador Don Gonzalo de Ulloa. Curiously enough, on one façade of this Baroque building, which now houses the presidency of the Andalusian Autonomous Government, a gallery of twelve illustrious Sevillians (among them, Velázquez, Murillo, and Fray Bartolomé de las Casas) was sculpted in 1895, creating another form of pantheon. The duke's gardens became part of the present-day Parque de María Luisa, where the monument to Bécquer memorializes the poet. The two statues, however, have vanished. By the 1870s they were in sorry physical state, according to the writer Blanca de los Ríos, who remembered playing in the gardens as a child.[52]

The transition from stage to garden, from make-believe play to historic palace, was a natural one. Notwithstanding the romanticized religious message of the play—salvation through profane, albeit etherealized, love—*Don Juan Tenorio* occupies the worldly realm of secular entertainment. And the pantheon in the play is already a garden. Montpensier's garden, with the statues of two fictional characters, simply completes the move toward secularization initiated in the early nineteenth century when people were no longer buried inside churches. Protestants had already adopted this practice by bringing back the freestanding mausoleum of antiquity in the seventeenth and eighteenth centuries. As Howard Colvin has remarked, "in pre-Reformation Europe the idea of a private place of burial unconnected with a consecrated church or chapel was unthinkable." Even more significant was the separation between the living and the dead that such a practice encouraged, intended as it was to counter the Catholic idea that the living could influence "the fate of a dead man's soul." Colvin points out that "burials in gardens were rare in Catholic countries." How could one perform religious services for the dead in a garden? The creation of large, public cemeteries in the nineteenth century and afterward marks the transition toward burial as, above all, a civic enterprise.[53]

None of this means that the religious component simply disappeared. It certainly plays a large role in *Don Juan Tenorio,* but one of the ironies of Zorrilla's work, often identified as Catholic and conservative, is how it reverses the relationship between the living and the dead noted above, by showing the contrary, how the dead influence the fate of the living. The phantom spirit of Doña Inés performs the religious conversion of the living in the personhood of Don Juan (though there is some debate among critics whether he truly is still among the living at this point in the play), thus saving his soul. For that purpose, Zorrilla, good showman that he was, knew he needed the proper setting, and that was the family pantheon.

To understand why this is significant, one needs to ask first why Doña Inés is buried in the pantheon of the Tenorio family, which also contains two other nonfamily members, Don Luis Mejía, erstwhile rival of Don Juan, and Doña Inés's father, the Comendador Gonzalo de Ulloa, both of whom the protagonist killed. Doña Inés died of love, after Don Juan abandoned her. The only other expressly mentioned person buried there is his father, though one assumes that the remaining tombs and niches are occupied by family. How could these three people be considered "family"? I would suggest that they have *become* family because of their intimate attachment to Don Juan and, more specifically, to his fame.

In explaining the institutions of society, Vico observed that "the family took its name principally from [the] *famuli*," vulnerable persons seeking refuge and protection among the stronger. They were servants and slaves, constituting the original household, and sustained by the strength and virtue of heroes. Vico also argued that the word *famuli* came from the fame of these heroes, though it appears that the origin of the term is unknown. It doesn't matter whether he is etymologically correct. What matters is the relation between family and fame that he suggests. Doña Inés, her father, and Don Luis are reflections of Don Juan's fame. Granted, this is *mala fama,* or notoriety, but fame initially referred to both the good and the bad kind, since it meant equally rumor and reputation. Doña Inés's role in saving Don Juan's soul cannot be separated from the kind of fame he has acquired in the first part of the play. Despite his poor behavior, he still performs the part of the hero in Zorrilla's work, however resistant he is to redemption until the very end. Correspondingly, if Doña Inés saves his soul, Zorrilla "saves" his fame, creating the ultimate symbolic memory space for it: a pantheon (not to mention the play itself). Like the famuli, and more broadly the "family," Doña Inés, Don Luis, and Don Gonzalo are inextricably linked to the hero's fame, which explains their place in the pantheon.[54]

The set up for the pantheon scene shows how aware the playwright was of its iconic value, because he introduced an innovative element into the Don Juan story: the part of the Sculptor, the creator of the pantheon. It is true that Giuseppe Gazzaniga thought of it first in his opera, *Don Giovanni Tenorio o sia Il Convitato di pietra* (1787), but the role is a fleeting nonspeaking walk-on. Zorrilla's Sculptor creates an entire meta-aesthetic in the work, as both Gustavo Pérez Firmat and James Mandrell have observed. Pérez Firmat points to the way the portrait of the artist prefaces both parts of the play and sees the pantheon as "an embedded creation." Mandrell views the Sculptor as Zorrilla's stand-in, and the pantheon as "a type of literary cemetery," in which the Sculptor's desire for artistic immortality correlates to literary fame for the playwright.[55]

The Sculptor's opening monologue stresses the artist's glory, incarnated in what he calls "my posthumous memory," the marbled likenesses he has created. Future generations, he boasts, will revere the generation to which he belongs, implying a kind of artistic rivalry with those to come. This attitude is of a piece with that of Don Juan's father, whose decision to transform the space into a pantheon arose from a desire to show up his own son, the final act of (past) rivalry between father and son. The Sculptor speaks of Don Diego finding glory in exposing his son's flawed character by erecting statues of his victims in the cemetery. In this manner, Don Juan's father declares his own superiority over his son, but he does so through art. (Ironically, the father also secures his son's fame with the creation of the pantheon.) Pliny reminds us of the origins of what were called *iconicae,* or portrait statues. The first of these were of the gods. "It was not customary," he wrote, "to make effigies of human beings unless they deserved lasting commemoration for some distinguished reason, in the first case victory in the sacred contests and particularly those at Olympia. . . . [T]hese statues . . . were modelled as exact personal likenesses of the winners." In other words, such statuary was born of "a most civilized sense of rivalry."[56]

Competitiveness lies behind the actions of both the Sculptor and Don Diego. Zorrilla's statues also speak to a second motive for their creation. Pliny wrote that it was "the custom for the state to confer this honour [of a statue] on those who had been wrongfully put to death." This is certainly the case for Don Juan's victims, whom Don Diego showcases, turning them into surrogates of his own future glory, thus combining both reasons for making likenesses in stone. Tellingly, there is no sculpture of Don Juan himself, even though the artist wanted to place him among his victims, but he could not find a portrait from which to model the work. Logically, he should not be there, however, as he is not yet among the dead, but symbolically and emotionally it makes perfect sense, because he already is.[57]

Fame as enduring memory sits squarely at the center of Zorrilla's pantheon, as it did for past representations of gods, heroes, and illustrious mortals of human history, but the motif of memory also runs throughout the play. Memorialization of Don Luis's and Don Juan's competing profane exploits and adventures occupies the first part of *Don Juan Tenorio,* turns aesthetic in the second half with the pantheon and, ultimately, spiritual in the culminating moment of salvation. Yet it is near impossible to separate these different kinds of memory work, because the entire play operates from the premise that everything—and everyone—is already posthumous. *Don Juan Tenorio* is itself a kind of pantheon, focused obsessively on being remembered, whether through forms of rivalry or love.

Like the physical setting in part 2, the work is also at once private and public. Its theatricality is exposed to all, but the drama is at heart familial, like the cemetery in which so many of the characters end up. The pantheon, while private in nature, makes a public statement about memory and fame, which also reflects the tenor of the play. In this sense, both the work and the pantheon are secular objects of aesthetic devotion, marking the transition from an ancien régime mentality to a modern one expressed through the exhibitionist rhetoric of romanticism in a bourgeois age. Like Zorrilla, his contemporary, the Romantic poet Carolina Coronado, also transformed her work into a pantheon. The second edition of her collected *Poesías* (1852) was typographically designed so that individual sections were akin to the niches of cemeteries, each page framed with different decorative borders, as families of verses, sometimes even in the literal sense. One section, for example, is titled "Salutaciones y despedidas" (Greetings and Farewells), directed toward relatives and friends, while another is dedicated to Alberto, an enigmatic, if undocumented, love evidently lost at sea. Larra described the autograph album (1835) as a pantheon filled with signatures anticipating posterity. Nearly a hundred years later, Ramón Gómez de la Serna, whose great aunt was Carolina Coronado, said people in the nineteenth century "pantheonized their things [and] shielded them from the pneumonia of time."[58]

This secularizing impulse, while inspired by the Enlightenment, retained traces of the sacred, unfolded in memory, among the dead, and found expression in a growing civic movement from the late eighteenth century on. Precisely because the civic turn was grounded on the dead—that is, on remembering the past, in its historical, national, individual, and popular forms—the sacred persisted. *Don Juan Tenorio* strikes me as an iconic example of a secularizing impetus that memorializes nonsacred objects, the statues of characters who are already an intimate part of a significant literary and historical past. Zorrilla placed them in a transcendent setting and mindset, having grasped intuitively the shrine that memory so often makes of loved persons and things. The cultivation of memory that Pierre Nora observed in the *lieux de mémoire*, the monumentalizing of history among other things, also needs to be situated within a similar affective geography.

Zorrilla already had in his memory kit Larra's funeral, where he read a graveyard elegy. Several months later, in November 1837, Parliament approved the creation of a national pantheon, attaching it to a law indemnifying victims of Fernando VII's despotic regime and thus politicizing an enterprise that, in any event, failed to launch. Having already made trips to visit Westminster Abbey and the Panthéon in 1833, the noted writer of customs, Ramón de Mesonero Romanos, was especially keen to have such a site; the ideal spot, he thought, was the San Francisco el Grande Basilica. He may very well have been the first to suggest the project. At the same time, in his zeal to promote Madrid as a symbol of both local and national culture, he also championed the first statue of Cervantes, erected in 1835, in front of the Parliament. As Álvarez Barrientos suggests, this monument, along with eighteenth-century efforts to recuperate other figures as well, including Calderón de la Barca and Lope de Vega, in editions and engraved portrait collections, paper pantheons in their own right, prepared the terrain for the idea of a national poet, a cultural symbol of the nation. Something similar was happening with Shakespeare in Great Britain.[59]

The more conservative Moderate Party threw out the progressives' project of the National Pantheon, along with the progressives themselves. The lack of historical, cultural, and political consensus would continue with the contentious opening of the National Pantheon of Illustrious Men in Madrid in 1869 (and afterward, in Lorca's time and since). Such ideological conflict rests on the same spirit of rivalry of which Pliny spoke and Zorrilla's play exemplified. A civic project if ever there was, after the September Revolution of 1868, the government took up the original proposal from 1837, with the San Francisco el Grande Basilica, an eighteenth-century neoclassical church, for this purpose, but within a few years it had been largely abandoned. The American Catholic Andrew Shipman expressed his disappointment in 1910, observing that the site was beautiful but not really what it claimed to be, since the illustrious personages deposited there had been disinterred and returned to their original resting places, "owing to the vigorous protests and threatened lawsuits of their descendants and their fellow-provincials."[60]

Writers buried in the pantheonized San Francisco el Grande included Calderón de la Barca, Francisco de Quevedo, Alonso de Ercilla, and Garcilaso de la Vega, as well as other historical and artistic figures. Many could not be found, such as Miguel de Cervantes, Lope de Vega, Gaspar Melchor de Jovellanos, Tirso de Molina, and Diego Velázquez. The National Pantheon was, at least for a time, a dead poets society. As the son of Mesonero Romanos remarked, the project failed in large part because of the lack of "prime matter": in a word, dead bodies. First, Calderón was exhumed, then one after the other till at length none were left. This prompted the journalist Mariano de Cavia to quip: "There is no profession more uneasy, more uncomfortable and insecure in this country than that of an illustrious corpse." Even before the Pantheon's inauguration, complaints were heard that "the revolution made on behalf of the living has ended up placing the dead into circulation." Echoes of such criticism persisted into the twentieth century. The fifteenth-century poet Juan de Mena had also been placed in the pantheon, but later returned to his original burial site in Torrelaguna. In 1944, under the Franco dictatorship, the daily paper *ABC* reported that the poet's tomb had been "opened by the reds" during the civil war, thus furthering the politicization of the dead.[61]

The idea goes back to the Roman Pantheon, but the real inspiration derives from Westminster Abbey, Santa Croce in Florence, and, most especially, the Panthéon in Paris. Like the French model, a product of revolutionary fervor, the Spanish one was closely attached to a political agenda. The language of the government decree creating the pantheon is both exalted and tendentious, blaming the old absolutist regime for having forgotten the glories of the nation. By contrast, the current government planned to awaken its citizens from the country's state of abjection and oppression and to educate them in the "new Spain," with the exemplary lives of its most celebrated men (no women yet) as pedagogical instruments.[62]

"The French Revolution," says the decree, "placed the Pantheon in contact with the heart of Paris; in time, the Spanish revolution will place its Pantheon in contact with the Parliament, the heart of the nation, by opening a new street so conceived that from one end where the national flag waves over the Congress one can see at the other end shining golden Fame proclaiming over the dome of the Pantheon the glory of our great men." Political and urban reform were one here. This symbolic linkage was never constructed, though opponents of the project clearly saw that its promoters wanted to establish a connection between the Pantheon and the new liberal constitution that was anathema to many Catholics and traditionalists because of its freedom of religion clause.[63]

The debate was especially intense in the newspapers. The monarchist *La Época* attacked the National Pantheon as an overreaching, centralizing move by the government and defended local and family rights respecting the disposition of the dead. (This last point finds an echo in the controversy over digging up García Lorca's remains, which I discuss elsewhere in these pages.) Unsurprisingly, the absolutist Carlist *La Regeneración* hated what it perceived as a secularizing impulse behind the project, observing the incongruity of associating the new constitution with the "apotheosis of so many Christian heroes and good Catholics." The paper considered the Pantheon a pagan idea.[64]

One of the most suggestive critiques was historically grounded. *La Época* considered the author of the decree, the progressive Manuel Ruiz Zorrilla, a poor historian, pointing out the inconsistency of attacking the history, religion, and monarchy of the old regime, while attempting to exalt national sentiment at the same time. How could one deny such history? "The National Pantheon," the paper concluded, "is a monstrous contradiction in the present circumstances." Similarly, the French Revolution aimed to wipe out the past, obliging promoters of the Panthéon to invent new historical memories. On the liberal side, *La Iberia* rejected *La Época*'s arguments as dogmatic and error-ridden—in a word, unenlightened. Each side was partisan, the tone frequently venomous. At heart, the dispute was about how the past was understood, as well as how the present was to be lived and governed. The two sides had a different past—and a different present—in mind. The controversy over Lorca's missing body—with the civil war as ever-present backdrop—is rooted in similar concerns over the past. And as with Zorrilla's play or Lorca himself, such issues are reenergized by symbolically bringing back the dead (or their substitute).[65]

Dead poets were part of a cultural patrimony, the cultural identity of a nation. This idea, which arose from the ashes of the French Revolution, was taken up by the liberal Romantic tradition in the early nineteenth century. Edgar Quinet believed that the dead housed in the Panthéon served a national educational purpose. But he also assumed that first there needed to exist "a moral edifice, that of the conscience, of the ideal country, of political liberty in the heart and home of every person." Without that inner pantheon, a real one was useless. In 1852, for example, Gabriele d'Amato published a two-volume work titled *Panteon dei martiri della libertà italiana* (Pantheon of the Martyrs of Italian Liberty). The book itself he considered to be a "monument" to the sacrifices of Italian patriots inspired by the "cry of universal redemption" begun in 1789. To communicate the heroism of their lives was "a sacred message" ("un codice sacro"), he wrote. Italian unification—the *Risorgimento*, resurgence or renaissance—was not achieved until 1871, but meanwhile d'Amato impressed upon his readers in high-flown language the national scope of his project, the educational uses of the past, and the inexorable march of human progress. D'Amato, who was also director of the Society of the Pantheon of Italian Martyrs, used the proceeds to help Italian emigrés and refugees abroad.[66]

A similar rhetoric infused not only the government decree establishing the National Pantheon in Madrid but the writings of the progressive Ángel Fernández de los Ríos, a key promoter of the project. Indeed, some of the phrasing in the decree can already be found in Fernández de los Ríos's *El futuro Madrid* (Future Madrid), published in 1868, and leads one to wonder what role he played in writing the document. At any rate, the idealism of these writings derived from a kind of secular religiosity that had replaced religion with civic passion. He described the inaugural ceremonies of the Pantheon as "the apotheosis of the nation [culminating] in what remains of its great men." Its foundation, he wrote, will be "tolerance for these great figures who may be weak in some respects, but who have served the dignity of man, and exemplified what more than anything else needs to be glorified in Spain: civic courage." An account of the opening ceremonies in the liberal paper *El Imparcial* also spoke of a "sacred duty" ("deber sagrado") toward these men, emphasizing the civic nature of the event.[67]

Fernández de los Ríos declared that the National Pantheon was *part of* the liberal revolution but hastened to add that the Spanish Revolution should not copy the French one. Nonetheless, the project was essentially Europeanist in design and purpose, and was viewed as a French import. The splendid procession to San Francisco el Grande, while largely secular and civic, still displayed traditional symbols of monarchy, and the Chariot of Fame was the same one used for Queen María Cristina's triumphant entry into Madrid in 1843, suggesting a yet-to-be-defined national identity. At least one observer thought the celebrations on the eve of traditional feast days held for SS. Peter and John were more genuinely popular than the ceremony for the pantheon.

Most significantly, the project failed to create consensus or a sense of unity in the Spanish nation, but, rather, continued to remind the country of unresolved political divisions. This result was not so very different from that of the French Panthéon (or the failed exhumation of Lorca). Here too, political conflict was built into the partisan nature of the project, which could never erase "the stain of the French Revolution," as Mona Ozouf observed.[68]

Nor was this the last of national pantheons in Spain. To my surprise, I discovered there actually is a current-day Pantheon of Illustrious Men in Madrid. In March 2015, I decided to check it out, along with the former site at the San Francisco el Grande Basilica. I had tried to visit the church several times over the years, since the 1970s, but it was always closed for repairs. I found out later that, because of a protracted process of restoration, it had been closed for the last third of the twentieth century. This time, I was lucky. The basilica has a rather plain façade, but is breathtaking inside, with an impressive dome and rotunda, exquisite frescos, and paintings by Goya, Zurbarán, Carducho, and others. I saw no traces of its earlier life as a pantheon. During the civil war it was one of several buildings that the Second Republic used to protect some fifty thousand art treasures, while the crypt, on the other hand, apparently served either as an arsenal or a bomb shelter or possibly both.[69]

There was no evidence of this past either, though an informed guide did point it out. On a more sinister note, it seems the basilica was also used to detain prisoners of the SIM, the Republic's dreaded secret police during the war, known for its summary tribunals, torture, and extrajudicial executions.[70] This forgotten, or repressed, history is a reminder that the narrative I am pursuing—the pantheon of illustrious men—is selective history (to which Lorca also belongs). That the religious and civic history of this building, so intimately situated "among the dead," might also have held other bodies, awaiting an unknown fate. Ironically, San Francisco el Grande was the church of preference of the Franco regime, though that, too, is submerged history. It receives approximately ten thousand visitors a year.

Leaving the basilica, I caught a cab for the National Pantheon. "There's a National Pantheon?" the taxi driver asked me. To a person, no one seemed to know there was one. Although I had been told the place would probably be deserted, there were a few people wandering peaceably among the tombs, all of them Spaniards except me. Annual attendance figures vary, from three thousand to an improbable twenty-one thousand visitors.[71] This National Pantheon arose from the ashes of the previous one but was conceived in very different terms. Designed to be part of a new basilica, in the neo-Byzantine style, only the Italianate campanile and a cloister, where the Pantheon is located, were built. (It is near the Basílica de Nuestra Señora de Atocha, constructed in 1951 on the site of the earlier seventeenth-century church and convent burned down during the civil war.)

Inaugurated in 1902, the Pantheon contained only politicians and military figures, four of them assassinated. Despite claims that there are no actual bodies on the premises except for Canalejas, only the mausoleums, that does not appear to be the case, although three of the generals did eventually go home: José Palafox, to Zaragoza, in 1958; Francisco Castaños, to Bailén, in 1963; and Prim, along with the tomb itself, to Reus, in 1971. Once again, local demands trumped national ones, although one observer complained, in a fit of disproportionate pique, that no one would think of making the same demand of Westminster Abbey. In at least one case, that of Prim, however, local jurisdiction did not mean better treatment, as one commentator remarked in 2012 that Prim's remains were now deteriorating and abandoned in his hometown.[72]

Despite the inclusion of both liberal and conservative politicians, this commemorative site, which was closely associated with the Army, the Monarchy, and the Church, was as partisan as the earlier pantheon, reaffirming long-standing political divisions. Both pantheons offer two different, politically charged narratives of national history. The presence or absence of bodies is not the point; the absence of national consensus is. Yet, strolling among the tombs of the National Pantheon, I was struck by the irrelevance of the place, even while admiring the artistic dexterity of the sculptures, especially Mariano Benlliure's tribute to the liberal statesman Práxedes Mateo Sagasta, the only one to provoke heated debate at the time for its inclusion of a stunning allegorical figure of the working classes holding a sword and wearing *alpargatas*, or espadrilles. Even in this case, Benlliure's representative of the pueblo, or people, his back to Sagasta, leaning casually on one elbow and gazing calmly into the distance, expresses nobility, an unruffled, self-possessed air. As one contemporary observer said, a funerary monument should evoke a sense of permanence and tranquility. Artistically, these monuments do that, but they also point to the inadequacy of art as an instrument of pedagogy.[73]

Art as "a form of civic education" is, no doubt, out of fashion in the late twentieth and early twenty-first centuries. Even some in the nineteenth century questioned how effective a pedagogy of the dead might be. In 1840, Ramón de Mesonero Romanos thought the French Panthéon was but "a political copy of the religious and historical Westminster Abbey, a true temple of glory open to all the celebrities of Great Britain." It lacked the element of the sublime because neither religion nor history could sanctify it. And no mere decree could make the kind of history that a pedagogy of the dead might inspire. Even the more liberal Carolina Coronado felt uneasy, her hostility spilling over, as she contemplated Voltaire's tomb in the deconsecrated church (St. Geneviève) now occupied by the Panthéon. "The Paris of the dead," she wrote somewhat flippantly in 1851, "may be the true Paris," if you wanted to find the wise men and heroes of France or the virtues of the République. When her guide began shrieking to demonstrate the presence of an echo, she concluded that she "had never seen the ridiculous and the sublime combined in such a bizarre fashion," likening herself and the other tourists to "a troupe of the dead . . . [dancing] in the Panthéon." The accomplishments of the men buried in these places are not the issue; the ability to use them to create or foster a national identity and unity is another question altogether. This same question is equally pertinent in the case of Lorca, as I argue later in this book.[74]

The current sensibility has, until recently, seen commemorative sites as places that "produce forgetting." We walk by sculptures and plaques and pay no attention to them (unless they become politically inconvenient). Maybe they did that, too, in the nineteenth century. Maybe only the pigeons value them, having no interest in the vagaries of history. Writing in 1898, Mesonero Romanos's son saw nothing but indifference and neglect, when he inspected the graves of illustrious personages in Madrid. He saved for the last those of his parents and brother in the Cementerio de San Isidro. His visits to their graves, he said, were the stimulus for his melancholy reflections, but also for his suggestion that the idea of a National Pantheon be revived. Filial devotion, his own private mourning, led him "naturally," he wrote, to reconsider the more public form of remembrance. Unlike Don Juan's rivalry with his father, the son of Mesonero Romanos seems not to have harbored a competitive streak with the man who engendered him. Even more telling is how he tied together fame and family, the public and the private, to a civic enterprise.[75]

So maybe the ritualistic purpose of pantheons, of remembering famous people, poets included, has no place in our lives today; but then we would have to conclude the irrelevance of ceremony and observance. I don't think that is the case: the very act of burial itself, which is at the heart of such rituals, is a sign of our humanity, as Vico noted. He considered burial "the second human institution" (the first was marriage). We are compelled to remember, not because of rituals, but because of our very nature that has devised them; rituals are ways of remembering. Specific rituals or forms of rituals may lose their power or their relevance, but not what provokes them in the first place: the need to bind ourselves to a community in the mutual act of remembering, an impulse contrary to the spirit of rivalry that appears elsewhere to inform the creation of memory sites. That makes such acts and the places in which they occur both private and public, insofar as individuals derive sustenance from participating in public observance.[76]

A dead poets society may be, first, a place of the mind, as well as a place of community for the boys who celebrate the poetry of companionship, in Peter Weir's film. But it is a place, of one kind or another. In that sense, it is not so different from a nineteenth-century pantheon. And it tells us one of the reasons why dead poets matter: because they create these places of the mind. They create places of community. There are no poets left in San Francisco el Grande, and there were never any poets in the National Pantheon of Atocha, but the cultural and human patrimony of dead poets such as García Lorca persists.

This is part of their afterlife. In a thoughtful meditation on the place of the dead in human existence, Robert Pogue Harrison suggested that "like human dwelling, the after-life needs places to take place *in*. If humans dwell, the dead, as it were, indwell—and very often in the same space." In a related vein, Wordsworth observed that a village churchyard "is a visible centre of a community of the living and the dead." This surely is the case for dead poets, but their place in human history is unlike that of most individuals, who remain private, in that the greatest of them attain a public profile that makes them deeply social, that gives them a lasting sociability because they share these places of the mind with us, their readers. This space—which is ultimately the point of contact between the living and the dead—is where the dead live within us. William Godwin had expressed something similar in 1809: "I wish to live in intercourse with the Illustrious Dead of All Ages. . . . They are not dead. They are still with us in their stories, in their words, in

their writings." In seventeenth-century Spain, Francisco de Quevedo wrote
with Baroque eloquence on the value of books, "I live in conversation with
the departed, / and I listen to the dead with my eyes."[77]

The nineteenth-century eulogizers of the National Pantheon understood something of this relationship, even if the lofty rhetoric with which
they expressed it strikes current readers as dated or over-the-top. In this
period, dead poets such as Garcilaso de la Vega and Quevedo were more
and more seen as part of that select historical and cultural category of beings
who are called great men, the existence of which has obsessed humans for
centuries. In the eighteenth century, Mona Ozouf wrote, "the great man was
neither a king nor a hero nor even an illustrious man," but he *was* self-made
and, in this sense, an exemplar. Over time the idea has become increasingly
democratized, but without ever losing its aura. Carlyle in 1841 saw Shakespeare and Dante as heroic because the Poet, or at least this caliber of poet,
was a hero. There was even a sacredness attached to the mere presence of
Shakespeare, he said. In 1869, a poem by Ventura Ruiz Aguilera titled "Apoteosis. El 20 de junio de 1869" (Apotheosis. The 20th June 1869) appeared
in a pamphlet celebrating the inaugural day of the National Pantheon. He
described those honored as "the dead who will live forever," observing that
"they were more than kings, they were men."[78]

This was the same apotheosis of the nation symbolized in the remains
of great men of which Fernández de los Ríos had spoken the year before.
And if one thinks about it, this same elevated language, in which the civic
is clothed in the sacred rather than opposed to it, was also used to remember
Federico García Lorca during the civil war and for many years afterward,
not in Franco's Spain where his name was met with silence but among Republicans and their supporters abroad. Thus, to give but one example, Lorca
"died . . . so that he would be resurrected with his people in history and in
immortality." The civic, public nature of Lorca's apotheosis as part of a national, and universal, cultural patrimony represented his pantheonization,
his membership in the Dead Poets Society. A community "among the dead."
And, one might add, among the "family" of poets, as Eliot would have appreciated. Or for that matter, Mallarmé, who returned to a genre closely
attached to the notion of literary community, the sixteenth-century *tombeau*,
with the purpose of creating a new poetic space for a trio of *poètes maudits*—
Poe, Baudelaire, and Verlaine—that he hoped might even reach beyond the
poets themselves.[79]

WHY DEAD POETS MATTER 67

A sonnet by Juan Gil-Albert (1937), which is dedicated to Lorca, evokes the Mallarméan idea, by combining fame and poetic community in his vision of Lorca's (missing) tomb from which "monsters flee in horror" (gesturing to Goya's *El sueño de la razón* [The Sleep of Reason]) and to which fame lays siege. Here, both "grief-stricken poets" and "the people" find comfort and even joy in what once was a wellspring of life. The shock of Lorca's death created a huge community of poets, in and beyond Spain, as Neruda suggested when he wrote, "we, the poets of Spanish America and the poets of Spain, will not forget and will never forgive [his] assassination . . . Never." He thought Lorca was "the greatest among us," occupying the place of angels. The poet's name, he said, was so "filled with significance" because it stood for "all those who fell defending the very substance of his song." The working-class English folk singer A. L. Lloyd, who joined the Communist Party around the same time as Neruda in the 1930s and translated Lorca's poetry, echoed the Chilean poet's words in a piece for the *Left Review*. Likewise, Machado's poem breathes with a similar democratic idealization of Lorca as the great man, that is, as man and poet, at once familiar and strange, in the one place any poet would die to get into: someone else's poetry.[80]

That community, however, is not necessarily immoveable or permanent, especially in the case of national poets, for whom, it appears, there is an expiration date. Does anyone still think of Zorrilla or Bécquer as national poets or as the symbol of poetry incarnate, whether Spanish or Andalusian? How quickly such images fade. Another question is what being a national poet meant. In 1883, the philologist-literary historian Marcelino Menéndez y Pelayo already believed the national poet an idea of the past. He saw the traditional singer of songs as closest to being one, because he was nearest to the people, "a solemn echo of the multitude who listened to him." "In an earlier period," he wrote, "there were national poets, singers of the folk, of religion, the first educators of the people." In contrast to the impersonality of the *cantor*, modern lyric poets who aspired to such standing could at most be considered civic, tempered as their poetry was by individual sentiment. He likened this kind of verse to the Italian tradition of *poesia civile*, a form of political poetry, with origins in Dante's *Commedia* and Petrarch's canzone "Italia mia," but reinvented and modernized in Foscolo, Leopardi, and others as a powerful personal expression of the Risorgimento movement. Even so, by the 1880s, for Menéndez y Pelayo, it was clear the poet was disappearing from the public sphere and those who remained—figures like Núñez de Arce and the earlier Quintana—saw the world "as a [Roman] arena or circus, filled with clamorous multitudes, upon whom they descend to test their athletic prowess."[81]

Although it is no longer fashionable to speak of Lorca as "the Poet" or as the people's poet (about which I have much more to say), claims of the Granadine writer's symbolic importance as the voice of the marginalized and oppressed, as the icon of Republican Spain, or as the symbol of the civil war dead, are still very much heard. These are updated versions of the Poet, tailored to fit the historical circumstances and emotional needs of twentieth- and twenty-first century Spain (and beyond). They feed into and blend two traditions, one ancient or at least premodern, to which Menéndez y Pelayo alluded, and the other far more recent, with roots in the nineteenth century and in the populist thinking of the left in 1930s Spain and Europe. In this context, Lorca can be considered as probably the last national poet of Spain, a civic presence echoing a much longer, contentious history of national issues of identity and consensus that continue to be worked out on the public stage. (Nor is Spain an exception in this instance, as the history and reception of France's Panthéon demonstrate.)

Nationalization of Lorca's iconic standing is, however, fraught. His afterlife has taken place in a rather noisy pantheon, in which family squabbles have often prevailed. By that I am not referring to the poet's own biological family, but to the larger national one in which Lorca occupies such a prominent place and to which his fame symbolically belongs. This national space of the dead among the living has much in common with Zorrilla's family pantheon in *Don Juan Tenorio*, for being grounded in deep and lasting antagonism and disconnected from Quinet's moral edifice that he called an inner pantheon. It reminds us as well of Mariano José de Larra's dark, conflictive vision of the two Spains killing each other off, in which he re-created Madrid as a vast cemetery, full of *hic jacet*s, "here lies," words that, in another context, would have strengthened the notion (and place) of a community of souls (arguably, Zorrilla's ideal space). Like the community of poets, this national space is situated among the dead, the same dead that Lorca once remarked were more alive in Spain than anywhere else. Only Lorca could have said that and meant it, because it issued from what I like to imagine were the unbounded recesses of the poet's own inner pantheon, his community among the dead.[82]

2. Lorca's Grave

In November 2009, the novelist-essayist Francisco Ayala died at the age of 103, and his ashes were buried in a biodegradable urn beneath a lemon tree at the Alcázar Genil de Granada Palace.[1] Federico García Lorca was thirty-eight when he was assassinated at the start of the Spanish Civil War in August 1936, and we do not know where his bones or his ashes are, although there is talk of an olive tree, a fountain, and a handful of gray earth. Both were from Granada and both supporters of the Second Republic. The ironies of these two deaths abound, with multiple possibilities for symbolic interpretation. But the killing of Lorca is not a postmodern phenomenon. It is a fact. A brutal fact, the product of the times, of savagery and malevolence all too sadly common.

At the same time, any commentary on his assassination must deal with the dual predicament created by his death, with the reality and the fiction of Lorca's wartime fate. His murder, along with his earthly remains, has been turned into something mythic, in which the meaning of history plays a large behind-the-scenes role. The search for Lorca's bones, which is ongoing, represents an effort to take possession of his myth and memory and to mold both to fit the desires of ideology and identity politics. More generally, the fate of Lorca and his remains compels us to further pursue what place poets have in the public arena—if indeed they do have one, given the modern view of poetry as a private matter.

It is Lorca's grave, or rather its absence, that interests me here, though we should bear in mind that, to extrapolate from Lorca's "Canción de jinete" (Rider's Song), no one ever makes it to Córdoba. "Ay, for death awaits me," wrote the poet, "before I get to Córdoba." His brother Francisco said, "for Federico dying is not arriving, because death surprises us always in the midst of our journey." We never get to Córdoba because we do not know what or where it is, in contrast to the Iraqi fable that Lorca appears to reinvent in the poem. A servant sees Death in Baghdad and runs to his master to beg for a horse and escape to Samarra. When the master inquires why Death threatened his servant, Death, dressed as a woman, replies: "I was surprised to see your servant there in Baghdad, because I have an appointment with him in Samarra." Samarra is the inevitable endpoint, the place of death, while Córdoba is an illusion, a not-arriving, from which, the poet says, death, alive in its towers, "keeps watch" on the rider. Death, then, is already a myth in Lorca's writings, and it is the *myth* we cannot escape. By this I am not referring to the cliché of Lorca's supposed premonition of his own death, but to a peculiar truth about the illusory character of death as being impossible to know. In this sense, the grave is always going to be empty.[2]

Not all readers may agree with this interpretation. Roland Grass asked, "Will the rider arrive at Cordoba? I think he will." And he concluded: "García Lorca, after all, did not write his poem for the dead." Franz Schneider took issue with his interpretation and summed up the poem as meaning "that a whole lifetime is not enough to ride to the next village." He also believed that "Rider's Song" presaged Lorca's own death, just as other critics have seen, or wanted to see, the poet's work as, in this sense, oracular. This is an immensely enigmatic poem, capable of sustaining all kinds of readings, though to say the rider will reach Córdoba is not, I believe, supported textually or aesthetically. His arrival would have deflated all the mystery of the poem. Grass's other comment, however, gave me pause. How do we know Lorca isn't writing for the dead?[3]

And if he is, maybe Schneider and others are not so far off course, not in the biographical sense but in the sense that all writing issues from a future grave and the ultimately unsayable nature of the poet's posthumous status and meaning. "Rider's Song," like other Lorca works, suggests that the spark of writing and all creativity, what he called *duende*, comes with an awareness of death surrounding us, that death is a precondition of poetry. Duende, Lorca said, "likes the rim of the well," defying catastrophe. Perhaps this is why, in its struggle with death, the poem, like the rider himself, hurls itself toward the future, which is a way of saying toward a poem that may never arrive, or may never get written. The point is, like the rider, the poem is bent on taking that risk.[4]

The future-directedness of this poem also links it to the augur, the priest in ancient Rome who read signs to understand the will of the gods and by extension predict what was to come. Portent is everywhere in "Rider's Song," just as it is in poems such as "Romance de la luna, luna" (Ballad of the Moon Moon) from *Gypsy Ballads*. But what do the signs mean? How do we read the black pony, the big moon (a red moon, in the next stanza), or the olives in the rider's saddlebag, when Lorca writes: "Jaca negra, luna grande, / y aceitunas en mi alforja?" Or "Córdoba / Distant and lonely" ("Córdoba. / Lejana y sola")? The poetic style is elliptic, as though the poet can only point to the objects in question, in this way intimating unspoken meanings in a universe still to be deciphered. Symbolism alone does not explain this kind of poetry, which is rooted in something far more primal, in a relationship between the human and nonhuman that we have largely erased.[5]

Like the practices of other early cultures, the augur's method was to look to the birds, as they swooped and sang, and read the signs therein. "How the nightjar sings! / How it sings in the tree!" Lorca wrote in "Ballad of the Moon Moon," two of his most haunting lines in the original Spanish: "Cómo canta la zumaya / ¡ay, cómo canta en el árbol!" I fell in love with Lorca's work when I read these verses for the first time. The sound alone is a winged word, the repeated vowel an *a* opening into flight. And look how the hard *c* of "cómo canta" trembles when spoken, even before we have the slightest idea of what it means or whether we can know what it means. The lines hover in mystery, like the nightjar in the tree.[6]

As with Córdoba's towers and the red moon in "Rider's Song," the *zumaya* is a portent of perplexity, because we have not fathomed its song. Similarly, the little boy's fate in the ballad is rich with uncertainty, forever open to interpretation. Is he asleep or dead? Where does the moon take him? In the ancient world, contact with the gods was prerequisite, without which the augury could not be completed. In "Rider's Song," the poetic voice tells us what will happen, but the paradox remains: we do not see the action completed. The rider is forever arriving. Have we or the rider really understood the signs? And where are the gods in all this? You could also say that if death is a not arriving in this poem, correspondingly, life is a never finishing, confirming Schneider's view. The poem is an empty grave.

This view of death as illusory, of the poet's death in particular, will never satisfy those for whom the quest for Lorca's missing bones is in psychic terms the desired reincarnation of the person he once was or at least the re-animation of a symbol that is both uncertain and overdetermined in its meaning. The quixotic search-and-rescue effort has consumed Lorca's biographer Ian Gibson. Lorca's family does not see it that way and prefers to leave the poet where he is, somewhere outside the city of Granada, with the other victims of civil war madness. The desire to dignify death is universal; the manner of implementing that desire is not. Hence the decision to bury the ashes of Francisco Ayala in a biodegradable urn beneath a lemon tree, with the idea that they will leave no trace, will disappear little by little as the ashes are gathered into the breast of the earth.

There is, however, nothing natural in our view of human death. Despite all efforts to accept the inevitability of our biological demise, we resist it by marking our disappearance. We leave signs, and those signs of death's singular artifice are found in the biodegradable urn, Gibson's obsessive search, the countless homage texts to Lorca, and my own words. Here, I return for further comment to Philip Levine's poem "The Search for Lorca's Shadow":

> Forgive the ants, they are merely ants,
> though they are alive and he is not,
> though they would surely eat him if they could,
> if in fact anything were left to eat—
> the bones are here as clean as porcelain,
> for the earth has long ago eaten all
> there was to eat.[7]

Lorca may seem to have disappeared, but the earth has not yet devoured the bones of this poem.

Levine begins his poem by saying: "I've seen the hillside. A soft wind moved / through the leaves of the olive trees." The opening is like a long shot in a film, after which he focuses on the physical qualities of the earth, its color, texture and occupants—metallic gray, with loamy dust, and ants. In ten lines the I/eye of his camera goes from long shot to close-up, from the hillside to the earth to the ants, in this way stressing the importance of perspective in the poem. The distance covered in space runs parallel with the distance covered in time, reminding us of the now considerable temporal gap between

1936 and 1998, when "The Search for Lorca's Shadow" was first published. He writes,

> The ants come and go
> doing their dull work. They are alive,
> they are going about the business
> of their lives, building their dwellings,
> providing, eating as best they can.
> They do not remember the victim.
> They did not even know his name.

Nature, as I noted earlier, is indifferent to Lorca's death. Several lines later, the poet asks us to forgive the ants, though it is not clear to whom Levine addresses these lines, given the cosmic irony conveyed. This is not to say the poem lacks feeling.[8]

Indeed, when Levine talks about Lorca himself, "his dark hair fallen across one eye, / his rages and jealousies," he brings the poet to life. In one of the loveliest details, he speaks of his body

> clothed in worn cotton garments sewn by hand.
> (Were he alive he could look carefully
> at the bloodstained shirt, count the stitches
> that attached the cuffs, and tell you, "No,
> that is not the work of my grandmother.")

These lines recall the way Nora in J. M. Synge's *Riders to the Sea* recognizes the stocking of her drowned brother Michael by the stitches: "It's the second one of the third pair I knitted, and I put up threescore stitches, and I dropped four of them." In both these works, we recognize the importance and specificity of such a small thing as a stitch because the stitch has so many unspoken things sewn into it: the love with which the garment is made, the loss that the ruined clothing entails, the living creature that once inhabited the stocking, the shirt. The deep connection with family and with the domestic labor memorized by the body's loss. The stitches that count the loss. While Nora makes the identification certain—it comes stitched to grief—in Levine's poem, Lorca appears to reject the identification, as though he were in denial over his own demise.[9]

Despite the reference to Lorca's rages and jealousies, the poem itself does not rail against the fate of the poet. And that is of interest, because Lorca's work had such a tremendous impact on Levine after discovering *Poet in New York* in the early 1950s. He asked, "how had [Lorca] mastered the language of my rage?" Reading Lorca was like being in the eye of a storm, the storm of chaos. The Granadine poet gave him "a validation of [his] own emotions." But in "The Search for Lorca's Shadow," fury and passion are useless, so you must forgive the ants. When I first read Levine's poem, I was not aware of his initial—and as it turns out, enduring—reaction to Lorca's poetry. Perhaps I was wrong, and there really is rage in the poem, but if so, it is sifted through the self-evident injustice of the poet's death, in the silence of the crime's witnesses that Levine mentions at the end of the poem. In any event, the American writer stages Lorca's earthly disappearance within two worlds, the natural one of soil, dust, and ants and the unnatural one of poetry (and, by implication, that of history). Forgiving the ants connects all worlds, while placing Lorca's unnatural death into the vanishing point of natural destruction.[10]

The bodies of other poets have also disappeared, though doubtless not so dramatically as Lorca's, a subject I explored in relation to the pantheonization of the dead. Cervantes's remains, for example, were only recently recuperated, having been lost in the very church in which he had been buried. He was identified in part by the initials on his coffin. It was not possible to do DNA testing, but the presence of a crippled left arm and ribs still showing the signs of bullet wounds from the battle of Lepanto convinced investigators this was their man. They apparently did not find his backbone, stooped over with degenerative joint disease, or the skull sporting a total of six teeth. As with Lorca, there was some controversy over disturbing his remains, though it was much more muted in Cervantes's case. The novelist Juan Goytisolo, for one, thought it best to leave him moldering in peace.[11]

It is worth noting here another instance of a lost body for its connection to the Granadine writer: one of the most brilliant poets of the Baroque age, Francisco de Quevedo. In 1639, after having attacked the king's favorite, the Conde-Duque de Olivares, Quevedo was imprisoned in the cold, dank bowels of the Convento de San Marcos in León (now an elegant state-run *parador*, or hotel, once a Francoist concentration camp), tormented daily by the proximity of the convent's constant bell ringing. Released after four years and in failing health, he died in 1645 and was buried in the Bustos family chapel of the church of San Andrés in Villanueva de los Infantes, despite his wish to be laid to rest in the Santo Domingo el Real church in Madrid.

In 1869, his remains were transferred to the short-lived National Pantheon in the capital, then returned, it is believed, sometime between 1888 and 1900. With it was a note saying that this was probably not Quevedo, because the subject had all his teeth and the skull looked female. Meanwhile, a black box with human remains designated as those of Quevedo showed up in 1920, so the local government in Villanueva held a proper burial ceremony but marked the spot as "Quevedo's apocryphal tomb." In 1955, it was discovered through excavation that the poet's remains had been transferred sometime during the eighteenth century from the Bustos family crypt to another one, along with 167 other bodies all jumbled together. Finally, forensic experts managed to identify parts of Quevedo, and he was reburied in May of 2007 in Villanueva. That begs the question, who on earth did they dig up in the nineteenth century?[12]

Quevedo's posthumous travails appear cut from the poet's own ironic imagination, a cadaverous journey mirroring in reverse the vagaries of the picaresque life that his own mordant tongue had dissected. Was Lorca aware of the seventeenth-century poet's zigzagging path through death? We do know that near the end of his life, Lorca gave an interview in which he spoke of Quevedo and how he planned to give a lecture on the poet during his trip to Mexico, the trip he would never make. He said: "My acquaintance with Quevedo dates back a few years. It was a melancholy rapprochement. In a journey through la Mancha, I stopped at the town of Infantes. The town plaza, deserted. The Tower of Juan Abad. And very close by, a gloomy church . . . Uneasy, I entered. And there was Quevedo, alone, entombed, perpetuating the injustice of his death. It seemed to me as if I had just been at his funeral." For Lorca, "Quevedo [was] Spain," a sentiment that others would apply to Lorca himself.[13]

Neruda also recounted this incident, stressing how strongly affected Lorca was, on seeing the great poet "lying there forever forgotten, in a forgotten church of a forgotten town." Clearly, mortality and fame had to be in the minds of Lorca and Neruda. Both moderns marked Quevedo's exit from life as something worth remembering, and in Lorca's case, as something personal, as though he *knew* him. He also saw his death as, in some sense, not natural, provoked by the unfortunate circumstances of his imprisonment. Ironically, forty years after Neruda's own death in 1973, his body was exhumed, following the accusation from his chauffeur and members of the Chilean Communist Party, to which the poet belonged, that he had been murdered by the Pinochet dictatorship in the wake of the coup against Allende.[14]

After a three-year forensic examination, experts concluded in 2017 that the poet, suffering from prostate cancer, did not die from the disease but from some other cause of a suspicious nature. They stopped short of saying the Pinochet regime poisoned him but noted the presence of an unexplained toxin. In 2013, however, investigators thought that he had indeed died of cancer. Meanwhile, Neruda was reburied (for the fourth time), and the forensic analysis continued. I suspect that, no matter the conclusions of experts, some will never accept the results, or the results will prove inconclusive, provoking skepticism and suspicion over a death mired in political and ideological strife.[15]

Lorca's real death was not natural either, nor was the repeated death inflicted on him symbolically and poetically. The poet has died countless times in poems, novels, history books, plays, films, and documentaries, and even online. In dying over and over he is also continually resurrected as if to say, oh well, what's one more death after all. On occasion, one recalls, he doesn't die at all, as in the novel *The Prodigious Light,* in which Fernando Marías imagined a wounded poet who cannot remember who he once was, or in a poem by Francisco Alarcón titled "The Other Day I Ran into García Lorca." In *The Ingenious Gentleman and Poet Federico García Lorca Ascends to Hell,* Carlos Rojas created an eternally dead—and thus alive—poet tormented by his memories and wandering "in the interminable wakefulness of [his] own death." And the playwright Nilo Cruz conceived various Lorcas, among them, Lorca as a Woman (played by a woman) and Lorca in a Green Dress (played by a man), in a waiting room called purgatory. Can there be anything original left to his death, to an understanding of it? His death is not simply an historical fact. It has proved to be a myth of great usefulness to those with an ideological agenda or those committed to identity politics. Lorca's multiple *exeunts* have made him even more of a public figure than he was in life, albeit a spectral one.[16]

The attempted exhumation of his remains turned into a colossal flop in the fall of 2009. Even so, there have been subsequent forensic forays since 2014, all of them failures. In one of the latest, investigators once again found nothing, but suggested, without any hard evidence, that the body could have been removed shortly after the poet's execution. The first crack at finding Lorca in 2009 appeared to be at once an effort at historical recovery and the kind of performance that for the poet's family always threatens to become a media circus. By sheer coincidence, the same day Ayala died in Madrid

(3 November), Gibson, who had gone with the director Juan Sella to document the physical destruction of the fertile plain called the Vega in Granada, found himself with the film crew at Fuente Grande, very near the excavation. He got swept into the spectacle when he was urged to check out the site, even though some plainly did not want him there. Gibson's keen desire to find Lorca's remains struggled with his sense of the unseemly.[17]

We know all this because he kept a diary, which he later published (more on the diary shortly). There is a rich irony of contrast between the great Republican exile Ayala's definitive death and the provisional status of Lorca's body, the scene of a continually dramatized death, as enacted in Gibson's encounter at Fuente Grande. The problem with Lorca is that he never stops dying and is repeatedly resuscitated as a political-cultural artifact in the unceasing struggle to possess his memory and myth. To paraphrase the former socialist prime minister of Spain, José Luis Rodríguez Zapatero, when asked if there was in fact an economic crisis, it seems to be "a matter of opinion if there is or is not a death" in the case of Lorca; such is the impoverishing effect of postmodernizing him.[18]

As an artifact, the poet has ended up symbolizing a variety of causes, ideas, and identities, from the Second Republic to the Spanish Transition toward democracy, from Republican trauma and victimhood to national reconciliation, from gypsyhood and southern Andalusianism to gay rights. This ability to represent different things to different people appears paradoxical, given Lorca's uniqueness, the incessantly stressed unrepeatable character of his personality and writing. As Jorge Marí observes, one of the latest reinventions of the poet identifies him as the "emblem of democratic Spain and foundational myth of the current-day autonomous Andalusia," although it seems to me that the roots of this symbol go back to the moment of Lorca's death, if not before, with the publication of *Gypsy Ballads* in 1928.[19]

The Statute of Andalusian Autonomy, approved in 2007, barely defines Andalusian identity, alluding to its "singular character" as "an essential part of Spain," one of pluralism and *mestizaje* (racial mixing), with the creation of an "Andalusian personality" fabricated on universal values. As Marí points out, it all boils down to the idea that the more Andalusian you are, the more universal, a formula no doubt taken from Lorca himself when he talked about "the truth, Andalusian and universal." One is reminded of the self-consciously bicultural William Carlos Williams's pithy phrase, "the local is the universal," borrowed in turn from John Dewey, who said "the locality is the only universal." For Dewey, the local wasn't provincial, it was "just local, just human, just at home, just where they live." Ironically, the minute you attach it to something universal, you turn the local into something else, whereby it assumes the archetypal.[20]

Couched in another way, maybe it is not so paradoxical that Lorca's unrepeatable individuality should serve a representative purpose. It is worth recalling what Thomas Carlyle and Ralph Waldo Emerson said about "representative men" and the "uses of great men" or "heroes," to try to understand the uses made of the poet and of his death. The nineteenth-century category of the great man or hero may very well not fit Lorca, but on the other hand, it seems to me that many of the master narratives of the poet aim to place him within an exceptional or extraordinary frame. For example, despite being a victim like thousands and thousands of other Spaniards during the civil war, he is *the* victim above all others. He is the deadest of the dead, or the most alive dead man you'll ever see, in a "country open to death." That exceptionality also recalls the fabricated account of his execution, which gained wide circulation in Spain and beyond, depicting Lorca in a heroic death march, even speaking to his executioners of "the people's Cause" before being gunned down. Like the great man, he is notable for his singularity, though one rarely hears of his excesses and insufficiencies.[21]

Emerson maintained that we recognize great men at once: "They satisfy expectation, and fall into place." Great men both stimulate and liberate us. At the same time, the essayist described them as representative, saying that "Men have a pictorial or representative quality . . . things were representative. Men are also representative; first, of things, and secondly, of ideas." The fascinating thing about this essay from 1850 is how Emerson, after idealizing the figure of the great man, bit by bit begins to whittle away at the image and ends up partly undermining his initial opinion.[22] The turning point is the moment when he says: "We are tendencies, or rather, symptoms and none of us complete." Then: "We swim, day by day, on a river of delusions." These notions, which underline our incomplete, illusory character, thus indirectly suggesting the necessity of the great man in order to feel complete and to feed our illusions, allow Emerson to introduce the idea of the "excess of influence of the great man." He writes: "His attractions warp us from our place. . . . We cloy of the honey of each peculiar greatness. Every hero becomes a bore at last. . . . There is . . . a speedy limit to the use of heroes. . . . The more we are drawn, the more we are repelled. There is something not solid in the good that is done for us. The best discovery the discoverer makes for himself." His Socratic conclusion is also classically American, because Emerson uses the great man as a way of defending the individual, stressing "the law of individuality": "Nothing is more marked than the power by which individuals are guarded from individuals."[23]

But the essay does not end there. Emerson returns to the great man because something of the figure remains, though diffuse, and that something is his effect. Perhaps for this reason Emerson writes in one of his most suggestive passages: "Once you saw phoenixes: they are gone; the world is not therefore disenchanted. The vessels on which you read sacred emblems turn out to be common pottery; but the sense of the pictures is sacred, and you may still read them transferred to the walls of the world." Was he remembering what his friend Carlyle had said some ten years earlier about Shakespeare? "For myself, I feel that there is actually a kind of sacredness in the fact of such a man being sent into this Earth."[24]

The great man's effect that Emerson talked about can be imagined as the wake (in both senses) of his death, the death, real or imagined or both things at once, of the great man or hero. Or of Lorca. I think it helps to link Lorca to the idea of the poet's trace—the empty grave—and the sense of his life's trajectory as something sacred, even if the person he once was is not, and his actual death a dismal fact. One early report referred to his murder as "an instant, sacramental drama" and the poet as "transcendent." The Lorca effect has always been felt as a kind of death, because everything that the poet is, is posthumous, as Kierkegaard once observed.[25] Lorca himself understood it in these terms and in his poetic capacity mythified the living illusion that death is in "Rider's Song" and other works. Death is a future filled with the past.

This effect has nothing to do with his possible usefulness to the reader, critic, or historian. Speaking of Dante and reflecting the Romantic spirit of his age, Carlyle writes: "The uses of this Dante? We will not say much about his 'uses.' A human soul who has once got into that primal element of *Song* . . . has worked in the *depths* of our existence; feeding through long times the life-*roots* of all excellent human things whatsoever,—in a way that 'utilities' will not succeed well in calculating!" The limits of the utilitarian, of the poet's or hero's uses, are on display in the efforts to exploit Lorca symbolically and ideologically, thereby losing what really matters with Lorca: the song, depths, and life-roots of poetic experience as the expression of the human condition. Tellingly, another member of what is now known in literary history as the Generation of 1927, José Bergamín, linked Carlyle's song to the Andalusian *cante jondo,* or deep song, and more broadly, to all poetry, which is the living spirit or word.[26]

The obsession with usefully situating Lorca in his proper place, or with his death, ends up burying him once more. You could say that the poet has been a victim, not once but twice: the first time is well known, but the second has occurred through a certain kind of exploitation that makes Lorca a pedagogical poster child, with a multitude of political and ideological meanings and identities. This impoverished view of the poet has also influenced how the circumstances of his death and his place in history have been understood. *El balcón abierto* (The Open Balcony) (dir. Jaime Camino, 1984), one of several documentaries on the writer, begins and ends in a classroom full of adolescents. We first see them selecting photos on the life and death of Lorca for a bulletin board and then, in the closing frames, looking at this same documentary and asking, "Why did they kill him?" The civic, educational impulse behind such efforts reminds us of a similar motivation that informed the nineteenth-century monumentalizing of great men, as illustrated in the National Pantheon of 1869.

Others bury Lorca under a pile of clichés. "Lorca is all the dead, and all the dead are Lorca." "We are all Lorca." Were his remains found, the poet "could become the greatest symbol of the long-awaited reconciliation of Spaniards." The writer's death can also serve as a "project that will give some kind of individual and collective relief." Lorca's missing body becomes part of a national "grieving process," essential "to working through trauma and elaborating a mourning process." A columnist claims, "Opening the grave sit[e] is therapeutic." And another says that until Lorca is found, "there is no modernity possible, or dignity, justice and atonement" for Spain. Declarations of this kind appear to harbor no doubts, and perhaps for this reason, paradoxically end up detaching us from the historical gravity of sites like the mass graves at Víznar, where a monolith engraved with "They were all Lorca" was raised in 2002 to remember what no words can say.[27]

These examples (and there are many), found in the press and even in scholarly articles, are intrinsically utilitarian. Such sentiments diminish Lorca as a person and a poet, making him the agent of someone else's desires or motives. They tell us much more about the people expressing them than about Lorca himself, who is turned into the vehicle for a political or ideological agenda. Examining the reception of Lorca in life and death, his inevitable transformation into a political and allegorical object, is certainly worthwhile, but no writer can withstand the heavy burden of significance that Lorca has been made to carry.

At the very least it seems naïve to believe that the bones of the poet can lead to national reconciliation or transcend the trauma of civil war. If, as Ángel Loureiro observes, it is true that "the dead resist leaving us" because they are so much a part of our identity and memory, it is also true that death puts us in our place, the place of oblivion.[28] More to the point, not everyone shares the same identity and memory. In the case of the Spanish Civil War, what hasn't always been sufficiently considered is the existence of different memory communities whose individual and collective values, beliefs, and experiences vary considerably and are often resistant to the smoothing out of ideological differences and the conflicting demands of historical reality. How can Lorca represent all Spaniards? Or all the dead? What does that mean?

From the moment of his death there was a struggle to take possession of his memory. In 1936 the idea of reconciliation or moving beyond trauma in the case of Lorca would have been inconceivable, above all because the pain of his loss was so real and immediate.[29] To speak of trauma or grief at this point in time, however, is of necessity unconvincing, inauthentic, not because the trauma and pain didn't exist but because we are now reduced to talking about the cultural mediation of mourning and trauma. Cultural critics tend to postmodernize grief and trauma, transforming them into a kind of simulacrum of what they are or once were. So, for example, in an otherwise suggestive article, Melissa Dinverno speaks of exhuming García Lorca "as a technology of memory—a mediatory space for the production of cultural memory, a site by which people articulate a relationship to the past."[30] At heart, it is assumed that cultural studies must necessarily be postmodern. What then is the role of history? Is history postmodern? That seems highly unlikely.

The assassination of Lorca (and so many others) was a vile, horrifying act. We risk trivializing, domesticating his death when it is subjected to a preestablished model like trauma theory. Appearing to transcend historical realities and the stupidity of human malevolence, such explanations, while ingenious in stressing the uncommunicable and sinister element of trauma, ironically end up communicating it. These are therapies to cure us of the damaging effects of history. Equally prefabricated is the vision of a Lorca teleologically marked by death.[31] None of this explains evil and violence, nor does it illuminate the figure of Lorca. On the contrary, these kinds of schema create yet another predigestible stereotype of the poet as victim.

Such uses of Lorca and his death serve rather to reaffirm the ideological posture or identity politics of the critic, a posture that is at heart moral, if not moralizing, in line with the current historical revisionism of the Spanish Civil War—of history as grievance, as Loureiro has argued.[32] Partisan politics has had a corrosive effect on the historical and cultural understanding of the civil war, not to mention the social fabric and civic community. A similarly narrow vision has cemented the iconic status of Lorca as an object of kitsch, like the angelic, adolescent image into which the painter Gregorio Prieto transformed him. Expressed another way, our age does not seem to know what to do with Lorca, bowing to the default mode, which is to make him accessible, domesticated symbolically and politically.

But neither did his own time. There is a tendency to idealize the period, emphasizing the aesthetic promise of the 1920s (Dalí, Picasso, Lorca, Rafael Alberti, Luis Cernuda, etc.) and the political promise of the Second Republic. José Moreno Villa, for example, recalled the era, and above all, the lively atmosphere of the Residencia de Estudiantes where so many artists, intellectuals, and writers congregated, as idyllic and full of youthfulness. Another prominent contemporary, Dámaso Alonso, faulted radical politicization for ruining what he perceived as an Edenic, conflict-free period of literary brilliance in the early 1920s, seemingly having forgotten the Primo de Rivera dictatorship (it should also be remembered that his remarks were published in 1948, under the ideological censorship of the Franco regime).[33]

Given the devastating losses of this period, it is not surprising that nostalgia has smoothed over imperfections and, in some cases, even depoliticized events. The partiality with which this timeframe is often viewed also occludes its contradictions, conflicts, insufficiencies, and insoluble problems. More fundamentally, it blinds us to the limitations and dangers of the idea of human perfectibility that was the basis for some of the more radical political thinking of the 1930s, thinking that tended to lead to a dystopian absolutism seen on both sides of the Spanish conflict. Few succeeded in escaping the straitjacket of ideology. The chaotic polarization and exclusivism of Lorca's time have trapped his image in a kind of stagnant catchment, where he is always the dying victim.

It is helpful to recall here what Carlyle said about three literary figures, Dr. Johnson, Jean-Jacques Rousseau, and Robert Burns, and their relation to the eighteenth century. For the essayist, these three represented the hero as the Man of Letters. Unlike Dante and Shakespeare, who illustrated the Poet as hero, they did not bring but sought the light, largely because the age in which they lived was one of skepticism, which for Carlyle signified "a chronic atrophy and disease of the whole soul." He also wrote: "They lived under galling conditions; struggling as under mountains of impediment, and could not unfold themselves into clearness, or victorious interpretation of that 'Divine Idea.' It is rather the *Tombs* of three Literary Heroes that I have to show you. There are the monumental heaps, under which three spiritual giants lie buried. Very mournful, but also great and full of interest for us." From those mountains of impediment, he singled out "that waste chaos of Scepticism in religion and politics, in life-theory and life-practice." Metaphorically, his own era heaped earth, the detritus of the age, on all three. By contrast, Carlyle never speaks of the tombs of Dante and Shakespeare.[34]

The deterioration, or disease of the soul, that Carlyle already saw in the eighteenth century, reached its nadir in the twentieth, something that Lorca imagined poetically as "water that goes nowhere" and "the eyes of statues [that] suffer the darkness of coffins." The poem from which these lines are taken is ostensibly about a girl drowned in a well, but it is set within the larger context of *Poet in New York,* which like the essayist's funereal image, was produced in a moment of waste chaos, of detritus, and disarray. Part of what makes the poem so striking, beyond the originality of its imagery, lies in the incongruity between the title and what follows. In calling his poem "Niña ahogada en el pozo" (Little Girl Drowned in the Well), Lorca evoked the kind of nineteenth-century poetry written to commemorate the deaths of children, their lives and promise cut short.[35]

The *corona poética,* or poetic homage, was a product of largely middle-class culture, expressed in the form of albums and other publications, such as the one that the liberal politician and entrepreneur Pascual Madoz paid for after his eight-year-old daughter drowned in the sea. Almost none of this poetry was memorable, since it was often composed by stringing together a series of clichés, as a favor to the grieving family. In this now obsolete genre, there were noteworthy exceptions. Carolina Coronado's brief and unadorned poem, which appeared in the Madoz publication, is titled "Tú pensaste que el mar era tu cuna" (You Thought the Sea was Your Cradle), and works off the cradle-to-the-grave conceit, but with a mournful, ironic twist: the little girl's cradle is now her grave. She sleeps "in tranquility," spared life's tears by drowning in the sea. Coronado reprinted the poem in the second edition of her *Poesías* (1852), when she added a depersonalizing note: "In a poetic album for a little girl who drowned in the sea."[36]

Lorca had a predilection for the faded artifacts of nineteenth-century culture, which he used to great effect in his play, *Doña Rosita la soltera, o El lenguaje de las flores* (Doña Rosita the Spinster, or, The Language of Flowers) (1935). All the objects of *cursilería*, of endearingly bad taste in the play, wither under the passage of time, in the same way the protagonist finds herself out of step in a modern world of alienating, programmed obsolescence. "Little Girl Drowned in the Well" is a modern reversal of the earlier period's mostly saccharine verses, meant to comfort family loss, because Lorca's poem offers no comfort at all, only anguish and a form of poetic paralysis. Not the swift currents of the sea, but the stagnant water of a well. In contrast to Madoz's daughter, the little girl is a fiction, suggesting that this poem isn't so much about a drowned child as a drowned existence symbolic of a culture that has lost its soul.

The poem is beautifully deceptive. The girl's voice says she is "tranquil in my memory, a star, circle, destiny." "Tranquil in my memory" ("tranquila en mi recuerdo") evokes Wordsworth's notion of poetry originating in "emotion recollected in tranquillity." The rounded images in the poem—a circle, ring, eye—appear to speak of perfection, eternity, thus buttressing the presence of tranquility, but do they here? The rest of the stanza suggests the contrary: "you weep by the shores of a horse's eye. / . . . that goes nowhere." The mantra—"[water] that goes nowhere"—is repeated at the end of every stanza. "Desembocar," the verb Lorca uses for this water, means to debouch, to emerge or issue, but it is also part of a set phrase, "desembocó en una tragedia" / "it ended in tragedy," to indicate resolution.[37]

The irony is that there is tragedy but no resolution, no catharsis, in Lorca's poem. The lyrical voice says to the dead girl, "you shudder forever, defined by your ring / that goes nowhere." Here is the paradox of death: it defines, as in a perfect circle, and is seemingly alive, but never debouches; it never reaches its destination. Death is stuck in the poem, as is the soul of the poor dead girl, as is the world that contains her. Death is a not arriving in this poem, just as it is in "Rider's Song." The last stanza reads:

> No, that goes nowhere. Water stuck on one point.
> Breathing unstrung with all its violins.

On a scale of wounds and empty buildings.
Water that goes nowhere!

While the poem can easily be imagined as a reflection of Lorca's alienated, tormented self, it says far more about a hollowing out of soul and society, as does *Poet in New York* overall, in the merging of private and public registers. The water doesn't sing, its pitch wounded, and emptiness prevails, as the image of deserted buildings intimates.[38]

Most significantly for my purposes, the water does not give up its dead, despite the townspeople's cries and the command to "rise from the water!" "But the well reaches out to you with small mossy hands," Lorca writes. He likens the little girl to an undine, or water nymph, who in the legend loses her immortality when she falls in love with a mortal. This undine, I would suggest, loses her soul, the self trapped in the stagnant circle of still water, burdened with a death that refuses to give her up but also struggles to surpass its own limitations. Like the little girl, death itself appears to yearn for liberation, to reach its terminus, which I take not only as Lorca's rewriting of Jorge Manrique's image of life as a river that ends in the sea, but the expression of an afflicted age in which "every point of light will leave you in chains."[39]

Speaking of Samuel Johnson, Carlyle said that "his time is bad," hence his desperate efforts to be genuine.[40] The essayist suggested that none of these writers achieved authenticity because they were in some sense beaten by their own time. We are reduced to studying their tombs, their valiant defeat, that which remains after the mortal fray. Something of this tremendous struggle against mountains of impediment can be glimpsed in the personal and historical circumstances of Lorca's work, his life and death. It may be less the skepticism that Carlyle perceived in the Age of Enlightenment than the waste, the remains of the eighteenth that have rivered their way into the futile confusion and extremism of our time.

The mythification of Lorca after his death is not surprising, for it is the result of the poet being transformed into his own grave. Metaphorically, he has become his own tomb. The insufficiencies and exhaustion of the present era have created a hunger for empty graves to be filled with some sort of transcendent meaning. Marx (Groucho, not Karl) was said to have remarked: "What should I care about posterity? What's posterity ever done for me?" thus comically emphasizing the fundamental irony of a posterity that only other people can enjoy. Lorca's transformation into the child of posterity began shortly after his assassination, a posthumous image that served an array of political and ideological purposes in the struggle to take possession of his myth.

Take, for example, the article by pro-Republican Antonio Sánchez Barbudo titled "La muerte de García Lorca comentada por sus asesinos" (The Death of García Lorca as Commented by his Assassins), which appeared in the celebrated wartime journal *Hora de España*. It is a commentary on another article, "A la España imperial le han asesinado su mejor poeta" (Imperial Spain's Best Poet Assassinated), published in the Falangist newspaper *Unidad*. For Sánchez Barbudo there were not enough words to denounce what was doubtless an absurd declaration by Luis Hurtado, that Lorca would have been the ideal poetic representative of Falangism.

Sánchez Barbudo called the piece "trashy and heavy-handed"; the author, one of those "pitiable writers, vile 'flatterers' of Franco"; and the style, "pompous, hollow, pathetically overblown" with "grandiloquent rhetoric, that masks a pedantic, coarse attitude," that seeks to be "signorial" but is only "tacky and dimwitted." To his indignation, Hurtado appropriated a line of verse from the poet Antonio Machado, "the crime was in Granada," a phrase, we recall, that also appeared in Republican poetic homages to Lorca: "This cannot be simply coincidence. The moment chosen and the tone employed leave no doubt: the line is from Antonio Machado and precisely from the deeply felt, beautiful poem dedicated to Federico on hearing of his death. His is a lament, a curse on his assassins; but the assassins have taken these words filled with authentic grief, this line from the celebrated poet, and they've used it without shame. Because they now need the pretense of grief to make people think of them as good and kind. But their crocodile tears don't fool us, they don't fool anybody." Sánchez Barbudo's infuriated tone makes it clear to whom or which side the memory of Federico García Lorca belonged.[41]

In May 1937 the passion and anguish over the death of the poet bled through the supercharged words and heightened emotion. Even so, the possessive note struck is palpable. The mere idea of a Falangist claim that Lorca would have shared the same sentiments drove Sánchez Barbudo crazy. Apart from there being no historical evidence pointing to the poet's Falangist politics, it seems to me that Sánchez Barbudo, in his defense of Lorca, in some ways unintentionally ended up once more extinguishing the life of the poet. His fury against the columnist was unable to move beyond the incivility of his time, as seen in these concluding remarks: "Those of us who truly mourn the poet's death, his friends, companions and disciples, the very people of Spain, those of us who truly desire Fatherland, Bread, and Justice for all, are well aware what crimes, what offenses, we can expect from that Falange, that Army, and that black Spain, with all its gaudy trappings, which assassinated Federico García Lorca." Here is not the place to review the undeniable brutalities to which Sánchez Barbudo alluded, or the accusations of criminality hurled against both sides. The withering, embittered tone in the middle of this waste chaos, the cry of despair, that permeated his prose, once again buried Lorca in the bone yard of time. Ultimately, this is less about the figure of the poet and more about reclaiming and possessing him.[42]

The process of mythifying Lorca intensified during the war. Like Sánchez Barbudo, Antonio Machado remembered the man of flesh and blood, though he already hinted at seeing him in an allegorizing mode, as achieved in his celebrated poem, but also visible in these words included in a wartime Republican propaganda pamphlet: "With the murder of Lorca Fascism has committed its most stupid, most abominable crime. García Lorca lived on the fringe of politics, but inside the real soul of the people."[43] Lorca as the voice, or soul, of the people almost immediately became a cliché, especially on the left, as I further explore in relation to the poet as a socially privileged señorito elsewhere in this book. The identity of the people is never defined here (as it is not in the later Statute of Andalusian Autonomy), in large part because the specific audience that the text addresses has already claimed it as theirs, ignoring the reality that not everyone viewed the concept of the people in the same way. Or that the mythification of the people, which is part of the Lorca myth, might engender not consensus but a conceivably insoluble problem, in not paying adequate attention to the complex and multiple constituencies that make up the people.

Similarly, from Latin America, José González Carbalho, the son of Galician emigrants and a friend of the poet, wrote in 1938, in *Vida, obra y muerte de Federico García Lorca* (The Life, Work, and Death of Federico García Lorca), that the poet represented "the finest of the soul and intelligence of the people," without explaining what that meant exactly. It would not be worth our while to examine more closely these worn-out images except that they remain in force today (as in turning everybody into Lorca), in part because they have become attached to another deep-rooted cliché: Lorca as a Republican martyr, a trope that appeared the moment his death was confirmed (and in at least one instance, even before). Indeed, claims that a refashioned image of the poet as a "luminous Christ-like figure nurturing the soil of Spain with his blood" is a feature of 1980s Spain fail to consider that this vision of Lorca had already saturated writings in the late 1930s, 1940s, and later. In this sense, there is nothing new, for example, in flanking the sacrificial figure of Lorca with two other victims as he walks to his death, in imitation of Christ and the two thieves, as Juan Antonio Bardem did in his film *Lorca, muerte de un poeta* (Lorca, Death of a Poet) (1987).[44]

Curiously, González Carbalho has said that the poet's death, "unhappily certain, has something of the phantom about it." This ghost is not the Freudian return of the repressed, as is sometimes applied to the repercussions of civil war, but the historical awareness of his missing body and of the Lorca effect, that wake of reverberation which has been observed so many times but especially in the immediate aftermath of his death. Then, as if it were of importance to counteract the ghostly with something more solid, he wrote that "above all, there is his death, which should be remembered more than his own work, because his death is the terrible document of an historic moment."[45]

Lorca, he continued, is "a martyr of the calamitous *señores*" (referring to the Falangists, or Spanish fascists) and a "martyr of the civil war." Like the traditional martyr, he leaves life-giving traces of himself with his blood: "Even his death is fertile. Now dead and buried in the earth where his bones are become ash, his blood has begun to run like an underground river, opening canals through which the generous passion of this new man whom they tried to annihilate will circulate. And the fields of Spain will flourish with wheat." Here, the representative man of his time is also archetypal, the earth itself; he is, moreover, solid as a document and ghostly as ash.[46]

In associating the image of the martyr with that of the earth, González Carbalho was echoing Republican rhetoric, in which the profoundly felt, intimate connection between people and land was exploited in posters, song, and other forms of propaganda. That which is martyred is the popular as embodied in Lorca. The double process of mythifying poet and people is also a way of laying claim to both, functioning as political signs of identity through a dual, mutually reinforcing unfolding of solidity and phantasmagoria. The myth made fruitful, giving life to another myth.

This topos reached a poetic and ideological paroxysm in the work of the exiled Republican and Communist militant Juan Rejano.[47] In *El poeta y su pueblo: Un símbolo andaluz; Federico García Lorca* (The Poet and His People:

An Andalusian Symbol; Federico García Lorca) (1944), Rejano wrote that "those who summoned death, dark and sordid, had lived detesting what Federico loved so dearly: the popular." Because, in effect, "people and poet were the same voice." Moreover, Lorca is the "intertwined bloody and spiritual symbol of salvation, the salvation of the true destiny of man." And then this: "García Lorca died at the hands of the enemies of the people, so that he would be resurrected with his people in history and in immortality."[48]

In the end, Rejano's rhetorical excess nearly loses sight of the poet, as an apocalyptic landscape in a ruined Andalusia and Spain looms over everything in "an abyss of abjection" under Francoism, in which civilization has been routed by barbarism, but with the hope of a clandestine resistance one of whose objectives is to avenge the death of Lorca. His last words are these, reminding us that his text was first read for the occasion of the eighth anniversary of the poet's death: "Commemorate? No. It is not enough to remember. It is not enough to reanimate for a moment the shadow of García Lorca— the shadow of so many who died—and then relapse into forgetfulness. The shadow we invoke now must be a living body, a real image, the image of the body of Spain . . . that seeks to join us together in one protest, in one struggle, to save each and everyone of us." As seen here, a transcendent metanarrative of martyrdom and salvation arose, fusing poet and people into one, in stark contrast to the brutal facts of his assassination.[49]

Lorca's death was not heroic, but sadly anonymous. At first, the myths created around the circumstances of his death made up for the lack of information Rejano and others complained about, especially in the 1940s. By 1948, one of the most fervent supporters of the Franco dictatorship, José María Pemán, would write: "The very rapid transformation of such a 'private' personality [as Lorca] into a 'public myth' is dangerous." I take this to mean that even a regime noted for its insularity was aware of, and no doubt alarmed by, the iconization of the poet. But even years later after multiple investigations by Brenan, Couffon, Penón, Auclair, and above all, Gibson, mythification appears to be unstoppable. The facts seem to have little influence on the need for myth. On the other hand, the desire to know absolutely everything about the last moments of the poet's life and to find his remains has produced a countermovement to mythification, relying on the power of documentation to dispel the mysteries of Lorca's fate.[50]

As we have seen, however, the solid and the spectral are not necessarily mutually exclusive in imagining Lorca and his death. The two impulses—the mythifying and the documentary—have something in common: an extraordinary obsession with Lorca. Illustrative of this tendency are two books I would like to comment on briefly here: *La fosa de Lorca: Crónica de un despropósito* (Lorca's Grave: Chronicle of a Travesty), by Ian Gibson (2010), and *Las trece últimas horas en la vida de García Lorca* (The Last Thirteen Hours in the Life of García Lorca), by Miguel Caballero Pérez (2011).

Gibson's book is a diary about what happened and what was written in the press during the failed excavation for Lorca's remains in the fall of 2009. As he himself confessed, "it is an obsessive document," thus demonstrating that to tell the story of Lorca is in reality the narrative of an obsession, especially if we bear in mind the number of books Gibson has written on the poet, at least twelve without counting studies on historically related figures like Salvador Dalí, Miguel Hernández, and José Antonio Primo de Rivera. He thought he had nothing more to say about the writer, while observing in the prologue: "It was not my intention to publish this chronicle, but I have come to believe that it is my obligation to do so."[51] From the beginning, the tone and direction of the book waver between chronicle and diary. This uncomfortable midway position affects the perspective of a book that is otherwise useful and informative. Most visible is the moral posture of the writing, shaped by the solemnity of the situation and by the defense that Gibson felt obliged to make, faced as he was with the controversy swirling around the exhumation and the number of disproportionate, personal attacks against him.

Although I disagree with some of his views and do not share his desire to continue seeking Lorca's bones, there is no doubt in my mind of the invaluable contribution he has made to biographical studies of the poet, especially with his first book, *The Assassination of Federico García Lorca*. The harsh criticism meted out against the Irish investigator (a Spanish citizen since 1984) during and after the excavation also struck me as uncalled-for. He was blamed for having mistaken the location of Lorca's grave, placing it at the site of the monument in the Parque de Alfacar, built to honor the poet. But Gibson never limited the possible location to the reduced area where the excavation took place, and he was never consulted by the forensic archaeologists during their preparations.

More unfortunate were the personal denunciations of Gibson, especially from bloggers. One said, "Gibson is not an historian. Gibson is an opportunist who has discovered in the figure of the assassinated Lorca a motherlode for his wallet and ego." After the team found nothing but rock, two cans of tuna fish, and a bottle of soda pop in the excavated zone, another blogger wrote in response: "The search is ended, and unless Lorca has the power to change into a can of tuna fish, the 60,000 euros budgeted by busybodies have served to bring to light the remains of Mr. Gibson's next-to-last bender in the environs of Alfacar Park." This comment appears as a unique twist on the remains of the poet being shoveled onto the compost heap of time.[52]

Even worse treatment came from Francisco Bejarano in an article from *Diario de Sevilla,* in which he alluded to "Gibson's ravings" and "the Lorquian fanaticism of a convert (*converso*), whom an ill wind from Ireland brought to Spain to join with leftists *du jour* and usurp the historian's place. Spare us the fate of *conversos,* spare us from those who make political hay even of the Holy Sacrament." Poor Gibson. These attacks, all discussed in his book, come wrapped in a view of Lorca and the civil war that claims to depoliticize them. The result is the very opposite. A language supercharged with historical and cultural associations like *converso* (referring to Jews compelled to convert under pain of expulsion) and *fanatismo* (referring to excesses like the Inquisition) ends up politicizing things as much as this commentary, with which Bejarano opened his piece: "The fear that García Lorca's remains would be found, transformed into secular relics and passed off as a symbol of resurrected and antiquated political ideas, made us reject a poet who represents nothing more than good poetry. . . . We have no interest in a partisan, shrunken Lorca in the hands of functional illiterates in public office. 'Lorca is one of us!' a bold-faced woman councillor of the Junta shrieked in the Andalusian Parliament, when the poet was quoted by the opposition." Such were the "dogs of politics scratching the earth to devour [Lorca's] bones."[53]

Likewise, declaiming vehemently "Lorca is one of us!" hardly exudes the voice of reason. More to the point, these commentaries demonstrate once again the degree to which Lorca's myth continues to be the object of an ideological and identity-laden struggle to possess his political and cultural capital. Even a book such as Gibson's, which aims specifically to document the vicissitudes of the search for the poet's remains by chronicling the press, ends up documenting the controversy and politicization of the excavation, thus losing sight of what is most important: Lorca himself. Paradoxically, the more documented Lorca is, the more ghostly and less knowable he appears, serving the pseudomyths of political interests that have also influenced the way he is seen historically.

The argument in favor of his exhumation maintains that Lorca belongs to everyone, that is, he is a public figure. Holders of this position tend to vilify the poet's family, who until recently were strongly opposed to the project of digging up his remains. In 2004, Andrés Soria Olmedo, married to his niece, Laura García-Lorca de los Ríos, attempted to unite public memory and private memory by speaking of the dead zone where Lorca lies as a *lieu de mémoire,* a collective memory place that, for him, also offers consolation to the private memory of the family. The idea of leaving the poet in the company of other victims of Víznar, most of them anonymous, is especially appealing to many writers. Francisco Ayala himself declared he was in favor of "leaving him alone." "We shouldn't mess with corpses. . . . There is no need to do anything." The poet Luis García Montero and the novelist Javier Marías share his view, as do the philologist Francisco Rico and the historian Santos Juliá. But obviously not everyone does, among them Ian Gibson. Antonio Muñoz Molina has observed that "Lorca's remains are not those of a private man, here the private and the public are mixed together, and García Lorca is the most universal figure we have. That is something that neither the family nor the public can avoid."[54]

In a commentary titled "El folklore de los huesos insignes" (The Folklore of Famous Bones), Marías opposed the exhumation: "Lorca's 'undeserving' burial is a necessary reminder of the undeserving death he suffered, and not to respect it would, in the long run, practically 'whitewash' his executioners." Defending the poet's family, he asked ironically: "are [the family] then against 'historical memory,' against the poet 'who belongs to everyone' being buried with honors (another cliché, I might add, by way of another falsehood: his poetry is available to anyone, but there is no reason his bones should be)?" Marías brings out the stereotyping and disingenuousness of the myth that the poet is a cultural possession (and artifact) belonging to everyone. If Lorca truly belonged to everyone, his exhumation would not be so hotly debated.[55]

The novelist also undermines a strawman argument of the controversy: the claim that the family's opposition and a politically incorrect position against "historical memory" and against the dignity of the dead are one and the same. To this end, Jon Lee Anderson in *The New Yorker* has cited another commentator, who complained that "any normal person with a close relative . . . who has been mysteriously disappeared, and is known to have been murdered, has to feel the minimal interest in where he might be. . . . Lorca isn't only the patrimony of one family but of all decent people of this world. Normal people want to know what happened. . . . But it seems that there are people who are not normal and are incapable of resolving their personal and family traumas." Here moral posturing barely hides the heavy-handed pressure laid on the Lorca family to conform to public opinion, an arena in which historical memory, whatever that might be, has become politicized, in a country that once chafed under stifling conformism of another ideological stripe.[56]

Such criticism ignores the reality that history and memory are not monolithic, nor is the manner of dignifying the dead. Manuel Reyes Mate maintains that historical memory is above all "political memory." The case of the Granadine poet is instructive here. The essayist confirmed his own point when he said, "The Lorca [matter] is a clear example of how family ideologies can coopt the rights of victims. To be identified and honored is Lorca's right as a victim beyond whatever his family says. It is a duty of society." Historical memory and political memory are difficult to separate in this statement. The duty of society comes out of an ideological position that sees in victimhood the reclaiming of history. But in speaking of "family ideologies" as opposed to human rights, Reyes Mate mixes apples with oranges, politicizing even more the historical circumstances of Lorca's death (not to mention ignoring the family's own rights).[57]

Maybe this is inevitable. Elsewhere, in referring to the anonymous burial pits of the Republican dead, I once wrote:

> One old man summed up things as a matter of geography: "In this village, there are more people outside the cemetery than inside." He meant of course more dead bodies. It is the place of these bodies, real and symbolic, that vexes Spaniards today: what place should these dead occupy in history? While individual families seek answers to particular questions, nations and societies are obliged to find a larger purpose in the largeness of many deaths. The tug of the particular and the general is taut with unresolved tension, especially when we speak of civil wars. Competing loyalties and creeds interpret the historic events of such conflicts in radically different ways. The meaning of the dead depends on whose dead we are talking about.[58]

This tension between the concrete and the general is evident in the debate surrounding the poet's body. I am struck by how the identity of this specific body is meant to define, however tentatively, not only the meaning of his death but the more general meaning of the history that produced it, situating it as a political and cultural possession. And yet to claim Lorca as belonging to all presupposes an underlying consensus concerning the war itself that simply does not exist. History stops us short.

Gibson reproduced Reyes Mate's commentary in his book in order to justify the exhumation along these lines: "Would the poet have wanted us to look for him? I believe so, and all the rest [of the victims]. Would he have preferred being an eternally disappeared person? I do not think so. Would it have made no difference to him? I do not think so. Have his heirs considered the matter from this perspective? It appears the answer is no." I confess that these speculations of Gibson leave me somewhat perplexed. How can the Irish investigator know what Lorca would have felt or thought? Not even his own family knows.[59]

Oddly enough, one of Lorca's last interviewers, the caricaturist Luis Bagaría, said to the poet: "It is so tragically painful to disappear forever. . . . In that tragic ending, I would only ask for one lasting thing: that my body be buried in a garden; that my afterlife, at least, be a fertile one." Lorca did not reply to his comment, choosing instead to ask a humorous question about the artist's political caricatures. A garden burial was not his end (though curiously, it was Francisco Ayala's), and the disappearance Bagaría ironically spoke of has nothing to do with the political status of a disappeared person. Clearly, Gibson sought a larger perspective than that of the poet's family, whose views he considered shortsighted. At heart he is suggesting that Lorca's place in the scheme of things appears to be that of History itself, or at least of a concrete history. The larger questions remain unanswered: To whom does this history belong? And which history is this?[60]

The Lorca case obviously offers the opportunity to relive and rethink the civil war and to consider its place in the democratic Spain of today. It also exemplifies the extremes to which the clumsy uses of great men can be applied: to fetishize his aura, his effect, to the point of converting Lorca into a usable lay relic, a public icon,[61] at the same time tends to favor a simplistic and unilluminating historical vision of the war that continues to sidestep its own partisanship. Lorca's aura is in the end nontransferable, as Emerson suggested when he spoke of the "virtues and powers not communicable to other men," as if God had written, "'*Not transferable*,' and '*Good for this trip only*,' on these garments of the soul."[62] The individual gift of personhood, however, cannot be transferred to the wretchedness of an execution. A sacralized Lorca is simply not compatible with the facts of his death.

Caballero Pérez's book demonstrates that unpleasant reality, as the earlier investigations of Gibson, Eduardo Molina Fajardo, and others had done. Unfortunately, the subtitle also reveals his disproportionate historical ambition. The full title is *Las trece últimas horas en la vida de García Lorca: El informe que da respuesta a todas las incógnitas sobre la muerte del poeta; ¿quién ordenó su detención?, ¿por qué le ejecutaron?, ¿dónde está su cuerpo?* (The Last Thirteen Hours in the Life of García Lorca: The Report That Provides Answers to All the Unknowns on the Death of the Poet; Who Ordered His Arrest? Why Did They Execute Him? Where Is His Body?). Such sensationalist claims recall the book by José Vila-San-Juan, published in 1975: *García Lorca, asesinado: Toda la verdad* (García Lorca, Assassinated: The Whole Truth). As far as I know, no one possesses all the truth and all the answers to the mysteries of Lorca's death. Nonetheless, *Las trece últimas horas*, which undoubtedly owes a large debt to Molina Fajardo and Gibson, adds something more to the story of his execution.

The book also brings home how difficult it is to separate the personal from the political in the circumstances that led to a violent death in a countryside already sown with many violent deaths. Lorca was killed most likely because he supported the Second Republic, because he was homosexual, because he alienated the well-connected bourgeoisie of Granada, and because his brother-in-law, also murdered, was the socialist mayor of Granada. Caballero Pérez repeats his earlier thesis that Lorca died partly because of a series of long-standing economic and political disputes that the poet's father, a wealthy liberal landowner, had with other members of the extended family.[63] He illustrates the thick web of relations connecting family members to executioners and others involved in the murder, including one of the assault guards who shot Lorca, Antonio Benavides Benavides. This last-named was first cousin to José Benavides Peña, the model for Pepe el Romano in *La casa de Bernarda Alba* (The House of Bernarda Alba), a work that apparently offended the Roldán Benavides and Alba families, who were related to the poet's father. The son of a landowner, Antonio Benavides enrolled in Falange on 18 July 1936, the day of the Franco uprising.[64]

Perhaps even more disheartening was the caliber of Lorca's executioners, according to Caballero Pérez. Benavides was described "as a cold-blooded person, with an assassin's vocation." A drunkard, he was accused of moral misconduct. Another member of the firing squad, "Salvaorillo" (Salvador Baro Leyva), was also called cold-blooded. It was said of the leader of the squad, Mariano Ajenjo Moreno, whose father was an agricultural laborer, that "the promise of promotion up the ladder and a material reward of 500 pesetas encouraged Mariano to join the squad." Like Benavides, two others were Falangists (or soon to be): Fernando Correa Carrasco, also a veteran of the African wars in colonial Morocco (an *africanista*) and the bastard son of a property owner father, and Salvio Rodríguez García, an *africanista* and civil guard, who joined Falange in 1938. The outside guard in the holding place for prisoners, La Colonia, where Lorca spent his last hours, Pedro Cuesta Hernández, also belonged to the party, though it is worth noting that he evidently refused to be part of the firing squad.[65]

Additionally, another outside guard and a Falangist, twenty-year-old Eduardo González Aurioles, "belonged to the most established bourgeois families of Santa Fe, related to García Lorca's father through social, economic, and family ties."[66] The poet had actually saved González Aurioles from drowning on one occasion. This is another example of how the personal and the political were intimately intertwined in the events leading to Lorca's death. At any rate, the political affiliation of some of those responsible, if indeed these are the poet's killers, contradicts the statements made by current *falangistas* that Falange played no role in the murder of the poet.

The Assault Guard (Guardia de Asalto) that carried out the shooting was not for the faint-hearted, as its general function was to impose a regime of terror on the population of Granada.[67] On the personal level, as Caballero Pérez observed, the executioners "were not refined or cultivated individuals, nor were they given to soul-searching or moral doubts." They were assassins neither before nor after the war, but rather had led respectable, ordinary lives. At least one member of the firing squad, Juan Jiménez Cascales, complied with orders out of fear, not duty, nervously saying that "this is not for me." It is not at all surprising, either, that, with an exception or two, the squad unit members came from humble backgrounds, given the kind of work they had been assigned.[68]

The investigator himself communicates all this in a tone and style redolent of an administrative report, as the novelist Muñoz Molina noted. The banal character of Lorca's murderers can be extended to other people who had something to do with his death, such as the ambitious and resentful Ramón Ruiz Alonso, who arrested Lorca, of whom the poet Luis Rosales said: "Federico died because he was the necessary piece to the political ambition of a cretin." Or the lawyer and businessman Juan Luis Trescastro, who also participated in the arrest and boasted, untruthfully, of having killed the poet, characterized by his "essentially violent nature." He too had a relationship with the Roldán family, demonstrating again that in at least some instances, "those responsible for the poet's death were persons either close or known to the family."[69]

The historical wretchedness of these circumstances is the very opposite of the mythifying, exalted image of Lorca's death. Whether or not some of these people are the poet's assassins and accomplices to his murder, there is an underlying, dismal truth to such baseness. By contrast, as Muñoz Molina has commented, it seems there is a need "to magnify" things and "to exaggerate the reach of the assassins' shadows, including the physical spaces that constituted the symbolic setting for the tragedy." The imagination fills the poet's grave with alien things, while the detritus of history continues to mount in slag heaps on his repeated burials. *There* is the monumental heap, as Carlyle said. The valiant defeat of the poet, not in the moment of his death, but in time. The dispute over his empty grave is nothing less than the struggle over the remains of history itself. If Lorca has become a myth of cultural possession, it is because history has turned into another, passionately reclaimed possession. The weight of that history piled on what remains of the poet needs to be recalculated, rethought, in the case of García Lorca.[70]

Lorca, I imagine, was probably not thinking about history in those last, unbearable moments of his time on earth. His line of vision would have been very reduced, very small, because the world that had brought him to this place had turned terribly small. Said another way, smallness killed him. Physically, the place of his death, or at least the place Caballero Pérez thought most likely, appears in a registry from 1906 as "a patch of land, unirrigated and uncultivated, useful only for the poorest-quality grazing." There is no mention in the registry of an olive grove. "At some point between 1906 and 1937," wrote Caballero Pérez, "this nearly worthless land was planted with olive trees."[71] It would be symbolically fitting were Lorca to be found in such strange and humble poetry of scarcity, possessed only by the earth, his last possession.

Subsequent excavations at the site came up empty. Like much information on the poet's final resting place, this hypothesis originated in oral sources. It is worth mentioning one more theory about a different location, also undocumented, stemming from a newspaper article published in 2008. In 1986, workers preparing the ground for the Parque Federico García Lorca in Alfacar dug up human remains near an olive tree, along with bits of a crutch, which might have belonged to the one-legged schoolmaster killed at the same time as Lorca. Under pressure to complete the project as quickly as possible, the workers placed the remains in a white plastic bag that once held fertilizer and reburied them elsewhere. No one knows if the poet really did end up as detritus, not of his age, but of ours, conveniently repurposed for the compost heap of history. What would Carlyle have said?[72]

3. The People's Poet and the Right

Federico García Lorca's violent death at the hands of the extreme right during the civil war has been remembered and imagined in a variety of ways, thus bringing the Republican poet back to life in a strange kind of afterglow and symbolically completing his earthly trajectory. The Republicans naturally declared him one of their own, as we have seen, but unexpectedly, a few on the right also professed ownership over Lorca. Here I focus on that claim as part of the aftermath of the poet's death, reexamining some of the early right-wing reaction to Lorca's death, which saw the poet in relation to the fascist leader José Antonio Primo de Rivera, subsequent commentary, and one especially pertinent case, that of the South African poet Roy Campbell. For additional contextualization of the period's left/right divide, I also bring in more discussion of the left's political-cultural uses of the poet, bearing in mind my earlier commentary on such figures as Machado, González Carbalho, Gil-Albert, Sánchez Barbudo, Juan Rejano, and a host of others.

Strangely (or not), Lorca's supposed connection to fascism has also resurfaced as an issue in the twenty-first century. As the assertion goes, the poet was little more than a señorito—an accusation with antecedents in the 1920s—whose values were conducive to those of fascism and who was incapable of understanding the working classes, contradicting an earlier insistence that Lorca was the people's poet. To dismiss such claims as unworthy of study and not subject them to scrutiny fails to shed light on the motivation or circumstances that produced them or on the ideological contentiousness that has so politicized Lorca's life and work. You can't even begin to explain what happened to Lorca or how his iconic status developed without looking at the extraordinary polarization of the period, although, as we shall see, even the black-and-white picture of the conflict requires nuance.

Lorca became a political football, and that alone should prompt us to reconsider the context and the major players behind such ideological strife. Moreover, the political tinderbox that set off the civil war continues to bedevil present-day Spain, as the debates over the Law of Historical Memory and resistance to exhuming Lorca's remains have shown. The unresolved nature of the conflict has shaped the cultural status of Lorca, underscoring the question of partisanship that goes back to the Second Republic and the war: whose side are you on? The expected answer—the Republican side—tends to foreclose further inquiry, ignoring a related question: Who does Lorca belong to? Should he? Why should he belong to anybody or any group with an axe to grind? One is reminded here of the classic dualistic conception of the two Spains pitted against each other, liberal versus conservative, radical versus reactionary, traditional versus modern. Yet, during the war and afterward, there undoubtedly was an even larger third Spain, as Andrés Trapiello observed, that had no interest in either ideological extreme. Lorca once jokingly said he was "an anarchist-communist-libertarian, a pagan-Catholic, a traditionalist and monarchist who supports Don Duarte of Portugal." He was of course a staunch Republican, but he belonged to no political party, disliked being used by any political group, and had friends across the political spectrum.[1]

News about Lorca's assassination filtered through slowly, followed by disbelief, rage, and anguish. The Nationalists, or Francoists, quickly understood that this was a public relations disaster. Lorca had gone home to Granada, a few days later the civil war erupted on 18 July 1936, and within a month he had been arrested and shot. It was believed most likely by the notorious Black Squad (Escuadra Negra), who worked hand in glove with the civil governor, José Valdés Guzmán, but now it seems by a group of Assault Guards. The Black Squad was filled with riffraff, including members of the fascist political party, Falange. Mostly it was filled with people who enjoyed killing. The firing squad responsible for Lorca's death also had Falangists and people of low character, according to Caballero Pérez. Valdés Guzmán himself was an "old shirt" member of the party, though evidently, he was away on the day of the poet's arrest, when Nicolás Velasco Simarro, an officer of the Civil Guard, substituted for him.[2]

The Falangist role in Lorca's death has been repeatedly denied by the party ever since. Caballero Pérez's investigation appears now to have put paid to such assertions. The Nationalists' immediate response was to blame the Communists. A false rumor also circulated that the execution was revenge for the murder of playwright Jacinto Benavente, whose apparent support for the Republic evaporated with Franco's victory. Another Nationalist, Merry del Val, incorrectly claimed Lorca was "executed after a trial by court-martial." Then the regime simply stonewalled—for decades. Very little about Lorca's death appeared in the Nationalist papers. Yet at least two pieces by Falangists did and are worth examining, especially since the first one published provoked a heated response from the Republican writer Antonio Sánchez Barbudo, an example of the kind of cultural possessiveness the poet prompted in his compatriots, noted elsewhere in these pages.[3]

The article "A la España imperial le han asesinado su mejor poeta" (Imperial Spain's Best Poet Assassinated), written by Luis Hurtado Álvarez, appeared first in *Unidad* (San Sebastián) on 11 March 1937, and was republished on at least four more occasions. Like other Falangist writings, this one insisted Lorca was at heart one of them, or at the very least was or might have been sympathetic toward the movement: "You would have been its best poet, because your sentiments were those of the Falange. You wanted Country, Bread and Justice for all." Hurtado also denied that the Falange or the army had anything to do with the poet's assassination.[4]

Sánchez Barbudo, who later went on, in exile, to a distinguished academic career in the United States, was infuriated over the piece. The title of his response, "La muerte de García Lorca comentada por sus asesinos" (The Death of García Lorca as Commented by his Assassins), drips sarcasm. Hurtado's homage, he said, was scurrilous and pompous, glorifying a victim of Falange, García Lorca, in a rhetorical style at once absurd and vulgar. He was particularly incensed over Hurtado's use of Antonio Machado's celebrated line, "the crime was in Granada," taken from the poem of the same name.[5]

Sánchez Barbudo's rage is understandable, but his rhetoric is as excessive as Hurtado's. Both articles show how little middle ground there was during the war, and how most rhetoric was propaganda of one sort or another. But what if Luis Hurtado (like Sánchez Barbudo) really meant what he said? What if he were sincere in his admiration for the poet? Aside from bad politics, he was more guilty of poor writing and poor judgment than anything else. There is some truly weird imagery in his homage. He speaks, for example, of Lorca's "gigantesque, pharaonic body" ("cuerpo gigantesco, faraónico") and of "100,000 violins of envy" ("cien mil violines de la envidia") as being responsible for the poet's death. (This last image probably echoes in part Lorca's "Casida del llanto" [Qasida of the Weeping].) Sánchez Barbudo comments acidly: "Those aren't daggers penetrating his body, they were only violins in all their glory." The metaphor of Lorca's larger-than-life body reflects, however, the Falangist cult of heroism, in which both rhetoric and ritual played a pronounced role. Thus, Ximénez de Sandoval explains in his novel *Camisa azul (Retrato de un falangista)* (Blue Shirt [Portrait of a Falangist]) how fellow Falangists handled a dead comrade's body "with religious solemnity," transforming "the corpse into the figure of a hero."[6]

Hurtado claimed to have known Lorca. He said the two of them enjoyed a good laugh reading mediocre poetry from an unnamed anthology that also contained some of Lorca's poems. Sánchez Barbudo rejected the claim, saying he was "absolutely unknown to the poet's true, intimate friends." Perhaps it was this friendship that allowed Hurtado to address Lorca directly, to speak of how he went searching for his poetry in bookstore after bookstore: "My pilgrimage was like a homage to your death." It was also common for Republican supporters to speak to the absent Lorca in poems and prose, in the same intimate way. Lorca had an enormous circle of friends, not all of them known to each other.[7]

As it turned out, Sánchez Barbudo was wrong. Hurtado, a university student in law and philosophy at the time, wrote at least two letters to the poet in 1935, using the second-person familiar and signing one of them "your good friend" ("tu buen amigo"). In the first one, he lambasted a scurrilous review of *Yerma* that had appeared a few days before in *Informaciones* (31 December 1934). In the second, he asked Lorca to autograph his copy of *Llanto por Ignacio Sánchez Mejías*, saying he called twice but the poet was sleeping. Copies of two other books affectionately inscribed to Hurtado— *Bodas de sangre* and one of the fifty limited edition copies of *Ode to Walt Whitman*—have turned up as well. It is also worth pointing out that Lorca's sister Isabel counted among her friends a "Luis Hurtado." Both were participating in the university summer program at Santander in 1935 when Lorca brought his theater troupe La Barraca to perform there for a week in August. Hurtado himself came from a theater family. His father, Luis Hurtado Girón, was an intimate friend and, later, secretary of Jacinto Benavente, and several siblings, as well as the father, became actors, known especially for performing in works by Benavente. In 1927, Benavente dedicated his magic play, *La noche iluminada*, to Luisito Hurtado Álvarez, who later became a theater impresario and director. (The first letter to Lorca quoted from Benavente.) With these connections, it makes perfect sense that Lorca knew Hurtado. Indeed, Benavente, a closeted homosexual, introduced Hurtado to the poet, at a bar much frequented by gays called Los Italianos.[8]

Hurtado's article was reproduced in the Falangist weekly, *Antorcha* (Antequera), in March 1937. A current Falangist website noted that the editor of *Antorcha*, Nemesio Sabugo Gallego, was detained by the Nationalist military authorities precisely because of the article. He was also questioned on the whereabouts of Hurtado. Sabugo Gallego (1888–1984), who later taught French at the secondary school level and became a local expert in the history of his hometown, Benavides de Orbigo, had taken courses with future Republican exiles Américo Castro and Tomás Navarro Tomás at the Council for Advanced Scientific Studies and Research (Junta de Ampliación de Estudios) in Madrid, an example of how freely people of ideologically diverse backgrounds (including Lorca of course) mixed with each other before the war.[9]

Was Sabugo Gallego detained? I don't know, but I am inclined to believe it after running across a document reproduced in Molina Fajardo's book on Lorca's last days. A little more than two weeks after the article was reproduced in *Antorcha*, the military governor of Antequera issued a complaint against Hurtado for slander against the army and requested information on how exactly Lorca had died. The statement is a bit confusing since it refers to "injurious opinions by the author Luis Hurtado Álvarez against the perpetrators of the assassination of an unnamed poet."[10]

The poet is, however, immediately identified as Lorca, since by April 1937 there was nothing anonymous either in the news of his death or in Hurtado's homage. The accusation against Hurtado is puzzling. He clearly defended the army (and Falange) against any perceived defamation. Moreover, if he really did slander the army, then why declare he offended the poet's assassins? You can only offend an assassin if he happens to be your man. The document amounted to an indirect admission of guilt, essentially equating the army with Lorca's assassins. I suspect this was unintended.[11]

Whatever the consequences were for Hurtado and Sabugo Gallego, these circumstances shed a different light on his article. Hurtado got into trouble for writing about Lorca. It was decidedly not smart for someone on the right to talk about the poet publicly and in such glowing terms. But it was especially risky to bring up his possible assassins. Indeed, as I have said, there is precious little praise or discussion of Lorca to appear in Nationalist publications during this period. Another example from the same time frame is worth noting, journalist Francisco Villena's piece titled "De una historia que vio la Alhambra" (On a Story that the Alhambra Witnessed), which was published in the Falangist daily, *Amanecer,* on 3 April 1937. The dedication reads: "To Federico García Lorca, in the Imperial immortality of his difficult paradise."[12]

Though Villena made no claim of friendship with Lorca, like so many, he speaks in the form of apostrophe to the absent poet: "It was, Federico, an August afternoon when they spoke to us of your departure."[13] The language is largely euphemistic, cloaked in Falangist rhetoric and Lorquian imagery. (Hurtado spoke more directly, saying he could not accept the poet's death: "you cannot die" ["tú no puedes morir"].) References to the poet's work and citational use of his words are found over and over among the hundreds of poetic and prose homages to Lorca. Villena alluded to the *Gypsy Ballads, Yerma,* and *Bodas de sangre* (Blood Wedding), for example. (Hurtado went looking for copies of the *Gypsy Ballads* and *Blood Wedding* in bookstores, just as the International Brigades volunteer Edwin Rolfe sought out the ballads in 1938 as he said in a poem written ten years later, though to different ideological ends.)

Moving away from the saccharine, Villena fixes upon the imagery of blood and gangrenous death found in Lorca's *Lament for Ignacio Sánchez Mejías,* creating parallels between Lorca's death and that of the bullfighter. His assassins have "metallic souls" ("almas de metal"), vaguely recalling similar imagery from the *Gypsy Ballads,* but they are also associated with what he calls "white Marxists" ("marxistas blancos") interested only in gold (a possible allusion to the Republic's gold reserves being shipped to the Soviet Union). They are "blind merchants" ("ciegos mercaderes"). Such terms remind us that Falangists were both anti-Marxist and anticapitalist. Unlike Hurtado, Villena played safe by implying Communist responsibility for Lorca's death, without mentioning the army or Falange.

Villena's Lorquian images and references are ultimately made to serve Falangist rhetoric, which dominates the final paragraphs. The poet "has gone, but he has left us the seed with which other poets will move our young Country forward." And this: "May our premiere Imperial poet march on ahead, blazing the path of our epic in blue. For the spring we will need to have soldiers who are poets with swords." The image of Lorca's seed relies on a martyr trope much favored by the Nationalists: "the blood of martyrs is the seed of Christians," which draws on the phrase attributed to Tertullian, "Sanguis martyrum, semen christianorum."[14] Lorca as a martyr for the Falangist cause has no basis in reality, but the sacrificial figure of the poet has deep roots, recalling the dismemberment of Orpheus at the hands of the Thracian maenads. Villena was not alone in imbuing Lorca with a transcendent aura. Hurtado promoted a similar vision by attributing Christ-like qualities to the poet (imagery also found in Republican homages). He saw Lorca as a kind of redeemer, capable of rescuing men from their unfortunate lives.

The most important trope for Villena is that of the poet himself as the standard bearer of the Falangist imperial dream. While the union of arms and letters has a long tradition, here the poet is to take up arms for a specific ideological purpose: to further the ambitions of the blue shirts (hence the "epic in blue" or "épica azul"). The militarized image of Lorca, while startling, is not unexpected, considering the context. Even Republican supporters used it to promote in equal measure the poet as heroic and the struggle as just. In a piece that employs the Nationalists' rhetoric against them, characterizing them as "vandalizing hordes" and the "anti-Spain," Raúl Roa writes, "[Lorca] fell vertically, like a genuine soldier of liberty, sealing with his pure blood the revolutionary holiness of the antifascist cause." The larger question is, why would Falangists even bother to make rhetorical use of the Granadine writer? Defending themselves against accusations of being accomplices in Lorca's murder does not explain why they would claim him as one of their own. There is some evidence that even Falangists, as well as other Nationalists, simply liked Lorca's poetry and plays. Second lieutenants were heard reciting verses from the *Gypsy Ballads* in the Nationalist frontlines. During the war, the Falangist soldier Antonio Zurita carried with him everywhere a kit filled with Lorca poems written out by hand. Falangists also imitated his poetry, often badly (so did many Republican supporters). This practice outraged the *falangista* Ernesto Giménez Caballero, who called such imitators "Reds and Lorquians." In stark contrast, Agustín de Foxá thought Lorca was a marvelously original poet, who had breathed new life into the traditional ballad form. One poet even produced a religiously inspired poem loosely based on "Ballad of the Moon Moon." Ximénez de Sandoval inserted a poetic inter-

Figure 3. José Antonio Primo de Rivera at a political rally, ca. 1935–36. Wikimedia Commons.

lude in dialogue verse form called "El falangista y la luna" (The Falangist and the Moon) into his wartime novel, *Camisa azul*. Both Foxá and Ximénez de Sandoval knew Lorca.[15]

For true believers, however, poetry had a political reason for being. The leader of Falange and the son of the dictator, José Antonio Primo de Rivera, founded the party in October 1933, saying: "Nations have never been moved except by poets, and woe betide the man who, faced with the poetry of destruction, does not know how to counter it with the poetry of promise!" His remarks on poetry come right after what he has to say about propaganda. In this view of things, propaganda becomes a kind of poetry, because propaganda should awaken strong emotion and passionate energy (fig. 3).[16]

Emotion links the two, turning poetry into politics. It is not surprising that Hurtado and Villena saw Lorca through a political lens, exploiting his person and poetry for ideological ends. (Republican supporters eagerly did the same.) Moreover, Primo de Rivera greatly admired Lorca's work. A rumor circulated that the two used to dine together in secret. Lorca seemed to know practically everybody, so it is conceivable the friendship existed, as the poet Gabriel Celaya claimed. That they were simply acquainted seems more likely. Nonetheless, current-day Falangists insist upon these two points of contact.[17]

The link between Lorca and Primo de Rivera goes beyond the anec-dotal. Only a few months after the poet's murder, José Antonio was executed by the Republicans in November 1936. His death turned him into a fascist martyr and a myth. He became "the Absent One" ("El Ausente") who was always "present," as all *falangistas* who had died for the cause were consid-ered since early 1934. Falangists spoke in the same breath of Absence and Ascension, to enshrine his "evangelical mission," as Ximénez de Sandoval remarked in *Camisa azul*. While the Franco regime did not declare him offi-cially dead until two years later, on 20 November 1938, rumors of his death abounded in the intervening period. The Republican zone of course knew he was dead; it seems improbable that the news had not filtered through to the other zone. The Falangist Rafael García Serrano observed it was an open secret that many rank-and-file *falangistas* refused to acknowledge, believing his death a metaphysical impossibility. He could not die, just as Hurtado wrote that Lorca could not. José Antonio had been in a Republican prison since March 1936, largely incomunicado by the end, so he was already absent in another sense. It was this particular "myth of his absence that finally died on 20 November 1938," as García Serrano has noted. Unquestionably, his mythification had already begun. The same play between absence and pres-ence appeared in many homages to Lorca, with a similar resurrectional im-pulse. Pointedly, Villena's dedication to the poet spoke of the "Imperial im-mortality of his difficult paradise." The Lorca family's lawyer made use of these very words to defend the poet posthumously before the Franco regime's Tribunal of Political Responsibilities in 1941. The best defense would have been Lorca's own works, the lawyer said, but he had none at hand.[18]

Villena's phrase self-consciously echoed something Primo de Rivera said: "Some days ago, I recalled before a small gathering a line of Romantic poetry: 'I want no paradise, but rest.' . . . Paradise is certainly not rest. Para-dise is against rest. In Paradise one cannot lie down; one is vertically like the angels. Well then: we, who have already led the lives of the best to the path of Paradise, want a Paradise that is difficult, erect, implacable; a Paradise where there is never rest, that has angels with swords lining the door posts." To be a Falangist is to be forever militant, to "remain standing," to "adopt before life and the dangers of life, a stance that is vertical, rigid, vigilant," the Falangist clerical Fermín Yzurdiaga observed.[19]

Villena's rhetoric places Lorca alongside Primo de Rivera without ever having to mention the Falangist leader directly. For both Villena and Hurtado, what is at stake is not so much Lorca as José Antonio, the sacrificed activist redeemer of men's souls. The man who could not rest yet sought a place in Paradise. Lorca is infused with the aura of the Absent One, who is ever-present rhetorically and emotionally in these pieces. The original source of poetry is José Antonio, the "poetry of promise." Falangists saw that promise cut short, the same way Republicans viewed Lorca's trajectory. In this sense, what is being completed here is not so much Lorca's brief life as José Antonio's. When Hurtado says to Lorca that "you would have been its best poet, because your sentiments were those of the Falange," he is symbolically filling in Lorca's life by projecting José Antonio's poetic presence and beliefs upon it. Indeed, followers envisioned José Antonio as an Orphic figure of poetry whose voice could sooth "the Marxist beast."[20] Moreover, it is probably not coincidental that both pieces were published shortly before Franco merged all political parties, despite their ideological disparities, into one National Movement on 19 April 1937, effectively diminishing the impact and independence of the Falange, as those opposed to the unification saw it. The fiction of a fascist Lorca, while offensive to Republicans, needs to be seen in the context of the claims and counterclaims to the poet as both an instrument of propaganda and a life-enhancing myth. The real Lorca remains an enigma.

Assimilating the poet to the Falangist leader made Lorca more acceptable to the extreme right. In the late 1940s and early 1950s, during the struggle to revivify the Spanish University Union (Sindicato Español Universitario, SEU), a Falangist student organization, one of the reforms proposed to raise SEU's intellectual profile bolstered its argument with the idea of being able to write on Lorca while still remaining ideologically pure. Despite these instances of admiration for Lorca, there is plenty of evidence to suggest how much other *falangistas* and rightists of similar minds in general disliked his poetry and his liberal politics. Mere months after the poet's death, the Marquis de Merry del Val claimed Lorca's "literary merits were outshone by his political zeal." He classified him among the "dangerous agitators who abused their talent and superior education to lead the ignorant masses astray for their own personal profit." It was said that José María Pemán reacted to his death by remarking, "Bah, no big deal!"[21]

Falangists, moreover, hated Lorca's version of Lope de Vega's classic seventeenth-century play *Fuenteovejuna,* which his government-funded traveling university players took round to rural audiences during the Second Republic. He had set the play in the 1930s and cut all references to the mon-

archy. More generally, *falangistas* like Giménez Caballero, who had once embraced aesthetic experimentation, thought the work of vanguard writers like
Lorca was decadent art. By contrast, for Pemán, Nationalist poetry *was* the
avant-garde, taken in the military sense, as it was written in the trenches and
on the march (as was Republican verse).[22]

Thus, the journalist Juan Aparicio bristled with unbridled hostility toward the literary avant-garde to which Lorca belonged, singling out "certain
little folkloric ballads, anemic and gypsified" and "the soulless, graceless
trifles" of "pure poetry." He also lashed out against Ortega y Gasset's "men-
dacious, treacherous theory of the dehumanization of art," the most influential text of the avant-garde. Those anemic and gypsified little ballads can only
be Lorca's *Gypsy Ballads*, published in 1928. Indeed, Aparicio denounced
1928 as the quintessential year of the Spanish *vanguardia*. With the war, he
said, all those "dehumanizers" and "pure poetry" enthusiasts have either fled
the country or joined the bureaucracy of the Horde, this last a much favored
Nationalist insult used along with "canaille" (*canalla*), or rabble, to characterize the Republican side.[23]

What is so strange about Aparicio's commentary is where it appeared:
as the prologue to fellow Falangist José María Castroviejo's wartime poetry
collection, *Altura* (Vertex). This occurrence by itself would not be worthy of
remark except that Castroviejo dedicated one of his poems to García Lorca.
Castroviejo came from a long line of Galician *carlistas*, who were ultramon-
archists and ultra-Catholics. In 1933 he joined Falange, after having been a
founding member of the Councils of National-Syndicalist Offensive (Juntas
de Ofensiva Nacional-Sindicalista, JONS), a national syndicalist organization that later merged with Falange.[24]

In the poem dedicated to Lorca, "Paso firme" (Steady Steps), Castroviejo speaks directly in the familiar second-person plural to the living and
indirectly to the dead. "Spain," he says, "is a fountain where corpses lie /
filled with the suns of justice and redemption made ample." The living be-
hold the dead, and the dead dictate to the living, urging unity and strength
against betrayal and infamy. The rhetoric is Nationalist, starting with the
title, which reminds us of the verticality of purpose that Primo de Rivera
espoused. Nonetheless, the image also appears in the Marxist-Leninist Raúl
Roa's declaration noted above. Castroviejo's dedication to Lorca makes the
ideological affiliation somewhat ambiguous. At the same time, the poem does
not speak directly to Lorca's death. The militant sense of urgency, reinforced

by the repetition of the phrase "it is necessary" ("es preciso"), along with imagery of destruction and violence, focuses on a collective mission demanding blood and sacrifice. The last stanza reads:

> But in heaven's bronze nothing can stop
> your hallowed madness earned inch by inch,
> among giant choirs of the proud and stubborn dead,
> who demand and demand again . . . it is necessary, it is necessary!

The language of command in which "death dictates its most profound poems," however eloquent, seems far removed from the hushed-up, cowardly execution of García Lorca.[25]

On the other hand, Castroviejo also speaks of "a future of brothers," albeit written in angles of blood. The imagery of brotherhood appears several times in *Altura,* as it does in Falangist rhetoric, notably in the poem that immediately precedes "Steady Steps." "El último hermano" (The Last Brother) is much more effective as a poem, with relatively little explicit Nationalist imagery. Here, the only thing that Castroviejo sees are the dead: "Dead, dead, dead" ("Muertos, muertos, muertos"). He speaks movingly not of enemies, but of brothers who have died:

> He was our brother. The brother who stood
> with his immense courage and the firmness of a flowering rock on the earth.
> He was that brother who was deep inside us
> while we always saw ourselves outside him,
> he was our brother, and now no more!
> He is no more our brother, not our blood, our bones, our hair, our fingers.

One could almost see Lorca as one of those brothers, bringing up once again the question: to whom does the poet belong? In such a reading, Castroviejo illuminates a troubling paradox: this brother now belongs only by virtue of his permanent and mortal estrangement. He was the brother who was once simultaneously inside and outside the community of which the poet speaks. Whatever claim to this brother that Castroviejo might have is not, apparently, ideological or aesthetic in the poem. In fact, he appears to understand how profoundly uncertain and impossible such a claim is. He says, "Let no one seek to deceive his dead brother!" A political reading of this sort speaks to the underlying ambivalent posture of Falangism toward the figure of García Lorca.[26]

Alas, the poem is not about Lorca. When I first came across "The Last Brother," I thought it was, having found it in two recent anthologies, which printed the text as dedicated to Lorca. Evidently, the first anthologist, Gonzalo Santonja, skipped a page and conflated this poem with "Steady Steps" by including the last three stanzas and the Lorca dedication of the second poem. "The Last Brother" is, instead, dedicated to a close friend of his, Captain Tomás Bolíbar Sequeiros, a civil engineer who was killed in action and, like Castroviejo, hailed from Galicia. In the first edition of *Altura* (1938), six of the people with poems dedicated to them had died, either in battle or through execution. By the second edition (1939), there were twelve. The dedications, marked with traditional crosses, create a visual and symbolic sense of solidarity, a thematic band of brothers that suggests the Nationalists had more in common with the Republicans than is generally thought. Falangists used the term "comrade" ("camarada"), which also appears in *Altura* (though far less than "hermano"), as meaning "brother." Moreover, the image of the brother and phrases of militancy like "it is necessary" are laced throughout the collection, connecting "The Last Brother" with other poems such as "Steady Steps," "Es preciso" (It Is Necessary), and "Oración a nuestro señor Santiago en el tercer año de la guerra de España" (Prayer to St. James the Great in the Third Year of the War in Spain). "Es preciso" is inscribed to Onésimo Redondo, one of the key figures of Falange. "Prayer," which is the last poem in the 1939 edition, begins with the phrase "it is necessary" and is dedicated to José Antonio. In the first edition, Castroviejo arranged "Steady Steps" to precede "It Is Necessary," thus reinforcing their rhetorical relationship, but in the second edition, the Lorca poem is immediately tied to "The Last Brother" (which does not appear in the first edition). All these linkages place Lorca in an odd series of relationships, not simply with Redondo, Primo de Rivera, Bolíbar Sequeiros, and other Nationalists, but with all the dead, who loom over *Altura* like a fatal cloud. He has become a peculiar kind of brother, the one Republican, amid a sea of Nationalists, perhaps the ultimate "last brother" after all. Lorca, who claimed in his final interview he was "a brother to all" and hated the idea of sacrifice in the name of an abstract nationalism, might well have found his place in *Altura* deeply ironic.[27]

Can there be anything more schizophrenic than the contrast between Aparicio's vituperative prologue and Castroviejo's dedication? The picture of the Lorca-Falange relation that begins to take shape is much more mixed, more blurred than we have been given to believe. Neither unmitigated Falangist hostility nor unadulterated admiration for Lorca fully account for the range of Falangist reactions to his death or his poetry. Undoubtedly, there were some *falangistas* who were attracted to the figure of Lorca and his work, but first they had to clear the hurdle of their own ideology in order to be able to talk about the poet or, in other cases, to try quixotically to bring him into the fold.

The period itself was a muddle politically. It was not uncommon for people to switch political allegiances, sometimes dramatically. Aparicio started out with Communist leanings only to gravitate toward Falangism. Castroviejo went from Carlist to Falangist. Ramón J. Sender veered from anarcho-syndicalist to Communist sympathizer, though he never joined the party, in the meantime becoming disillusioned by the party's cynical wartime opportunism. Moreover, while many writers of the avant-garde were on the left, others turned rightward, such as Giménez Caballero, Ramón de Basterra, and Edgar Neville. The right shared elements of vanguard experimentation with the left, most notably in aestheticizing politics. The left, it has been said, politicized aesthetics, while the right did the opposite, aestheticizing politics (though one can certainly also find the former among the right). But their ultimate effects are not terribly different, mixing politics and art so intimately and so messily that their various incompatibilities could only lead to divorce, that is, disillusionment or indifference. (The postwar histories of any number of Republican exiles and Falangists frozen out of power by the Franco regime bear closer examination in this respect.)[28]

This brings me to another point that must be made. Lorca knew many of these people. Many of them were his friends. Some of them, like the Rosales brothers who were all *falangistas* save one, tried to rescue him from the madness of civil war. There is a tendency to see the Second Republic and the war as so completely polarized, in such Manichean terms that each side possessed its own exclusive version of heaven and hell. Without question the war forced people to take sides; no one could remain on the fence, but this didn't mean that everybody wanted to take sides. Here is that "third Spain" again, which must have been an uncomfortable, awkward, even dangerous place to be in the 1930s.

Consider, for example, the case of two friends of Lorca, who were both intimately associated with the avant-garde and joined the Falange. The first, Joaquín Romero Murube, was part of a second-tier group of writers of the Generation of 1927, to which better known poets like Lorca, Alberti, Cernuda, and Aleixandre belonged. Beginning in 1932, the friendship between Lorca and Romero Murube was so close that they stayed at each others' family homes in Madrid and Seville. Shocked by Lorca's murder, Romero Murube privately printed in 1937 a little book titled *Siete romances* (Seven Ballads) in a limited edition of 237 copies. As an editor of a most welcome reprinting of this rare text, originally published in the Nationalist zone (Seville), remarked, "I believe that if *Siete romances* had fallen into the hands of the military censors, they would have shot [Romero Murube] straight off." The book bears this dedication: "To you, in Vízna[r], close to the big fountain, become earth now and the eternal murmur of hidden water!" We know that Romero Murube went with a friend to Granada in August 1936 to ascertain if the rumor of Lorca's execution was true. The editors say he was unable to find out anything, but the dedication suggests otherwise. At some point he had already acquired a rough idea of the location where Lorca had been shot.[29]

Lorca's influence is transparent throughout the book, but only one ballad, "Romance del crimen" (Ballad of the Crime), alludes to the poet's death. This poem originally appeared under a different title and context in 1929. With this and other small changes, Romero Murube turned the text into a stylized denunciation of Lorca's assassination. The style and imagery are Lorquian, imbued with the spirit of the vanguard. Like many other homages, it is in the manner of, after Lorca. Thus, "On the asphalt slither / serpents of green blood," recalling the Granadine poet's celebrated use of the color green in "Romance sonámbulo" ("Sleepwalking Ballad") and these verses from "Reyerta" ("The Feud"): "Sliding blood moans / the mute song of the serpent." The poem ends with the lines:

> And everywhere the press
> will deliver in great detail
> to honorable homes
> five columns of blood.

The irony is thick here, since the Nationalist papers were largely silent on Lorca's death, and at that point almost no one knew very much about the murder. The newspapers' "five columns of blood" play on the allusion to the five wounds of Christ, an image that appears in Lorca's poetry. They also recall the image of five red roses of blood found in the Falangist hymn "Cara al sol" (Face to the Sun). Five red roses were ritually placed at the feet of a murdered martyr, as illustrated in the Falangist novel *Camisa azul*.[30]

But there is a far more impressive poem by Romero Murube that appeared in the *Antología poética del Alzamiento, 1936–1939* (Poetry Anthology of the Uprising, 1936–1939), sometimes referred to as *Poetas del imperio* (Poets of Empire), in 1939. "No te olvides . . ." (Do not Forget . . .) begins by saying: "Do not forget, brother, there was an August / when even the oleanders turned to blood." While the poem contains no dedication or specific reference to Lorca, these lines evoke the poet's death in August 1936, a death filled with the bitter scent of oleander found in so many Lorca texts. Romero Murube's images describe a country bleeding with the cartloads of death, the tormented cries of the condemned, the pardon to which a deaf ear is turned, and the terror of flight amid a forest of bullets. For everything you cannot say with words, brother, he writes, cry deep, cry to heaven: Spain! This Spain with which the poem ends is not necessarily or exclusively Nationalist. ("¡Arriba España! or "Long Live Spain!" is much more typically Francoist.) Republicans too used the same rhetorical device during this period, as the editors of *Siete romances* point out. This is not a Nationalist Spain or a Nationalist Lorca, and it is to Romero Murube's credit that he wrote a poem so unlike the usual triumphalist, partisan verse of his compatriots.[31]

The other friend of Lorca I want to talk about is one of the most interesting figures of the period, Edgar Neville. A wealthy aristocrat, Neville was a premier humorist of the Generation of 1927, a film director, and member of Spain's diplomatic corps. During the Second Republic, he joined Manuel Azaña's political party, the Republican Left (Izquierda Republicana). He spent a few years in the United States during the Primo de Rivera dictatorship, where he worked on Spanish-language versions of American films, hobnobbing with Charlie Chaplin and Douglas Fairbanks. Returning to Hollywood for two months in the spring of 1936, he arrived back in Madrid the very day rightist politician José Calvo Sotelo was murdered. The war broke out a few days later.[32]

In 1937 Neville affiliated himself with the Falange. How did a man of liberal and agnostic tendencies, a man known for his cosmopolitan and bon vivant lifestyle, become a Falangist? Like a lot of people in civil war Spain, he was anxious to save his own skin, but less cynically, he was unhappy with the chaotic, deteriorating situation produced under the Second Republic's Popular Front. No radical, he preferred a sense of order to anarchy. His liberalism was not so much ideological as a reflection of his fundamentally open-handed attitude toward life, one biographer observed. He also belonged to a certain social class, many of whom supported the Nationalists. Indeed, the diplomatic corps of which he was a member was largely staffed with people of upper-class backgrounds. Many ended up defecting to the Nationalist side. Not a few, like Neville, played both ends against the middle in those first few months of the war, collecting a salary from the Republican government while privately declaring allegiance to the other side.[33]

Neville was eventually dismissed from his diplomatic post, and a few months later became a *falangista*. He did not, however, have an easy time regaining his diplomatic status under the Nationalists, who viewed him as ideologically suspect. He spent years submitting papers, affidavits, and other documents to the Francoist Commission for the Purification of the Diplomatic Corps (Comisión Depuradora de la Carrera Diplomática) and was only readmitted in 1940. Essentially, he was erasing his Republican past.

To my knowledge, Neville, who died in 1967, did not publish anything on Lorca until 1966, as part of a special issue of the Madrid daily, *ABC*, the first significant Francoist homage to the poet. No doubt the relative liberalization and relaxation of prior censorship, granted under the new Press Law and approved that year, played a role. Two things are worth noting about "La obra de Federico, bien nacional" (Federico's Works, a National Treasure). First, Neville displaced blame for Lorca's death away from the regime and onto the bad behavior of unknown individuals and the initial disorder of war. It was a crime of country rubes, most likely an act of personal revenge, he said. More than anything, Lorca's murder, like so many others, was incredibly stupid.[34]

Neville also made a trip down to Granada, part of a pilgrimage, he wrote, to find whatever trace of Lorca was left. His was not the first, or last, journey south. Romero Murube had gone right after the poet's death, and many more would come, some as friends to mourn like Dámaso Alonso in 1940, some as literary detectives (Gerald Brenan, Claude Couffon, Agustín Penón, Gibson) to solve the riddle of his disappearance. Some simply looked for him in his works, in bookstores, the way Rolfe and Hurtado had. Like so many others, Neville found nothing. The villagers were unfriendly and no doubt afraid to talk, as Brenan also discovered in the late 1940s.

Neville concluded by urging Lorca's remains be reburied in the Alhambra, in a ceremony of national unity in which everyone would participate. Similarly, his poetry and plays should be above politics, and only the politics of reconciliation should prevail. Earlier he said that "the idea of the monument to the fallen of both sides is a noble idea." These words have been interpreted as a request for such a monument, but it is also possible to read them as a guardedly positive allusion to Franco's Valley of the Fallen, inaugurated in 1959, which puts a somewhat different spin on what he wrote. The Valley, where both José Antonio and Franco are buried (Franco's body was removed in 2019), is a Nationalist monument, built largely with the labor of Republican prisoners, though it was touted by some as honoring both sides. The cautious ambiguity of the sentence is a reminder that all writers were subject to censorship in this period.[35]

In 1966, this message was considered sufficiently innocuous that the Franco regime did not object to the article, though some of Neville's friends did. In April 2010, however, Andrés Trapiello revealed that Neville had also written a very strong letter sometime in 1967, unpublished till now, urging that further investigation of the Lorca murder be pursued. We're talking about, the letter said, "a bunch of contemptible creatures whose intellectual level was sufficiently high to know the value of their prisoner, to know he was totally innocent and politically harmless." These were men who took pleasure in blowing the brains out of a person "full of ideas, beauty and goodness."[36]

This was not everything Neville had to say about Lorca. Little observed are two other writings of his on the subject. One of them is simply called "García Lorca," a revised version of the 1966 article. It appeared posthumously in 1969, but internal evidence shows that Neville himself made the changes, some of which are significant. At times he simply substituted or added another word or phrase, but even here he modified the tone and intention of the article. In 1966, he referred to the Franco regime's "error of allowing people who weren't even friends of the poet to exploit the poet's corpse." In "García Lorca," he wrote of "the foolishness of allowing the Movement's enemies, people who weren't friends of the poet, to exploit the poet's corpse." An "error" has become "foolishness," and an underlying political agenda becomes more transparent with reference to the Movement, that is, the sole political party that was legal in Franco's Spain. Clearly, Neville was interested in making sure that the regime would maintain control of the narrative.[37]

On the other hand, he added something astounding, appearing to reflect the contents of the unpublished letter. He said that in Granada people know who killed Lorca, but that the names cannot yet be released. Had the regime punished the murderers during the war, anti-Francoists would have had less reason to exploit the poet's death politically. Then he wrote: "At the end of the war everything possible was done to bring to trial, judge, and punish criminals, while the death of Federico continues unpunished, and this is the distinguishing fact that I deplore, not in the spirit of revenge, since so many years have passed, but because it offends me that we appear to be turning a blind eye, which is practically like making common cause with the guilty."[38]

The "criminals" punished at the end of the war were Republicans, some of whom probably did commit criminal acts (as did many Nationalists), but most were executed or sent to prison simply because they were on the losing side. Neville appeared unaware of the disproportion and difference between the two kinds of crimes entertained in his article. And as we have seen, his arguments were meant at least in part to benefit the regime. Nonetheless, it took some courage to speak so bluntly of a topic that was still pretty much taboo and addressed only with great caution: Lorca's death and the fact that those responsible had gotten away with murder.

Neville returned to the same subject in a poem. "Su último paisaje" (His Last Landscape) must have been written around the same time as his article for *ABC*, but before he wrote the letter, which refers to it. It speaks of following in the footsteps of Lorca's last moments and describes some of the landscape that the poet would have traversed. Like the prose piece, the poem literally goes after Lorca, seeking him out on the road to Víznar. Going after Lorca, however, merely brings home that this trajectory is really a depiction of Lorca's afterlife. In many homages to the poet there is an extraordinary, intense desire to visualize his last moments on earth. Neville's poem is no exception.

He drives home that point by citing the opening lines of Machado's elegy to Lorca at the beginning of his own poem. Machado was one of the first to imagine how Lorca met death. Neville continued that tradition, not only by alluding directly to Machado, as other writers have done, but by imitating in a kind of secular *imitatio Christi* Lorca's trajectory:

> And today, Federico my friend,
> in passing through Granada,
> I have wanted to follow that road
> through which your executioners must have brought you
> on that terrifying last day,
> on your last morning.[39]

The topography through which he passes turns to blood,

> blood spilt, blood hidden
> by cowardly peasant silence,
> from those witnesses "who know nothing."

This, he said, is "silent Víznar," this is "the most unjust crime of my country," this is Granada "pierced by shame."[40]

I have searched for you, Neville wrote, I have gazed upon the last landscape you saw. I am

> your school companion
> in Roman Law . . .
> Companion in the songs of *soleares*,
> and in the songs of the forge.
> The friend of first nights and café causeries.

While there are few references to Neville in the Lorca correspondence, testimonials, or secondary literature, Neville obviously considered himself a friend, as did Lorca himself and Isabel García Lorca in her posthumously published memoirs. Interviewed by Marino Gómez Santos in 1962, he spoke warmly of his friendship with Lorca, whom he met in 1920 in Madrid, most likely at one of Ramón Gómez de la Serna's literary gatherings at the Café Pombo. Lorca gave him a private reading of what was to be his first produced play, *El maleficio de la mariposa* (The Butterfly's Spell). In June 1922, Neville traveled down to Granada with the poet for the Cante Jondo Festival organized by Manuel de Falla. The Lorca Foundation archive contains two letters and a postcard from Neville to the poet. In one letter dated 22 August 1928, using the second-person familiar address, he wrote enthusiastically about the *Gypsy Ballads* and added that he wanted to make a film of the poems on Antoñito el Camborio and "La casada infiel" (The Faithless Wife), recording the poet's voice as he recited them. The project, alas, apparently never got off the ground. More importantly, as Lorca's friend, he identified himself emotionally with the poet and wrote himself into Lorca's life with these lines from "His Last Landscape."[41]

The poem appeared in 1967, in the collection *Poemas*, but it was also published in a limited edition of two hundred copies the year before, along with two other poems and graced with one of Lorca's drawings of a sailor (it is not reproduced in *Poemas*). The "Note to the Edition" emphasizes Neville's friendship with Lorca, observing that in Granada he had explored the terrain where the poet met his end, photographing the mountains, hills, and gullies of its topography. This experience evoked memories and nostalgia in Neville, but also "a noble desire for rebellion and protest," the note says.[42] Neville was able to get away with a more open denunciation of Lorca's death in this small edition precisely because it had little distribution and was less likely to come to the attention of the authorities.

None of this explains why he waited until 1966 to write about Lorca or to visit the place of his execution. His health was failing in his last years, so perhaps he felt he could wait no longer, and the *ABC* homage provided an opening. I do not know. At one point, in 1952, he alluded somewhat obliquely to Lorca in his film, *Duende y misterio del flamenco* (Duende and Mystery of Flamenco), in which the scene of a funeral procession for a beloved singer and favorite poet set in the Granadine neighborhood of Sacromonte is followed immediately after by that of a horseman and a voiceover reciting the opening lines from "Rider's Song": "Córdoba / Distant and lonely." (Though the allusion to the Sacromonte, the singer and the poet only appears in the version with English subtitles, for distribution in North America.) But thirty years after Lorca's death, he was still bothered by the poet's murder. These pieces show him trying to come to grips not only with the murder but with his own feelings, feelings so strong that he was finally compelled to go to Víznar and see for himself. Significantly, he relied partly on the words of an iconic Republican poet, Antonio Machado, to express what he felt. He not only opened but closed the poem with lines from "The Crime Was in Granada":

> And only a cold, clandestine wind
> murmurs:—"The crime was in Granada,
> know this, poor Granada! in his Granada."

The note to the 1966 edition suggests that Machado's presence here gave the poem "its deepest value," implicitly politicizing it.[43]

To cite from one of the strongest supporters of the Second Republic was to make a political statement. Neville certainly understood it this way, since he was careful not to quote the last lines of "The Crime Was in Granada" in his *ABC* article, which had a wide readership. It was safer to use lines from Machado in a poem, with a much more limited audience. Moreover, he chose the adjective *clandestine* to describe the voice of the wind reciting Machado's verse, a term with political implications in 1966, given the Franco regime's outlawing of the Second Republic. Only the opposition to Franco was labeled clandestine.

Neville appears to have dropped his Falangism along the way and resumed his cosmopolitan lifestyle, but that does not mean he stopped supporting the Franco regime, to judge from these writings. Rather, the personal and the political are hard to separate. The private quest for Lorca's trace was mixed up with public desire to make things right for Nationalist Spain, when it came to the dead poet, even if it meant airing dirty laundry. His comment about not "making common cause with the guilty" speaks of an underlying, lingering sense of shame, if not for himself then for the country. Recall too a Granada "pierced by shame" in his poem. There is almost a penitential air, most likely unconscious, in Neville's passage through Lorca's death march.

Lorca, in dying once again on paper, glows in that strange afterlife of poetic purgatory in which he resides. Neville himself seems caught in a similar limbo, unable to articulate fully what is bothering him. Something has been left unsaid, undone. His revisions to the 1966 article suggest he was not satisfied with the original piece, and we now know there was an angry letter about Lorca written after he published the *ABC* article. Whether he wanted to publish the letter, to which he gave the title "Otra vez Lorca" (Once More Lorca), is not clear to me, but in it he admitted that the 1966 article did not express everything he wanted to say. For whatever reasons (perhaps censorship, whether external or self-imposed), he removed some material, in his mind undercutting both the clarity and thesis. People were right to accuse him of being lukewarm in his defense of the poet, he said. In any event, completing the poet's final journey on earth was completing history, symbolically speaking, filling in the gaps and questions. Neville was unable to do so, but he took it personally, as did so many.

The ways people on the right saw Lorca were not monochrome, and distinctions should be made among them. By the 1960s drawing implicit parallels between Lorca and Primo de Rivera was not a high priority (though Giménez Caballero made a stab at it in 1966). Neville seemed entirely uninterested in making that case. But in the heat of war, neither did Romero Murube and Castroviejo, in striking contrast to Hurtado and Villena. An underlying ambivalence toward Lorca, however, can be detected among nearly all these writers, given their political allegiances and the circumstances of the poet's death. Making Lorca one of their own, as Hurtado and Villena attempted to do, was a stretch. By the 1940s the poet had become invisible in

Figure 4. Roy Campbell, 1951.
Photo by Jane Bown, © The Jane
Bown Literary Estate / National
Portrait Gallery, London.

Spain, and it was not until 1954 that the regime allowed publication of his complete works.

Shortly after the war, the Falangist writer de Foxá published an article called "Los Homeros Rojos" (Red Homers), in which he excoriated "Red poetry" as "chemically pure, dehumanized" and fated to end in Marxism. He did not name Lorca, but the poet's friends and fellow *vanguardistas*, Rafael Alberti, Luis Cernuda, Miguel Hernández, and Manuel Altolaguirre, were mentioned in the piece. "El olor marxista" (The Smell of Marxism), by Wenceslao Fernández Flórez, appeared in the same issue of *ABC*. In such a hostile, explosive atmosphere, it is small wonder that Lorca vanished from view.[44]

The same ideologically charged understanding of the poet and his times infused the writings of another man of the right, one of the most fascinating figures of the English-speaking literary world and a gifted poet, Roy Campbell (fig. 4). Campbell, a South African, was among the few non-Spanish writers to support Franco during the war. Like Lorca himself, he was larger than life, full of vitality and mesmerizing to many. There was "something big and generous seemed to flow out of the man in that firm clasp, that forthright look and Roy's whole intensely alive, eager bearing." He was "born on fire."[45]

He was also a deeply conflicted man, filled with contradictions. Hating authority, he embraced the Francoist authoritarian regime. Early in life he had anticlerical views, only to convert to Catholicism while living in Spain. Yet in a drunken moment he confessed to not believing in anything, to being a complete anarchist. His language and views were sometimes violent in nature, he himself rarely, though he did punch poet Stephen Spender in the nose once for calling him a fascist.

His inner unease came partly from being an outsider.[46] A wild dominion boy, he fit awkwardly into British culture, especially the Bloomsbury literary set of which he was briefly a part. His wife Mary's affair with the sexually voracious Vita Sackville-West (also Virginia Woolf's lover at the same time) nearly wrecked his marriage and turned him passionately against Bloomsbury. His own two fleeting homosexual affairs as a young man surely played a role here. Literary Britain never forgave him for lampooning progressive, effete Bloomsbury in his satire, *The Georgiad*.

More than anything, Campbell was ambivalent about modern life. He had been raised in a culture that valued the individual and individual worth, and the things he cherished had to do with a life of action, as well as the love of nature and rural life. He loved hunting, jousting, horse breaking, even bullfighting, and yet he was also a bookish man, which meant that when he returned home to South Africa on visits, he was also an outsider there. In this, he had something else in common with Lorca. Both were nature poets, with roots planted deep in country life. Lorca's antipathy to the urban frenzy of New York City is matched by Campbell's ferocious disdain of Bloomsbury sophistication. In his autobiography, he admitted London fascinated him, while feeling all along there was a minotaur "lurking here in the fogs," "a sort of psychic miasma which I slew in the *Georgiad*." Like Hemingway, he too "had a romantic love-affair with Spain," as Robert Graves observed, though it was not necessarily the same Spain each man had in mind.[47]

The Spanish Civil War was a turning point in Campbell's life and work. Conversion to Catholicism while living in the volatile and polarized Spain of 1935 inevitably colored his perception of things. His fervent new faith was also a political statement, visible in *Flowering Rifle*, a long narrative poem in heroic couplets that he composed during a frenzied two-week period, as a paean to the Nationalists in 1939. Despite flashes of verbal brilliance, the poem is a failure, badly structured, tedious, and full of political spleen. Spender wrote, "There are several passages in this book which make me feel physically sick." The poem is as much a continuing attack on the British literary left, Campbell's bête noire, as it is propaganda for Franco.[48]

My interest in *Flowering Rifle* centers on what he has to say about Lorca. Campbell, who never met him, also wrote a book on the poet (published by Yale University Press) and translated four volumes worth of his work, which merit comment as well. Here, first, are the lines from *Flowering Rifle:*

> And what if Garcia Lorca died for this [godlessness]
> Caught bending over that forlorn Abyss
> For some mephitic whim his soul that spliced,
> As once he boasted, with the Antichrist?
> This weary Faustian hunger for the void
> An age of intellectuals has destroyed;
> In him another Marsyas sang and died,
> The victim of the God that he defied:
> Was Spain to let an enemy escape
> Vowed to her Foe though in an angel's shape
> And lovely as Lalanda with his cape?
> It was his fate with his own age to die—
> That of the fevered sin and languid eye,
> And let the new-fledged eagle take the sky.[49]

The Republicans, for Campbell, are a godless lot, and so Lorca, associated with the satyr Marsyas whom Apollo flayed for his hubris, is "the victim of the God that he defied." Some of the imagery is, additionally, very suggestive. The poet is associated with the "fevered sin" and "languid eye," phrasing that calls to mind Campbell's virulent antihomosexual attacks in other parts of the poem. The allusion to bullfighter Marcial Lalanda, celebrated for his invention of the *mariposa* pass, may also contain the same innuendo, implicated in the homosexual slang meaning of *mariposa*. Curiously, those three lines (from "Was Spain to let . . . " to "with his cape") were struck from the revised version of *Flowering Rifle*. One cannot help wondering whether Campbell's own sometime bisexuality and anguish over his wife's lesbian infidelity played a part in these lines.

Significantly, the image of "the new-fledged eagle" (a Francoist emblem, borrowed from the Catholic monarchs) allowed Campbell to make the transition to a key figure in the book, Primo de Rivera, right after the passage on Lorca. Here though, unlike Hurtado and Villena, he established not an implicit parallel but a stark contrast. José Antonio is the

> One (whose Absence fills the land entire
> With one mad love to emulate his fire)
> At the same moment, to the firing squad
> Spurning his body, launched his soul to God,
> Whose epic line (no flourish of the pen)
> Was life and rapture, and whose words were men.[50]

In *Flowering Rifle,* the Nationalists are "men"; the Reds turn tail and run away.

From these words you might think Campbell was a fascist or Falangist. He wasn't, though he certainly supported Franco and seemed to revel in the cult of heroes. When World War II broke out, he immediately volunteered for British military service. Like Lorca, he never joined a political party; and he hated group think. Indeed, he had no coherent set of political beliefs, "only personal likes and dislikes," as his biographer observed.[51] José Antonio fit Campbell's image of the heroic individual. Lorca did not.

In the revised edition of *Flowering Rifle,* Campbell added a long footnote to the Lorca passage:

> The amazing amount of paper wasted over this almost unique stain on Nationalist arms [the murder of Lorca] is typical of the Anglo-Saxon Press. When the Nationalists entered Granada the unbelievable babooneries perpetrated by the Reds made them trigger-happy as they rounded up and shot all corrupters of children, known perverts and sexual cranks. A natural reaction, considering that the week before the Reds had slaughtered and tortured anyone who was under suspicion of any sort of decency at all. Maeztu, Calvo Sotelo, Muñoz Seca, Padre Eusebio (about to be canonised) and [José] Antonio Primo de Rivera were all killed not for their vices but for their virtues. They were intellectuals on a higher scale, and died better than the cowardly Lorca. If the author of this poem, a better poet than Lorca, so Borges the leading S. American critic points out, had not been resourceful, he would have died, like Lorca, but at the hands of the Reds.[52]

One hardly knows where to begin. Both Republicans and Nationalists no doubt persisted in denying the atrocities committed by their own side, although Campbell's rhetoric ratchets up the ante considerably, calling the

Nationalist response "a natural reaction" and seemingly lumping Lorca among the "corrupters of children, known perverts and sexual cranks." One suspects, too, that most people would prefer not to be killed either for their virtues *or* their vices. For Campbell, Nationalist intellectuals simply knew how to die better than Republicans, and the worst insult was to be called a coward. Poor Lorca: not only a coward, but an inferior poet as well. Having enshrined heroism as part of their ideology, Falangists too were obsessed with cowardice, but the South African's preoccupation with it drew upon a different, more personal source, which was deeply attached to the history and culture of his homeland and to the values of individual worth and courage.[53]

If these deplorable views were the only thing Campbell had to say about Lorca, I would not bother to discuss him here. It is not clear to me when he made the revisions to the poem, but we know that he had corrected the proofs for the volume of his *Collected Poems* in which it was to appear, in January 1957. On 23 April, he was killed in a car crash near Setúbal in southern Portugal. What is so odd about these vituperative and intemperate comments is that they would appear in print *after* Campbell had published his largely glowing book on Lorca's poetry in 1952 and had translated much of his work into English. How to reconcile such wildly divergent treatment of Lorca?

A clue to this puzzle lies in his translations of Lorca, which Faber & Faber, under T. S. Eliot's aegis, was keen to publish. Four volumes of translations were ready in early 1950, but according to Campbell's biographer, they never appeared with the press "because of copyright difficulties." His wife Mary said he "translated nearly all the works of García Lorca." They were even advertised as in preparation between 1946 and 1949 in *The New Statesman* and in *Poetry London*. What happened? Letters from 1946 between fellow Republican exiles Arturo Barea, his wife Ilsa and Guillermo de Torre and between de Torre and Lorca's brother Francisco, fill in some of the details. Barea, who informed de Torre of the impending translations, felt strongly that it would be "a beastly thing" were Campbell, a pro-Franco supporter, to publish them.[54]

In a letter to de Torre dated 17 July 1946, Francisco explained that his mother authorized his brother's old friend, Rafael Martínez Nadal, to make the arrangements, a contract had been signed and an advance given. "How could I have imagined," he wrote, "that Nadal was going to entrust the translation of Federico's works to a Francoist writer, and that the Roy Campbell I had heard about was the author of poems in honor of Franco."[55]

Barea eventually met Campbell over drinks, where the South African "unexpectedly displayed anxiety lest he be misinterpreted by our [Republican] side." He said he felt honored and obliged to do the translations and believed the family, through Martínez Nadal, had given him permission. Barea thought Martínez Nadal manipulative and Campbell naïve. He was also afraid Campbell might somehow present Lorca as a Nationalist writer and mistakenly identified him as having been a volunteer in Franco's army. Campbell never fought in the civil war, however, although he sometimes gave that impression. Like Lorca, he enjoyed making up stories, especially about himself. His wartime experience was limited to a few days as a correspondent in the Nationalist zone.[56]

In the end the contract was rescinded, which must have been a huge disappointment to Campbell and a huge relief to the Lorca family. Barea believed Campbell was a Falangist, which was not the case, but his pro-Nationalist views were enough to kill the project. There is no mention in the correspondence of the specific verses on Lorca from *Flowering Rifle*, and one can only imagine the Lorca family's horror had they seen the revised version of the poem. His biographer's reticent explanation of "copyright difficulties" barely suggests what was really happening behind the scenes.

Yet I am struck by what Barea had to say about meeting with Campbell in an English pub, which is that the South African was anxious not to be misunderstood by the Republicans. This insecurity was of a piece with Campbell's conflicted nature. He obviously valued Lorca's poetry; otherwise he would not have translated so much of it, or written *Lorca: An Appreciation of His Poetry*. At one point he also wrote that the translations were partly "an expiation of the indelible stain on Nationalist arms resulting from the dastardy murder of Lorca." Then, why did he add such a hateful annotation to the revised *Flowering Rifle?* Was this a delayed angry reaction to the Lorca family's rejection of his translations? Was it a renewed immersion in the heated wartime atmosphere that first produced the poem? One can only speculate. His friend Charles Ley recalled in his memoirs that Campbell, still upset in 1951 over the translation debacle, took pleasure in hearing the Falangist Eugenio Montes trash Lorca as a playwright.[57]

One thing is certain. He was not about to treat Lorca as a martyr. Only heroes like José Antonio were martyrs for a righteous cause, and Lorca was José Antonio's complete opposite for Campbell. In 1946 he published this ditty titled "On the Martyrdom of F. Garcia Lorca":

> Not only did he lose his life
> By shots assassinated:
> But with a hatchet and a knife
> Was after that—translated![58]

As a translator himself, he was keenly aware of the lethal effects of bad translation, though here I think the intent goes a bit further in satirizing the stereotypical martyr image attached to Lorca.

Tellingly, his 1952 study of Lorca's poetry begins with these words: "The time is past when Lorca's steadily growing popularity could be ascribed to the dramatic circumstances of his murder during the Spanish Civil War. The memory of the wave of publicity on which his name was first launched as a martyr for communism would by now have caused a reaction against him in English-speaking countries if the worth of his work had not transcended all political emotions."[59] Campbell was right to play down the martyr role for the poet. By 1952, the times had changed, passions were largely spent, and Lorca's murder, while still mysterious, no longer uniquely defined who he was. Arguably, though, his death always lurks in the shadows, even now. More to the point, the politics behind his murder was the original catalyst for the subsequent twists and turns that Lorca's image and meaning would acquire over the years. In this respect, Campbell was no different from earlier commentators who politicized the poet. His rejection of one set of political ideas—those of the far left—issued not only from his own political views but from the Cold War context in which he was writing at this time.

Campbell was a vehement anti-Communist, as he had already made clear in *Flowering Rifle*. A Nationalist supporter remarked that the poem "serves also to condemn the Red shadow of Communism and its allies, who are legion." The opening paragraph to *Lorca* also referred to the now classic book on leftist disillusionment with communism, *The God That Failed*, published in 1949 and containing the essays of six writers/intellectuals—André Gide, Richard Wright, Ignazio Silone, Stephen Spender, Arthur Koestler, and Louis Fischer. Campbell would have gone straight to that of Spender, with whom he had had a turbulent personal and literary relationship. Spender singled out the crude Communist propaganda used to exploit the murder of Lorca, saying: "The fact that Lorca was not a Communist, but a Catholic who in fact fled to Franco territory at the beginning of the War, made his assassination by Fascists the more useful to the Communists." Whether the poet was Catholic or not is debatable. Nor did he go to Granada at the beginning of the war, but a few days before it began (and before Granada fell into Franco's hands). Spender's point, however, is well taken. He added: "I noticed when I was in Spain that most of the Spanish poets felt a certain shame about the propaganda that had been made from Lorca's death." In his autobiography, he wrote that the Communists canonized the poet, turning him into an "ex-officio Marxist saint."[60]

The left, like the right, certainly made ideological use of Lorca. John Wheelwright, an American socialist poet with Trotskyist tendencies, wrote in 1937 that Lorca was killed "because he was political," and then went on to say that "even as the death of De Bosis [an anti-fascist poet and aviator] in Italy showed that Fascism cannot long command the allegiance of creators, so the death of Garcia Lorca in Spain shows that creation impels the service of socialism." The poet's work, he said, "is important as propaganda." Writing in the *Daily Worker*, A. L. Lloyd declared that the Spanish fascists think "they are dispelling the spectre of Communism from Spain," but Communists like himself and Rafael Alberti "'are proud to call this spectre 'comrade,'" even though Lorca wasn't a party member. Campbell's initial politicization of the poet in *Flowering Rifle* was harpooned in 1957 by the Marxist Scottish poet Hugh MacDiarmid, in verses far more aesthetically impoverished than Campbell's:

> Bah! Any poet worth his salt would liefer die
> With Lorca, Campbell, than survive with you.
> And Fascism must needs treat any poet worth the name
> As it treated Lorca.

Sinking to a new low, he accused the South African of being "an accomplice" in Lorca's murder.[61]

Campbell claimed Lorca was apolitical, with "no political tub to thump." He rejected the label of martyr precisely because it reduced the poet to that of a "'world-message.'" Lorca's current detractors have been unable to spin him any longer as a political symbol, he said, and have now taken to calling him regional, provincial and "'a very minor poet, after all.'" Campbell's reevaluation, which was primarily an aesthetic one, insisted on the poet's regional character as the source of his universal appeal. By contrast, Lorca "is never more parochial and provincial than when he is self-consciously trying to be 'cosmopolitan.'" Campbell was half right and half wrong. He was wrong about Lorca's politics and right about his poetry being largely free of a narrowly ideological "'world-message.'"[62]

Spender, who reviewed the book, objected to Campbell's saying that the poet's name had been "launched as a martyr for communism" and that "as far as England is concerned, no book about Lorca has so far appeared which has not tried to use him as a political symbol." Not true, he said, and brought up Martínez Nadal's protesting the "use of Lorca's name for purposes of propaganda" as proof, though Nadal's statement in truth buttressed Campbell's opinion. Astonishingly, Spender appears to have forgotten what he himself wrote in 1949 about crude communist propaganda exploiting the poet's death.[63]

Another reviewer thought Campbell overstated "the left-wing idolisation [of Lorca] and the reaction which has followed." The precise source for Lorca as "'a very minor poet, after all,'" with no "'world-message,'" was not given, though Campbell said he was quoting the poet's "former admirers and present detractors." I found the put-down of Lorca, but it came from a Falangist writer, Manuel Iribarren, not from the left, and appeared within months of the poet's death: "The ultramodern poets have turned all moral values upside down. García Lorca—a minor poet after all—sported the title of Pontifice, flaunting his phony Andalusianism under the gray skies of the North, like a professional cliché of Spanishness." Apparently, Borges was not alone in seeing Lorca as "a professional Andalusian." It is certainly quite possible that a left-minded critic might also have had similar views of the Granadine poet's reach (if not his moral values). Iribarren, who was from Navarra, however, also went on to say that the morally and spiritually superior North would redeem Lorca's South, thus pitting one region against the other. Was Campbell misremembering or projecting? Ironically, the South African's book was praised elsewhere for introducing readers to "a minor genius."[64]

In rejecting the image of Lorca as a martyr for communism, Campbell reminds us of the parallel Falangist view of the poet as a martyr for imperial Spain, like Primo de Rivera, as envisioned in Hurtado and Villena. This view did not prevail in postwar Spain, even as the Franco regime eventually found it politically attractive to recuperate an apolitical Lorca whose death could not be blamed on the regime but on anonymous, chaotic forces. Campbell seems to follow a similar line, saying that the poet's murder "was but one of tens of thousands of deaths which were due to the settling of personal accounts behind the smoke-screen of civil strife." None of this makes for martyrdom of any sort. A "private grudge," as Campbell calls it (much like Neville), or "an unfortunate, vile episode" ("un episodio vil y desgraciado"), as Pemán wrote in 1948, is not good material for a martyr narrative. Campbell had already excluded Lorca from heroic death in *Flowering Rifle*, a death reserved only for men like Primo de Rivera, "whose phoenix blood in generous libation / With fiery zest rejuvenates the nation."[65]

Yet in 1952 he also had this to say about the poet: "In the repeated wrestling with the idea of death, Lorca generally increases the stature of life, and intensifies it. All those people who repeatedly seek out death to risk their lives do so chiefly because they are overflowing with a surplus of life." Whether he thought Lorca also sought out death remains ambiguous. What is certain is that Campbell saw himself in this light, and in that sense, he discovered himself in Lorca's poetry, sharing with him the "surplus of life" so many people observed in both writers. In that respect, Dudley Fitts said "it would seem almost that Roy Campbell was born to write this explosive little book."[66]

Yet like others on the right whose lives were conditioned by war and the ideological strife of the 1930s, Campbell had some difficulty coming to grips with who Lorca was and where he fit in the South African's scheme of things. The poet is branded a coward, a product of fevered sin and languid eye, in one book, only to be aesthetically and existentially redeemed in another. Which part is and is not García Lorca? Campbell's reaction to Lorca was almost as schizophrenic as the mystifying contrast between Aparicio's contempt for the poet and Castroviejo's dedication to Lorca appearing in the same book. It is hard to reconcile the exquisite sensitivity with which Campbell talks about Lorca's poetry and the vulgar vilification of his character elsewhere. How is it possible to speak disapprovingly of the poet's "Faustian hunger for the void" on the one hand and, on the other, praise his capacity for "static inward illumination, lit up even by one's own sorrow"?[67]

If some on the right sought to complete Lorca's trajectory either by reinventing him as a Falangist martyr or reenacting his death march, Campbell seems to have responded to the poet in a deeply individual manner, alternating between revulsion and ecstasy, to judge from his writings. As one observer remarked, the South African finds in Lorca, "or imagines that he finds," those qualities that are his own.[68] But the paradox and the mystery remain: for a man so full of life as Lorca, why do so many people feel compelled to fill in that life with their own narrative of who he was?

As personal as Campbell's view of the poet was, it too is part of a larger story, a national and even supranational perspective, to which the narrative of Lorca and Primo de Rivera as martyrs, whether Falangist or not, also belongs. In an age of bitter divisions and debilitating uncertainties, when totalitarian mass movements like fascism and communism were sweeping away the very foundations of society, the cult of the individual refused to die, bolstering in some cases the same mass movements. José Antonio and Stalin are examples from opposite ends of the political spectrum, responding to the times and serving emotional and ideological needs that are often hard to disentangle. This last point is also true of Lorca.

One of those needs was expressed in the strong identification supporters of the Republic and others made between Lorca and the people, or pueblo. Unsurprisingly, the same thing happened with José Antonio, though the meanings of pueblo diverged. In both cases, this relation with the pueblo is intimately linked to the view of these figures as "poets," to how they were poets (notwithstanding José Antonio's reputation as a political writer). After a public recital of his "Ballad of the Spanish Civil Guard" in October 1935, Lorca received a wildly enthusiastic reaction from a massive, largely working-class crowd in Barcelona, who cried out, "Long live the poet of the people!" In a letter to his parents, he said he was so moved by their affection and fervor, by contact "with the real people," that he nearly choked up. Afterward, he shook hands with everyone for the next hour and a half. The event, to which I will return, commemorated the failed social revolution in Asturias only the year before, the significance of which Lorca fully understood, as he thought that the right would pounce on his presence there. No one, he wrote, could remain neutral in Spain anymore. Emotion and politics enveloped the moment, just as José Antonio's speeches fired up crowds.[69]

This enduring, if by now clichéd, image of the people's poet, which is largely a Republican narrative, continues to shape perceptions of Lorca, despite all attempts to eradicate or dismiss it. Ironically, the poet himself was a señorito, a member of the privileged classes, supported mostly by his father's generosity. Books by Republican exiles and sympathizers like Arturo Barea, Juan Rejano, and José González Carbalho in the late 1930s and 1940s effectively championed the close identification between Lorca and the popular, but what did "the people" mean in this instance? This word, along with señorito, a concept inseparable from pueblo, has a long and rich history in Spain. By the time of the Second Republic and the civil war, both terms had acquired complex political resonance, even as pueblo retained the aesthetic folkloric quality promoted in the nineteenth century.

In death, Lorca's connection with the pueblo turned into a symbol of the Republican cause. Pueblo as a category, however, was rarely examined, or it was absorbed into the working classes, urban and rural, while the poet's own social class was elided or smoothed over. A similar class awkwardness appeared in the case of his iconic contemporary, José Antonio, a señorito who claimed to espouse the working classes. Lorca's social affiliation led at least one twenty-first-century Marxist critic, José Antonio Fortes, to call the poet a Gramscian "organic intellectual of the bourgeoisie," whose work laid down the ideological conditions for fascism in Spain. This assertion in turn drew a heated response from the poet Luis García Montero—a dispute which, astonishingly, ended up in court. With this characterization of Lorca, Fortes used the opportunity to contest his iconic status and the value of his work, calling it nil. Lorca was a señorito, he said, whose social origins made it impossible for him to appreciate the life of the working classes. His views are a reminder of the politics of celebrity and fame, but also of the remarkable capacity of Lorca to set off firestorms even decades after his death. Fortes's allegation also allows us to position the poet with the other prominent señorito (and celebrity) of the period, José Antonio, while clarifying the degree to which the Marxist critic has misconstrued the Granadine writer ideologically and historically. As we will see, his class critique also has an antecedent of sorts in the 1920s. Lorca's afterlife is rooted in his past.[70]

To contextualize this after-image of the poet, we should first reexamine the understudied relation between pueblo and señorito as a cultural-historical opening into the evolving complexities of class and the fate of poetry in the fallen world of politics. As Tierno Galván has observed, the señorito, a term used initially by servants to characterize their young masters, is largely of nineteenth-century origin, a development of the new middle classes in Spain from the 1830s on, and ubiquitous in plays and realist novels. The classic example is Juanito Santa Cruz in Galdós's *Fortunata y Jacinta*. Nonetheless, the negative connotations attached to the figure—entitled, self-important, and idle, among other traits—already appeared by the late eighteenth century

in a well-known work of the stage by Tomás de Iriarte, *El señorito mimado*
(The Spoiled Señorito) (1787). The title character is described as

> self-willed, effeminate,
> superficial, insolent,
> an enemy of work,

and bears more than a *soupçon* of resemblance to the dandy figure of the *pe-timetre*. Almost a century later, Armando Palacio Valdés satirized the type in
his novel *El señorito Octavio* (1881), as a somewhat effeminate, provincial
snob and socially self-conscious bourgeois, in a word, *cursi*. A *señorito cursi*
was what Tierno Galván ironically called a fallen señorito, rather like a lapsed
Catholic who's slipped out of grace (though Tierno didn't take it that far).[71]

In most accounts of the type and the accompanying phenomenon of
señoritismo, a degraded señorito is redundant, as superfluous as José Ortega
y Gasset's "self-satisfied señorito" ("señorito satisfecho") outlined in his *La
rebelión de las masas* (Revolt of the Masses) (1929). Ortega removed the figure from the confines of the historic social class to which he belonged and
reimagined him as an example of mass man, "the spoiled child of human history," whose inheritance is the fruits of civilization. Today, we would call him
entitled. Essentially, Ortega appropriated the Spanish context of the señorito
and projected it onto a global scenario, hispanizing the world by retaining the
specific negative character of the type. Life, he wrote, is struggle, unending
effort to become oneself, with no guarantees, the very opposite of existence
as the señorito knows it. The señorito plays at life, indulges in every whim,
and signals his inauthenticity like a rhetorical flourish. Two years later, he
wrote that "it is necessary to do battle with life," which he saw as difficult and
serious. "Anything else is *señoritismo*." One cannot help thinking of his characterization of the avant-garde as essentially nonserious, nontranscendent art
at play in his earlier essay *La deshumanización del arte* (The Dehumanization
of Art). Is this, too, señoritismo, albeit in aesthetic form?[72]

Ortega's imaginative analysis also sheds light on a larger concern of
the period: the effort to make society productive as a measure of the meaningful life. This notion stems from Enlightenment principles, many of whose
representative thinkers waged war on the idle classes and elevated work as a
virtue and sign of progress. Ortega turned the productive into a philosophical principle rather than an economic-moral one (without altogether elimi-

nating these elements), but others saw it differently. In 1933, at the height of the Second Republic (and before the right's electoral victory in November), Marañón called the señorito a "tremendous plague in Spain" that was now diminishing, presumably because of new, harsher economic realities, declaring: "let no one live off the efforts of others." Tellingly, he found the type in all social classes. Like Ortega, the eminent physician and sexologist also saw life as a serious endeavor, and the "sportive spirit" ("espíritu deportivo"), in its largest sense, as unproductive, detrimental to "the noble and manly activity of creative labor." By contrast, in 1932, the manifesto at the heart of Lorca's theater group, La Barraca, declared that same spirit fundamental to its genesis.[73]

During the civil war, Antonio Machado also believed that the señorito phenomenon reached into all sectors of society, though with the coming of the conflict, the type, he said, had suddenly disappeared. (George Orwell observed something similar in Barcelona but saw later they were just lying low.) At the same time, the faces of ordinary militiamen seemed infused with "noble dignity" ("noble señorío"). Echoing Ortega, Machado wrote, "there are no señoritos, but rather, 'señoritismo,' one of several forms of degraded manhood, a particular version of not being a man." The infamous dauphins of Carrión in the *Poem of the Cid* were thus anachronistic "felonious señoritos," representative of a deeply corrupt aristocracy. By contrast, in a Heideggerian vein, "only man, never the señorito, man as intimately human and destined for death (*Sein zum Tode*), can look death in the face." Machado's stance in all these comments was at once idealistic and political, unsurprising in a war of such stark contrasts, passionately held beliefs, and mutual dehumanization of the enemy.[74]

The figure of the degraded señorito turned explicitly political with Lorca's assassination. The poet Eduardo Blanco Amor raged against the "shitty señoritos" ("mariconadas de los señoritos"), charging them (and all the bad actors of Spanish history) with the murder. Max Aub did the same, calling them "plague-ridden" and monstrous, with a similarly harsh accusation coming from José Mora Guarnido. Less than a month after Lorca's death, a newspaper article blamed "savage clericalism and pretty-boy señoritos" for the execution, calling out "the boastfulness and bloody exhibitionism of a degenerate señoritismo." In the same month, another Republican journalist reported secondhand on the conversation of an aristocratic señorito in Granada responding to the mistaken communiqué of playwright Jacinto Benavente's murder: "While the reds do such things, we've respected García Lorca, knowing as we know, that he bats for the other team. We will have to take action." To bat for the other team—"[ser] de la cáscara amarga"—can mean at least two things here (and probably both): to be on the left or gay. In the heightened atmosphere of civil war and coming from a señorito, these words appeared to convey a vague threat. There would be no respect, though plenty of action.[75]

As a class term with inevitable political associations, the señorito also made incursions into cultural-literary territory. The Republican exile Juan Climent juxtaposed the Falangist José María Pemán, whom he called "a poet-señorito" ("poeta señorito"), to the poet of the people, García Lorca. Pemán's verse was contrived, he said, pitched to the "tastes of a corseted public." For the rightist José María Carretero, the bullfighter-playwright Ignacio Sánchez Mejías, a doctor's son (and close friend of Lorca), was a señorito. Of all the members of the fabled Generation of 1927, most of whom could be considered señoritos for their social origins, only José María Hinojosa was singled out for his wealth and privileged position as "an Andalusian señorito" and mocked by his contemporaries (and supposed friends) as both a provincial snob and "a bohemian with a checking account," despite (or perhaps because of) his generous support of his fellow poets and their pet projects.[76]

Tellingly, if in a somewhat lighthearted vein, in 1926 Gerardo Diego alluded to the group to which he belonged as the "generation . . . of señoritos." At the time he was organizing a celebration of Luis de Góngora, an event indicative of the regard young writers like himself had for the seventeenth-century poet. Nearly a year later, the group would come in for harsh criticism from Ernesto López-Parra, who called them false innovators and young señoritos with reactionary ideas (anticipating Fortes's views decades later). Instead, he praised another group of young people, modest folk struggling to keep alive liberal values and beliefs. A similar juxtaposition of two different kinds of youth had already appeared three weeks before in the same newspaper, El Liberal. Mariano Benlliure y Tuero, son of the celebrated sculptor, never used the word señorito, but the terms with which he described the two groups—one frivolous, interested only in play, unwilling to work, and the other idealistic, committed, willing to sacrifice themselves—places the first kind of youth squarely among the class of señoritos who have invaded contemporary art, literature, and politics, according to his analysis.[77]

López-Parra and Benlliure leaned left, as did many, though not all, critics of the señorito and señoritismo, and would experience firsthand the consequences of war and dictatorship. A freemason, Benlliure was detained at least once by the Primo de Rivera dictatorship on charges of conspiracy, prosecuted by the Franco regime, and died an exile in France in 1951. A onetime *ultraísta* poet, López-Parra boasted of having been arrested twenty-one times by the Primo de Rivera regime and died of tuberculosis in a Francoist prison in 1941 while serving a politically imposed life sentence. In "Los innovadores," he was responding to a tongue-in-cheek, invented interview with Gerardo Diego that Ernesto Giménez Caballero had cooked up, in which he portrayed Diego as a fascist, at least in aesthetic terms (though it is impossible to separate the aesthetic from the political here). López-Parra failed to get the joke, but clearly didn't think much of the vanguard poets in any event.[78]

The only innovative writer was Góngora, he said, while Diego's cohort exuded an "air of bourgeois vulgarity found in provincial 'señoritismo.'" Literature was a sport to "this horrid wave of rearguard señoritos [señoritada] invading Madrid, nearly all of them having come from the provinces, like a singular form of leprosy." Somewhat contradictorily, he also slammed them as an elite group of university-educated intellectuals. This class critique of a literary group was at once aesthetic and political, obsessively focused on the distinguishing trait of provincialism and indirectly echoing a long-standing division between center and periphery in Spanish cultural and political life. Many of the Generation of 1927, such as Alberti, Cernuda, and Lorca, did indeed hail from the provinces, just as López-Parra's own solid middle-class family came from Talavera de la Reina. But Diego's witty riposte turned the tables on López-Parra's critique, when he replied that the brilliant and ingenious Góngora "was a señorito, a voluntary member of the aristocracy, a provincial, and—in the sense that you imply—most assuredly a sterile intellectual elitist, a man of elegance."[79]

Attacks on the señorito and señoritismo also came from the opposite side of the political spectrum. The vanguard writer Giménez Caballero, who had been steadily moving rightward, linked the aesthetic and the political in a single analogy between surrealism and marxism: "Those señoritos who surrealize [superrealizan] their poetry are the same as those other señoritos who communize [comunistizan] their political ideas. They devour their own social class, [leading to] the collapse of their standing, or *señorío.*" In 1933, two years after these remarks were made, Primo de Rivera delivered his inaugural speech on the founding of Falange, the Spanish fascist party. Acutely aware that his upper-class origins could prove fatal for some and wishing to appeal to the working classes, he declared the defense of privilege anathema. He said, "yes, we wear ties; yes, you could say that we are señoritos," but he insisted that the new party wanted to benefit all classes. A few months later, he clarified further his point of view and that of Falange in a piece titled "Señoritismo": "The 'señorito' is the degeneration of the 'señor,' or the 'hidalgo.' ... But the señorito, unlike the señor, believes that his social position relieves him from any obligation. It relieves him from work, sacrifice, and solidarity with other mortals." Like Marañón and Machado, he thought the type doomed as a class. There are considerable ironies of history in contemplating how devastatingly correct that prognostication proved for both Primo de Rivera and García Lorca.[80]

José Antonio's protestations aside, the moniker of señorito persisted even in death. Fellow Falangists like Pedro Laín Entralgo denied he was a señorito, because he did not fit the classic definition, while in life Primo de Rivera's rival, Ramiro Ledesma Ramos, always thought he was one. In an interview from the late 1980s, a fervent supporter put it this way: "They could not understand him: many from below, because he was a *señorito* of the aristocracy; and the aristocracy repudiated him because he was socially advanced and defended the worker."[81]

The image crafted of José Antonio the martyred icon rested partly on erasing, or at least downplaying, his status as a señorito, while associating him with the people, or pueblo, a concept that Falangists distinguished from the plebe and the masses. For Raimundo Fernández-Cuesta, the pueblo was responsible for "the great enterprises of [Spanish] history"; it was a "cosmic force," completely removed from the idea of popular sovereignty, which Falangists rejected. Moreover, the pueblo linked to José Antonio was rooted mainly in the countryside and the peasantry, despite his appeals to both the urban and rural worker. Fernández-Cuesta emphatically declared that José Antonio loved the people, not the plebe or the masses, while Antonio Tovar singled out the Falangist leader's sympathy for the peasantry, whose enemies, he said, were urban culture and high capitalism. The transcendent symbolism of the land and rural life as deeply Spanish infused Nationalist ideology in general, though an intimate connection to the land was also part of Lorca's image as a poet of the people and of Republican ideology, as I have observed elsewhere in this book.[82]

The señorito can only be fully understood in relation to the pueblo, as Eugenio Noel suggested in 1916, bluntly stating that the lower classes needed a master and only a revolution would change that dynamic. Like other commentators, he saw the Andalusian señorito as the archetype and the "product of an immense degeneration," not as a literary invention. The señorito was the younger version of the classic *cacique*, or local boss, as plentiful as olive trees, but diseased. A man of strong convictions and humble origins, Noel believed the pueblo was stirring from its long sleep. Others were saying similar things, even in venues as ephemeral as the ever-changing offerings of theater fare. In a monologue from 1905, we read that the señorito's days are numbered and the peasant class is rising. In the melodramatic *El señorito Arturo* (1900), the title character seduces a young woman from the lower classes, and her boyfriend kills the señorito at the end of the play.[83]

In 1922, Luis Antón del Olmet and Alfonso Vidal y Planas cowrote the theatrical production *El señorito Ladislao,* in which things spiral out of control after the drunken son of a Castilian cacique shoots a working-class man. The brother of the dead man's girlfriend refuses to shake the cacique's hand and rejects the familiar form of address customarily used with those considered social inferiors at the time. The people en masse demonstrate against the cacique and his family, and when the señorito gets off scot-free, the same brother kills him. Antón del Olmet was a political opportunist, but Vidal y Planas felt genuine sympathy for the downtrodden, perhaps in part because his bohemian lifestyle brought him so close to them. Astonishingly, one year later, for personal and professional reasons that remain somewhat clouded, Vidal y Planas shot his erstwhile collaborator dead during a theater rehearsal.[84]

A loaded term even in the nineteenth century, the señorito was increasingly associated with violence by Lorca's time. In a remarkable painting first titled *Self-Portrait,* then *Accident* (1936, Museo Nacional Centro de Arte Reina Sofía, Madrid), Alfonso Ponce de León depicted a señorito with matinee-idol features lying on the ground, a single car headlight focused on his body (fig. 5). He is awkwardly positioned, appearing not dead but oddly removed from his own surroundings, with one surreal eye staring mysteriously at an implied spectator. His head and one hand are against a rock, and the other hand clutches what appears to be dried thistle, amid lush greenery evocative

Figure 5. Alfonso Ponce de León, *Accident* (also known as *Self-Portrait*), 1936. Courtesy of Museo Nacional Centro de Arte Reina Sofía, Madrid.

of Le Douanier Rousseau's work framing the figure. The light emitted is both artificial and lunar, while a sign is posted with the words "it is prohibited" partially cut off. Reflecting magical realism and surrealist influence, the painting is at once enigmatic and ironic, resolutely unsentimental in the face of an apparently fatal car accident.[85]

There is no sense of victimhood or martyrdom in the figure. The body could just as easily have represented an extrajudicial execution, with the light visually targeting the figure, but in any event the entire picture demonstrates in aesthetic terms the effects of violence, symbolized in a classic object of modern life and its destructive tendencies, the automobile. The painter himself had experienced just such an accident, and the features of the man are modeled on the artist's own. Ponce de León never suggests that he intended to single out the señorito as his primary focus, but he didn't have to, as any contemporary observer would have recognized the type immediately. In fact, only a few years earlier, Ortega y Gasset had explicitly connected the señorito to the proliferation of luxury cars in a piece titled "La moral del automóvil en España" (The Morality of the Automobile in Spain), arguing against them on moral grounds as nothing but objects of social prestige.

The painter himself came from an upper-class background, with noble antecedents in his family history. Like the figure in the painting, he dressed with dandy flair and was teased for being a señorito. By the time he painted this picture he had joined Falange and was shot for his Falangist activities a month after Lorca was killed. Both were also tortured, Ponce de León, at the *checa,* or people's tribunal, installed in, of all places, Madrid's Círculo de Bellas Artes. (His father and two of his brothers were also executed, and his mother subsequently killed herself.) For this reason, the work has sometimes been read as prescient of his own destiny, in the way some interpret the Granadine poet's obsession with violent death in his poetry and plays. As was so often the case in this period, Ponce de León was friends with people across the ideological divide, including Lorca, for whom he designed the costumes and sets for two theatrical productions of La Barraca, and contemporaries like Edgar Neville, Dionisio Ridruejo, and Primo de Rivera. They often coincided at *tertulias,* or social gatherings, in places such as the Granja del Henar Café, where the painter, Neville, Luis Buñuel, Eduardo Ugarte, and Lorca socialized. Ponce de León met his future wife, Margarita Manso, also a close friend of Lorca, at the Academia de Bellas Artes de San Fernando where both were studying art, along with Emilio Aladrén, García Lorca's lover.[86]

You would have thought the painter's violent death choice material for Falangist martyrdom and future Nationalist celebrity, but that didn't happen. In truth, he was completely forgotten until the 1990s, with a revival of his work culminating in an exhibit and catalog in 2001. One small attempt to turn him into a martyr for the cause appeared in an undated, but probably wartime, article, but it seems failed to fire up more propaganda. He was depicted in stereotypically heroic fashion giving the Falangist cry as bullets were flying, reminding us of similar imagined and idealized portraits of Lorca meeting his end. I suspect that Ponce de León was too closely associated with the avant-garde, to appeal to political hard-liners. Neglect of his work since Franco's death is harder to explain but may perhaps be attributed to baked-in attitudes from the opposite side of the ideological compass stemming from the time of the Popular Front, as Stradling suggests.[87]

Whatever the reasons, the artist's lack of iconic status stands in stark contrast to the celebrity of Lorca or even of Primo de Rivera, as dimmed as the latter's burnished halo is in the present day. The aura that still clings to Lorca and once did to Primo de Rivera is probably another word for "poet," in the very broad, and not necessarily literal, sense that people appeared to have understood, in their presence and in the immediate aftermath of their deaths. "Poet" in this context goes back to the Romantic notion of seer or visionary. Agustín de Foxá said José Antonio was "our premier poet" ("nuestro primer poeta"). Another *falangista* declared he was poetry incarnate, reminding us that the founder of Falange believed nations (pueblos) were only moved by poets. To call José Antonio a poet was also another way of eliding his social position as a señorito.[88]

While the señorito meets a violent dénouement in Ponce de León's painting, the work doesn't include any allusion to the pueblo. As a Falangist and therefore anticapitalist, the artist opposed working-class exploitation, but the painting makes no class statement of that sort (nor does it need to). It does achieve something else, however: it projects onto the ironic figure of the señorito the aura of art itself through the combined defamiliarizing and alienating techniques of magical realism and surrealism. This aura is rooted in the same Romantic source as "poet," and both—poet and art—can be understood as cultic in this sense. The señorito possesses iconic status in this painting, sharing in a kind of celebrity distinction like that of Lorca and Primo de Rivera. His matinee-idol face, literally spotlighted and the central focus of the painting, emphasizes a glamor that no amount of irony can altogether extinguish, seeming to enclose the señorito's inauthenticity within poetry's purview.

Ponce de León's painting reminds us of the enduring power of this poet-aura. In the Romantic era, the poet's visionary gifts were also married to his ability to represent a certain spirit that was attached to something larger than himself, a collective *Geist* that crystalized in the notion of pueblo, as both people and nation. It is important to recognize that in Lorca's time, especially, both left and right exalted the pueblo, even if ideological aims differed. Figures such as Lorca and Primo de Rivera were emotionally invested as bearers of the pueblo's transcendence, though this symbolic transference was far more potent and lasting in Lorca's instance than in José Antonio's. A case could be made that pueblo became just as iconized as the two men precisely for its significance being funneled through their singular status. Like them (but also separately from these two figures), pueblo became enshrined, and in this sense, set in stone and unquestioned.

The pueblo's significance is at once aesthetic and political. From the very beginning, with its origins in nineteenth-century romanticism and nationalist identity movements, pueblo was both, as was the poet-spokesman of the pueblo. The liberal-minded Agustín Durán, for example, collected hundreds of anonymous *romances*, or ballads, but he also adapted popular legends and stories, explaining how he forgot about his own personality and felt transported to another time and place while writing them: "I was no longer then a man fed and nourished by the art taught in school; I wasn't the poet endowed with a specific name: rather, I was the universal spirit inspired by the wandering troubadours, who spread hither and yon the anonymous ideas that belonged to everyone." The Krausist reformer, Francisco Giner de los Ríos, declared that popular poetry was "the highest manifestation that nations can express of themselves. . . . [I]n [popular poetry], the poet is the patria." He looked for "the genius of peoples [pueblos] [to flow spontaneously] into the poet's own genius."[89]

But it was the poet Antonio Machado's father, Antonio Machado y Álvarez ("Demófilo"), who condensed the earlier *Volksgeist* in a progressive vision of the pueblo that his son, García Lorca, José Bergamín, and others would embrace. For Demófilo, the pueblo was the "great anonymous poet." "The cultured poet's mission," he wrote, "is . . . to elevate the production of the multitudes." While he greatly appreciated the beauty of form in popular literature such as the *romances*, its aesthetic qualities were inseparable from the pueblo's history and fundamental character, analogous to the land itself, that its forms revealed. (This assimilation of land and pueblo would later reappear in writings, documentaries, posters, and other kinds of cultural-political expression during the civil war.) He also was convinced that the recuperation of this literature was critical to regenerating Spain, perceived by more advanced nations as inept and politically picayune. Anxious to "lift and reanimate the country's despondent spirits," to have it rejoin the larger community of civilized nations, he looked to popular literature, which he called "authentic fossils of earlier civilizations," as generators of symbolic meaning.[90]

The anthropologist Honorio Velasco Maillo astutely observed that Demófilo's stance exemplified the paradox of progressivism, as the nation's progress, or modernity, depended on a fossilized, premodern foundation predicated on the postulates of cultural evolutionism. Like the study of folklore, national revival issued from a profound feeling of nostalgia for everything that contradicted the ideal of modernity but also seemed doomed to disappear. Demófilo insisted, on the one hand, that no one from the educated classes really knew the pueblo, but on the other, he defined "the man of the pueblo" ("el hombre del pueblo") as less cultured, less individual, and less refined than his contrary. Nonetheless, only in such a representative type and in its anonymous cultural production, could one hope to find multitudes, the life held in common.[91]

In this way, the pueblo was conceived through the lens of modernity, as a product of modern thinking, and depending on one's perspective, either the pueblo or modernity could be understood as deficient, as missing some component that the other one possessed. An accompanying sense of loss, impending or actual, resided in the heart of the modern. For intellectuals like Demófilo, the appeal of this idealized, quasi-sacred image of the pueblo was immense, even if it could only be understood in a secondhand way, with the aid of the educated classes, or as he said, of scientific investigation. Unamuno's exhortation "to immerse our selves in the pueblo" issued from a similar deeply emotional source, attempting to reconnect with "the substance common to all classes of people." This ultimately problematic relationship between intellectual-writer and pueblo reminds us that a similar phenomenon defined the uneasy position of other left-wing members of the bourgeoisie with respect to the people, specifically to the working classes, in Europe and the Americas. In *The Road to Wigan Pier*, George Orwell, for example, was acutely aware that nothing he did could erase the markers of class, despite living for months among a group of coal miners. Like other committed men of the left, he joined the Republican cause in Spain partly in the hope that such differences would disappear. The image of Lorca as the people's poet must be understood in that context of desired social erasure.[92]

The lack of precision in defining the pueblo made it protean, susceptible to differing interpretations, serving different needs and purposes, and lending itself at times to ideological and political conflation. If, for example, both Unamuno and Nationalist ideology elevated the presumed living tradition of the pueblo, what was the difference? None, if one ignored the elasticity of the term. In Lorca's time, debates over the pueblo, especially in relation to art and politics, continued unabated into the civil war, when both sides laid claim to the people. Lasting echoes of these arguments are still heard within the differing memory communities of present-day Spain to which I alluded earlier.

Clear traces of the nineteenth-century Romantic view of the pueblo persisted in a talk given in 1930 and published three years later by Lorca's friend and fellow writer, José Bergamín. Singling out what he called authentic illiteracy ("analfabetismo verdadero"), he said it was "the generative spirituality of a language, which is the creative spirit of a people." As with Machado y Álvarez's "authentic fossils," "authentic illiteracy" was a plea for a return to origins, as deeply Romantic and utopian as the earlier notion. In this case, metaphorically, Bergamín was arguing for the recuperation of the child's imaginative, preliterate vision of the world, which he assimilated to the pueblo, observing: "The something that a people has of the child and that a person may have of the people, which is to say that which preserves something of the child, is precisely what it has of the illiterate." Illiteracy, a very real concern of the Second Republic, is not to be taken literally here, but inspired by Bergamín's Romantic-Christian tendencies, signifies a poetic condition that is "a state of nostalgia [found in the child or the people]" and, ultimately, the yearning for paradise.[93]

All of this may seem rather removed from the historic labor movements, revolutionary action, and social-economic protests of anarchists, socialists, and communists spreading throughout the cities, towns, and countryside of Spain in Lorca's time. Víctor Fuentes has pointed out, however, that both the folkloric and the political-revolutionary views of the pueblo were represented in contemporary writings. As we have seen, the folkloric tradition was already steeped in liberal Romantic thinking, but significantly, what one might call the "hard" ideological version of the pueblo (as opposed to the "soft" or poetic one) also invested in its own form of poetry, thereby imbuing the pueblo with larger-than-life, nearly mythic qualities. This is to say that both tendencies, the poetic and the political, were on numerous occasions intertwined in enveloping the pueblo with an aura of cultlike status. Many civil war posters, for example, depicted the redemptive symbolism of the land for the pueblo, recalling Demófilo's correspondences between land and people. "The produce of the peasant is as sacred to everyone as the worker's wages" was declared in one Republican poster.[94]

Thus, too, the Communist César Arconada would write in a transcendent vein, "I believe in you, Pueblo" ("Creo en ti, Pueblo").[95] Lorca's quasi-sublime experience of working-class fervor during the recital of his "Ballad of the Spanish Civil Guard" in Barcelona is equally illustrative of what I mean. To a lesser degree, this same interchangeability and fusion of aesthetics and politics occurred on the right, as Primo de Rivera's insistence on the emotional and propagandistic power of what he called "the poetry of promise" to motivate nations, or peoples, suggested. In this sense, it hardly seems to matter whether we speak of a Benjaminian aestheticizing of politics or a politicizing of aesthetics, when the effects, if not the meanings, are so similar, especially in the mythification of overdetermined entities like the pueblo.

Antonio Machado's wartime writings updated his father's thinking. He wrote, "When Juan de Mairena [Machado's alter ego] was asked if the poet and, in general, the writer should write for the masses, he answered: Beware, my friends. There exists the man of the pueblo, who is, in Spain at least, elemental, essential man, closest to the universal, the eternal in human terms. Mass-man does not exist. Human masses are an invention of the bourgeoisie, a degradation of the multitudes of men, based on a disqualification of man that aims to leave him reduced to that which man has in common with the objects of the physical world." Machado reutilized his father's expression, "man of the pueblo," within a more radicalized context of anticommodification and anticapitalism, as he elaborated a few lines later, targeting the capitalist bourgeoisie as exploiters of the people. Mass-man is the language of the enemy, he wrote, although ironically, on the right, Falangists, at least, also rejected the concept for similar reasons. Machado was especially concerned that the left not use the term, but of course many of them did, and that included the mission of creating art for the masses. "To write for the masses is to write for no one," he said, because it diminishes "every man" who forms a part of the pueblo. He considered himself "an incorrigible *demófilo* [a lover of the people and his father's pseudonym] and an enemy of all cultural señoritismo."[96]

At the same time, his man of the pueblo is deeply ahistorical, essentialized, a near universal abstraction that detaches it from both a Romantic *Volksgeist* and the historical-political particularities of the time, thus converting the pueblo into modern myth. Machado's political beliefs were sincere, if in wartime especially susceptible of propagandizing effects, but also consistent with earlier attitudes of the poet. So, for example, in a poem titled "El quinto detenido y las fuerzas vivas" (The Detained Conscript and the Powers-That-Be), he wrote, "Oh, the saintliness of the pueblo! Oh, the saintly pueblo!"[97]

The cultural señoritismo he rejected no doubt represented a similar target for those on the left such as Wenceslao Roces, Juan Rejano, and José Díaz Fernández, who were associated with the politically committed avant-garde journal *Post-Guerra* (Madrid, 1927–28), which repeated in every issue:

"Under the pretext of militating in literary schools of the avant-garde and modernism, numerous young aesthetes defend the political ideals of reactionaries. Literary dilettantism is another type of political reactionism." In the 1920s Spanish communists took a hard line against "intellectual señoritos" dabbling in working-class movements. Some of these attitudes would soften during the war. Rejano, for one, would go on to write an enthusiastic hagiographical treatment of one of those young aesthetes, Lorca himself, whom he portrayed as a Republican martyr and poet of the people.[98]

In life, Lorca was already associated with the pueblo, through poetry collections like the *Gypsy Ballads*, despite its avant-garde treatment of a traditional form, and his own affection for the popular classes. In 1935, one commentator dubbed him, not only the "son of a peasant from Fuentevaqueros," but "the future great poet of the working class." During the Second Republic, his traveling theater group brought classical Spanish plays to places and people who had rarely, if ever, been exposed to them. La Barraca, he said, wasn't for señoritos, but for the working classes, the humble, the young, and students. He was acutely aware of his own social status as a "rich kid in a backwater town," though that didn't stop him from taking advantage of his privileged position (anachronistically irrelevant as this comment is). After his murder, the image of Lorca as the people's poet just exploded in the rush to remember, praise, and exploit his memory during the civil war and for many years afterward. Vestiges of this image remain today in the effort to see him as a symbol of the Second Republic and of a lost cause (after the fact), reminding us, once again, of the mantra, "we are all Lorca," as a journalist said in 2009, when the fevered quest for the poet's bones was heating up.[99]

In the aftermath of his death, it would be impossible to separate the folkloric (aesthetic) and the political uses of this image. For the exiled Republican playwright Alejandro Casona, he was the "poeta-pueblo," though not merely folkloric. Pedro Garfias wrote, "You lived your life as a poet fully / as the people's poet." "Your death is life for the pueblo." M. J. Benardete said he "incarnated the folk tradition of Spain." Echoing the sentiments of many at the time, he went on to write, "It was because he was with the people and worked for them that the Fascists assassinated [Lorca]." In 1938, a wounded volunteer in the Abraham Lincoln Brigade picked up a book of verse (probably the *Gypsy Ballads*) and, in a letter written on the back of a civil war poster, called Lorca "the poet of the Spanish people. He is much revered by all Spain."[100]

I could cite many more of these kinds of comments, but this sampling should suffice. Two, however, are worth mentioning for their connection to Fortes's present-day attack on Lorca as a señorito and bourgeois intellectual, in effect, an "intellectual señorito," in the parlance of the time. In a radio broadcast from Madrid, in November 1937, Langston Hughes spoke of Lorca as the "martyred people's poet of Spain," touting Rafael Alberti's popular edition of the *Gypsy Ballads* while quoting liberally from his prologue to the book. "Housewives, workers, school-children, and soldiers buy it," he said. "And at many public gatherings Lorca's poems are read and applauded." At an orphanage for the sons and daughters of militiamen, the children recited his ballads. Illiterate militiamen in the trenches learned them by heart. Alberti himself read Lorca's *Lament for Ignacio Sánchez Mejías* at a benefit in September 1936. It was not the poem he planned to read that night, but when he strode onto the stage of the Teatro de la Zarzuela, he came with terrible news: confirmation that Lorca had been murdered. A young American dancer, Janet Riesenfeld, witnessed the moment, the words "alive, strong, transcend[ing] the death they spoke of, transcend[ing] even Lorca's death . . . as Lorca held the people under his spell."[101]

Alberti's "Palabras para Federico" (Words for Federico), dated May 1937, speak directly to the Granadine poet, as so many homages did. He observed that "in ten months of warfare, nearly a thousand [ballads] have been collected. You . . . seem to have influenced almost all of them. Your voice, hidden under other voices, is heard in our struggle. But that which speaks to us the loudest is your blood . . . like an immense fist, clenched in accusation and in protest." The prologue was reprinted more than once and appeared in English, translated by Hughes himself, in January 1938.[102]

Fortes took aim at the Alberti prologue, for what he perceived as an attempt to proletarianize Lorca, the "Andalusian señorito," and transform him into the sacred icon that eventually became an object of consumption or trademark after Franco's death. There is certainly some truth to this latter claim. His assertion that Alberti was the first to sacralize the poet, thereby encouraging others to do the same, however, is off the mark. One of the first reports of Lorca's death, one remembers, called it "an instant, sacramental drama." Homages, in prose and poetry, had already been published during the fall of 1936 and in early 1937, not to mention numerous commemorative public acts that took place in working-class clubs and athenaeums, union meetings, gatherings in theaters and movie houses, and so on. The papers were full of such notices. In 1936, two poems by friends of Lorca, Emilio Prados and Manuel Altolaguirre, appeared in *El Mono Azul,* the pro-Republican journal supported by the Alliance of Antifascist Intellectuals in Defense of Culture and under the direction of Alberti (though this was largely a collaborative effort). Colleagues from Latin America and other parts were even quicker than Lorca's compatriots to produce homage issues and books in 1936 and 1937, some of them with contributions from Spaniards as well. There were at least twelve to appear in this period alone in Lima, Santiago de Chile, Bogotá, La Paz, Buenos Aires, Paris, Valencia-Barcelona, and elsewhere.[103]

Lesser lights from the provinces also published poems in the same week of September 1936 as that of Prados. They are of interest mainly for the presence of motifs that immediately became iconic Lorca clichés. Fernando Guerrero's "Responso (Al llorado poeta Federico García Lorca)" (Funeral Oration [For the Lamented Federico García Lorca]) anticipated the folkloric gypsy-poet theme, which Rafael García Velasco's elegy took even further, connecting it to the poet as a friend of the poor:

> Ay, how the gypsies
> weep over your death!
> Ay, how the poor, your comrades,
> weep and weep!

Lorca was already part of the pueblo in a poem that gestures toward myth.[104]

Prados's lovely "Llegada" (Arrival) is unsurprisingly far more personal, hardly daring to give credence to the rumor of his death, but even here he linked his friend with the working-class red kerchiefs of gypsies and fishermen. At the same time, he placed the poet in a cosmic setting, in which the olive trees moan and the moon "goes looking for him, / slowly circling in the sky." The mythic and the social are part of the same poetic space. Altolaguirre's poem is politically more explicit. Dedicated to Saturnino Ruiz, the blue-collar printer who produced the books for Altolaguirre's small press, it appeared three weeks after "Llegada." Lorca is not, apparently, the subject of this poem; nevertheless, he dominates much of it. A book of his (it would have been *Canciones*) is the initial conduit in the poem, passing from the poet to the printer and linking together all three, after which Altolaguirre creates a series of parallel verses between Lorca and Saturnino Ruiz. Thus,

> If with you I was a printer,
> he was a poet with me;

> if they killed him in Granada,
> you fell in Somosierra,
> and you've both come
> glorious into my presence.
> He, with the martyr's palm,
> you, like a hero of war.
> He, asking me for vengeance,
> you, giving me strength.
> If he makes the cause just,
> you make victory certain.

He goes on to say that Saturnino is a "brave hero of the working class." Both figures are converted into icons.[105]

Significantly, the poem, by sympathetic approximation, joins Lorca to this exemplary member of the laboring classes, while merging the two cultures, popular and learned. Lorca's own social status is quietly elided. That is especially striking when this poem is juxtaposed to another one on the same page of *El Mono Azul*, titled "Traición y muerte del señorito Cañero" (Treachery and Death of the Señorito Cañero). The author was the same Ernesto López-Parra we saw before, still railing against the señorito, this time explicitly as the enemy of the people. Here, he lumps together in one compost heap of degeneration former bullfighters, pederasts, thieving landowners, flamenco priests, gypsies, and others as representative of the señorito class or associated with it. Lorca seems positively proletarian by contrast.[106]

Above all, and well before Alberti's prologue, as I have pointed out, it was Antonio Machado's poem "The Crime Was in Granada," which appeared a short time after the publication of these poems (17 October 1936), that had a major impact, in Spain and beyond, on the sacralization of Lorca, transforming him into myth. The poem was recited at the front and distributed as a pamphlet at the Spanish Pavilion during the 1937 International Exposition in Paris, where a huge photograph of Lorca hung opposite Picasso's *Guernica*. It was quickly reprinted, appearing in many Republican newspapers and journals, and translated, while lines and images were inserted into countless other poems and writings. Indeed, even Alberti referenced the text in the very first line of his prologue, by emphasizing, with quote marks, the crime committed against the poet "in 'your Granada,' in your own Granada" ("en 'tu Granada,' en tu propia Granada"), mirroring Machado's emblematic phrase, "in his Granada" ("en su Granada").[107]

Only Lorca's own poetry was recycled more than these verses of Machado. The one thing he does not do in an elegy striking for its accusatory stance is bestow the label of people's poet on Lorca, unlike so many other writers who did. That included Alberti, whose prologue no doubt exercised significant influence in propagating the image. By contrast, in a gesture at once lyrical and civic, Machado turned Lorca into something deeply popular, encircling the poet in an aura of martyred heroism and death-defying fortitude (historical inaccuracy aside), without needing to name him a *poeta-pueblo* as such. Alberti's prologue pays homage not only to Lorca but to Machado's vision of him.

Fortes is on shaky ground when he asserts Alberti launched Lorca's sacralized image, as this effort was, in the end, over all a collective one, but what about his claim that Alberti made propagandistic hay of the *Gypsy Ballads*, promoting the book "as if it were . . . revolutionary, proletarian"? Were that so, he would be right to criticize him, but what did Alberti really say about the *Gypsy Ballads* in his prologue? After singling out "Romance sonámbulo" (Dreamwalking Ballad) as the poet's best poem, he observed its mysterious nature, our inability to explain or narrate it. Lorca, he wrote, created a "strange and strong" form of balladry, built on the earlier tradition. This is the standard view of the *Gypsy Ballads*, nothing startling here. He does point out how the editions are multiplying ("se multiplican"), concluding that Lorca's poet friends, along "with the same sad and magnificent people [pueblo] of your poems," remember and celebrate him "with the fervor that the poets of old held toward the young Garcilaso de la Vega." Perhaps it was this last sentence that provoked Fortes, but in that case, where does the exquisite Garcilaso de la Vega fit into Alberti's presumed proletarianizing of Lorca's poetry? He doesn't. If anything, the parallel between Lorca and Garcilaso recalls another one, that between the Renaissance poet and José Antonio Primo de Rivera, as at least one hagiographical account from the same period maintained, along imperialist lines. Indeed, Francoists considered Garcilaso their own "imperial poet." Alberti unwittingly furthered the correspondences among all three figures when he waxed indignant over Falange attempting to transform Lorca into a poet of "imperial Spain." This appears to be an allusion to Luis Hurtado's article from 11 March 1937. The same Hurtado who, like Alberti, also referenced Machado's poem. What strange bedfellows poetry makes.[108]

The inexpensive edition, which was printed again in 1938, was heavily promoted, read and recited at the front and among civilians. Lorca's book of verse and the poet himself possessed cultural and political capital, and Alberti was eager to exploit the value they brought to the Republican side, in this sense backing up Fortes's claim of Alberti's propagandizing efforts. In this vein he wrote that "your name and your poetry continue to march, now and forever, on the lips of the fighting people in the ranks of Spain's antifascist forces." It is hard, however, to see in this kind of boiler-plate war rhetoric a proletarian Lorca. When Alberti said, "your voice [is] hidden under other voices" and "heard in our struggle," he was really talking about a Lorca-pueblo, the pueblo seen through the image of Lorca, that is, the very opposite of what Fortes finds in this prologue.[109]

It isn't Lorca being proletarianized, but the pueblo being lorquianized. Stated another way, the culture of the people (keeping in mind the expansive understanding of these terms in this period) was sifted through the broader culture that Lorca possessed and translated into such compelling poetry. More generally speaking, Republicans believed themselves to be the unique bearers of Spanish culture and western values, a stance that encouraged a top-down, elitist approach geared toward imparting high culture to those unfamiliar with it, while embracing those popular, folk elements of tradition compatible with the goals of the Second Republic. Lorca's execution was therefore seen as an assault on culture, exemplary of the struggle between civilization and barbarism. Referring to the political stance of the Nationalists, Vicente Sáenz wrote, "Culture and the intellectuals who create it must be shot. That is why Federico García Lorca died outside Granada, his Granada."[110]

Of course Lorca was not pueblo. He was a poet who connected with the people, and whose death, Cernuda incisively pointed out, was experienced like that of untold numbers of anonymous victims among the pueblo. Or as one of his translators, the working-class folk singer and collector A. L. Lloyd put it, the popular world was "not really his world, but he was able to steal over the walls of class-distinction and book-learning." These distinctions are of little interest to Fortes, whose understanding of culture rests entirely on social class. Closer to his line of thought was another of Lorca's friends, Pío Fernández Muriedas, himself from the laboring classes, who traveled throughout Spain reciting both classic and avant-garde poetry, including Lorca's. In 1934 he wrote that Lorca was "the best poet of the bourgeoisie," but that, "in an era of ferocious class warfare," his poetry did not speak to the working classes. Nonetheless, he collaborated with La Barraca and participated in homages to Lorca.[111]

From Fortes's standpoint, Lorca and nearly everyone else associated with the Generation of 1927 are elitist "señoritos of literature" ("señoritos de la literatura"), dismissed as mere *gongorinos*, imitators of the worst reactionary of all, the Baroque poet Luis de Góngora.[112] As we have seen, none of this is new, as López-Parra, the writing staff of the journal *Post-Guerra*, and others had all taken similar potshots at the group during the 1920s, although it is not clear to me whether Fortes was aware of their criticism. His strident views are of little importance when taken in isolation, but they point to larger underlying issues that go back to Lorca's own time. The only thing surprising here is to find these accusations repeated in the twenty-first century.

Or perhaps not. The ideological conflicts of the 1920s and 1930s have never really been resolved in modern Spain (or elsewhere). The pueblo was claimed by both sides, because in large part what was truly at stake was its future, the kind of people Spain would become. The politicization of Lorca was of a piece with the politicization of the pueblo, which had also been hopelessly aestheticized since the nineteenth century. These same attributes were applied to Lorca, or rather, to the myth that was being constructed of his posthumous image for the use of others. If a poet never utterly belongs to himself, to whom or what does he belong? Similarly, to whom or what does the pueblo belong?

There was never a clear understanding of what pueblo meant and attempts to limit it to specific social categories run up against an idealizing counter tendency to romanticize the pueblo because pueblo is not a neutral term, so closely associated is it to the idea of nation. Moreover, as a concept, pueblo is not sufficiently rigorous to apply it to social classes. Fortes, however, critiques the notion of the "spirit of the pueblo," not so much because it is unquestionably nonobjective, but rather because he ties it uniquely to the right, specifically to fascism.[113] This leaves figures who like Lorca, or Unamuno, to name but two, elevate the pueblo's living tradition, in an awkward spot, to say the least. What would the progressive Demófilo have made of all this? Or his son the poet?[114]

The uncritical, elastic manner whereby pueblo was used in Lorca's time, and especially by both sides during the civil war, allowed Falangists to associate Primo de Rivera above all with an idealized peasantry, while making sympathetic claims on the urban working classes. At the same time, the spirit of the people, symbolized in the "great enterprises of [Spanish] history," was transparently imperialist. José Antonio was a martyr for imperial Spain, an image that Falangists such as Hurtado and Villena tried to project onto Lorca, as improbable as that is. Others on the right, notably Romero Murube and Neville, mourned the loss of a friend, visualizing a martyr, among other things, in their poetry, while the Nationalist supporter Roy Campbell was riven with contradiction and ambivalence, magnifying José Antonio but irresistibly drawn to Lorca. From an ideologically opposite position, Fortes aimed to crush the poet's iconic status, the aura so closely linked to the cult of the individual, by imagining the poet as a bourgeois intellectual and an Andalusian señorito, who had more in common with the right than with the left. And by so doing, he not only unwittingly brought these two figures, Lorca and Primo de Rivera, together once more, but in an unconsciously ironic gesture, returned Lorca's afterlife to the past in which it is found.

PART TWO

PART TWO

4. Fabulous Fag (I), or the Politics of Celebrity Murder

If few poets are assassinated, an even smaller number of them are gay murdered poets. Being homosexual and the victim of a violent death are invariably associated with Lorca. Is this how you get to be a gay icon? Is Lorca a gay icon? And what does it mean to be one? What are the connections between being gay, murdered, and famous? In the immediate chaotic aftermath of his execution, almost no one spoke of his homosexuality, at least not publicly, though one Nationalist paper alluded to his "vacillating sexuality." The postwar dictatorship made it near impossible to do so, but even abroad, little was said out of discretion or ignorance. Merely hinting at his sexuality threw Ángel del Río into a tizzy in 1954, as he contemplated what to write in his introduction for the soon-to-be-released Ben Belitt translation of *Poet in New York*. Lorca's good friend Cipriano Rivas-Cherif was an exception, in his account of the poet's confession that he had only slept with men. He also recalled learning that the poet José María Pemán had spoken with contempt of Lorca, Rivas-Cherif, and the actress Margarita Xirgu as "inverts" on the Falange's National Radio during the war. This three-part piece, published in Mexico in 1957, created a firestorm among Rivas-Cherif's fellow Republican exiles, who questioned its accuracy and thought it slanderous, the long-winded and euphemistic style notwithstanding. Only the year before, Jean-Louis Schonberg (Baron Louis Stinglhamber) stunned the literary world by claiming, without a shred of evidence, that Lorca was the victim of a homosexual revenge plot. The Franco regime predictably exploited what for them amounted to a whitewashing of Nationalist guilt in the killing. Decades after the civil war, evidence surfaced that Lorca's homosexuality did play a role in his execution, but so did his Republicanism even more. The accuracy of Schonberg's book aside, the link he forges between the poet's murder and his homosexuality is an early example of how his death becomes a transformative event in the creation of Lorca's iconic status.[1]

Like so many deaths on both sides of the conflict, Lorca's was a political murder, and in this sense, meant that his homosexuality also became politicized. Even in life, attacks on his sexual identity surfaced, and in the days before his death, he apparently suffered antigay insults and physical affronts. Infamously, a local Granadine figure boasted he had shot him "twice in the ass for being a faggot." (Lorca was already known as "the queer with the bowtie" in Granada ["el maricón de la pajarita"].) In July 1932, the rightist journal *Gracia y Justicia* published an anonymous piece with the title, "Federico García Loca o cualquiera se equivoca" (Federico García the Loca, or Anyone Can Equivocate). Terms like *loca* and *equívoco* ("ambiguous" and "equivocal") were part of the gay subculture (and clearly known to those outside it).[2]

Comments on the poet's retinue of young men, replete with "sweetly languid voices," members of his theater group La Barraca, were politically tied to "Don Fernando el Laico," Lorca's close friend, Fernando de los Ríos, the socialist minister of public instruction responsible for the creation of the group. Similarly, another rag, *El Duende,* turned its venom on Lorca and the entire Barraca and suggested the government was subsidizing sodomites, by associating them in a verbal cheap shot with "Cipri . . . ano Rivas Cherif, their 'protector'" (and brother-in-law of the Republican politician-statesman, Manuel Azaña). Lest readers think this kind of thing only happened in Spain, in 1926 the *Chicago Tribune* called Rudolph Valentino a "pink powder puff" and a "painted pansy." As an antigay act of censorship, in 1931 "the very words 'pansy' and 'fairy' were banned from use in RKO vaudeville establishments, and in January 1933 pansy acts were banned from public entertainment venues in Atlantic City."[3]

Following the controversial premiere of his play *Yerma* in late December 1934, an equally crude anonymous attack appeared: "La cofradía del apio," or "The Confraternity of Fags." Here too, loaded terms of the period like *cofradía* and *apio* introduced even more marked innuendo targeting some of Lorca's fans in the audience, young men described as having stereotypically high-pitched voices and excessive hand gestures. (An article in *La Voz* from the same period also referred to the poet's retinue of young men.) The charge of moral degeneration in the piece cannot be divorced from the paroxysms of political rage against the play. Opening night, a right-wing claque hurled cries of "lesbian" at the star and "queer" at the playwright.[4]

On the very day of the military revolt against the Second Republic, an affectionate caricature by Manuel del Arco was coincidentally published in the pro-Republican daily, *El Heraldo de Madrid*, depicting Lorca as "a cute kid, pride and joy of his mother." He was drawn as a bit of a brat, faintly ridiculous, with a candle in one hand and a feminine bow around his arm. The image was reproduced on 8 September when the paper reported his death, calling it a monstrous crime. By no means deliberately antigay, the mama's-boy image nonetheless lent itself to misinterpretation.[5]

By the late 1980s and early 1990s, Lorca's homosexuality was more out in the open and more accepted in Spain, propelled partly by Ian Gibson's biographical work (and preceded by Marcelle Auclair's) and furthered, since then, by the scholarly contributions of Ángel Sahuquillo, Daniel Eisenberg, Paul Julian Smith, Anthony Geist, David Johnston, Alberto Mira, Carlos Jerez Farrán, Javier Herrero, and others. The publication in 1983 of the eleven poems that came to be known as the *Sonetos del amor oscuro* (Sonnets of Dark Love), initially in a clandestine edition, sparked more debate about the poet's sexual identity and its presence or nonpresence in the sonnets. A brilliant production of *The Public* in 1986–87 also broke more taboos on the subject. Gibson saw him as secretly anguished by unfulfilled homosexual desire in a repressive, homophobic society. Writing to Louise Bogan in 1938, Rolfe Humphries, who was finishing up his translation of *Poet in New York*, thought "that [Lorca] was more and more having a hell of a time with his homo impulses." That is the prevailing view. There is certainly truth to this account, backed up by antigay attitudes and Lorca's own conflicted words in works like the "Ode to Walt Whitman" and *The Public*. But the picture is a good deal cloudier, more ambiguous, and at times the very opposite of grim and depressing, when the poet is placed within his own time. Much of the 1920s and early 1930s in Spain had more of a live-and-let-live attitude toward sex and sexual identity, at least among certain circles and groups, according to Lorca's friend Rafael Martínez Nadal.[6]

The kind of gay you were also depended to some degree on which circles you frequented. And of course, nobody was gay but homosexual, and

Figure 6. Federico García Lorca,
1919. Photo by Rogelio Robles
Romero-Saavedra, courtesy of
Archivo de la Fundación Federico
García Lorca, Centro Federico
García Lorca, Granada.

even then, barely so since the term was only beginning to be used and com-
peted with a plethora of categories such as invert, third sex, uranian, intersexual, and even hermaphrodite, in an era alternatively fascinated and repulsed by the hybrid and ambiguous. The word *hybrid* itself could also refer
to homosexual. Thus, for example, the public for a drag queen was labeled a
"caravan of hybrid types." As seen in this naming frenzy, the temptation to
stereotype, when faced with challenges to the norm, was overwhelming. Even
Gibson's privately tormented Lorca feeds into a cliché of the homosexual
writer as a variation of the *poète maudit*. Similarly, one could also fit him into
the related Wildean mold, an odd sort of Andalusian dandy figure, less elegant
sartorially than Oscar but extroverted and performance-driven, bordering on
Jorge Luis Borges's disdainful epithet of "professional Andalusian."[7]

An iconic photograph of a young Lorca, much reproduced, portrays
him staring pensively into the camera, his face resting on his hand, with two
fingers curled downward, another just touching his ear, and thumb under his
chin (fig. 6). I projected this image on a large screen for a talk in front of a

lively group of Yale alumni, nearly all of them couples and most of whom were over sixty. As I was setting up, a white-haired woman came up to me, gestured toward the photo, and asked me whether Lorca was gay. This woman knew nothing about Lorca, but somehow, she knew he was gay. What did his face communicate to her? Or had she simply matched his face and gesture to what she understood was homosexual? This too speaks to the convenience of stereotype.

The moment that the label of gay icon is attached to someone specific like Federico García Lorca, stereotype follows, turning into inconvenience. The association between his homosexuality and his death, between martyrdom and being gay, which is part of his iconicity, for example, is now completely banal, history and facts notwithstanding. Lorca's image has been thoroughly domesticated, through familiarity and repetition. Calling him a gay icon says less about Lorca himself or his work, than about the public need for icons and readily available images to signal and even explain changing cultural and historical realities. Paradoxically, modern icons continue to draw on the sacred origins of such representations while deconstructing the very mystery that makes figures like Lorca so irresistible.

I've called this chapter "Fabulous Fag," along with its sequels, not to disparage but to provoke. I cannot resolve what some might see as an uneasy tension between *fabulous* and *fag*, a tension exacerbated if *fag* is only allowed its habitual pejorative sense. The two words together, however, suggest a third entity, of indeterminate significance, perhaps, but also richly taut and located in the realm of the marvelous, anticipated in 1919 with Álvaro Retana's finely calibrated creation of "El apio maravilloso," or The Marvelous Fag, as observed in the next chapter. This realm is that of the iconic. I am not even certain if I understand what it means to call Lorca a gay icon. What is "gay" here? Are you a gay icon if you are "out"? Lorca was never out, though he has certainly been outed. Allen Ginsberg spotted him in a California supermarket, "down by the watermelons," along with Walt Whitman "eyeing the grocery boys." Was Lorca eyeing the grocery boys, too? One critic sees this setting and imagery as a form of commodification, but I think she misses the larger point. Ginsberg placed both poets in ordinary surroundings, shopping in a grocery store. Is it consumerism? Sure, but what about those peaches and penumbras? And "Aisles full of husbands! Wives in the avocados, babies in the tomatoes!" The poet also understands the extraordinary found in the ordinary.[8]

Ginsberg asked: "Where are we going, Walt Whitman? The doors close in an hour. Which way does your beard point tonight? (I touch your book and dream of our odyssey in the supermarket and feel absurd)." Lorca knew which way his beard pointed: "toward the pole" ("hacia el polo"), as he wrote in "Ode to Walt Whitman." The delight Ginsberg took in "dreaming of [Whitman's] enumerations" as he shops for images is equally blessed with irony and marvel. One outing is turned into another kind of outing, but most importantly, in asking which way Whitman's beard points tonight, he left the poem open, akin to Whitman's open road, in the midst of Ginsberg's "dreaming of the lost America of love." Like the wayward pointing of the poet's beard, all directions are possible, leaving sexual identity fluid, unfixed. In linking Lorca to the fabled Whitman, this poem also works toward transforming Lorca into a gay icon. At the same time, Ginsberg astutely intuited that modern icons are by their very nature seemingly accessible, consumable like peaches and avocados, even if he chose not to affix a specific name brand or label to either poet.[9]

If being out is not necessarily a feature of a gay icon, is there a definition or image of gayness that lends itself to being fetishized? Evidently not: just imagine Pedro Almodóvar's flamboyance alongside Lorca's dislike of the stereotypical flaunting he attached to fairies, or maricas. There are any number of differing iconic gay images of artists and writers, ranging from Oscar Wilde, Álvaro Retana, and Ocaña to Whitman, Lorca, André Gide, and Allen Ginsberg himself. Focusing on distinct categories of gay icons draws us away from what connects them: celebrity itself, and in some instances enduring fame.

Lorca had a complicated, ambivalent relationship with celebrity, and at the same time, he was fascinated with fame, to judge from his extraordinary elegy on his close friend, the lionized bullfighter Ignacio Sánchez Mejías. The publication of *Gypsy Ballads* in 1928 cemented his reputation in ways that both flattered and irritated him. He hated being called a gypsy poet. First, it was untrue; and second, it was a cliché. I doubt he would have liked any better being seen as a gay poet, as it fueled his dread of what he considered the most stereotypical: external displays of homosexuality. His "Ode to Walt Whitman" envisions at its center a gay icon surrounded by lesser, impure forms of being gay.

An avant-garde poet, Lorca sought new, fresh images to startle and delight his readers. "I hold fire in my hands," he wrote, refusing to say what poetry was. And this: "I shall burn down the Parthenon by night only to begin again to raise it up the next morning and never finish it," the perfect expression of the Nietzschean idea of creative destruction. He also insisted upon something else: the idea of never finishing. Lorca embodies this paradox of a creation that never ceases to come undone only to make itself anew once more, even though, ironically, an image that appears modern is ancient in origin, harking back to the myth of the phoenix. Expressed another way, Federico suggests that poetry, or literary creation, is a dangerous thing. It is fire in an artist's hands, unending destruction that is always in a state of becoming, of re-creation. What poetry isn't is stale and domesticated. Neither was Lorca himself. That untamed Lorca, full of the marvelous, can never be entirely explained, but should we even try?[10]

His fundamental strangeness interests me far more, and that difference began in his own time. Ambiguity, oddness, and indefinability were repeatedly associated with homosexuality in his day, though clearly the latter has no monopoly over such characteristics. Rather, it is homosexuality that stood in for something larger than itself, for the bewildering strangeness of modernity, to which Lorca belonged. Being gay was and is not an explanation of his poetry or his person; being gay was one of the newly modern expressions of the marvelous that was both disquieting and exhilarating, just as the surrealist notion of the marvelous produced a similar reaction. For André Breton, this was "the shadow of the marvelous that no one has ever seen."[11]

In Spain, Rafael Cansinos-Asséns saw something similar in what he perceived as renewed sexual forms of the hybrid and ambiguous, monstrous forms that partake of the marvelous and inhabit the deepest part of the human imagination. The aura of the marvelous, or its shadow, as Breton called it, has a secondhand connection with celebrity and iconicity, insofar as the iconic status of a figure like Lorca possesses something of the same aura, as a reflection of modernity's own unsettling strangeness and its media-driven propensity toward the display of the fetishized self. Lorca after life still reverberates in the air of the marvelous that he once inhabited, though we have yet to grasp fully what that means. In this sense, Lorca was a gay icon before he was a gay icon; we simply haven't shown enough of a defamiliarizing light upon the depths of the marvelous in the poet and his era.[12]

The domestication of Lorca's poetry is personified in imitators, hackneyed performers of his poetry and poetic homages, reductive critical approaches to his work, and, as Jonathan Mayhew has pointed out, in the way some U.S. poets have Americanized him in their own writing. The man himself has also been made into an overly familiar figure, a ubiquitous, overdetermined symbol of multiple causes and identities, as I have noted before. Even the mystery of his poetry and his person seems a worn-out mantra in desperate need of reexamination. Similarly, Lorca the gay icon shortchanges our understanding of the man and his work, failing to address the elusive, complex nature of both. By this, I do not mean that it is not worth examining Lorca's homosexuality and its relation to iconicity. Or that being gay is irrelevant to his work. On the contrary, Lorca's complexity, his elusiveness, can in part (though only in part) be attributed to his homosexuality, to being gay in a specific time and place. Being gay has also occupied a place in the public sphere—as Lorca himself divined with his play *The Public* and with the "Ode to Walt Whitman"—marked especially as performance driven in the modern period since the appearance of the inimitable Oscar Wilde, whose dandy figure achieved both celebrity and scandal.

This particular context—the poet's homosexuality—has been fruitfully explored in recent years (Sahuquillo, Gibson, Mira, Jerez-Farrán, and others), as I have noted, but I don't think anyone believes we know enough about the period or even about the poet's life to have the final word on the subject, and this book certainly makes no claims to doing that. For the most part, the standard high-culture model that isolates the Generation of 1927, to which Lorca belonged, from the rest of cultural production, from other forms of being gay or of being a celebrity, and from the larger social body has prevailed. Gay writers like Lorca, Luis Cernuda, and Vicente Aleixandre are almost completely segregated from non-avant-garde contemporary gay writers of the era like Antonio de Hoyos y Vinent, Pedro de Répide, and Álvaro Retana, who appealed to a larger reading public, even though all of them occupy the same time and space in the small literary world of early twentieth-century Madrid. Their histories are treated separately, as are their circles of friends and acquaintances, this despite the fact that certain people acted and circulated as hinge figures between the groups, such as Edgar Neville, Jacinto Benavente, Hoyos y Vinent, Cansinos-Assens, Ramón Gómez de la Serna, and César González Ruano.

Lorca's celebrity and its subsequent association with a gay identity (among other things) merit a closer look in this larger literary-cultural setting, which also extends to situating and reexamining writings like the "Ode to Walt Whitman." For readers today, the brightest name in the constellation of gay writers and icons is Lorca, but in early twentieth-century Spain, that wasn't the case. The big gay celebrity then was the flamboyant Álvaro Retana, known for his erotic kiosk fiction, who also worked as a music-hall set and costume designer and song writer. His work and persona were almost totally forgotten at the time of his death in 1970 and, since the 1990s, have slowly been recuperated. Despite the obvious differences in writing and lifestyles, these two figures have more in common than one might expect, providing both a wider scope for understanding and situating Lorca and a strategy to break down a few more of the artificial barriers that critics have erected between high and low culture in the period, especially in the case of the Generation of 1927.[13]

Before addressing this rich local history, however, there is an even larger one that cannot be ignored: that of iconic gay writers as a whole and their relation to celebrity. The limitations of this book make it impossible for me to deal with this subject in all the depth that it deserves, but it is worth considering Lorca in the context of that select group of other gay writers who died under violent or unnatural circumstances. British playwright Joe Orton was bludgeoned to death by his lover, but suicide and self-destructive behavior are more common. Yukio Mishima committed seppuku, after a failed coup attempt. Suffering from end-stage AIDS, Reinaldo Arenas killed himself, lamenting his inability to write and continue his struggle against the Castro regime. Booze, drugs, and exhaustion destroyed Rainer Werner Fassbinder.

The suicides of Mishima and Arenas can be understood as both personal and political, but political murder of gay writers is hard to find, which is partly why Lorca's assassination has reverberated for so long. He wasn't, however, the only writer executed during the Spanish Civil War. He wasn't even the first. That dubious honor belongs to the Communist poet Manuel Gómez del Valle, executed on 11 August 1936, a week before Lorca (Gómez del Valle's mother was doused with gasoline and burned alive). Writers were shot on both sides of the conflict, none of them gay, to my knowledge. Among the Republicans: Eduardo Barriobero y Herrán, Javier Bueno, Manuel Ciges Aparicio, and Pedro Luis de Gálvez. A bullet wasn't always necessary. In poor health, Antonio Machado died in exile a month after fleeing to France. Miguel Hernández died under deplorable conditions in a Francoist prison, as did Hoyos y Vinent, a gay aristocrat who turned leftward. Among the Nationalists: Ramiro Ledesma Ramos, Pedro Muñoz Seca, and Ramiro de Maeztu. Two right-wing poets affiliated with the vanguard literary movement were also shot: Francisco Valdés and José María Hinojosa. Both were from prosperous landowning families, with deep rural roots and agrarian traditionalist leanings. Little known today, Valdés lived for a time in the Residencia de Estudiantes and contributed to the avant-garde magazine *La Gaceta Literaria*, but turned against the Republic. It is not clear to me what kind of a relationship he might have had with Lorca, Cernuda, Alberti, Buñuel, and other members of the Generation of 1927.[14]

Hinojosa, however, was closely connected to them. He became friends with Lorca in Granada during the early 1920s, worked with Emilio Prados and Manuel Altolaguirre on the literary journal *Litoral,* which he also supported financially, and frequented the Resi on an almost daily basis, even though he didn't live there. In truth, he belonged to the same literary generation; yet his work was excluded from the celebrated anthology *Poesía española contemporánea.* After visiting the Soviet Union with José Bergamín in 1928, Hinojosa turned rightward. Along with his father and one of his brothers, he was shot three days after Lorca. Until the 1970s, his name was for the most part forgotten. He had been scrubbed from literary history, despite producing provocative poetry and the first book of surrealist poetry in Spain, *La flor de California* (The Flower of California), in 1927.[15]

Various contemporary accounts suggest he was seen above all as a *señorito andaluz,* as a well-to-do young man from Andalusia (but so of course was Lorca), not to be taken seriously, and as José Moreno Villa rather meanly said, "a country bumpkin poet dazzled by prolonged stay in Paris," this after having been one of his closest friends. Alberti claimed the workers on his family's estate killed him, a false narrative that depicted him as an enemy of the people. The truth is that he and forty-nine others were executed in a Málaga cemetery as payback for the Nationalists' bombing of the Campsa petrol tanks. There is little doubt that Hinojosa's politics played a role here and in his subsequent erasure from Spanish literary history. A Carlist and agrarian traditionalist, he did not fit the Republican mold of a Lorca or Alberti, but as a surrealist and experimental poet, he did not sit well with the other side, either, just as the assassinated Falangist painter Alfonso Ponce de León's association with the avant-garde may have proved problematic. (On the other hand, Franco embraced Salvador Dalí, but he was already a huge celebrity, appearing on the cover of *Time* magazine in December 1936.)[16]

There is nothing iconic about Hinojosa, he wasn't gay, and his poetry will never match Lorca's, but it is important to see these two political murders together. In one case, politics dug a deep memory hole, even as in the other, it became enshrined in the politics of memory. For the longest time, no one wanted to talk about Hinojosa because he was an embarrassment for both sides of the political and literary divide. Cernuda remarked that no one among his group would mention his terrible death, and Bergamín apparently even denied knowing him at one point. Years later, Pepín Bello, an intimate of both Lorca and Hinojosa, linked their deaths—and their assassins— together. Before Lorca was a murdered gay poet, he was simply another dead writer. Famous certainly, but one who shared the violent fate of so many others, among them, writers, intellectuals, and artists. Contemporary politics singled him out as the Republican martyr of martyrs, but the later politics of identity has turned him into something else, so that it is nearly impossible to forget he was both gay and assassinated. A documentary from 2017, *Bones of Contention*, for example, has Lorca as the centerpiece for an investigation into the Franco regime's persecution of gays. But the narrator also observes that the poet is "the ultimate countercultural gay symbol, as though there were only room in the cultural register for one queer icon at a time."[17]

He is not alone in his current iconic standing as a murdered gay poet. Pier Paolo Pasolini (1922–75) immediately comes to mind. Pasolini and Lorca may not appear to have much in common, considering the Italian writer-director's open flaunting of his homosexuality. Yet both have been viewed as late expressions of the Romantic tradition, of the *poète maudit*, and linked to figures as disparate as Christ, Don Quixote, Rimbaud, and Mishima. Pasolini embraced scandal, as it fed into his obsession with public martyrdom, unsurprising in someone who perceived "the language of the world [as] essentially a spectacle." (The martyr figure, especially Christ, already appears in Lorca's early work.) A book on Pasolini could also easily be titled "Pasolini After Life," like this one on Lorca, not only for the way his presence endures in Italian culture but for his insistence on the significance of death as the completion of life. "Man . . . expresses himself," he wrote, "primarily by his action. . . . But this action lacks unity, that is, meaning, *until it has been completed*." He went on to say:

> It is therefore absolutely necessary to die, *because, so long as we live,*
> *we have no meaning,* and the language of our lives (with which we
> express ourselves, and to which we therefore attribute the greatest

importance) is untranslatable; a chaos of possibilities, a search for relations and meanings without resolution. *Death effects an instantaneous montage of our lives;* that is, it chooses the truly meaningful moments (which are no longer modifiable by other possible contrary or incoherent moments) and puts them in a sequence, transforming an infinite, unstable, and uncertain—and therefore linguistically not describable—present into a clear, stable, certain, and therefore easily describable past. . . . *It is only thanks to death that our life serves us to express ourselves.*[18]

In this same essay, Pasolini likened life to an infinite sequence shot in film, where death is the ultimate editor of life. Elsewhere, he continued to link cinema and life, by seeing film time as "complete." "Time in this context," he said, "is not that of life when it lives, but of life after death; as such it is real, it is not an illusion, and it can very well be that of the story of a film."[19] One might also consider this to be the fate of literature, of a kind of life after death that only death can at once finish off and explain. Most evocative is Pasolini's sense of completion, which Lorca by and large resisted. The incomplete defines, to the extent it can, the Andalusian's life and work, incomplete in the most obvious sense for being cut short by his murder, but also so for the very resistance with which he opposed finality. Death is a not arriving in "Rider's Song." The Parthenon is burned down, only to be remade but never finished. Real death is a pool of stagnant water, as in "Little Girl Drowned in the Well," or a paralyzed sea in "Asesinato" ("Murder"). Real death stops time and, perhaps, the poem.

Equally haunted by death, Pasolini, like Lorca, has attained a near mythic status, in part because these were public deaths, despite the paucity of witnesses to their murders, and public deaths come inscribed in symbolism; they must be explained. They did not die in bed, or in obscurity. But they are also contested deaths (as are their lives), putting into question Pasolini's notion that death can create "a clear, stable, certain, and therefore easily describable past." Perhaps in these cases, that certainty can only be attained if one understands what kind of death each man suffered, but that can never be known, since their deaths no longer belong to them alone.

Pasolini's real death, on 2 November 1975, was painfully sordid. Openly gay, he cruised nightly the wild, impoverished Roman shantytowns, or *borgate,* for street boys. When they found his body, it was first mistaken for trash. He had been badly beaten, hit repeatedly with a wooden board, and run over by his own car, which proved fatal, crushing his thorax. A seventeen-year-old hustler, Pino Pelosi, confessed to the crime, claiming self-defense, but years later retracted his words and, implicating the Mafia, said three persons with Sicilian accents set upon Pasolini. Police contamination of evidence, conflicting accounts by Pelosi and others, and the immediate sensationalizing of the murder have made it impossible to know for certain what happened, or how and why. As with Lorca, there is a paradoxical obscurity about such a conspicuous act. For all we do know about their deaths, a core of darkness envelops them.[20]

Unsurprisingly, conspiracy theories mushroomed, given Pasolini's gadfly presence in Italian culture. With enemies on the right and the left, he was never comfortable in any single political or ideological identity, spotting conformism on all sides. A Communist, he was thrown out of the party for being a homosexual. Some immediately concluded his murder was a "typical homosexual crime" and nothing more, akin to the way Schonberg imagined Lorca's death, with little attention paid to the possibility of homophobic motives. Indeed, by the end of the 1950s a *pasolini* was synonymous with *finocchio* (lit. "fennel"), or slang for "queer."[21] Whatever the truth, politics and gay sex were inextricably interwoven in Pasolini's murder. He picked up Pelosi for one purpose and took him to the kind of place he preferred: a desolate open field sometimes used to play soccer on the outskirts of Ostia (not to be confused with the tourist attraction, Ostia Antica).

Pasolini once shot film there and described a similar wasteland in his poem, "Le ceneri di Gramsci" (The Ashes of Gramsci). Contemplating the Protestant English cemetery in Rome, where Gramsci is buried, he wrote of "the grayness of the world," in which "you are dead and we are likewise dead." The poem, which is civic in nature, also addresses political death, alluding to the Marxist thinker's demise as an assassination, though strictly speaking, he died while in prison, deprived of adequate medical attention. Pasolini makes Gramsci's death personal, ending with these lines: "But I, with the conscious / heart of one who lives only in history, / can I ever act with pure passion again, / when I know that our history has ended?" The sense of paradox, of the tension between living in history and dying in it, of needing history in order to "act with pure passion," all of this makes the poem deeply political yet intimate and suggests how much death, for Pasolini, was not simply existentially felt but inserted into a political dimension, without which, perhaps, death, at least in this poem, cannot be understood.[22]

In some ways, it almost doesn't matter whether Pasolini's murder was in fact politically motivated or not, because the writer himself was already political, meaning his death lent itself to politicized interpretations. Maria-Antonietta Macciocchi is a case in point. Like Pasolini, she also ended up being expelled from the Italian Communist Party (in 1977), though for supporting Maoists in Bologna. In a strongly worded, hyperdramatic statement, she wrote: "Crime is political. Pasolini was assassinated by society in a savage act of self-defense, a society which could not bear his defiance (of sexual, political, and artistic prohibitions), his undisguised equation of commitment and life. The hatred unleashed against him was expressed in the staging of the crime: a public execution, at high noon, so that everyone might see and learn." She goes on to quote Philippe Sollers: "'Pasolini was killed so that the repressed homosexual center of society would remain so, sealed by the blood of someone able to *speak* of it. A ruthless sentence of aphasia.'" A feminist, she lambasted the Communist Party as the Male party, "the self-constituted grey State of order," for dictating sexual norms and thereby banishing the writer for his homosexuality. By contrast, Pasolini represented "the first heretic of the Marxist religion." She doesn't let the extreme right off the hook, either, and denounces the fascists for stalking the writer. Her own ideological blindness aside, Macciocchi fed into the widely disseminated martyr image of Pasolini as a kind of dissident saint, a new version of the *poète maudit,* sexually, aesthetically and politically blessed. Lorca's own politicized mythification isn't far behind.[23]

Giuseppe Zigaina, a painter and close friend of Pasolini, took to heart the writer's dictum of death as the ultimate sequencer of meaning in one's life. He spoke of the filmmaker's "death project," suggesting that he "'made poetry' with his death." In this view, Pasolini can be understood as encrypting his approaching death in his own work and orchestrating his end as a sexualized passion play. Zigaina's reading of the writer-director's life and death only seems unhinged if one ignores Pasolini's penchant for martyrdom. It represents a more elaborate, self-consciously wrought version of earlier prophetic interpretations of the deaths of other writers as foreseen in the work itself, but in this instance further extended to Pasolini's collaboration in his own fate. Or as one newspaper headline phrased it: "Pasolini Killed Where He Would Have Shot the Film of His Own Death." Lorca is the most obvious example of this kind of anticipated martyrdom.[24]

Whether conspiracy or complicity, such deaths are indeed like stagings, with the scandal of sex added. Both Pasolini and Lorca met death in the open air, in a field, but they died with secrets attached, with unanswered questions that demanded public revelation. The murders of these figures are part of their celebrity, with an impact on the collective imagination akin to that of Marilyn Monroe's suicide or James Dean's fatal car accident. Death becomes a strangely twisted halo illuminating the after-effects of life as a matter of public interest. It seems to me that Pasolini's understanding of death is intimately linked to the idea of the writer as a public persona. In seeing death as an "instantaneous montage of our lives," he imagines it as something visual, to be shown like a film. This sequence shot is played out in full view, in the same way Pasolini played out his own life. For Alberto Moravia, he was "a poet in the grand European tradition that celebrated the civic man." Frequently reviled, he spoke of the ills of Italian society, even when the country did not want to listen. Like Gramsci in his poem (and in the Protestant English cemetery), he remained an outsider, imprisoned in a world not of his choosing.[25]

This sense of being in the public sphere, in life and in death, cannot be separated from his celebrity. The language of the world as spectacle practically invites celebrity, which the Italian filmmaker-poet viewed as a form of falsification. The same is true of García Lorca. But not everything was necessarily public. For Pasolini, his gayness was a personal matter, not to be hidden but to be lived as a kind of "private Calvary." He did not back gay rights, for fear of erasing part of what made him (and other homosexuals) so different and, even more important for him, so alienated. He didn't even call himself a homosexual, but rather a pederast in the Gidean vein. Pasolini's fierce individuality was bound to be resisted, attacked, and misinterpreted. Death may complete life, giving it meaning; yet what lies beyond is also opaque, as Pasolini recognized: "Death lies not / in not being able to communicate / but no longer being understood." This being Pasolini, he deliberately undercut his own message by saying to an interviewer later in the poem that "this is just some flimsy thought that came to me / on the way back from Fiumicino!" It is not clear to me if he means simply that death is no longer understood, or that the fact of being dead means *we* are consequently no longer understood (or perhaps both). But was he even understood in life?[26]

This essential opacity was even more foregrounded in two notorious murders of the sixteenth and seventeenth centuries: those of Christopher

Marlowe and the Conde de Villamediana. Marlowe was stabbed to death on 30 May 1593, it was said, in a tavern brawl over a bill or "reckoning." In another version, the fight was over a rent boy. In the Elizabethan world of continual intrigue, of plots and counterplots, however, nothing is ever that simple. Later reconstructions of Marlowe's end have questioned early accounts, observing, first, that he did not die in a tavern, but in the widow Bull's house at Deptford Strand. Charles Nicholl, for example, suggested that he was a pawn in a Crown plot against Sir Walter Raleigh, and he completely rejected the theory that he was murdered because of his homosexuality. "Entertaining," he said, "but [it] is no more than a novelistic convenience."[27]

There are so many explanations for his violent death that you can take your pick, but nearly all of them are rooted in the complicated politics of the day, in which his own aggressive temperament and comportment also played a determining role. The son of a Canterbury cobbler, Marlowe possessed a self-assured, flashy persona, with a proclivity for Sturm und Drang. Indeed, the entire Marlowe family proved to be "a quarrelsome tribe." He also had a reputation as an atheist and blasphemer, with evidence of criminal behavior. Was he homosexual, and did that figure into his murder? This is a trickier question for a period in which homosexual practice rather than identity prevailed, and homosocial bonding confusingly blended with homosexual affection. Bed sharing among men, for example, was common, in part because beds were in short supply. David Riggs observes, "The question of whether or not Marlowe was a homosexual is misleading. Marlowe's contemporaries regarded sodomy as an aspect of seditious behaviour rather than a species of person. The crime of sodomy became visible in connection with other offences—blasphemy, treason, counterfeiting, sorcery—that activated the heavy hand of the law. Marlowe avoided this predicament until the final weeks of his life, when he was accused of atheism, coining and crypto-Catholicism."[28]

The striking thing here is the elusive slipperiness of homosexuality, on one hand as a category, on the other as a practice when contemplated as an independent or isolated entity, which is how we tend to see it today because we have named it. Politics in the largest sense of the word gave homosexuality a heightened contour in Marlowe's world, situating it in association with those acts that could be explained or understood, juridically or otherwise, thus conferring significance upon other acts like sodomy, itself a term of broad applicability. Without the political scheming of the Elizabethan period in which

Marlowe was so deeply embedded, homosexuality appears to have a diminished meaning. Homosexuality in this sense and context doesn't exist without the political frame. This is to say that without the politics, the intrigue, or his violent death, perhaps we wouldn't even be talking about Marlowe as homosexual (a term he wouldn't have recognized, in any case). This is a "gay politics" very unlike what late modernity imagines. What kind of an agenda would a Marlowe serve in the public arena today? Could he be viewed as a gay icon? For that, wouldn't we have to know first who he was?

To complicate matters, some of the Elizabethan's own work reflects homosexual themes, such as *The Tragedy of Dido, Queen of Carthage,* which opens with Jupiter and his cupbearer Ganymede (known also as Catamitus) canoodling. The very first line, "Come, gentle Ganymede, and play with me," recalls the celebrated line from "The Passionate Shepherd to His Love": "Come live with me, and be my love." The scene ends with this exchange, as the youth Ganymede says:

> I would have a jewel for mine ear,
> And a fine brooch to put in my hat,
> And then I'll hug with you an hundred times,

to which Jupiter replies: "And shalt have, Ganymede, if thou wilt be my love." These gifts have a parallel in the poem, which boasts a gown of the finest wool, slippers, and buckles of gold. The lover of the passionate shepherd could be male or female, though it is worth noting that in the myth Ganymede was tending sheep before becoming Jupiter's cupbearer. Neither character reappears in *Dido,* but tellingly, the Queen of Carthage compares her lover Aeneas, bearing the crown and scepter she has given him, to "immortal Jove," saying: "O where is Ganymede, to hold his cup?" Marlowe's parallel is ambiguous, seemingly associating Aeneas with a different kind of love, while raising his status to that of Jupiter.[29]

The jewel and brooch coveted by Ganymede, moreover, lend themselves to an interpretation that unsettles or puts an additional spin on the gifts. Riggs writes that "the distinction between eroticized male friendship and sodomy turned on cultural rather than exclusively sexual criteria [and that] [t]he stigma of sodomy attached to the base interloper who traded sex for reward and threatened the marital alliances that maintained class privilege."[30] In these cases, the younger man was seen as effeminate, and referred to as a catamite or Ganymede. Ganymede is called a "female wanton boy" in the play. He clearly supplants Juno, characterized as a shrew and bully, for Jupiter's affection, while Jupiter steals his wife's jewels to give to his boy lover.

Yet the erotic nature of their relationship seems to be based, at least in part, on a form of economic exchange, which in turn makes it more difficult to know how to interpret the passage. To what degree is this a different kind of love? Or is this merely a fluid continuum, in which both Jupiter and Dido can bestow gifts, and lovers are not so much defined sexually but rather singled out as the recipients of their largesse? Is Jupiter gay, or simply wearied of his wife? Is Aeneas straight or a stand-in for Jupiter, and what would that point to? The terms are meaningless, not to mention anachronistic, since we do not altogether understand what sex signified in the Renaissance. In any event, whatever "gay politics" this play might hold is entirely unclear, as is any possible insight into Marlowe himself other than to reveal how adept he was at deflection.

The mystery surrounding Marlowe's death also envelops his life because of his death. Rather than explain his life, his death simply deepens the enigma. This is also true of Federico García Lorca (and of Pasolini). As with the Spanish poet, Marlowe's violent end threw a veil of obscurity over his life, a life that was already a puzzle. The politics of murder for all these writers is embedded not only in cultural-historical criteria but in personal conundrums. This same uncertainty about their lives (and deaths) extends into the intricate loops and folds of the psyche, suggesting how pointless it is to assume we can ever know anything of Lorca's inner life or his sexual complexity. The bewilderingly contradictory lives of Pasolini and Marlowe shed an oblique, if precarious, light on the Granadine poet's own entangled persona.

The same could be said of Juan de Tassis y Peralta, second Count of Villamediana, the last example of an assassinated poet to be briefly considered here before returning to Lorca's own time. Villamediana also brings us much closer to home, at least geographically, for Lorca himself. Like Marlowe and Pasolini (and perhaps Lorca), he appears as pure performance, as though modeled on Zero Mostel's exuberant cry in *The Producers:* "That's it, baby, when you got it, flaunt it! Flaunt it!" Villamediana possessed the same aggressive, intemperate personality as Marlowe (and Pasolini). His life was full of scandal, marked by dissipation, periods of banishment, whore mongering, excessive gambling, and debt.

All these figures are larger-than-life personalities, who attracted as many enemies as friends (Lorca no doubt had fewer enemies, but those few were deadly). Villamediana went out of his way to create enemies by attacking powerful members of the court in his satires. Looking backward, it is also difficult for us to penetrate the façade of public behavior in a setting dictated by court etiquette and a seventeenth-century presentation of self profoundly enmeshed in political intrigue and deceit, when the political was personal and not the reverse. As with Marlowe, this nobleman's private life is something of an enigma, and his literary work, filled as it is with concealment, ambiguity, and silence, does little to dispel that mystery.[31]

Death met Villamediana at night on a street in Madrid on 21 August 1622. The likely weapon, a crossbow or something similar, assailant unknown. The bolt pierced his chest so deeply it came out the other side. He was hastily buried in a hanged man's coffin, the gravesite lost to time. Why was he killed? All explanations are, in one form or another, political in nature, as either his satirical poetry or his person gave offense to the court, possibly even to the king. In a nineteenth-century reconsideration of his life and work, Juan Eugenio Hartzenbusch observed that Villamediana's contemporary celebrity as a satirist was superseded by the celebrity of his death, which turned into infamy when accusations trained on the poet's sexual practices surfaced. A secret proceeding against Villamediana and several others for the charge of presumed homosexuality was apparently underway at the time of his murder. Four months later, five men, including two servants of his, were burned at the stake for sodomy, an act considered as serious as heresy and lèse-majesté in seventeenth-century Spain and indicative of the merging of crime, sin, and politics in the period. The secret investigation erupted into scandal. By the nineteenth century, Hartzenbusch barely insinuated the presence of *el pecado nefando* (the abominable sin), or sodomy, while Emilio Cotarelo y Mori made no mention of it at all in his biography of the count.[32]

Interest in Villamediana sparked again in Lorca's day, with the publication of Narciso Alonso Cortés's book on the poet's assassination in 1928. It was, he said, a delicate matter, but nonetheless he felt obliged to speak of Villamediana's sexuality, convinced that this was the reason for his murder and not his political satires or his rumored love for the queen. He gave two alternate accounts for the nobleman's presumed homosexual orientation: "Whether modern psychopaths and sexualists can explain and even justify, if that is possible, the Villamediana case, or whether others seek the connection that might exist between such excesses and periods of decadentist art, in order to see in the count a representative figure of Gongorism, it will always remain true that his tragic death, once seemingly that of another Macías [the lovestruck troubadour], was on the contrary joined to the lowest and most detestable of circumstances."[33] Both these explanations are rooted in contemporary issues of early twentieth-century Spain, in the first instance, sexology and psychiatry, and in the second, literary history. It isn't clear that Alonso Cortés altogether understood the incongruity of juxtaposing psychopaths with sexualists, this latter term referring either to someone who uses sexuality as an explanation of phenomena or a botanist who follows Linnaeus's sexual classificatory system. His references to Magnus Hirschfeld, J. E. Meisner, Ivan Bloch, and Gregorio Marañón indicate familiarity with some of the research of the period. The term *psychopath* is loosely used here, most likely reflecting the broad spectrum of sexual *psychopathias* outlined in Krafft-Ebing. By associating these contemporary, apparently disparate concerns of sexuality and Gongorism in the same paragraph, Alonso Cortés suggested a common genealogy of degeneration, one psychosexual and the other literary.

The link is not farfetched. Góngora had been attacked as a poet of sodomy in his own day, a homoerotic veil seemingly cast over the verses of his extravagant *Soledades* (The Solitudes). (Both Góngora and his archrival Quevedo wrote scabrous satires on homosexual practices.) The critic's allusion to decadentist art, which he associated with Villamediana's *gongorismo* and thus with a particular ornate style of the Baroque (and nonconformism), also evokes the more immediate excesses of fin de siècle decadentist literature and art, equally fixated on style and transgressive modes (Ramón María del Valle-Inclán, Oscar Wilde, Aubrey Beardsley). He united the two periods by calling Villamediana the "seventeenth-century's Oscar Wilde." Like Wilde, the count enjoyed such great success as a writer of wit and verve and a figure of elegance that his fall from grace stunned contemporaries. Observing that in the last several years Wilde's case had attracted a great deal of attention, from Marc-André Raffalovich to Lord Alfred Douglas, André Gide, and Frank Harris, he went on to say that the record on the seventeenth-century poet was far sketchier.[34]

In this manner, Alonso Cortés turned Villamediana into a contemporary. His own twentieth-century mindset had some difficulty in reconciling the count's manliness ("fué *todo un hombre*" / "he was *every inch a man*") with his sexual behavior. The solution was to declare him not a homosexual but bisexual, recalling the nobleman's reputation as a womanizer. "He wasn't, therefore," he writes, "a born Uranian . . . but a degenerate of vice." Marañón would later refer to his "ambivalent instincts." Alonso Cortés himself does not offer enough clarity, referring first to his bisexuality, then to what appear to be acquired vices. Like Marlowe, Villamediana is ultimately unreadable, but here it seems he was unreadable precisely because he was being read as a modern, in a period when the understanding of sexual identity was in flux.[35]

The poet's Gongorism is also made modern by association with later forms of decadentism, but in addition Góngora himself was part of the literary currency in the 1920s, having been championed by writers such as Lorca, Gerardo Diego, and Dámaso Alonso. Only a year before Alonso Cortés's book appeared, these same poets, along with José Bergamín, Jorge Guillén, Rafael Alberti, and Juan Chabás, all part of what would later become the literary construction known as the Generation of 1927, had gone to Seville, coinciding with the third centenary of his death (though in truth the gathering promoted their own work far more than Góngora's). Was Alonso Cortés alluding, however obliquely, to them as well? That seems unlikely. More significant is his making Villamediana relevant to the critic's own time, by attaching him to concerns and subjects such as homosexuality, Góngora, and Wilde that were of great interest in the 1920s. In "La imagen poética de don Luis de Góngora" (Góngora's Poetic Image), from 1926, Lorca wrote of "the delicate Gongorine Marquis of Villamediana [felled] by the king's sword." But in 1930 he revised the reference to read, cut down "by the sword of his dark love," using the multivalent word *oscuro* with its homosexual connotations, as in his *Sonetos del amor oscuro*. Was he by then familiar with Alonso Cortés's book, as Gibson suggested?[36]

There is yet another reason for considering Villamediana's case in the light of Lorca's. His good friend and fine poet in his own right, Luis Rosales, wrote a book on the seventeenth-century poet. First delivered as his acceptance speech for the Royal Spanish Academy in 1964, *Pasión y muerte del conde de Villamediana* (Passion and Death of the Count of Villamediana) appeared, revised and considerably enlarged, in 1969. The study is notable for its solid documentation, subtlety of interpretation, and impassioned stance toward Villamediana. Rosales's posture led one scholar to say dismissively that his "arguments were mostly tendentious, and need not detain us." Rosales vehemently rejected the Alonso Cortés thesis of Villamediana's homosexuality (or his bisexuality) and maintained, among other reasons, the poet's undisguised love for the queen provoked the king's displeasure, hence his death. In an earlier draft of the book, he also observed that the motivation for personal conduct and in history was complex and contradictory, the whys and wherefores for one's behavior "often unknown even to ourselves."[37] The circumstances of the murder remain murky, as does Villamediana's sexuality, enough to suggest he may very well have done some dipping into both wells.

The passion with which Rosales defended the seventeenth-century poet is striking, even bearing in mind his hesitation over how to address such a delicate subject in 1960s Spain without offending anyone's sensibilities. Yet he felt compelled "to vindicate the count's memory" for having been "unjustly condemned," a preliminary statement he dropped from the 1969 Gredos publication. Nonetheless, his fervor is just as transparent in the longer study, in which he set out to prove Villamediana's innocence, ending with this flourish: "Calumny is not always accompanied by defamation, nor is it the ultimate verdict."[38] Calumny is the key word here, though it is not altogether clear to me what Rosales meant when he spoke of the count's innocence. That he did not deserve to be murdered is self-evident. What was his presumed crime or, perhaps more apt, his sin? There appears to be none, in Rosales's judgment. What really bothered him was the stain on Villamediana's reputation, having gone from being celebrated as gallant and generous-spirited, if unruly and intemperate, to depraved.

Why should the death of a poet in 1622 provoke such indignation in 1964, almost 350 years later? To understand Rosales's reaction, you really have to go back to Granada, the summer of 1936. Rosales and his family harbored Lorca in their home, as the poet was being targeted (and was ultimately shot) by the Nationalists. (The Rosales, it must be said, gave refuge to many other Republicans as well during the civil war.) This event—the death of Lorca—shaped the rest of Rosales's life in the most definitive and radical way.[39] Rosales, who like all but one of his brothers had joined the Spanish fascist-style party, Falange, was later accused of having denounced and betrayed Lorca to the Nationalists. Gibson, Molina Fajardo, Félix Grande, and others have long since put paid to the charge, but Rosales was smeared repeatedly over the years. Tellingly, Grande called his book on the subject *La calumnia: De cómo a Luis Rosales, por defender a Federico García Lorca, lo persiguieron hasta la muerte* (Calumny: How Luis Rosales Was Persecuted till the End for Having Defended Federico García Lorca). Slander, which carries a strong juridical thrust, is also a very personal offense, difficult to shake off, impossible to forget. It strikes at the very core of a person's sense of self and at the same time produces a false, public version of the self that totally contradicts what one knows to be true. Slander is a form of shaming of the innocent.

In my view, Rosales, in his book on Villamediana, was remembering not only the injury to himself, but the disinformation campaign and unfounded accusations laid against Lorca during the war and in the Franco era. Robert Stradling has another take. As Villamediana for some is the prototype of the classic Don Juan figure, he reasons, his gayness constitutes the heart of the Don Juan myth. Alonso Cortés's research appeared to confirm his homosexuality, although subsequently the papers he used to make his point vanished from the archives. Stradling speculates they disappeared because a gay Don Juan was culturally unacceptable. (It should be remembered that Alonso Cortés hedged by calling the count bisexual, while Marañón brought up his ambivalent instincts.) Rosales's book can thus be understood as aiming to puncture that gay myth, further contributing to the "cultural cover-up" that began with the disappearance of the documents. In parallel fashion, Lorca, Stradling says, could now be thought of as a modern-day gay Don Juan, especially after it became common knowledge that he was killed at least in part for being homosexual. "Since Rosales presumably knew about Lorca's sexual orientation," he suggests, "further suspicions are inevitably evoked about the case which he tried so obviously to explain away."[40]

Rosales did indeed know that Lorca was gay, as did many of his friends. (Unsurprisingly, others were completely in the dark, in a period when few homosexuals were out of the closet.) In conversations with Ian Gibson, he recalled having met Emilio Aladrén, a former lover of Lorca, in 1934 or 1935. By that time, he already knew about the relationship. Even more telling, Rosales teased the poet, saying "you have a very virile head but underneath you're a fairy," and delighted Lorca by bestowing upon him the phrase, *machihembrista*, a combination of the feminine and the masculine echoing in parodic fashion the Platonic ideal. Rosales also had in his possession an inscribed copy of *Ode to Walt Whitman*, one of only fifty printed.[41] In the 1950s and 1960s, however, to speak openly (and favorably) of Lorca's homosexuality not only would have been unacceptable during the Franco regime; it would have been used to prop up some of the more scurrilous attacks against the poet. And no one in Spain would have seen Lorca as a gay Don Juan at the time Rosales published his book on Villamediana.

Stradling's argument is nonetheless of interest because it links Villamediana to Lorca and both to the status of gay icon, though I doubt Rosales was thinking of either poet in this way. The first question to ask is why he wanted to write about Villamediana to begin with. His enthusiasm for the seventeenth-century Baroque poet went back to the 1930s, a passion he shared with Pablo Neruda at the time, as he recalled in an undated letter to the Chilean writer (but probably from the very early 1970s). In the same letter, he appeared to reference his own book on Villamediana, saying it might be thought of as "a poetic indictment against violence," though he wasn't sure if he had succeeded in conveying that aim; one can't help thinking of Lorca's assassination in this context as well. Neruda himself wrote admiringly about Villamediana, calling him "a great seigneur of poetry and of life, a great assassinated poet."[42] His homage-poem to Villamediana, "El desenterrado" (lit., The Disinterred), was first published in July 1935, along with a selection of Villamediana's poetry, in the journal *Cruz y Raya* (also as a *separata*), and finally in *Residencia en la tierra* (Residence on Earth).

Some of the imagery appears to mirror that of the "Ode to Walt Whitman," believed to have been written in 1930, and making its first appearance in a noncommercial Mexican edition in 1933. The aims of this book do not allow me to analyze in detail the two poems together, but they share certain images such as mist (*niebla*), ash (*ceniza*), ear/spike of corn or wheat (*espiga*), and the beard (*barba*) of both Whitman and Villamediana. Thus, for example, Neruda, who had a close relationship with Lorca, wrote: "Sweet Count, in the mist," while Lorca described the American poet as an "old man, beautiful as the mist." Even more striking, the Granadine poet compared Whitman to a bird "with its sex pricked by a needle." Neruda's lyric voice says to Villamediana, "your murdered sex rises up." There is no allusion to the count's sexual identity, but the two lines speak to each other, evoking a common thread. Is Walt Whitman at one remove outing the count? Probably not. Years later Neruda made clear that, like Rosales, he believed Villamediana's love for the queen led to his murder. It is also worth noting that Neruda's resurrection of the flesh in "The Disinterred" contrasts strongly with Lorca's struggle between flesh and spirit in the "Ode to Walt Whitman."[43]

Nothing in Rosales's book suggests he was trying to cover up Villamediana's sexual identity. On the contrary, he appeared absolutely convinced that Alonso Cortés was wrong. The moral thrust of his argument attacked mainly what he considered slander. That there might be other motives for his posture cannot be discounted. He reacted, for example, very strongly to Quevedo's insinuation of the count's homosexuality, calling it vile. And he viewed Villamediana's posthumous trial on the charge of sodomy as pure defamation, observing that witnesses protested the proceeding. "The death of Villamediana," he wrote, "was ordered by the powers from above. . . . The truth cannot be hidden. . . . It is useless to lie and try to falsify history. There is always evidence. The truth is the bridge that brings everything together." Whatever the truth about Villamediana, a sense of outrage overflows here, pointing to an underlying motive that remained unspoken in 1960s Spain.[44]

In denying Villamediana's homosexuality, was he also denying Lorca's? This seems unlikely. Rosales's revulsion derives much more from the perceived stain on Villamediana's reputation than anything else, for what he considered to be lies. His reference to powers from above and the falsification of history resonates in the context of Lorca's murder and the real coverup, that of the Nationalists. The poet was accused of being a red spy and of the ideological crime of associating with the socialist intellectual-politician, Fernando de los Ríos, among other things. (As Gregory Woods observed, there was already "widespread paranoid association of homosexuality with espionage" in many parts, to which communism was added in the 1930s, reflecting a perception of gays as less patriotic and more cosmopolitan in their loyalties.)[45]

Realizing too late the enormity of their error, the Nationalists tried to distance themselves from the assassination. Worse, supporters of the Franco regime even suggested that it was Lorca's own fault, vaguely insinuating he was mixed up in something sordid. Pemán wrote in 1948 that the poet's death was "a vile, unfortunate episode" and completely unrelated to any official actions. In a propaganda pamphlet from 1953 aimed at the English-speaking world, the Francoist government continued to deny culpability and assigned blame to "some irresponsible elements because of their own personal quarrel." Schonberg, as we know, was more explicit in suggesting a homosexual rivalry, in which he said Rosales was also implicated, a plot evocative of an updated Elizabethan revenge tragedy or of the fate of Marlowe and Villamediana.[46]

In 1961, Gonzalo Fernández de la Mora characterized the traditionalist Ramiro de Maeztu's wartime death as heroic by way of comparison with Lorca's: "He didn't die like the fragile Lorca, a victim of a dark crime of passion in a time of uncertain confusion." This comment provoked a response in 1963 from Ramón de Garciasol, in a damning critique of the Franco dictatorship for the prestigious journal *Cuadernos Hispanoamericanos*. The regime promptly censored it, withdrawing the issue from circulation and substituting another essay for its later appearance. Rosales, who happened to be editor-in-chief at the time, resigned. All this drama formed the immediate backdrop to his book on Villamediana.[47]

Rosales himself was subjected to a whisper campaign, which became public in late December 1949 while he was on a tour of poetry readings in Latin America. Someone in the audience yelled out, "Murderer!" and he was pelted with tomatoes and rotten eggs. In Cuba, Nicolás Guillén and Juan Marinello had already made the charge in a local newspaper. It also probably didn't help that comments on Lorca's death, mentioning Rosales as the poet's protector and absolving the Falangists from all blame, coming from Franco's brother-in-law and former righthand man, Ramón Serrano Suñer, had appeared in a Mexican newspaper the year before. The accusation of having been complicit in Lorca's assassination never really went away, resurfacing, for example, when he won the Cervantes Prize in 1982.[48]

Sometime in the fall of 1977, he also received an anonymous letter from a splenetic rightist, branding him a homosexual, or *maricón*, like Lorca and at the same time claiming Rosales was exploiting the poet's death. "García Lorca died, alongside the enemies of Spain," he wrote, "because he was a queer." Lorca's fate, he also said, would have been different had he associated with gays from the right rather than the left! This libelous, incoherent letter would scarcely merit any attention, did it not confirm that homophobia wielded as a weapon of slander was still very much alive in the late 1970s in Spain, and that both Lorca and the civil war were still a flash point. In an interview from 1979, Rosales said he had received "anonymous letters, threats, and insults against [himself] and against the figure of Federico, who was treated in the vilest manner." He also noted that "they killed [Lorca] because of a slur [*calumnia*]," without specifying what that slur was.[49] It seems less likely that Rosales thought the fact of Lorca's homosexuality in itself constituted slander, but rather that the innuendo and insults focused on his sexual identity were patently contemptible.

These attacks from both the left and the right were devastating for Rosales. When even his fellow Falangists blamed him for Lorca's death, his disillusionment with *falangismo* and politics in general was complete. More than anything, one suspects that the politicization of Lorca's murder had to have reverberated, in Rosales's mind, with that of Villamediana's. He detested how both the Spanish Communist Party and Falange used Lorca as propaganda for their causes.[50] None of this tells us very much about the count's own sexuality, or whether Rosales's vehement defense of his hetero-sexuality was misguided, or at the very least overstated (though I am in-clined to think it was). Nor was he alone in rejecting Alonso Cortés's thesis.

In 1961 the poet Gerardo Diego, friend to both Lorca and Rosales, thought the same and remained unconvinced of the possibility that Villame-diana might have shared what he termed "the abjection of an Oscar Wilde." It pained him to think that his old maestro, Alonso Cortés, espoused such an idea. Both Diego and Rosales held a Catholic view of the world, which surely shaped their insistence on Villamediana's "normalcy," as Diego put it. Like Rosales, he saw the seventeenth-century poet as a victim of calumny. He also linked the legend that grew up around Villamediana and the subsequent ob-scuring of historical truth to that of another assassinated poet who remained unnamed, though the reference to Federico García Lorca seems clear.[51]

By contrast, in 1969 Juan Manuel Rozas said Villamediana's sodomitic practices were "almost a certainty."[52] As with Marlowe's time, however, we do not altogether grasp how sexuality was understood or how it was situated then. Significantly, for highly visible figures like Marlowe and Villamediana homosexual conduct attained meaning partly through the political frame that set the stage for such acts. Is it any different for Lorca or Pasolini, bearing in mind the discrete historical and cultural contexts I have laid out for all these writers? What distinguishes Villamediana is the cultural amnesia that buried his work and his life until the mid-nineteenth century. The recovery of both also revived what he shares with Lorca, Pasolini, and Marlowe: his celebrity, his importance as a public persona, even when that celebrity turned into in-famy, whether deserved or not. In all these cases celebrity also made their lives, and sometimes their work, more opaque, in part because the aura of myth and legend overtook and colored the historical record, in part because the demands of performance were intrinsic to celebrity, throwing a veil of mystification over life and work.

The presence of homosexuality complicates the picture of celebrity in interesting and surprising ways, and indeed modern celebrity could be said to be understood at least in part through the impact certain homosexual figures have had in shaping it, above all Oscar Wilde. Wilde's extravagant personality embodied modern celebrity as an exuberant form of performance, literally enacted in his wildly successful lecture tour of America in 1882. *The Wasp* satirically depicted him as the "Modern Messiah," bearing a sunflower

Figure 7. Oscar Wilde as *The Modern Messiah*. Cartoon by George
Frederick Keller, *The Wasp*, 31 Mar. 1882, San Francisco.

with a dollar sign and mounted on a donkey with calla lilly ears, a simultane-
ous burlesque of the aesthetic movement and crass commercialism (fig. 7). In
such enterprises, he made explicit the performative nature of celebrity itself,
but he also suggested how celebrity obscured who he was by focusing on his
public persona, himself as performance, as above all a feminizing dandy figure, who sported flowers as decor. As Rhonda Garelick has pointed out, "dandies are among the earliest celebrities." Wilde went further, erasing the "distinctions between private and public, life and work, artist and celebrity."[53]

He made people think about him as something extraordinarily out of
the ordinary, while hiding his sexuality in plain sight. In this case, performance itself links celebrity and homosexuality, highlighting the ephemeral-
ity of the first and the elusiveness of the second. Celebrity slips away, while
homosexuality is simply slippery, acting out an unstated gayness that only the
law managed to define years later with devastating clarity for Oscar Wilde.
Modern celebrity is, in this sense, gay, even when the person isn't, though
what that gayness is often seems indeterminate in the late nineteenth and
early twentieth centuries.

The undecidable quality about Wilde remained part of his persona, at
least for his public, until suddenly it wasn't. One could argue something similar for Villamediana and Marlowe, though in their cases that ambiguity
seems permanent, embedded as it is in a history and culture alien to us. Political intrigue (and murder) brought to the surface something we might never
have otherwise learned or considered, but these very circumstances are also

suspect precisely because they *are* political. In any event, apart from their unquestionable literary value, celebrity for these writers has become at once political and sexual. It rests on a few related questions: Who and what is gay? Is it any different for Lorca and Pasolini? What does calling them gay icons tell us about them?

5. Fabulous Fag (II), or the Celebrity of Sex

What did a gay icon or celebrity look like in Lorca's day? For that you need to dig into popular culture and an extraordinary personality who, to my knowledge, is never talked about in the same breath as Federico García Lorca: Álvaro Retana (fig. 8). Only in linking them to the same culture, and thus decentering Lorca as a solitary star unattached to this particular writerly constellation, can you also see something of the range and variety of what it meant to be a gay writer, what was attached to it, and what being gay might have signified in early twentieth-century Spain. It also allows me to examine further, in this chapter and the next, the relation between celebrity and being gay in a period when the two were not necessarily viewed in tandem. Lorca's afterlife is firmly rooted in the past, as latter-day reimaginings of the poet's iconic gay status, such as those of Edouard Roditi and Jaime Manrique, suggest. Manrique, who places him among a group of "eminent maricones," including Manuel Puig, Reinaldo Arenas, and himself, wrote, "the minute the bigots who killed Federico put an end to his earthly life, they gave birth to the myth."[1]

Álvaro Retana (1890–1970) was never a myth, but he was once famous. That he isn't anymore had as much to do with the cheaply produced kiosk literature he wrote as with the nature of celebrity. One of the things that kiosk literature, as a sign and instrument of mass culture, generated *was* celebrity. Perhaps the first to attain such widespread familiarity with a mass readership in this period was Felipe Trigo (1864–1916). Like Trigo, Retana earned a great deal of money writing erotic fiction but little prestige. Unlike Trigo, he appeared relatively unaffected by his less than stellar place in the

Figure 8. Álvaro Retana. Drawing
by Guillén, 1924. *Flor del mal,*
by Álvaro Retana, p. 14.

literary world. While some critics praised his work, by and large he exploited
celebrity as the next best thing to literary reputation. He went even further
and made celebrity sexy.[2]

The reverse could also be argued: he turned sex into a kind of celebrity
culture. Retana's work and life are worth a second look, precisely for what he
can tell us about the changing conception of the modern writer, the creation
of a mass readership, and the reinvention of sex in all its permutations as an
ambivalent sign of modernity in early twentieth-century Spain. Retana promoted a highly sexualized celebrity as part of the fabric of both his writing
and persona, and like Wilde, erased the distinctions between his literary production and his own life. For many of his readers, his books *were* Álvaro
Retana. He incorporated celebrity into his books the same way he inserted
himself into his writing. Celebrity encouraged admirers of the famous to
blur the line between writer and work, a phenomenon observable in the case
of Lorca. The slippery line between documented fact and literary fact is fertile territory for the birth of celebrity.

Retana was also a creature of another celebrity scene: the early twentieth-century music halls of vedettes and *cupletistas,* or cabaret singers, who would shortly be joined by the *transformista,* or male imitator of women and women entertainers. As a popular composer of *cuplés,* a set and costume designer, and confidant to several women artistes, he knew this special world intimately, re-creating it in one of his early successes, *La carne de tablado* (Theater Flesh) (1918). In reviewing the novel, Antonio Zozaya counted himself among those "fortunate and rare mortals who only know from afar such celebrated artists." But he wrote, "no one knows how real the prestige of glory not seen close up is." *Theater Flesh* tore away that veil of illusion for Zozaya, who, like Retana, understood that celebrity was a fabrication and better experienced from afar.[3]

At the same time, Retana intentionally drew both his characters and his readers into the self-enclosed realm of celebrity, in some ways updating and surpassing the function of the society reporter by showing what the society chronicler, constrained by convention, could not talk about: sex among the favored few. Their sexual practices, polymorphously perverse, speak above all to the performative, to the display of sex and sexual identity as a form of celebrity, as the form that celebrity assumed in his works. This relation between sexual identity and celebrity is germane to Lorca, in considering his status as a gay icon.

Retana also re-created himself as a celebrity in his books. In an Artemio Precioso prologue to *Flor del mal* (Flower of Evil) (1924), the novelist claimed that the Princess Raffalovitch was a frequent visitor to his home and regaled him with gifts, such as a pianola. "I await her somewhat theatrically," he continued, "because my eccentricities amuse her, and after five o'clock tea she will drive me around in her automobile exhibiting me on la Castellana like some fantastic creature." Moreover, "Álvaro Retana" is a major character in *Flower of Evil,* and like his other characters, the novelist is a singular personage of exceptional temper. Unlike them, he experiences celebrity as a burden, as Retana observed, in an ironic, self-conscious gesture: "I needed to continue being the libertine artist in my books and maintain the disquieting halo my figure radiates." It is this sexualized aura that is imagined as celebrity.[4]

Here I need to foreground the significance of celebrity as something modern in early twentieth-century Spain, in order to best situate both Retana and Lorca. Painting in broad strokes, Richard Schickel maintained "there was no such thing as celebrity prior to the beginning of the twentieth century." In contrast to "fame," which was associated with deeds, excellence, honor, and the quality of *virtù*, celebrity, while more often attached to achievement than not, was no longer constrained by talent (or by *virtù*). Fame derived from the Latin for rumor, *vox populi*, and public opinion (and its earlier Greek origins), which established a close connection between renown and reputation as seen through the estimation of others. Fame could be good or bad, whereas the self-promoting effect of celebrity, even when infamous, was always "good."[5]

Media-driven, modern celebrity also appears to do away with the traditional barriers between the favored and the ill-favored, creating the "illusion of intimacy" with the celebrated person, along with the delusion of future celebrity for those not blessed by VIP status. In a comic vein, the British actor, Leslie Howard, once found himself on the receiving end of mistaken familiarity when a jocular theatergoer barged into his dressing room postperformance. Bewildered, grease paint clouding one eye, Howard says, of course, he remembers Wilfred; of course, he remembers little Alice Fraser to whom he is supposed to have done something or other. "Two things I would like to know," Howard wrote in 1925. "Where on earth did I encounter Wilfred and exactly what did I do to little Alice?" A modern celebrity is a peculiar thing: a projection of mass-produced desires, yet seemingly singular.[6]

At the same time, the contemporary phenomenon of literary modernism, understood in the broadest sense of the word, enthroned the author's uniqueness, seen as personality and duplicated as style. Jonathan Goldman pairs modernism and celebrity together as two phenomena that issue out of the same fetish of self. Similarly, the flamboyant Valle-Inclán equated modernism with "an intense yearning for personality," writing about "my profession of modernist faith: seeking myself in myself and not in anyone else." The quintessential writerly figure was Oscar Wilde, who made himself into an international public image well before the period Schickel claimed for the creation of modern celebrity. Wilde's thirst for fame made him a celebrity. Even more significantly, his was the model, dandified and vaguely aristocratic, the living performance of authorship, for subsequent writers like Antonio de Hoyos y Vinent, Retana, and, self-confessed or not, perhaps even García Lorca, to the degree his Andalusian persona was also receptive to other forms of self-fashioning, particularly after the extraordinary success of *Gypsy Ballads* in 1928. By the time of his Latin America tour in 1933–34, uncontrollable, publicized fame, to which Lorca had contributed his share, had made the poet ubiquitous, as I explore in the next chapter.[7]

The Wilde model of celebrity faintly echoes earlier representations of the artist as hero, linking it to the tradition of arms and letters and the Carlylean inner heroism of the genius. In Spain, the Renaissance poet Garcilaso de la Vega embodied the nobility of blood and spirit in the tradition of *armas y letras,* as Gustavo Adolfo Bécquer's 1870 meditation eloquently reminds us. But Garcilaso possessed fame, not celebrity. He was celebrated, but not a celebrity. Covarrubias (1611) placed *celebridad* and *festividad* together, while noting that one celebrates something said or done, something worthy of being observed or honored. Vélez de Guevara (1641), for example, equated the toasting of the king, the festivities of a bullfight and jousting with canes to a *celebridad,* that is, a celebration. From the sixteenth into the nineteenth centuries, *celebridad* retained that meaning, as well as its association with the classical notion of fame, which was still in use in Ramón López Soler's *Los bandos de Castilla* (The Bands of Castile) (1830), when he referred to a "youth of such celebrity and lineage" and to "the pure bloodlines and celebrity that are ennobling."[8]

In 1877, Benito Pérez Galdós associated fame and celebrity together, remarking that the liberal politician General Rafael del Riego was mediocre at best, "living proof of the follies of fame and usurper of a celebrity more befitting other personages and names." By the 1880s, the meaning of celebrity was changing, loosely approximating the modern, mass-mediated notion of the term marketed in the early twentieth century. In 1881, Emilia Pardo Bazán spoke of the then controversial French literary school of naturalism by observing that "one now attains celebrity by way of scandal and talent, rather than talent alone."[9]

By 1924, José Ortiz de Pinedo was writing about the sins of celebrity, noting that very few people are "famous without a reason" ("célebres gratuitamente"). He went on to say, a "writer may think, with melancholy, that here no one enjoys the glory he deserves, only the kind he can manage to grasp or that others allow him to acquire." The side effects of celebrity were sometimes unexpected. Pointedly and to humorous effect, the Colombian writer Baldomero Sanín Cano observed in 1914 that the big-game animals Theodore Roosevelt bagged in Africa, as he himself was being relentlessly pursued by reporters and movie cameras, would gladly have foresworn his celebrity. Roosevelt, like William Jennings Bryan and Charlie Chaplin, embodied the larger-than-life personality that newspaper moguls like William Randolph Hearst exploited by making names the news. This practice of personification spread everywhere in the media world.[10]

Celebrity had sex appeal, as the endocrinologist Gregorio Marañón, well known for his sexology studies in the 1920s, recognized. It was also associated with the flourishing nightlife of big cities, which is to say with the sexual mores of its denizens, a heady mixture of lowlifes and the slumming upper classes. Thus, the novelist Alberto Insúa (1922) describes the Count Virama as "handsome, elegant and a millionaire [who] in a matter of months became a celebrity of Madrid by night." (In the same work, *El negro que tenía el alma blanca* [The Black Man with a White Soul]), the main character attains celebrity as an entertainer, a celebrity that is at once complicated and enhanced by race.) Such celebrity sometimes signified notoriety, as with the real-life case of the Marqués de Hoyos y Vinent, who trolled for rent boys in the Puerta del Sol and other Madrid locales, a practice Cansinos-Asséns clucked over with barely contained gleeful malice in his memoirs. Even more scandalous in his day was the Infante Luis Fernando de Orleans, a Bourbon prince who lost his title in 1924, after a sailor mysteriously died during one of his drug-filled gay parties in Paris.[11]

The link between aristocracy, homosexuality, and celebrity, which strikes me as key for the period, is especially relevant for Álvaro Retana. Aristocratic characters abound in his fiction, and many of his friends, gay and straight, came from the same class, such as Hoyos y Vinent and Edgar Neville (Conde de Berlanga de Duero). He didn't hesitate a moment in 1928 to solicit the protection of the Duke of Vistahermosa, who belonged to the League against Public Immorality (Liga contra la Pública Inmoralidad), when he was being prosecuted as a pornographer. At the very same time, he shamelessly asked the duke his help in placing one of his lovers, Ricardo Berdejo, in a government post! Retana even claimed his grandfather was a grandee. While there is no doubt he grew up in an upper-class, privileged home and socialized with members of the aristocracy, some of whom were most likely related, the grandee in his family was probably a flourish of Retana's imagination.[12]

His father Wenceslao also provided a model of sorts for this linkage, with his own novel *La tristeza errante* (Errant Sadness) (1903), a satire of the aristocracy highlighting the perils of prestige and the celebrity of sex. It is useful to recall that the society reporter was still a ubiquitous figure in the prewar period 1900–1914, which was also the swansong of high society. And not just in Spain. Edith Wharton, of privileged patroon stock, wrote in 1905 of "a world where conspicuousness passed for distinction, and the society column had become the roll of fame." Even as society chroniclers endeavored to maintain the special aura of the aristocracy, while peddling such singularity for mass consumption in their columns, other observers were harsher. In 1901, Rubén Darío criticized the Spanish aristocracy's indolence, their pampered existence, and what he saw as the palpable degeneration of the nobility. "Tell me how you create a country with such elements?" he asked. Several years later, the Jesuit Julio Cejador y Frauca, himself of noble origin (the Cexadores de Ateca), said the old lineages were rotten to the core. "The new aristocracy is one of talent and work. When talent and work are injected into the trunk of ancient lineages, we see them revive." Ironically, he was writing about one of the most scandalous figures of the period, the flamingly gay Marqués de Hoyos y Vinent, whose elevated social status afforded him protection. It didn't, however, prevent him from falling, or possibly being pushed, down the subway stairs at the Plaza del Progreso, a nocturnal haunt for hookups, and raising eyebrows.[13]

Culturally and socially, throughout Europe, a popular, long-standing perception of the aristocracy associated it with homosexuality. Real scandals reinforced it, such as the marriage of the homosexual son of the Duques de la Torre in 1880, which became food for gossip when his wife sought a divorce in Paris and a papal annulment. This was not the kind of celebrity that the Duquesa de la Torre, apparently obsessed with it, craved. Dueling books on the matter turned it into a political and medical issue, given that his father was General Francisco Serrano, a key politician-statesman of the period, while the court went so far as to investigate his son's sexual make-up. Ironically, Serrano was once a lover of Isabel II, whose own marriage was awash in rumors of her husband's homosexuality.[14]

The society chronicler not only paved the way for the erotic novel in Spain; it provided one of the basic staples of the genre, a continuing fascination with the aristocracy, in a period when high society was about to become irrelevant. It could be argued that the erotic novel briefly made the aristocracy relevant again, at least symbolically, as a form of modern, if largely decadent, celebrity for a mass readership. The aristocrat was already highly visible in fin de siècle decadentist literature, not to mention the romantic serial novel and the even earlier chivalric tradition, but none of these earlier genres conceived the aristocratic figure as a celebrity. There is, however, a link between decadentist literature and the author as celebrity, as a kind of vaguely pseudo-aristocratic personage who appears to have stepped out of his own books, as embodied in Oscar Wilde. Tellingly, Artemio Precioso called the eternally youthful-looking Retana a modern Dorian Gray, and some of his characters are also seen as Dorian Grays for the same reason. The novelist even self-styled himself a latter-day version of Oscar Wilde.[15]

Retana's fabricated Wildean persona fascinated many readers but provoked disdain and homophobic hostility in others, sometimes privately sometimes not, such as Cansinos-Asséns and the Chilean Joaquín Edwards Bello, who was familiar with the Madrid literary scene. Years later, the same disgust dripped from José Alfonso's pen as he recalled the novelist's physical appearance—plucked eyebrows, painted lips and eyes—on magazine covers. He was photographed at work sometimes in a kimono, sometimes in a white dressing gown, or with an infantilizing black satin apron, white socks and patent leather shoes. And early in his career, he cross-dressed on at least one occasion. Other observers played along with Retana's deliberate exploitation of a sexually charged, ambivalent image of himself, in both visual and verbal venues. He was "ambiguous," accepted code for gay, surrounded by an entourage of "guayabitas y guayabitos" ("attractive young men and women"), recalling Lorca's retinue of youthful male followers in the theater.[16]

Flesh-and-blood readers waxed ecstatic over his physical appearance, calling him a living Adonis, Dionysian perfection. "I find myself looking at an extraordinarily beautiful youth," one of them wrote, commenting on the photo Retana sent him, "like a Byzantine ephebe or a Venetian page from the Renaissance." The novelist's inveterate use of photographs, as part of his books and his dealings with admirers, demonstrates the degree to which he understood how such visuals—functioning like the close-up in film—created a virtual, seemingly personal relationship with his readers, which in turn promoted his celebrity. (As with other celebrities, such as the dancer Tórtola Valencia, magazine shoots also photographed him in domestic settings, thus furthering the illusion of intimacy.) Retana himself confused readers, warning them not to equate a feminine man with an effeminate one, but mostly he left the door open to his sexual identity.[17]

In a word, Retana excelled as something of a Rorschach poseur, who could mean different things to different people, which is the essence of modern celebrity, circumstances that are also relevant in Lorca's case. He continually distanced his persona from the intentionally pumped-up immorality of his characters, while often inserting himself as an apparently active participant into the same scandalous worlds of his books. He was an attention-grabber, whose gender performances made it difficult to separate reality from fiction. The sexual personage he promoted in real life and in his books was enormously attractive to readers. It was an attraction made doubly so for the social risks attached to such publications in some quarters. Retana's novels were devoured surreptitiously, his fans fearful of being caught reading red-handed.[18]

Intended for a wide readership, much of his work was printed on cheap paper, in massively produced series. He made no bones that writing for him was a money-making business. And like celebrities today, he saw nothing incongruous in plugging a cognac that had just been named after him, an early example of product placement. He even thanked his readers for the numerous gifts they showered on him, from expensive jewelry and a Russian coffeemaker to a box of oranges, candy, and flowers. At one point, he broadly hinted how much he would love one of those miniature train sets that you could find in Almacenes Rodríguez on the Gran Vía. In this way, Retana managed at once to highlight his own celebrity—his specialness—and to draw his readers closer to that same celebrity in a calculated gesture of intimacy.[19]

In a word, his celebrity also became a celebration of mass culture. Retana's relationship with his readers was very different from that of most high-culture writers like Pérez de Ayala, Valle-Inclán, or Unamuno. Some, antagonistic to this kind of commercial enterprise, were quick to point out how much more money he (and writers like José María Carretero, who went by the name El Caballero Audaz, Alberto Insúa, and Joaquín Belda) made, while poor Cansinos-Asséns struggled to survive as a translator and Gabriel Miró was a paltry civil servant. Masses of readers flocked to Retana and company, while serious writers were left with relatively few, but equally significant is the nature of that readership, which a novelist like Retana deliberately cultivated and created. His own persona, largely invented, depended on another invention: a readership that embraced the fantasy of sex he was selling.[20]

We know that readers were eager to establish a relationship with Retana because some of the letters they wrote to him survive. (Like Byron, he saved his letters from fans.) Tellingly, many were from the provinces. One young man, Fernando Rodríguez, from Almería, explained in his first letter, dated 26 January 1932, that Retana's *Mi novia y mi novio* (My Girlfriend and My Boyfriend) (1923) inspired him to write the novelist. His letters were peppered with references to Retana's characters as potential role models, with questions about the writer's life and plans to meet him in Madrid. Is Rafael in *Flower of Evil* a real person, he asked? How many letters do you receive daily? What is your entourage like? Are you propositioned, do they want money? These are the kinds of questions asked of a celebrity. Fernando said he did not believe the stories about Retana's notoriety, but his curiosity was all-consuming.[21]

We shouldn't be surprised: Retana's Wildean reputation preceded him, incessantly promoted in his own books, in interviews, and articles. Even his friends sometimes participated in burnishing the aura of celebrity. In 1918, Hoyos y Vinent, for example, relished describing a wild costume party at Retana's new quarters, where attendees imbibed champagne with ether and took hash with dessert, the gay dress designer José de Zamora danced an oriental capriccio, and the multimillionaire Eduardo Burnay trashed all the guests, calling them "*ratés*, leftovers from the Wildean era, and phony muses, *all very Montmartre*." Hoyos claimed that Burnay disappeared with a Pierrot figure of "fugitive, small gestures" into another room and shot him, having mistaken him for a woman, after which the corpse was dumped in the street. Hoyos's imagination was working overtime here, as these kinds of embellishments blurred the line between the real lives of celebrities and fiction.[22]

So did some readers, to judge from these letters. Alternatively, maybe admirers like Fernando didn't really confuse fiction and reality at all, contrary to what is generally believed. Initially a fan, Fernando quickly moved to flirtation. Reading between the lines, it becomes evident that some sort of brief relationship developed between them. The letters stopped after Retana discovered that Fernando had also had a liaison with a member of his male entourage. His admirer remarked more than once that the novelist didn't behave like a celebrity: "your letter seems more like that of a friend of many years than of a writer as celebrated as you are." Then he added: "and the fiction would have been complete if you had used the familiar *tú* in the letter." Here is that illusion of intimacy with celebrity of which Richard Schickel spoke, though with a twist. First, the barrier between the favored and the ill-favored was later breached in this instance. And second, before that breach, the admirer disclosed to what degree he was aware of the illusion, while happily participating in it.[23]

Later Fernando imagined what his first encounter would be like with Retana, in a full-blown sexual fantasy that reads like something out of one of his novels. While the writer continually, if ironically, made distinctions between his flesh-and-blood self and the persona he paraded in public and in his books, his readers did not always do so, nor in this case did he. Fernando saw Retana through the sexualized aura of celebrity, which enhanced the novelist's singularity while paradoxically making him accessible as a prefabricated fantasy, anticipating Ginsberg's vision of Whitman and Lorca as consumable as peaches and avocados. His celebrity was meant to transfer, vicariously or otherwise, to the uncelebrated, akin to what Walter Benjamin observed of the newsreel effect: "the newsreel offers everyone the opportunity to rise from passer-by to movie extra. In this way any man might even find himself part of a work of art." This is quite different from Emerson's notion that the great man's uniqueness was nontransferable. Fernando's association with the novelist provided him, albeit briefly, with the simulacrum of celebrity. A pseudo-aristocratic model, modern celebrity nonetheless also speaks to a democratic wish fulfillment. The sense that anyone could *be* Lorca is a natural outcome of such a mindset.[24]

Retana evidently had encounters, of different sorts, with other readers, too, though not all of them produced the same results. One young man named Luis declined to meet him in Madrid, explaining that he did not share the same sexual tastes but was not offended. Yet another admirer from Almería, Ricardo Berdejo, talked about the effect Retana had on his life, as he had decided to "go gay" ("pasear el plumero"). Amid complaints of the stupidity and tedium of provincial life, he told Retana how much he remembered the writer and his home, fantasizing nostalgically over his experience in Madrid. The letters, written between 1928 and 1932, show an ever-deepening despair in Berdejo, trapped in a dull existence and now seriously considering marriage, even though it would likely bring unhappiness for "men like us" ("los hombres como nosotros"). He signed the letter, apparently the last one, using the feminine form, "your old friend" ("tu antigua amiga"), and adding: "the great Almería cocotte" ("la gran cocotte almeriense").[25]

Berdejo called Retana his confidant and most intimate friend. Whether the reverse was true is impossible to tell, as we do not have the novelist's letters, though I think it doubtful that Retana saw Berdejo in the same light. Berdejo was one among several fleeting affairs the writer had; and as with other admirers, he also asked favors, namely help in relocating to Madrid. What seems clear here is the great attraction celebrity held for provincials like Fernando and Ricardo precisely because it wasn't provincial. Retana's celebrity was inconceivable without the modern, cosmopolitan setting. His lifestyle and his books provided an alternative world for some readers, an imaginary world clothed in an idealized, unreal halo, but no less appealing, especially for closeted gay readers who may have seen Retana's celebrity (and his books) as a form of coming-out. In this respect, the pervasive gay and bisexual themes and characters of his fiction cannot be divorced from the ubiquitous presence of celebrity. Retana's flashiness, the way he flaunted his persona and his work, was part of his celebrity, but it was also part of his gay performance. Celebrity, as seen in his lifestyle and books, offered the novelist a way to come out without coming out, because celebrity was also a performance. The way Lorca also enacts a performance of celebrity will be taken up in the next chapter.[26]

Modern celebrity tends to be democratizing, as it "denotes a new form of social status that is dependent neither on rank [n]or institutional achievement."[27] Yet it seems clear to me that the aura of celebrity, which may initially have arisen in part out of the need to find a substitute for the gradual social loss of aristocratic prestige and influence, provides a kind of pseudo-aristocracy in the public sphere. Mass media made modern celebrity possible because it created a mass readership capable of bestowing widespread recognition upon a select few, who were already singled out through the heavily reproduced, fetishized image. Moreover, the mutual craving for celebrity feeds the demand for unique forms of the self, forms that lend themselves to a kind of eroticized radiance (this is certainly true of Lorca). Modern celebrity is, however, ambivalent by nature. Its fleeting character can produce notoriety, as well as fame.

Significantly, Retana's first full-length novel, *Al borde del pecado* (On the Edge of Sin) (1916), focused on the downfall of a celebrity. Retana seems to have already grasped the risks of celebrity, but he also knew the risks of being gay in a less than tolerant society. Being gay placed him in an even more vulnerable position than celebrity itself. Instead of retreating, he flaunted both, turning sexual audacity, whether gay or straight or something inbetween, into a form of celebrity culture. Not everyone saw it his way, and the excesses others perceived in his work twice landed him briefly in jail, under the politicized system of censorship during the Primo de Rivera dictatorship. (Far worse awaited him after the civil war, when the Franco regime first sentenced him to death, then imprisoned him for nine years and denounced him publicly as homosexual in the infamous Causa General, the official Francoist investigation of "red crime.") The bitterness he felt at being abandoned by his friends during these prosecutions, precisely when he was most vulnerable, seeped into his 1931 critique of erotic and pornographic literature, *La ola verde* (The Pornographic Deluge), written under the pen name, Carlos Fortuny. Cynically, he observed that writers cultivated literary pornography, not out of conviction or depraved instincts, but because it "paid better and brought them celebrity more quickly."[28]

Retana's ability to reinvent himself, using celebrity as a springboard to fetishize the self in an endless striptease of performance, suggests a certain paradox: the gayness of apparently not being gay, which also works in reverse. The novelist threw off veils as fast as he replaced them. His flair for showmanship, in which an ambiguous sexuality was key, may seem far removed from Lorca's stated dislike of an extroverted, extravagant homosexual persona, but another way to view the poet's stance is to see it as a refusal to be pinned down, to be defined as one thing only. And in that he has much in common with Retana, not to mention Pasolini, who hated the same kinds of restrictions. Still, Lorca seems to have felt uncomfortable not only with celebrity, but, for at least some of his life, with homosexuality itself in some respects.

For someone like Lorca, being a celebrity and being gay are two sides of the same thing, in their disturbing effect on his inner life and on his sense of privacy. By contrast, Retana relished being in the spotlight; yet he was ultimately every bit as elusive as Lorca in being *identified* as gay (as opposed to really being gay). Social taboos do not altogether explain the intricacies of being Álvaro Retana and Federico García Lorca in their day. And indeed, despite the presence of homophobia, this period is remarkable for the growing visibility of a gay subculture in Spain and elsewhere. A commonplace is to say how awful it was to be homosexual for Lorca in the 1920s and 1930s, but one could also argue that this was a truly interesting time to be gay.

It has been observed more than once that the changing perception of homosexuality since the 1890s represents a distinguishing trait of modernity. This is the era "in which homosexuality *came out* as a major cultural influence, and in which homosexuality was itself one of modernity's major cultural constructions." In a humorous vein, the openly gay dress designer, writer, and dancer José de Zamora wrote to Retana, whom he had known since their school days, mentioning a female ski champion who had become a man. He suggested the two of them compose a novel exploiting the latest trend of "sex changes." The letter included a funny, mildly obscene cartoon of the going market for various body parts. Retana himself spoke of the lesbian chanteuse Olimpia d'Avigny as possessing a *"very modern"* aura, and he added, "we all know that the word *modernity* justifies everything."[29]

In an unpublished, tongue-in-cheek gay manual, "Guide for the Perfect Kept Man," he offered this advice: "Take every opportunity to repeat to your lover that you do not consider him an invert, but rather a modern man." Clearly, gay men like Zamora and Retana were already aware of the nexus between modernity and homosexuality, even if the shadow of homophobia had not disappeared. Their irrepressible funny bone is a dead give-away. Once things are spoofed, you know they've become part of the cultural scene, in the same way Cary Grant, cross-dressed in a lady's marabou-trimmed négligée in *Bringing Up Baby* (1938), jumps wildly into the air and exclaims to a mystified grande dame wondering why he's wearing those clothes: "Because I just went gay, all of a sudden!" (His ad-libbed remark might also have been a dig at rumors he and his then roommate, fellow actor Randolph Scott, were an item. In any event, the studio left it in the film.)[30]

Contrast this with the shock of a provincial audience in 1933 upon hearing a woman say *maricones* while reciting lines from a production of Lope de Vega's *Fuenteovejuna* for Lorca's traveling university players. That same audience erupted into wild applause afterward. The year before, the Second Republic had decriminalized homosexuality, reversing the legal stance of the Penal Code of 1928 during the Primo de Rivera dictatorship. A parody of the regime's antigay crackdown appeared in a kiosk novella, *El club de los queridos* (The Lovers' Club) (ca. 1930–31), written by the pseudonymous Barón de Montenegro. A vast group of gigolos, pimps, gays, bisexuals, and those in between, all of whom figure in police files, decide to band together in self-defense, a project the narrator calls "worthy of a modern nation." In no time at all, the entire enterprise is shut down, after the police raid a mass meeting and jail the attendees for creating a public scandal. The result? The police files have now grown from twenty-three thousand to seventy thousand names! The piece also pokes fun at contemporary explanations and categories of homosexuality. We're not miscreants, they say, call us sick maybe or just misunderstood. Are they low-lifes or victims? Such niceties of distinction seem beside the point in a work that suggests at once an increasingly more open society and unease at such openness.[31]

The association between gayness and modernity in these examples ex-

Figure 9. José de Zamora and
Antonio de Hoyos y Vinent.
Caricature by César Abin, 1917. *El
año artístico*, by José Francés, p. 28.

tends to far more negative perceptions as well. Even as the new Penal Code
of 1928 was being prepared and debated, the Peruvian writer Felipe Sassone,
who spent much of his life in Spain (he was married to actress María Palou),
took potshots at various types that he found objectionable. "The effeminate
today," he wrote in a kiosk novella, "don't go to bars or to cabarets. They
prefer to make Dadaist verses or to take hip baths like their Paris professors."
The modern here is European (and avant-garde), as it so often was for Spain,
but so too is homosexuality in this example. This is also the case when Sassone uses a French colloquialism for ponce, *maquereau*, to characterize two
blond men sitting together in a bar.[32]

Later, when the exotic dancer Tórtola Valencia walks into the same bar,
she is accompanied by "a dancer who looked like a decadent avant-gardist
and a decadent avant-gardist who looked like a dancer." These two figures
were probably José de Zamora and Antonio de Hoyos y Vinent, as Valencia
was often seen in their company, trolling the underbelly of Madrid (fig. 9).
Sassone made no mention of her rumored and almost certain lesbianism. Significantly, he mixed different worlds in bringing together avant-gardists and
decadentists, dance and literature, the frivolous and the serious, but right-

fully so, because these groups did know each other. Hoyos wasn't really part of the avant-garde, but he certainly knew much of the literary-artistic scene in Madrid, frequenting Ramón Gómez de la Serna's celebrated gatherings at Pombo (as did Zamora, Tórtola Valencia, and García Lorca), Cansinos-Asséns's rival group, and the seemingly unending series of banquets and homages in this period. Tórtola Valencia possessed popular appeal, but was especially favored by the cultural elite, including Gómez de la Serna, Valle-Inclán, Pío Baroja, and others who sang her praises in poems and novels. Zamora designed costumes for Mistinguett and Moulin Rouge, but also for Diaghilev's Ballets Russes and Valle-Inclán's play *Farsa y licencia de la Reina Castiza* (Farce and Misrule of the Castilian Queen).[33]

This *was* the modern world. It was also transparently gay, or read as gay, in many instances. Sassone lampooned the avant-garde, signaling their snobbery—they don't go to bars and cabarets, he claimed—but also tarnished them (in his view) by labeling them effeminate, or gay. The terms decadent and avant-garde are also loaded, by being associated with a male dancer. Inconsistently, these same apparent snobs also show up in the bar in which Sassone as narrator finds himself. They belong to the same set of "exquisites" and "aesthetes" that Cansinos-Asséns found so unwelcome in his memoirs and that Gómez de la Serna urged him to meet at the poet-translator Ricardo Baeza's social get-togethers.[34]

Liberalizing attitudes aside, for centuries homosexuals had been viewed as freaks of nature. A writer like Retana worked toward disarming hostility and disapproval by transforming a negative image into something he sometimes called eccentric and sometimes monstrous. He turned his persona and his fiction into an extravagant, ironic display, while performing the role of showman. The same could be said of the extroverted public behavior (and dress) of artists and writers like Tórtola Valencia, barefoot and draped in gauzy veils, and Hoyos y Vinent, a dandy embellished with raised heels, a flaming gold watch and monocle. They reveled in being walking spectacles, the embodiment of the fabulous. This too was part of their celebrity.

The monstrous and the eccentric are joined to a similar constellation of qualifiers of uniqueness, singularity, and anomaly. In using such qualifiers, especially the monstrous, Retana appeared to embrace a status seen today as unwanted and undesirable, but, as I argue here, the aesthetics of oddness he fashioned reveals even as it occludes an early twentieth-century homosexual subculture in Spain that was far more visible than previously thought.[35] Retana also allows us to consider qualities and aspects that, to my knowledge, have been largely overlooked in a period marked by great social, cultural, and political change and fluidity: a renewed and modern sense of the marvelous, as reenvisioned through the ambiguous forms of the monstrous and the eccentric, a sense of the marvelous we may only have glimpsed in other writers and artists of pre–civil war Spain, most particularly, in the case of García Lorca, who also demonstrates his own aesthetics of oddness.

This self-image as monster or eccentric can be traced back to the Romantic artist's envisaging "the monstrous as a metaphor for the *unique*" and art as "a monstrous progeny," of which Mary Shelley's creature in *Frankenstein* is an archetype. Fin de siècle literary decadence further sexualized the monstrous with tropes of ambiguity. Rachilde's *Monsieur Vénus* (1884) immediately comes to mind for its representation of gender confusion and cross-dressing reversals. A self-confessed admirer of decadent literature, Retana linked monstrous uniqueness to the symbolic doubled figure of the hermaphrodite, a classic figure of monstrosity in early modern treatises on monsters and later medical textbooks, which takes on new life when reimagined narratively as forms of the bisexual and the ambiguous. The novelist tended to use terms such as ambiguous and androgynous, rather than hermaphrodite, but the exhibition of the doubled self draws on the tradition of the hermaphrodite as display and entertainment. In so doing, he recalled the links that were made between the hermaphrodite and homosexuality in medicine and society, associations that expressed uncertainty and confusion over sexual identity and blurred gender roles but also linked homosexuality to the realm of the marvelous. These associations continued to persist in Lorca's time.[36]

Like homosexuals, monsters were considered freaks of nature; both were viewed as something unnatural, against nature, albeit produced in the natural world. In time, this awkward positioning allowed an opening for gays to argue in favor of homosexuality as part of nature, as André Gide wrote, following Goethe, that it was "natural, that it resides in nature, even if it proceeds against nature." An analogous turn took place in the perception of monstrosity, when human monsters were demythologized in the eighteenth century, removed from the world of the marvelous, and brought into the realm of science and thus to some degree naturalized. The nineteenth century's pathologizing of homosexuality and human monstrosity retained an underlying moral posture, but paradoxically also attempted to rationalize both.[37]

It is worth thinking of them as interrelated, conjoined in more ways than one, especially in the rhetoric of literary decadence of the late nineteenth century. Decadentism continued in the enormously popular phenomenon of the erotic novel, of which Retana was a prime example in the early twentieth century. Like the equally outré gay writer Hoyos y Vinent, he was especially drawn to the double-sided figure of the hermaphrodite, as imaginatively construed through bisexuality and the seeming transformation of men into women and women into men. Indeed, I would argue that Retana brought back the marvelous through the sexual fantasies he provided to readers who avidly devoured his fictions.

In sideshows, the half-man/half-woman sex attraction played off the duality of the hermaphrodite, by presenting one side of the body as masculine, the other as feminine. As with the classification of homosexuality, which was divided into congenital and acquired, human oddities were either born or made. The lines between the congenital and the acquired, however, were often blurry, in the opinion of Havelock Ellis, perhaps the most influential of the fin-de-siècle sexologists in Spain and elsewhere. Ellis thought both sexes were "latently hermaphrodite," suggesting that there was "a general undefined homosexuality," in addition to what was then called sexual inversion. He also observed that "the bisexual group is found to introduce uncertainty and doubt."[38] Likewise, part of the allure of the hermaphrodite as oddity relied on uncertainty, on not knowing what it is, or whether we are seeing a true freak of nature or a marvelous fraud. Many half-woman/half-man entertainers were female impersonators.

Retana was intimately familiar with the world of female impersonators, who were known as *transformistas,* a term emphasizing the appearance of sexual transformation, however illusory. In some instances, such as the artiste Freddy, he created costumes for them. As a songwriter, he provided material to one of the most popular cross-dressers, Egmont de Bries (Asensio Marsal), who also appears in his novel *Las "locas" de postín* (The Posh Fairies) (1919) (fig. 10). An imitator of female music-hall stars, he generates great enthusiasm among the "representatives of the indecisive sex, for what there is . . . of the ambiguous and propagating effect" in his artistic efforts. Thus, his performance art serves "the cause of the third sex." While some female impersonators were heterosexual (like Barry Humphries, creator of his comic alter ego, the incomparable Dame Edna), many were gay.[39]

The heterosexual *transformista* protagonist of El Caballero Audaz's *La*

Figure 10. Egmont de Bries, drag
queen. Photo by Rapide.

pena de no ser hombre (The Agony of Not Being a Man) (1924), angst-ridden
when his public is convinced that he is homosexual, brings out the divided
self that resides in the metaphorical, latent figure of the hermaphrodite,
whether dressed in drag or not. Retana is much more lighthearted and playful (though awareness of the difficulties that homosexuals experienced in this
period can certainly be detected beneath the surface). Unattached to the vanguard, he nonetheless wears the same mask that García Lorca displays, and
like the poet, he slips it on and off. The doubled nature of sexual identity—a
figurative half-man/half-woman—in his work allowed him at once to declare and deny he was gay, in this sense, to impersonate what he said he was
(or his characters claimed to be). Thus, for example, his eccentricity, which
identified him as an outsider, as equivocal, also made him fascinating, if not
necessarily transparent, to his readers.

Whether Retana drew on the tradition of the sideshow as well as the drag spectacles of his day I have not been able to ascertain, but it would not be surprising. As we will see, the sideshow image also appears in Lorca as part of an aesthetics of oddness and performance. There is a long tradition of human monsters as entertainments, recalled in Velázquez's paintings of the dwarves who occupied a complicated place in the royal court of the Hapsburgs, and in circuses, fairs, anatomical museums and collections, both traveling and permanent, where human anomalies, natural and fraudulent, were shown, including an apparently true case of a hermaphroditic "intersexual" at a fair in 1928.[40]

Exhibits of oddities, including racial and ethnographic displays of colonial peoples at parks and zoos, were announced in the newspapers and could be viewed at the Circo Hipódromo, Circo Colón, and Circo Price, or Dr. Velasco's Museo Anatómico y Universal de Curiosidades (now the Museo Nacional de Antropología) in Madrid, or in one of some twenty anatomical collections and museums documented in Barcelona between 1849 and 1938. In 1859, Adolfo de Castro meticulously described the pathological specimens of the anatomical cabinet in the Facultad de Medicina of Cádiz, including a "model of monstrosity." P. T. Barnum initially called his world-famous enterprise the Grand Traveling Museum, Menagerie, Caravan, and Hippodrome. The line between dime museums and more high-minded anthropological and ethnographic collections was not as clear-cut as it might appear today.[41]

Circus acts and spectacles, which Enrique Sepúlveda in 1886 called "great attractions" and "monster debuts," appealed to a broad swath of the population. The same observer noted that the celebrated impresario Felipe Ducazcal promoted all kinds of spectacles, from operetta (zarzuelas) to magic plays, from acrobats and clowns to wild animal tamers and monsters or freaks ("fenómenos"). The aristocratic closeted protagonist of Hernández-Catá's El ángel de Sodoma (The Angel of Sodom) (1927) is aroused sexually at a circus, while the equally closeted Nobel Prize winner Jacinto Benavente, a good friend of Retana (and theater colleague of Lorca), was a circus impresario in his youth.[42]

Another friend, Hoyos y Vinent, directly linked the sideshow to a display of sexual nonconformity. The prologue to his collection of novellas, El secreto de la ruleta (The Secret of Roulette) (1919), begins with these words: "I have often found them at the world's fair—that fair where God, like an omnipotent Barnum, has delighted in gathering together all the monsters and all the deformities—and the smile that was meant to be ironic has turned so doleful that it's more like a grimace of pity." He goes on to describe these creatures "with their bodies impossibly maintained, thanks to massages and corsets, beneath the lace, silk, furs, and pearls, with their painted faces, made-up and powdered. . . . They made sensational appearances, flirting like queens [*locas*]." If Hoyos's pronounced allusion to *locas,* meaning fags, hasn't tipped off the reader, his conclusion makes it clear that he is speaking of cross-dressers, when one of them begins to recount an experience at a drag ball ("un bal travesti").[43]

Hoyos's transvestites are not, strictly speaking, hermaphrodites, but they are expressive of that diffuse cultivation of the ambiguous and the impersonated that we see in Retana's fiction, of what is male but also female, of what is performance but also real when the mask is dropped and they are "truly themselves" ("ellas de verdad") (whatever that might be).[44] That these transvestites belong to the same world as the hermaphrodite is suggested in an earlier text of Hoyos, "Hermafrodita," from the collection, *El pecado y la noche* (Sin and Night) (1913). At an upper-class social gathering set in the nineteenth century, one of the *habitués* enthralls the prudish Doña Recareda, who bears the ironic feminine version of a Visigothic king's name, with the myth of the double-sexed Hermaphroditos.

Mythology is seen as full of youth and vitality, but then the conversation veers toward more scandalous subjects, and another character begins to talk about "monstrous transformations, bizarre caprices of Nature; he revealed horrible monsters, cases of madness. . . . [T]hey came and went strangely turmoiled, these absurd beings, hybrid creatures that contorted themselves, emerging from the grotesque only to cross over into the painful." Doña Recareda, endowed with a mannish voice and features, is terribly flustered and rushes out into the street, where she is taken for a man in women's clothing. Harassed and about to be arrested, she has a (comic) epiphany in Madrid's Plaza Mayor, realizing that she too is "one of those fabled ambiguous beings, unsexed and hybrid," and, eyes flashing, declares herself the reincarnation of Hermafrodita. Removed from the privacy of an aristocratic *soirée,* she has also become a public spectacle.[45]

Clearly, the marvelous has not been completely expelled here. As an early attempt to naturalize monstrous creatures such as the hermaphrodite by linking them to reproduction and minutely describing them, Ambroise Paré's influential *Monsters and Marvels* (1573) nonetheless insisted that "there are divine things, hidden, and to be wondered at, in monsters—principally in those that occur completely against nature." "On Hermaphrodites or Androgynes" comes early in the treatise, as the sixth section, immediately followed by "Memorable Stories about Women Who Have Degenerated into Men," thus linking the double-sexed with sexual metamorphosis (unsurprising, given the influence of Ovidian myth). Defining *monstro*/monster, Covarrubias (1611) limited himself to the physical deformities of human monstrosities, as "against the natural order and rule." In the entry for *ermaphrodito*/hermaphrodite, he first summarized the myth, then gave a morphology, alluding to Pliny's belief in hermaphrodites as a distinct race. Mateo Alemán (1599) cited the case of the monster of Ravenna, whose two sexes signified "sodomy and bestial brutishness," a reminder of the long-standing association between hermaphroditism and sodomy (which included a panoply of sexual practices).[46]

For Antonio de Fuentelapeña (1676), the hermaphrodite was neither "perfect man, nor perfect woman." While a monster, it is to be distinguished from the sex that is called "neuter," considered even more abhorrent. A monster, he wrote, is nothing less than a "sin of nature," though elsewhere, he suggested that such beings no doubt consider so-called normal people equally monstrous. In a book filled with as many invisible creatures like ghosts, imps, and other spirits, or *duendes*, as visible ones, Fuentelapeña also stressed the divine presence illuminating such prodigious entities.[47] By the nineteenth century, there was considerable skepticism as to whether true hermaphroditism existed, with apparent or pseudo-hermaphroditism clouding the picture.[48] The physician Pedro Felipe Monlau (1853) denied it, saying: "What we have, at any rate, are a number of monstrosities; what we have are many anomalies that simulate, convincingly or not, the amalgam of both sexes in one individual." With startling bluntness, he called them *maricas* (fags) and *marimachos* (butches). His use of the term *vicios de conformación* echoes the prevailing view of monstrosity as an anomaly, which was deemed either congenital or acquired.[49]

In a series of late nineteenth-century aphoristic fragments, José de Letamendi deemed hermaphroditism atavistic; all "erotic aberrations," in his view, proceeded from the inherent hermaphroditic condition of human beings, from what he called "militant hermaphroditic vestiges." Associating homosexuality with this genealogy, he maintained that "all unions between individuals of the same sex are reduced to a simulacrum of an incomplete hermaphroditism." In this way, he approximated the notion of psychic hermaphroditism, as opposed to an anatomical one. In 1912, Max-Bembo divided hermaphroditism into the categories of physical (very rare), psychic (seen in geniuses), and sexual (known as bisexualism). Later, Martín de Lucenay equated psychic hermaphroditism with "moral bisexuality" and Marañón's "intersexual states," an indication of the inconsistency, confusion, and uncertainty over how to define the undefinable. The same could be said of the taxonomies of monsters, particularly germane in the case of hermaphrodites, in the effort to medicalize what once was folklore and fantasy.[50]

So, in the very period that encompassed the decadent and erotic flowering of all kinds of imaginative aberrations, from Rachilde to Jean Lorrain, Oscar Wilde to Aubrey Beardsley, from Hoyos y Vinent to Álvaro Retana, and yes, even Federico García Lorca, science attempted to pin down this strange, once-marvelous creature, in classifications, both verbal and visual, that were meant to demythify. As Leslie Fiedler has observed, however, the aura of the older mythology clings to the word itself, even if the taxonomies and the photographs are entirely devoid of previous mystery.[51] Yet, in truth, medicine had merely refocused its attention on the very elements that made hermaphroditism and all such variations monstrously prodigious: the atavistic and the psychic as new forms of the marvelous.

One could even argue that the intricate, detailed taxonomies sprouted like luxuriant vegetation nearly as wildly as the creatures in any erotic or decadent fiction of the fin de siècle and early twentieth century. Moreover, there is as much display in some of these taxonomies as in the extravagant presentation of the double-sexed in literature, the arts, and the actual spectacles of monstrosities. The "hermaphrodism of the soul," as Foucault called it, anticipated in psychic hermaphroditism, or in the aphoristic musings of Letamendi, would be mapped onto the figure of the homosexual, paradoxically making him visible but also endowed with the marvelous. Thus, hermaphroditism "remained as a 'ghost category' in the construction of sexual inversion and homosexuality," according to Cleminson and Vázquez García. Iterations of homosexuality as a form of hermaphroditism, with vaguely Platonic resonances—the Uranian, the third sex—characterized the period. The homosexual presence in works like the "Ode to Walt Whitman" or *The Public*, or even *Once Five Years Pass*, with its protagonist's elusive psyche projected onto other characters, however, is slippery, sliding from one position to another, thus defying classification. The construction of sexual identity that Cleminson and Vázquez García see is, it seems to me, always in question.

In this sense, the hermaphrodite as symbolically challenging, difficult to categorize, is an apt term for understanding Lorca's work, without defining it or calling it as such.[52]

That same "hermaphrodism of the soul" appears allegorized in Oscar Wilde's 1891 depiction of Dorian Gray's "monstrous soul-life," the portrait as the aesthetic display of a secretly divided soul, who believes himself "tainted with the monstrous maladies of the dead." This familial atavism is extended to his "ancestors in literature" as well. Among these ancestors is Théophile Gautier's poem "Contralto" (1852), which Dorian recalls with the phrase "charming monster" ("monstre charmant"), an allusion to the hermaphrodite sculpture that is the subject of the poem. Unlike Gautier's sculpture-poem, the portrait gradually loses all identifiable form, until the very end, when Dorian Gray's death restores the picture's original beauty, while making the loathsome deformity of his own visage unrecognizable.[53]

The figure of the hermaphrodite is central to Rachilde's *Monsieur Vénus*, described as "two different sexes in a unique monster." The exhibitionist nature of Rachilde's text and characters, which Maurice Barrès in his prologue called the "spectacle of a rare perversity," is apparent. Ironically, despite Wilde's own extroverted personality, *The Picture of Dorian Gray* occludes the unnameable monster of sex at the heart of the novel, working against one of the suggested etymological meanings of monster, as derived from the Latin *monstrare:* to show or to display, because the terrifying painting of the protagonist's inner life cannot be publicly exhibited. On the other hand, the word as currently derived from *monere*, to warn, points to monsters as signs, prophecies of catastrophe, a meaning that Dorian's fantastically imbued portrait embodies.[54]

The built-in signifiers of the term monster suggest why the monstrous is inherently a spectacle, as display and sign, but is it representable? This same question has occurred to Roberto González Echevarría in his analysis of Calderón de la Barca's *La vida es sueño* (Life Is a Dream) (1635), in which monstrosity offers a key to Baroque aesthetics and, by extension, to art as "monstrous by nature." As he observes, the monster appears to make a "mockery of mimesis." Monstrosity does not conform to what we expect in nature, despite what Diderot (1769) (and others) claimed: "Man is nothing but a common effect—the monster but a rare effect; both [are] equally natural, equally within the universal, general order of things. . . . And what is astonishing about that? . . . [A]ll beings circulate within each other, and conse-

210 THE CELEBRITY OF SEX

quently all species . . . everything is in a perpetual flux." Diderot's own
words belie his point: if everything is in a perpetual flux, how is monstrosity,
already observed as a "rare effect," captured (never mind the natural)? That
which astonishes does so because it is a rare effect, something that defies expectations and norms, a point worth bearing in mind in considering works
such as the "Ode to Walt Whitman" or *The Public*.[55]

According to Antonio Santos, both popular usage and etymology indicate that the word can only be applied to the most serious of anomalies, to
those which produce "*entities* more or less *amorphous*, more or less *viable*."
The monstrous lacks a definable shape. Similarly, the hermaphrodite is deemed
ambiguous, hybrid, unsexed, as Hoyos (and many others) observed, and is
thus troubling because it upsets expectations of what a "true sex" is.[56] Significantly, it is hard to represent. The restrictions in making visible such things
as hermaphroditism and homosexuality are not simply social, cultural, and
even legal, especially in this period, but more profound, striking at the heart
of the matter, at that formlessness which threatens the boundaries between
the human and the not human. Despite all the taxonomies, hermaphroditism,
and by extension homosexuality, could not be delimited, hence their perceived
monstrousness. Psychic hermaphroditism pointed to an inner monster in
perpetual flux, as Dorian Gray's ever-changing, dissolving portrait signifies
(or Lorca's fluid image of Walt Whitman).[57] The difficulties in representation
are conveyed in the secrecy, the invisibility, with which the portrait becomes
wrapped.

At the same time, only the artifice of art enables Wilde and his readers
to frame the picture's boundless horror, to put it on display. I have dwelled
on Wilde's novel because along with Rachilde and other decadent writers, he
offered a model of monstrosity that Álvaro Retana and others found attractive, a model of uniqueness, inherited from Romanticism, as I noted earlier,
but also a model of dissolvent, yet proliferating ambiguity. This same indeterminate ambiguity in some ways could be said to threaten that very uniqueness, just as the trope of monstrosity enhances originality as a thing against
nature.

In Retana's and Lorca's day, Rafael Cansinos-Asséns, a key figure of
the intellectual world in the pre–civil war period, was illustrative of the contemporary obsession with the hybrid and the ambiguous, especially in its
sexual manifestations (one has only to think of the fascination with the androgynous). Ernesto Giménez Caballero, for example, wrote a story titled

"Aventura con hermafrodita" (Adventure with Hermaphrodite) (1928), in which *both* main characters are hermaphroditic. In ironic, antigay commentaries that pepper the pages of Cansinos's memoirs, a parade of ambiguous types, ephebes, and effeminate creatures is displayed in a gay spectacle, suggesting a voyeuristic enthrallment with the homosexual world, as Alberto Mira observed.[58]

But Cansinos was also the author of the book *Ética y estética de los sexos* (Ethics and Aesthetics of the Sexes) (1921), one of the most subtle, thought-provoking, and singularly forgotten essays on this theme. Although Mira does not mention it (it appears to be a text ignored by practically everyone), the book affirms what the critic maintains: the presence of homophilia and homophobia in the same individual. The nuanced position Cansinos assumes in the essay contradicts the sarcastic, often contemptuous tone of his memoirs. (A similar conflict can be detected in Lorca's "Ode to Walt Whitman.") It is as though actually coming into contact, however fleetingly, with someone gay provoked a form of social anxiety in Cansinos that, in another context, the abstract beauty of the imagination, largely melted away. Perhaps because the imagination was a lot safer to play in than the real world. Or because the imagination freed him from the real world of social conformity and received notions. Then again, both attitudes may simply have been equally genuine, and irreconcilable, expressions of the self. Lorca's "Ode" is illustrative here, as we will see.

While it is true that Cansinos emphasized the desired perfect union between a man and a woman in the creation of progeny, what really stands out here is the indeterminate, the indecisive, and, suggesting clear Platonic echoes, the impossibility of two sexes uniting ideally into one or of incorporating one sex within the other. On the other hand, he also wrote of a "principle of inversion in the excessive love for the opposite sex" and of "the yearning for an inverse experience." Gregorio Marañón popularized an idea that was already much disseminated by the 1920s, in Freud and others, that of "'the other sex' that accompanies us." The phantom of the other sex was in the blood, not the imagination, he said in 1926. For Marañón, who admitted the existence of intermediate types, what was truly important was "to make men more manly and women more womanly." By contrast, Cansinos described something that above all inhabited the imagination: "like a larva, or a specter, the hybrid is introduced into the dreams of normal human beings." In this indeterminate zone of sex exists the hybrid, "the ambiguous throng of androgynes and hermaphrodites," whose mysterious presence, like fauns, "fills a great part of the forest of the night."[59]

One's sex, he said, "isn't simply a material representation perfectly defined in space, a topographical reality . . . it is, above all, a nexus of mental representations, of affective states, a medium of the most tenuous suggestiveness, infinitely variable." A little later he declared that sex "was once a unique attribute, irreplaceable and immutable. But see it now flutter like a marvelous bird over human trees. The words male and female no longer possess an unquestioned meaning. In between the lines of duality gracefully slip in with an evasive air, women endowed with virile attributes, men with supple waists and disturbing hollowed out hips, beings adorned with double attributes." At heart, Cansinos appeared to suggest the desire to go beyond the two sexes, recognizing, in a utopian gesture that recalls such German Romantics as von Humboldt, the hybrid as something future-minded: "And in this zone of the sexes, the monster is a new interpretation, a desire for liberation and originality."[60]

While he seemed ambivalent about the normality or abnormality of the beings he described, he was also entranced with their possibilities, describing them in Promethean, heroic terms. They are aware of their transgression and what the essayist considered their tragic condition, but "at the same time in their faces, astonished at their marvelous discovery, they express the ecstatic, serene joy of being at peace with the intimate truth. Because what seems monstrous in all this is their truth."[61] Cansinos embraced the monstrous by returning it to the territory of the marvelous and the unique.

It appears that Cansinos was speaking of two different things at the same time: of the hybrid as an inescapable part of our imaginary and the hybrid as a concrete phenomenon in the real world. In my view, his somewhat vague, poetic language does not clarify precisely who these strange creatures are. Are they a new being formed from the two sexes that will ultimately reconcile their differences? Or are they something else, the monster or hybrid within us that we do not recognize? Breton's "shadow of the marvelous that no one has ever seen" seems to hover in anticipation over them. Cansinos's evasive technique, I believe, is intentional and, doubtless, characteristic of many writings of the period. A homosexual interpretation, or at least an androgynous one, of these marvelously monstrous creatures who fascinated him is certainly a possibility.

The confusion over the metaphorical and the real is never resolved in

Cansinos, but then, neither is it settled in the writings of Álvaro Retana, who was familiar with *Ethics and Aesthetics of the Sexes*.[62] Cansinos's remarks remind us that Retana's use of the monstrous has a long Spanish pedigree, especially notable in the sixteenth and seventeenth centuries. Forms of the hybrid appear, for example, in the plays of Calderón. In *Life Is a Dream*, Rosaura calls herself "a monster of two appearances"; and in *El monstruo de los jardines* (The Monster in the Garden) (1667?), a character describes himself as a "a monster, then, in two images / am I: your lady by day and by night / your suitor." Lope de Vega sometimes uses hermaphrodite to mean belonging first to one sex, then to another, rather than being endowed with two sexes.[63]

In other words, there are probably far more metaphorical hermaphrodites present in literature than anatomical ones. Moreover, the looseness with which the term is used suggests that writers not only understood the phenomenon as metaphorical, but also found its hybrid instability engaging and full of social, psychological, and sexual implications in order to express the indeterminate, the ambiguous, and the impossible to define. Thus, in 1835 Larra disapproved of an anomaly he calls the *mujer-calavera*, or female roué, whose (uncharacteristic) boldness unsexes her, making her more of a man. "It's the confusion of the sexes, Nature's only hermaphrodite."[64]

One of the most fascinating comments on the subject appeared in a letter from the poet Salvador Rueda to Leopoldo Alas (internally dated July 1900), in which he described his astonished reaction to the decadent-symbolist D'Annunzio's *Il trionfo della morte* (The Triumph of Death) (1894). Having originally imagined the writer as "a sickly, effeminate, complicated creature, unelevated, weak, lacking an artistic sex, or with an intermediate sex, in short, an aesthetic hermaphrodite," he now saw him as quite a guy (*un tiazo*), "in whom there is a woman, a man, a child, a psychologist, a poet, a *creator of a modern idiom*" and much more.[65] Writers seemed less interested in a strictly anatomical hermaphroditism than in a slippery, ever-changing inner hermaphroditism, or, in Rueda's case, a hermaphroditism of aesthetics, but which was still inward in nature.

Retana was no different here, though the strategy he employed took him in another direction. His writing and his persona became fused, and the apparently frivolous way he appeared to identify himself and some of his characters as metaphorically and monstrously double-sexed turned his fictions into doubled readings as well. Sexual ambiguity was flaunted as a kind of eccentricity that allowed the writer to claim and deny at the same time who he was, or how his characters should be identified and read. The human monsters on view serve not as warnings (*monere*), but as displays (*monstrare*), and moral posturings, notwithstanding some ambivalence, are nearly always deflated by irony and humor. Thus, we recall how he sees himself as a fantastic creature, or monster, whose idiosyncrasies (*excentricidades*) amuse the Princess Raffalovitch. He is, in a word, a performance.

This self-aggrandizement (of which he was an expert) cleverly off-sets negative connotations of the monstrous by associating it with the eccentric and the fantastic. For Gloria Fortuny, one of the novelist's fans in the Baudelairean titled *Flor del mal,* Retana, who appears as a principal character, is "the most adorable of monsters." But Gloria's own "delicious monstrosities" pressure Retana and another male character, Rafaelito, into a fake homosexual relationship, none of which prevents the novelist from considering Rafaelito the perfect gay lover or falling for Gloria. If Retana is an exhibit for the princess, he in turn delights in showcasing himself publicly with Gloria ("exhibirme públicamente").[66] The entire novella is an exhibition, in private and in public venues like the theater, carnival, banquets, taxis, and automobile rides, of role-playing, of assuming a bisexual identity, or what Max-Bembo called sexual hermaphroditism.

The use of the words *eccentric* and *eccentricity* is of special interest. An astronomical and mathematical term meaning not concentric, or not central (Gr. *ekkentros* [out of the center] = ek "out" + kention "center"), *excéntrico* was registered in the nineteenth century as a Gallicism (*excentrique*), taken from the English, signifying "extravagance," "caprice," and "originality" in 1855, while Onions said it was from the French. Baralt retained the older ridiculing sense of "original" as extravagant and even monstrous. (*Exhibirse,* in the sense of to show oneself in public, was also considered Frenchified, with connotations linking it to eccentric [ek = out] and extravagant [extra = outside of]). In another meaning stressing display and the performative, eccentric was also said of a circus artist who does "original or strange exercises."[67]

As far as I can tell, under the entry for *excentricidad,* the 1925 *Diccionario de la Real Academia Española* was the first to list, after the initial definition of "oddity or extravagance of character," a secondary one that says, "a peculiar, abnormal saying or act." In the 1927 edition, the term *anormal* was removed from the secondary definition. It was back for the 1936 and 1939 editions;

gone again, in 1950. In 1956, *anormal* was back! And it remains as of the 2001 edition. This apparent struggle over one word—*anormal*—suggests some disagreement over the meaning of *excentricidad*. Its initial association with eccentricity in 1925 situated this specific connotation in the same period as the heyday of the erotic novel and the stirring of interest in sexology and psychoanalysis in Spain. *Anormal* itself first appeared in a Spanish dictionary in the mid-nineteenth century, it seems, as did *normal*, around the same time as the nonastronomical or nonmathematical use of *excéntrico*. Baralt viewed it as akin to *anómalo* (anomalous), which as we have seen elsewhere, was associated with monstrosity. By 1925, "abnormal" was widely linked to homosexuality, bisexuality, and other kinds of sexualities considered deviant.[68]

The terms *excéntrico* and *excentricidad* also showed up in Spanish literature and other written sources. Ramón de Mesonero Romanos, for example, referred to the bohemian artist figure as eccentric (1851) and, in his memoirs (1881), to Goya, the Romantic writers of El Parnasillo, and even political parties. In 1866, the physician Pedro Mata associated the term with abnormality in a case of homicidal monomania. None of the references I found implied anything sexually abnormal about being eccentric, but a brief allusion in Luis Coloma's *Pequeñeces* (Trifles) (1891) hinted at it, when he described a young woman's "manly and determined allure," along with her "eccentric genius."[69]

Both the eccentric and the abnormal, which were sometimes seen as synonymous, represented a deviation. The abnormal diverges from the normal. A word much associated with the English, especially in the nineteenth century, eccentricity is a "deviation from a centre," as James Kendall observed in 1859, in his humorous defense of the character trait. In the same year, John Stuart Mill also defended eccentricity as nonconformity, an antidote to the tyranny of opinion, abundant "where strength of character has abounded" and "proportional to the amount of genius, mental vigour, and moral courage" of a society. One is reminded of Cansinos's monster as a new interpretation, a "desire for liberation and originality." The eccentric was closely attached to the aesthetic realm, especially to genius. It was widely applied, however, not only to all kinds of out-sized, quirky personalities but to oddities, including the physically deformed, as well. Thus, people looked at eccentrics with a certain ambivalence, and still do.[70]

As a deviation that was at the same time considered part of the normal, eccentricity could be accepted and even admired. By the early twentieth century, homosexuals had been heavily medicalized as pathological specimens in the museum of human oddities. A counternarrative emerged in gay writers like Gide and Edward Carpenter, who highlighted eccentricity as genius in historical homosexual figures. Alberto Nin Frías, also homosexual, took a similar tack in *Alexis* and *Homosexualismo creador* (as the title, Creative Homosexuality, illustrates), ambivalently likening the image of homosexuality to a coin: on one side, "anomaly, aberration, perversion, and on the other side, it is equally possible to make out the divine sublimeness and transparency of human greatness." Nature abhors the absence of variation, he argued, but humans tend to flatten differences, such as the "excentricidad," or "eccentricity," that homosexuality displays, observing that "the pearl is the product of a disease." To complicate matters, he also said that "the abnormality of the Uranian doesn't reside in him, but in those who do not participate in his sui generis mode of being." It appears that Nin Frías wanted to have it both ways, ascribing the abnormal to something intrinsic to gays but also categorizing it as imposed from without.[71]

The aesthetic oddness of eccentricity, perhaps even its diseased underbelly, as Nin Frías seems to suggest, has a double-sidedness here, revealed in the coin's two faces and the bivalvular source of beauty, the pearl. Eccentricity is, in this sense, possessed of a kind of psychic hermaphroditism, or the hermaphroditism of aesthetics that Salvador Rueda discerned in D'Annunzio. Cansinos-Asséns said androgynes and hermaphrodites "belong more to aesthetics than to biology," but represent real desires. He also remarked that androgynes and hermaphrodites have "a decorative reality." We have already seen that genius is linked to eccentricity but also to psychic hermaphroditism. This "decorative" element can be observed as attached to both. Nin Frías's "pearl" as a metaphor of the aesthetics of oddness is a statement on homosexuality that seeks not to reconcile the two sides of the image but to flaunt both in the same way that the term fabulous fag does. And this, it seems to me, is extraordinarily significant for understanding works like Lorca's "Ode to Walt Whitman." It doesn't matter that the poet never uses the word *eccentric,* because eccentric is simply a signpost to a larger aesthetics of oddness that takes the modern forms of the marvelous and iconic exceptionalism. Such signposts are part of an early twentieth-century conversation reshaping the image of homosexuality along lines that eventually appeared to merge with other strands, those of a nascent celebrity culture.[72]

Unlike Lorca, Retana does use the word. In his novella, *La hora del pecado* (The Moment of Sin) (1923), the sexually ambiguous sensation-seeker Lolina possesses a seductive attractiveness described as eccentric. She permits all sexual practices so long as they are aesthetically justified ("una razón estética") and occur in "a decorative, eccentric, and luxurious setting" ("ambiente decorativo, excéntrico y lujoso").[73] Like Cansinos's hermaphrodites and androgynes, the eccentric is demonstrably visible, or decorative. In other words, eccentricity is a form of display, or performance, perhaps even an aesthetics implicating the oddness of the aesthetic itself in these instances.

The aestheticizing of what was considered aberration is a constant in Retana's work. In *Mi alma desnuda* (My Naked Soul), eccentricity has two faces—the elegant and the grotesque—though both are deviations from the norm. Both are hybrid, sharing in the monstrous. The negative counterpart is exemplified by an over-the-hill dress designer-dancer, whose physical appearance and attire resemble a "musical eccentric" and whose mind is "diseased with eccentricity." Identified as "that hybrid" ("aquel híbrido"), the effeminate, aging queen embarrasses his guests by dancing in front of them. "These degenerates are the ones discrediting Vice," says the aristocratic and bisexual bohemian Santiago Vilar. "We ought to knock off these types, not for their sexual perversion, but because they're grotesque. Elegant and decorative aberrations, discreetly disguised, deserve our respect because they don't make things look ridiculous."[74]

By contrast, Vilar claims, it is not heterosexuality, but bisexuality that is the counter-narrative to the "comic and antiquated inversion of these survivors of Sodom who live as slaves of the joke Nature has played on them." Heterosexuality, he says, is mere normality. "Perfection lies in those of us who bat for both sides. The most refined erotic sensibility is that which makes us vibrate interchangeably [or indistinctly] with one or the other sex. I could give you a really interesting lecture on the subject, backed up by textbooks of forensic medicine, but I fear I might scandalize Retana, who has lately been behaving like an angel." Vilar's reference to the medical literature on bisexuality reminds us that in this period the lines drawn between male and female were increasingly blurred and uncertain. As Cleminson and Vázquez García note, the "concern about hermaphroditism," from the turn of the century to the start of the civil war, can be seen "as a symptom of the crumbling frontiers of the genders." The use of the word *indistintamente* ("indistinctly") also points in the same direction.[75]

The perspective in these passages is a bit complicated, filled as it is with irony, reflecting a certain ambivalence and perhaps a changing perception of the fairy's visibility, such as George Chauncey documented for New York between 1890 and 1940. Chauncey also observed, "At the turn of the century, however, *bisexual* referred to individuals who combined the physical and/or psychic attributes of both men and women. A bisexual was not *attracted* to both males and females; a bisexual *was* both male and female." The bisexual as both male and female is embodied in the figure of the hermaphrodite, whether manifested physically and/or psychically.[76]

Retana, however, defies Chauncey's clear-cut distinction, not only in his work but his life. A somewhat effeminate-looking man, he had affairs with both men and women. *My Naked Soul* is the most autobiographical of his books, though one can never take his presentation of self prima facie. The novel centers on the equal attraction that Retana, the first-person narrator-character, feels for a pair of twins, Tito and Graciela, his "boyfriend" and his "girlfriend." The twinning effect of this attraction, however, suggests projection as well, the two sides of the narrator himself.

The author as character describes himself as a "young, beautiful monster," who possesses a kind of aura, which is linked to his celebrity. He disguises his identity to the twins in hopes of escaping his reputation and presenting himself as he really is. But even he admits such frankness is impossible, seeing himself metaphorically as a Salomé of the seven veils dancing on the world's stage. No one is permitted to see him as he truly is, because the veils remain. There is a certain irony in recalling the mocked fairy figure of the dancing dress designer, who duplicates through parody, Retana's own dancing figure, with its Wildean homoeroticism and psychic hermaphroditism. (Cansinos-Asséns in 1919 called Wilde's monstrous Salomé androgynous and "an ephebic dancer.")[77]

These erotic displays are enhanced with the introduction of Don Juan Ambiguo into the text, who is, in turn, a bisexual parody of the classic Don Juan Tenorio. Retana anticipated the debate on this figure unleashed by Marañón, who tied him to the state of intersexuality and the blurring of the sexes. Don Juan Ambiguo is described as a "victim of modern decadent literature," suffering from "the poison of the decorative sin." While it is not clear to me what particular sin this is, the reappearance of the word *decorativo* in this context is noteworthy and can be linked to the extroverted figure of the Wildean dandy and, by extension, to homosexuality, just as Cansinos associated it with the hermaphrodite. In similar fashion to Don Juan Ambiguo, the narrator is also "poisoned by literature and eccentricity."[78]

My Naked Soul is a vehicle for the novelist's deceptive and singular display of self, for his eccentricity and monstrosity, which is projected over nearly the entire cast of characters. Like Santiago Vilar, when he finds other transgressions banal, he too dedicates himself to the ultimate monstrosity: himself. This same exhibitionism appears in *El octavo pecado capital* (The Eighth Deadly Sin), embodied in the polymorphously perverse character of Baby, who is similarly described as monstrous and eccentric. She possesses, for example, "an air of original eccentricity." An "eccentric woman," she plays at being a man and wears the mask of an "ambiguous personage," "an amoral or eccentric type, dressed in a flamboyant and inappropriate fashion." Declaring herself a monster, she gives her newest lover the classic books of aberration—Wilde, Lorrain, Sacher Masoch, Barbey d'Aurevilly—to corrupt him. Baby is a walking textbook of decadent literature.[79]

Her first appearance is as a classic Pierrot during the upside-down world of carnival, in which her confusing, ambiguous gender attracts and repels the other protagonist, Enrique Salazar. The traditional commedia dell'arte character type lent itself to an androgynous representation in this period, though at the same time, it also suggested an underlying homosexual reading, to the extent androgyny and hermaphroditism are veiled figures of homosexuality. Verlaine had already suggested this meaning. The image had crossover appeal, as it showed up in both popular erotic fiction and avant-garde literature and art. Dalí's *Pierrot jouant de la guitare* (Pierrot Playing the Guitar) (1925) (Museo Nacional Centro de Arte Reina Sofía, Madrid) contains the shadow of Lorca in it, while the Granadine poet drew a series of such figures, including a priapic Pierrot (ca. 1932–36). (Priapus is also linked to Hermaphroditus in myth.) He even doodled the image on a letter. The figure occupies center stage in one of Lorca's earliest writings, "Pierrot. Poema íntimo" (Pierrot. An Intimate Poem) (1918), in which "an exotic, distant virgin and a muscular, strapping man dance inside me," suggestive of the hermaphrodite. Lorca associated the Pierrot with a secretly painful inner life ("interioridades dolorosas") that no one could divine. His Pierrot wears a permanent mask, even as it becomes first Harlequin, then Columbina. A letter from the same year revealed how much the young Federico had imbibed Verlaine, reading his own conflicted sexuality into the French poet.[80]

Raised as a boy, Retana's Baby continues to use the masculine forms of grammar for herself, even after she reveals her feminine sex to Salazar, though on occasion she slips and turns to the feminine, suggesting a certain instability and slipperiness between what she thinks she is and what she plays at being. She seems poised more between genders and sexual identities, in flux rather than identifiable. The equivocal costume of the Pierrot is only one of several clothing changes that display one sex, while pointing to the flimsily disguised signs of the other one. As in *My Naked Soul,* the decorative is an exhibitionist device that occludes even as it reveals.

When Baby puts on a transparent Greek tunic, Salazar says she looks like a *marica,* or fag, and "an invert, poisoned by literature and much too vicious" because at this point he now thinks she is a man.[81] (The tunic recalls a similar practice of sartorial androgyny in ancient Greece.) Metaphorically, Baby appears to transform herself from one sex to another and back again, while retaining both. Even after he finally realizes her presumed true sex, it hardly matters because she continues to refer to herself in masculine terms, insisting on the double nature of her identity, an identity that is always on display, but never resolved, thus calling into question Salazar's own identity as well. Her ultimate costume is the cloak of literature she wears in an unending performance of decadent monstrosity.

In the second part of the novel, which opens with a section called "The 'Monster,'" the narrator observes that sometimes "Nature appears to delight in the creation of monsters, on land and at sea" to terrorize ordinary mortals. Baby is one of these terrifying monsters, who lives *"in her mind* a fabulous and strange existence." Salazar likens Baby's strange figure to that of "an extraordinary creature, having seemingly leapt out of some mythological garden." Subsequently, he says to himself: "Happily, Baby is a woman; we are no longer in the time of Adonis and Hermaphroditos, who have disappeared forever; a man could never possess such heights of beauty."[82] Salazar, however, is mistaken. The world of myth may have disappeared, but another monster has taken its place: the monster of sex. Retana shrewdly exploited the sexual fantasies of his readers in the creation of the hermaphroditic Baby, who is as much a human oddity as any sideshow creature, real or feigned, put on display for public amusement. The marvelous as entertainment has not disappeared. It has simply been transformed.

The ultimate exhibition of spectacular, double-sided ambiguity is Retana's presentation of "El apio maravilloso," or "The Marvelous Fag," meaning the *transformista* Egmont de Bries, as well as the parade of flaming gays in *The Posh Fairies*. Feigning outrage, the novelist claims in a mock prologue that he has nothing to do with the "equivocal adventures" and "monstrous aberrations" of his characters. He has merely documented the codes, manners, and feminine-inflected speech of these "pseudo men," members of the third sex, whose unfortunate vices are the very opposite of that normality to which the writer and his readers belong. What follows completely and comically undermines the prologue, even parodying the image of monstrosity when a character proposes the project of a gigantic-sized urinal ("urinario monstruo"), big enough for six hundred people, to be installed near the Plaza de Toros, as a gift to the state.[83]

Like *Flower of Evil*, this novel is an exhibition-text, here demonstrating the visibility of a homosexual subculture in pre–civil war Spain. Investigators such as Max-Bembo, Bernaldo de Quirós and Llanas Aguilaniedo had already begun to document that reality, descriptively and taxonomically. Retana parodies their efforts in a very funny passage, in which he classifies the various *locas*, or gays, attending a performance of the cross-dresser Egmont de Bries, as though they were specimens on display, such as "the *locas* out of conviction," "the professional *locas*," "the suspected *locas*," "the scandalous *locas*," "the embarrassed *locas*," "the romantic *locas*" and several others, including the "embryonic *locas*" and "the inevitable troop of *amphibian*s, or bisexuals."[84]

As a well-known imitator of female music-hall entertainers, Egmont de Bries is given star treatment in Retana's novel, with his performance described in some detail, part of which includes the customary back-and-forth banter between the *transformista* and his audience.[85] Spectators of sideshows also habitually laughed, jeered, and hurled insults, but the freaks often gave as good as they got. In *The Posh Fairies*, Egmont de Bries is the target of name-calling, mostly antigay slurs, some of which, however, is taken as a joke (and to which I return in the next chapter). To the charge of being gay—*mariposa, goloso, apio*—he replies with a witticism: "How utterly tacky! Nobody says *apio* [lit. 'celery'] anymore! You say *vidrio* [lit. 'glass']!" Even though in real life the performer denied he was gay, it didn't matter. Audiences saw female impersonators as homosexuals, and a recent biographer of de Bries believes he was. Retana does nothing to persuade them otherwise, but at the same time, he makes it clear that he does not share the spectators' insults. More importantly, he does not dispel the ambiguities surrounding a figure like Egmont de Bries or the ambivalence with which some characters perceive him. The character remains as much an impersonator as the impersonated, to the degree we rarely get past his performance, or the mask that the novelist affixes to nearly all his characters, including his alter ego.[86]

Retana's humor and the constant note of frivolity, it could be argued, make light of the presence of homophobia; conversely, it could also be said he uses the comic as an effective weapon for disarming hostility, just as Egmont de Bries does during his performance. In this sense, the narrative perspective of *The Posh Fairies* internalizes the equivocal point of view and status of eccentric figures like the very *locas* and the *transformista* Retana puts on display, just as he showcases himself as a fantastic monster, thus creating an aesthetics of oddness as spectacular and unique as the fabled hermaphrodite.[87]

Retana as sexual display is also another way of highlighting the author as celebrity. His vaunted oddness was inseparable from his celebrity, as both were predicated on forms of exhibition. In the same way modern celebrity aims to recover something of the aura of aristocracy (whether real or not hardly seems to matter), the modern forms of homosexuality (or their veiled substitutions) revive a reimagined sense of the marvelous. I've dwelled on Retana, his self-image as a fantastic monster of sex and celebrity, because there is much here that evokes García Lorca (and much that doesn't). As different as these two are in temperament and artistry, they are at the same time representative of a period that for Gregorio Marañón was worryingly obsessed with sex and for others a promising time of liberation. Marañón himself undoubtedly helped fuel this obsession with his prolific writings on the subject.[88]

Neither of these characterizations comes close to giving us a nuanced, layered understanding of early twentieth-century Spain, but there is some truth to both views. In his *Invertidos célebres* (Famous Inverts) (1933), the sexologist Martín de Lucenay, who profited hugely from his popularizing books on sex in the early 1930s, claimed that "in Spain, around the year 1925, a homosexual writer, who was the object of persecution by the [Primo de Rivera] dictatorship, made homosexuality and all the literature pertaining to it fashionable."[89] This statement is no doubt impossible to back up, but worth noting for three reasons.

First, it reflects some of the contemporary perceptions of the growing visibility of homosexuality in Spain. Second, it comes from a source unfavorably disposed toward homosexuality (which partly explains the tenor of his comment), but which nonetheless affirms a new reality. And finally, the gay writer he refers to is most likely Álvaro Retana himself, who was among a number of people prosecuted as pornographers, but the only one to serve time in 1926 for his novella *El tonto* (The Jerk) (1925), and again in 1928. Small wonder that other homosexuals such as Lorca thought discretion the better part of valor. Being fashionable wasn't worth going to jail, and Oscar Wilde's trials had not been forgotten either.

Looking back, in his memoirs Francisco Ayala saw the post–World War I period as one marked by "artificial worldliness," or cosmopolitanism, with its musical reviews, gaming casinos, and cabarets frequented, he said, mostly by out-of-towners and not the locals. (To judge from the popularity of such places, there must have been an awful lot of these visitors.) He called the writings of Retana, Hoyos y Vinent, El Caballero Audaz, Pedro Mata, and Joaquín Belda "monstrosities," still seeing them as pornographic, though he recognized not all of them were insignificant, some appearing in the same publications as the canonical Unamuno and Valle-Inclán.[90]

Ayala's memory of the era joined two forms of worldly entertainments, both having to do with sex or profane pleasures, but he also gave the impression of two distinct and separate cultures, high and low, despite overlapping publication venues in the one instance and shared social experiences in the other. The picture, however, is more mixed than this. Retana's *The Pornographic Deluge*, for example, is a fascinating examination of early twentieth-century Spanish erotic literature, in part because it represents an insider's view (Retana's), in part because it deals with authors not ordinarily discussed together, ranging from serious writers like Pérez de Ayala and Cansinos-Asséns to more commercially minded ones like Hoyos y Vinent, El Caballero Audaz, and Vidal y Planas. Literary history now separates these figures, but this was not always the case in the 1920s and 1930s.

Even on a personal level, the ghettos of artists and writers, high and low, avant-garde and popular (and later, right and left), artificially created by critics and literary historians, were more permeable than is normally thought, as the memoirs of César González-Ruano and Cansinos-Asséns made clear. While Retana and Lorca apparently did not know each other and generally moved in different circles, there were other personalities who moved easily between groups and locales.[91] Edgar Neville, who was a very good friend of both, is a good example. As I noted earlier, Neville, who had been an intimate of Lorca since 1920, was also part of the avant-garde.

Like Hinojosa, he too, for example, worked with the small press Sur, created by Altolaguirre and Prados in Málaga. This enterprise produced the literary magazine *Litoral* and other publications, including Lorca's *Canciones*. Neville, however, appears to have been excised from some of the memories of that time, apparently for his politics. Yet his name is sprinkled throughout the pages of Gómez de la Serna's record of his *tertulia* at the Café Pombo, banquets and homages. Along with Lorca, Neruda, Salinas, Jorge Guillén, and many other notable personalities of the prewar period, he too frequented the home of the Chilean diplomat Carlos Morla Lynch. On more than one occasion, after a party or a social or cultural gathering, Lorca, Morla Lynch, and others would pile into Neville's automobile, prolonging the enjoyment of each other's company.[92]

But Neville also hung out with Álvaro Retana, who dedicated the libertine novel *Una niña "demasiado moderna"* (A "Too Modern" Girl) (1919), to the future filmmaker. Neville even appeared as a character in one of his novellas, *El vicio color de rosa* (The Rose-Colored Vice) (1920), in which his alter ego Alberto Reyna's studio serves as "a sacred temple . . . [for] all the pleasures of a false paradise." A mix of high and low, Reyna's friends are, above all, "ambiguous people" who indulge in the ritual of an English tea, after which the aristocratic Edgar Neville carefully prepares opium pipes for everyone. Fiction or reality? That's hard to say. In a series of interviews from 1962, he claimed that he never took drugs during the Roaring Twenties, characterizing himself as a bohemian with a healthy lifestyle. It would not, however, be the first time the filmmaker had cleaned up his past. The cosmopolitan Neville, who had also worked in Hollywood, was well known for his freewheeling ways and he loved to party.[93]

The hedonistic lifestyle was evidently not just for out-of-towners. With World War I and Spain's neutrality, a more open, tolerant society burst onto the scene, at least in large urban centers like Madrid and Barcelona. Drugs, sex, gaming, and risqué entertainments defined the period. Retana spoke of "the mad desire to drink in all the decadence imported by the world war," while González-Ruano remembered going to the first American-style bar in Madrid, Maxim's, where the doorman sold tiny glass vials of cocaine procured from Merck. Neville recalled how bouncers at the most popular cabarets "used to sell a fine white powder at exorbitant prices, that more often than not turned out to be bicarbonate of soda."[94]

For others, the war was responsible as well for the arrival on scene of "that ambiguous, intelligent and perverted fauna" of gays, bisexuals, and other, even more indeterminate beings, according to Santiago Ibero. "The war of 1914," wrote Retana, "was for Spain the apotheosis of gambling, narcotics, and the love that dare not speak its name." He was known to have initiated quite a few friends, including the recently ordained (and gay) priest, Pedro Badanelli, into the nightlife of cabarets, music halls, and private parties where drugs, sex, and cross-dressing flowed freely. He was also credited for having introduced jazz into Madrid, symbolic of the cosmopolitanism and modernity to which so many were drawn, including Lorca, who loved the new American music.[95]

High culture, to which Lorca belonged, was not so detached from low, or popular, culture. Indeed, one form of cosmopolitanism fed into another. It just depended on your point of view. Retana was no less cosmopolitan than Lorca, nor did the vaunted sophistication of the Generation of 1927 exist in a vacuum, whether literary, social, or cultural. So, for example, the avant-gardist Gómez de la Serna was known to deliver a series of lectures astride an elephant or swinging on a trapeze, but Retana, too, devised entertainments in which he lectured, played the piano, told anecdotes, painted costume designs, and paraded a line of models on stage. In a piece on Barcelona nightlife, Retana described with equal relish the drag performers of the Cabaret Catalán and the scantily dressed women entertainers of the Excelsior down the street, exclaiming: "All this is called cosmopolitanism, tolerance, and modernity!" Like Lorca, Retana was much interviewed. In a publication called *Celebridades de Varietés*, one interviewer declared that he was "always exquisite and above all modern." A poem reproduced in the same piece said he was "like the fox-trot and morphine, / a product of civilization."[96]

Significantly, the more open society of the pre–civil war era also made homosexuality, in all circles and groups, more visible, and at the very least in literature, a sign of modernity. In Retana's *A Sodoma en un botijo* (To Sodom by Slow Train) (1933), gay aristocrats take tea, then dance together and later do so in drag, with lower-class lovers dressed as Pierrots, thugs (*apaches*, in the popular French parlance) or in male formal attire. At the poet Vicente Aleixandre's soirées, young gay men did the same (though not, apparently, in drag). Concha Méndez, however, recalled the hilarity over seeing Lorca, draped with a serviette as costume, dance in imitation of a female cabaret singer, perhaps evoking drag queens like Egmont de Bries who did the same (or did it mean something different for Lorca?). Hard to think he could have mimed a *cupletista,* a supreme example of popular culture in Spain, without having already seen one. On another occasion, the Granadine poet brought a working-class fellow he met at a bar to Aleixandre's gathering, thinking he might find him of interest, but Aleixandre declined (though Cernuda did take him up on the offer). Both Aleixandre's home and that of Morla Lynch served as discreet meeting places for such encounters. How much different were they, really, from what Retana depicted in his kiosk fiction (and no doubt practiced)?[97]

Another hinge figure, César González-Ruano, knew both Lorca and Neville, but also Retana and Hoyos y Vinent, neither of whom appeared to have much in common with the avant-garde. Retana was once asked whether he was a vanguardist, to which he replied: "I have not been honored with the friendship of any of them, but I follow with great admiration the work of Giménez Caballero . . . Claudio de [la] Torre, and naturally, Ramón Gómez de la Serna . . . who is the true leading light for modern writers." None of this prevented him from burlesquing ultraism, a short-lived avant-garde movement, several years earlier in the novel *My Naked Soul.* The exquisite Santiago Vilar recites several poems including one titled "Boudoir galante," in which a urinal makes an ironic appearance and an ambidextrous gigolo doubles as a bidet, prompting a character to declare: "My goodness, this ultraism is terribly convenient! . . . You can make the most atrocious things rhyme." In the same interview from 1930, he mentioned several authors who interested him a great deal, among them the *vanguardista*s Benjamín Jarnés, Antonio Espina, Valentín Andrés, and González-Ruano. Yet he did know at least two avant-garde writers: González-Ruano, who began his writing career as an *ultraísta,* and Neville.[98]

Although he made no mention of Retana in his memoirs, González-Ruano composed a poem, "Álvaro Retana," and penned a prologue to one of his novels in 1924; Retana dedicated his novella *El encanto de la cama redonda* (Three-Way Delights) (1922) to him. Conversely, González-Ruano and Lorca never hit it off, sharing a mutual antipathy. Despite having many of the same friends, he thought Lorca was unattractive and vulgar, calling him a tackily dressed "queer from the South." (Though he also called him a great poet, to which he added his deep admiration for *La zapatera prodigiosa* [The Shoemaker's Prodigious Wife].) This seemingly homophobic attitude, however, should be weighed against his friendship not only with Retana but with the notoriously gay Hoyos y Vinent, whom he met around 1920. Rejecting what he saw as bourgeois, provincial prejudice, he discovered "a secret, low-life Madrid [that was] truly fabulous," with the aristocratic Hoyos, who introduced him to masked balls and bawdy cabarets among the plebes.[99]

By some accounts, González-Ruano, who was something of a scoundrel, with a later reputation as a con artist, collaborator, and anti-Semite in occupied Paris, had a complicated relationship not only with the truth but with his own sexuality. His dislike of Lorca may have had more to do with his own insecurities. He admired Hoyos for his *épater le bourgeois* attitude, in a word for his snobbery, appearing to overlook his homosexuality, and even congratulated himself for daring to brave the general condemnation of Hoyos as a public spectacle. He took to heart something the Colombian writer José María Vargas Vila told him: "If you don't have a horrible, monstrous legend, you'll never amount to anything."[100]

On the other hand, Lorca himself was also something of a snob, repulsed as he was by the outward behavior of more flamboyant gays, but how removed was he really from the "confraternity of fags," as one anonymous reviewer crudely labeled some of the attendees at the opening night of *Yerma?* One of his many admirers, Alberto Nin Frías, created his own small gay confraternity in a book he self-published, *Ensayo sobre tres expresiones del espíritu andaluz* (An Essay on Three Expressions of the Andalusian Spirit) (1935), which looked at three exemplars of that spirit, Juan Francisco Muñoz Pabón, Pedro Badanelli, and García Lorca. This was a very different understanding of Lorca from that of Rejano and others, who saw the poet as a martyred symbol of the Andalusian people.

If Willy in *The Third Sex* (1927) produced a kind of "gay Baedeker" of homosexual haunts in France, Italy and Germany, Retana fashioned a similar world in his fiction, which was at least partly reflective of certain circles and practices in the real world. Many gay Spaniards visited Paris in the 1920s and early 1930s, including the royal Luis Fernando de Orleans y Borbón, self-styled "king of the queers," whom Willy spotted in the Léon Bar near Les Halles, taking an apéritif with a hotel bellhop. By contrast, Nin Frías's literary-artistic coterie is purely symbolic in nature, suggesting the degree to which such worlds also exist as conscious mental constructions (as they do in this book). The constellation of these three writers (Muñoz Pabón, Badanelli, and Lorca) comprising this Andalusian spirit is totally artificial.[101]

What was the relationship among them? As far as I can tell, there was none. Muñoz Pabón, a canon from the Catedral de Sevilla and a regionalist writer who died in 1920, didn't know Badanelli or Lorca. Nin Frías knew none of the three, although he was soon to become friends with Badanelli in Argentina. He tried to meet Lorca during his Latin American tour, requesting an appointment with him in a brief letter, but was unsuccessful. Lorca knew that his name had appeared in one of Nin's books, mistakenly thinking it was *Homosexualismo creador,* though it was really *Alexis,* published in 1932, in which Nin alluded to "signs of Uranianism" in Lorca.[102]

Had Badanelli, a homosexual priest and author of the gay novel *Serenata del amor triunfante* (Serenata of Love Triumphant) (1929), met the poet? Possibly. Badanelli did have in his possession a copy of *Gypsy Ballads,* dedicated to him and signed by Lorca. Tellingly, in a letter to Retana written decades later, Badanelli identified himself (and Retana) as belonging to a gay fraternity ("la Cofradía"), along with the celebrated pianist Antonio Lucas Moreno (to whom he dedicated his book *Bengalas* [1928]), another pianist Felipe Campuzano, the poet and song writer, Rafael de León (a friend of Lorca), and Nin Frías (who died in the priest's arms).[103]

To situate the three writers, Nin equated what is Andalusian with the Arab-Andalusian qualifier (*lo arábigoandaluz*), introducing early Arab-Andalusian texts into the book. Emilio García Gómez had made this literature fashionable with the publication of *Poemas arábigoandaluces* (Arab-Andalusian Poetry) in 1930, which contained poetry of a homoerotic tradition that conveniently fed into the trending subject of contemporary homosexuality. (Lorca, who owned a copy of the book, began writing the poems for *Diván del Tamarit* [The Tamarit Divan] not long after its publication.) Fragments of poems found in the anthology adorn Nin's book. Nin added to his analysis a Hellenizing element, that in combination with the Arab-Andalusian ingredient, produced an interpretation of this invented literary community as a homosexual brotherhood. This reading is not altogether convincing in the case of Muñoz Pabón, presented as "the perfect woman-spirit . . . [who] never appears effeminate in his writings." On the other hand, Nin praised Muñoz Pabón's descriptions of male beauty, which reminded him of a similar tradition of al-Andalus "in the Muslim anthologies of a marked Uranian character."[104]

Along analogous lines, he said of Lorca, "the most Gypsy of poets," that "the pathos of his *cante jondo,* and above all his surprising, magical brush strokes, with a Greek-style instrumentation and an architecture of sighs, in strikingly Uranian harmonies, evoke in the soul emotions akin to the medieval enchantment of the al-Andalus poets." He saw Lorca and Badanelli as "carried away by the divine Hellenism of their respective imaginations, living to catch sight of the Andalusian *young man* and capture him on their canvases." Badanelli, who was from the Southern city of Sanlúcar de Barrameda, possessed an "Arab-Andalusian" soul, he observed, enriched with an Oscar Wilde temperament. "The best of Badanelli," the playwright Jacinto Benavente wrote Nin, "is to be found in the genuine poetry of his own life." This notion of an individual life as a form of poetry incarnate is reminiscent of Oscar Wilde's remark: "I put all my genius into my life; I put only my talent into my works." Even more pointedly, this was how many saw the charismatic persona of García Lorca.[105]

It is striking that Nin only cites in passing Badanelli's *Serenata of Love Triumphant,* choosing not to allude explicitly to the defense of homosexuality in the novel, which would have provided him with the strongest argument of all for including him in his gay-themed fraternity. I suspect that he based his characterization partly on Benavente's observations, which in turn stemmed from his own close friendship with Badanelli. Nor is it surprising that Nin did not appear to be familiar with Lorca's "Ode to Walt Whitman," given its limited availability, but rather, he focused above all on the *Gypsy Ballads*. The "Ode" would have bolstered his case for a homosexual reading of Lorca, but perhaps not for a homosexual brotherhood. In any event, neither one of these works (the "Ode" and *Serenata*) fit into the Andalusian frame that served as the ultimate marker of gayness in Nin's book. They would not have been sufficiently Andalusian for Nin.[106]

By attaching gayness to an "Andalusian spirit," Nin was reiterating something many already believed: that this was a culture long associated with homosexuality. With this presumed affinity, he accomplished two not necessarily compatible goals. First, he enveloped his gay brotherhood within the protective folds of the more acceptable aspects of Andalusian culture, accentuating the latter but not the former, in an era when it was not easy to talk openly about such things, especially in relation to contemporary personalities. At the same time, this blending of the two meant that the homosexual character he saw in these three writers also bordered on long-standing stereotypes drawn from hackneyed views of an exoticized Andalusia. Lorca as the quintessential gypsy poet, embodied in the "pathos of his *cante jondo*," is a good example.

Second, it was plainly not his intention to conventionalize any of the three, but rather, to singularize them, borrowing in part from the aura of an imagined Andalusian culture whose legend was and is always at risk of lapsing into cliché. This singularity is yet another variation of the "marvelous fag," made even more so by being linked to the veiled erotic mysteries of an al-Andalus poetic pedigree. Like Retana, Nin Frías converted what was insult into something more desirable, through the aestheticizing of a perceived aberration. In this way, Andalusia became less a culture and more an aesthetic, starting with the homoerotic Arab-Andalusian poetry of the Middle Ages and proceeding to Muñoz Pabón, Badanelli, and Lorca. In a word, he transformed his unique constellation of gay writers into stars, visiting upon them an iconicity of the marvelous. But only Lorca would have an enduring after life.

6. Fabulous Fag (III), or a Face in the Crowd

You could say that Nin Frías was the first to see Lorca as a gay icon. By that I mean Lorca as a prefabricated fantasy, a fetishized image that fulfills someone else's desires and needs (much as we saw with Retana). Nin's strategy was to transfer the aura of al-Andalus—its "medieval enchantment"—to the poet, though Lorca was, from nearly all accounts, already a charismatic figure. He also blurred the distinction between man and poet in the cases of both Badanelli and Lorca, emphasizing that they lived "to catch sight of the Andalusian *young man* and capture him on their canvases." The poet's singularity ends up fetishizing homosexuality as well, a gesture also visible in some of Lorca's own work, notably in the "Ode to Walt Whitman."

Nin's outing of Lorca remained an exception for decades to come, confirming his view of homosexuality as both anomaly and eccentricity, as he wrote in *Alexis*. And yet, the only difference between Nin's portrait of the poet's star quality and those of many other commentators was identifying that quality as gay. So we are faced with what might now be called a belated gay icon, but one that also stemmed at least in part from Lorca's fabled uniqueness and the manner in which that personal aura, exploding like an eroticized radiance, attached to his work. There is no evidence, however, to indicate that the poet intentionally presented himself as gay in public.

Instead, I am arguing, first, that the celebrity status and fame he attained in life (and afterward) need to be resituated within the growing culture (and cult) of celebrity and alongside the heightened visibility of figures like Retana, Hoyos y Vinent, Wilde (and, one might add, Whitman), which I have already commented on. This peculiar status must also be seen in relation to its public—to the crowd, both material and virtual, that creates celebrity. And second, that his charismatic presentation of self in life and, by implication, in his work exhibited traits of the marvelous, the monstrous, and the hybrid, which other writers of his day such as Retana and Cansinos-Asséns saw as both a gay (or ambiguous) and modern phenomenon inextricably linked together. Expressed another way, Lorca built into works such as "Ode to Walt Whitman" and *The Public* a poetry of performance grounded in iconic exceptionalism, in a poetics of the marvelous that can be read on at least one level as gay, symbolically or otherwise.

This is to say that, like Retana, Lorca, whether intentionally or not, fed the desires of his readers, especially his gay readers, to see in his persona and work a form of personal validation. Nin Frías may have been the first to view the poet's work as imbued with a "strange and equivocal flavor," which can be understood as a poetics of oddness, but he certainly wasn't the last.[1] (The phrase recalls Lillian Smith's controversial *Strange Fruit* [1944], which used a slang term referring to the lynching of African-Americans but also to lesbianism in her novel.) His endeavor to place Lorca within a specific coterie, an Andalusian homosexual fraternity, also needs to be seen alongside the poet's own conflicted attitude toward other gays, especially in the "Ode to Walt Whitman," and the creation of subsequent gay communities attached to Lorca and his work.

No other writer or artist of his generation, with the possible exception of Salvador Dalí, came even close to his unprecedented visibility. There were numerous testimonials of Lorca's enormous vitality and larger-than-life persona, rarely linked to his being gay, but crucial to his transformation into an icon. By contrast, being gay was more often associated with something unsavory, with the underbelly of celebrity. In Granada especially, his "very special way of being," said one of his contemporaries, repulsed some, who saw Lorca's "ambiguous fame" ("fama equívoca") as the wrong sort. José Moreno Villa remembered how some in the Residencia de Estudiantes avoided him, having "sniffed out his defect," he wrote. No one, however, could resist for long the poet's charm and his gift for piano and song, though Luis Buñuel's homophobia nearly wrecked his friendship with Lorca. Unsurprisingly, many of the most glowing accounts came from friends. Of more significance is the degree to which they have endured, preserving the poet's image in amber, like the fossilized tail of a feathered dinosaur.[2]

Jorge Guillén, for instance, wrote, "Everyone knows it, that is, about this, the entire world: Federico García Lorca was an extraordinary creature. 'Creature' means here more than simply being a 'man.' Because Federico put us in touch with creation . . . [he] was above all a wellspring, a fountain burst of radiance, the very clarity of the world's origins, freshly created and yet so ancient. In the presence of the poet—and not simply in his poetry—one breathed an aura illuminated by his own light. . . . A creature of Creation, immersed in Creation." Bathed in Guillén's effusions, Lorca is unearthly, practically divine, akin to a religious icon. For Vicente Aleixandre, he was "fabulous and mythic," "passing magically through life," and for Cernuda, "legend." Pedro Salinas said, "Federico was more than a person, he was a climate. He irradiated power and an atmosphere of vitality and cordiality." At the turn of the nineteenth century, Gustave Le Bon called this kind of charisma the "personal prestige" of certain individuals, a power that "fills our soul with astonishment and respect." All these attributes also resonate with the way celebrities are perceived. There is a "numinous aura of the godly" bestowed upon modern-day idols and icons, as, for example, when a fan called Retana a living Adonis. Others might call it sex appeal.[3]

Lorca was viewed "a bird as rare upon the earth as a black swan," or so Juvenal thought (about virtuous women). But black swans do exist. Mythical plumage aside, Lorca as a chimerical creature can be documented, first, visually in some of his pen and ink self-portraits that are joined to the image of a "fabulous animal" ("animal fabuloso"), but especially in the form of growing fame and celebrity, in Spain and abroad. The poet himself contributed significantly to that perception, though he sometimes joked about it, likening his celebrity at one point to that of a bullfighter. When he became too full of himself, he burst his own balloon with laughter. He found fame more often disconcerting, when not a downright nuisance. "Stupid fame," he wrote a friend, for invading his privacy. And yet he courted recognition just the same. At least one critic believed Lorca "never had any interest in fame and success," but almost all accounts, including his own correspondence and the mountain of interviews he did, suggest otherwise.[4]

By the 1920s, one of the staples of mass media, the celebrity interview, often illustrated with photos, was well established in Spain. Perhaps the most influential practitioner of the art, José María Carretero (El Caballero Audaz), oddly enough, appears not to have interviewed Lorca. Nor did José López Pinillos (Pármeno), whose early death in 1922 no doubt prevented him from doing so, in a period when Lorca was still largely unpublished (though known among a growing coterie of admirers). The title of his book, *Los favoritos de la multitud: Cómo se conquista la notoriedad* (The Favorites of the Crowd: How to Win Notoriety) (1920), gives a snapshot in time of the changing perceptions of fame. *Fama* is, in its origins, "the talk of the multitude." To be famous is to be *thronged*. At the same time, the verb *conquistar* evokes the oldest model of fame, unparalleled military prowess, embodied in the first such person to acquire lasting, universal renown, Alexander the Great, who in turn relied on the model of Homeric heroism. López Pinillos, however, used the word *notoriedad*, not fame or celebrity.[5]

While it is true that the two terms (fame and notoriety) can be and are used synonymously in Spanish, notoriety has, since the seventeenth century, also acquired a negative connotation of ill fame. Interviewing a mixed bag of politicians, writers, actors and actresses, singers, composers of *zarzuelas*, and even a female lion tamer, López Pinillos barely paused to reflect on what celebrity meant, though in several instances, he focused on how the people interviewed rose from humble beginnings to the pinnacle of their profession. This is a classic life history, with its own self-justification. If someone makes it to the top, then fame has got to be good because it is earned.

Still, the term *notoriety* gives pause, as does *multitude*, especially when used together, hinting at the currying of favor, outsize ambition, and an accompanying lesser value in the celebrity attained. Most plainly, López Pinillos's book largely highlighted popular, even mass, culture. One exception was the iconoclastic Ramón del Valle-Inclán, who immediately asked him if he thought a writer's life really interested the public in Spain. Pármeno responded, absolutely, even with someone "so aristocratic in taste, who hate[d] playing to the masses as much as [Valle-Inclán] did." This exchange pointed to a certain uneasiness toward celebrity in early twentieth-century Spain, emphasized by the word "notoriety," and specifically with someone representing high culture. Even so, Valle didn't turn down the interview, reminding us of how he obsessed over "an intense yearning for personality" at the turn of the century, the kind of thing celebrity fetishized. Oscar Wilde was no different in this respect. And neither was Lorca.[6]

The whiff of snobbery detected in Valle-Inclán's attitude reaches back to the Romantic era and forward to the avant-garde, rooted in the artist's "superior soul" and social-cultural alienation. That disdain, however, sometimes wobbled, in part, because the thing against which the Romantics, the modernists, and then the vanguardists revolted was a constantly moving target, continually swallowing up their own territory and thus forcing them to stake out newer, more radical claims of originality and antibourgeois rebellion. Another way of looking at this much-observed phenomenon allows us to see that these same artists and writers never occupied one single world, the world of "against," because *their* world was part of the larger one; it was an alternative expression of it. There was no escaping their own time, even if, on the surface, they appeared to be taking a stance against the kind of celebrity that would debase their achievements. By 1931 the vanguardist Giménez Caballero believed the movement was already dead and buried, and he signaled that demise by pointing to the supposedly posthumous fame and mock funeral of Pablo Picasso. He parodied the artist's fabulous commercial success by suggesting he do the only thing left to redeem his avant-garde bonafides: exhibiting his work to "the great unwashed" at a popular *verbena,* or street festival, a mere penny the price of admission.[7]

Here, the crowd is traditional and identified with the people, or pueblo. This kind of crowd shares common ground with the nameless multitudes to whom the equally nameless *cantor* of old sang. This was the same anonymous condition of poetry, of being one with the people, that the nineteenth-century poet José Zorrilla emulated in vain. "I am nothing in the world," he wrote, as though this statement had anything to do with the obscurity of the masses now wending their way through history. What Zorrilla really wanted was to be legend, like the folk of myth and tradition and the singer of songs, that is, famous without saying so. And for a time, he was, approaching celebrity status as the national poet of Spain.[8]

The throngs of modern celebrity are a distinct phenomenon, insofar as a symbiotic relationship develops between the singularity of the celebrated and the crowd. The multitudes create and legitimize a celebrity, while the celebrity projects their dreams. Celebrities often arise from the very depths of the legions that empower them, as Elia Kazan's film *A Face in the Crowd,* explored to unsettling effect in 1957. Andy Griffith's raw, magnetic performance as Lonesome Rhodes, a singer with folksy humor and personality who turns on his own fans, transparently drew inspiration from humorist Will Rogers's "man of the people." Both were equally fabrications, and both spoke to nostalgia for an earlier time in American culture. As Budd Schulberg wrote in the story that served as the basis for the film, "America, in this complex age of supergovernment, overtaxation and atomic anxieties, was harking back to the simple wisdoms that had made her great, said *Life*. The mass swing to Lonesome was a sign of this harking." Schulberg's cynical narrator —Lonesome Rhodes's female assistant—punctures the hollowness of the dream, but she cannot help feeling drawn to him in the same libidinized way the crowd is. (Kazan cast a superb actress for the part in Patricia Neal. Her husky voice and intelligent gaze projected both skepticism and sex.)[9]

It is no surprise that celebrity as we know it today flourished in a period when the study of crowds also began to emerge, in a line stretching from Charles Mackay to Le Bon, Ortega y Gasset, and beyond. Writing in 1895, Le Bon saw his age as the start of "the era of crowds," manifested, above all, in the political power of the masses. The future president of the Second Republic, Manuel Azaña, echoed that sentiment in 1900. Three years earlier, the novelist Benito Pérez Galdós expressed the belief that the crowd, which he also called a characterless mass and amorphous agglomeration, was the result of the decomposition of the popular and aristocratic classes, recognizing that a new phenomenon had arisen.[10] Not that anyone altogether understands the meaning or character of crowds, given the fluid complexity of such phenomena. Context is everything. A lynching mob has little in common with an arena full of rock fans, except for the fact that in each case an object or figure of attention has become the focus of an emotional investment, one in hate, the other in lust. Similarly, the crowd, in one form or another, imbues a celebrity with an aura of specialness that may not necessarily be intrinsic to the person.

In this manner, the working-class audience of Barcelona listening intently to Lorca's recital of the "Ballad of the Spanish Civil Guard" in 1935 read into the poem and the poet something that I suspect a reading in 1928, at the height of the avant-garde movement, would not have produced: a growing intensity of feeling that they were witnessing the embodiment of a national consciousness on this occasion and in this poet. As we have seen, Lorca felt it, too. Lorca was introduced as the people's poet at the event, which was also broadcast over the radio. Tellingly, the journalist Juan Olmedilla saw in the packed audience, which was filled with many Republican supporters and not a few Communists, a socially symbolic gathering. He felt that poet and people fused in the moment Lorca read from his *Gypsy Ballads*. Another observer reported that the crowd began to murmur among themselves when it was announced that the poet would recite the "Ballad of the Spanish Civil Guard," a work of harsh social critique centering on an institution—*la guardia civil*—much despised by the working classes, rural and urban.[11]

By this time, public events such as the failed revolution in Asturias and the short-lived revolt in Catalonia, amid deepening political tensions, had overtaken personal circumstances. Lorca was already closely identified with the Second Republic because of his theater work with La Barraca. And he was famous. You might call the kind of emotional investment that led a working-class crowd to declare Lorca, son of a landowner, the people's poet a libidinized political act. No doubt Lorca himself, who was a gifted performer of poetry, contributed to the exalted atmosphere, all of which exemplifies the complex dynamic that runs like an electric current between crowd and celebrity.

It may seem strange to think of multitudes and Lorca together, because we are so accustomed to seeing him either as part of an elite literary movement, the Generation of 1927, or as an Andalusian poet with "an agrarian complex," to use Lorca's half-joking self-characterization. Spain's heavy dependence on agriculture, the prevalence of rural life, and hackneyed, outdated views of the country as premodern and exotic have masked to some degree the growth of urban culture and changing demographics in the early twentieth century. The first chapter of Ortega y Gasset's *Revolt of the Masses* (1929) was about "the fact of agglomeration," the presence of crowds of people everywhere. "The cities," he wrote, "are full of people. Houses, full of tenants. Hotels, full of guests. Trains, full of travelers. Cafés, full of consumers. Promenades, full of pedestrians."[12]

This remark provided Ortega with an entrée into the rest of his book: separating the social body into masses and elites, while noting that mass man could be found across the class divide. Politically, mass mobilizations, in the form of fascism and communism, defined the era. More interesting is to consider that the agglomeration of people he observed in places they may not have occupied in an earlier period, such as theaters, trains, and hotels, meant the inevitable convergence and mingling of different social classes, a democratizing move that the Second Republic in particular would soon promote. The crowds Ortega found so preoccupying welcomed Lorca in Barcelona. Over five thousand saw his adaptation of Lope de Vega's *La dama boba* (Lady Nitwit) in Madrid's Retiro Park.[13] They applauded cuplé singers and sparred with cross-dressing entertainers like Egmont de Bries, Mirko, and Freddy in theaters and cabarets, and they read, massively, novels by Álvaro Retana, El Caballero Audaz, Rafael López de Haro, and other kiosk writers, that you could buy for practically nothing at newsstands.

This was mass culture, a phenomenon with roots in nineteenth-century urbanization, technological-commercial advances, and a growing democratic mindset, just as celebrity itself arose from the same social and historical conditions. In that vein, Pérez Galdós remarked in 1870, "the participation of all in public life" promoted the belief that everybody already had "one foot in the temple of fame."[14] That poets might be conceived as occupying more than a unique sphere separate from, or opposed to, the rest of culture expands our understanding of both literature and society. Poets, from the Romantics to the avant-gardists, may have viewed themselves as above the social body, but all risked having their aura, or halo, dragged through the mud in the "moving chaos" of modern city life, as Baudelaire observed with his customary ironic flair, and some never had one to begin with. The advantage to not having one, he said in "Perte d'auréole" ("Loss of Halo"), was going incognito, swimming in the same morass as everyone else, free to do as one pleased. But "at least you should put up a notice or report the loss to the commissioner," exclaims his interlocutor.[15] Tellingly, the language Baudelaire used is both legal ("faire réclamer par le commissaire") and commercial ("faire afficher") in nature, bringing his aura (or his insignia, as he also calls it) down to earth and, to some extent, monetizing it. In any event, he placed its value squarely in the social sphere, the collective ethos of the day. What he doesn't do is explain how the aura got there in the first place. The halo could just as easily be the perishable glow of celebrity. Why else go incognito? Its meaning derives from its relation to society as a whole and especially, to the kind of modern democratizing culture Paris represented in mid-nineteenth century, a culture in which poets and plebes could mix indiscriminately.

This is not to suggest that poets unthinkingly embraced mass culture. Lorca's position is both ambiguous and ambivalent in this respect, paralleling his reaction to fame. His prefatory remarks for the Barcelona recital are illustrative of what I mean. Observing the huge audience in the Teatro Barcelona, he expressed misgivings whether his poetry would be well received in such surroundings. Poems, he said, are meant for intimate gatherings. No doubt his words were in part intended to ingratiate himself with the classic *captatio benevolentiae,* by conveying modesty to his public, but the note of sincerity is undeniable. Whether or not this was the largest group of people before whom he had spoken, as he claimed, the size and setting clearly made an impression on the poet. "Here we are, gathered together," he remarked, "and as I do not have the technique or the range of an actor and I see this great theater filled with a different, expectant public, I am somewhat apprehensive that my poems, whether because they are intimate or obscure or too stark, . . . will end up petrified with fear under this dome, like those trembling alley cats children stone to death in city slums."[16]

Lorca possessed a brilliant public persona, along with an actor's instincts for drama, so everything he says here should be taken with a grain of salt. You would have thought the image of children stoning cats offensive to the crowd, implying, as it did, a public bereft of understanding, but the poet immediately gained their trust, saying: "My love for others, my deep affection and rapport with the people has led me to write a theater meant for everyone, to intertwine and merge myself with everyone, and it has led me here on this warm Barcelona morning to read before a great public what I consider the most personal part of myself." Then came a dazzling move. Lorca tapped into the public's imagination, by having the crowd think of themselves as intimate friends of the poet ("amigos íntimos todos"). Forget about the theater's vast recesses, the deluxe velvety décor, and imagine, he said, "a small room where a poet, in all his modesty and simplicity, is going to give you, without any fuss or ego, the best, the deepest part of himself." In a word, the poet offered them the illusion of intimacy, precisely what the celebrity creates with his fans.[17]

He went on to say that reading poetry is "an intimate act," "the very opposite of public speaking. In oratory, the speaker works and reworks one idea familiar to the public . . . cheered on enthusiastically by the multitude."[18] He likened such oratory to the flourish of flag waving. With these initial remarks, Lorca at once embraced the mostly working-class audience and schooled it in the appreciation of poetry. He insulated poetry from the lowest-common-denominator standards of crowd-pleasing oratory, but also transformed his verse into a mass event, with his performance transmitted through radio and loudspeakers into La Rambla, homes, bars, workingmen's clubs and athenaeums. In the end, the audience stood up and hailed him the people's poet. Though it is certainly true that Lorca controlled and manipulated the crowd into being something less and something more than what it was, his own poetry and the reading itself ultimately enthralled them. What's more, Lorca hadn't lost his aura by contact with the masses. On the contrary, they had given him one of their own.

Lorca and his public mutually defined one another through virtual intimate contact, transferring what one possessed to the other in a fluid, if illusory, dynamic. The current of celebrity ran through the people, even as the current of the people ran through the poet. This is heady stuff. Olmedilla captured some of the electric atmosphere, observing how the moment Lorca appeared he "ratcheted up the energy level of everyone's enthusiasm." In a piece titled "El poeta y la multitud" (The Poet and the Multitude), another reporter wrote that "the people place its seal on the pages [of poetry] reserved for the elites, when they are read before great assemblies." Significantly, he also said the audience was "eager to identify with the poet."[19]

Lorca had already had experience with the crowd before his reading organized by the People's Encyclopedic Athenaeum. More precisely, he had experienced crowds of a size and character unheard of in Spain. These were the masses of people he encountered in New York, just as he was in the throes of a personal crisis, crushed by a failed love affair and restless in spirit. Some of his poetry and correspondence together suggest an accidental kind of hybrid letter-poem of multitudes that speaks not only to the complex juxtaposition of being at once privately and publicly grounded, but to the weirdly unsettling prodigiousness of modernity itself (not to mention that of the poet). Writing home to his family in June 1929, he gave his first impressions of what he called "the most daring and modern city of the world," including the streaming "jumbled multitude of colorful jerseys and bold handkerchiefs, the clamor of cars . . . [and] radios" and the dazzling light show of commerce. A few days later, he visited Coney Island and marveled at the sheer numbers packed like sardines on the beaches and milling about the sideshows and rides of the amusement park. "The crowd fills everything," he wrote, "with a sweaty babble of sea salt, a mass of Jews, blacks, Japanese, Chinese, mulattos, and blond yankees. It's a stupendous, if excessive, spectacle, enough to see once, because it's too popular. This is the people's people of New York" (fig. 11).[20]

Lorca's uneasiness over this crowd is patent and later appeared most visibly in two poems from *Poet in New York:* "Landscape of a Pissing Multitude (Battery Place Nocturne)" and "Landscape of a Vomiting Multitude (Dusk at Coney Island)." Although, roughly speaking, the masses he observed and wrote about in New York share with the working-class crowd in Barcelona the attribute of being the common people, there are also profound

Figure 11. Crowd on the Boardwalk, Coney Island, NY. Undated postcard, ca. 1928–29, Manhattan Post Card Publishing Co.

differences, as there are in the relationship between poet and people. For one thing, Lorca was totally anonymous in his first glimpse of mass-man, though less so in the poems. "I, poet without arms, [am] lost," he wrote, "among the vomiting multitude" of Coney Island. The poem begins, however, not with the I but with the fat lady, a staple of sideshow attractions, the first of a series of images issuing from an aesthetics of oddness. To his family he described, in a jumbled enumeration, "incredible roller coasters, enchanted lakes, grottos, music, human monsters, sprawling dances, menageries of wild beasts, gigantic ferris wheels and swings, the fattest women on earth, the man with four eyes, and so on and so on, and then thousands of ice cream stands, sausage, fried foods, buns, sweets, in a fantastic variety."[21]

This same disordered excess of the letter appears in the poem, as "the fat lady [comes] / scratching out roots and moistening membraned drums" and "turns dying octopuses wrong-side-out." She leaves "tiny skulls of pigeons in the corners / and [fires] up the furies of centuries-old feasts." Just as the poet is lost in the vomiting multitude, the fat lady is closely associated "with the crowds from the ships, taverns, and gardens." The poem astonishes us with its unpredictable, disturbing connections and imagery, linking the exuberance of carny with death and decay. Clouds and desserts rot, and kitchens in sorrow are

> buried beneath the sand.
> These are the dead, the pheasants and apples of another time,
> shoved into our throat.

The staff of life brings asphyxiating death, the fat lady invoking "the demon bread." "It can't be helped, my son, vomit!" The poem is so visceral it practically chokes the reader's breath. In lines uneven in length and, at times, abrupt, we are pushed to the limits, until we, too, like "the entire city," in the end, "pushed against the railings of the boardwalk." Like much of *Poet in New York,* the poem is driven to escaping itself.[22]

At the same time, there is nothing more alive than this poem. It overflows with excess, like the flesh of a fat lady. What drew Lorca to write about Coney Island was plainly an attraction-repulsion he felt compelled to recreate. "The fat lady came first," he wrote, which is to say he began with a sideshow exhibit and moved on to a performance. Then he added the crowd, "rumors from the jungle of vomit / with empty women, with hot wax children." And the poet in the poem? In torment, he wrote, "This look on my face was mine, but now isn't mine." Mutilated, trapped in the crowd, he can think of nothing else but to defend himself. "I, poet without arms." Is there anything more exhibitionist than this image of the sacrificial poet drawing attention to his presence, the counterperformance to the fat lady's? The poet without arms is no less a sideshow curiosity than the fat lady in the poem, as though he were part of Hoyos y Vinent's world fair of rare creatures, whose ringmaster is God masquerading as P. T. Barnum.[23]

Lorca's relation to the crowd, to its stupendous spectacle, as he remarked to his family, was deeply ambivalent, even fearful, in this poem. But also astonished. In this, he appears, then, "to be surprised, to wonder," which for Ortega y Gasset, "is to begin to understand." The intellectual, he wrote, "[gazes] upon the world with eyes opened wide by strangeness. Everything in the world is strange and marvelous for eyes wide open." He is "the visionary perpetually made drunk with the world," the dazzle of shock and awe blinding his sight. Is the poet any different? Tellingly, Ortega's remarks appeared in the very same section on crowds in *Revolt of the Masses,* in which this "fact of agglomeration" represented both a historical reality and an amazing phenomenon. Ortega's disquiet over the masses, over what he called their "brutal empire," prevails in his essay, but he also recognized it as "the era of the colossal," akin, you could say, to the excess and spectacle of Coney Island and of popular culture in the United States that so impressed (and unnerved) García Lorca. The large, public nature of such things is the very opposite of the private, invented world that the poet had imagined only a few, short years ago in the *Gypsy Ballads,* where "the night became as intimate / as a village square." Nonetheless, Lorca stresses smallness ("pequeña plaza") and intimacy ("íntima") in a public space, in these lines from "Sleepwalking Ballad," recalling for us his paradoxical insistence on the private performance of reading poetry in the heart of a huge crowd.[24]

Lorca wrote home that his first poem would deal with a Hungarian child he met on the ship, a child, he said, about to enter the belly of New York. That poem has never surfaced, but New York itself was already in the letter, as in the belly of a whale (or maybe a mother), like the child in the city. Also in that first letter to his family is his observance of the advantages to growing fame, when a group of Spaniards greeted him at the dock. "Landscape of a Vomiting Multitude" is not about a writer's celebrity, but about mass culture and the poet's place in a public sphere unimaginable within Spain during this period. Not for the first (or last) time, Lorca's anguished poetic figure bears the mutilated mark of martyrdom, here, lost in the tidal wave of Coney Island's grotesque exuberance. The frenzy that runs through the entire poem is first made visible in the twisted, death-dealing bacchanalia of the fat lady, setting the stage for the poet's sacrifice. Perhaps the most proactive sideshow exhibit to be encountered in poetry, she sows a trail of destruction, flinging about verbs that yank, tear, turn insides out, and stir up the furies, the feasts of yesteryear jammed down throats. By contrast, the poet conceived as a curiosity wields none of her intimidating energy, but is nonetheless part of the same performance, the same show, which is the poetry in action of modernity itself.

Not precisely a figure of celebrity here, no, but something that needs a public to be understood, much as the fat lady herself or any luminary does. If modern fame is "a way of defining oneself, making oneself known," this poem appears to signal the very opposite, a terrified vulnerability to, and fear of, public exposure:

> This look on my face was mine, but now isn't mine.
> This naked look trembling in alcohol

244 A FACE IN THE CROWD

> bids farewell to incredible ships
> through the anemones of the piers.

The line in which the poet's gaze "bids farewell to incredible ships" faintly evokes Christopher Marlowe's "face that launch'd a thousand ships." Thus the image appears as Lorca's backhanded gesture toward fame, assimilating the figure of the poet to Helen of Troy (who shows up as well in the gender-bending play *The Public*). Backhanded, because he is also busy defending himself "with this look / that springs from waves where the dawn dare not go," as he stands surrounded by the virtual crowd of the vomiting multitude. The delirium of mass culture is both backdrop and proscenium, or perhaps better said, theater in the round, defining and undefining the poet, but also making him *known* to us. A face in the crowd.[25]

Without being a poem about celebrity, "Landscape" nonetheless simulates a relationship between the swarms of people and the poet, setting the stage for the "frenzy of renown" that would shortly engulf García Lorca in his wildly successful Latin American tour. Reporters and fans besieged him everywhere. He did countless interviews, reaching virtual multitudes larger than any audience in the flesh. The nature of these interviews and encounters with his public is crucial to grasping how Lorca became "Lorca," the fabulous creature who occupies the brightest spot in a constellation of equally marvelous (and gay) personalities such as Antonio de Hoyos y Vinent, Álvaro Retana, and Tórtola Valencia, all of whom knew how to exploit the value of publicity.[26]

The dancer Tórtola Valencia, for example, was interviewed and photographed incessantly (fig. 12). Like Retana, she understood how both forms of visibility enhanced her aura, while seemingly bringing her persona into close contact with an enthralled public. She made massive use of the camera, disseminating exotic poses that one admirer styled a photographic museum. Even in interviews, Tórtola physically framed herself in spaces, converting her possessions into mute commentaries on her special status. On one occasion, as Carmen de Burgos waited to speak with the performer, her things transformed an ordinary hotel room into something strange and uncommon, like a fortune-teller's parlor. A dozen hats appearing like stylized fetishes, four or five pairs of slightly worn shoes, a large doll, papers, and cigarette boxes were strewn about. Postcards, fans, and drawings festooned the walls, and a mantel clock was draped with odd-looking metallic necklaces and ban-

Figure 12. *Tórtola Valencia mime danzante*. Drawing by Xavier Guerrero, 1918.

gles. Tórtola emerged from the bathroom, wearing a loose-fitting robe, her head wrapped in a snood of white lace. There was something serpentlike in this domestic sorceress, de Burgos thought. At the same time, she remarked on the feeling of intimacy in which the interview, conducted in 1917, took place.[27]

In 1927, Margarita Nelken had a similar experience in the dancer's home. Her article, which appeared in the popular illustrated weekly magazine *Blanco y Negro*, contained several photographs of a variously costumed Tórtola in different rooms, in effect positioning her public persona in a domestic setting. Was this "really a home?" a female friend asked Nelken. To have a home like Tórtola's, filled with antiques, tapestries, tiger skins, jewels and fans, she replied, you first "have to become Tórtola." Her exuberantly decorated home struck another journalist as overwhelming and strange, more like an overstuffed antique shop, an impression that simply confirmed the performer's highly publicized eccentricities.[28]

In Latin America, Lorca received star treatment, with huge throngs of fans and journalists awaiting his arrival. The poet seemed overwhelmed by the enthusiastic reception, which was of a magnitude he was not expecting. One of the first photographs taken in Buenos Aires captured him in bed, exhausted but toasting his visitors with sherry. "I'm like one of those worn-out, gouged bullfighters," he said, "after a legendary struggle, smiling at the photographers from his bed." Joking aside, Lorca was already mythifying himself, though with a good deal of help from his admirers. In Montevideo, when a woman implored him to kiss her little boy, Enrique Amorim jested that he had achieved a bullfighter's triumph. Another image, that of the prodigy, the boy wonder, for example, spontaneously spreading his poetic gifts far and wide, also appeared in newspaper accounts, accompanied by photographs of his "round, luminous face." Lorca himself pointed out that all this frenzy of publicity was preceded by his own poet-friends building the Lorca myth, so that Latin America already was familiar with his image before the tour even began.[29]

At the same time, as with Tórtola, Retana, and other celebrities, the poet invited a false sense of intimacy, by greeting interviewers at different times in bed, in a bathrobe, and even showering. He was "pajama guy," for one journalist. As Carmen de Burgos did for Tórtola Valencia, another interviewer gave his readers glimpses of Lorca's hotel room, the nightstand heaped with "cigarettes, books, pencils, sheets of paper, an empty bottle, and the loose change of different countries," while a typist, struggling with Lorca's handwriting, yelled questions as the writer showered and yelled back. A typical poet's room, the journalist opined. Lorca capped off the moment with a theatrical entrance, loudly flinging open the bathroom door. It would be hard to say who was orchestrating the scene more, the interviewer or the poet.[30]

For someone who professed not to like interviews, Lorca seemed to go out of his way to accommodate the press. In another encounter, he greeted Narciso Robledal as he was shaving in his pajamas. "'I'm shaving,'" he said, "waving his Gillette razor blade like a baton." "I'll be ready in a moment, dressed in my blue overalls." This working-class outfit, which he adopted as he toured Spain with his traveling theater troupe, at once made him appear different and one of the boys. He boasted it only cost him twenty-five pesetas (a male farm worker's average daily wage was three pesetas, circa 1930). The photographer shot him in his overalls, with a drawing of an implike creature hovering over him, for a piece titled "El duende se hizo carne" (The Duende Made Flesh). Lorca was shaping his own image, as much as the press was. He invited the illusion of intimacy, presenting himself as down-to-earth, like everyone else. I shave! I wear overalls! He even fraternized at night with journalists in Buenos Aires. Robledal, however, draped him in the aura of celebrity, merging poet and duende into the figure of charisma incarnate. Lorca, he said, yearned for "the winged language of angels." And this, after the poet had pulled the reporter's leg, making up an absurd story of having seen a nocturnal vision of an elflike duende, swimming through the air, growing feathered appendages, and dissolving into a cloud.[31]

Before long, Lorca was so much in demand that, according to one humorous account, all he wanted to do was escape, it was so tough being famous. "With so much radio, press, and mass media," Antonio Soto ("Boy") wrote, "the truth is that at present the personal situation of anyone who falls into the circle of fame is unenviable." Lorca, it seemed, was everywhere: "García Lorca in the café terrace. García Lorca at the piano. García Lorca backstage. García Lorca at a writers' hangout. García Lorca reciting. García Lorca putting on his tie. García Lorca learning how to steep mate. García Lorca signing a photo. And with all this, in the middle of all this, as a physiological consequence of all this, García Lorca staring at his hands, striking his forehead, hiding here, fleeing there, the poor kid not knowing what to do or where to go to avoid the onslaught of journalists, photographers, sketch artists, impresarios, and admirers." The mantra of the poet's name embodies Hearst's strategy of making names the news, the net effect surrounding it with an aura. By 1930, it was already "enough to say his first and last name," wrote Miguel Pérez Ferrero. In hot pursuit of this elusive mythical creature, Soto sought him everywhere, but there was no sign of Lorca. Somebody spotted him in the hotel bar, another on the stairs, there he was on the street, attempting to extricate himself from a small army of female autograph hunters. Finally, he caught up with him in the hotel's underground entrance. Don't ask me, Lorca said, to sing, recite, play the piano, read from my newest play, sign photos, or give you a piece of my sailor shirt. "And for heaven's sake, don't ask me to write down what I think!" Feeling overwhelmed and under siege, the poet wrote home that you would have thought he was the Prince of Wales, a humorous reminder of the pseudo-aristocratic standing of celebrity. Complaints aside, Lorca's letters were littered with the crumbs of fame. He autographed twenty albums in one morning, he wrote to his family on the dorso of a photo. He had been photographed more than two hundred times and, in a gesture of excess, he said there were hundreds of articles written about him. Amid such fevered attention, he wound up hiring a personal assistant to handle the publicity (and back in Spain, a news agency to send him the slews of press clippings).[32]

Lorca was sharply aware the more public his persona, the larger his fame, but he could not bear, he said, to see his name exhibited. There it was "big as the sky, exposed to the world," on a theater billboard advertising one of his plays in Buenos Aires. The very idea made him cringe, as though he had been stripped naked before the crowd's inquisitive eyes. "My name was on every corner, the object of curiosity for some and indifference for others. And it was my name! . . . Something that was so much mine, out there like that, for everyone to use! . . . It was as if I had ceased to be myself. . . . But I bow to the inevitable, my friend!" Resigned to the necessity of publicizing his work, Lorca nonetheless rebelled against commercialization of his name, vaguely evoking Baudelaire's tainted halo. There is more, however, than the shimmer of fame, or its loss, in his remarks.[33]

Celebrity threatened his sense of self, the closeted inner life Lorca guarded so fiercely. The name, shivering under public scrutiny, personified the poet himself, who imagined two selves warring within, as if, he said, there were "a second person, my own enemy, mocking my timidity from all these billboards." Was this simply a histrionic gesture? Quite possibly, but the expression of vulnerability also echoes that of the poet's naked look of his face and his defenselessness as the poet without arms in "Landscape of a Vomiting Multitude." Lorca's reluctant exhibitionism evokes parallels with another media myth, his contemporary T. E. Lawrence, whose "genius for backing into the limelight" war correspondent Lowell Thomas first publicized. He was also the first to sensationalize the image of Lawrence in flowing Arab robes, feeding into the Englishman's conflicted desire to be a hero even as he craved anonymity. Unsurprisingly, the Lawrence persona was cloaked in a complicated sexuality. And as with Lorca, his apparent omnipresence was gently burlesqued, the New York Times dubbing him "Lawrence the Ubiquitous," when Russia accused him of being somewhere that he wasn't, namely Afghanistan.[34]

Lorca's fame followed him back to Madrid. One interview reproduced the same paragraph from "Boy" I referred to above, in which the poet was seemingly everywhere. The journalist in question, Miguel Pérez Ferrero, was astonished at the "veritable mountain of press clippings" the writer had accumulated. That, perhaps, explains how he was able to cite verbatim from Antonio Soto's piece, as one suspects Lorca must have provided the source. Lorca, he said, was now as famous as Einstein, Keyserling, and Ortega y Gasset, his personality having captivated everyone. In any event, it wasn't simply reporters but a host of fans who trailed after the poet, bathing in his afterglow.[35]

As one journalist witnessed at the Plaza de Catalunya, all around him there was "an ample circle of people struck dumb, ecstatic at simply being there, hanging on his pronouncements, caught up in the verbal magic of the poet who speaks the way he writes, his imagination on fire, his words luminescent." Lorca himself was "radiant with joy," his natural exuberance overflowing. When a young woman sat down with them, she immediately called the writer by his first name, but was also amazed that the rest of the group was able to see him every day. A kind of synergistic energy appeared to connect poet, journalist, and admirers, enveloping everyone in the same aura, described as "the misty glow" of the poet's warmth, a moment condensed in the adoring young woman's instant pseudo-intimacy with Lorca. It would be hard to say how much of the aura was manufactured, how much not, in this and similar pieces, while allowing for both Lorca's own charisma and propensity to dramatize his life. At the same time, the trite images milked what was by this point a stereotypical view of the poet.[36]

Growing adulation (and success) produced a small backlash, as when, for example, the journalist José Luis Salado explicitly criticized the languid young men who seemed to follow the playwright everywhere during rehearsals for *Yerma*. That, he said, was "the only bad thing about Lorca." In Buenos Aires, Pablo Suero received nasty anonymous missives, after he wrote about the poet's "transcendence," how he was revitalizing the theater. Those same writers, he said, publicly fawned over Lorca, while being eaten up by envy. Even before leaving for Latin America, after the triumph of *Gypsy Ballads* and *Blood Wedding*, Lorca knew he could not trust the flatterers and hangers-on, who professed to love him. In the remaining two years of his life, he was fêted and interviewed nearly nonstop, to such a degree that his friend Sebastián Gasch hardly recognized the life Lorca was leading, "fully submerged in a mundane literary atmosphere that was frivolous and superficial." The last time he ran into him, at the opening night of *Doña Rosita the Spinster,* Lorca was nervous and preoccupied and they exchanged only a few meaningless words. He never saw him again.[37]

Personal antipathy toward Lorca appears to have motivated some protestations, such as those of Borges and González-Ruano, but annoyance with his fame has also played a role and even extended to his work years after his death. In 1997, for example, Roger Wolfe called him a fossil and quite possibly "the most overrated Spanish poet of the twentieth century and maybe of all time." Were there no other poets in Spain, he asked? There is certainly some truth to his observation that, outside Spain, Lorca is the only poet with near universal name recognition. For Wolfe, his fame seemed disproportionate to his achievements. Wolfe's own views overstate his case. The most overrated Spanish poet of the twentieth century and maybe of all time? All such blanket judgments are always debatable, but what gets lost are the more interesting questions: why Lorca's celebrity did not fade, but rather turned into durable fame, what it says about poetry's role in the public sphere, and why it matters to us in the first place, as I have been exploring in these pages.[38]

Lorca's fame today cannot be fully understood without initially looking at what celebrity meant during his lifetime, because to a significant degree we have inherited the celebrity he enjoyed then, which in turn has been shaped by his persona, his death, his homosexuality, and his own work. Not to mention the poet's own manipulation of his public image. If Lorca was perceived, for example, at one point as a gypsy poet, despite his claims to the contrary, it was because he relied in part on Andalusian stereotypes that buttressed the intense originality of *Gypsy Ballads.* Admirers of "The Faithless Wife" especially were entranced with the potent male gypsy presence of the poem, identifying it with Lorca himself, and ignoring the subtle ironies undercutting the surface machismo of the text. Although he came to detest the poem and by 1935 refused to do public readings of it, the poem circulated widely in Spain and Latin America. Equally noteworthy, as C. Brian Morris has observed, are the grandstanding traits of both the male gypsy and the rhetorical flair of the text. Along similar exhibitionist lines, as we have already seen, Lorca also allowed (perhaps even encouraged) at least one reporter to equate the poet with the figure of the duende, ultimately trivializing both.[39]

To be sure, he was no doubt often misquoted and misrepresented as the subject of interviews. Worse still, he felt caricatured, but continued to talk to reporters. On one occasion, he stressed the difference between an individual's public life and private life. One is like a calling card used to present the self to others, he said; the other, a gray inner life, tortured and secret, "like an ugly sin." Then he went on to speak about his childhood, recounting the story of how he heard the poplars murmur his name, "Fe . . . de . . . ri . . . co . . . " The effect was to emphasize, and not for the first time, the image of Federico as childlike, yet another favorite device to singularize him, much as the exoticizing, if stereotypical, view of Lorca as a gypsy (he wasn't), as an Andalusian or Granadine did. The anecdote is lovely and imaginative, as we would expect, but it also illuminates how Lorca himself contributed to the perception of his own uniqueness, creating an aura around his very name. He was literally making his name the news, as Hearst might have said, while marching in the procession of his own legend. He furthered that impression by pointing to a hidden life but was careful not to reveal its contents.[40]

From that closeted existence and time, it is not surprising that almost nothing of his sexuality came to light in public statements. In one interview, he alluded to the limited edition of the "Ode to Walt Whitman" that had just been published in Mexico, calling it exquisite. And in another, the futurist poet Alfredo Mario Ferreiro re-created the day he spent with Lorca and Enrique Amorim on the Uruguayan coast, where the poet recited the "Ode" as waves crashed against the rocks. Ferreiro's narration begins with the poet changing into a sailor's shirt, a gift from Amorim, in his hotel room, while Amorim finished dressing in the corridor as they were leaving. The details are trivial but also intimate. Then, on the Atlántida beach, he writes, "You should have heard that ode to Whitman! It's the best of García Lorca, if García Lorca can be admitted to being classified as having produced some things better than other things of his. It is the funeral oration for all the queers of the world; the defense of that man, hands hanging at his sides, who walked along the East River, with his great beard filled with butterflies, playing with the boys, talking with them, while the sun sang through their navels, beneath the bridges."[41]

The two men were absolutely mesmerized. This same moment was remembered much later somewhat differently by Amorim in an unpublished memoir, where he omitted Ferreiro's presence entirely and transformed the scene into a romantic twosome. As the interview makes clear, however, the only intimacy came at the beginning, with the barest suggestion of a possible relationship between Amorim and Lorca. Intentionally or not, Ferreiro made intimacy, sexual and literary, part of his chronicle of that day, by linking them through the "Ode to Walt Whitman."

At the same time, he also stressed Lorca's exceptional nature through the poetry itself. The poetry *was* Lorca. Biography didn't simply trump literature; it was one and the same. This perception goes against all the prescriptions of current literary criticism, of the way we understand poetry. It says to us, not that we should read his life through the poetry, or that the poetry can explain his life, but that poetry seeks out life: green desire exploding, the relentless *verde que te quiero verde,* fire held in the poet's hands. The fusion between Lorca and his poetry is found over and over in the interviews. In effect, journalists were creating a biographical legend, but they were also reading poetry as a life-affirming experience because Lorca himself appeared to embody that experience. Were the reporters wrong to see the poet (and poetry) in this light, however inadequately they sometimes expressed it?[42]

"A glorious day," Ferreiro wrote, as the two men listened with "intense joy, flowing from the precipitous torrent of words." He continued, "And nothing more than words. Not even images. As with great music, nothing more than notes. But what words! Eternal and solid. Even when he was saying 'column of ash,' the words stood erect with the perennial confidence of these dazzling poems." It is also safe to say that Lorca's performance of those words, spoken against the dramatic backdrop of a roiling sea, lent form, apparent solidity, to the column of ash in "Ode to Walt Whitman." What else is a "funeral oration for all the queers of the world" but a poetry of performance? Or the defense of the American poet?[43]

Along with *The Public,* the "Ode to Walt Whitman" is one of the most bedeviled works Lorca ever wrote. What I want to single out here is its extraordinary iconic effect, in both the literal and metaphorical senses. The poem is closely attached to the perception of Lorca as a gay icon, in large part, because that image is sifted through the biggest gay icon of all, Whitman himself. I doubt this was Lorca's intention, but tell that to Allen Ginsberg eyeing both poets among the peaches and penumbras of a California supermarket. Or Jaime Manrique, who constructed his own biography alongside that of Lorca as one of his "eminent *maricones*" reading himself through Whitman. This is by no means the only interpretation of a poem that was, first, deeply personal for Lorca, so personal that some have seen it as unvarnished autobiography. In one of the least felicitous—and plainly mistaken—considerations of the "Ode," Jean-Louis Schonberg used the poem as evidence

to explain Lorca's death, ascribing motives of homosexual revenge and jeal-
ousy to the "vile queers" supposed to be responsible for killing the poet. They
were like the *maricas* from Sevilla, Málaga, Alicante, and Cádiz that Lorca
enumerated in a list of slang terms from the poem, he said. A textual witness
to the murder, the "Ode" became the basis for Schonberg's revenge fantasy,
which in turn furthered a warped version of the poet's iconic status.[44]

The poem is, at its most unproblematic, a celebration. The "Ode"
shimmers with the Apollonian aura of Whitman, icon of the marvelous. The
American poet is "beautiful as the mist," with "Apollo's virginal thighs" and
a "beard full of butterflies." He is also the "Adam of blood, Macho," the
"lover of bodies under the rough cloth." Whitman both transcends and embodies the flesh in Lorca's poem. An "unbodied gazelle" in one passage, elsewhere he moans "like a bird, / its sex pricked by a needle" and arouses groans
"in the flames of [his] hidden equator." Lorca's exaltation of Whitman followed an established tradition. The Nicaraguan modernist poet Rubén Darío
called him a prophet and priest, as "beautiful as a patriarch," Olympian, with
the "face of an emperor." Even the more restrained Borges believed Whitman
revealed the "unexpected and elusive quality of the world," its very random-
ness a gift. Neither Darío nor Borges, however, emphasized his sexuality.[45]

After his death in 1892, he was practically divinized, especially by his
friends and admirers, as was the case for Lorca. His eventual biographer,
Horace Traubel, who paid daily visits to the poet in his final years, wrote:
"We thought we had buried him. But he eluded the darkness and the pall. He
reappeared in us." Another eulogized him, saying "he walked . . . with the
unconscious majesty of an antique god." Across the pond, Edward Carpenter spoke of his charisma, "a certain radiant power in him, a large benign
effluence and inclusiveness, as of the sun, which filled out the place where
he was—yet with something of reserve and sadness in it too, and a sense of
remoteness and inaccessibility." This, in a chapter on Whitman as prophet,
whose "arrival in the morning was as exhilarating as a fine sunrise." Similar
things, we know, were said of the fascination Lorca exercised over others.[46]

Whitman was also attacked. Some disliked the cult of Whitmaniacs
or judged his poetry overrated, though by the turn of the century, the focus
moved to his sexuality. In 1907, the *New York Times*, for example, observed
that the German writer Eduard Bertz, who some twenty years ago once defended the poet, now saw him as a degenerate, abnormal. In that intervening period, theories of decadence and sexual pathology by men like Nordau,

Lombroso, and Krafft-Ebing "materially changed the angle of observation for many students of mankind." Bertz also felt Whitman had manipulated his own image. By 1913, the subject was being more and more openly discussed. W. C. Rivers called the poet's homosexuality an "anomaly," relying heavily on the poems, on an invented guilt by association with Wilde, John Addington Symonds, and others, and on Whitman's presumed feminine qualities, for his interpretation.[47]

The issue exploded in the pages of the *Mercure de France*, when Guillaume Apollinaire claimed that pederasts came en masse to Whitman's funeral, while drunkenness, violence, and arrests marred the event. There was an enormous reaction to the piece, which Apollinaire later retracted. Was it a hoax, as has been said? If so, the flurry of letter writers defending and attacking the French poet's position seemed unaware and were dead-serious about the matter. The first to respond was Stuart Merrill, the American symbolist poet, much of whose work appeared in French. He completely rejected the picture of a rowdy, debauched funeral. Whitman was "normal," he wrote, as "pure as nature herself." Whitman "detested with all his being the small perversities of sick persons and maniacs." Merrill pointedly disputed the idea that Whitman's camaraderie with tram and omnibus drivers was suspect. Apollinaire had mistakenly identified the American poet's close friend Peter Doyle, a streetcar conductor, middle-aged in 1892, as a twenty-something Peter Connelly, surrounded by pederasts at the burial. He also brought up the memory of Doyle and Whitman sitting on a sidewalk curb and eating watermelon together. The sexual innuendo was clear.[48]

Coachmen and conductors had on various occasions been associated with homosexual acts, dating at least from the nineteenth century. In the early 1880s, the Duke de la Torre's son, for example, was accused of paying for sex with coachmen, purchasing their silence handsomely. In Retana's *The Posh Fairies* (1919), two gays in an open carriage hear homophobic insults from the street but declare the coachman to be the target. Lorca appears to reflect such a perception in the "Ode," when he alluded to the faggots (*maricas*) "trembling between the legs of chauffeurs." He wrote as well of "a friend [that] eats your apple / with a slight hint of gasoline," which evokes the watermelon shared by Whitman and Doyle. (Ginsberg used the same watermelon image in "A Supermarket in California," but attached it to Lorca.) Lorca also disassociated Whitman from scenes of drunkenness, presenting the author of *Leaves of Grass* as an "enemy of the satyr, / enemy of the vine." Above all, like Merrill, he embedded Whitman in the natural world, with butterflies and mist, rivers and birds. By contrast, the maricas were "packed at bars" or found "spinning, high on absinthe." Did the *Mercure de France* polemic influence the Spanish poet, as Gari Laguardia, who observed these points of contact between the "Ode," Apollinaire, and Merrill, suggested? Possibly.[49]

Even more relevant are the implications of the polemic for Lorca's poem (and for the writer himself). A Whitman scholar wrote that his burial may have had "the atmosphere of an old-time tent meeting," with jubilant crowds, but it was far from scandalous. Dignified or not, what ultimately mattered to Whitman's friends and admirers was his reputation, not his funeral rites. Here, the record is ambiguous. In a subsequent letter, Merrill contested claims by two other participants in the *Mercure de France* exchanges, Eduard Bertz and Harrison Reeves, that Whitman was a sodomite. There was no shame or abomination in sexual anomalies, he said. Indeed, Merrill tried to free Oscar Wilde, convicted of the crime of "gross indecency" (homosexuality) in 1895. Because an accusation of this kind was so defaming at the time, with such serious consequences, he was especially concerned not to see Whitman's memory "dragged through the mud." He went on to refute a series of what he considered slanderous allegations, "anonymous calumnies that go after the honor of a poet." Merrill's attempt to clear the poet's name by attacking calumny itself as the true culprit calls to mind Luis Rosales's tortured defense of the Count of Villamediana, under whom lay the shadow of García Lorca, as in a Dalí painting.[50]

There is nothing straightforward about Apollinaire's position either. In his retraction months later, he thought that Merrill "confuse[d] unisexuality with the most revolting debauchery." Apollinaire believed that many unisexuals, or gays, were chaste and engaged only in Platonic friendships, an opinion that others in the period shared. Whitman's homosexuality was common knowledge, he said, even among his devotees. He ended his brief commentary on a rather surprising note. "Since the barbaric and unjust legislation of certain countries harshly condemns unisexuals, does not Monsieur Merrill think that it is of the greatest interest to demonstrate that men of genius can be found among unisexuals? Wouldn't the prestige of these men help undo the barbarism and injustice of [such] legislation?" Apollinaire's initial homophobic attitude (joke or not) seems to have vanished here, though like Merrill, he too carefully built a wall between Whitman and less acceptable forms of homosexuality of the time.[51]

This is also why it was so important to Merrill that no hint of scandal be attached even to Whitman's funeral. In first claiming crowds of pederasts swarmed the event, by extension Apollinaire gave a name to the poet that few wanted to publicly admit. As Laguardia and others have observed, Lorca had the same problem. It wasn't so much "the love that dare not speak its name," but the name itself that became such a deeply psychological and social stumbling block. "The faggots, Walt Whitman," he wrote, "point you out. / He's one, too! He's one of us!" Indeed, it could be argued that however one defined such love, Lorca passionately argued for it. In private conversation with Rivas-Cherif, he believed love should have no limits. Love's total freedom was "what Walt Whitman called for," he said. For such advocacy, he needed Whitman to be in his poem, or perhaps better said, Whitman's exceptional reputation, his oversized iconicity. In a word, only Whitman could transcend the shaming effect of a name—what Rosales and Merrill called calumny—because Whitman was the greatest faggot of all: the father of all such fabulous fags. Lorca's poem is, in this sense, founded on fame, the American poet's enduring celebrity. He certainly couldn't have used the figure of poor Oscar Wilde, ruined and disgraced, to make his case.[52]

The *Mercure de France* polemic lingered into the early 1920s, though in a subdued venue, it seems, notably in Henry Saunders's book *A Whitman Controversy*, from 1921. He wrote in his introduction that the book was "'privately printed' for a few friends, in a limited edition of thirty-five copies (none for sale), signed and bound by myself," though the text I read appeared to be a typed manuscript. It consists of translations of the thirteen letters that appeared in *Mercure de France* in 1913–14, along with Saunders's occasional parenthetical comments on the letters. That it was privately circulated speaks for itself. A Whitman admirer, Saunders dismissed the idea of orgies at his funeral, but had more trouble coming to grips with the poet's sexuality.[53]

While he used the term "sexual inversion" twice in the introduction and homosexuality once, he also said, "In regard to sexual inversion, the fact that there are all grades of humanity, from those completely one-sexed to others with the physical form of one sex and the mental characteristics of the other, that to take an individual with slightly abnormal mental attribution and say exactly where he should be placed is most difficult." He appeared unable to decide what to call or how to deal with "Whitman's alleged sexual inversion," which he acknowledged "having probably a partial background of truth." Saunders' reluctance to categorize Whitman's sexual identity can be read in at least two different ways.[54]

On the one hand, he maintained that his poetry "transcends one-sided interpretations of isolated passages . . . relied on chiefly, by those who want to prove homosexuality in Whitman." He came down heavily on Eduard Bertz's claim that one poem alone, "Hours Continuing Long," was enough to demonstrate Whitman's "homosexual sensibility." He especially disliked what he saw as a proclivity in scientific minds toward labeling and pigeon-holing "cases," with "no deviation from certain rules." The argument for a broader, open-ended understanding of the poet has also been used for Lorca. On the other, Saunders seemed to hesitate between acceptance and rejection of Whitman's homosexuality. He saw "partial background of truth" to the question, but proof, he implied, was elusive. Or perhaps feared. Saunders's language cautiously picked a path through the minefield that classification—naming Whitman—represented for him in the *Mercure* controversy. Here, too, the poet's reputation remained a concern.[55]

The power of names to harm, but also to illuminate, comes to the fore in a startling passage of Lorca's "Ode," the enumeration of slang terms for gay:

> Always against you,
> *Fairies* of North America,
> *Pájaros* of Havana,
> *Jotos* of Mexico,
> *Sarasas* of Cádiz,
> *Apios* of Seville,
> *Cancos* of Madrid,
> *Floras* of Alicante,
> *Adelaidas* of Portugal.

This inventory of names is a parade of maricas, or fags, flaunting and performing their identity as they do in the rest of the poem, the very beings who out Whitman in another section of the "Ode": "He's one, too!" For all Lorca's efforts to distinguish the American poet from the faggots surrounding him, he allows Whitman to be branded with the same word, in what appears to be a gesture of libidinized aggression. Lorca's tormented response to the maricas in his poem has been read as internalized homosexual self-loathing. The list of slang terms for fag could also, however, be taken as a critique of gay stereotypes, a kind of domestication that lends itself to a false sense of familiarity. One interpretation does not rule out the other one in this conflict-ridden text.[56]

The shock of seeing these words comes partly from the lexical register to which they belong. Contrary to the coded significance that Ángel Sahuquillo has sought in other gay-inflected Lorca images to suggest an initiation "into a distinct and secret world," there are no hidden meanings here. You don't expect this eruption of popular culture in a poem of such fiercely stated elegance and lyrical power, even though previous use of the term marica has laid the groundwork. The words practically slap you in the face. Not even translators are able to deal with their colloquial and geographical specificity, preferring generally to leave them alone. Words like these are intimate wounds. You hear them as festering insults in the accusatory poetic voice, in the "faggots of the world" that Lorca calls "murderers of doves" and the "bedroom bitches" of women, right after enumerating his list. The laser focus on effeminate men—as opposed to Whitman's virile beauty—may distract discomfited readers from appreciating just how remarkable this poem is, not simply for its verbal and cultural daring, but for its full immersion in the world. From the start, Lorca plunges us into the same visceral depths as these words intimate, opening the poem with a Whitmanian image of laboring men, "singing, displaying their waists, / with the wheel, oil, leather, and hammer."[57]

Like Whitman, Lorca jumbles together low and high culture, but the mix is not indiscriminate. There is a pecking order, with Whitman at the top and the maricas at the bottom. Even so, the Floras, Jotos, and Fairies can also be viewed as a parody of high culture, given the peculiarities of their naming. They are the Floras of Alicante, the Jotos of Mexico, and the Fairies of North America, just like the protagonist of *Don Quixote of La Mancha*, which in turn burlesqued the characters of chivalric novels such as Amadís of Gaul, Lisuarte of Greece, and Florisel of Niquea. Despite being "always against" them, the poetic voice lends them comic flair, paying a backhanded compliment to their odd specialness as a coterie of unacceptable persons.

Lorca's treatment of the maricas calls to mind Retana's mock presentation of the same group in *The Posh Fairies*, noted earlier. I doubt that he was familiar with Retana's novel, though one never knows. More relevant is the common territory both works share: the significance of naming and the community—wanted or unwanted—that naming creates. Retana's juxtaposition of the "posh fairies" with the cross-dresser Egmont de Bries also bears functional resemblance to Lorca's Whitman-maricas opposition, especially if one considers the celebrity of both de Bries and Whitman, however different in kind and permanence that fame was. The relation between community and celebrity is key, because all celebrities have a double identity that is at once individual and communal. Their singularity can only be fully grasped in the light of the aura that the crowd bestows on them or recognizes in such persons. Lorca and Retana, who were already celebrities in their time, set apart two figures, each acclaimed in his own way and marked ambivalently in their relationship to the crowd, here, the enclave of maricas, in both works.

The insults hurled at Egmont de Bries come from an assorted group of gays and straights among the audience of the Teatro-Circo de Price, a popular venue of the period. As a form of inside joke, they consist mainly of slang words for gay, especially of the effeminate kind, but mixed in are nonsensical or irrelevant words that apparently have nothing to do with homosexuality. Egmont is called *mariposa* and *apio*, but also *goloso*, or sweet-toothed. As noted before, he mocks the colloquial use of *apio*, literally celery, for being outmoded. The new word, he says, is *vidrio*, or glass, thus cleverly disarming the power of insult but also revealing the playful arbitrariness of language. Later, pranksters fling more of "the classic adjectives" at the drag queen: *sape*, *bribón* (*pícaro*, or rogue), *sarasa* (faggot), and *fuego* (fire). Only one of these, *sarasa*, is pertinent, though *sape*, which I have been unable to find in any dictionary, might also be. In another scene, *apio* is associated with *escarola* (chicory) and *brecolera* (cabbage), a verbal vegetable stew, or gastronomical reductio ad absurdum.[58]

The two words found in both Retana and Lorca are *sarasa* and *apio*. These and the other terms from the "Ode" have a cultural and historical context, if not always traceable. To my knowledge, all save *flora*, *canco*, and *adelaida* appear in dictionaries: *marica* (1620), *fairy* (1895), *joto* (1917), *sarasa* (1918), *apio* (1992), and *pájaro* (2001). (*Homosexual*, which is not in Lorca's poem, showed up in 1917.) In his memoirs, the novelist Pío Baroja registered *canco* as a slang word he had never heard of before, at the turn of the century. The word also appears in Retana's novel *Ninfas y sátiros* (Nymphs and Satyrs) (1918), a text with several gay characters and references, such as *marica* and *apio*. And a friend, Santiago Ontañón, told Lorca that maricas were called *floras* in Alicante. Clearly, oral usage predates documented appearances. It is, nonetheless, surprising to find such a late dictionary entry for *apio*, when the word was already current by the early twentieth century, in Lorca, Retana, Cansinos-Asséns, and anonymously. Retana had even thought of writing a novel with the title *El apio maravilloso (Historia de un modisto-dibujante-bailarín)* (The Marvelous Fag [Story of a Fashion Designer-Illustrator-Dancer]). It was announced as in preparation in 1918. He planned to dedicate it to his friend, the fêted designer-dancer José de Zamora, who appears, thinly veiled, as Pepito Rocamora in *The Posh Fairies.*[59]

Sarasa has the richest chronicled history. In an 1883 account of what was probably the first big homosexual scandal in nineteenth-century Spain, Luis Carreras's *Un casamiento infame* (An Infamous Marriage), the Duques de la Torre's son Francisco, in the middle of a very public divorce, was outed as gay. Medical-legal commentary and press coverage offered conflicting reports of his condition, which included impotency and hermaphroditism. *An Infamous Marriage* and Carreras's first book, *Los duques de la Torre y el casamiento de su hijo* (The Duke and Duchess de la Torre and their Son's Marriage), both published in Paris where the case was being heard, were instrumental in publicizing the affair in Spain and throughout Europe. In the first book, he mostly hinted at Francisco's homosexuality, citing one opinion that it was impossible to know if he was a man, a woman, or some mythological hybrid of the two. In the second, Carreras wrote, the duke's son "is an unfortunate young man, rather contemptible, who has learned nothing but how to properly pronounce the word queer [sarasa]." "The only thing he [thinks] about are grooms and coachmen." He went on to say, "Although Paquito Sarasa pays his dear coachmen well, he takes care not to owe them money, because, in that case, everyone knows what the dear coachman can do: the purse shut, goodbye earthly paradise!"[60]

There seemed little clarity on how to categorize the duke's son. Calling him a hybrid or a hermaphrodite suggested either unfamiliarity with same-sex practices or a way of evading the social-moral constraints of a taboo subject, or possibly both. By contrast, the openly coarse language targeting Francisco as a *sarasa* points in the opposite direction. Readers knew what the word meant. The name was intended to shame not just socially but politically. Carreras, who was a staunch Republican, milked the scandal for what it was worth, depicting the aristocracy as corrupt and degenerate (he had plenty of material). What would neighboring countries think of us, he asked his fellow Spanish journalists, many of whom had remained silent. For Carreras, it was a matter of national honor.[61]

The other notable homosexual scandal occurred in 1898 and took place in the Andalusian city of Cádiz, producing national and even international repercussions. The civil governor was accused of issuing health cards for male prostitutes and, it was said, profiting from it. Only female prostitution was regulated, with bordellos and working girls alike obliged to pay for weekly medical inspections. Extending such services as health cards, or sanitary certificates, to *maricas de burdel* (bordello queers), including the servants in such establishments, outraged the Conservative Party in particular. The governor belonged to the Liberal Party then in power and had family connections with the leadership. The national crisis spilled over beyond the country's borders, as the Treaty of Paris was being negotiated to end the Cuban conflict between the United States and Spain at the same time. For many, the scandal in Cádiz exposed the nation to ridicule and disgrace, to being perceived as weak and degenerate in Europe and abroad. "In complete decay," as one journalist put it. *El Siglo Futuro,* an ultra-Catholic newspaper, went apocalyptic, declaring that Cádiz had "converted that horrendous abomination [sodomy] into a legal industry." The satiric publication *Gedeón* issued a cover-page color cartoon, depicting the politicians involved on one side and two effeminate gays with exaggerated hand gestures and body posture on the other, with the words, "girl, what have we done!"[62]

The press was merciless. As Francisco Vázquez García has remarked, these events fixed in stone the idea that Cádiz was a "city of inverts." Years later, when all this history had been forgotten, that single image persisted, encapsulated in Lorca's phrase "*Sarasas* of Cádiz." Even though several different terms were bandied about—*mariquilla, pericón, esteta, efebo, afeminado,* even *coridón*—*sarasa* stuck more than most. One anonymous piece of the time said it all, with the title, "El Reino de Sarasa" (The Kingdom of Queers). *Sarasa,* however, does not appear in the text. Instead, the journalist used *estetas,* or aesthetes, out of discretion, he said. This same term popped up in other accounts as well. In a satiric poem, *pericones* (lit., a large fan used in flamenco performances) became a barely disguised reference to *maricones,* who embrace the "aesthetic life" ("vida de la estética"). The flamenco artist Pericón de Cádiz recalled how, in 1936, "the audience made fun of his name by pronouncing 'Cádiz' in an exaggeratedly effeminate manner."[63]

Words like *sarasa* and *esteta* were not uniquely restricted to Cádiz. The

262 A FACE IN THE CROWD

dictionary entry for *esteta* included "sodomite" in 1917, and in 1918, "effeminate man," with no regional distinctions. López Pinillos used *sarasa*, along with an entire constellation of homophobic terms in his novel, *El luchador* (The Fighter) (1916), set in Madrid: among them, *invertido, homosexual, sodomita, mignon, efebo,* and *andrógino.* His narrator sarcastically claims that being "a wretched sodomite" ("un sodomita desdichado") enhances a writer's reputation. Unsurprisingly, he links queerness to a fin de siècle decadentist aesthetic. Thus, the *sarasa* Luis, who writes "deliquescent" verses, adores Verlaine, Lorrain, Mirbeau, and Oscar Wilde. During the same period, Cansinos-Asséns privately registered in his memoirs *esteta* as code for gay in a section titled "Exquisitos" (Exquisites). In an antigay vein resembling that of López Pinillos, he also used *sarasa, invertido, efebo,* and *mignon,* as well as *semi-hombre/semi-mujer* and *maricón,* to describe certain elements of the Madrid literary-artistic scene. In one entry, he noted that Carmen de Burgos called homosexuals a "social plague" ("plaga social") and was planning to write something on it. The subsequent novella, *El veneno del arte* (The Poison of Art) (1910), was a free-wheeling satire of both aristocrats and writers, embodied in the protagonist Luis, who in turn was probably based on the openly gay, decadentist writer, the Marquis Antonio de Hoyos y Vinent.[64]

As Vázquez García has observed, these are different homosexual social groupings. The *estetas de burdel* were distinct from aesthetes like Hoyos y Vinent found in high society or among literary-artistic bohemians, which is not to say they didn't mix. The mingling of high and low, found in Lorca's "Ode," is also class- and culture-conscious, indirectly reflecting the sexual exchanges between men of unequal social rank—"trembling between the legs of chauffeurs"—common to many homosexual subcultures of the period. The queers "emerging in clusters from the sewers," the "crowds of howls and gestures" in the poem, are an urban phenomenon deeply embedded in the degraded, prostituted world Lorca envisioned in *Poet in New York.*[65]

The differences, however, are not simply social or cultural, but aesthetic. Both the contrastive lexical registers in describing the American poet and the queers and the opposition between beauty (Whitman) and ugliness (maricas) are inherently aesthetic arguments projected onto social-cultural poetic constructs. And yet, the faggots are entwined with Whitman himself, landing on his "luminous chaste beard," imaged earlier as full of butterflies. Here, the wordplay between *marica* and *mariposa* (butterfly) is unmistakable, as *mariposa* is also slang for fairy, for an effeminate-looking homosexual. (Lorca planned to include in *Poet in New York* a photomontage of Whitman, butterflies in his beard.) Lorca is unable to keep them apart, despite distinguishing between the American poet's Apollonian purity and the maricas' stained fingers and frozen saliva. Another way of putting it: one aesthetic feeds into another. The exquisite imagery portraying Whitman as androgynous, a blend of feminine and masculine associations—his "virile beauty," his "Apollo's virginal thighs," the "beard full of butterflies"—recalls *modernista* poetry, whereas the images for the maricas—"trembling between the legs of chauffeurs," "spinning, high on absinthe," "tumescent flesh and foul thoughts"—evoke decadentist tropes. Both *modernismo* and decadentism, however, issue from the same fin de siècle aesthetic movement. And in both instances these aesthetic phenomena—whether attached to texts or to persons—have been read as gay. The history of words like *sarasa* and *esteta* points to this underlying association.[66]

Another (and ultimately related) reason Lorca's queers cannot be permanently segregated from Whitman is because they are part of the multitude, the very demos that he embraced in *Leaves of Grass* and in his life. Even Lorca acknowledges Whitman's democratic tastes as the "lover of bodies under the rough cloth." The Whitmanian aesthetic was all inclusive. He took ordinary people and elevated them into the ranks of the extraordinary, in part by wrapping himself around the lives of others. He donated himself to what is common, and he drew into himself what is ordinary, portraying both as heroic acts of the democratic soul in which every American shares. You can't read his poetry without wondering which part of Walt's persona is his and which part belongs to that vast forest of common life called *Leaves of Grass* he draws into himself. What looks like sheer narcissism in the poet's "song of myself" opens into the larger unfolding of life. This is because Whitman so closely identified himself as "the poet of comrades." In "Song of Myself," he announces, "I am of old and young, of the foolish as much as the wise"; "Through me many long dumb voices"; "I do not ask the wounded person how he feels, I myself become the wounded person." In "Starting from Paumanok," he writes,

> I am the credulous man of qualities, ages, races,
> I advance from the people in their own spirit,
> Here is what sings unrestricted faith.

The I is never simply the poet's voice; it is everyone else's voice as well.[67]

The word Whitman favored was "common," not "ordinary"; "ordinary" never appears in *Leaves of Grass*. He sang in "Song of Myself," "What is commonest, cheapest, nearest, easiest, is Me."

> Of every hue and caste am I, of every rank and religion,
> A farmer, mechanic, artist, gentleman, sailor, quaker,
> Prisoner, fancy-man, rowdy, lawyer, physician, priest,

in "this the common air that bathes the globe." He spoke of "slow-stepping feet, common features, common modes and emanations." And most famously: "Do I contradict myself? / Very well then I contradict myself, / (I am large, I contain multitudes)." He also wrote:

> Walt Whitman, a kosmos, of Manhattan the son,
> Turbulent, fleshy, sensual, eating, drinking and breeding,
> No sentimentalist, no stander above men and women or
> apart from them,
> No more modest than immodest.[68]

The Southern Agrarian and Imagist poet John Gould Fletcher considered him "the supreme, the only democratic poet the world has ever possessed." In 1920, as he rode in a bus down New York City's Fifth Avenue, seeing crowds of workmen, Fletcher had an epiphany: "At that moment, as I was borne past them . . . all these lives, all these faces, became mine; I felt bowed down in worship to the unseen life-force that was pressing in and through them to some unknown end; and I understood in a flash of perception . . . the meaning of the poet who had walked these same pavements years before; the one unique, authentically great American poet: Walt Whitman." He saw the fusion between poet and crowd as key to *Leaves of Grass*. "Whitman felt himself," he wrote in 1924, "to be a member of the crowd . . . but primarily he knew that his function to the crowd was to be their poet, their interpreter." Whitman said, "Just as any of you is one of a living crowd, I was one of a crowd." The crowd is shorthand for the astounding variety and display of ordinary people, "all the shows of laboring life," that Whitman addressed. In a theatrical vein, he called it

> this drama of the whole,
> this common curtain of the face contain'd in me for me, in
> you for you, in each for each.

What complicates and deepens *Leaves of Grass* is the beauty of the ordinary, though its source be equivocal. To whom does such beauty belong? To ordinary people or to Whitman himself?[69]

For all his talk of the common, Whitman magnified himself. He acquired a celebrity status of sorts by manipulating the celebrity culture of his time, as David Haven Blake has argued. He wrote anonymous favorable notices of the first edition of *Leaves of Grass*, flaunted a facsimile of his autograph in the book, and used staged photos of himself, such as one in which he gazes at a cardboard butterfly poised on his hand. Recalling Retana's commercial instincts, he even endorsed cigars in his name (though not a calendar adorned with his poems) (fig. 13). The readers to whom he spoke so intimately were woven into the fabric of his poems. They are the crowd, ordinary folks, made partners in the poet's promotion of himself. In this way, Whitman was like the powerful politician who adopts a folksy demeanor. The effect is not to bend down but to raise up. Because at the same time, Whitman was really saying that they were not ordinary. How could they be if he, too, was part of the crowd? "Just as you feel when you look on the river and sky, so I felt," he wrote in "Crossing Brooklyn Ferry." And in "By Blue Ontario's Shore," he affirmed, "We are the most beautiful to ourselves and in ourselves." From the same poem: "Produce great Persons, the rest follows." "I am he who tauntingly compels men, women, nations, / Crying, Leap from your seats and contend for your lives!"[70]

The transformation of people's lives Whitman urged was to be achieved, tellingly, through the advice of the poet himself. Over and over in "Song of Myself," for example, he flings himself enthusiastically into the role of life-coach. "I dilate you," he writes, "with tremendous breath, I buoy you up, / Every room of the house do I fill with an arm'd force, / Lovers of me, bafflers of graves." He also says,

> Not I, not any one else can travel that road for you,
> You must travel it for yourself.
> It is not far, it is within reach,
> Perhaps you have been on it since you were born and did not know,
> Perhaps it is everywhere on water and on land.

And in the penultimate stanza, he observes:

> You will hardly know who I am or what I mean,
> But I shall be good health to you nevertheless,
> And filter and fibre your blood.[71]

Figure 13. Walt Whitman and his butterfly. Photo by W. Curtis
Taylor, 1877, courtesy of the Library of Congress, Prints and
Photographs Division, LC-USZ62-124410.

Blake points out that Whitman's pep talk to his readers works like patent medicine. He brings "good health," strengthening the fiber of our blood.
It's also a form of self-advertising for the poet, but his poetry goes beyond
the promotion of self. By identifying so closely with his readers, with ordinary folk, Whitman the kosmos suggests a sense of community, the blending
of the I with the whole. At the same time his own extraordinariness is made
visible through the ordinary lives of others, he seems to be saying the reverse,

that the ordinary is in truth extraordinary. Through the technique of accumulation (an innovative use of the classic *amplificatio*), his celebrated enumerations of different kinds of persons, labor, things, geographies become repeated affirmations of unity in variousness, a modern prayer to a chain of being to which all belong. Significantly, Whitman's arrangement of the universe in *Leaves of Grass* rests on the individual himself, a surcharged personality that dilates and buoys us up.[72]

In this way Whitman also anticipated the current-day obsession with celebrity, the fetish of individualism, precisely through his gregarious hyping of the ordinary. Conflating the ordinary with the extraordinary carries grave risk. "Song of Myself" begins, "I celebrate myself, and sing myself, / And what I assume you shall assume." That is a remarkable presumption, perhaps unavoidable as part of the democratic proposition to which Whitman was devoted, which may be why individualism, the cult of celebrity, and a pervasive belief in greatness latent within everyone are very American. But it assumes no liabilities, no enduring debts or incurable defects on Whitman's part (or that of the reader either). Turning your life into an endless selfie, however, was not Whitman's aim. Elevating the vigor of a common life was. Above all, American life. Yet the tension between celebrity and community that runs through *Leaves of Grass* persists. Celebration of "common features, common modes," of the "common curtain of the face," is inevitably wrapped up in self, in Whitman's personality, but also in something he sees, or when war has divided the nation, wishes to see in American life: the combined boosterism of the life held in common *and* the self. He aestheticizes ordinary life, not simply because he is writing poetry, but because he places ordinary people within the same aura as himself.[73]

As a poet, Whitman courted the crowds. He was as much in love with them as with the gay lovers in the Calamus poems intimated in another register. Lorca, however, had another take, writing that "no one can imagine precisely what a multitude in New York is like, though Walt Whitman knew, seeking solitude in it." He went on to speak of his own solitude, how no one can conceive of what it is like for a Spaniard, and worse, for an Andalusian, to experience such aloneness. "If you fall," he wrote, "you'll be trampled. . . . The sound of that terrible crowd completely fills Sunday in New York." In the same text, a lecture-recital centered on his New York poetry, Coney Island is a vast orgy of loud people, food, booze, trash, vomit, and urine. Whitman is one with the crowd; Lorca is not, in the "Ode." Barely out of adolescence, in 1918, he wrote a friend that he wanted "to be all things." And as we have seen, at the Teatro Barcelona in 1935, he spoke warmly of how his love for others led him "to intertwine and merge myself with everyone."[74]

These sentiments have something in common with Whitman's inclusivity, but it's important to see the differences, too. In the first instance, the oceanic feeling of wanting "to be all things" was still colored with a lingering romanticism in the young Lorca, in a letter full of personal anguish and uncertainty. In the second, the crowd whom he addressed in 1935 was much closer in spirit and character to the pueblo than to the crush of people at Coney Island. Both were representative of mass culture, but the Barcelona public, politically motivated and having chosen to attend the reading, had a relationship with Lorca, while the chaotic, amorphous throngs of New York did not. In the "Ode," another anonymous multitude emerges in bunches, like tainted grape clusters ("racimos"), it howls and gesticulates, "flesh for the whip, / the boot, or the bite of the lion tamers." These are the maricas, seemingly set apart from Walt Whitman and, by extension, from Lorca himself through his poetic I.[75]

Lorca's identification with the American poet, with his exceptionality, only works by segregating the other gays in the poem. He can't really sustain that posture, however, for at least two reasons. First, because Whitman's celebrity, his iconicity, is matched by the fetishization of homosexuality elsewhere in the "Ode." When the maricas exclaim, "He's one, too!" their fingers point back at themselves as well. As with all deictic usage, context is crucial, which in this case is one of marking. Lorca singles out not only Whitman but the queers of his poem. They are a veritable sideshow, filled with performative power like the fat lady (and the poet without arms) in "Landscape of a Vomiting Multitude" or Retana's drag queen, Egmont de Bries. Being "flesh for the whip, / the boot, or the bite of the lion tamers," "spinning, high on absinthe," or "opening in plazas fevered with fans" are theatrical displays of oddness. Even when he speaks disparagingly of types—*sarasas, jotos, apios, pájaros*—he also differentiates them geographically, parodically dubbing them knights of a peculiar confraternity.[76]

Which brings me to my second point. The crowd of gays is also a community, but an enclave that refuses to stay in the ghetto. They spill into practically everything, even Whitman's beard, as part of the fallen world of modernity. By denying their legitimacy as a group, however, Lorca weakens his defense of the all-inclusive Whitman. Almost as though aware he's devised a trap of his own making, he carves out exceptions, explicitly pointing them out to the American poet. He doesn't "raise [his] voice"

> against the little boy who writes
> a girl's name on his pillow,
> nor against the boy who dresses like a bride
> in the darkness of the closet,
> nor against the solitary men in casinos
> who drink revulsed the waters of prostitution,
> nor against the men with that green look
> who love other men, with lips that burn in silence.

All these examples are striking for being clandestine or silent in nature, the very opposite of the maricas' flash and clamor. Homosexual desire happens in secret places like bedrooms and closets, or in the mute recesses of solitary, green-eyed men. The exceptions are even exceptions to Whitman's own singularity. Innocence rubs up against prostitution, in Lorca's tortured effort to remove such beings from the freak show of the maricas.[77]

Whitman devotees did the same for the American poet. In 1926, William Sloane Kennedy, for example, thought the reproduction of the poet's autopsy report in a homage volume "grewsome." (At the very least, it was certainly more information about the poet than we needed to know.) Overall, he felt *In Re Walt Whitman*, despite its sincere tone, left the poet vulnerable to being viewed as an exhibit to the anti-Whitmanites, who could then say: "'Gentlemen, walk up and view the greatest poet on earth. We've captured him here in Philadelphia. We'll give his dimensions in inches, cut him open and show his anatomy; and we've got a phonographic report of his talk. We show the whole animal, gentlemen.'" Blake astutely observed that "Whitman the icon becomes Whitman the freak show," his privacy invaded by editors who "had put the poet on display; as in an autopsy, they had opened him up to public view." It could also be argued that icons are always on display and therefore easily lend themselves to being regarded as freaks.[78]

This sense of discomfiting, revealed intimacy is also crucial to the "Ode." Lorca appears, on the one hand, to struggle against such familiarity; on the other, to embrace it. The passage cited above, with its profoundly personal annotations, is emblematic of the poet's conflicted attitude. Secret lives are unveiled but remain thwarted confessions. Whitman, the icon, is himself placed on a pedestal, but descends into more human realms at the same time, feeding the poetic I's craving to know him more intimately. That desire is part and parcel of Whitman's iconic celebrity. Celebrities belong to others, or at least their admirers seem to think so. Thus, Lorca imagines him "sleeping like a river / with that comrade who would leave in your breast / the small ache of an ignorant leopard." Or moaning "like a bird / with its sex pricked by a needle." Or he thinks of "the flames of your hidden equator." In an entirely different (but not unrelated) register, one recalls how Retana's readers wrote him fan letters, fantasizing about his sex life. The nature-related images, which lend transcendence to Whitman the icon on one level, also humanize him on another, stressing the "small ache" or the birdlike moan, his most privately lived experience.

The risk (or is it the challenge?) of opening up Whitman in this way lies in exposing him to being associated with the maricas, who, like the poetic I, also want to know him, jumping all over his beard. This is the crowd, which resembles the invasive multitudes that so impressed and confounded Lorca in New York, but here seen as the throngs that flock to, and identify with, celebrity, with Whitman's luminosity, in an ironically manifested frenzy of renown. A reverse reading points to something else: the American poet's being threatened with contamination by close contact with the maricas, deemed "mothers of mud" ("madres de lodo") in the "Ode." You could call this a potential loss of aura, such as we saw mired in Baudelaire's imagination. That is always the vulnerability of celebrity or fame. Lorca skirts around such peril by separating Whitman the icon from the maricas, but he also ends up cutting off the American poet's communal identity, which defined him as a writer and a celebrity. Either Whitman is queer, or he isn't. Either he is part of that specific group, or he isn't. Whitman embraced a cosmic belonging, but the terms of Lorca's "Ode" pit him against a distinct community that is crucial to the presentation of Whitman.

The poetic I is as much a fan of Whitman as any crowd of admirers. In this sense, Lorca's voice in the poem can be conceived as part of the multitude itself, whether the poet recognizes it or not. The problem is, Lorca never could entirely sort through his feelings about crowds, as we have seen, either in his life or his work. In the "Ode," he is hell-bent on maintaining Whitman's protected status, on keeping him away from the multitude. Whitman's exceptionality is expressed not only in images of purity but of ineffability and fluidity. What else is a "column of ash" but impossible to grasp? Or Whitman dreaming "of becoming a river and sleeping like a river" and looking "for a nude who was like a river" but sheer flow and mutability? Poetry's power to metamorphose its chosen subject already embraces a poetics of the marvelous. Add to this the fluidity of sex, an unstable sexual identity, and you also get a queer interpretation of the marvelous in the "Ode" that almost seems ready-made for current-day queer theory. But it is equally important to recognize the obsession with hybridity and ambiguity in Lorca's own time, which, certainly in some cases, saw such creatures as fabulous and unique, as undefinable, in the same way monsters are.[79]

Cansinos-Asséns, one recalls, returned them to the territory of the archaic imagination and myth. "The zone of sex," he wrote, "appears to us as a zone of imprecise flourishing. All the intermediate forms that we could imagine flourish here. . . . The multitude of hybrids is as numerous perhaps as that of the fauns, feminine and masculine." There was nothing immutable about them, he said, as the feminine and masculine "no longer possess an unquestioned meaning." Their unfixed nature he saw in relation to the ability of the gods to change sex or form. Whitman's transformation into a river, his butterfly-beard, his slipping away unbodied into ash, mist, and gazelle, reinforce how extraordinary he is. His mutability ties him closely to the constantly metamorphosing, hybrid world of the gods, without necessarily privileging either the feminine or the masculine traits found in the "virile beauty" Lorca attached to the figure of Whitman. But did the gods really care about such things? What was feminine or masculine to them?[80]

The boy-bride and the little boy with the name of a girl speak further to the ambiguous beings of whom Cansinos-Asséns wrote and Retana put on full exhibit. And the maricas? Where do we place them? The hermaphrodite and the androgyne, often taken to be veiled references to homosexuality, as a way to talk about homosexuality without naming it, were forms of the eccentric, an aesthetic and biological deviation, that Nin Frías praised and compared to the way disease could produce a pearl. Like them, the maricas broadcast an aesthetics of oddness, except that, in contrast to Nin Frías and Retana, Lorca found such extravagant display profoundly unwelcome. You could say their very difference defined them too clearly by eliminating all other possibilities of being for the poet. He far preferred Whitman's fluid nature in the "Ode" or the changeable, astonishing creatures in *The Public*, where "Romeo can be a bird, and Juliet, a stone. Romeo can be a grain of salt and Juliet can be a map." "Do Romeo and Juliet necessarily have to be a man and a woman?" asks a character. In another scene, First Man can go behind a screen and a woman emerge dressed in black pajamas, carrying eyeglasses on a handle "covered by a blond mustache." Setting aside for a moment Lorca's distaste in the "Ode," isn't this, too, an expression—and performance—of an aesthetics of oddness, an inventive instance of the monstrous doubled figure of the hermaphrodite? The hermaphroditic sculpture in Gautier's "Contralto" is both Romeo and Juliet. Lorca's creations spring from a renewed sense of the marvelous that we also see in Hoyos y Vinent, Retana, and Cansinos-Asséns, all of whom are variously rooted in a re-visioning of the archaic as part of the modern world.[81]

Or take from the same period as these two works, the example of Lorca's pen-and-ink line drawings composed as self-portraits, to which fabulous animals are attached. Mario Hernández says they are polymorphic, though one could also call them shape-shifters, in the same way Walt Whitman is in the "Ode." In the best-known of these, *Self-Portrait in New York,* four of these creatures border the central figure, a pearlike balloon face, with thread-like arms and defensively held elongated hands (fig. 14). Do they belong to external urban threats, posed by the surrounding skyscrapers, or to obscurely felt internal projections (or quite possibly both)? Three of the animals are black, and the fourth is half inked-in, half not, while overlapping with part of the human figure's extended filaments. Their coexistence suggests that all four animals, springing into being like psychic quicksilver, are simultaneously wanted and unwanted manifestations of Lorca's self-representation, an expression of all that is monstrous within. The whorls of manes and tails, evoking those of the sea anemone, are also fluid, like the pliable, amorphous image of the human face in the drawing. As rare as black swans, they astonish by appearing in the very heart of the modern world. Are they at the same time part of the modern? Or do they tell us instead how thin the veneer of modernity is, how deep myth?[82]

At least one of Lorca's untamed animals, kicking up its hind legs, strikes us as more unruly than the others, but all possess a kind of strange wildness, which is a fundamental part of their fabulous nature. Fabulous as in mythic, archaic, or unreal, but also extraordinary. Irreducible. This same quality adheres to Whitman in the "Ode," and in this sense, resembles what Cansinos-Asséns saw in those mysterious creatures in the forest of the night. Despite not severing Whitman entirely from urban life, however corrupted, in the end Lorca places him in the most transcendent, ineffable realm conceivable, that of "the kingdom of grain," essentially, a vague kind of Second Coming

Figure 14. *Self-Portrait in New York.* Pen-and-ink line drawing by
Federico García Lorca, ca. 1929–31.

to counter a degenerate, materialist civilization. His beard is "toward the
pole" and his hands are "open." This ultimate swerve away from Whitman
as the ideal model of homosexual toward something more universal goes
beyond Lorca's labored strategy of segregating the American poet from the
maricas, but it also means the poem, as remarkable as it is, lacks cohesiveness.
Cernuda, who elsewhere wrote directly about Lorca's homosexuality in a
moving elegy, was one of the first to observe how confusing and contradictory the "Ode" appears. He thought that Lorca betrayed his own emotions,
though it could be said that the poem faithfully reflects the complexity of his
feelings as an insecure mass of confusion. At any rate, Cernuda, who was
also gay, likened the work to an unfinished sculpture "because the block of
marble contained a flaw." Much more recently, another gay poet, Luis Muñoz,
begged to differ, seeing in the inconsistency of the "Ode" an invigorating
openness and vulnerability, and this, despite fighting with the poem "every
time [he] reads it." Beginning in his adolescence, Muñoz found in Lorca not

only a poetic exemplar but a personal one, precisely for the inner battles the poet endured in order "to speak out from a homosexual standpoint."[83]

The one thing Lorca maintains to the end in the "Ode" is Whitman's iconicity. Said in a different way, Whitman is another one of the poet's un-domesticated, fabulous animals, as much on exhibit as the pictorial represen-tations of Lorca's pen-and-ink drawings. He is no less legend than the fabled hermaphrodite. And, like Retana or Egmont de Bries, he possesses a sexual aura that is part and parcel of his celebrity. As sexual display, he also shares common territory with the much-detested maricas of the "Ode." An aesthet-ics of oddness is not restricted to the queers, since in many ways Whitman is as fetishized as they are in Lorca's poem. More than anything, Whitman allowed the poet to revitalize a sense of the marvelous in what could be called a fantasy of homosexuality, in the same way the American poet is made to dream himself becoming a river.

None of what I have said does away with Lorca's conflicted attitude in the poem, nor should one try to do so. Whitman's exceptional status only functions through exclusion of the very beings whose multitudes are part of his fame. And whose behavior is as uncontrollable as that of Lorca's fabulous animals. On one level, the litany of names they bear may make the maricas more definable, and apparently more segregated, but on another their actions make them proliferate, as they tremble, spin, howl, or murder doves, invad-ing every urban space imaginable. Yet Whitman, who serves as the poetic I's advocate, seems to exist in a metaphorical and cultural vacuum, carefully removed from the community surrounding him and from the calumny of a name. This positioning of Whitman reminds us how Merrill, Saunders, and others similarly attempted to protect the American poet's image even in death, against the claims of crowds of pederasts (and orgies) at his funeral.

How did gay writers and artists react to Lorca's intensely ambivalent, even negative, feelings toward other homosexuals in the "Ode"? What did Lorca mean to them? I have mentioned Cernuda and Muñoz, but there are others as well. I am less interested in tracing literary-artistic genealogy or influence than in further understanding how the poet as gay icon shaped his after life, how his celebrity created posthumous relationships and communi-ties, of which Nin Frías's imagined gay Andalusian constellation was a pre-cursor. Just as fame helps explain and infuses the "Ode to Walt Whitman," the same can be said of how fame fashioned Lorca's life and work and those who came in contact with him or his writing. Even during his lifetime, he had an impact on gays. The copla singer and dancer Miguel de Molina (1908–93), celebrated for his renditions of "Ojos verdes" and "La bien pagá," first ran across Lorca in 1922, at the Cante Jondo Festival in Granada. While he was delivering telegrams, and shortly before beginning work as a houseboy in a bordello, someone lent him a book of Lorca's poetry. In his memoirs, he wrote that even as an untutored, working-class adolescent "Federico's image and poetry burrowed deep inside me." Lorca's name pops up regularly in the book, interwoven with the larger narrative of Molina's coming-out. He began reading the poet's work at age fifteen; by eighteen he knew he was gay. He didn't meet the poet until 1932, at the Café Ivory, which he frequented with the sole purpose of getting to know Lorca.[84]

Was he dazzled by the poet's fame? Absolutely. He dropped out of a show over a low billing dispute, a show partly inspired by Lorca, and had always regretted having lost the opportunity for his name to be professionally associated with the poet's. But it wasn't all about fame. Molina had his most intimate (and last) encounter with Lorca in December 1935, after the Barcelona opening of the play *Doña Rosita the Spinster*, when the poet and song writer, Rafael de León (also a closet gay), Lorca, and Molina spent a couple of hours in lively conversation. At the time de León was composing his most famous song, "Ojos verdes" (Green Eyes). Lorca teased him, saying his celebrated line, "Verde que te quiero verde" ("Green, I love you green") from "Dreamwalking Ballad," obviously inspired him. Although Molina doesn't mention it, we now know that the original lyrics of "Green Eyes" referred to homosexual love. That version was never released.[85]

Lorca's assassination devastated Molina. He had felt for him not only deep admiration but "something like an impossible love." As was the case for so many people, the civil war would have a tremendous impact on him, beginning with the extinction of "a human being so important for me as Federico García Lorca." Because Molina had entertained the Republican troops in Valencia, he was targeted by the Franco dictatorship. But it was more than that. Shortly after the war ended, he was arrested and at that moment thought of Lorca's fate. He was thrown to the ground, pistol-whipped, his hair yanked out, nose and teeth broken, and forced to drink castor oil mixed with vaseline. Why were they doing this? he asked. Because you're "a faggot and a red! We're getting rid of all the queers and communists. One by one!"[86]

By 1942, demoralized and fearful, Molina decided to pursue his career in Buenos Aires and there, too, under the Perón regime, he was persecuted for being homosexual, accused of causing a public scandal and organizing orgies in his home. A newspaper denounced him for promoting "the exhibitionist debauchery of 'the love that dare not speak its name.'" For some, he became "the local version of the Oscar Wilde case." Molina's trademark extravagant blouses also singled him out as effeminate, even though he did not see himself that way. "The idea was," he wrote, "not to cross dress, but definitely with a bit of a feminine air." On the other hand, his performances had no "ambiguous or feminine movements."[87]

Without necessarily drawing a straight line between himself and Lorca in his autobiography, the singer found validation but also an object lesson in the poet. You could be a gay performer while not saying so, but you could also get killed for being gay. Molina never spoke explicitly of Lorca as homosexual, though he did mention his "ambiguous relationship" with the bullfighter-playwright Sánchez Mejías, but there wasn't any need to spell it out. It was understood. Lorca, he said, was utterly captivated by the bullfighter's alpha male personality. At the same time, Molina distanced himself from being perceived as a marica, much as the poet did. Little good it did either one of them.[88]

Significantly, the singer's "impossible love" for Lorca places him in the position of both a fan and fellow gay. Only a fan bathes in the warm illusion of celebrity intimacy. This kind of adoration is common to modern fame. The strong identification Molina felt with the poet had more, however, to do with what they shared than mere fandom. Lorca's iconic status, already visible in life, was like a magnet for many, prompting real and imagined relationships, as we saw, for example, with Nin Frías's fantasizing a contemporary gay al-Andalus brotherhood or, later, with Ginsberg's having Lorca and Whitman roam the same California supermarket. Molina's experiences are obviously more personal; he, after all, knew Lorca. The idea of a community does not, however, appear in his memoirs. Like the singer, both Nin Frías, who wrote Lorca in hopes of meeting him, and Ginsberg, who imagined himself walking alongside Whitman, while asking which way his beard pointed tonight (in a clear reference to the "Ode"), also imagined a close relationship with the poets they coveted, remote figures who represented, you could say, an "impossible love."

They were not alone. In the same period as Ginsberg's "Supermarket," Jack Spicer was working on a series of poems for a book titled *After Lorca* (1957). He, too, sought a chimerical intimacy with Lorca, though in the end he broke it off, metaphorically speaking, in the last of several interspersed letters addressed to the Spanish poet. He wrote to the phantom-Lorca, "It is over, this intimate communion with the ghost of Garcia Lorca, and I wonder now how it was ever able to happen." "The poems are there," he went on to say, "the memory not of a vision but a kind of casual friendship with an undramatic ghost who occasionally looked through my eyes and whispered to me." As with the other letters, he signed this one "Love, Jack."[89]

The merging of perspectives—Lorca looking through Spicer's eyes— springs from the language of lovers, whispered into the poet's ear. The hoped-for friendship is anything but casual, starting with the title itself, as Spicer chases after the Spanish poet in more ways than one. In the ironic introduction to the book, the posthumous Lorca nails it when he calls out Spicer's epistolary attempts to woo him in a "singular tryst." This impossible courtship can only be expressed as a linguistic and poetic belatedness, through different kinds of emulation. What Spicer cannot do is *be* Lorca. Lorca's writerly renown, his iconic originality, stands in the way, but his personal celebrity also comes into play here, as the American poet pursues him as if he were a fan attaching himself, however illusorily, to an object of devotion. Like Ginsberg, Spicer also shapes and contributes to Lorca's fame, namely, his status as a gay icon.[90]

At the same time, Spicer created a collective ethos behind a broadly conceived form of translation in *After Lorca*, revitalizing the idea of writing as translation. The book contains translations, both real and apocryphal, of Lorca's work, which Spicer claims belong to both poets. They are "our poems," he wrote, highlighting the blurry line between the two writers. This comment comes at the end of a letter in which he complains how hard it is to find an audience for his poems. It's that "first night," when you've just finished the poem, "when I leave my apartment almost breathless, searching for someone to show the poem to," he said. Forget about his fellow poets or poet-apprentices. They're either not interested or only self-interested. As for friends, there are only two, and neither one is available. So, he concluded, "All this is to explain why I dedicate each of our poems to someone."

In this way, Spicer linked his imagined intimate relationship with Lorca to a larger community, found among the dedications, nearly all of whom were gay, friends, exlovers and poets living in the San Francisco Bay Area. This local identity reminds us, curiously, of the regional specificity Lorca assigned to his enumeration of homosexual epithets in the "Ode," though there is no pejorative intent in Spicer's dedications. This, too, brings the two poets closer together. Significantly, the epistolary language eroticizes the relationship by making the poems *become* a kind of sexualized object, a substitute for the desired connection with Lorca (though not simply with the Spanish poet). In the same letter, Spicer wrote, "some poems are easily laid . . . [whereas] the quiet poems are what I worry about—the ones that must be seduced."

Then there's that "first night," a phrase that he associates with the thrill of finishing a poem and showing it to someone, but it also evokes two lovers coming together. Later, he says, "when you are in love there is no real problem. The person you love is always interested because he knows that the poems are always about him." This is when his "poems have an audience." Expressed another way, for Spicer readers are potential (and real) lovers, and what the American poet seeks is a conversation that lasts the whole first night. And while he dances around whatever he really expects from Lorca in his "singular tryst," "Lorca" himself looms larger than life—and larger in death —than ever before because he comes "after," posthumously libidinized like an idolized celebrity would-be lover.

The yearning for dialogue in Spicer's work spills over into the translations in the book. Daniel Katz observes, "Spicer, rather than simply becoming the vehicle for Lorca's ghostly and Americanized voice, will in fact 'talk back' to 'Lorca' in a series of letters signed 'Jack.' Translation, crucially, is refigured . . . as epistolary dialogue—a series of entirely mediated messages and transmissions passed back and forth across borders of language, death and the earth's cover." Jack talking back to Federico is especially jolting in his translation of the "Ode to Walt Whitman" because of the gay lexicon Spicer employed, including such words and phrases as "cocksucker," "prick," "sucked-off," and "opening their flies." As with the use of *marica, sarasa,* and other slang words for queer, these terms possess a certain shock value.[91]

Spicer was far more direct than Lorca, however, in linking the figure of Walt Whitman to the faggots (cocksuckers) in his rendition of the poem. Using the same explicit language, he speaks, for example, of Whitman's prick and his "tight-cocked beauty." On the one hand, he follows Lorca in speaking openly of homosexuality, but on the other, the English version diverges by subverting the very kind of vocabulary and poetic stance Lorca used to denigrate queer behavior in public. One line especially deliberately misrepresents the original. Lorca wrote, "los maricas, Walt Whitman, te señalan," which translates as "the faggots, Walt Whitman, point you out." Spicer rendered it as "the cocksuckers, Walt Whitman, were counting on you," which gives the line a very different meaning, intended to join Whitman to this specific gay community rather than segregate him from it. Spicer retained much of Lorca's harsh position toward the maricas, but as seen here, not always. His translation conveys a tension, which is both external and internal, between the English version and the original, between a gay community of cocksuckers and a ghettoized group of *maricas, sarasas, pájaros,* and others.[92]

After Lorca weaves together a collective and individual vision of being gay and being a poet. Being part of a community and being alone. Spicer called himself Lorca's "special comrade," evoking the language of Whitman. But in his last letter, he wrote, "saying goodbye to a ghost is more final than saying goodbye to a lover. Even the dead return, but a ghost, once loved, departing will never reappear." That is not altogether true here, because "Lorca" will never leave the pages of Spicer's book. And love, when gone, haunts us forever. "Today, alone by myself," Spicer reflected, "it is like having lost a pair of eyes and a lover." Yet Lorca remains as an aura, an apparition of the inseparability of love and poetry. Isn't that what Whitman was about? And Lorca's "Ode," with all its contradictions?

That aura points to Lorca's personal and poetic iconicity, the very thing that draws one in, a luminosity, as though lover to lover, real or not, offering validation in the same way lovers do. A ghost-lover, he attests to his own extraordinary nature, as fabulous as Walt Whitman. In some ways, Spicer's vision of the poet anticipates another gay writer's idea of Lorca, that of Jaime Manrique, in a poem titled "My Night with Federico García Lorca" and in the book *Eminent Maricones.* Born in Colombia, Manrique (1949–) currently lives in New York City and writes in both English and Spanish. *Eminent Maricones,* published in 1999, is a mix of personal essay and memoir, in which the lives and works of Manuel Puig, Reinaldo Arenas, and García Lorca intertwine with Manrique's. David William Foster called it a queer manifesto, even though most of its programmatic content only appears in the last chapter, which serves as a kind of coda. Here, Manrique explains why he chose the title, first, as a homage, however ironic, to Lytton Strachey's *Eminent Victorians.* But more significantly, because its bilingual character "sums up what I am—a bilingual, bicultural writer—and because of the oxymoronic quality it acquires when these two words stand next to each other. *Maricón* is a word used to connote something pejorative; by implication a maricón is a person not to be taken seriously, an object of derision. Without exception, maricón is used as a way to dismiss a gay man as an incomplete and worthless kind of person." His book aims to deconstruct a long-standing negative stereotype.[93]

In that sense, Manrique takes Lorca's conflict-ridden ambivalence in the "Ode" and revalorizes it as something positive by joining "eminent" to *maricón*. Spicer does something similar, though not consistently, at least not for the "Ode," since he is constrained, for the most part, by what Lorca wrote. Manrique's initial view of the Spanish poet's work was not especially favorable. He knew his earlier poetry, notably the *Gypsy Ballads*, and even publicly recited it, but he thought the poems were old-fashioned and tied to conventional rhymes. In Colombia, Lorca, by far, was the most popular choice in poetry performances. His theatricality, Manrique wrote, provided "a safe way of being a drag queen without having to cross-dress." A few years later, he ran across *Poet in New York*. Sparked by Ginsberg's outing of the Spanish writer in his "Supermarket" poem, he returned to the "Ode" with a new sense of who Lorca was and what his poetry meant. "The first time I read [the "Ode"]," he said, "I was shocked by its in-your-face explicitness. Reading it as a forty-year-old man, it was hard for me not to read into it Lorca's internalized homophobia and self-hatred." Lorca's anguish spoke to Manrique intimately, as a gay man in Colombia and then in the States, when the deaths of friends like Manuel Puig and Reinaldo Arenas forced him to wrestle with his own inner demons.[94]

Reexamination of his life, racked by years of drug and alcohol abuse, went along with a new perspective on Lorca. It led, I would argue, to a sense of personal validation, partially fueled by the imaginative power of gay icons—eminent maricones—like Lorca, Puig, and Arenas, to see oneself as exceptional, as a dissenter and visionary, in Manrique's eyes. These attributes appear as the logical outcome of Nin Frías's interpretation, alongside that of others such as Gide, Carpenter, and Retana, of homosexuality as eccentric and anomalous. A dissenter feels or thinks things differently, as its Latin roots indicate (*dis*- [differently] + *sentire* [to feel, think]). The eccentric and the anomalous are deviations from the center and the regular, respectively. Lorca's "strange and equivocal flavor," to recall Nin's expression, begins to take on another coloration, a stamp of approval for being divergent.

In 2013, one Spanish blogger in an anachronistic gesture even coopted the poet on behalf of "the indignant" (*los indignados*), protesting the austerity measures prompted by the 2008 economic crisis. Lorca, too, was indignant, he said, up in arms over fascism, classism, racism, and homophobia. At the height of the movement, a bronze statue of Lorca in Madrid's Plaza Santa Ana sported a poster urging people to be incensed and get involved. The fact that he is depicted, in suit and tie, calmly standing with a dove in his hands, apparently was lost on the protesters. The poet's celebrity at once encourages and justifies the fashioning of such images, made to answer the needs and desires of others. A celebrity is like an emotional Rorschach and can be anything people want him to be.[95]

The evolution of Manrique's thinking is not surprising in this instance, given his life story. He was born illegitimate and mixed-race. His father was already married when he fell in love with Manrique's mother (and eventually abandoned her). The search for recognition runs through the narrative, starting with his birth and extending to his sexual identity. Legitimation of who one is and who one loves strikes me as crucial to *Eminent Maricones*, explaining to a significant degree the presence of Lorca in the book. For that we also need to look at the poem, "My Night with Federico García Lorca," which had appeared a few years earlier and is reproduced in *Eminent Maricones*.

In 1988, Manrique crossed paths with the by then elderly American poet, Edouard Roditi (1910–92), who recounted a one-night stand he had with Lorca in Paris, while the poet was en route to New York in 1929. The poem is a secondhand reelaboration of that encounter, one that had been whispered about for decades. There is some doubt whether the two really met. Maurer and Anderson point out that the day in question had a full itinerary and Fernando de los Ríos accompanied Lorca nearly everywhere. Roditi also said he was introduced to the poet in the painter Gregorio Prieto's Paris studio, but Prieto was in Rome during that period. On the other hand, C. Brian Morris, who consulted Roditi's unpublished memoirs, stresses how deeply etched the experience was in the American writer's psyche. For my purposes, the biographical facts are less important than the emotional truth the poem seeks to convey.[96]

Manrique's poem became "a sort of signature piece," speaking to many gay readers. Significantly, "My Night" is important to *Eminent Maricones* because it drew him back to Lorca, just as Ginsberg's "A Supermarket in California" had earlier. Roditi, who himself had also written poems about the Spanish poet, in remembrance of the love he felt for him and the death that crushed it, acts as a conduit for Manrique to produce a close encounter of the third kind, with Lorca as reanimated creature. The title, which includes the parenthetical "*as told by Edouard Roditi*," points to two voices in the poem, a merging of Roditi and Manrique that seemingly blurs their identities, recalling Spicer's blended voices. Whose night with Federico García Lorca is it really? Biographically, Roditi's, but poetically, it is also Manrique's, as he ventriloquizes the speech of another man's experience.[97]

The style is deliberately prosaic, evoking that of an interviewer who's recorded (and then edited) his subject's words. Manrique, however, subtly modifies the "as told to" technique, making it "as told by," which stresses Roditi's active role as narrator of his own story. The poem begins with:

> It happened in Paris.
> Pepe asked me over to dinner
> to meet a guy named Federico
> who was on his way to New York.

The anecdotal approach brings out the small details you expect from someone's recollection of a memorable, if distant-in-time, experience. It also conforms to the five *w*'s of journalistic writing, corresponding to the who, what, when, where, and why of a story. The title and initial lines answer everything but why. Roditi then goes on to point out the age difference between himself and Lorca, who was eleven years older. He mentions the poet's failed relationship with Emilio Aladrén (referred to as "a sculptor"), "who had been rotten to him," and says he "hated promiscuous queens." "We were both Gemini," he adds, which leads to the supposed why. "Since astrology / was very important to him," he says, "Federico took an interest in me." By the end of the second stanza, readers also know about Roditi's double-minority status as not simply a gay man, but one of Sephardic Jewish origin.[98]

After this set-up, the remaining three stanzas briefly relate what took place that night and afterward. The last one sums up the experience:

> All this happened in Paris
> almost sixty years ago.
> It was just a night of love
> but it has lasted all my life.

The anecdotal, journalistic style lends a kind of material credence to Roditi's story, while the conclusion speaks to the poem's emotional truth as something that "has lasted all my life." Readers, I expect, took home that message as a universal expression of love's endurance. There is more, however, to this poem than its being personally relatable, or validating, for that matter. I was just a blip in Lorca's life, Roditi seems to be saying, but it meant something to me. The fellow he slept with may have been only "a guy named Federico" in 1929, but not in the 1990s. Lorca's fame hangs over the poem and changes the context and meaning correspondingly.[99]

Unlike most poems about Lorca, this one ostensibly focuses more on his private life and very little on his public persona or his symbolic and historical significance. "In the morning," after a night of drinking and sex, Roditi recalled,

> when I woke up,
> his head lay across my nipples.
> Hundreds of people
> have asked me for details:
> Was Federico fabulous in bed?
> I always give them my standard answer:
> Federico was emotional
> and vulnerable; for him,
> the most important thing wasn't sex
> but tenderness.

Manrique, however, undercuts the intimacy of these lines with the question, "Was Federico fabulous in bed?" Why would hundreds of people ask? Clearly, Lorca's celebrity, his mythic status, lies behind such curiosity, the avid interest of the crowd. Roditi's response blocks the obsessive desire to know the hidden emotional life of the poet: "I always give them my standard answer." This is an ironic nonanswer, a tactical device to avoid saying whether he was fabulous in bed or not. How can there be a standard answer when it comes to someone like Lorca?[100]

Manrique's quasi-journalistic style aside, the Colombian-American poet is really saying we cannot know who Lorca was. (Or Roditi, for that matter, who hides behind the same standard answer.) The deceptively prosy quality of the poem functions like a Hitchcockian Macguffin of misdirection, becoming irrelevant in the end, because that's not what the poem is about. It's not about the real Lorca, or the facts of his life (or even of Roditi's experience). The poem is an admission that there is no such thing as the real Lorca, because the myth has overtaken everything else, challenging even the strategy of deconstructing the myth through anecdotal, plain style. The secondhand nature of myths and celebrity is made manifest with the "as told by" technique italicized in the title. This is not a live broadcast of Lorca—*en directo,* in Spanish—a self-evident impossibility in any event, but a voiced reanimation. Which is probably why the poem never talks about his death. Manrique has ended up creating another fiction of the poet, attesting to the fascination Lorca continues to hold. This is as good an example as any of Dos Passos's legend in one's mind becoming the only literary fact of consequence.

The why of the story is never really explained, but it probably doesn't matter. The presence of Federico García Lorca overwhelms everything else, swallowing up reasons, just as it has in so many other ways in the years since his murder. Like Oscar Wilde, his persona has become part of his work for many people, but it also inhabits the writing of others, in an imagined relationship with the poet. "It was just a night of love / but it has lasted all my life." The life referred to is Roditi's, but who is to say it is not Manrique's as well? Miguel de Molina and Jack Spicer saw Lorca as their phantom lover, and they were not alone. The Spanish poet Dionisio Cañas read Manrique's book of poems *My Night with Federico García Lorca* and told him, "I *almost* had a night with Federico: I went to bed with Philip Cummings!" He did so "because it was as close as he could come to being with Lorca," as Cummings, who met the poet in 1928, actually was his lover for a brief moment in time. It isn't just fans fascinated with Lorca.[101]

Not all gay writers have heeded the siren call of Lorca's seductive aura, as Cañas himself has pointed out, most especially in the case of the Puerto Rican poet, Manuel Ramos Otero (1948–90). Ramos Otero took issue with what he perceived as the closeted, conflicted image of homosexuality in the "Ode to Walt Whitman," although, in other ways, as I have argued, the poem is remarkably open. This question arose earlier with Spicer's use of a provocative gay lexicon in his translation of the "Ode," which could be read as an outing of the poem itself. One of the most important figures of the San Francisco Renaissance, Robert Duncan, responded to the "Ode" saying, "I too must be one of those *maricas de las ciudades* Lorca inveighs against, for in my purest moods there will always appear some imp of a sexual jokester, persona of a possible cheerful lewdness. . . . I know your ardor, Garcia Lorca, but it does not burn pure in me, it is ever mixed with life-greediness, an avidity."[102]

Ramos Otero similarly rejected the purity line promoted in Lorca's image of Whitman. "I will be my own, promised man," he said, "when pools of blood dawn / mingled with oblivion and twilight." In response to the section of the "Ode" on clandestine homosexuality, he wrote, "Here I am dressed as a bride." And: "I am the Queer of Creation / and I murder doves to swarm the wind." "You're better dead than alive," he declared to Lorca, so as not to spoil the bacchanal. These lines of Ramos Otero, who lived in New York for half his life and died of AIDS in 1990, reflected a post-Stonewall age, jubilation in this period having given way to sober realism and anguished militancy. Manrique's meditation on his departed friends and fellow writers acknowledged a similar change. "I came to terms with my own internalized homophobia only after Manuel [Puig] and Reinaldo [Arenas] and other close friends died of AIDS. In a way, I can say that it was because of AIDS that I finally learned to love gay men as soul mates."[103]

Like Nin Frías and Spicer, Manrique creates a gay community, this one full of dead souls. Lorca is not only a full-fledged member, but a founder as well. *Eminent Maricones* is a dead poets society, whose afterlife Manrique continues in his book, just as his poem, "My Night with Federico García Lorca," quickens the ghost-lover's spirit that once was Lorca. Roditi's recollection is also tinged with the knowledge that he could only have acquired years after his single encounter with the poet. He mentions, for example, how "the second love / of his life was murdered / defending the Republic," a clear reference to Rafael Rodríguez Rapún, who died in August 1937. Biographical detail—Lorca's rejection of "promiscuous queens," his failed relationship with Aladrén—is meant to put flesh on the dead poet.[104]

More importantly, the poem is infused with the sense and awareness of the posthumous, of the iconic status that Lorca had by then achieved. It would be pointless, or at most a personal exercise of memory, to write about a one-night stand with someone anonymous as lasting an entire lifetime. An enduring remembrance of this kind is made meaningful because of the poet's subsequent image as a gay icon. Fame underwrites the poem, starting with the title itself. With the help of Edouard Roditi, Manrique builds on Lorca's celebrity, by projecting to his readers the very thing that star power dangles before individuals and crowds (those "hundreds of people") alike: the illusion of intimacy, the answer to the question, was Federico fabulous in bed? This is just what adoring gay fans of Álvaro Retana wanted to know as well. Talking about Lorca's imagined prowess in bed reminds us why people needed to believe in the gods of antiquity. When the gods disappeared, so did the marvelous, the Dionysian power to transform the universe. The capacity to make something last your entire life. Lorca not only created Breton's shadow of the marvelous in his work, he inhabited it. What is even more remarkable: he made people believe they could, too.

Postscript

In 1989, a fourteen-year-old schoolboy named Víctor Fernández Puertas wrote a letter to the poet Luis Rosales, in which he described himself as a simple *lorquista*, or Lorca devotee, working on a class assignment. He had just one question for Rosales: "How do you remember your friend, Federico García Lorca?" Fernández Puertas, who hailed from Molvízar, in the province of Granada, also mentioned that his grandfather knew one of Rosales's brothers. Then he recounted how he called up the son of the civil governor at the time of Lorca's arrest and murder, the Falangist José Valdés Guzmán, who played a large role in the brutal repression that terrorized Granada during the war. His son's wife answered the phone but refused to engage in conversation. "Everything they say is a lie," she responded. "His father did not kill García Lorca." And that was that. The letter also included a drawing titled *Lorca in the Mind of Don Luis Rosales*, which imagines an inward-looking Rosales, pen in hand, and Lorca's face looming large in a cartoon bubble (fig. 15). This is a wonderful illustration of Dos Passos's legend, as viewed through the eyes of another.[1]

Rosales, struggling with poor health, did not reply. I came across the letter among the poet's papers in the Archivo Histórico Nacional and wanted to know more. What had prompted this fourteen-year-old schoolboy to write it? Homework doesn't usually motivate adolescents to send letters to distinguished poets. This was, among other things, a fan letter, and doubly so, expressing admiration for both Rosales and Lorca. "There is," he said, "a *je ne sais quoi* that I like in your poetry." You can also spot a budding journalist competing for space with the apprentice Lorca scholar. As it turns out, Fernández Puertas did become a journalist and writer and ended up publishing a good deal on Lorca, especially for the daily newspaper *La Razón*. He has also produced books and editions on Lorca, Dalí, and Picasso.[2]

Figure 15. *Lorca en el pensamiento de Don Luis Rosales.* Drawing by Víctor Fernández Puertas, 11 Mar. 1989, courtesy of Archivo Histórico Nacional, Madrid, and Víctor Fernández Puertas.

Fernández Puertas didn't just write to Rosales or telephone Valdés Guzmán's son. Some, like Ian Gibson, Rafael Alberti, and Pepín Bello, answered, others didn't. "This was the moment," he recalled, "when I first felt a passion for Lorca. I was a kid, looking for extra credit, so I picked Lorca. It got out of hand because I contacted a whole bunch of people." While the abortive interview with Francisco Valdés's wife no doubt appeared impertinent to her, others probably were charmed that a fourteen-year-old would go to such lengths for a school project on the poet. Fifty years after the end of the civil war, Lorca, the poet and man, was still drawing people in, as Fernández Puertas's life-long fascination and love for the Granadine writer illustrate.[3]

Already a *lorquista* at fourteen, he didn't stop at interviews, reportage, or editing correspondence, but, along with Ian Gibson, forensic anthropologist Francisco Etxeberría, lawyer Enrique Ranz, and Luis Avial, an expert in ground penetrating radar, went back to the 1986 account, in which workmen were said to have discovered human remains while completing the Parque Federico García Lorca in Alfacar. After some delays, in December 2018, four

specialists from the University of Granada's Instituto Andaluz de Geofísica
(Andalusian Institute of Geophysics) finally examined the site, using geo-
radar, and came up empty-handed, but the spot they chose appeared not to
correspond to the two areas—the fountain and the perimeter fence—where
an earlier report found indications that something had been buried there.
Accusations of bad faith immediately surfaced. Lorca had gone missing once
again.[4]

Whether this latest investigation is the last opportunity to locate the
poet's bones, as some believe, remains to be seen. Throughout the preparation and writing of this book, which took far longer than I ever anticipated,
I have thought a great deal about Lorca's absent body and why it should
matter so much, as it obviously does to a lot of people. Even those who op-
pose his exhumation do so because it matters. More than anything, I have
wondered what would happen if the relics of his earthly existence were
found. After all the ballyhoo and press coverage, after the dredging up of old
wounds, after everyone had their say and showed up for the ceremonies,
what then? Everyone would pack up their things and go home. And perhaps the aura of the unattainable, signified by Lorca's terrible disappearance,
would as well. Should we then choose to follow the interlocutor's advice in
Baudelaire's "Loss of Halo" and "put up a notice or report the loss to the
commissioner?"

That concern, I think, is premature. Lorca's missing body is seen as
symbolic of far greater losses brought home by civil war that can never be
sufficiently commemorated or conveniently archived in the memory hole of
unwanted history. We think of him as buried beside three other men, a one-
legged schoolteacher and two bullfighter assistants, or *banderilleros,* but in a
larger sense if not in fact, he lies within a vast multitude of the dead, some of
them poets and most of them ordinary people. His dual citizenship in both
communities, that of literature and that of history, is part of what makes him
a world-poet, a poet who speaks posthumously to the crowds following the
parade that have taken up permanent residence with readers and admirers.
This world-making capacity is probably what drew so many to him in life
and after, seeing him initially in the guise of the Poet and the people's poet.
It was a makeshift way of acknowledging not simply his connection to ordinary folk but his ability to make them believe they were part of his world,
that they *were* the world. In death, this same view of Lorca is wrapped up in
the mass graves of history, in the people who sleep beside him.

But the gods themselves are never merely asleep, because they are always dreaming of us. "And you, lovely Walt Whitman," Lorca wrote,

> sleep along the Hudson's banks
> with your beard toward the pole, hands open.
> Soft clay or snow, your tongue calls for
> comrades to keep watch over your unbodied gazelle.

Allen Ginsberg woke him up entirely, asking "Where are we going, Walt Whitman? The doors close in an hour." That's what poets do, they wake up the gods, in their dreaming, and make us remember the shadow of the marvelous in this world. They announce the arrival of the kingdom of grain. This, too, is world-making, and more pointedly, is part of the modern world, expressed in the marvelous as an aesthetics of oddness amid the growing visibility of celebrity culture and homosexuality.[5]

Lorca of course was only mortal, divinely flawed, as was Whitman, whose tongue in the "Ode" speaks as much to his afterlife as to his comrades, because each goes hand in hand. Lorca's "comrades" also keep watch, forming at the same time an invisible cortège responsible for the anecdotes, death notices, and elegies of which Dos Passos spoke. That procession—call it an aura, fame, or celebrity—is "disembodied, triumphant, dead," but announces "what comes after me," wrote Whitman. (What else are his enumerations but an endless cavalcade of things to come?) The American poet is really talking about a kind of fulfillment, his afterlives as a dream of completion. For that, he needed the multitudes, as much as they appeared to need him. Something similar can be said of García Lorca, whose own sense of being unfinished is personal and historic in nature. Writers and ordinary people alike have filled in the missing parts, seeing in him what they wanted to find: in communion with the dead, or with the people, with the great and the gay, or with history itself, to name just a few of Lorca's various afterlives.

This posthumous sequel to the performance of self in life is what we call fame. Fame, however, is not solitary, but actually quite crowded, as I have argued here. A figure like Lorca has both an individual and communal identity, rooted not only in personality but in history and culture. A writer or an artist may be a star yet is always part of a constellation of other stars, some of them older like Marlowe, Zorrilla, and Bécquer and some newer like Pasolini, spread across a vast darkness that sometimes shoots off comets of disruption. Lorca's celebrity must also be viewed as a mass-culture phenomenon and as a product of his time and ours. As a myth of cultural possession, he takes his place in history, even as history itself is hotly contested. The struggle over that place—where and to whom Lorca belongs—has often been personal to those who have a stake in the poet's ultimate significance in the scheme of things. You could say the illusion of intimacy that celebrity fosters also spills over into the domain of history, to judge from the passion with which people seek meaning in Lorca, an ersatz closeness standing in for resurrectional impulses. "How do you remember your friend, Federico García Lorca?," Fernández Puertas asked. Tomaševskij's "literary fact," the biographical legend, is to be found in an entire pantheon of cultural-historical consequence, the individual and collective threads so tightly plaited as to wonder whether or why we ever thought we could fully grasp who Federico García Lorca was.

Notes

Introduction

1. The edition of Spicer's *After Lorca* I have used lacks pagination. My warm thanks to Wan Sonya Tang, Daniel García Donoso, Laurie Lomask, Evelyn Scaramella, Tanya Romero–González, Nicole Mombell, Diego del Río Arrillaga, José Antonio Simonet, José Ramón Sabín Lestayo, Luis Bautista Boned, Veronica Mayer, and Sarah Glenski for their assistance at different points in time in locating some of these materials.

2. Levine, "Search" 31; Molina Fajardo 63 (gray earth).

3. García Lorca, "Juego y teoría" (*OC* 3: 151): "'Todo lo que tiene sonidos negros'"; García Lorca, "Fábula y rueda de los tres amigos" (*OC* 1: 515): "Cuando se hundieron las formas puras / bajo el cri cri de las margaritas / comprendí que me habían asesinado. / Recorrieron los cafés y los cementerios y las iglesias. / Abrieron los toneles y los armarios. / Destrozaron tres esqueletos para arrancar sus dientes de oro. / Ya no me encontraron. / ¿No me encontraron? / No. No me encontraron." Unless otherwise stated, all translations are mine; and articles without pagination are electronic publications. Any italicized quoted material is reproduced from the original source.

4. Gibson, *La fosa de Lorca* 114.

5. García Lorca, "Poética" 485 (Parthenon); García Lorca (in Pinto 268): "Cuando comienzo a corregir las pruebas, experimento la sensación inevitable de la muerte; que el poema ya no vive, que para que viva, debe poseer otra arquitectura, más nervio, mayor claridad, total simplicidad y limpieza." Mario Hernández suggests that Lorca's unwillingness to publish was a myth, "fed, in part, by the poet himself" (Prologue xxi).

6. García Lorca, *Así que pasen cinco años* (*OC* 2: 332, 333). See also Kierkegaard in *Repetition* (1843), who wrote, "what is recollected has been, is repeated backwards, whereas repetition properly so called is recollected forwards" (33).

7. Benjamin, "Work of Art" (aura); "Task" 71.

8. Benjamin, "Task" 71.

9. Braudy, *Frenzy* 592. See Fernández Cifuentes, "La verdad de la vida"; Smith, *Theatre* 105; and Dinverno, "Raising the Dead" 31, 45 for the confusion between Lorca's life and work; also, Bonaddio, "Introduction" 1–15, for the impact of Lorca's personality on the interpretation of his work.

10. Qtd in Junquera.

11. Rothenberg 88, 90 (the ampersand is Rothenberg's); Mayhew, *Apocryphal Lorca* 173, 117.

12. Rothenberg 85–86, 87.

13. Tomaševskij 55, 49 (Byron); Boym 24 (blurred line), 27–29 (cultural myth); see also Kris and Kurz.

14. I am indebted to the work of a long list of fine Lorca scholars and enthusiasts, many appearing in this book, a number of whom have also written about the poet's fame, the reception of his work, and the symbolic weight of his death and person, including María Delgado, Melissa Dinverno, Laura Dolfi, Derek Gagen, Anthony Geist, Ian Gibson, Antonio Gómez López–Quiñones, Jonathan Mayhew, Silvina Schammah Gesser, Christopher Maurer, Antonio Monegal, Christian de Paepe, Stefan Schreckenberg, Paul Julian Smith, Andrés Soria Olmedo, Guillermo de Torre, Sultana Wahnón, Viki Zavales, Andrew Samuel Walsh, and others. For the sake of readability, I have confined most of my references to scholarly and critical work to the endnotes.

15. Ramos Espejo; and Anon., "Fuente Vaqueros conmemora" (commemorations in Fuente Vaqueros). Alberti first came to Granada in 1980 for the annual Lorca observance, where he apparently felt so unwelcome that he walked off in the middle of the ceremony, according to Ian Gibson (Gibson, *Un irlandés* 140).

16. Anon., "Más de 12.000 visitas."

17. Mendelssohn 2–3 (Wilde); Blake 22 (Whitman); Zamostny, "Tórtola Valencia" 311 (Valencia); Valis, "Celebrity" 137 (Retana); see Delgado, *Federico García Lorca* 192–201, for more examples of the branding and commercialization of the Lorca image.

18. Dos Passos 109–10.

19. Dos Passos 110, 108.

20. Dos Passos 109; Schickel viii–ix, 4.

21. Delgado, *Federico García Lorca* 196 (*El Universo de Lorca*) (see also the website; and *El universo de Lorca*, which contains the script and soundtrack of the planetarium program); Prados 4: "La luna lo anda buscando, / rodando, lenta, en el cielo."

22. Pemán, "García Lorca" 3: "No debe ser cosa tan deleznable la poesía, cuando los políticos y gobernantes vivos, con toda la fuerza, a la espalda, de un Estado, tienen que lidiar todavía con los poetas muertos."

23. Whitman, "So Long!" *Complete Poems* 511, 514; Blake xii (*Leaves of Grass*).

24. Noel 98 (exhibitionism), 100: "Quieren ser hombres públicos, domar la esquivez de la fama."

25. Eliot 49.

26. Romacho ("We are all Lorca").

27. Levi 2, 236 (Mozart); Goebbels 259, 260; Vaill 229–31 (Gerda Taro).

28. Alonso Cortés 85.

29. González-Ruano, *Diario íntimo* 445: "porque de cada diez anécdotas que se cuentan de mí, seis o siete son absolutamente apócrifas"; Machado, "Crime" 263 (trans. Alan S. Trueblood); "Crimen" 331: "Se le vio, caminando entre fusiles, / por una calle larga, / salir al campo frío, / aún con estrellas, de la madrugada."

30. Monegal, "Releer" 79, 80.

31. Del Río xxx (*Manhattan Transfer*). See Pollin for more on Lorca's familiarity with the poetry of Walt Whitman; also, Martínez Nadal, *Federico García Lorca* 174. The multiple translations of the "Ode to Walt Whitman" have unquestionably helped create and reinforce Lorca's status as a gay icon (see Walsh 133).

32. See Goldman for the relation between modernism and celebrity; Blake for more on Whitman's obsession with fame; and Fiedler's classic essay, "Images of Walt Whitman," for his fluctuating reputation in the United States.

33. See Braudy's magisterial study, *The Frenzy of Renown*. Nin Frías's imaginary gay community is found in his *Ensayo sobre tres expresiones del espíritu andaluz* (1935).

34. "El *Romancero gitano* de Lorca" (video). Now that Lorca's works have been in the public domain since 2017, projects like this illustrated edition of the *Gypsy Ballads* have been easier to undertake.

1. Why Dead Poets Matter

1. Lerner, *Leaving* 37, 38, 143. "Poetry makes nothing happen" is a line from Auden's "In Memory of W. B. Yeats" (1939) (*Selected Poems* 82). Yet in Lerner's essay *The Hatred of Poetry* (2016), he says, "'poetry' is a word for the meeting place of the private and the public, the internal and the external" (12), though at the same time he appears to question the unifying power of poetry.

2. Harrison 14, 15.

3. Zambrano 63; Eliot 49, 59; Borges, "Kafka y sus precursores" 148: "cada escritor *crea* a sus precursores. Su labor modifica nuestra concepción del pasado, como ha de modificar el futuro." Like Lorca, Antonio Machado also attained national iconic status, especially for his close identification with the Second Republic.

4. Strand 106; Wordsworth, "Upon Epitaphs (I)" 129 and "Upon Epitaphs (III)" 182.

5. Strand 107; Whitman, "O Living Always, Always Dying" (*Complete Poems*) 464; Bécquer, "Enterramientos" 1053 (on Garcilaso): "una época de poesías y combates."

6. See Bowra; and Fussell (World War I); Apollinaire, *"Poet Assassinated"* 66, 68; Cervantes 74: "y no huuo nada" (see also Ayala's commentary, "El túmulo"). Germán Labrador Méndez argues for a return "to a consideration of poetry as a *civil religion*, as a type of language related to civic experience" (243).

7. Monegal, "Releer" and "La verdad" (life-work inseparability); Gibson, *Assassination* 51–54 (Lorca's politics). Gibson, *Asesinato* 309–20, 322–44, reproduces the various left-leaning manifestos and other statements to which Lorca lent his name.

8. Levine, "Poet in New York" 19; see also Laffranque, *Les idées esthétiques* 221–28, who stresses Lorca's sense of solidarity ("the community of mankind") in works like *Poet in New York;* and Predmore. By referring to Lorca as a civic poet in the largest sense of the word, I do not advocate for the politicization of a writer whose complexity cannot be reduced to ideological concerns. In this vein, see Acereda's comments on Antonio Machado.

9. García Lorca, "Nueva York" (*OC* 1: 556): "Los patos y las palomas / y los cerdos y los corderos / ponen sus gotas de sangre / debajo de las multiplicaciones"; "los interminables trenes de leche, / los interminables trenes de sangre / y los trenes de rosas maniatadas / por los comerciantes de perfumes." Von Koppenfels sees *Poet in New York* as the textual attempt "to establish . . . a burial rite" (22).

10. García Lorca, "Nueva York" (*OC* 1: 557): "¿Qué voy a hacer? ¿Ordenar los paisajes? / ¿Ordenar los amores que luego son fotografías, / que luego son pedazos de madera y bocanadas de sangre?"; *OC* 1: 556: "Óxido, fermento, tierra estremecida"; *OC* 1: 555: "que lleva las máquinas a las cataratas"; *OC* 1: 556: "Tierra tú mismo que nadas por los números de la oficina"; *OC* 1: 556: "Yo denuncio a toda la gente / que ignora la otra mitad"; *OC* 1: 557:

"Yo denuncio la conjura / de estas desiertas oficinas / que no radian las agonías, / que borran los programas de la selva."

11. García Lorca, *OC* 1: 557: "y me ofrezco a ser comido por las vacas estrujadas"; Perloff 62 (Rimbaud); García Lorca, *OC* 1: 556: "un mundo de ríos quebrados y distancias inasibles" and "el Hudson se emborracha con aceite"; García Lorca, "The Gypsy Nun" 561 (*Collected Poems*) (trans. Will Kirkland); "La monja gitana" (*OC* 1: 424): "¡Qué ríos puestos de pie / vislumbra su fantasía!"

12. Bowra 4 (Victor Hugo); Pemán, "García Lorca" 3: "un poeta de ideas, de entonación civil y social"; Dué (Athenian democracy).

13. García Lorca, "Oda" (*OC* 1: 567): "Quiero que el aire fuerte de la noche más honda / quite flores y letras del arco donde duermes, / y un niño negro anuncie a los blancos del oro / la llegada del reino de la espiga"; García Lorca, "Rey" (*OC* 1: 520): "Es la sangre que viene, que vendrá / por los tejados y azoteas, por todas partes"; Bowra 17 ("the more personal note").

14. Godwin 47. Matthews observes that in the nineteenth century there was "an effort to restore poetry to its place at the centre of British cultural life" (2).

15. Godwin 141, 140; Weston 657 (moral significance); Westover 307; Schickel (intimacy and celebrity).

16. Spender and Lehmann 13, 7, 8, 9, 10, 13 (see also Rogers 180–84); Serrano Plaja, "Ponencia colectiva" 91 (my thanks to Susanne Zepp-Zwirner for this reference) (Communication 1 May 2019) (see also Meyer-Minnemann et al.); Antonio Aparicio (qtd in Trevor 460). As with *Poems for Spain*, another anthology, *Cancionero de la guerra civil española* (1937), edited by Ildefonso Pereda Valdés, devoted a separate section to Lorca, "El poeta asesinado." The headliner was Machado's poem. Cunningham's Penguin anthology of *Spanish Civil War Verse* also has a small section called "The Crime Was in Granada," including, of course, Machado's text.

17. See Castro, *Versos;* Poeta; and Clúa, *El crimen,* for examples of homage-poems to Lorca; Machado: "con un destino cultural" (qtd in Whiston 51); Iarocci 186 (poetry as action); Whiston 69; Whiston 67 ("witnesses"); also Sánchez Barbudo, *Los poemas* 448–51. See Lecointre, for a discussion of how the crime against Lorca was perceived as "the paradigm of all crimes" during the war (250). Machado's poem is nearly always seen as iconic, but not universally so. See, for example, Aldo Garosci, who also knocked the clichés found in a good number of the homage-poems to Lorca (34–35, 40).

18. Machado, "Crime" 263 (trans. Alan S. Trueblood); "Crimen" 331.

19. Trueblood 265 (in Machado, *Selected Poems*); Whiston 67 (addition of

298 NOTES TO PAGES 39–42

"sabed"). Labrador Méndez calls Lorca and Miguel Hernández "civic representatives of the anonymous collective of the Republican dead" (228).

20. Machado, "Crime" 265; "Crimen" 333: "Se le vio caminar . . . / Labrad, amigos, / de piedra y sueño, en el Alhambra, / un túmulo al poeta, / sobre una fuente donde llore el agua, / y eternamente diga: / el crimen fue en Granada, ¡en su Granada!" Lorca *can* be found outside the Alhambra, in the virtual sense, at Dead Poets Society Memorials: Waymarking, www.waymarking.com/waymarks/WMPPG0_Federico_Garcia_Lorca_Alhambra_Granada_Spain (accessed 12 Mar. 2021).

21. Vidal Corella (in Gibson, *Assassination* 221) (newspaper account): "con magnífica serenidad"; "Allí quedó el poeta insepulto, frente a su Granada" (in Gibson, *La represión* 143). Vidal Corella's piece appeared, under different titles and unsigned, in such publications as *ABC* (Madrid) ("Un testigo presencial"), *Solidaridad Obrera* ("Pasión y muerte"), and *Claridad* (Anon., "El asesinato de García Lorca. 'Allí quedó el poeta insepulto, frente a su Granada.' Relato de un testigo presencial" [17 Sept. 1937: 4]). I have not been able to locate this last-named paper. See also Gibson, *Assassination* 218–23 for more information on this account.

22. Gil-Albert, "La poesía" 488: "una voz serena y entrañable"; "'hecho histórico'"; "Los sobrios versos de Machado patentizaban que aquello que 'parecía mentira' era cierto"; Machado, *La guerra* 323: "la expresión poco estéticamente elaborada de un pensar auténtico"; "implica una acusación a Granada"; Gil-Albert, "La poesía" 488: "intensa precipitación de un destino común"; "precisa lentitud"; "la finura y penetración y esa especie de delirio de la sensibilidad que anteceden a las conmociones históricas y a los más violentos trastornos de los pueblos."

23. Machado's poem was included in *Homenaje a Federico García Lorca, contra su muerte.*

24. Sánchez Barbudo, "La muerte" 392; Alberti, "Palabras" 261.

25. Bergamín, "¿Su muerte?" 112: "Y *el crimen fue en Granada, en su Granada.* La voz de otro poeta, maestro, pudo, por vez primera, precisarnos al sentimiento la verdad temida; la realidad negada, rechazada"; 113: "Te mataron por eso, por ignorarte. Como matan al pueblo. Por ignorarlo . . . Pero esa ignorancia es el peor crimen"; 114 (imagining his death).

26. Garfias 216: "El crimen fue en Granada, / dijo el maestro Antonio"; de Torre 70, 71; Rejano, "Para un aniversario" 20 (later incorporated into his book); Rejano, *El poeta y su pueblo* 11–13 (along with Machado, Miguel Her-

nández's "Elegía" to Lorca is also included [77–82]); Serrano Plaja, "En la muerte" 397. Garfias's poem was reprinted in 1938, alongside two other poems of his, "Guerrilleros" and "Teniente Ruperto Ceballos," in which this latter poem appears to be in dialogue with "A Federico García Lorca" ("Héroes"). For more examples of the presence or echo of Machado's poem in other poetry, see: Rojo León ("Fue en tu Granada") (1962), Romera (who uses Machado's final stanza as an epigraph and includes Machado as a voice in his poem) (1960), Pineda Novo ("En la noche sensual de su Granada") (1996), and Ruiz Amezcua (" . . . En Granada, ¡en su Granada!") (2019); in prose, see: Couffon; and Vázquez Ocaña, for the use of Machado's key phrase as chapter titles.

27. Trevor 460 (Rogers 188, 268 n79 mistakenly attributes the comment to Edgell Rickword); Namorado 488; Ibarbourou 253; Parrot 89–90; Brenan 136; Couffon 59–123.

28. Levine, "Search" 32.

29. Levine, "Search" 31; Wardropper 169.

30. Roncagliolo 13–15, 281–91.

31. Alonso, "La Fuente Grande" 95 (see also Gagen, "'De vivos y de muertos'" 35–36); García Lorca, "Sueño," *Libro de poemas* (*OC* 1: 110); Roncagliolo: "[Amorim] fue el primero que supo de la importancia del cuerpo de Lorca" (qtd in Corroto).

32. Rubio Jiménez, "Un marco"; Carrete Parrondo (elegiac art forms); Motherwell (qtd in Flam 22). Mayhew sees Motherwell's work as the "fossilization of elegy" (*Lorca's Legacy* 112–14).

33. Nancy 110; Pekron 331–32 (*tombeau* revival; Mallarmé); Mallarmé 71–73. In a moving variation on Lorca's missing body, the Portuguese poet Sophia de Mello Breyner Andresen wrote: "E por mais que te escondam não ficas sepultado" (And no matter how much they hide you, you do not stay buried) (28). My thanks to Susanne Zepp-Zwirner for pointing out this reference (Communication 1 May 2019).

34. Bécquer, "Enterramientos" 1054: "¿Había visto, en efecto, el sepulcro de Garcilaso? ¿O era todo una historia forjada en mi mente sobre el tema de un sepulcro cualquiera?"; 1054–55 (paragraph).

35. Rodríguez Alcayna (Garcilaso's remains); González Domínguez (Panteón de Sevillanos Ilustres).

36. For this account, I have relied on Brown; Rubio Jiménez, *La fama;* and Palenque, *La construcción.*

37. Rubio Jiménez, *La fama* 53; Gestoso y Pérez. For the scandal surrounding the portrait, see Palenque, *La construcción* 21–25. *Rimas* VIII and LXXIII were singled out as religiously suspect.

38. Palenque, *La construcción* 12 (myth); Gestoso y Pérez 15, 51 (crowds).

39. Bécquer, *Rimas* 48: "Podrá no haber poetas; pero siempre / habrá poesía"; Durán, *Leyenda* 3: "Et sin haber un poeta / De todos fue su poesia"; 3–4 (oral literature).

40. Anon., "Gustavo Adolfo Bécquer": "Bécquer es nuestro pueblo, artista, y por lo mismo, dichoso y desdichado. . . . Es el poeta. Ninguno concibió como él el tenue claro oscuro del sentimiento, de la frase. Nadie expresó como él esas cosas menudas, *inmensamente* menudas del alma" (reproduced in Palenque, *La construcción* 75–76; orig. *El Liberal* [21 Jan. 1901]); García Lorca, "Paraíso cerrado" (*OC* 3: 80): "La estética genuinamente granadina es la estética del diminutivo, la estética de las cosas diminutas"; 79: "diminutivo asustado como un pájaro, que abre secretas cámaras de sentimiento y revela el más definido matiz de la ciudad. El diminutivo no tiene más misión que la de limitar . . . traer a la habitación y poner en nuestra mano los objetos o ideas de gran perspectiva."

41. Martínez Sierra [7]; Cernuda, "El Poeta" 56; *Bécquer desconocido* (offerings).

42. García Lorca, "*Romancero gitano*" (*OC* 3: 179).

43. Bécquer, "La feria de Sevilla" 1231–33. For more on the relation between Lorca and local culture, see Valis, *The Culture of Cursilería*, chapter 8, "The Culture of Nostalgia, or the Language of Flowers." In 1936, Jesús Escartín would draw parallels between Lorca and Bécquer, as sharing the same "intense philosophical melancholy" (Inglada, *Palabra* 450) (orig. in *Norte: Revista Mensual Ilustrada* [Bilbao] No. 8 [Feb. 1936: 10]).

44. Nemoianu (national literatures and poets); Pemán, "García Lorca" 3. Gillis observes that modern memory is "born not just from the sense of a break with the past, but from an intense awareness of the conflicting representations of the past" (8).

45. Pastor Díaz 15 (Larra's funeral); Palenque, *El poeta* 242; Álvarez Junco 243–46, 386–87 (Zorrilla's values and the Spanish past).

46. Zorrilla de San Martín 1: "Zorrilla es más que un poeta: es el poeta"; "el alma de España"; Anon., "Madrid a Zorrilla" 1: "¡palpitaba el alma del Pueblo y triunfaba el espíritu del Poeta!"; Rodríguez Gutiérrez 183, 185 (Zorrilla as *cantor* of the multitudes); Zorrilla, "Introducción" xvi; Anon., "La última visita" 2 (fifty thousand mourners); Anon., "D. José Zorrilla" 1 (thirty thousand mourners); Anon., "Madrid a Zorrilla" 1 and Anon., "La última visita"

2 (social classes at funeral); Anon., "Madrid a Zorrilla" 1 and Anon., "El entierro de Zorrilla," *El Liberal* 2 (behavior of the crowds). Lorca's first publication, "Fantasía simbólica" (1917), appeared in a homage honoring Zorrilla's centenary (Gibson, *Federico García Lorca* 1: 124–26).

47. Anon., "El entierro de Zorrilla," *El Siglo Futuro* 2 (doctor from heaven); Anon., "Última hora. Zorrilla" 2 (hawking of newspapers); de Navarro 196; Anon., "At Dickens's Funeral"123.

48. See Fernández Almagro 159–70, 176–80 for the historical context; Anon., "Madrid a Zorrilla" 1 (official homage versus the masses); Cavia, "Plato" 2 (San Francisco el Grande).

49. Eneas 1 (Zorrilla as traditionalist); Anon., "El entierro de Zorrilla," *El Siglo Futuro* 2 (Centro Instructivo del Obrero).

50. Anon., "El testamento de Zorrilla" 1.

51. Colvin 328 (theater and garden; "sepulchral farces"); Anon., "Perspectiva teatral" 145–46 (print of pantheon). See Pérez Firmat and Mandrell for the symbolic importance of the pantheon in Zorrilla's play.

52. See Fernández Cifuentes, 304 nB, in his edition of *Don Juan Tenorio*, for more on the use and kind of funerary statuary found in the play; García Rodríguez, *Montpensier* 92 (statues in San Telmo gardens); Márquez Villanueva 63–64 (Blanca de los Ríos); de los Ríos 551. My thanks to José Carlos García Rodríguez for pointing out these references to Blanca de los Ríos and Márquez Villanueva (Communication 27 Aug. 2018).

53. Colvin 283, 296, 331, 374; see also Pereiro Otero.

54. Vico §18, §555.

55. Gazzaniga 21; Pérez Firmat 18, 24; Mandrell 110. Lorca played the part of the Sculptor in a production of *Don Juan Tenorio* at the Residencia de Estudiantes, in Madrid (Gibson, *Federico García Lorca* 1:375).

56. Zorrilla, *Don Juan Tenorio* 110, 112; Pliny 139 (also Braudy, *Frenzy* 198); Pérez Firmat 16–31 (father-son rivalry).

57. Pliny 145; Zorrilla, *Don Juan Tenorio* 114 (portrait of Don Juan).

58. See Valis, "Introducción" to Coronado's *Poesías,* 38–39, for more on the poet's familial paper pantheon; Larra, "El álbum" 330 (also Mandrell 110–11; Valis, *Culture of Cursilería* 91–98); Gómez de la Serna, *Mi tía Carolina;* Gómez de la Serna, "Lo cursi" 38: "panteonizaban sus cosas, las cuidaban de la pulmonía del tiempo"; also Valis, *Culture of Cursilería*, chapter 7, "The Margins of Home: Modernist *Cursilería*." Philippe Ariès observed that from the end of the eighteenth century on, visiting the graves of loved ones "is a private cult, but also from its very origins, a public one" (73).

59. Álvarez Barrientos 42–44. Álvarez Barrientos and Géal provide context for earlier efforts by Martín Sarmiento, Antonio Ponz, Francisco Mariano Nifo, and José I to create various kinds of sculptural spaces and similar projects.

60. Shipman 18; for more on the National Pantheon of 1869, see Fernández de los Ríos, *Guía de Madrid;* Pastor Mateos; Boyd; and Assier.

61. M. Mesonero Romanos, *Goya, Moratín* 6; de Cavia, "Huesos" 31: "No hay en este país profesión más intranquila, incómoda é insegura que la de cadáver ilustre"; Anon., "Parte política" 2 (3 June 1869): "la revolución hecha para los vivos pone en movimiento a los muertos"; Anon., "La sepultura" 14: "abierta por los rojos."

62. Prieto y Prieto 3–4.

63. Prieto y Prieto 4–5: "La revolución francesa puso el Panteon en contacto con el corazon de París; la revolución española pondrá, andando el tiempo, el Panteon en contacto con el palacio de las Córtes, el corazon de la patria, abriendo una calle destinada á que desde el extremo en que ondee sobre el Congreso la bandera nacional, se vea brillar al otro extremo la fama de oro que sobre la cúpula del Panteon pregone la gloria de nuestros grandes hombres." See also Fernández de los Ríos, *Guía de Madrid; Españoles ilustres;* Boyd; and contemporary reportage in *La Época, El Imparcial, La Regeneración,* and *La Iberia.*

64. Anon., "Parte política" (7 and 15 June 1869) (*La Época*); Anon., "El Panteon" 1 (3 June 1869): "la apoteosis de tantos héroes cristianos y buenos católicos" (*La Regeneración*).

65. Anon., "Parte política" 1 (7 June 1869): "El Panteon Nacional es una contradiccion monstruosa en lo presente"; Huet, *Mourning Glory* 132–33 (French Revolution and memory); *La Iberia* (10 and 12 June 1869); also, *La Época* (10 and 12 June 1869).

66. Díaz Viana 75 (liberal romantic tradition); Quinet 670: "un édifice moral, celui de la conscience, de la patrie idéale, de la liberté politique dans le coeur et la maison de chaque homme"; d'Amato 2: xx: "grido di universale redenzione."

67. Fernández de los Ríos, *El futuro* 222: "el apoteosis de la patria en los restos de sus grandes hombres"; 337: "la tolerancia para las grandes figuras que, aunque débiles en algun concepto, hayan servido la dignidad del hombre, y dado ejemplo de lo que mas falta hace glorificar en España: el valor cívico"; Anon., "Panteon Nacional" 1 (21 June 1869).

68. Fernández de los Ríos, *El futuro* 334; Assier (pantheon as imported model;

Chariot of Fame); Díaz Benjumea 201 (feast days); Boyd 38 (political divisiveness); Ozouf 345.

69. Bonet Salamanca 903 (prolonged restoration). By 1911, the only sign of the basilica's earlier role as a pantheon was the inscription on the façade: "Spain to her illustrious sons" ("España a sus preclaros hijos") (Labra, "El Panteón de los doceañistas" 14). For more on the basilica's civil war history, see Montoliú; Bruquetas Galán 211–12; the photos in Argerich and Ara 295–97; and *Las cajas españolas*.

70. Anon., "Consejo de Guerra" 8 (SIM prisoners).

71. Anon., "El Panteón" (14 Nov. 1981); Prieto Pérez 41; Anon., "Las tumbas."

72. For more on the Pantheon, see Pastor Mateos; and Serra; Martínez Olmedilla 7 (Westminster Abbey); Anon., "El Panteón de los Políticos Ilustres" (Prim's remains). Prim's corpse was also submitted to the indignity of not one, but two forensic investigations, in 2012 and 2013, to prove how exactly he died, more specifically whether he was strangled or not, after having been shot multiple times, in a political assassination. The results were inconclusive. See Anon., "El general Prim fue estrangulado" and "El general Prim no murió estrangulado"; García Rodríguez, *Montpensier* 248, 355 n177.

73. Boyd 32, 38; also, Pastor Mateos (Pantheon as partisan); Alpuente (*alpargatas*); Picón (permanence and tranquility). This is not the only pantheon of celebrated individuals in Spain. There is also one in Madrid's Cementerio de San Justo, created by the Asociación de Escritores y Artistas in 1902, where Larra, Espronceda, Gómez de la Serna, Sara Montiel, and others are buried (see Porpetta); as well as more local sites, such as the Panteón de Sevillanos Ilustres, the Panteón de Personas Ilustres (Santander), and the Panteón de Ilustres Granadinos. Not all such enterprises prospered. Republican Rafael M. de Labra tried in vain to establish a pantheon honoring the men responsible for the first modern Spanish constitution produced at the Cortes of Cádiz (1810–12). See Botrel for more examples of pantheons, successful and unsuccessful.

74. Ozouf 333 (civic education); R. Mesonero Romanos, *Recuerdos* 311: "remedo político de la religiosa e histórica abadía de Westminster, verdadero templo de gloria abierto a todas las celebridades de la Gran Bretaña"; Coronado, *Un paseo* 107: "el París de los muertos es acaso el verdadero París"; Coronado, *Un paseo* 125, 126: "Nunca he visto lo ridículo y lo sublime combinados de una manera más extraña" and "una tropa de difuntos que había salido a danzar en el Panteón." By contrast, in an earlier unsigned piece on

the Panthéon (1837), Mesonero Romanos referred admiringly to the echo (10).

75. Gillis 16 ("produce forgetting"); M. Mesonero Romanos, *Las sepulturas* 116.

76. Vico §12, §337.

77. Harrison x; Wordsworth, "Upon Epitaphs (I)" 134; Godwin 98, 104; Quevedo, "Retirado en la paz de estos desiertos . . ." 105: "vivo en conversación con los difuntos, / y escucho con mis ojos a los muertos."

78. Ozouf 327, 328, 330; Carlyle 150; Ruiz Aguilera: "son muertos que viven"; "Más que reyes; fueron hombres" (in *Españoles ilustres* 57, 58).

79. Rejano, *El poeta y su pueblo* 47: "murió . . . para resucitar con su pueblo a la historia, a la inmortalidad"; Pekron 328–29, 343 (Mallarmé).

80. Gil-Albert, "Dos sonetos" 163: "monstruos huyen espantados"; "poetas desolados" and "la gente"; Neruda, "Federico García Lorca" 238: "nosotros, los poetas de América Española y los poetas de España, no olvidaremos ni perdonaremos nunca el asesinato [de Lorca] . . . Nunca"; 238: "el más grande entre nosotros"; 228: "tan atravesado de significaciones" and "todos los que cayeron defendiendo la materia misma de sus cantos" (see also Lecointre 240–41); Lloyd, "Lorca" 72. Ozouf observes, "The great man was both familiar and strange: familiar because he was a man, strange because he was great; given a choice between the two, the eighteenth century preferred to conjure with familiarity" (333) (see also Braudy, *Frenzy* 400–401).

81. Menéndez y Pelayo 276, 280: "eco solemne de la multitud que le escuchaba"; "En otro tiempo había poetas nacionales, poetas de raza, de religión, primeros educadores de su pueblo"; Pala 199 (*poesia civile* tradition); Menéndez y Pelayo 290: "como palestra o circo, henchido de multitud clamorosa, al cual descienden para hacer prueba de sus músculos de atleta"; see also Rodríguez Gutiérrez.

82. Larra, "El día de Difuntos de 1836" 392–99; Harrison 17–36 ("hic jacet") (also Westover 311); García Lorca, "Juego y teoría" (*OC* 3: 156): "Un muerto en España está más vivo como muerto que en ningún sitio del mundo." See also Labrador Méndez, who examines what he calls "an association of *poets of the dead* . . . who are dedicated to preserving the memory of the [civil war] dead by evoking their provisional and inadmissible burial" (236). In 1939, Francisco Ayala wrote a powerful elegy to the anonymous dead of the war, observing: "But all of that is neither mausoleums, nor arches, nor laurels, nor columns, nor gravestones, nor hymns. It is neither marble nor bronze. It is not a pantheon" ("Dialogue" 167) (trans. Carolyn Richmond) ("Pero todo eso no es ni mausoleos, ni arcos, ni laurel, ni columnas, ni lápidas, ni

himnos; no es mármol ni bronce; no es panteón") ("Diálogo de los muertos" 254).

2. Lorca's Grave

1. See Anon., "Cenizas" for more on Ayala's last resting place.
2. Francisco García Lorca 279; Federico García Lorca, "Canción de jinete" (*OC* 1:369): "¡Ay, que la muerte me espera, / antes de llegar a Córdoba"; "está mirando." This poem has always had a great effect on readers. On his deathbed, the modern-day jongleur, Pío Fernández Muriedas, who knew Lorca and had declaimed his poetry, asked a close friend to recite "Rider's Song" to him (Madariaga de la Campa 58).
3. Grass 45, 47; Schneider 141, 143.
4. García Lorca, "Juego y teoría" (*OC* 3:159): "el duende gusta de los bordes del pozo."
5. García Lorca, "Canción de jinete" (*OC* 1:368). Robert Havard calls Lorca a "seeker of signs who is constantly interpreting the primitive, material world . . . every image is an omen . . . everything carries meaning, everything is portentous" (13).
6. García Lorca, "Romance de la luna, luna" (*OC* 1:416); see Sibbald's illuminating commentary on the *zumaya*.
7. Levine, "Search" 31.
8. Levine, "Search" 31.
9. Levine, "Search" 31; Synge 58.
10. Levine, "Poet in New York" 19, 20; Kan (Levine's reaction to Lorca).
11. For more on Cervantes's reburial, see Fraguas; Frayer; Mayordomo (Goytisolo's opinion).
12. See Merino for more details on Quevedo's remains.
13. Morales 461 (orig. in *La Voz* [Madrid] [7 Apr. 1936]): "Mi amistad con Quevedo data de pocos años. Fue un acercamiento melancólico. En un viaje por la Mancha, me detuve en el pueblo de Infantes. La plaza del pueblo, desierta. La Torre de Juan Abad. Y muy cerca, la iglesia oscura. . . . Entré sobrecogido. Y allí estaba Quevedo, solo, enterrado, perpetuando la injusticia de su muerte. Me parecía que acababa de asistir a su entierro"; "Quevedo es España." The notion that Lorca embodied Spain was widespread after his death; see, for example, Larrea, for the case of Argentina.
14. Neruda, *Viajes* 34–35: "yacía ya olvidado para siempre, en una olvidada iglesia de un olvidado pueblo."

15. See Montes Rojas for more on the forensic examination of Neruda's body.

16. C. Rojas, *The Ingenious Gentleman* 68; C. Rojas, *El ingenioso hidalgo* 70: "en el desvelo interminable de [su] propia muerte." For a sampling of the different ways Lorca (and in particular, his death) has been reimagined, see Bardem (*Lorca, muerte de un poeta*) (film); Bonet (graphic novel); Golijov (opera); Hernández and El Torres (graphic novel); Herrick (novel); Manrique, "My Night" (poem); Morrison (*Little Ashes*) (film); Reina (novel); Roffé (novel); Thornton (novel); Vilallonga (novel); and the poetry anthologies of Nelson, Clúa, Poeta, Breda, and Castro.

17. Gibson, *La fosa* 66–67; Ruiz Mantilla, "García Lorca"; Anon., "Federico García Lorca podría"; Anon., "Ultiman un informe"; also, Gibson, *Asesinato* 216–17.

18. Anon., "Es un tema opinable si hay crisis o no hay crisis."

19. Marí 212. See also Paul Julian Smith, "The Lorca Cult" and *Theatre;* and Delgado, *Federico García Lorca,* for Lorca's heavy symbolic presence in the Spanish Transition period to democracy.

20. Marí 213 (Statute), 214 ("universal"); see also Schreckenberg; García Lorca, "*Romancero gitano*" (*OC* 3: 179): "la verdad andaluza y universal"; W. C. Williams 233; Dewey 684, 687.

21. García Lorca, "Juego y teoría" (*OC* 3: 156): "país abierto a la muerte"; Vidal Corella 220–21 (fabricated account). See Gibson, who provides an English translation of Vidal Corella's article, for the impact the piece had in Spain and Latin America (*Assassination* 218–23). Vicente Sáenz helped disseminate it in Latin America. But it also popped up in English-language speeches and publications, such as Langston Hughes's radio broadcast ("Spain's Martyred Poet") and Lloyd Mallan's article, "Granada, Oh! Granada," which appeared on at least three different occasions, once under the title, "Death of a Spanish Poet. A True Story," in *The Daily Clarion,* a newspaper of the Communist Party of Canada; see also Valis, "Lloyd Mallan." Vidal Corella's account was published as well anonymously in *The Volunteer for Liberty,* the organ of the International Brigades ("Death").

22. Emerson 13, 14.

23. Emerson 24, 25, 31, 32, 33.

24. Emerson 38–39; Carlyle 150.

25. Anon., "Picota" (qtd in Díez de Revenga 5) (orig. in *Nuestra Lucha* [30 Aug. 1936]). Robert Pogue Harrison observes that to write constitutes "a gift of the dead to the future," hence "the intrinsically posthumous character of the

literary voice" (14, 15), an echo of Kierkegaard, in *Either / Or* (1843); see also Tambling.

26. Carlyle 134; Bergamín, "La decadencia" 76.

27. See Francisco Rico (qtd in Cruz) ("all the dead"); Romacho ("We are all Lorca" / "todos somos Lorca"); Gibson, "El Estado" ("greatest symbol"); Dinverno, "Raising the Dead" 34,41 ("project," "grieving process," and trauma); Ruiz Mantilla, "Abrir" ("therapeutic"); Garí ("no modernity"), who echoes that "all [the dead] are Lorca" ("todos ellos son Lorca"); also Gibson, "Federico, símbolo de reconciliación."

28. Loureiro, "La vida" 151.

29. See Loureiro, "Pathetic Arguments," who writes that "the very idea of reconciliation with respect to the past is suspect because it assumes an unchanged nation populated by unchanged people" (226).

30. See Dinverno, "Raising the Dead" 32 ("cultural mediation"; and "technology of memory").

31. Marí 216.

32. Loureiro, "Pathetic Arguments" 233.

33. In his memoirs, Moreno Villa titled one chapter, "En presencia de la eterna juventud" ("In the presence of eternal youth"); Alonso, "Una generación" 670; see also Harkema, "'Felices años'" 227–29.

34. Carlyle 233 ("chronic atrophy"); 212 ("galling conditions"); 245 ("waste chaos"). In Spain, José Bergamín was a close reader of Carlyle's essay, making use of the Man of Letters notion in his "La decadencia del analfabetismo" in order to critique the excesses of turning culture into literature (68–69).

35. García Lorca, "Niña ahogada en el pozo" (*OC* 1:544–45): "agua que no desemboca," "estatuas [que] sufren por los ojos con la oscuridad de los ataúdes"; see Valis, *Culture of Cursilería* 172–74, for more on the *corona poética* tradition.

36. Valis, *Culture of Cursilería* 172–76; *Corona poética;* Coronado, "Tú pensaste que el mar era tu cuna," *Poesías* 119: "En un álbum poético para una niña que se ahogó en el mar."

37. García Lorca, "Niña ahogada" (*OC* 1:544): "Tranquila en mi recuerdo, astro, círculo, meta, / lloras por las orillas de un ojo de caballo. / . . . que no desemboca"; Wordsworth, "Preface" 68.

38. García Lorca, "Niña ahogada" (*OC* 1:544–45): "tú lates para siempre definida en tu anillo / . . . que no desemboca"; "No, que no desemboca. Agua fija en un punto, / respirando con todos sus violines sin cuerdas / en la

escala de las heridas y los edificios deshabitados. / ¡Agua que no desemboca!"

39. García Lorca, "Niña ahogada" (*OC* 1:544): "¡Levántate del agua!"; 545: "Pero el pozo te alarga manecitas de musgo"; 544: "¡Cada punto de luz te dará una cadena!"

40. Carlyle 237, 238.

41. Sánchez Barbudo, "La muerte" 391: "encanallado y enfático," "escritores lamentables, esos envilecidos 'cantores' de Franco," "pomposo, lumínico, tristemente barroco," "frases grandilocuentes y retóricas, [que] ocultan una actitud grosera, pedante," "señorial," "que es sólo cursilería, cursilería y zafiedad"; 392: "No cabe pensar en una coincidencia casual; el momento escogido y el tono empleado no dejan lugar a dudas: el verso es de Antonio Machado y precisamente del sentido y bello poema que éste dedicó a Federico al enterarse de su muerte. Es un lamento, es una maldición a los asesinos; pero los asesinos cogen estas palabras de dolor auténtico, este verso del célebre poeta, y lo utilizan sin remordimientos. Porque necesitan ahora fingir dolor para que los crean buenos y sensibles. Pero no nos engañan, no engañan a nadie, sus lágrimas de cocodrilo."

42. Sánchez Barbudo, "La muerte" 392: "Los que nos angustiamos de verdad con la muerte del poeta, sus amigos, compañeros y discípulos, el pueblo entero, los que queremos de verdad Patria, Pan y Justicia para todos, sabemos claramente qué crímenes y qué ultrajes pueden esperarse de esa Falange, de ese Ejército y de esa España negra, vestida de luces, que ha asesinado a Federico García Lorca." Accusations of criminality appeared in the writings of both sides. See, for example, Fernández Almagro, "Genealogía" (in Gibson, *El hombre que detuvo* 217–21 [orig. *La Vanguardia* (Barcelona) (6 May 1939)]: 3).

43. Machado (qtd in *Intellectuals* 27).

44. González Carbalho 74: "era lo más selecto del alma y de la inteligencia del pueblo"; Anon., "Se confirma el asesinato" 7 (Republican martyr trope); Delgado, "Memory, Silence" 185 ("luminous Christ-like"); Smith, *Theatre* 112 (Bardem scene). See Medina 44–46, for González Carbalho's friendship with Lorca. On the image of martyrdom: in 2004, Benjamín Prado, for example, argued for Lorca's exhumation as a way to counter "that bitter and unjust amnesia [the result of amnesty and the political pact of the Transition], owing to the strong symbolic character that the figure of Lorca possesses, as an emblem of all the martyrs of fascism in Spain." Even before the poet's death was confirmed, the martyr trope was in the air, as the title of

Joaquín Béjar's piece suggests: "¿Un mártir más? F. García Lorca" (2 Sept. 1936).

45. González Carbalho 14: "desdichadamente cierta, ha tenido algo de fantasmal," "ante todo, estará su muerte, más de recordarse que su obra misma porque su muerte es el documento tremendo de un momento histórico."

46. González Carbalho 15, 77: "un mártir de los funestos señores," "mártir de la guerra civil"; 81: "hasta su muerte es fecunda. Ya muerto y hundido en la tierra para que su materia se haga ceniza, su sangre ha empezado a correr como un río subterráneo, abre canales por los que circulará la pasión generosa de este hombre nuevo que se pretendió aniquilar. Y los campos de España se llenarán de trigo." Some of González Carbalho's religious spirit is evident in this last passage; see Requeni 11.

47. Another classic, and influential, example of this approach is Arturo Barea's *Lorca: The Poet and His People* (1944; 1949); see Zavales, chapter 3, for more information.

48. Rejano 18: "convocaron a la muerte oscura y sórdida, quienes habían vivido odiando lo que Federico amaba entrañablemente: lo popular," "pueblo y poeta eran una misma voz"; 23: "ensangrentado símbolo espiritual enlazado, para salvarse y salvar los verdaderos destinos del hombre"; 27: "García Lorca murió a manos de los enemigos del pueblo, para resucitar con su pueblo a la historia, a la inmortalidad."

49. Rejano 40: "un abismo de abyección"; 73 ("clandestine resistance"); 75–76: "¿Conmemorar? No, no basta con el recuerdo. No basta con reanimar en un instante la sombra de García Lorca—la sombra de tantos que cayeron—, y luego darnos al olvido. La sombra que convocamos ahora ha de ser cuerpo vivo, imagen real, la imagen del cuerpo de España . . . que nos quiere apretados en un clamor, en un solo combate, para salvarse y salvarnos." As we read in *El poeta y su pueblo*, Rejano ceded "his author rights so that the sale of copies is to go entirely to the aid of the heroic patriots who are fighting inside Spain against the Franco regime." This was not the first time Rejano commemorated Lorca's death. In 1940, he was scheduled to deliver a radio talk on the subject in Mexico City, but the station preferred he not mention the poet's death, so he withdrew ("Para un aniversario" 20). Indeed, he steadfastly marked Lorca's death year after year ("García Lorca" 36).

50. Rejano 17 ("lack of information"); Pemán, "García Lorca" 3: "Es peligrosa la transformación, tan rápida, en 'mito público' de una personalidad tan 'privada'"; for more on the proliferating mythification of Lorca, see Marí 215; and Paepe, "F. García Lorca" 80.

51. Gibson, *La fosa* 14: "es un documento obsesivo"; 9: "No fue mi intención publicar esta crónica, pero he llegado a creer que es mi obligación hacerlo."

52. Qtd in Gibson, *La fosa* 102 ("not an historian"); 163 ("can of tuna fish"). The Executive Vice-president of the conservative party, Partido Popular (PP), Antonio Ayllón, declared that the excavation had been carried out by "the economic interests of some Hispanists and historians who do not deserve to be in Granada, despite calling themselves Lorca experts" ("El PP pide").

53. Bejarano: "delirios de Gibson"; "su fanatismo lorquiano de converso, a quien unos malos vientos irlandeses trajeron a España para encontrarse con el izquierdismo de salón y usurpar un puesto de historiador. Líbrenos el destino de los conversos, líbrenos de quienes hacen ideología hasta del Santísimo Sacramento del Altar"; "el temor de que se encontraran los restos de García Lorca para convertirlos en reliquias laicistas y pasearlas como símbolo de anticuadas ideas políticas resucitadas nos había causado el rechazo por un poeta que no representa más que a la buena poesía. . . . Había dejado de interesarnos el Lorca parcial y empequeñecido en manos de analfabetos funcionales con cargos públicos. '¡Lorca es de los nuestros!,' se atrevió a gritar en el Parlamento andaluz, cuando fue citado por la oposición, una consejera de la Junta"; "perros de la política escarbando en la tierra para comerse sus huesos."

54. Soria Olmedo, "Lorca en Víznar"; the remaining opinions are taken from Juan Cruz, "García Lorca es todos los muertos."

55. Marías, "El folklore": "La 'indigna' sepultura de Lorca es un recordatorio necesario de la indigna muerte que sufrió, y no respetarla sería, a la larga, poco menos que 'blanquear' a sus verdugos"; "¿ . . . es que están en contra de la 'memoria histórica' y de que el poeta 'que es de todos' (otra cursilería, por cierto, amén de otra falsedad: sus versos están al alcance de cualquiera, pero no tienen por qué estarlo sus huesos) sea sepultado con honores?"

56. J. Anderson 48.

57. Reyes Mate (qtd in Rodríguez Marcos).

58. Valis, "When the Dead" 710; Kolbert 70 ("in this village").

59. Gibson, *La fosa* 62: "¿Querría el poeta que le buscasen? Creo que sí, y a todos los demás. ¿Preferiría ser un eterno desaparecido? Creo que no. ¿Le daría igual? Creo que no. ¿Han planteado alguna vez el asunto desde esta perspectiva sus herederos? Parece que la respuesta es negativa."

60. Bagaría, "Diálogos" 637: "Es tan trágicamente doloroso el desaparecer para siempre. . . . En el trágico fin, sólo desearía una perduración: que mi cuerpo

fuera enterrado en una huerta; que, por lo menos, mi más allá fuese un más allá de abono." The last interview with Lorca, conducted shortly before his fatal journey to Granada, was posthumously printed. Antonio Otero Seco's piece appeared in *Mundo Gráfico* (24 Feb. 1937); see Otero Seco, *Écrits*.

61. On the treatment of Lorca as a secular relic, see Marías, "El folklore"; and Bejarano, who politicizes the image.

62. Emerson 33.

63. *Historia de una familia*, by Caballero Pérez and Góngora Ayala, provides dense documentation of the conflictive atmosphere in Granada that surrounded the life of the poet's father.

64. Caballero Pérez 184 (Benavides Benavides).

65. Caballero Pérez 186–87 (Benavides); 190 (Salvaorillo); 177 (Ajenjo Moreno); 196–97, 204, 206 (Correa Carrasco, Rodríguez García). According to Caballero Pérez, there was "an order from Captain Nestares in which he indicated that the forces of Falange Española were obliged to participate in the firing squads" (171). Others who played a role in the poet's death and who belonged to Falange were Federico Martín Lagos, who participated in the arrest; Rafael Martínez Fajardo, among those who transferred Lorca to Víznar; and José María Nestares, in charge of the Víznar front and a man of great charisma by all accounts, who considered Lorca's execution a "despicable act" (*canallada*) (Molina Fajardo 337; and Caballero Pérez 149).

66. Caballero Pérez 168,171–72 (González Aurioles).

67. Police and civil guards in the civil government worked with the assault guards, compiling "lists of persons to be eliminated" and forming "'black squads' to help in this task of elimination of fellow citizens" (Caballero Pérez 146; see also Gibson, chapter 7: "The Repression," *Assassination*).

68. Caballero Pérez 215 ("refined or cultivated individuals"); 194 (Jiménez Cascales).

69. Muñoz Molina, "Burocracia" ("administrative report"); Molina Fajardo 234 ("Federico died"); Caballero Pérez 111–12 (Trescastro; Roldáns; "those responsible"). There is also a connection between Ruiz Alonso and the Roldán family: "the patriarch of the Roldán family . . . was Alejandro Roldán Benavides, a shareholder of the publisher of the daily *Ideal*, the Editorial Católica, where Ruiz Alonso worked" (Caballero Pérez 88).

70. Muñoz Molina, "Burocracia": "agrandar las sombras de sus asesinos, incluso los espacios físicos que constituyeron el escenario simbólico de la tragedia." On Lorca's death, he writes: "And the poet, petrified with fear, understanding little by little that in this place without relief and among these faces, both

known and ordinary, filled with contempt and petty hatred, with likely sarcasm for the vulnerability of a celebrated compatriot, now humiliated—*who does he think he is*—was living the last hours of his life" ("Burocracia").

71. Caballero Pérez 216 (registry); 217 ("olive trees").

72. López and Chirino; also, Gibson, *Asesinato* 221–23, 299. For the latest attempt to find Lorca's remains, this one in 2018 and stemming from the workmens' story, see Camacho; Cappa; and Rodríguez.

3. The People's Poet and the Right

1. Stainton 425–26 ("anarchist-communist"); Gibson, *Asesinato* 38, noted that Lorca especially disliked being pressured to join the Spanish Communist Party. Opting for discretion, the poet also asked his good friend, Adolfo Salazar, to surreptitiously remove an answer on communism and fascism from his written responses to an interview with Luis Bagaría (letter dated early June 1936) (see *Epistolario* 823–24; also, Gibson, *Asesinato* 40–41). See Dennis 170–89, for an overview of Lorca's political views and the political context of his time.

2. See Gibson's classic study, *The Assassination of García Lorca*, for these and other details of the poet's death; also, Caballero Pérez, for the identification of the firing squad as filled with Assault Guards (chapter 9) and the role of Velasco Simarro (chapter 2).

3. Merry del Val 368. For more on the Nationalist reaction to Lorca's death, see Gibson, *Assassination*, chapter 14; K. Schwartz 569; Dolfi. Rumors about the deaths of various intellectuals and writers circulated on both sides. Vicente Sáenz, for example, mistakenly reported that Republicans José María Morón, Enrique Azcoaga, and José Rial had all been killed (355).

4. Hurtado's piece was reprinted in *Antorcha* (Antequera) No. 16 (28 Mar. 1937); *La Falange* (Segovia) 2, No. 24 (2 Apr. 1937), 3; *Arriba España* (Pamplona) (2 Apr. 1937) (titled "Duelo por Federico García Lorca"); and *Voz de las CONS* (5 Apr. 1937), 4 (CONS stands for Central Obrera Nacional Sindicalista, a Falangist organization for the working classes); also reproduced in Gibson, *Asesinato* 262–64; Hurtado: "Tú hubieras sido su mejor poeta, porque tus sentimientos eran los de Falange. Querías Patria, Pan y Justicia para todos." "Country, Bread, and Justice" was a Falangist slogan originally coined by *jonsista* Ramiro Ledesma Ramos (Ximénez de Sandoval, *José Antonio* 140 n1; Payne, *Fascism in Spain* 100).

5. Sánchez Barbudo, "La muerte" 392.

6. Sánchez Barbudo, "La muerte" 392: "No son puñales los que entraron en su cuerpo, fueron sólo los violines de la gloria"; Ximénez de Sandoval, *Camisa azul* 42: "con seriedad religiosa la transformación del cadáver en la figura de un héroe."

7. Sánchez Barbudo, "La muerte" 392: "[un] absoluto desconocido para los verdaderos e íntimos amigos del poeta"; Hurtado: "Mi peregrinación era como un homenaje a tu muerte." Nelson, "Literature as Cultural Studies" 91, also notes how often American poets spoke directly to Lorca in elegies dedicated to his memory.

8. Paepe 242–43; and COA-477 and -478, FFGL [Fundación Federico García Lorca] (Hurtado letters); Fernández (inscribed books); I. García Lorca 182–83; Sánchez Estevan 269, 284, 332 (Hurtado family) (see also Anon., "El actor Luis Hurtado" 67); "Don Luis Hurtado Álvarez" (Esquela) 95; Castro Jiménez; Fernández (Benavente introduction). In 1961, Hurtado Álvarez's father, Luis Hurtado Girón, a beneficiary of Benavente's estate, ended up in a lawsuit with the playwright's daughter, Rosario Benavente Martín, over the inheritance (Anon, "¿Cuánto vale la obra de Benavente?" 66).

9. *Falange Auténtica* (18 Oct. 2008); Fernández (whereabouts of Hurtado); Sabugo Gallego 11–12, 173.

10. Molina Fajardo 478: "conceptos injuriosos por su autor Luis Hurtado Álvarez contra los autores del asesinato de un poeta anónimo."

11. The army did not shoot Lorca, though there is strong evidence to suggest that General Queipo de Llano also played a role in his murder.

12. Villena: "A Federico García Lorca, en la inmortalidad Imperial de su paraíso difícil" (reprinted in García de Tuñón Aza, *José Antonio* 67–69).

13. Villena 67: "Fue, Federico, una tarde de agosto cuando nos hablaron de tu marcha."

14. Villena 68: "el poeta se ha ido, pero nos ha dejado la semilla con la que otros poetas moverán a nuestra joven Patria"; "Nuestro primer poeta Imperial que marche delante marcando la ruta de nuestra épica azul, que para la primavera tenemos que tener soldados que sean poetas con espadas"; Valis, *Sacred Realism* 203, for seed imagery.

15. See Cano Ballesta 27–38 on the Falangist imagery of empire; Albert 423 on the Falangist rhetoric of the soldier/poet; Sáenz 354 (Lorca as hero); Roa 42: "cayó verticalmente, como un soldado genuino de la libertad, sellando con su sangre pura la santidad revolucionaria de la causa antifascista"; Ríos Carratalá, *Una arrolladora simpatía* 20 (second lieutenants) and also Escobar

97 on requests for Lorca's repertory among Carlist *requetés;* Ortiz Lozano (Zurita); Martín 139–40 (imitations); Clariana 283 (Giménez Caballero); Foxá, *Madrid* (1938) 141; Ximénez de Sandoval, *Camisa azul* 179–90; Paepe 188, 506, for Foxá and Ximénez de Sandoval's friendship with Lorca (Lorca's copy of Foxá's *El toro, la muerte y el agua* [1936] is inscribed: "For Federico, Premier Poet, in love with Spain, with admiration, Agustín" [Paepe and Fernández–Montesinos 64]). See also Martín 139, 143 n23 ("Romance de la luna"), who cites from a religious poem titled "Por aquel huerto de olivas," attributed to José María de Iruna and published in *Fotos* No. 5 (27 Mar. 1937), which I have not been able to see. Evidently the same poem, with the title "Las cruces de los cordeles," written by P. Iglesias Caballero, appeared before the war in *Blanco y Negro* (5 Apr. 1936). In any event, the poem is modeled on Lorca's "Romance de la luna, luna" and was reproduced in a publication whose early numbers were Falangist-oriented (*Fotos*). Years later, Franco's grandson went so far as to claim that the impromptu recitals of Lorca's verses at private gatherings of the dictator proved such activities were not prohibited during the regime (Franco Martínez-Bordiú 141).

16. Primo de Rivera, "Discurso de la fundación": "A los pueblos no los han movido nunca más que los poetas, y ¡ay del que no sepa levantar, frente a la poesía que destruye, la poesía que promete!"

17. Ortiz Lozano; García de Tuñón Aza, *José Antonio* 64–66; Alcocer 118. Gibson, however, is highly skeptical of the supposed Lorca-Primo de Rivera friendship (*En busca de José Antonio* 214–21); see also Ximénez de Sandoval, *José Antonio* 349, 427. The latest effort to draw Lorca and Primo de Rivera together—Cotta's *Rosas de plomo*—is long on rhetoric and speculation, but short on facts.

18. Burgos, "Balada" 172–75 and Serna 177–78 ("the Absent One"); Payne, *Fascism in Spain* 106 ("present"); Ximénez de Sandoval, *Camisa azul* 396; García Serrano 506–8 (also Ximénez de Sandoval, *José Antonio* 515–20); Payne, *España* 323 (mythification of José Antonio); Molina Fajardo 497–98 (Lorca family lawyer). Ximénez de Sandoval, *José Antonio* 517–18, says the Republicans silenced the news of Primo de Rivera's death, remarking that all sorts of contradictory notices did, however, reach the Nationalist zone. The Republican newspaper *El Día* (Alicante) reported his death sentence (reprinted in *Dolor y memoria* 293–94), and very brief statements of the execution, though apparently no detailed account, subsequently appeared in the Republican press ("¡¡José Antonio!!" 293–94; and "Comentario" 319–20).

19. Primo de Rivera, "Discurso sobre la revolución española": "Hace unos días

recordaba yo ante una concurrencia pequeña un verso romántico: 'No quiero el Paraíso, sino el descanso' . . . es cierto, el Paraíso no es el descanso. El Paraíso está contra el descanso. En el Paraíso no se puede estar tendido; se está verticalmente como los ángeles. Pues bien: nosotros, que ya hemos llevado al camino del Paraíso las vidas de nuestros mejores, queremos un Paraíso difícil, erecto, implacable; un Paraíso donde no se descanse nunca y que tenga, junto a las jambas de las puertas, ángeles con espadas"; Yzurdiaga Lorca 12: "estar en pie"; "adoptar ante la vida y los peligros de la vida, la postura vertical, rígida, vigilante." "I want no paradise, but rest," to which Primo de Rivera alludes, is from Byron's *The Giaour* (1813) (389). Did he find it there, or as quoted in Alarcón's novel, *El escándalo* (1875) (2: 270)?

20. Ximénez de Sandoval, *Camisa azul* 390 (Orphic figure); see also Albert 418–19.
21. Jordana Fuentes 241 (SEU); Merry del Val 368; Anon., "Un caracterizado fascista granadino" 5: "'¡Bah, bah, no se ha perdido nada!'" (Pemán reaction).
22. Wahnón 411–13, 417–18 (Falangist enmity); Holguín 105–7 (*Fuenteovejuna*); Giménez Caballero, "Decadencia" 15 (also Foxá, "Homeros" 4); Pemán, *Bestia* 917.
23. Aparicio 9: "ciertos romancillos folklóricos, exangües y agitanados"; "las naderías sin crisma y sin alma"; "la teoría mendaz y traidora de la deshumanización del arte." Aparicio's prologue appeared in the 2nd edition of *Altura* (1939), from which I also cite Castroviejo's poems.
24. See Aparicio 10–11; García de Tuñón Aza, "Castroviejo"; also, Estévez 46, who sees Castroviejo as leaning traditionalist.
25. Castroviejo, "Paso firme" 39: "España es una fuente donde abrevan cadáveres"; "Paso firme" 40: "Pero en cielos de bronce nada impedir podrá / vuestra locura santa ganada metro a metro, / entre coros gigantes de altivos tercos muertos, / que ordenan y que ordenan . . . ¡es preciso, es preciso!"; "la muerte dicta sus profundos poemas." Franco himself used rhetoric like "con paso firme y seguro" or "con paso firme" (see Franco, "El mensaje de Franco" and "Discurso de Unificación"; also Anon., "17N" for current-day Falangist use of the term, in commemorating José Antonio's death). The phrase "es preciso" also appeared in fellow Falangist (and Galician) Álvaro Cunqueiro. "Paso firme" is among the very few non-Republican homages to Lorca (Ridruejo, Entrambasaguas) included in Eduardo Castro's excellent anthology and speaks to the paucity of such texts.
26. Castroviejo, "Paso firme" 40: "La sangre escribe en diedros un futuro de hermanos" (a "diedro" is an angle at which the port and starboard sides of

an airplane are inclined upwards: a clear war reference here); Castroviejo, "El último hermano" 37: "Era el hermano. El hermano que quedaba / con su valor inmenso y su firmeza de roca en flor sobre la tierra. / Era aquel hermano que estaba tan dentro de nosotros / que siempre nos creíamos fuera de él, / era el hermano ¡y ahora ya no es! / No es hermano, ni sangre, ni huesos, ni pelo, ni dedos nuestros ya"; "¡Que nadie pretenda engañar a su hermano muerto!"

27. Anon., "Recuerdo y homenaje" 8, and García de Tuñón Aza, "Castroviejo" (Bolíbar Sequeiros) (Castroviejo was married to María Francisca Bolíbar Sequeiros); García Serrano 470–73 ("comrade"); García Lorca (in Bagaría 468). An incomplete version of "El último hermano" is reprinted in Santonja and in Castro: the last twenty-four lines of the poem are missing in both anthologies, with the final three stanzas of "Paso firme" additionally attached to the poem, in Santonja. My most sincere thanks to Eduardo Castro and Manuel Antonio Estévez for their invaluable help in clearing up the publishing history of this poem.

28. See Benjamin, "Work of Art" 241–42; also, Caudet, "Aproximación" 160; Rodríguez Puértolas, "Fascismo y poesía"; and Albert 358–60.

29. García (qtd in Anon., "Romero Murube"): "creo que si *Siete romances* llega a manos de la censura militar, directamente lo fusilan"; Romero Murube: "¡A ti, en Vizna[r], cerca de la fuente grande, hecho ya tierra y rumor de agua eterna y oculta!" See García and Martínez for more details on the Romero Murube–Lorca relationship, and Paepe 433–34, for correspondence from Romero Murube to Lorca; Trapiello, *Las armas y las letras* 582, suggests Romero Murube may have gone at Franco's request to investigate the poet's death. We know that the Generalissimo sent agents to Granada for that purpose, but they found out nothing evidently and appeared uninterested in any event (Penón 545–46). Penón also notes that a military man, Emilio Moreno Olmedo, carried out a secret inquiry in October 1936; he too knew Lorca (543–45; also, Pozo 193). And Giménez Caballero says he went sometime during the war, accompanied by his wife, Colonel Víctor Martínez Simancas, and Luis Rosales, to investigate the poet's death in Granada ("Lorca" 166).

30. Romero Murube, "Romance" 47: "Por el asfalto resbalan / serpientes de verde sangre"; García Lorca, "Reyerta" (*OC* 1: 419): "Sangre resbalada gime / muda canción de serpiente"; Romero Murube, "Romance" 48: "Y en todo el mundo la prensa / llevará con gran detalle / a los hogares honrados / cinco columnas de sangre"; Albert 414 (five red roses); Ximénez de

Sandoval 42 (*Camisa azul*). "Romance del crimen" is reprinted in Clúa. It first appeared with the title "Las aleluyas del crimen" in *Mediodía: Revista de Sevilla* (14 Feb. 1929) (García and Martínez 12–13).

31. Romero Murube, "No te olvides" (65; reprinted in García and Martínez 27–28; see also García de Tuñón, "Romero Murube"): "No te olvides, hermano, que ha existido un agosto / en que hasta las adelfas se han tornado de sangre" ("agosto" also means "harvest"); García and Martínez 28 n21 ("España"), also Caudet, "Aproximación" 165, for Nationalist use of "España." See Santonja's fine anthology for more examples of non-sectarian civil war poetry. Romero Murube also wrote a sonnet, "A un amigo muerto," in memory of Lorca (*Canción del amante andaluz* [1941], in *Verso y prosa* 88). The poem is dedicated to Alfonso García Valdecasas, a Republican turned Falangist, who accompanied him to Granada in August 1936 (García and Martínez 25).

32. I have relied on Ríos Carratalá's excellent study of Neville, for these details. See also Burguera Nadal; and Espín.

33. Ríos Carratalá, *Una arrolladora simpatía* 61, 72, 94, 124; also, Ayala 223 (diplomatic corps).

34. Neville, "La obra de Federico" 4. "La obra de Federico" was reprinted in *Las terceras de ABC*. See also Ríos Carratalá, *Una arrolladora simpatía* 31–35; and Dinverno, "Raising the Dead" 32–33.

35. Neville, "La obra de Federico" 4: "La idea del monumento a los caídos de ambos lados es una idea noble"; Anon., "Trapiello" and Ríos Carratalá, *Una arrolladora simpatía* 33–34. Neville says it was Antonio Machado's wish that Lorca be reburied in the Alhambra, which appears to reflect the final lines of "El crimen fue en Granada" (not quoted in the article).

36. See Ríos Carratalá, *Una arrolladora simpatía* 34, for criticism by Neville's friends, including Rafael García Serrano, of his dream of reconciliation (also Gibson, *Asesinato* 287); Trapiello, "Causa general"; Neville (in Trapiello, *Las armas y las letras* 569): "unos cuantos miserables cuyo nivel intelectual era lo bastante elevado para saber el valor de su presa y su total inocencia e inocuidad política"; "llena de ideas, de belleza y de bondad." Neville's letter, which he addressed to the journalist Miguel Pérez Ferrero, is printed in its entirety in Trapiello, *Las armas y las letras* 569.

37. Neville, "La obra de Federico" 4: "error de dejarse arrebatar la bandera de su cadáver por gentes que no eran ni amigos del poeta"; Neville, "García Lorca" 815: "insensatez de dejarse arrebatar la bandera de su cadáver por los enemigos del movimiento, por gentes que no eran amigos del poeta."

Ruiz-Castillo, "Preámbulo del editor" xiii, observes that Neville was personally involved in the preparation of his *Obras selectas*. The changes Neville made in "García Lorca" could only have come from him. For example, he modified the date of his last encounter with Lorca from the 15th to either the 15th or 16th July 1936 (Lorca, however, left Madrid on the 13th; see Gibson, *A Life* 444). He added another line to what the goatherd told him, when asked where Lorca might be buried. He talked as well about being unable to respond to an article by García Serrano. Giménez Caballero, by then Spain's ambassador to Paraguay, who was still whipping up the misbegotten image of Lorca as a Falangist martyr in 1966, alluded approvingly to Neville's *ABC* article ("Conmemoración" 473) (orig. publ. in *La Tribuna* [Asunción] [4 Dec. 1966: 7, 11]). (Giménez Caballero appeared to have forgotten his own earlier, acidic comments on the decadence of vanguard writers.)

38. Neville, "García Lorca" 816: "al final de la guerra se hizo todo lo posible por procesar, juzgar y castigar a los criminales, mientras que la muerte de Federico sigue totalmente impune, y éste es el hecho diferencial que yo deploro, no por espíritu de venganza, pues han pasado muchos años, sino porque me hiere lo que pueda parecer cerrar los ojos, que es casi como hacer causa común con los culpables."

39. Neville, "Su último paisaje" 37: "Y hoy, Federico amigo, / al pasar por Granada, / he querido seguir ese camino / por donde tus verdugos te llevaran / en aquel espantoso último día, / tu postrer madrugada."

40. Neville, "Su último paisaje" 38–39: "una sangre vertida y ocultada / por silencios cobardes campesinos, / de esos testigos, 'que no saben nada'"; "Víznar 'la callada'"; "crimen más injusto de mi patria"; "transida de vergüenza."

41. Neville, "Su último paisaje" 40: "tu compañero de aulas / y Derecho Romano . . . / Compañero en el cante por soleares, / y los cantes de fragua. / Amigo en los estrenos y tertulias"; Ríos Carratalá, *Una arrolladora simpatía* 35 (Lorca correspondence); García Lorca, *Epistolario* 351, 740; I. García Lorca 273, 294; Gómez Santos 327–29; Franco Torre 44, 50; Paepe 361–62; and COA-727, -728, -729, FFGL (Neville letters and postcard). In the second letter, undated, Neville complained, with affectionate humor, of Lorca's inability to keep appointments. In his memoirs, the humorist Miguel Gila refers to Neville's "great friendship" with Lorca (295–96). Of what remains of Lorca's personal library, there is one book by Neville, *Música de fondo* (1936) (Paepe and Fernández-Montesinos 103).

42. "Nota a la edición" (Neville, *Su último paisaje*): "un noble afán de rebelión y protesta." There is a copy of this publication in the Fundación Federico

García Lorca (Caja IV-162 [16 y 17]), with a dedication to Francisco and Isabel García Lorca.

43. Franco Torre 273, 366–67 (*Duende y misterio*); Neville, "Su último paisaje" 40: "Y solo un viento clandestino y frío / murmura: —'En Granada fue el crimen, / sabed, ¡pobre Granada!, en su Granada'"; "Nota a la edición": "su más honda valoración."

44. Foxá, "Homeros" 4: "poesía roja"; "químicamente pura, deshumanizada"; Fernández Flórez 3. (Both Foxá and Fernández Flórez articles are reprinted in Rodríguez Puértolas, *Literatura fascista española* 2: 972–76.)

45. Uys Krige (qtd in Alexander 120) ("big and generous"); and Laurens van der Post (qtd in Alexander 121) ("born on fire"). I have relied on the excellent accounts of Alexander, Pearce, and D. Wright, for my discussion of Campbell's life and personality; see also his autobiography, *Light on a Dark Horse*, fascinating though not always factually reliable.

46. Wright said: "Among colonials he was a European and among Europeans a colonial" (38). See also Bergonzi; and Akerman.

47. Campbell, *Light* 194; Graves 6.

48. Alexander 152: "Belief in God, in Spain at this time, was itself a political act" (see also M. E. Williams 100); Spender, "The Talking Bronco" 442.

49. Campbell, *Flowering Rifle* 93 (1939 ed.). Lorca had a copy of the French translation of Campbell's *Adamastor* in his library, but the book remained unopened (Paepe and Fernández-Montesinos 42).

50. Campbell, *Flowering Rifle* 93.

51. Alexander 144.

52. Campbell, *Flowering Rifle, Collected Works* 1 (1957 rev. ed.) 671–72; see also Southworth on Campbell's view of Lorca (91–95).

53. See Ximénez de Sandoval, *Camisa azul* 204–5 and Albert 430–31 on the theme of cowardice in Falangist ideology; also, Fernández-Morera and Hanke, for Campbell's affinities with the heroism of Don Quixote (184–85).

54. Alexander 226–27 (copyright difficulties); M. Campbell, Preface, to R. Campbell's *Collected Poems* 3 (1957) 13; Letter from A. Barea to G. de Torre (24 June 1946), in Eisenberg, "Nuevos documentos" 87. A selection of Lorca poems eventually appeared in Campbell's *Collected Works* 2 (Poetry Translations). The manuscript notebooks are housed in the National English Literary Museum, Grahamstown, South Africa (*CW* 2:482). I am most grateful to Joseph Pearce for responding to my inquiries about the Campbell translations. See also Maurer, "Lorca, from Country to City" 36–37, for overtures to New Directions to publish the translations; and Walsh 84–97.

55. Letter from F. García Lorca to G. de Torre (17 July 1946), in Eisenberg, "Nuevos documentos" 90: "Cómo iba a imaginarme que Nadal iba a confiar la traducción de las obras de Federico a un escritor franquista, y que el Roy Campbell de quien yo tenía noticia era autor de poemas en honor de Franco." See also Isabel García Lorca's unflattering portrait of Martínez Nadal (166–67).

56. Letter from Ilsa Barea to G. de Torre (20 Aug. 1946), in Eisenberg, "Nuevos documentos" 91: "mostró un ansia inesperada de no ser mal interpretado por nuestro lado"; Alexander 172–73 and Pearce 269–72 (wartime experience); see also Ley 111, who says Campbell, while visiting in postwar Spain, was careful not to boast of fighting alongside the Nationalists. One Nationalist supporter suggested, incorrectly, that Campbell "fought in Franco's forces from the day of the Relief. This enables the reader to realise that Roy Campbell's poem is something real and experienced" (Arteaga de León 140). Campbell embellished even more to Robert MacGregor of New Directions, claiming he was conscripted, condemned to death, and tortured by Spanish Republicans (letter dated 27 Sept. 1954, qtd in Maurer, "Lorca, from Country to City" 37).

57. Campbell to Robert MacGregor (letter dated 27 Sept. 1954, qtd in Maurer, "Lorca, from Country to City" 37) ("an expiation"); Ley 124. Ironically, Francisco García Lorca and Donald M. Allen chose to include two of Campbell's translations in *The Selected Poems of Federico García Lorca* (1955).

58. Campbell, *Talking Bronco* 70; see also Campbell, "¡Banderillas de fuego!" 418, for his put–down of the inadequacies of Lorca translators, above all A. L. Lloyd. Campbell's English versions of St. John of the Cross won the Foyle Prize for Poetry in 1951.

59. Campbell, *Lorca* 1; also, Rogers 193–95. In a brief piece from 1949, Campbell says that Lorca's "reputation has been spread like wild-fire throughout the world by means of communist propaganda" ("Federico Garcia Lorca" 319). Walsh sees Campbell's book "as less of an *appreciation* of Lorca's poetry and more of an *appropriation* of the work of a writer who had by then been adopted by the international Left as the quintessential martyr of the Spanish Republican cause" (84). But others, too, had tired of the political manipulation of his image. See, for example, this comment of Warren Carrier from 1956: "And if Lorca is not forgotten long after the intellectuals deserted and the Communists betrayed political liberalism, it is because, despite his popularity as a martyr and a 'people's' poet in those dated days, he is a great poet who opened his arms to the world" (303).

60. Arteaga de León 140 ("Red shadow") (see also Pujals 68); Spender, in Crossman 226–27; Spender, *World within World* 251. Campbell refers to *The God That Failed* on at least two more occasions; see "A Decade in Retrospect" 312 and "Poetry and Experience"430, in *Collected Works* 4.

61. Wheelwright 167, 169; Lloyd, "Spain's Poet" 4 (I have been unable to find Lloyd's source for the Alberti quote); MacDiarmid 14, 16. See Gagen, "Lorca" 165–67 for more on MacDiarmid-Campbell; also, Pearce 388–89. MacDiarmid's poem appeared shortly after Campbell's death.

62. Campbell, *Lorca* 1–3.

63. Campbell, *Lorca* 2; Spender, "Speaking" 19; Martínez Nadal xxvii; see also Garosci 34 and Walsh 61–101 for more on the use of Lorca as wartime propaganda.

64. Brereton 456 ("idolisation"); Iribarren 405 (orig. publ. in *Jerarquía* No.1 [1936]): "Los poetas ultramodernos han trast[r]ocado todos los valores morales. García Lorca—un poeta menor después de todo—detentaba el título de Pontífice, llevando su andalucismo de ballet bajo los cielos grises del Norte, como un profesional de la españolada"; Burgin 109 (Borges's view of Lorca); Fitts, "Voice" 4 ("minor genius"). My thanks to Kevin Foster and the late Derek Gagen, who also searched for the source of Campbell's quotations.

65. Campbell, *Lorca* 2; Pemán, "García Lorca" 3; Campbell, *Flowering Rifle* 93. Franco's brother-in-law Ramón Serrano Suñer insisted in 1948 that "out-of-control" elements, unaffiliated with Falange, killed Lorca (Gibson, *El hombre que detuvo* 160).

66. Campbell, *Lorca* 47; Fitts, "Voice" 4.

67. Campbell, *Flowering Rifle* 93 ("void"); Campbell, *Lorca* 50 ("illumination").

68. Fitts, "Voice" 4 (qualities).

69. García Lorca, *Epistolario* 816: "¡Viva el poeta del pueblo!"; "con el pueblo auténtico"; García Lorca, *Epistolario* 817 (the right and "neutral"). See also Maurer, "Sobre 'joven literatura'" 313–14, for more on the context of this letter.

70. Fortes, "Populismo"; Fortes, *Intelectuales* 132–33; Fortes, *La ideología mata* 32, 77, 84, 188; García Montero, "Lorca era un fascista." The conflict between Fortes and Luis García Montero, both professors at the Universidad de Granada at the time, erupted at a faculty meeting and later in the press. In an unconvincing defense, some of Fortes's students claimed he never said Lorca was a fascist, but that his works "contribute[d] to the ideological formation crucial to fascism" (Colectivo de Alumnos). García Montero, the

poet's family, and many others strongly objected to Fortes's views of Lorca. See Cortés; Soria Olmedo, "Lugares"; Anon., "Opiniones de Fortes."

71. Tierno Galván 90; Ortiz (realist novels); Iriarte 146 (in his notes for the play, he characterized the protagonist in similar terms; see 139 n2); for more on *El señorito Octavio*, see Valis, "Palacio Valdés' First Novel"; Tierno Galván 93 (fallen señorito). For representative plays centered on the señorito, see Mozo de Rosales (1869), Ramos Carrión (1874), Sánchez Pastor (1900), González Rendón (1905), and Antón del Olmet and Vidal y Planas (1922).

72. Ortega y Gasset, *Rebelión* 150: "el niño mimado de la historia humana"; Ortega y Gasset, "Los problemas" 1: "es forzoso apencar. Lo demás es *señoritismo.*" See also Sinclair for a discussion of the relation between the avantgarde, especially the Generation of 1927, and the *pueblo*.

73. Marañón, *Raíz y decoro* 43, 44, 37: "gran plaga española"; "que no viva nadie del esfuerzo de los demás"; "la noble actividad viril del trabajo creador"; Inglada, *Ponce de León* 86 (La Barraca). The prologue to Marañón's book is dated August 1933.

74. Orwell, *Homage to Catalonia* 113; Machado, *La guerra* 78, 79, 89: "no hay señoritos, sino más bien 'señoritismo,' una forma, entre varias, de hombría degradada, un estilo peculiar de no ser hombre"; "señoritos felones"; "sólo el hombre, nunca el señorito, el hombre íntimamente humano, en cuanto ser consagrado a la muerte (*Sein zum Tode*), puede mirarla cara a cara"; see also Whiston 90–91, for more on the pueblo/señorito dichotomy in Machado's wartime thinking.

75. Blanco Amor 134 (orig. 1937); Aub 73: "carcomidos de peste"; Rocca and Roland 118 (Mora Guarnido) (I have not been able to locate the original source, "Odio y envidia en el asesinato de García Lorca," *España Democrática* [Nov. 1937]: 5); Anon., "Federico García Lorca" (in Dolfi 137; orig. *La Prensa* [Gijón] 10 Sept. 1936): "el clericalismo montaraz y los señoritos guapos" (see also Anon., "Se confirma el asesinato" 7); "el señoritismo degenerado, en sus alardes y sanguinolentos exhibicionismos"; and de la Villa (in Dolfi 143; orig. *Estampa* [Madrid] [26 Sept. 1936]): "uno de los señoritos insinuó: 'Mientras eso hacen los rojos, nosotros hemos respetado a García Lorca, sabiendo, como sabemos, que es de la cáscara amarga. Vamos a tener que tomar alguna medida.'" From the Republican side came the promise to exact revenge for the murder of Lorca (see Anon., "Se confirma el asesinato" 7).

76. Climent 3: "el gusto de un público encorsetado"; Carretero, "Ignacio Sánchez Mejías" 343; Juan Ramón Masoliver: "señorito andaluz"; and "un bo-

hemio con cuenta corriente" (qtd in Ruiz Gisbert 192); for more on Hino-josa, see Duque Gimeno and Ruiz Gisbert.

77. Diego: "generación . . . 'de los señoritos'" (qtd in A. Anderson, *El veintisiete* 36); López-Parra 5; Benlliure y Tuero 3. Diego's comment appeared in a letter to Alfonso Reyes dated 28 Aug. 1926. In a different context, the libertine novelist Álvaro Retana was viewed as the "most fervent singer of youth" (González-Ruano, "Álvaro Retana visto" 17).

78. L., "Carta de Madrid" 176 (Benlliure detention); see P. Rojas, for more on López–Parra; López-Parra 5; Giménez Caballero, "Visitas literarias" 1; also, Harkema, *Spanish Modernism* 170–72.

79. López-Parra 5: "un tufillo de vulgaridad burguesa de 'señoritismo' provinciano"; "esta señoritada hórrida de retaguardistas que invade Madrid nos vino de provincias como una lepra distinguida"; Diego, "Crónica" 6: "Góngora fue un señorito, un voluntario de la aristocracia, un provinciano, y—en el sentido en que usted lo implica—seguramente también un estéril y un selecto intelectual, un elegante."

80. Giménez Caballero, "Nosotros los señoritos" 4: "Esos señoritos que super-realizan sus versos son lo mismo que esos otros señoritos que comunistizan sus ideas políticas. Devoradores de su propia clase social. Derrumbamiento de su 'señorío'"; Primo de Rivera, "Discurso de la fundación": "sí, nosotros llevamos corbata; sí, de nosotros podéis decir que somos señoritos"; Primo de Rivera, "Señoritismo": "El 'señorito' es la degeneración del 'señor,' del 'hidalgo.' . . . Pero el señorito, al revés que el señor, cree que la posición social, en vez de obligar, releva. Releva del trabajo, de la abnegación y de la solidaridad con los demás mortales."

81. Laín Entralgo 20; Ximénez de Sandoval, *José Antonio* 141 n1 (Ledesma Ramos); Enders 383 (fervent supporter). In Sender's acclaimed novel *Réquiem por un campesino español* (Requiem for a Spanish Peasant) (1953), the murderous Falangists who sow terror and mayhem in an Aragonese village are simply called señoritos.

82. Fernández-Cuesta 56 (plebe/masses); 56: "las grandes empresas de nuestra historia"; 57: "fuerza cósmica"; Tovar 24–25, 26.

83. Noel 40 (dynamic); Noel 41: "producto de una inmensa degeneración"; Noel 87 (cacique); González Rendón 10 (monologue).

84. Compare these plays with three earlier, more lighthearted ones. Mozo de Rosales's *El señorito de pueblo* (1869) is a farce, in which the title character plays against the country bumpkin stereotype assigned him and assumes different roles. Ramos Carrión's *Los señoritos* (1874) satirizes middle-class

social pretensions, advising children be educated "for something more use-ful than simply being señoritos" ("para algo más útil que ser sencillamente unos señoritos") (54). In Jackson Veyán's one-act *pasillo cómico-lírico* (music by El Maestro Chapí) (1891), the señorito is listed as a "professional loafer" ("vago de profesión") and, in the original production, played by a woman!

85. See Carmona's sharp analysis of irony in Ponce de León's *Accident* (147-48).

86. Inglada, *Ponce de León* 38 n7 (señorito); Gómez Santos 336 (Granja del Henar Café). I have relied on Inglada's study for the biographical details of Ponce de León's life and work; also, Stradling, "Inspired Neglect?" 199 (mother's suicide). Stradling characterized the figure in *Accident* as "a ste-reotypically handsome señorito" (200). Other artists besides Ponce de León were also killed: Baltasar González Fernández, Camilo Buenaventura Díaz Baliño, Felicia Browne, and, under the most horrific circumstances, Lorenzo Aguirre, who was tortured and then garroted in one of Franco's prisons (Sáenz 355; Anon., "Lorenzo Aguirre").

87. Anon., "Vieja guardia" 194 (in Inglada, *Ponce de León*) (Ponce de León as martyr); Stradling, "Inspired Neglect?" 201. Stradling (199) also spotted an allusion to the artist as a Falangist underground resister or fifth columnist in director Carlos Arévalo's Falangist film, *Rojo y Negro* (Red and Black) (1942).

88. Foxá, "José Antonio" 96; Redondo 151 (poetry incarnate).

89. Durán, *Leyenda* xxiii: "Entonces no era yo el hombre alimentado y nutrido por el arte enseñado en las escuelas; no era el poeta que tiene un nombre determinado: era sí el espíritu universal inspirado á los trovadores ambulan-tes, que por do quier difundian las ideas anónimas por ser de todos"; Giner de los Ríos 97: "la más alta manifestacion que hacen de sí las naciones ... en ella, el poeta es la pátria"; 94: "se vierte el génio de los pueblos más espon-táneamente con el génio mismo del poeta."

90. Machado y Álvarez, Prólogo 13, 19: "[el] gran poeta anónimo"; "la misión del poeta culto es ... la de enaltecer las producciones de la muchedumbre"; Machado y Álvarez, *Estudios* 223: "levantar y reanimar el abatido espíritu de esta nación"; 216: "verdaderos fósiles de civilizaciones primitivas"; see Fer-nández-Medina 52–60 for more on Demófilo.

91. Velasco Maillo 125–26; Machado y Álvarez, *Estudios* 214. Like Machado y Álvarez, Unamuno 141 also asserted that the educated classes had yet to dis-cover el pueblo.

NOTES TO PAGES 143–146 325

92. Unamuno 143: "chapuzarnos en pueblo"; "la masa común a todas las castas"; Orwell, *The Road to Wigan Pier* 145; see also K. Foster 215–16.

93. Bergamín, "La decadencia" 94: "la espiritualidad generadora de un lenguaje, que es el espíritu creador de un pueblo"; 65: "Lo que un pueblo tiene de niño y lo que un hombre puede tener de pueblo, que es lo que conserva de niño, es, precisamente, lo que tiene de analfabeto"; 70: "un estado de añoranza infantil o popular"; "añoranza paradisíaca." See also Harkema, *Spanish Modernism* 220–22.

94. Fuentes 22; Tisa 40 and Carr 66 (Republican posters).

95. Arconada (qtd in Fuentes 227).

96. Machado, *La guerra* 129: "Cuando a Juan de Mairena se le preguntó si el poeta y, en general, el escritor debía escribir para las masas, contestó: Cuidado, amigos míos. Existe un hombre del pueblo, que es, en España al menos, el hombre elemental y fundamental y el que está más cerca del hombre universal y eterno. El hombre masa no existe; las masas humanas son una invención de la burguesía, una degradación de las muchedumbres de hombres, basada en una descalificación del hombre que pretende dejarle reducido a aquello que el hombre tiene de común con los objetos del mundo físico"; 130: "escribir para las masas no es escribir para nadie"; 130: "nosotros, demófilos incorregibles y enemigos de todo señoritismo cultural." In the mid-nineteenth century, Agustín Durán used the term *popular masses* ("masas populares") interchangeably with pueblo, in a nonpejorative sense (Prólogo, *Romancero general* xxv). For more on the relation between art and the masses in early twentieth–century Spain, see Bozal. Edgar Neville had another take on the turn-of-the-century señorito and economic exploitation: "The 'señoritos' did not exploit the people. In ruining themselves, they fulfilled a social mission of redistribution of wealth. Those who did exploit the people, the provocateurs of hate, were . . . the industrial class who made them work from dawn till dusk for a miserable salary, without sharing with them even the barest minimum of their profits, without attending to them in sickness or old age" ("Sobre la nostalgia" 124–25).

97. Machado, "El quinto detenido" 390: "¡Oh santidad del pueblo! ¡Oh pueblo santo!"

98. *Post-Guerra:* "Bajo el pretexto de militar en escuelas literarias de vanguardia o modernistas, numerosos jóvenes estetas defienden los ideales políticos de la reacción. El diletantismo literario es una modalidad de reaccionarismo político" (qtd in Fuentes 56); Fuentes 54–55 (intellectual señoritos) refers to

326 NOTES TO PAGES 146-148

an article, "Señoritos e intelectuales en movimiento obrero," *Comunismo* (1 May 1922), which I have not been able to see.

99. Anon., "Federico García Lorca habla" (Inglada, *Palabra* 407, 408) (orig. "Federico García Lorca parla per als obrers catalans," *L'Hora Setmanari d'Avançada* [Palma de Mallorca] No. 52 [27 Sept. 1935: 4]): "hijo de un campesino de Fuentevaqueros" and "el futuro gran poeta de la clase trabajadora"; Chabás 330 (La Barraca); Giménez Caballero, "Itinerarios jóvenes" 28: "un niño rico en el pueblo"; Romacho ("all Lorca"); see also Caudet, "Lorca." La Barraca was promoted as popular culture during the war (see M.M. 12).

100. Casona; Garfias: "Viviste plenamente tu vida de poeta, / de poeta del pueblo"; "tu muerte es vida para el pueblo" (in Castro, *Versos* 216); Benardete 25, 26; Salazar 14 (wounded volunteer). My thanks to Antonio Fernández Insuela for bringing the Casona article to my attention.

101. Hughes 1 (I cite from the original typescript housed in the Beinecke Rare Book and Manuscript Library, Yale University. The piece was first published in *Good Morning, Revolution* 114–19); Ecroya 6 (children reciting Lorca); Barea 7 (militiamen) (also Plenn 170; Rejano, "García Lorca. Raíces" 3, for similar comments); Riesenfeld 199–200 (see also her Lux Radio Theatre interview). The daughter of the composer Hugo Riesenfeld, she later became an actress, under the name Raquel Rojas, and as Janet Alcoriza, a screenwriter in Mexico, alongside her husband, the director-screenwriter Luis Alcoriza, a frequent collaborator of Luis Buñuel.

102. Alberti, "Words" 240; "Palabras" 259: "En diez meses de lucha llegan a cerca del millar los recogidos. Tú . . . andas por debajo de casi todos ellos. Tu voz, velada, a través de otras voces, se escucha en nuestra guerra. Pero lo que más resuena es tu sangre . . . como un inmenso puño de acusación y de protesta." The English translation is by Langston Hughes, from *New Masses: An Anthology of the Rebel Thirties* 239–41 (originally published in *New Masses* [11 Jan. 1938], 38–39). My thanks to Evelyn Scaramella for her helpful information on these sources.

103. Fortes, *La ideología mata* 84, 96; Anon., "Picota" (qtd in Díez de Revenga 5) (orig. in *Nuestra Lucha* [30 Aug. 1936]) ("sacramental"); Juliá 59 (public acts); Castro, *Versos* 565–73, provides a list of several Lorca homages published between 1936 and 1986; see also Rosenbaum 276–79. The Chilean diplomat and close friend of the poet, Carlos Morla Lynch, recounted in his wartime diary having attended one of these commemorative acts in the

Salamanca Cinema, with recitation, dances, and songs honoring the poet (*España sufre* 315).

104. Guerrero (in Castro, *Versos* 230–31; orig. published in *El Liberal* [Murcia] [13 Sept. 1936]); García Velasco: "¡Ay, cómo lloran tu muerte / los gitanos y gitanas! / ¡Ay, cómo lloran y lloran / los pobres, tus camaradas!" (in Castro, *Versos* 215; orig. published in *El Liberal* [Murcia] [18 Sept. 1936]); also Santa Cruz, "A Federico García Lorca, muerto" (1936) (in Castro, *Versos* 390–94); and Díez de Revenga, who first came across the poems published in *El Liberal* (Murcia).

105. Prados's poem is reprinted in Castro, *Versos* 353–56, who notes its publishing history (though not its first appearance in *El Mono Azul* 4); Altolaguirre 5: "Si contigo fui impresor, / él fue conmigo poeta; / si a él lo han matado en Granada, / tú has caído en Somosierra, / y los dos habéis venido / gloriosos, a mi presencia. / Él, con palma de martirio; / tú cual héroe de la guerra. / Él pidiéndome venganza; / tú dándome fortaleza. / Si él hace la causa justa, / tú haces la victoria cierta"; "valiente héroe de la clase obrera." Alberti included both poems in his *Romancero general de la guerra española* (1944).

106. López-Parra, "Traición" 5. Antonio Cañero was a Nationalist bullfighter, horseman, and military man accused of wartime acts of atrocity. His figure used as propaganda on both sides, he died in 1952, not in 1936; see Casado Salinas.

107. Holguín 174 ("Crimen" recited); E. Martín, "Antonio Machado" 240–41 (pamphlet); Gibson, *Asesinato* 262 (reprints of poem); Alberti, "Words" 239; "Palabras" 258. Hughes's translation fails to transmit the Machado echo: "in your own Granada." Machado's poem first appeared in *Ayuda* (Madrid, 17 Oct. 1936); see Rosenbaum 278, for its partial publication history covering the years 1936–40.

108. Fortes, *La ideología mata* 84: "como si fuese . . . revolucionario, proletario"; Alberti, "Words" 240; "Palabras" 259: "rara y fuerte"; "Words" 241; "Palabras" 262: "con ese mismo pueblo dolorido y magnífico de tus romances"; "con el mismo fervor que a un Garcilaso de la Vega sus poetas amigos"; Redondo 151 (hagiographical account); Saz 2 (Garcilaso as Francoist imperial poet); Alberti, "Words" 240–41; "Palabras" 261.

109. Alberti, "Words" 241; "Palabras" 261: "tu nombre y tu poesía andan ya, y de modo perenne, en los labios de nuestro pueblo combatiente, de todos los antifascistas españoles." Machado observed that Lorca's pueblo was "not

precisely the one that the International sings" ("no era precisamente el que canta la Internacional") (*La guerra* 323), while Cernuda thought his image as a "messianic bard" ("bardo mesiánico") was a complete deformation of the poet ("Federico García Lorca [Recuerdo]" 230).

110. Sáenz 355: "Cultura e intelectuales que la crean tienen que ser fusilados. Por eso murió frente a su Granada Federico García Lorca." The title of Gordón Ordás' article, "Los intelectuales asesinados," reflects the Republican view of Nationalists as anticulture. Space does not allow me to pursue further the complicated, sometimes contradictory attitudes of Republicans and the Second Republic toward culture. See Faber and Holguín for more on this subject.

111. Cernuda, "Federico García Lorca. *Romancero gitano*" 272, 273; Lloyd, "Preface" xii (1953) (his initial preface from 1937 was entirely rewritten in 1953; see also Rogers 187, who mistakenly identifies this later preface with that of 1937) (see also Lloyd, "Spain's Poet"); Fernández Muriedas (in Inglada, *Palabra* 316) (orig. in *La Región* [Santander] [19 Apr. 1934: 1]); Madariaga de la Campa 29, 30 (on Fernández Muriedas). Fernández Muriedas was affiliated with the Spanish Communist Party during the Republic and the war. The right-wing poet Pemán was instrumental in saving his life, after being condemned to death in a Francoist court (Madariaga de la Campa 23, 33, 46).

112. Fortes, *La ideología mata* 33, 70.

113. Fortes, "Populismo." This article and his *Intelectuales de consumo* anticipate his critique in *La ideología mata*. Fortes also wrote a poem on Lorca in 1976, published in 1986 in a homage volume to the Granadine poet (and reprinted in Castro, *Versos* 184–85).

114. Machado has a generally inclusive (if rather loose) understanding of the term *pueblo*. See Whiston 88–89 on this subject.

4. Fabulous Fag (I), or the Politics of Celebrity Murder

1. Anon., "Ya se matan" 1: "sexualidad vacilante"; Maurer, "Lorca, from Country to City" 40 (del Río), who references del Río's letter to Ben Belitt, dated 6 Dec. 1954; Gibson, *"Caballo azul"* 343 (Rivas-Cherif); Rivas-Cherif (13 Jan. 1957): 4; Schonberg 106; Anon., *"Le Figaro Littéraire* confiesa" 1. An unsigned report from 1965 described Lorca as a mason, socialist, and homosexual, reasons presumably given for his execution. See Anon., "Los documentos"; Anon., "Asunto"; Bueno; and Olmedo. Pro-

Nationalist Roy Campbell insinuated Lorca was gay in his long poem *Flowering Rifle* (1939).

2. Gibson, *"Caballo azul"* 305, 368–69, 371 (homophobic insults; faggot); Gibson, *Vida, pasión* 608 ("maricón de la pajarita"); Anon., "Federico García Loca."

3. Anon., "No hay crisis teatral" (*El Duende*); Woods 282, 283 (antigay censorship).

4. Anon., "La cofradía del apio" (undated; reprinted in Gibson 2:338); Salado 345 (orig. in *La Voz* [Madrid] [29 Dec. 1934]); Woods 294 (claque).

5. Toll 344–45 (del Arco caricature reprinted in Toll 346).

6. See bibliography; Eisenberg, "Reaction" (debate on *Sonetos*); Humphries, Letter to Louise Bogan, dated 4 Oct. 1938 (in Gillman and Novak 152); Martínez Nadal, *Federico García Lorca* 58–59. Sahuquillo's study began as a dissertation (1986) and then came out as a book (1991); it was translated into English in 2007. Paul Binding's book *Lorca: The Gay Imagination,* while reductive and analytically deficient, also appeared in the 1980s.

7. Anon., "Edmund de Bries" 2 ("caravana de tipos híbridos"); see Umbral for a view of Lorca as a *poète maudit;* for Borges's opinion, see Burgin 109 and Bioy Casares 588, 595, 752.

8. Delgado, *Federico García Lorca* 192 (commodification of Lorca); Ginsberg, "A Supermarket in California" (*Collected Poems* 144) (dated Berkeley 1955).

9. Ginsberg, "A Supermarket in California" 144; García Lorca, *OC* 1:567. In a note to his poem, Ginsberg cited lines from Lorca's "Ode to Walt Whitman" (*Collected Poems* 768–69). In "Death to Van Gogh's Ear!" (from 1957), he wrote, "Franco has murdered Lorca the fairy son of Whitman" (*Collected Poems* 175). See also Mayhew, *Apocryphal Lorca* 42–44.

10. García Lorca, "Poética" 485: "Yo tengo el fuego en mis manos"; "Quemaré el Partenón por la noche para empezar a levantarlo por la mañana y no terminarlo nunca"; Valis, "Prólogo/Prologue" 9, from which I have taken the comments on Lorca's "Poética." See also J. Marías, "Lorca, Untamed," who comments on two photos, the first one showing Lorca's "somewhat rustic, untamed appearance" and his enigmatic gaze (31).

11. Breton 63.

12. Cansinos-Asséns, *Ética y estética* 128, 167, 169.

13. For studies that consider high and low culture, see Fernández Cifuentes; Sieburth; Valis, *Culture of Cursilería;* and Bellver. Zubiaurre juxtaposes high and low through Miguel de Unamuno and Álvaro Retana as examples of "the two Spains—the chaste and the erotic" (6–8). For the reevaluation and

recuperation of Retana, see: Villena; Toledano Molina; Cruz Casado; Barreiro; Mira; Heuer; Ezpeleta Aguilar; Vernet Pons; Sánchez Álvarez-Insúa; Zamostny, "Faustian Figures," "¡Todos a bordo!" and "Virtual Álvaro Retana"; Zubiaurre; Coste; and Toro Ballesteros.

14. Alonso Montero 22 (Gómez del Valle; his mother); Trapiello 546, 591 (Gómez del Valle; Valdés); Bernal 19; Viola and Bernal 11, 13–14 (Valdés).

15. A. Anderson, *El veintisiete*, has usefully documented how poets like Hinojosa have appeared and disappeared in literary histories and anthologies of the Generation of 1927.

16. Moreno Villa 139; Alberti, *La arboleda perdida* 190; Lluch Fabado Valls 50, 54; and Canales 90 (Campsa; Hinojosa execution); Anon., "José María Hinojosa" and Hyeronimus (Carlist). Years later, Moreno Villa (563) softened his stance on Hinojosa, but still echoed Alberti's erroneous account of the poet's death. Altolaguirre peddled a similar story of his murder (Belausteguigoitia). Hinojosa's proverbial generosity toward other poets also extended to the least privileged in his hometown Campillos and elsewhere (Anon., "José María Hinojosa"; Hyeronimus; Ruiz Gisbert 196). The extant holdings of Lorca's library include one of Hinojosa's books of poetry, *Poema del campo* (1924) (Paepe and Fernández-Montesinos 78); it was unopened.

17. Cernuda, "Historial" 495; Ruiz Gisbert 197 (Bergamín); Alós (Bello); also, Sánchez Rodríguez; Hinojosa; and *Bones of Contention*.

18. Gordon, "Pasolini's Murder" 155 (Romantic tradition); Martín, *Federico García Lorca* (Lorca and martyr figure); Pasolini, *Heretical Empiricism* 236–37, 239.

19. Pasolini, *Heretical Empiricism* 243.

20. See Barth David Schwartz's superb biography for more on Pasolini's death; also, Schwenk and Semff; Anon., "Documents"; and Rich.

21. Gordon, "Pasolini's Murder" 156 (homophobic motives); Woods 232 (*pasolini/finocchio*).

22. Pasolini, *Selected Poetry* (trans. Stephen Sartarelli): "il grigiore del mondo" (166, 167); "tu, morto, e noi / morti ugualmente" (168, 169); "Ma io, con il cuore cosciente / di chi soltanto nella storia ha vita, / potrò mai più con pura passione operare, / se so che la nostra storia è finita?" (186, 187). The poem is dated 1954.

23. Macciocchi 11, 12, 13–14, 15, 18. Gordon, "'To Speak Oneself'" 56, also focuses on the notion of the scene of death.

24. Zigaina 29, 30; Gordon, "'To Speak Oneself'" 60 (headline).

25. B .D. Schwartz 89 (Moravia).

26. B. D. Schwartz 12, 69–70, 377–78; Pasolini, *Selected Poetry:* "La morte non è / nel non poter comunicare / ma nel non poter più essere compresi" (332, 333); "ch'è una fiacca pensata / fatta tornando da Fiumicino!" (336, 337).

27. Nicholl 415, 432.

28. Riggs 349 (the Marlowes); Riggs 76 (homosocial bonding); Nicholl 431–32 (bed-sharing); Riggs 77 (Marlowe's homosexuality).

29. Marlowe, *Dido* 330–31, 361; Marlowe, "The Passionate Shepherd" 434.

30. Riggs 123.

31. For accounts of Villamediana's life and death, see Hartzenbusch; Cotarelo y Mori; Rozas; Stradling, "The Death of Don Juan"; and Rosales; for the concealment, ambiguity, and silence found in his work, De Armas, "'The Play's the Thing'"; Leopold; and Weich.

32. Hartzenbusch 44, 88 (Villamediana's celebrity; sodomy).

33. Alonso Cortés 84: "Expliquen los modernos psicópatas y sexualistas, y hasta justifiquen, si ello es posible, el caso Villamediana; busquen otros la relación que puede haber entre tales extravíos y las épocas de arte decadentista, para ver en el conde una figura representativa dentro del gongorismo: siempre resultará que la trágica muerte que hasta ahora pareció la de un nuevo Macías, estuvo acompañada, por el contrario, de las más bajas y odiosas circunstancias."

34. De Armas, "Embracing Hercules" and A. Martín (Góngora and sodomy); Alonso Cortés 85–86. For Oscar Wilde's presence in Spanish literature, see Constán.

35. Alonso Cortés 84 ("*todo un hombre*"); 85: "No era, pues, un uranista ingénito . . . sino un perturbado del vicio"; Marañón, *Don Juan* 105 ("instinto indeciso"); also, Mira, *Para entendernos* 747–48.

36. Neira Jiménez 197 (Góngora and Generation of 1927); García Lorca, *OC* 3: 76: "cae atravesado por las espadas de sus amores oscuros"; 1331: "cae atravesado por las espadas del rey"; Gibson, *"Caballo azul"* 24, 26. Lorca's phrasing for Villamediana evokes his image of Walt Whitman's "sexo atravesado por una aguja" in the "Ode" (*OC* 1: 564).

37. Stradling, "The Death of Don Juan" 16; Rosales, "Borradores mecanografiados."

38. Rosales, *Pasión y muerte* (1964) 6: "para reivindicar la memoria del Conde de Villamediana," "condenado injustamente" (these phrases were originally in the draft of the 1969 book [see "Borrador"]); Rosales, *Pasión y muerte* (1969) 247: "La calumnia no siempre va acompañada de difamación, ni es el último veredicto." The academician-priest López de Toro echoed this motif

of calumny in a mock verse-letter to Rosales, "Carta del Conde de Villamediana." Long out of print, Rosales's book really deserves a new edition, something he looked into during the late 1980s. See the Balcells correspondence.

39. Grande 99 (Rosales home as refuge to Republicans); Rosales, "Carta" 14
(effect of Lorca's death).

40. Stradling, "The Death of Don Juan" 17.

41. Gibson, *Caballo azul* 262, 344: "'Tú tienes una cabeza muy viril pero por
debajo eres maricón'"; *Federico García Lorca / Biblioteca* 29–32 (Rosales's
copy of *Oda a Walt Whitman*). The Biblioteca de Andalucía acquired Luis
Rosales's library.

42. Rosales, Letter to Pablo Neruda, undated, Archivo Histórico Nacional,
Diversos—Luis Rosales, 15, N. 56: "un alegato poético contra la violencia";
Neruda, *Viajes* 45: "un gran señor de la poesía y de la vida, un gran poeta
asesinado."

43. A. Anderson, "Introducción" 59 (composition of "Oda a Walt Whitman");
Neruda, "El desenterrado" 128: "Conde, dulce, en la niebla," "tu sexo asesinado se incorpora"; García Lorca, *OC* 1: 564: "anciano hermoso como la
niebla," "con el sexo atravesado por una aguja"; Neruda, *Viajes* 46 (Villamediana's love for the queen).

44. Quevedo, *Grandes anales* 212; Rosales, *Pasión y muerte* (1969) 93–94, 140–
41: "la muerte de Villamediana fue ordenada desde el poder. . . . La verdad
no se puede ocultar. . . . Es inútil mentir y pretender falsificar la historia.
Siempre quedan indicios. La verdad es el puente donde todo se une."

45. Woods 7, 27 (espionage; cosmopolitan).

46. Pemán "García Lorca" 3; *64 Questions* 14 ("personal quarrel"). Delgado
(*Federico García Lorca* 177) suggests Rosales was a closet homosexual but
offers no documentation. Such a claim, if substantiated, would certainly
complicate even more the Rosales-Lorca relationship, as outlined here.

47. Fernández de la Mora 3; Garciasol 131–32; Eisenberg (in Garciasol 129)
(Rosales's resignation); see also Grande 342–43.

48. Cabañas Bravo 703, 704 (Latin American reception; N. Guillén and Marinello); Gibson, *Asesinato* 269–73, reproduces Serrano Suñer's comments.
Auclair 443 and Grande 278 say the tour took place in 1948, but Cabañas
Bravo observes that the government-sponsored junket, which served both
cultural and propagandistic aims and included Leopoldo Panero, Agustín
de Foxá, and Antonio de Zubiaurre, began in late December 1949 and ended
by March 1950. Rosales reached Cuba on 21 December 1949 and was back
on Spanish territory by 10 March 1950 (see Rosales, Passports).

49. Grande 213, 214: "'García Lorca, murió, por su mariconería, al lado de los enemigos de España'"; Ramos Espejo 116: "'Lo mataron por una calumnia'"; 117: "He recibido anónimos, amenazas, insultos contra mí y contra la figura de Federico, calificada de forma soez" (Rosales interview). The anonymous letter is reprinted in Grande 212–14 (Gibson, *El hombre que detuvo* 213–15, also reproduces it). For other attacks against Rosales, see Grande 281, 284, 290–305, 344–47, 395–97.

50. Montetes-Mairal y Laburta 133 (Rosales's disillusionment); Ramos Espejo 116 (Lorca as propaganda).

51. Diego, *La estela* 124, 126–27. Julio Neira also thought Diego was referring to Lorca (*La estela*, 220 n69). In his warm appreciation of Alonso Cortés from 1972, Diego made no mention of his maestro's work or thesis on Villamediana. In a 1948 piece, written twenty years after Alonso Cortés's book, he spoke forcefully against the attempts of Villamediana's "modern accusers" ("modernos acusadores") to "stain a reputation [that was] unequivocally virile" ("manchar una reputación bien viril e inequívoca") (*La estela* 120).

52. Rozas 15. In an otherwise highly favorable review of Rosales's book, Edward M. Wilson nonetheless wasn't altogether convinced that "a homosexual episode in [Villamediana's] life" could be ruled out (167).

53. Garelick 11 (dandies), 128 (distinctions).

5. Fabulous Fag (II), or the Celebrity of Sex

1. Manrique, *Eminent Maricones* 102.

2. For more on Trigo's reputation, see Valis, "Society Reporter"; on the lack of prestige of the erotic novel, see Villena, *El ángel* 35–36.

3. Zozaya: "afortunados y raros mortales que no conocemos a tan celebradas artistas sino de oídas"; "nadie sabe hasta dónde llega el prestigio de las glorias que no se ven de cerca."

4. Precioso, "A manera de prólogo" (in Retana, *Flor del mal*) 4: "La espero un poco teatralmente, porque a ella la divierten mis excentricidades, y después de merendar me llevará en su 'auto' a exhibirme en la Castellana como un monstruo fantástico"; Retana, *Mi alma desnuda* 30: "Yo necesitaba seguir siendo el artista libertino en mis libros y sostener la aureola inquietante que nimba mi figura." Artemio Precioso's prologues were instrumental in promoting Retana's celebrity (Martínez Arnaldos 54–59).

5. Schickel 23, 24; Corominas, "Fama"; *Diccionario* (1732); *Online Etymology*

Dictionary. See also Retana's novel, *La mala fama* (1922), which turns on the benefits of a bad reputation.

6. Schickel 4; Howard 17; also, Inglis.

7. Valle-Inclán, "Breve noticia" 18, 19: "un vivo anhelo de personalidad"; "mi profesión de fe modernista: buscarme en mí mismo y no en los demás"; Soto ("Boy") 276–77 (Lorca's Latin America tour) (orig. in *El Plata* [Montevideo] [12 Feb. 1934]). See also Paul Julian Smith, on the current-day perception of Lorca's ubiquity (*Theatre* 105).

8. Vélez de Guevara 124, 154; López Soler 2: 250, 255: "un joven de tal celebridad y linage"; "de la limpia cuna y de la celebridad que os ennoblecen." López Soler also refers to the "celebrity of wit, or talent" ("celebridad de los ingenios") (1: 58). Corominas (2: 19) cites a 1629 reference (G. del Corral) to *celebridad* as *frecuentación*, or frequentation, and *celebración*, but a perusal of the Real Academia Española's database, CORDE, shows sixteenth-century appearances of the word, with one in the fifteenth being the earliest. *Celebrare* was initially a religious term. A similar occurrence appears in English, according to Onions (156), though elsewhere, the word is dated to the late fourteenth century, as celebration or multitude, fame; the "condition of being famous," ca. 1600, and "famous person," 1849 (*Online Etymology Dictionary*).

9. Pérez Galdós, *El terror de 1824* 61: "prueba viva de las locuras de la fama y usurpador de una celebridad que habría cuadrado mejor á otros caracteres y nombres"; Pardo Bazán 8: "antes se llega a la celebridad con escándalo y talento, que con talento solo." The violinist Ventura in Leopoldo Alas's *Las dos cajas* (The Two Coffins) (1883) does not become a "European celebrity," much to his father's disappointment. Nor does Galdós's Tristana in her continually evolving artistic apprenticeship (*Tristana* 180) (1892). In Alas's *Su único hijo* (His Only Son) (1891), Bonifacio Reyes can be viewed as a kind of "groupie" of an opera company's stars, who craves his own celebrity (see Herda 79, 90–91).

10. Ortiz de Pinedo 23: "El escritor piensa, acaso, melancólicamente, que aquí nadie tiene la gloria que debe, sino la que puede, la que le dejan tener los demás"; Sanín Cano 172; Schickel 30 (personification).

11. Marañón, *Ensayos* 203–4; Insúa 133: "guapo, elegante y millonario, se convirtió, en unos cuantos meses, en una celebridad del Madrid nocturno"; Cansinos-Asséns, *La novela* 1: 211–12; García Rodríguez, *El infante maldito* 15–17, 112, 135.

12. In a questionnaire from 1966, Retana said that his friendships were found among the "world of the aristocratic and the erotic" ("mundo aristocrático

y galante") (Pérez Sanz and Bru Ripoll, *La erótica* 1100); Pérez Sanz and Bru Ripoll, *La sexología* 15 (Duke of Vistahermosa); Pérez Sanz and Bru Ripoll, *La erótica* 2410 (Ricardo Berdejo). The family on Retana's paternal side was related to the Marqués de Cerralbo (Pérez Sanz and Bru Ripoll, *La sexología* 5) and the Marqués de Flores Dávila (Cano, "La cara oculta" 277). The Marqués de Goicoerrotea (Ramón) was Álvaro's uncle (*Mi alma desnuda* 36). I am most grateful to Maite Zubiaurre for making the Pérez Sanz–Bru Ripoll materials (*La erótica*) available online at her *Virtual Wunderkammer* site. My thanks to Luis Bautista Boned for his help in locating some of Retana's now difficult to find works.

13. See Valis, "Celebrity, Sex" 134–35, for more on *La tristeza errante;* Wharton 225; Darío, "La joven aristocracia" 288: "decidme si se puede 'hacer patria' con tales elementos"; Cejador y Frauca 24: "La aristocracia nueva es la del talento y la del trabajo. Cuando el talento y el trabajo han sido injertados en los troncos de añeja alcurnia, hemos visto revivir los linajes"; Cansinos-Asséns 2: 399 (Hoyos's fall). Edwards Bello (and others) believed Hoyos's accident a robbery gone bad (191), but as Cansinos suggested, an antigay attack cannot be ruled out.

14. Max-Bembo (pseudonym for José Ruiz Rodríguez) 43 (popular perception of aristocracy); Carreras, *Los duques de la Torre* 6 (Duquesa and celebrity); also Carreras, *Un casamiento infame;* Serrano y Domínguez and Chinchilla; and Cleminson, Fernández, and Vázquez García, for more on the scandal of the Duques de la Torre's son and his marriage.

15. Rivalan Guégo, *Fruición-ficción* 86–91 (erotic novel and aristocracy); Precioso, "A manera de prólogo" (in Retana, *El encanto*) 5 (Retana as modern Dorian Gray); Valis, "Celebrity, Sex" 135–36, for more on Retana's self-image as an Oscar Wilde (also Cansinos-Asséns 3: 79, who considered him Wildean). For characters, see *Mi alma desnuda* 164, where the singer Chelito's youthful appearance is compared to that of "the character of a celebrated novel by Oscar Wilde" ("el personaje de una célebre novela de Oscar Wilde"). In *A Sodoma en tren botijo* 163, Nemesio thinks he deserves "to inspire a novel and be loved like Dorian Gray" ("inspirar una novela y ser amado como Dorian Gray") (see also Zamostny, "¡Todos a bordo!" 58). Retana also exploited, in an ironic, light-hearted way, the topos of the decadent aristocrat, most notably, in *Las "locas" de postín,* a novel that has received recent critical attention.

16. Cansinos-Asséns 1: 372–73, 3: 79; Edwards Bello 182–84; Alfonso 86–87; Campoy, "El novelista ambiguo" 2040; Fernández Vieites 1710 ("guaya-

bitas y guayabitos"); see also Anon., "El novelista más guapo" 2047–48, in which the journalist says Retana is no ephebe, but admitted that others thought he was gay.

17. Pérez Sanz and Bru Ripoll, *La erótica* 2447–48 (Modesto Huescas Ruiz): "me encuentro con un joven bellísimo, como un efebo bizantino o un paje veneciano del Renacimiento"; Schickel 35 and MacCabe (virtual relationship with readers); Retana, *Las mujeres de Retana* n. pag. (feminine / effeminate man).

18. See Zamostny, "Faustian Figures," for a reading of Retana's gender performances as queer, thus evading categorization. Alberto Mira ("After Wilde") gives Retana a camp interpretation. On his fans, see Campoy, "Álvaro Retana, el novelista" 1682; Pascua 1642; and Zamostny, "Virtual Álvaro Retana," for current-day enthusiasts. Pascua comments on the febrile joy of devotees, who also feared that reading Retana was a mortal sin. "You will find these books," he says, "carefully hidden in desk drawers" ("Hallaréis estos libros cuidadosamente escondidos en los cajones de las mesas de trabajo") (1642).

19. Retana, "A manera de prólogo" 6, 8, 15–18. See Rivalan Guégo, *Lecturas gratas* 167–68 on the use of advertisements and the porous border between writing and commerce. The cognac was produced by the Casa Luis Hidalgo, in Sanlúcar de Barrameda. One wonders whether Retana's close friend, the *sanluqueño* Pedro Badanelli, might have had something to do with the endorsement. In 1929, Badanelli published a gay novel, *Serenata del amor triunfante* (see my edition of 2016).

20. Edwards Bello 183 and Alfonso 85 (high-culture writers and their readership).

21. Braudy, *Frenzy* 408 (Byron). The letters to Retana may be found in Pérez Sanz and Bru Ripoll, *La erótica* 2379–95; included is Fernando's letter to Miguel, who was part of Retana's entourage (2393–94). See also González-Ruano, "Álvaro Retana visto" 12, for his comments on the novelist's fan mail.

22. Hoyos y Vinent, ["Vidas literarias"] 2038–39: "*ratés*, rezagados de la era Wildeniana y falsas musas, muy *montemartre*"; "gestos fugitivos y menudos." The plot line of Retana's *El octavo pecado capital* includes a mysterious Pierrot figure of indeterminate gender.

23. Fernando Rodríguez, Letter to Álvaro Retana (31 Jan. 1932) 2380: "su carta me ha parecido más bien la carta de un amigo de muchos años, que la de un escritor tan célebre como usted lo es"; "la ficción hubiera sido completa si en ella me hubiese tuteado." Villena believes Retana's life was pretty close to that of his characters (*El ángel* 47).

24. Fernando Rodríguez, Letter to Álvaro Retana (8 May [1932?]) 2385–86: "Will you receive me in bed? ... What I want is to really find you sleeping, so that I can come in and awaken you and when you do, it will be nothing less than you in your bedroom with a stranger" ("¿Me recibirás en la cama? ... Lo que yo deseo es que efectivamente, te encuentre durmiendo, para entrar a despertarte y cuando lo hagas te encuentre nada menos que en tu alcoba con un desconocido"); Benjamin, "Work of Art" 231.

25. Pérez Sanz and Bru Ripoll, *La erótica* 2402 (Luis), 2412–13, 2420, 2423, 2425, 2426 (Berdejo, letter dated 6 Jan. 1932).

26. Pérez Sanz and Bru Ripoll, *La erótica* 2419.

27. MacCabe; see also Braudy, *Frenzy* 348, 427 and Inglis, chapter 8.

28. Labrador Ben et al. 283–92 (censorship under Primo de Rivera); *Causa General* 249 (Ríos Carratalá, *El tiempo* 84, suggests that Retana's political posture during the war was considered suspect by both sides); Fortuny, *La ola verde* 301: "se cotizaba mejor y concedía rápidamente más celebridad." Retana's book is often contradictory and incoherent in its position, not to mention self-serving, but, nonetheless, indispensable for understanding erotic literature and the period.

29. Woods 29 ("homosexuality *came out*"); José de Zamora, Letter to Álvaro Retana (undated), in Pérez Sanz and Bru Ripoll, *La erótica* 2064; Retana, *Crítica frívola* (typed manuscript), in Pérez Sanz and Bru Ripoll, *La erótica* 1956: "Ya sabemos que con la palabra *modernidad* se justifica todo." In an interview with Carmen de Burgos, Olimpia d'Avigny said she "debuted in Naples as an eccentric" ("Olimpia" 237).

30. Retana, "Manual del perfecto 'entretenido'" (typed manuscript), in Pérez Sanz and Bru Ripoll, *La erótica* 2095: "Aprovecha cuantas ocasiones se presenten para repetir a tu amante que no le consideras invertido, sino simplemente un hombre moderno"; Russo 47 (*Bringing Up Baby*). Retana also advises, "Never demean your lover in a quarrel by calling him an invert" ("Nunca denigres a tu amante cuando surja una disputa entre vosotros, con el calificativo de invertido") ("Manual" 2095).

31. Sáenz de la Calzada 67 (*Fuenteovejuna*); El Barón de Montenegro 6: "digno de un país moderno"; 33, 36 (categories of homosexuality).

32. Sassone 15: "Los afeminados del día no van ni a los 'bars' ni a los 'cabarets'; prefieren hacer versos dadaístas o tomar baños de asiento como sus profesores de París"; 16 (*maquereau*).

33. Sassone 22: "La seguían un bailarín que parecía un decadente vanguardista, y un vanguardista decadente que parecía un bailarín"; Gómez de la Serna,

Pombo 101–3, 106–8, 110–11, 139–41 and *La sagrada cripta* 359, 444–45, 488, 528–33, 536–37. For more on Tórtola Valencia and José de Zamora, see: Clayton; Queralt; Villena, "Una tribu dorada" and Prólogo to Zamora, *"Princesas de aquelarre."*

34. Cansinos-Asséns, *La novela* 1: 376.

35. See Mira; Cleminson and Vázquez García, *"Los Invisibles"* (homosexual subculture).

36. Huet, *Monstrous Imagination* 10, 161 (monstrous; monstrous progeny); Cleminson, "El libro *Homosexualidad"* 975–76 (blurred gender roles).

37. Gide, *Corydon* 91; Vázquez and Cleminson, "El destierro de lo maravilloso" and Flores de la Flor 84–85 (demythologized monsters).

38. The documentary *Freaks: The Sideshow Cinema,* an extra feature of the DVD for the film *Freaks* (1932), discusses the popular sideshow attraction of the half-man/half-woman, focusing on the historical figure, Josephine-Joseph. See also Fiedler, *Freaks* 178–94; and Adams 96–97, 124–26; Ellis 82–83 and Bogdan 8 (congenital/acquired); Zubiaurre 45 (Ellis as influential); Ellis 80, 83, 88 (latently hermaphrodite; inversion; uncertainty). The collection of essays, *Freakish Encounters* (2018), edited by Sara Muñoz-Muriana and Analola Santana, is an indication of the growing interest in this subject within Hispanic cultural studies.

39. Thomson 2 (Freddy); Usó 36–37 (material for de Bries); Retana, *Las "locas"* 111: "representantes del sexo indeciso, por lo que hay . . . de ambiguo y propagador"; 112: "la causa del tercer sexo." Women also attended drag performances (Usó 47). For the close association made between being gay and a drag queen in 1920s Spain, see Madrid 65, 69.

40. Ravenscroft; González Echevarría 102–3; and Moreno Villa, *Locos, enanos* (monsters as entertainments); Sánchez Gómez; Agulló y Cobo 4: 116, 428 and 5: 160; Almagro San Martín 215–16, 233; Marañón, "Un caso" 4 (intersexual).

41. March 34 (exhibits, collections, etc.); Castro 89; Adams 30–31, 39, 50 ("line between dime museums").

42. Sepúlveda 213, 408; Hernández-Catá 16–19; Sánchez Estevan 38 (Benavente) (also Peral Vega 17–18, for Benavente's interest in the circus). Almagro San Martín marveled how the Spanish aristocracy remained enthusiastic about the circus as late as 1900, long after their peers in France and Great Britain had apparently lost interest (167–68).

43. Hoyos y Vinent, Prólogo 7: "Yo las he hallado muchas veces en la feria del mundo—esa feria donde, Dios, como un Barnu[m] omnipotente se ha complacido en reunir todos los monstruos y todas las deformidades—y la son-

risa que iba a ser irónica se ha hecho tan triste que más ha sido mueca con-miserativa"; 7: "con sus cuerpos que se mantenían inverosímiles, gracias a los masajes y a los corsés, bajo los encajes, las sedas, las pieles y las perlas, con sus rostros pintados, maquillados, estucados. . . . Hacían entradas sensacionales, flirteaban como *locas;* 9 ("bal travesti").

44. Hoyos y Vinent, Prólogo 9 ("ellas de verdad").

45. Hoyos y Vinent, "Hermafrodita" n. pag.: "fenómenos de transformación, raros caprichos de la Naturaleza; descubría monstruos horribles, casos de locura. . . . [I]ban y venían en raras zarabandas seres absurdos, criaturas híbridas, que se contorsionaban saliendo de lo grotesco para entrar en los linderos de lo doloroso"; "uno de aquellos seres ambiguos, insexuados, híbridos, de la fábula." See also Hoyos y Vinent, "La última encarnación de Hermafrodita" 55–72.

46. Paré 73; Covarrubias 812: "contra la regla y orden natural"; Covarrubias 530–31 (*ermaphrodito*) (see also his *Emblemas morales,* Centuria II, Emblema 64); Alemán 1: 71: "sodomía y bestial bruteza"; also, Moreno Mengíbar and Vázquez García 95; Paré 6–7; and Fiedler, *Freaks* 24–25.

47. Fuentelapeña 165: "perfecto hombre, ni perfecta muger"; 181 ("neutro"); 167 ("pecado de naturaleza"); 141 (normal people); 80 (divine presence). Nearly a century later, the 1780 *Diccionario de la lengua castellana* of the Royal Spanish Academy continued calling the hermaphrodite a monstrosity and somewhat elliptically noted that the term "by extension is said of other things" (524).

48. For a helpful overview of the changing medico-legal understanding of hermaphroditism, especially in Spain, see Cleminson and Vázquez García, *Hermaphroditism* 1–28. In eighteenth-century Spain, some questioned the authenticity of hermaphrodites, but cases continued to be reported in the press (Flores de la Flor 97–98); see San de Velilla 125–35, for a twentieth-century example of the continuing interest in the subject, especially false hermaphroditism.

49. Monlau 140: "Lo que hay, en fin, son algunas monstruosidades; lo que hay son muchos vicios de conformación que simulan con mas ó menos verdad la amalgama de los dos sexos en un solo individuo"; see also Ballano 3: 879 and Santos 338, 340, 347, on the question of anomalies. *Vicio* can be either a physical or a moral defect, though Covarrubias (1611) lists only the moral definition (1004). By the early nineteenth century, we have gone from Fuentelapeña's "pecado de naturaleza" in the seventeenth century to a "vicio de conformación" (which does not mean, however, that the earlier meaning had disappeared).

50. Letamendi 119, 120: "los restos hermafrodíticos militantes"; "toda unión entre individuos de un mismo sexo se reduce á simulacro de hermafrodismo incompleto"; Cleminson and Vázquez García, *"Los Invisibles"* 52 (psychic hermaphroditism); Max-Bembo 70; Martín de Lucenay, *Homosexualidad* 13; San de Velilla 132 (the undefinable); Angell (taxonomies).

51. See Fiedler, *Freaks* 192–94, esp. the 1942 photograph of hermaphrodite subjects, now classified as intersex; and for a contemporary taxonomic and visual example, Bernaldo de Quirós and Llanas Aguilaniedo (1901) 248–63, 267.

52. Foucault, *History* 43 ("hermaphrodism of the soul"); Cleminson and Vázquez García, *Hermaphroditism* 3.

53. Wilde 254, 165, 167, 190; Gautier 56.

54. Rachilde 189: "deux sexes distincts en un unique monstre"; Barrès (in his prologue to Rachilde) viii: "spectacle d'une rare perversité"; Huet, *Monstrous Imagination* 6 (*monere*).

55. González Echevarría 96, 102, 107, 113 (see also Valis, *"Ángel Guerra"* 32–33); Diderot 269: "L'homme n'est qu'un effet commun—le monstre qu'un effet rare; tous les deux également naturels, également dans l'ordre universel et général. . . . Et qu'est-ce qu'il y a d'étonnant à cela? . . . tous les êtres circulent les uns dans les autres, par conséquent toutes les espèces . . . tout est en un flux perpétuel."

56. Santos 344: *"entes* mas ó menos *amorfos,* mas ó menos *viables"*; Foucault, "Introduction" vii ("true sex").

57. The nineteenth-century French case of the conflicted hermaphrodite Herculine Barbin also suggests "a form of monstrosity within the self" (Webb 159). Pedro Mata describes this case in the fourth edition of his *Tratado de medicina y cirugía legal* (1866) (1: 474–75). It is worth reiterating that Baroque forms of the monstrous should be distinguished from this later notion of a constant dissolving, psychic flux of monstrosity, anticipated in Diderot and manifested from the Romantics on (see González Echevarría 254 n20).

58. Mira, "Modernistas, dandis" 67–68. See, for example, Cansinos's comment on Hernández-Catá's novel: *"El ángel de Sodoma* hizo llorar de emoción a todos los invertidos de la literatura y le valió a su autor felicitaciones agradecidas de los Pepito Zamora y los Pepito Ojeda, que ahora ostentaban el cartel wildiano tan descaradamente como Antonio de Hoyos y Répide al comienzo del siglo" (*La novela* 2: 360–61).

59. Cansinos-Asséns, *Ética y estética* 172: "un principio de inversión en el excesivo amor al sexo contrario"; "anhelo de una experiencia inversa"; Marañón, *Tres ensayos* 168: "'otro sexo' que nos acompaña"; 169 (the blood);

"hacer muy hombres a los hombres y muy mujeres a las mujeres" (92, 141, 168–69); Cansinos-Asséns, *Ética y estética* 171: "como una larva, el híbrido se introduce en los sueños de los seres normales"; 128, 167: "la turba ambigua de los andróginos y los hermafroditas"; 167, 171: "sus misterios llenan gran parte del bosque de la noche." See also Giménez Caballero's comment on the contemporary fascination with androgyny ("Anteprólogo" 6); and Carpenter, *Intermediate Sex*. Cristóbal de Castro declared that "the world is populated only with intermediate beings."

60. Cansinos-Asséns, *Ética y estética* 113: "un sexo no es sólo una representación material perfectamente definida en el espacio, una realidad topográfica . . . es, sobre todo, un nexo de representaciones mentales, de estados afectivos, un medio de tenuísimas sugestiones, variables hasta lo infinito"; 128: "era antes un atributo único, insustituible e inmutable. Mas vedlo ahora revolotear como un pájaro maravilloso sobre los árboles humanos. Las palabras de varón y mujer no tienen ya un sentido indudable. Por entre las líneas de la dualidad, graciosamente se deslizan con un aire evasivo mujeres dotadas de viril atributo, varones de grácil talle, en cuyas caderas se marcan hoyos turbadores, seres ornados con un doble atributo"; 129: "el monstruo es una interpretación nueva, un anhelo de liberación y de originalidad."

61. Cansinos-Asséns, *Ética y estética* 129: "al mismo tiempo en sus rostros, atónitos del maravilloso hallazgo, expresan el júbilo estático y quieto de su reconciliación con la íntima verdad. Porque lo que en ello parece monstruoso es su verdad."

62. Fortuny, *La ola verde* 118. He did not, however, think highly of Cansinos-Asséns's narrative talents, calling him too "cerebral" (*La ola verde* 119–21; also, Montero Alonso). Retana possessed a large library, including books by Havelock Ellis, Freud, Nin Frías (*Homosexualismo creador*), Colette, Verlaine, Lorrain, and Cocteau (Pérez Sanz and Bru Ripoll, *La erótica* 2098–99). He parodied Marañón's theories of sexuality in *A Sodoma en tren botijo* (1933) (202–3).

63. González Echevarría 100–101 (long Spanish pedigree), 81–113 (Calderón); Calderón, *La vida* 93: "monstruo de una especie y otra"; Calderón, *El monstruo* n. pag.: "monstruo, pues, de dos especies, / tu dama de dia, y de noche / tu galán" [Eng. trans. González Echevarría]; Lope de Vega, *La Dorotea* 247, 333 n144 (also Entrambasaguas 279–80).

64. Larra 345–46: "Es la confusión de los sexos el único hermafrodita de la naturaleza." Bretón de los Herreros satirized the proliferation of geniuses in 1839, saying: "One is a male *genius* / The other, a female *genius* / And I

presume there are / *Hermaphrodite*s as well" ("El uno es *genio* varon, / El otro es *genio* mujer, / Y presumo que los hay / *Hermafroditas* tambien") (281). Pedro de Alarcón (1875) sardonically called the cross-dressers of Carnival "hermaphrodites" (11); and in Leopoldo Alas's 1891 novel, *Su único hijo*, Bonifacio Reyes, described as somewhat feline but not effeminate, thinks of the ministrations and massages he performs on his capricious, demanding wife as belonging not to the "natural aptitudes of an overly-pious or fussy hermaphrodite, but the romantic exaggeration of a quixotic love" ("aptitudes naturales de un hermafrodita beato o cominero, sino la romántica exageración de un amor quijotesco") (71).

65. Rubio Jiménez and Deaño Gamallo 94: "un ser enfermizo, afeminado, complicado, sin altura, sin vigor, sin sexo artístico, o con sexo intermedio, en fin, un hermafrodita estético"; "dentro del cual hay una mujer, un hombre, un niño, un psicólogo, un poeta, un *creador de idioma moderno.*"

66. Retana, *Flor del mal* 33: "el más adorable de los monstruos"; 52, also 64: "monstruosidades deliciosas"; 43 ("exhibirme").

67. Baralt 229–30, 231–32 (*exhibirse*), 398; also, Zerolo; Onions 299 (and *Online Etymology Dictionary*); Babbit 187 ("original" as extravagant); *Diccionario* (1927) 909 (circus artist): "ejercicios originales o extraños." Space does not allow me to consider how the widespread eighteenth-century use of the word *capricho* might have served a purpose partly related to the later appearance of *excentricidad* (see Ilie; and Dowling).

68. *Diccionario* (1925): "rareza o extravagancia de carácter"; "dicho o hecho raro, anormal"; Baralt 44–45. In English, the mid-seventeenth-century word *eccentric* meaning odd or irregular antedates the early nineteenth-century medical use of the term *abnormal* (*Online Etymology Dictionary;* Onions 299; Gregory 83).

69. Mesonero Romanos, "Contrastes" 498, and *Memorias* 1: 100, 223, 240; 2: 56; Mata 1: 264; Coloma 20: "*allure* varonil y decidida" and "excéntricas genialidades." See also Bretón de los Herreros's "El genio—Los genios" for a reference to one dubious genius as an "eccentric youth" ("excéntrico doncel") (282) (the poem first appeared in the *Revista de Madrid*, 2nd series, 1 [1839]: 255–60; then in *Obras: Poesías* [Madrid: Imprenta Nacional, 1851], *Obras escogidas*, vol. 2 [Paris: Baudry, Librería Europea, 1853], and in *Obras* 1884, from which I am citing). Campoamor (1875) called the poet Heine eccentric, in a piece on originality and plagiarism (245). And in 1886, Alas humorously suggested that a critic's severity might be viewed as eccentricity, or quixotic, given the general tendency to lavish unmerited praise (*Un*

viaje 9). At the end of the nineteenth century, the Italian quick-change artist, who appeared dressed as a woman, among other roles, Leopoldo Fregoli, advertised his creations in Barcelona as "comic-musical-eccentric" (Usó 11).

70. Gregory 83, also Foucault, *Abnormal* 72–73 and Schreck (deviation); Kendall 27; Mill 83; Gregory 84, "Biographie des excentriques," attributed to Baudelaire [1850]; and Brix (oddities).

71. Gregory 83 (eccentricity as deviation and normal); Cleminson, "El libro *Homosexualidad*" 971 (counternarrative); Nin Frías, *Alexis* 189: "anomalía, aberración, perversión, y sobre cuyo reverso es posible asimismo otear la excelsitud y la diafanidad divinas de la grandeza humana" and "la perla es el producto de una enfermedad"; Nin Frías, *Homosexualismo creador* 17: "La anormalidad del uránico no está en él, sino en quienes no participan de su modalidad *sui generis*."

72. Cansinos-Asséns, *Ética y estética* 134: "antes pertenecen a la estética que a la biología" and "una realidad decorativa"; Max-Bembo 37 (psychic hermaphroditism).

73. Retana, *La hora* 51 ("eccentric"); 67. Richard Cleminson links both Retana and Cansinos-Asséns (*Ética y estética*) to a literary-artistic bohemia marked by sexual dissidence and ambiguity ("La antorcha extinguida" 58).

74. Retana, *Mi alma desnuda* 113, 114, 115: "excéntrico musical," "enfermo de excentricidad," and "Estos degenerados son los que desacreditan el Vicio. Estos tipos debiéramos matarlos, no por su perversión sexual, sino porque son grotescos. Las aberraciones elegantes y decorativas, discretamente disimuladas, merecen el respeto de la gente porque no ponen en la vida una nota ridícula"; Retana, *La hora* 67.

75. Retana, *Mi alma desnuda* 115: "inversión cómica y anticuada de estos supervivientes de Sodoma que viven esclavos de la burla que les jugó la Naturaleza"; 116: "La perfección está en las personas que hacemos 'a pluma y a pelo.' La sensibilidad erótica más refinada es la de quienes pueden vibrar indistintamente con uno y otro sexo. Podría darles a ustedes una conferencia interesantísima sobre el tema, apoyándome en textos de Medicina legal; pero temo escandalizar a Retana, que de algún tiempo a esta parte se expresa como un ángel"; Cleminson and Vázquez García, *Hermaphroditism* 230.

76. Chauncey 13, 358, 49.

77. Retana, *Mi alma desnuda* 195: "un monstruo bello y joven"; 196: "mostrarme tal cual soy"; 209 (Salomé); Cansinos-Asséns, *Salomé* 46: "efébica danzarina."

78. Retana, *Mi alma desnuda* 80: "víctima de la moderna literatura decadente"

and "el veneno del pecado decorativo"; 54: "envenenado de literatura y de excentricidad." The same passage on Don Juan Ambiguo also appears in *El veneno de la aventura* (1924) (72–75), as does the phrase, "a pluma y a pelo," though the remarks here are in response to a third-rate *transformista* who mangles his female imitation and not to an aging fairy in the shape of a dress designer (65–66). Retana was not above recycling material from one text to another.

79. Retana, *Mi alma desnuda* 83 (ultimate monstrosity); Retana, *El octavo* 36: "aire de excentricidad inédita"; 47, also 41, 49: "mujer excéntrica"; 74: "personaje equívoco," "tipo amoral o excéntrico, vestido en una forma aparatosa y poco digna"; 49, 61 (monster).

80. Hernández 207 (priapic Pierrot); Anon., "Una carta del poeta" (undated letter to Melchor Fernández Almagro, prob. 1920s); García Lorca, "Pierrot" (*OC* 4: 833): "una virgen exótica y lejana y un hombre muscular y acerado danzan en mí"; 831, 832 (inner life), 833, 834 (mask); Letter to Adriano del Valle (May 1918) (*Epistolario* 47). Reflecting the influence of Verlaine, the Pierrot appears in other early texts of Lorca: "Crepúsculo espiritual," "Carnaval: Visión interior," and "Los cipreses" (*Poesía inédita*); see also Benavente's pantomime, *La blancura de Pierrot* (1898) and Peral Vega 18. Retana designed several Pierrot costumes for female music-hall entertainers, as well as Harlequin and Columbina outfits (see Peláez Martín). In *La mala fama* (1922), Retana's alter ego, Alberto Reyna, pulls out a heap of postcards stamped with his image, one of which shows him dressed as a Pierrot (131).

81. Retana, *El octavo* 71: "invertido, envenenado de literatura y demasiado vicioso."

82. Retana, *El octavo* 115: "la Naturaleza parece deleitarse en la creación de monstruos terrestres o marinos"; 116: "*in mente* una doble existencia fabulosa y pintoresca"; 86: "una criatura extraordinaria, al parecer fugada de los jardines mitológicos" (also 108); 126: "Felizmente, Baby es una mujer; no estamos ya en tiempo de Adonis y Hermafrodita, que desaparecieron para siempre, y nunca un hombre podrá adquirir semejantes grados de belleza."

83. Retana, *Las "locas"* 32: "aventuras equívocas" and "monstruosas aberraciones"; 34–35: "seudohombres"; 120: "urinario monstruo." Readers were clearly aware of the specific geography of the gay world; see also Max-Bembo 48–49 and Madrid (64–68), for the homosexual subculture in Barcelona in the early twentieth century.

84. Retana, *Las "locas"* 113: "*locas* por convicción," "*locas* profesionales," "*locas*

en entredicho," "*locas* escandalosas," "*locas* vergonzantes," "*locas* románti-cas," "*locas* en germen," "el inevitable grupo de *anfibios*." Cleminson and Vázquez García see Retana's work "as a protest against . . . the medicaliza-tion of homosexuality" (*"Los Invisibles"* 243–44).

85. Fortuny, "Nacimiento, esplendor" 25 (banter). During the Franco regime, without fanfare, Retana managed to slip in a section of *transformistas* into his book on female entertainers, *Historia del arte frívolo* (1964) (136–40). He also wrote a short book on Egmont de Bries, which is filled mostly with the lyrics of songs that de Bries performed in drag (*Egmont de Bries. Su vida. Sus amores. Su arte. Sus canciones*). The artist's name has been variously spelled; I have adopted Retana's usage, "Egmont de Bries."

86. Adams 12–13 (sideshow spectators); Retana, *Las "locas"* 124: "¡Ay, qué cur-sis! ¡Ya no se dice apio! ¡Se dice vidrio!"; Mira, *De Sodoma* 150 (performer denied he was gay); Usó 45 (de Bries as gay); Retana, *Las "locas"* 127 (am-biguities of Egmont de Bries). See Retana, *Egmont de Bries* 9–10 and Usó 26, for more on the insults and mockery de Bries sometimes received. He was temporarily banned from performing in Madrid in 1921 (Usó 48–50). In Ar-gentina, authorities were so incensed by his cross-dressing they proposed legislation to prohibit the practice (Usó 70–71; Anon., "Edmond de Bries" 2).

87. For a view of eccentricity as a non-Spanish stereotyping of the perceived marginality and extravagance of Spain, see Ayala, "La excentricidad his-pana" 22–23.

88. Marañón, "Psicopatología" 76 (first published as "Notas para la biología de Don Juan" in 1924); and S. Wright 717, 721; see also Rioyo.

89. Martín de Lucenay, *Invertidos célebres* 34: "En España, allá por el año 1925, la persecución de que fue objeto por la dictadura un escritor homosexual puso de moda la homosexualidad y toda su literatura."

90. Ayala, *Recuerdos* 82–83.

91. Citing Javier Rioyo, Maite Zubiaurre suggests Retana and Lorca knew each other, but I have been unable to confirm the observation (7).

92. Ríos Carratalá, *Una arrolladora simpatía* 42 (Altolaguirre apparently ex-cised Neville from his memory) (also Neville, "Una especie de ángel," who recalled Altolaguirre fondly); Gómez de la Serna, *Sagrada cripta* 472–73; Morla Lynch, *En España* 270.

93. Villena, *El ángel* 49 (Retana and Neville); Retana, *El vicio* 10: "un templo sagrado . . . [para] todos los placeres de los falsos paraísos" (Alberto Reyna's studio is a "temple of Mortal Sin" ["un templo del Pecado Mortal"], in *Una niña "demasiado moderna"* 79); 35 ("gentes ambiguas"); 37–38 (Neville); Ríos

Carratalá, *El tiempo* 86–87 (Retana-Neville friendship); Pérez Sanz and Bru Ripoll, *La erótica* 1611 (*Una niña*); Gómez Santos 324 (Neville and drugs).

94. Retana, "Historial documentado de "*La carne de tablado*": "un ansia loca de apurar las decadencias importadas por la guerra mundial" (in Pérez Sanz and Bru Ripoll, *La erótica* 1589) ("mad desire") (see also Santiago Ibero [pseudonym for José Sánchez Moreno] 10–11); González–Ruano, *Memorias* 69–70 (Maxim's) (Retana also mentions the use of cocaine ["Historial" 1589]); Gómez Santos 324 ("fine white powder"). For the easy availability of cocaine in Barcelona, see Francisco Madrid (1926) (103–7).

95. Santiago Ibero 10–11: "esa fauna ambigua, inteligente y pervertida"; Retana (in Pérez Sanz and Bru Ripoll, *La erótica* 1955): "La guerra de 1914 fue para España la apoteosis del juego, de las drogas estupefacientes y el amor que no puede decir su nombre"; Valis, introduction to Badanelli, *Serenata del amor triunfante* 13 (nightlife); Davidson 6, 13, 43, 55–61 (jazz and drugs); Marín Abeytua and Marín Abeytua 39 (Retana and jazz).

96. Santiago Ibero 15–16 (Retana's entertainments); Retana, "Barcelona de noche" (June 1935) (in Pérez Sanz and Bru Ripoll, *La erótica* 1533): "¡Cosmopolitismo, tolerancia y modernidad se llama todo esto!"; Santiago Ibero 5: "siempre exquisito y sobre todo moderno"; Campoy (in Santiago Ibero 4): "como el fox-trot y como la morfina, / un producto que trajo la civilización."

97. Retana, *A Sodoma* 179, 219–20; García Posada 203–4, 206–7 (Aleixandre's soirées; Morla Lynch home); Ulacia Altolaguirre 88 (Lorca as *cupletista*).

98. Valverde (Retana interview) (in Pérez Sanz and Bru Ripoll, *La erótica* 964): "No me honro con la amistad de ninguno de ellos; pero sigo con muchísima admiración la labor de [G]iménez Caballero . . . Claudio de [la]Torre, y, naturalmente, Ramón Gómez de la Serna . . . el verdadero faro de los escritores modernos"; Retana, *Mi alma desnuda* 88–89, 90: "¡La verdad que esto del ultraísmo es comodísimo! . . . Permite rimar las mayores atrocidades." Vilar's study is also decorated in a purported ultraist style (95).

99. Pérez Sanz and Bru Ripoll, *La sexología* 185, 187 (González-Ruano and Retana) (also Villena, *El ángel* 55–56); González Ruano, "Álvaro Retana" (poem) (1923) (in Villena 55–56) (the novel, for which González-Ruano wrote a prologue, is *El infierno de la voluptuosidad* [1924], a reincarnation of *La hora del pecado* [1923]); González-Ruano, *Memorias* 205–6 (Lorca); González-Ruano, "Bajo la sonrisa" (in Inglada, *Palabra* 50) (orig. *Crónica* [Madrid] [11 Jan. 1931: 5]) ("great poet"); González-Ruano, *Memorias* 85–87 (Hoyos y Vinent).

100. Vargas Vila (qtd in González-Ruano, *Memorias* 160): "Si no tiene usted una leyenda monstruosa, horrible, no será nunca nada." For more on González-Ruano, see Sala Rose and Garcia-Planas; also, Castillo Cáceres; Cansinos-Asséns 3: 225–34; and Moga. On his equivocal sexuality, Sala Rose and Garcia-Planas 23, 88; and Cansinos-Asséns 3: 226. Pedro Salinas declared González-Ruano an expert shameless bastard, though he also found merit in a poetry anthology he had prepared (Moga 4; A. Anderson, *El veintisiete* 198 n11).

101. Schehr x (gay Baedeker); Willy 60 (Orleans y Borbón). Retana's stand-in Alberto Reyna is especially taken with the writings of Willy, along with Jean Lorrain and Rachilde (*La mala fama* 49).

102. Nin Frías, Letter to FGL (1 Nov. 1933); Nin Frías, *Alexis* 181–82; Gibson, *Federico García Lorca* 2: 285–86 (Nin Frías).

103. Armando Vites (Antiquarian), Communication with Noël Valis (20 June 2013) (Badanelli and *Gypsy Ballads*); Badanelli, Letter to Álvaro Retana, dated 30 May 1969 (in Pérez Sanz and Bru Ripoll, *La erótica* 2464–65).

104. Mira, "Modernistas, dandis" 72–73 (*Poemas arábigoandaluces* and trending subject); García-Posada, in García Lorca, *OC* 1: 953 (*Diván*); Nin Frías, *Ensayo* 32–33: "un perfecto espíritu de mujer . . . [que] jamás resulta afeminado en sus escritos"; 33–34: "en las antologías musulmanas de marcado tinte uránico."

105. Nin Frías, *Ensayo* 76: "el gitanísimo poeta"; "su patetismo de *cante jondo*, y sobre todo sus sorprendentes y mágicas pinceladas, con instrumentación a lo griego y arquitectura de suspiros, con sonoridades marcadamente uránicas, ponen en el alma emociones que no son ajenas al conjuro medieval de los poetas arábigos andaluces"; 45: "afiebrados en el divino helenismo de sus respectivas imaginaciones, viven como acechando al *mocito* andaluz para estamparle en sus lienzos"; Nin Frías, *Ensayo* 42: "'donde hay que buscar lo mejor de Badanelli es en su propia vida que es donde está su verdadera poesía'"; Gide, *If It Die* 302 (Wilde remark).

106. Nin Frías, *Ensayo* 25 (reference to *Serenata del amor triunfante*); for Badanelli's friendship with Benavente, see the six letters from Benavente (1939–49), no doubt part of a much more extensive correspondence. In a pro-Franco publication, the poet Eduardo de Ory praised Badanelli's novel but was silent on its content. Ory also referred to Nin Frías's comments on Badanelli but without mentioning that Nin's study included Muñoz Pabón and, most significantly, Lorca ("Zahorí" 3).

6. Fabulous Fag (III), or a Face in the Crowd

1. Nin Frías, *Ensayo* 64: "extraño sabor equívoco."

2. Molina Fajardo 181: "su manera de ser tan especial" and "fama equívoca"; Moreno Villa, *Memoria* 109; Gibson, *"Caballo azul"* 117–20 (Buñuel's homophobia); Buñuel 61–62. Despite his open admiration for Lorca, the poet Pedro Salinas could not stop himself from reproving his behavior in private: "Federico as usual has made himself scarce, as he's with those friends of his, *du côté de Charlus*" ("Federico siempre huido, entre esos amigos du côté de Charlus") (*Correspondencia* 133) (letter to Jorge Guillén, dated 21 Feb. 1931). See also Herrero 241–44 for similar criticisms from other friends of Lorca.

3. Guillén xvii: "Lo sabe todo el mundo, es decir, en esta ocasión el mundo entero: Federico García Lorca fue una criatura extraordinaria. 'Criatura' significa esta vez más que 'hombre.' Porque Federico nos ponía en contacto con la creación . . . era ante todo manantial, arranque fresquísimo de manantial, una transparencia de origen entre los orígenes del universo, tan recién creado y tan antiguo. Junto al poeta—y no solo en su poesía—se respiraba un aura que él iluminaba con su propia luz . . . criatura de la Creación, inmersa en Creación"; Aleixandre 1829, 1830: "fabuloso y mítico" and "pasaba mágicamente por la vida"; Cernuda, "Líneas sobre los poetas" 66 ; Salinas, "Federico García Lorca" (1972) 173; Le Bon 130, 132 (also Weber); Boone and Vickers 903 ("numinous aura"); see also Rojek, for the link between celebrity and religion. Le Bon had already noted in 1895 what he called the "religious shape assumed by all the convictions of crowds," including the worship of leaders and other special figures (72–73).

4. Juvenal 97; Hernández, *Libro de los dibujos* 129–30 ("fabulous animal"); García Lorca, Letter to his family (20 Oct. 1933) (*Epistolario* 772) (bullfighter); Salinas, "Federico García Lorca" (in Castro, *Versos* 383–84) (too full of himself); García Lorca, Letter to Jorge Zalamea (Aug. 1928) (*Epistolario* 577) ("stupid fame"); Dudgeon 107 ("interest in fame"); Stainton, chapter 11 ("Celebrity: 1927") (157–75). In 1929, however, Lorca's fame had not yet spread to the United States. Sofía Megwinoff recalled she could not find any of his books in New York bookstores or libraries at that time (letter to Daniel Eisenberg, mid-1970s, in Maurer and Anderson 185).

5. Boone and Vickers 904 ("talk of the multitude"); Blake 27 (thronged); Braudy, *Frenzy* 38–39 (Alexander the Great); see also Inglis.

6. López Pinillos, *Los favoritos* 153: "Aunque el escritor sea tan aristocrático y odie tan furiosamente la populachería como usted [Valle-Inclán]." A pop-

ular series of the day titled "Los favoritos de la fama" (The Favorites of Fame), from the publishing house Rafael Caro Raggio, centered on celebrities, as, for example, was the case with Álvaro Retana's book on the cross-dresser Egmont de Bries (1921).

7. Giménez Caballero spoke of "las gentes populares españolas" ("the popular classes in Spain") and "el pueblo ignorante y genial de España" ("the great unwashed of Spain") ("Fama póstuma" 2).

8. Zorrilla, "Introducción" v: "nada soy en el mundo."

9. Schulberg explicitly used the phrase, "man of the people," and compared Lonesome Rhodes to Will Rogers (9, 12); Schulberg 27–28. Will Rogers is also evoked in the film.

10. Le Bon 14, 15; Azaña 44; Pérez Galdós, "La sociedad" 178.

11. J.J. 2 (people's poet); Olmedilla, "Rutas mediterráneas" 16 ("simbología social"); J.J. 2 (crowd reaction to "Ballad of the Spanish Civil Guard"); García Lorca, "Lectura de poemas" (OC 3: 174–77); also Anon., "En el Barcelona" (in Laffranque, "Federico García Lorca" 17) (orig. in Día Gráfico [Barcelona] [8 Oct. 1935]).

12. Ortega y Gasset, Rebelión 50: "Las ciudades están llenas de gente. Las casas, llenas de inquilinos. Los hoteles, llenos de huéspedes. Los trenes, llenos de viajeros. Los cafés, llenos de consumidores. Los paseos, llenos de transeúntes."

13. Olmedilla, "Ayer se celebró" 8 (La dama boba).

14. Braudy, "Knowing the Performer" 1071 (nineteenth-century mass culture and celebrity); Pérez Galdós, "Observaciones" 128: "la participación de todos en la vida pública"; "un pie en el templo de la fama."

15. Baudelaire, "Perte d'auréole" 155: "Vous devriez au moins faire afficher cette auréole, ou la faire réclamer par le commissaire."

16. García Lorca, "Lectura de poemas" (OC 3: 175): "Estamos aquí reunidos y como yo no tengo la técnica ni el paisaje del actor y veo este gran teatro lleno de un público distinto y expectante, tengo cierto miedo de que mis poemas o bien por íntimos o bien por oscuros o bien por demasiado escuetos . . . pueden quedar ateridos bajo esta bóveda temblando como esos gatos sucios que los niños matan a pedradas en los arrabales de las poblaciones."

17. García Lorca, "Lectura de poemas" (OC 3: 175): "Mi amor a los demás, mi profundo cariño y compenetración con el pueblo, como me ha llevado a escribir teatro para llegar a todos y confundirme con todos, me trae esta tibia mañana de Barcelona a leer ante gran público lo que yo considero más entrañable de mi persona"; "una pequeña sala donde un poeta con toda su

modestia y sencillez va a daros sin desplantes ni orgullo lo mejor, lo más hondo que tiene."

18. García Lorca, "Lectura de poemas" (*OC* 3: 175–76): "un acto íntimo"; "todo lo contrario a la oratoria. En la oratoria, el orador estira una idea ya conocida del público . . . que la multitud acoge con entusiasmo."

19. Olmedilla, "Rutas mediterráneas" 16: "puso con sólo aparecer, en alta tensión el entusiasmo de todos"; J.P. (in Laffranque, "Federico García Lorca" 1): "Pone el pueblo su sello en las cuartillas reservadas a los escogidos, cuando son leídas en grandes asambleas"; "ávido de identificarse con el poeta" (orig. in *Día Gráfico* [Barcelona] [10 Oct. 1935]).

20. García Lorca, *Epistolario* 616–17 (Letter dated 28 June 1929): "la ciudad más atrevida y más moderna del mundo"; "la multitud abigarrada de jerseys de colores y pañuelos atrevidos, las bocinas de los autos . . . [y] las radios"; 621 (Letter to his family, dated 6 July 1929): "La muchedumbre lo llena todo con un rumor sudoroso de sal marina, muchedumbre de judíos, negros, japoneses, chinos, mulatos y rubicundos yankis. Es un espectáculo estupendo, aunque excesivo, y con una vez basta, porque es demasiado popular. Es el pueblo más pueblo de Nueva York"; see also García Lorca, ["Un poeta en Nueva York"] (*OC* 3: 169); Yahni; and Morris, *Lorca entre la muchedumbre*.

21. García Lorca, "Paisaje de la multitud que vomita" (*OC* 1: 528): "Yo, poeta sin brazos, perdido / entre la multitud que vomita"; García Lorca, *Epistolario* 621 (Letter to his family, dated 6 July 1929): "montañas rusas increíbles, lagos encantados, grutas, músicas, monstruos humanos, grandes bailes, colecciones de fieras, ruedas y columpios gigantescos, las mujeres más gruesas del mundo, el hombre que tiene cuatro ojos, etc., etc., y luego miles de puestos de helados, salchichas, frituras, panecillos, dulces, en una variedad fantástica."

22. García Lorca, "Paisaje de la multitud que vomita" (*OC* 1: 527): "La mujer gorda venía delante / arrancando las raíces y mojando el pergamino de los tambores"; "vuelve del revés los pulpos agonizantes"; "dejaba por los rincones pequeñas calaveras de paloma / y levantaba las furias de los banquetes de los siglos últimos"; "Paisaje" (*OC* 1: 528): "con las gentes de los barcos, de las tabernas y de los jardines"; *OC* 1: 527: "enterradas bajo la arena. / Son los muertos, los faisanes y las manzanas de otra hora / los que nos empujan en la garganta"; "demonio del pan"; "Sin remedio, hijo mío, ¡vomita!"; *OC* 1: 528: "la ciudad entera se agolpó en las barandillas del embarcadero" (see Koppenfels 50 on the convulsive movement of the poem). In

another context, Walker Percy asked, "Is it possible to live without feasting on death?" (354).

23. García Lorca, "Paisaje" (*OC* 1: 527): "La mujer gorda venía delante"; "los rumores de la selva del vómito / con las mujeres vacías, con niños de cera caliente"; "Paisaje" (*OC* 1: 528): "Esta mirada mía fue mía, pero ya no es mía"; "Yo, poeta sin brazos"; Hoyos y Vinent, Prólogo 7. Anthony Geist interprets the armless poet as poetically and sexually impotent and a transvestite Venus de Milo; and the fat lady as a "perverse inversion of the Statue of Liberty" ("Las mariposas" 557); Morris, "Fat Body," considers the poet "participant and captive, victim and judge," while the "fat woman . . . becomes, literally, a leading lady," at the head of the crowd (52, 60). See also José Antonio Llera, who focuses on the unsettling excess of *Poet in New York* as a form of the abject, and along these lines, views the figure of the poet as a monster and freak (46, 48).

24. Ortega y Gasset, *Rebelión* 51: "Sorprenderse, extrañarse, es comenzar a entender"; "[mira] el mundo con los ojos dilatados por la extrañeza. Todo en el mundo es extraño y es maravilloso para unas pupilas bien abiertas"; "lleva al intelectual por el mundo en perpetua embriaguez de visionario"; 59: "el brutal imperio de las masas"; "la época de lo colosal"; García Lorca, "Sleepwalking Ballad," *Collected Poems* 559 (trans. Christopher Maurer); "Romance sonámbulo" (*OC* 1: 422): "La noche se puso íntima / como una pequeña plaza."

25. Braudy, *Frenzy* 14 ("a way of defining"); García Lorca, "Paisaje" (*OC* 1: 528): "Esta mirada mía fue mía, pero ya no es mía. / Esta mirada que tiembla desnuda por el alcohol / y despide barcos increíbles / por las anémonas de los muelles"; "Me defiendo con esta mirada / que mana de las ondas por donde el alba no se atreve"; Marlowe, *Doctor Faustus* 154. Marlowe 146–47 also highlights the fame of Alexander the Great, whose spirit Doctor Faustus conjures up.

26. Braudy notes he found the phrase, "the frenzy of renown," in Matthew G. Lewis's novel *The Monk* (1796) (*Frenzy* 14). On the idea of a virtual, dispersed crowd, see Le Bon 24.

27. Burgos, "Retratos" [14] (photographs of Tórtola Valencia) (also García Sánchiz 5, for the impact of photography on Tórtola's celebrity); Burgos, "Tórtola Valencia" 185–86; see also Zamostny, "Tórtola Valencia," who observes how Hoyos y Vinent's "friendship with Tórtola was mutually beneficial for stoking their celebrity" (302). In 1954, when César González-

Ruano tried to conduct an interview with her, she acceded but refused to be photographed, so he called it off (González-Ruano, *Diario íntimo* 629).

28. Nelken 98, 101: "verdaderamente una casa" and "llegar a ser Tórtola"; Carretero, "Tórtola Valencia" 38; Zárraga 27 (Tórtola's eccentricities); see also Clúa, *Cuerpos de escándalo* 122–26.

29. Erre 170 (throngs) (orig. in *El Diario Español* [Montevideo] [14 Oct. 1933]); Anon., "Llegó anoche" 156 (Lorca overwhelmed) (orig. in *La Nación* [Buenos Aires] [14 Oct. 1933]); Anon., "'Vengo de torero'"148 (orig. in *Crítica* [Buenos Aires] [14 Oct. 1933]): "'Estoy como esos toreros postrados, desgarrados, después de la lucha mitológica, que sonríe a los fotógrafos desde el lecho'"; Rocca and Roland 93 (Amorim); Pinto 268 (boy wonder / "niño prodigio") (orig. in *La Mañana* [Montevideo] [6 Feb. 1934]); Anon., "Llegó anoche" 155: "circunferente y luminosa"; Anon., "Llegó anoche" 157 and Pinto 266 (poet-friends) (also Rocca and Roland 75). See also Maurer's excellent prologue to Inglada, *Palabra de Lorca* vii–xx.

30. Rivas 186 ("pajama guy") (orig. in *La Razón* [Buenos Aires] [21 Oct. 1933]); Rodríguez Lence 190 (orig. in *Correo de Galicia* [Buenos Aires] [22 Oct. 1933]): "cigarros, libros, lápices, cuartillas, una botella vacía y monedas sueltas de diversas naciones"; Rodríguez Lence 191 (hotel scene).

31. Robledal 208 (orig. in *Aconcagua* [Buenos Aires], No. 47 [Dec. 1933]): "'Estoy afeitándome'"; "enarbolando la 'gillette' a modo de batuta"; Conze 12, 130 (farm worker's wage); Robledal 208 (fraternizing; and "el lenguaje alado de los ángeles"), and 209 (photograph, "El duende se hizo carne"); Robledal 212–13 (Lorca's duende dream). Barthes observed, "Far from the details of [the writer's] daily life bringing nearer to me the nature of his inspiration and making it clearer, it is the whole mythical singularity of his condition which the writer emphasizes by such confidences" (31).

32. Soto ("Boy") 276 (orig. in *El Plata* [Montevideo] [12 Feb. 1934]): "Con tanta radio, tanto periódico y tanto elemento de comunicación colectiva, la verdad es que en nuestros días resulta poco envidiable la situación personal del hombre que cae en el círculo de la fama"; 276–77: "García Lorca en la terraza. García Lorca en el piano. García Lorca entre telones. García Lorca en una peña. García Lorca recitando. García Lorca poniéndose la corbata. García Lorca aprendiendo a cebar mate. García Lorca firmando una foto. Y a todo esto, en medio de todo esto, como consecuencia fisiológica de todo esto, García Lorca mirándose las manos, golpeándose la frente, escondiéndose por aquí, huyendo por allá, sin saber el pobre muchacho qué hacer ni dónde meterse para esquivar los golpes del asalto del periodista, del fotóg-

rafo, del dibujante, del empresario, del admirador"; Pérez Ferrero, "Voces" 38 (orig. in *El Heraldo de Madrid* [9 Oct. 1930]): "Basta decir su nombre y sus apellidos"; Soto 278 (autograph hunters); 279 (don't ask me); 280: "Y sobre todo, ¡por lo que más quiera! No me pida que le escriba un pensamiento"; García Lorca, *Epistolario* 773 (Prince of Wales); *Epistolario* 772 (twenty albums) (Letter to Clotilde García Picossi, dated Oct. 1933); *Epistolario* 776 (photographs and articles) (Letter to his family, dated 20 Oct. 1933, on the back of a photo) (also *Epistolario* 772–73); *Epistolario* 772 (personal assistant); Maurer, "Lorca, de viva voz" vii–viii.

33. Luna 305 (orig. in *Crítica* [Buenos Aires] [10 Mar. 1934]): "en grande, expuesto al público"; "Mi nombre estaba en las esquinas, ante la curiosidad de unos y la indiferencia de otros. ¡Y era mi nombre! . . . ¡Eso, tan mío, puesto así, para que todos se sirvan de él! . . . Era como si dejara de ser yo . . . ¡Es una cosa que no puedo evitar, amigo mío!"

34. Luna 305: "una segunda persona, enemiga mía, para burlarse de mi timidez desde todos estos cartelones"; "genius for backing into the limelight," a Turkish saying, attributed to Lowell Thomas; Yardley 156–58, 227 (Lowell Thomas); Anon., "Lawrence the Ubiquitous" 29.

35. Pérez Ferrero, "Los españoles" 311 (orig. in *El Heraldo de Madrid* [14 Apr. 1934]): "una verdadera montaña de recortes de Prensa."

36. Guasp 399 (orig. in *El Mercantil Valenciano* [22 Sept. 1935]): "un amplio corro de atónitos, gozosos de poder estar, callados, prendidos en el prodigio de la palabra del poeta que habla como escribe, con la imaginación caliente, con el verbo encendido"; "deslumbrante de gozo"; "la niebla encendida"; Soria Olmedo, "Introducción" 18 (dramatize his life).

37. Salado 345: "lo único malo de Lorca"; Suero, "Los últimos días" 478, 479 (orig. in *España levanta el puño* [Buenos Aires], 1937) (for the Suero-Lorca relationship, see Larrea 35–36; and Mansilla and López Alfonso 32–35); García Lorca, *Epistolario* 758 (letter to Eduardo Rodríguez Valdivieso, dated Apr. 1933); Gasch 14: "sumergido de lleno en un epidérmico, superficial, ambiente literario-mundano."

38. Wolfe 25: "el poeta español más sobrevalorado del siglo XX, y tal vez de la historia."

39. Wolfe 25 and Torrecilla 243 (stereotypes); Fernández Cabal and Pérez Herrero 131, who observed that Lorca himself was seen as "the one who took her to the river" ("el que se la llevó al río"), in many towns and villages, thus identifying the poet with the male gypsy in "The Faithless Wife" (orig. in *La Mañana* [León] [12 Aug. 1933]); Gibson, *Federico García Lorca* 2: 85

(circulation of "The Faithless Wife"); Morris, *Son of Andalusia* 345. Gibson notes at least two specific occasions when Lorca read "The Faithless Wife" in public (*Federico García Lorca* 1: 514, 2: 285); also, Stainton 185.

40. Jou 424 (caricatured) (orig. in *La Humanitat* [Barcelona] [6 Oct. 1935]); Luna 298: "como un feo pecado"; 299 (public/private; poplars); also, Maurer, "Lorca de viva voz" x, xi.

41. Suero, "Crónica" 166 ("Ode") (orig. in *Noticias Gráficas* [Buenos Aires] [14 Oct. 1933]); Ferreiro 258 (orig. in *El Pueblo* [Montevideo] [1 Feb. 1934]): "¡vieran ustedes esa oda a Whitman! Es lo mejor de García Lorca, si García Lorca admite que se le clasifique como productor de cosas mejores que otras suyas. Es el responso a todos los maricas del mundo; es la defensa del hombre aquel, de las manos caídas, que andaba por East River, con su gran barba llena de mariposas, jugando con los muchachos, hablando con ellos, mientras el sol cantaba por sus ombligos, debajo de los puentes." Ferreiro also published a second version of his day with Lorca in 1945 (Inglada, *Palabra de Lorca* 496–517).

42. Roncagliolo 51–52, 167–69 (Amorim account).

43. Ferreiro 257, 258: "jornadas de gloria"; "una angustia de alegría, manada en el despeñadero de aquel torrente de palabras"; "Y nada más que palabras. Ni imágenes siquiera. Como en la gran música, nada más que notas. Pero ¡qué palabras! Eternas y macizas. Aun cuando decía 'columna de ceniza,' se encrespaban la seguridad perenne de estos poemas geniales." In a letter to Lorca, dated Feb. 1935, Enrique Amorim also brought up the "column of ash," mentioning it in the same breath as two words invented by Lorca: *epente* (code for gay) and *chorpatélico* (playful, or nonsensical) (in Rocca and Roland 193).

44. Schonberg 107, 113.

45. García Lorca, "Oda a Walt Whitman" (*OC* 1: 564–67): "hermoso como la niebla," "tus muslos de Apolo virginal," "barba llena de mariposas," "Adán de sangre, Macho," "amante de los cuerpos bajo la burda tela," "gacela sin cuerpo," "igual que un pájaro / con el sexo atravesado por una aguja"; Darío, "Walt Whitman" 119: "bello como un patriarca," "rostro de emperador"; Borges, "El otro Whitman" 54: "inesperado y elusivo es el mundo."

46. Traubel 438; Robert G. Ingersoll (cited in Traubel 450) (antique god); Carpenter, *Days with Walt Whitman* 6, 24. After W. B. Yeats's death, Auden wrote that "he became his admirers" ("In Memory of W.B. Yeats" 81).

47. Ende 146; Rivers.

48. Apollinaire, "Un témoin" 658–59; Erkkila 199 (hoax); Merrill, "Une lettre"

891: "pure comme la nature elle-même"; 891: "qu'il répugnait de tout son être aux petites perversités des malades et des maniaques"; see Murray for more on the Peter Doyle–Walt Whitman relationship.

49. Carreras, *Los duques de la Torre* 75 (see Chauncey 108–9 for gay sex with train conductors); Retana, *Las "locas"* 56; García Lorca, "Oda" (*OC* 1: 565): "temblando entre las piernas de los *chauffeurs*"; 565: "el amigo come tu manzana / con un leve sabor de gasolina"; "Oda" (*OC* 1: 564): "enemigo del sátiro, / enemigo de la vid"; "Oda" (*OC* 1: 565): "agrupados en los bares"; 565: "girando en las plataformas del ajenjo"; Laguardia 543–44. Lorca owned two books by Apollinaire: *32 poemas* (1929), untrimmed and probably unread; and *Alcools: poèmes* (1920), with pencil markings and underlined passages (Paepe and Fernández-Montesinos García 28).

50. Reynolds 589 (atmosphere) (see also Traubel 438); Merrill, "La question" 330: "c'est traîner dans la boue"; 336: "des calomnies anonymes qui attentent à l'honneur d'un poète."

51. Apollinaire, "La vie anecdotique" 864: "il confond l'unisexualité avec la débauche la plus crapuleuse"; 865: "Puisque la législation barbare et injuste de certains États condamne avec séverité les unisexuels, M. Merrill ne pense-t-il pas qu'il est du dernier intérêt de montrer qu'il a pu y avoir des hommes de génie parmi les unisexuels? Le prestige de ces hommes ne peut-il aider à défaire la barbarie et l'injustice [de telles] législations?"

52. Laguardia 545 (see also Jerez-Farrán, "Transvestism" and "García Lorca, el espectáculo," who argues for conflicted, internalized homophobia in Lorca); García Lorca, "Oda" (*OC* 1: 565): "los maricas, Walt Whitman, te señalan. / ¡También ése! ¡También!"; Rivas-Cherif (13 Jan. 1957): 4: "la que pedía Walt Whitman"; see also Mayhew, *Lorca's Legacy* 149–53, who observes that "Whitman [in the "Ode"] has become the guiding spirit for the *maricas* themselves, the founder of their own social movement" (149).

53. Saunders iv.

54. Saunders iii.

55. Saunders iv, 18 (his comment on Bertz letter, published in *Mercure de France* [1 July 1913]), iii ("cases"). See McDermid for the brief in favor of Lorca's universality over a uniquely homosexual reading (2, 110).

56. García Lorca, "Oda" (*OC* 1: 566–67): "'Fairies' de Norteamérica, / 'Pájaros' de La Habana, / 'Jotos' de Méjico, / 'Sarasas' de Cádiz, / 'Apios' de Sevilla, / 'Cancos' de Madrid, / 'Floras' de Alicante, / 'Adelaidas' de Portugal."

57. Sahuquillo 131; see Hiller 26–28 for more on how these slang terms resist translation; García Lorca, "Oda" (*OC* 1: 567): "¡Maricas de todo el mundo,

asesinos de palomas!"; "perras de sus tocadores"; "Oda" (*OC* 1: 563): "los muchachos cantaban enseñando sus cinturas. / Con la rueda, el aceite, el cuero y el martillo." Lorca used the diminutive form, *mariquita*, in "Canción del mariquita," which Philip Cummings translated as "The Song of the Fairy Lad" (García Lorca, *Songs* 74–75) and Alan S. Trueblood as "Song of the Fairy" (*Collected Poems* 493).

58. Retana, *Las "locas"* 124, 126, 56. The *transformista*, or drag entertainer, in Carretero's *La pena de no ser hombre* (1924) is also called a *sarasa*, even though, ironically, he happens to be straight (22). There was also a *cuplé*, "¡Sarasa!" (1913), sung by the legendary Fornarina (music by Quinito Valverde; words by José Juan Cadenas), that Retana later modified to get it past Franco-era censorship (see Retana, *Estrellas del cuplé* 63–64).

59. Franciosini (*marica*); *OED* (*fairy*); Alemany y Bolufer (*joto*); Rodríguez Navas y Carrasco (*sarasa*); *DRAE* (*apio*); *DRAE* (*pájaro*); Alemany y Bolufer (*homosexual*); Baroja 664; Retana, *Ninfas y sátiros* (244 [*canco*]; 246, 251, 252 [*apio*], 251 [*marica*]); Ontañón y Moreiro 115; Retana, *Las "locas,"* chapter 9: "El apio maravilloso" (*apio*); Cansinos-Asséns, *La novela* 2: 248–49 (*apio*); Anon., "La cofradía del apio" (in Gibson, *Federico García Lorca* 2: 338); Cruz Casado, "La moda femenina" 231 (*El apio maravilloso* project). See also Valle-Inclán, *La corte de los milagros* (1927), who reproduced satirical verses targeting Isabel II's husband, Francisco Asís de Borbón, as a namby pamby, that is, effeminate: "Paquito Natillos / es de pasta flora . . . / Y orina en cuclillas / como una señora" (233). I do not know if the colloquial phrase, "de pasta flora" (to be of bland character), bears any relation to the "Floras de Alicante."

60. Carreras, *Los duques de la Torre* 92 (hybrid); Carreras, *Un casamiento infame* 88: "no ha aprendido otra cosa que á pronunciar bien la palabra sarasa"; 89: "no pensaba sino en *grooms* y cocheritos"; 121: "Aunque Paquito Sarasa pague bien á sus cocheritos, no llega hasta deberles dinero, porque, en estos casos, ya se sabe lo que un cocherito puede hacer: cerrada la bolsa, ¡adios paraiso terrenal!" See Cleminson, Fernández, and Vázquez García for more on this scandal.

61. Carreras, *Los duques de la Torre* 144 (national honor).

62. Anon., "El suceso del día" 3; and Anon., "Situación interina" 1 (Treaty of Paris; national ridicule); Anon., "En plena descomposición" 1 (decay); Equis 1: "convertido en industria legal aquella espantosa abominación"; *Gedeón* (27 Oct. 1898): "¡Ay, hija, lo que hemos hecho!" For a discussion of the so-

ciohistorical context of the Cádiz controversy, see Cleminson, Fernández, and Vázquez García; and Vázquez García.

63. Vázquez García 21–23; Anon., "El Reino" 1; Anon., " . . . Y armas" 3; Anon., "Nuestra adhesión" 1; Anon., "Refranes" 4 (*esteta*); San Rafael 1 ("aesthetic life"); Moore 170 (Pericón de Cádiz). Vázquez García notes that the use of *coridón* for homosexual predates the publication of Gide's *Corydon* (17 n104).

64. Alemany y Bolufer (*esteta*/sodomite); Rodríguez Navas y Carrasco (*esteta*/effeminate man); López Pinillos, *El luchador* 146 ("sodomita desdichado"); Cansinos-Asséns 1: 212, 231, 334, 340 (Burgos), 373, 376 (*esteta*).

65. Vázquez García 12–13; García Lorca, "Oda" (*OC* 1: 565): "saliendo en racimos de las alcantarillas," "muchedumbre de gritos y ademanes."

66. See Caparrós Esperante 382–84, for more on the photo-montage of Whitman (also A. Anderson, "Introducción" 126–33); García Lorca, "Oda" (*OC* 1: 564, 566): "hermosura viril"; "de carne tumefacta y pensamiento inmundo"; Mira, "Modernistas, dandis" 64 and *Para entendernos* 523–25 (aesthetic phenomena as gay).

67. Whitman, "These I Singing in Spring" 151; "Song of Myself" 79, 87, 102; "Starting from Paumanok" 54 (*Complete Poems*).

68. Whitman, "Song of Myself" 75, 80, 86, 108, 123 (*Complete Poems*).

69. Fletcher 355, 358; Whitman, "Crossing Brooklyn Ferry" 191 ("living crowd"); "Outlines for a Tomb" 402 ("laboring life"); "Out From Behind This Mask" 403 ("common curtain") (*Complete Poems*).

70. Blake xi–xiii and introduction; Whitman, "Crossing Brooklyn Ferry" 191; "By Blue Ontario's Shore" 362, 363 (*Complete Poems*).

71. Whitman, "Song of Myself" 109, 118, 124 (*Complete Poems*).

72. Blake 127–30.

73. Whitman, "Song of Myself" 63 (*Complete Poems*). The first edition of *Leaves of Grass* (1855) opens with "I celebrate myself." See Fiedler's "Images of Walt Whitman," for more on Whitman's partially self-created legend.

74. García Lorca, ["Un poeta en Nueva York"] (*OC* 3: 169): "Nadie puede darse cuenta exacta de lo que es una multitud neoyorquina; es decir, lo sabía Walt Whitman que buscaba en ella soledades"; "si te caes, serás atropellado. . . . El rumor de esta terrible multitud llena todo el domingo de Nueva York"; Letter to Adriano del Valle (19 Sept. 1918), *Epistolario* 52: "¡Quiero ser todas las cosas!" See also Bordier 188–89, who observes that the crowd was an "inspiration" for Whitman and Lorca, conflating, however, the people with the multitude, without making any distinctions.

75. García Lorca, "Oda" (*OC* 1: 565): "carne para fusta, / bota o mordisco de los domadores."

76. García Lorca, "Oda" (*OC* 1: 567): "Abiertos en las plazas, con fiebre de abanico."

77. García Lorca, "Oda" (*OC* 1: 566): "no levanto mi voz . . . / contra el niño que escribe / nombre de niña en su almohada, / ni contra el muchacho que se viste de novia / en la oscuridad del ropero, / ni contra los solitarios de los casinos / que beben con asco el agua de la prostitución, / ni contra los hombres de mirada verde / que aman al hombre y queman sus labios en silencio." Mayhew observes that "this category of silent sufferers unsettles the binary opposition between the pure and the impure" (*Lorca's Legacy* 155). See also Perriam 161–66 for the complicated ways in which masculinity in Lorca's work can be seen.

78. Kennedy 85–86; Blake 139; see Longaker for the autopsy report and Whitman's personal daily observations of his physical decline.

79. García Lorca, "Oda" (*OC* 1: 565): "un desnudo que fuera como un río"; see Mayhew, *Lorca's Legacy* 139–42, who believes that "the overemphasis on the biographical author" has impeded a fully developed queer theory of Lorca's work.

80. Cansinos-Asséns, *Ética y estética* 167, 171: "la zona del sexo se nos aparece como una zona de florecimientos imprecisos. Todas las formas intermedias que pudiéramos imaginar florecen aquí. . . . La muchedumbre de los híbridos es tan numerosa acaso como la de los faunos y faunesas, y sus misterios llenan gran parte del bosque de la noche"; 128, 165 (unfixed nature).

81. García Lorca, *El público* (*OC* 2: 283): "Romeo puede ser un ave y Julieta puede ser una piedra. Romeo puede ser un grano de sal y Julieta puede ser un mapa"; 314: "¿es que Romeo y Julieta tienen que ser necesariamente un hombre y una mujer?"; 287: "cubiertos por un bigote rubio"; Gautier 58 ("C'est Roméo, c'est Juliette"). Lorca also drew a male figure, with a beard reminiscent of Whitman's, on at least six copies of the privately printed edition of the "Oda a Walt Whitman." See Yagüe Bosch's commentary, who describes the beard as fluvial (213–14).

82. Hernández, *Libro de los dibujos* 129 (polymorphic), 136 ("Autorretrato en Nueva York").

83. García Lorca, "Oda" (*OC* 1: 567): "reino de la espiga"; "con la barba hacia el polo y las manos abiertas"; Cernuda, *Estudios* 217: "porque el bloque de mármol encerraba una grieta"; Muñoz 63, 78, 83, 216: "una toma de la palabra de carácter homosexual"; "cada una de las veces que lo he leído" (En-

glish trans. Juan Santana Lario, slightly modified). For a different reading of the last lines, see Nandorfy, who argues that these verses "do not resuscitate Whitman but bury him deeply within the chaos that will erase all traces of his grave" (161).

84. Molina 44: "la imagen y la poesía de Federico se adentraban en mí."

85. Molina 109; Calero Carramolino 56, 61 (original version of "Ojos verdes").

86. Molina 129: "algo así como un amor imposible"; 131: "un ser humano tan importante para mí como Federico García Lorca"; 152–55 (arrest and abuse); 153: "¡Por marica y por rojo! Vamos a terminar con todos los maricones y los comunistas. ¡Uno por uno!"

87. *Noticias Gráficas* (31 July 1943) (qtd in Acha and Ben): "la voluptuosidad exhibicionista del 'amor que no osa decir su nombre'" (Buenos Aires scandal); Acha and Ben: "versión local del caso Oscar Wilde"; Molina 85–86, also 113 (trademark blouses): "Mi propósito no era vestirme de mujer, pero sí con una pizca de aire femenino," "ningún movimiento equívoco ni femenino." In his memoirs, Francisco Ayala recalled what a sensation Molina's performance created in Valencia during the war (231). Ayala's brother Eduardo also recounted a wickedly humorous episode in which a military officer accused Molina of making a pass at him. The singer denied it, but later got his revenge, when Eduardo saw the same officer intimate with Molina in a hotel room (Ayala, *Recuerdos y olvidos* 232).

88. Molina 91–94 (Lorca and Sánchez Mejías). Decades later, during the Spanish Transition, the cross-dressing performance artist Ocaña would invoke Lorca, while singing in a cemetery (see *Ocaña, retrat intermitent*).

89. In the pages that follow, I am indebted to the work of such Spicer critics as Daniel Katz, Burton Hatlen, Clayton Eshleman, Michael Davidson, Lori Chamberlain, and Eric Keenaghan; see also Mayhew, *Apocryphal Lorca* 106–21 and Walsh 135–40.

90. Bloom's anxiety of influence inevitably comes to mind, with questions of belatedness.

91. Katz 87. In a poem on Lorca's assassination from 1973, Harold Norse ventriloquized the voice of Ramón Ruiz Alonso, responsible for the poet's arrest, using words like "queer" and "goddam fag."

92. García Lorca, "Oda" (*OC* 1: 565).

93. D. W. Foster, "Jaime Manrique" 8 (queer manifesto); Manrique, *Eminent Maricones* 112. See also D. W. Foster, "El gay como modelo cultural," for a discussion of Manrique's re–vision of the term "maricón" (121–25).

94. Manrique, *Eminent Maricones* 29, 30, 73.

95. Aguiló ("the indignant" and Lorca).

96. Maurer and Anderson 9 n3; Morris, "Brief Encounter" 339, 343. Manrique's "My Night with Federico García Lorca" first appeared in a gay magazine, *Realidad Aparte* (New York), which I have not been able to find, and then in *My Night with Federico García Lorca* (1995; 1997). It has been reprinted in Lassell and Georgiou (*The World in Us*) 187–89 and Nelson (*The Wound and the Dream*) 280–81. I am citing from *Eminent Maricones*.

97. Manrique, *Eminent Maricones* 72–73; see Roditi, "Three Laments. I" and "Poem for L." (*Poems* 113, 137).

98. Manrique, "My Night" 71, 72.

99. Manrique, "My Night" 72. In an interview from 1986, Roditi observed, "[W]hen I was nineteen I had this extraordinary one-night affair with [Federico] García Lorca, which was rather like a flash of lightning in my life. I didn't realize what a great poet he was. Who did in 1929?" (R. C. Smith 85).

100. Manrique, "My Night" 72.

101. Manrique, *Eminent Maricones* 82 (Cañas). For more on the Lorca-Cummings relationship, see Cañas, "Aquella relación" and "Lorca era muy infantil."

102. Cañas, *El poeta* 136–39 (Ramos Otero) (also, "Epístola," which is an appreciation of both Manuel Ramos Otero and Philip Cummings); Keenaghan 274–75 (Spicer's gay lexicon) (also, Katz 96–97, who disagrees with Keenaghan's view that Spicer "deliberately undermined Lorca's ideal of 'gay invisibility,'" noting that the homosexuality of Lorca's Whitman is highly visible); Duncan (qtd in Keenaghan 286).

103. Ramos Otero 45: "yo seré justamente mi hombre prometido / cuando charcos de sangre amanecida / me integren al olvido y al crepúsculo"; "Ahora mismo estoy vestido de novia"; "Soy Maricón del Mundo / y asesino palomas para invadir al viento"; 46: "¡Qué bueno que estás muerto Federico!"; Manrique, *Eminent Maricones* 70.

104. Manrique, "My Night" 72.

Postscript

1. Fernández Puertas, Letter to Luis Rosales, dated 11 Mar. 1989, Archivo Histórico Nacional, Diversos—Luis Rosales, 6, N. 35: "¿Cómo recuerda a su amigo Federico García Lorca?"; "todo es mentira"; "Su padre no mató a García Lorca"; *Lorca en el pensamiento de Don Luis Rosales*. My thanks to Christopher Maurer for his help in locating Fernández Puertas.

2. Fernández Puertas, Letter to Luis Rosales: "Vd. tiene un no sé qué, que me gusta en su poesía." Fernández Puertas' publications include *Picasso y yo, Cartas de Vicenta Lorca a su hijo Federico, Querido Salvador, Querido Lorquito,* and his collaboration on the book project, *Palabra de Lorca,* as well as *Dalí y el Quijote.*

3. Personal communication with Víctor Fernández Puertas (1 Sept. 2019) (Fernández Puertas recollections): "Fue el momento en el que me entró Lorca en las venas. Era un colegial y para hacer un trabajo sin más pretensión que subir nota me centré en Lorca. Se me fue de las manos porque hablé con mucha gente."

4. For more information on the forensic search at the Alfacar Federico García Lorca Park in 2018, see Camacho; Cappa; Rodríguez; and Anon., "Un informe de la UGR."

5. García Lorca, "Oda" (*OC* 1: 567): "Y tú, bello Walt Whitman, duerme a orillas del Hudson / con la barba hacia el polo y las manos abiertas. / Arcilla blanda o nieve, tu lengua está llamando / camaradas que velen tu gacela sin cuerpo."

Bibliography

Acereda, Alberto. "Antonio Machado, ¿poeta cívico?" *Libertad Digital* (17 Feb. 2005).

Acha, Omar, and Pablo Ben. "Dossier: Género y peronismo; Amorales, patoteros, chongos y pitucos; La homosexualidad masculina durante el primer peronismo (Buenos Aires, 1943–1955)." *Trabajos y Comunicaciones.* 2ª época. Nos. 30–31 (2004–5): n. pag. http://sedici.unlp.edu.ar/bitstream /handle/10915/11506/4939-7718-1-PB.pdf.txt;jsessionid=E0C0D75EC 44F86ADCD0C54504D716042?sequence=2 (accessed 10 Mar. 2021).

Adams, Rachel. *Sideshow U.S.A.: Freaks and the American Cultural Imagination.* Chicago: University of Chicago Press, 2001.

Aguiló, Antoni. "Lorca, indignado y comprometido." *Público* (Madrid) (4 June 2013).

Agulló y Cobo, Mercedes, ed. *Madrid en sus diarios.* Vols. 4 (1876–90) and 5 (1891–99). Madrid: Instituto de Estudios Madrileños, 1971–72.

Akerman, Anthony. "Dark Outsider: Writing the Dramatic Life of Roy Campbell." *English in Africa* 30.1 (2003): 5–20.

Alarcón, Francisco X. "The Other Day I Ran into García Lorca" / "El otro día me encontré a García Lorca." *From the Other Side of Night / Del otro lado de la noche.* Bilingual edition. With a selection of translations by Francisco Aragón. Tucson: University of Arizona Press, 2002. 39.

Alarcón, Pedro Antonio de. *El escándalo.* 2 vols. Edited by Mariano Baquero Goyanes. Madrid: Espasa-Calpe, 1973.

Alas, Leopoldo (Clarín). *Las dos cajas.* In *Pipá.* Edited by Antonio Ramos-Gascón. Madrid: Cátedra, 1976.

———. *Su único hijo.* Edited by Carolyn Richmond. Madrid: Espasa-Calpe, 1990.

Albert, Mechthild. *Vanguardistas de camisa azul.* Translated by Cristina Díez Pampliega and Juan Ramón García Ober. Madrid: Visor, 2003.

Alberti, Rafael. *La arboleda perdida*. Barcelona: Bruguera, 1984. (Orig. 1959.)

———. "Palabras para Federico." *Federico García Lorca (poeta y amigo)*. Introduction by Luis García Montero. Granada: Biblioteca de la Cultura Andaluza, 1984. 258–62.

———. "Words for Federico García Lorca." *New Masses: An Anthology of the Rebel Thirties*. Edited by Joseph North. Introduction by Maxwell Geismar. New York: International Publishers, 1969. 239–41.

———, ed. *Romancero general de la guerra española*. Buenos Aires: Patronato Hispano Argentino de Cultura, 1944.

Alcocer, José Luis. *Radiografía de un fraude: Notas para una historia del Frente de Juventudes*. Barcelona: Planeta, 1978.

Aleixandre, Vicente. "Federico." In *Obras completas*. By Federico García Lorca. 16th edition. Edited by Arturo del Hoyo. Prologue by Jorge Guillén. Madrid: Aguilar, 1971. 1829–31. (Orig. 1937.)

Alemán, Mateo. *Guzmán de Alfarache*. 5 vols. Edited by Samuel Gili Gaya. Madrid: Espasa-Calpe, 1942–53.

Alemany y Bolufer, José. *Diccionario de la lengua española*. Barcelona: Ramón Sopena, 1917. In *Nuevo Tesoro Lexicográfico del Español* (Real Academia Española).

Alexander, Peter. *Roy Campbell: A Critical Biography*. Oxford: Oxford University Press, 1982.

Alfonso, José. *Siluetas literarias*. Valencia: Prometeo, 1967.

Almagro San Martín, Melchor. *Biografía del 1900*. 2nd edition. Madrid: Revista de Occidente, 1944.

Alonso, Dámaso. "La Fuente Grande o de las Lágrimas (Entre Alfacar y Víznar)." In Castro, *Versos* 95.

———. "Una generación poética (1920–1936)." *Obras completas*. Vol. 4. Madrid: Gredos, 1975. 653–76. (Orig. 1948.)

Alonso Cortés, Narciso. *La muerte del Conde de Villamediana*. Valladolid: Imprenta del Colegio Santiago, 1928.

Alonso Montero, Xesús. "Manuel Gómez del Valle, poeta, comunista e mártir (1906–1936)." *Madrygal* 2 (1999): 21–29.

Alós, Ernesto. "Pepín Bello rememora a sus amigos de juventud." *El Periódico de Aragón* (3 June 2007).

Alpuente, Moncho. "'Sic transit gloria mundi.'" *El País* (Madrid) (15 July 2000).

Altolaguirre, Manuel. "A Saturnino Ruiz, obrero impresor." *El Mono Azul* (Madrid) 1.7 (8 Oct. 1936): 5.

Álvarez Barrientos, Joaquín. "Ramón de Mesonero Romanos y el Panteón de hombres ilustres." *Anales de Literatura Española* (Alicante) 18.8 (2005): 37–51.

Álvarez Junco, José. *Mater Dolorosa: La idea de España en el siglo XIX.* 7th edition. Madrid: Taurus, 2003.

Amato, Gabriele d.' *Panteon dei martiri della libertà italiana.* 2 vols. 2nd edition. Turin: Stabilimento Tipografico Fontana, 1852.

Anderson, Andrew A. "Introducción." *Poeta en Nueva York,* by Federico García Lorca. Edited by Andrew A. Anderson. Barcelona: Galaxia Gutenberg / Círculo de Lectores, 2013. 7–138.

———. *El veintisiete en tela de juicio: Examen de la historiografía generacional y replanteamiento de la vanguardia histórica española.* Madrid: Gredos, 2005.

Anderson, Jon Lee. "Lorca's Bones." *New Yorker* 85.18 (22 June 2009): 44–48.

Angell, Katherine. "Joseph Merrick and the Concept of Monstrosity in Nineteenth-Century Medical Thought." In *Hosting the Monster,* edited by Holly Lynn Baumgartner and Roger Davis. Amsterdam: Rodopi, 2008. 131–52.

Anon. "El actor Luis Hurtado." *ABC* (Madrid) (22 Mar. 1967): 67.

———. "Asunto: Antecedentes del poeta Federico García Lorca." *El Blog de Sato* (28 Apr. 2015).

———. "At Dickens's Funeral." *Tennyson: Interviews and Recollections.* Edited by Norman Page. London: Macmillan, 1983. 122–23. (Orig. 1911.)

———. "Un caracterizado fascista granadino, insospechadamente horrorizado de los crímenes de su gente, huye de España y escribe horrorizado." *El Diluvio* (Barcelona) (5 Aug. 1937): 5.

———. "Una carta del poeta García Lorca se vende por 28.400 euros en una subasta." *El Mundo* (Madrid) (3 July 2007).

———. "Las cenizas de Francisco Ayala, depositadas bajo un limonero en su fundación." *El Mundo* (Madrid) (4 Dec. 2009).

———. "La cofradía del apio." In Gibson, *Federico García Lorca* 2: 338.

———. "Comentario a la noticia dada en la prensa roja sobre el fusilamiento de José Antonio." In *Dolor y memoria de España* 319–20.

———. "Consejo de guerra contra el jefe del S.I.M. de Madrid." *ABC* (Madrid) (23 Feb. 1940): 8.

———. "¿Cuánto vale la obra de Benavente?" *ABC* (Madrid) (7 June 1961): 66.

———. "Death of a Spanish Poet." *Volunteer for Liberty* (Madrid) 1.17 (4 Oct. 1937): 3, 8.

———. "17N—Marcha de la Corona en Homenaje a José Antonio Primo de Rivera: 71 Aniversario de su asesinato; 71 años presente en el corazón de los falangistas." *La Falange Informa* (21 Nov. 2007).

————. "Los documentos sobre la muerte de Lorca." *Cadena Ser* (22 Apr. 2015).

————. "Documents Cast New Light on Murder of Italy's Pasolini." *The Independent* (6 June 2010).

————. "D. José Zorrilla." *El Correo Español* (Madrid) (25 Jan. 1893): 1.

————. "Edmund de Bries constituye actualmente la preocupación de los legisladores argentinos." *El Imparcial* (Madrid) (19 Nov. 1924): 2.

————. "En el Barcelona. Lectura de poemas por Federico García Lorca." In Laffranque, "Federico García Lorca" 338–39.

————. "En plena descomposición." *La Época* (Madrid) (22 Oct. 1898): 1.

————. "El entierro de Zorrilla." *El Liberal* (Madrid) (26 Jan. 1893): 1–2.

————. "El entierro de Zorrilla." *El Siglo Futuro* (Madrid) (26 Jan. 1893): 2.

————. *La estrella de oro*. Drama de magia, en cuatro actos y en prosa. Madrid: Imprenta de I. Sancha, 1838.

————. "Es un tema opinable si hay crisis o no hay crisis." *El País* (29 June 2008).

————. "Federico García Loca o cualquiera se equivoca." *Gracia y Justicia* (Madrid) 47 (23 July 1932): 10.

————. "Federico García Lorca." In Dolfi 137–38.

————. "Federico García Lorca habla para los obreros catalanes." In Inglada, *Palabra de Lorca* 407–13.

————. "Federico García Lorca podría haber sido exhumado." *ABC* (Madrid) (15 Feb. 2017).

————. "*Le Figaro Littéraire* confiesa: ¡En fin, la verdad sobre la muerte de García Lorca!" *La Estafeta Literaria* (Madrid) 2ª época, No. 65 (13 Oct. 1956): 1.

————. "Fuente Vaqueros conmemora el 120 aniversario del nacimiento de Federico García Lorca." *Ahora Granada* (5 June 2018).

————. "El general Prim fue estrangulado y suplantado por sus asesinos." *La Vanguardia* (Barcelona) (11 Feb. 2013).

————. "El general Prim no murió estrangulado, según un estudio de la Complutense." *La Vanguardia* (Barcelona) (18 Dec. 2013).

————. "Un informe de la UGR descarta la presencia de restos humanos en el entorno de la fuente del Parque Lorca de Alfacar." *eldiario.es* (21 Jan. 2019).

————. "Joaquín Romero Murube, el falangista que escondió a Miguel Hernández." *Memoria Azul* (19 Sept. 2006).

————. "¡¡José Antonio, condenado a muerte!!" In *Dolor y memoria de España* 293–94.

———. "José María Hinojosa Lasarte: tradición política y vanguardia artística." *El Matiner Carlí* (20 Aug. 2010).

———. "Lawrence the Ubiquitous." *New York Times* (11 Dec. 1928): 29.

———. "Llegó anoche Federico García Lorca." In Inglada, *Palabra de Lorca* 155–60.

———. "Lorenzo Aguirre: Una vida apasionante y una muerte horrenda." *alicantevivo.org* (4 June 2009).

———. "Madrid a Zorrilla." *El Liberal* (Madrid) (26 Jan. 1893): 1.

———. "Más de 12.000 visitas mensuales consolidan la web Universo Lorca como referente sobre Federico." *Ahora Granada* (15 July 2019).

———. "No hay crisis teatral." *El Duende* (Madrid) (10 Feb. 1934): 14.

———. "El novelista más guapo." *Mundo al Día* (Bogotá) (1924). In Pérez Sanz and Bru Ripoll, *La erótica* 2047–48.

———. "Nuestra adhesión en lo que se refiere á la cuestión Ribot." *La Época* (Madrid) (21 Oct. 1898): 1.

———. "Opiniones de Fortes indignan a familia de García Lorca." *Letralia* (Cagua, Venezuela) 13.209 (4 May 2009).

———. "El PP pide explicaciones por el 'ridículo mundial' de la fosa de Lorca." *Público* (Madrid) (28 Dec. 2009).

———. "El Panteón de Hombres Ilustres, de Atocha, un mausoleo desconocido para la mayoría de los madrileños." *El País* (Madrid) (14 Nov. 1981).

———. "El Panteón de los Hombres Ilustres." *La Regeneración* (Madrid) (3 June 1869): 1.

———. "El Panteón de los Políticos Ilustres." At www.ciao.es (2 Aug. 2012). Defunct website.

———. "Panteón Nacional." *El Imparcial* (Madrid) (21 June 1869): 1.

———. "Parte política." *La Época* (Madrid) (3 June 1869): 2.

———. "Parte política." *La Época* (Madrid) (7 June 1869): 1.

———. "Parte política." *La Época* (Madrid) (10 June 1869): 2.

———. "Parte política." *La Época* (Madrid) (12 June 1869): 2.

———. "Parte política." *La Época* (Madrid) (15 June 1869): 3.

———. "Pasión y muerte de Federico García Lorca." *Solidaridad Obrera* (Barcelona) (21 Sept. 1937): 6.

———. "Perspectiva teatral. *Panteón ducal* en la *Estrella de oro.*" *El Panorama* (Madrid) 2ª época, No. 10 (7 Mar. 1839): 145–46.

———. "Política." *La Iberia* (Madrid) (12 June 1869): 1–2.

———. "Política: Justicia." *La Iberia* (Madrid) (10 June 1869): 1.

———. "Recuerdo y homenaje a los compañeros caídos." *Revista de Obras*

Públicas (Madrid). Número especial 1936–1939 dedicado a la guerra (1940): 4–14.

———. "Refranes gamacistas." *Gedeón* (Madrid) (27 Oct. 1898): 4.

———. "El Reino de Sarasa." *El Nacional* (Madrid) (17 Oct. 1898): 1.

———. "Se confirma el asesinato de Federico García Lorca." *ABC* (Madrid) (8 Sept. 1936): 7.

———. "La sepultura del gran poeta nacional Juan de Mena." *ABC* (Madrid) (18 Nov. 1944): 14.

———. "Situación interina." *La Época* (Madrid) (23 Oct. 1898): 1.

———. "El suceso del día." *La Época* (Madrid) (21 Oct. 1898): 3.

———. "El testamento de Zorrilla." *El Liberal* (Madrid) (25 Jan. 1893): 1.

———. "Un testigo presencial relata cómo asesinaron los facciosos al inmortal García Lorca." *ABC* (Madrid) (17 Sept. 1937): 7.

———. "Trapiello: 'Edgar Neville sentó las bases de la Ley de Memoria Histórica.'" *Terra Noticias* (6 May 2010).

———. "Las tumbas de Cánovas, Canalejas y Sagasta se podrán visitar de noche." *El Confidencial Autonómico* (17 Oct. 2015).

———. "Última hora: Zorrilla." *El Correo Español* (Madrid) (25 Jan. 1893): 2.

———. "Ultiman un informe para pedir a la Junta exhumar los restos de la posible fosa de García Lorca en Granada." *EFE* (28 July 2018).

———. "La última visita: En la capilla ardiente." *El Liberal* (Madrid) (25 Jan. 1893): 2–3.

———. "'Vengo de torero herido a dar cuatro conferencias.'" In Inglada, *Palabra de Lorca* 147–51.

———. "Vieja guardia: Alfonso Ponce de León; Breve historial falangista de un intelectual." In Inglada, *Ponce de León* 194.

———. " . . . Y armas al hombro." *Gedeón* (Madrid) (20 Oct. 1898): 3.

———. "Ya se matan entre ellos. ¿Ha sido asesinado Federico García Lorca?" *Odiel* (Huelva) (10 Sept. 1936): 1.

Antón del Olmet, Luis, and Alfonso Vidal y Planas. *El señorito Ladislao*. Drama en tres actos. Madrid: Sociedad de Autores Españoles, 1922.

Aparicio, Juan. Prologue ("Una biografía poética"). In Castroviejo, 2nd edition. 9–12.

Apollinaire, Guillaume. *"The Poet Assassinated" and Other Stories*. Translated by Ron Padgett. Manchester: Carcanet, 1985.

———. "Un témoin des funérailles de Walt Whitman." *Mercure de France* (Paris) No. 379 (1 Apr. 1913): 658–59.

———. "La vie anecdotique: À propos de Walt Whitman." *Mercure de France* (Paris) No. 396 (16 Dec. 1913): 864–65.

Argerich, Isabel, and Judith Ara, ed. *Arte protegido: Memoria de la Junta del Tesoro Artístico durante la Guerra civil.* Madrid: Instituto de Patrimonio Histórico Español / Museo Nacional del Prado, 2003.

Ariès, Philippe. *Western Attitudes toward Death: From the Middle Ages to the Present.* Translated by Patricia M. Ranum. Baltimore: Johns Hopkins University Press, 1974.

Arteaga de León, J. "Roy Campbell through Spanish Eyes." *Spain* (London) No. 85 (18 May 1939): 140.

Assier, Mathilde. "Le Panthéon de San Francisco el Grande (1869–1883): L'échec d'un monument à la gloire de la civilisation espagnole." At www.thes–arts .com (4 May 2010). Defunct website.

Aub, Max. Nota to *"Así que pasen cinco años* (Escena inédita: romance del maniquí)." *Hora de España* (Valencia) No. 11 (Nov. 1937): 67–74.

Auclair, Marcelle. *Enfances et mort de García Lorca.* Paris: Éditions du Seuil, 1968.

Auden, W. H. *Selected Poems.* New edition. Edited by Edward Mendelson. New York: Vintage, 1989.

Ayala, Francisco. "Diálogo de los muertos." *Los usurpadores.* Edited by Carolyn Richmond. Madrid: Cátedra, 1992. 247–54.

———. "Dialogue of the Dead: A Spanish Elegy." *Usurpers.* Translated by Carolyn Richmond. New York: Schocken Books, 1987. 159–67.

———. "La excentricidad hispana." *La imagen de España.* Madrid: Alianza, 1986. 19–25.

———. *Recuerdos y olvidos (1906–2006).* Madrid: Alianza, 2006.

———. "El túmulo." *Obras completas.* Vol. 3. *Estudios literarios.* Edited by Carolyn Richmond. Prologue by Ricardo Senabre. Barcelona: Galaxia Gutenberg / Círculo de Lectores, 2007. 676–87. (Orig. 1963.)

Ayguals de Izco, Wenceslao. *El Panteón Universal: Diccionario histórico.* 4 vols. Madrid: Imprenta de Ayguals de Izco Hermanos, 1853–54.

Azaña, Manuel. *La responsabilidad de las multitudes.* Introduction by Gabriel Moreno González. Seville: Athenaica, 2018. (Orig. 1900.)

Babbit, Irving. "On Being Original." *Literature and the American College.* Washington, DC: National Humanities Institute, 1986. 186–201. (Orig. 1908.)

Badanelli, Pedro. Letter to Álvaro Retana (30 May 1969). In Pérez Sanz and Bru Ripoll, *La erótica* 2464–65.

————. *Serenata del amor triunfante.* Edited by Noël Valis. Seville: Renacimiento, 2016. (Orig. 1929.)

Bagaría, Luis. "Diálogos de un caricaturista salvaje." In Inglada, *Palabra de Lorca* 464–71.

Balcells, Carmen. Letter to Julio Calonge (26 June 1987). Archivo Histórico Nacional (Madrid), Diversos—Luis Rosales, 2, N. 7.

————. Letter to Luis Rosales (26 June 1987). Archivo Histórico Nacional (Madrid), Diversos—Luis Rosales, 2, N. 7.

El balcón abierto. Dir. Jaime Camino. Madrid/Barcelona: Televisión Española (TVE) / Tibidabo Films, 1984.

Ballano, Antonio. *Suplemento al Diccionario de medicina y cirugía.* Vol. 3, 2nd part. Madrid: Imprenta de Brugada, 1823.

Baralt, Rafael María. *Diccionario de galicismos (Voces, locuciones y frases de la lengua francesa).* Madrid: Visor, 1995. (Orig. 1855.)

Barea, Arturo. *Lorca: The Poet and His People.* Translated by Ilsa Barea. New York: Grove Press, 1949. (Orig. 1944.)

Baroja, Pío. *Memorias: Desde la última vuelta del camino. Obras completas.* Vol. 7. Madrid: Biblioteca Nueva, 1949.

Barón de Montenegro, El. *El club de los queridos. La Novela Sugestiva* (Madrid) No. 7 (ca. 1930–31).

Barreiro Bordonaba, Javier. "Álvaro Retana en la erotografía del primer tercio de siglo: un acercamiento a los textos del cuplé sicalíptico." *Cruces de bohemia: Vida y Planas, Noel, Retana, Gálvez, Dicenta y Barrantes.* Zaragoza: Una Luna Ediciones, 2001. 89–122.

Barthes, Roland. *Mythologies.* Selected and translated by Annette Lavers. 19th printing. New York: Hill and Wang, 1987.

Baudelaire, Charles. "Biographie des excentriques." *Oeuvres posthumes.* Paris: Société du Mercure de France, 1908. 363–72.

————. "Perte d'auréole." *Petits poèmes en prose (le Spleen de Paris).* Introduction by Marcel A. Ruff. Paris: Garnier–Flammarion, 1967. 155.

Bécquer, Gustavo Adolfo. "Enterramientos de Garcilaso de la Vega y su padre." *OC* 1049–55.

————. "La feria de Sevilla." *OC* 1231–33.

————. *Obras completas (OC).* Prologue by Joaquín and Serafín Álvarez Quintero. 11th edition. Madrid: Aguilar, 1964.

————. *Rimas.* Edited by José Luis Cano. 13th edition. Madrid: Cátedra, 1987.

Bécquer desconocido. Dir. Manuel H. Martín. Seville/Madrid: La Claqueta / Canal de Historia / Televisión Española (TVE), 2010.

Béjar, Joaquín. "¿Un mártir más? F. García Lorca." *El Diluvio* (Barcelona) (2 Sept. 1936): 2.

Bejarano, Francisco. "Lorca reencontrado." *Diario de Sevilla* (7 Jan. 2010).

Belausteguigoitia, Santiago. "Un poeta rechazado por todos." *El País* (Madrid) (1 Sept. 1999).

Bellver, Catherine G. *Bodies in Motion: Spanish Vanguard Poetry, Mass Culture, and Gender Dynamics.* Lewisburg, PA: Bucknell University Press, 2010.

Benardete, M. J. "Why Did They Kill García Lorca?" *New Republic* (Nov. 1937): 25–26.

Benavente, Jacinto. *La blancura de Pierrot: Argumento para una pantomima. Teatro fantástico.* Madrid: Imprenta de Fortanet, 1905.

———. Six letters to Pedro Badanelli (1939–49). RES/262/199, Biblioteca Nacional de España (Madrid).

Benjamin, Walter. "The Task of the Translator." *Illuminations.* Edited by Hannah Arendt. Translated by Harry Zohn. New York: Schocken Books, 1969. 69–82.

———. "The Work of Art in the Age of Mechanical Reproduction." *Illuminations.* Edited by Hannah Arendt. Translated by Harry Zohn. New York: Schocken Books, 1969. 217–51.

Benlliure y Tuero, Mariano. "Las dos juventudes." *El Liberal* (Madrid) (10 July 1927): 3.

Bergamín, José. "La decadencia del analfabetismo." *Cruz y Raya* (Madrid) No. 3 (15 June 1933): 61–94.

———. "¿Su muerte?" In Castro, *Versos* 112–14.

Bergonzi, Bernard. "Roy Campbell: Outsider on the Right." *Journal of Contemporary History* 2.2 (1967): 133–47.

Bernal, José Luis. "Introducción." *Letras: Notas de un lector.* By Francisco Valdés. Badajoz: Editora Regional de Extremadura, 1993. 9–47.

Bernaldo de Quirós, Constancio, and José María Llanas Aguilaniedo. *La mala vida en Madrid: Estudio psicosociológico con dibujos y fotografías del natural.* Edited by Justo Broto Salanova. Huesca/Zaragoza: Instituto de Estudios Altoaragoneses / Egido Editorial, 1997. (Orig. 1901.)

Binding, Paul. *Lorca: The Gay Imagination.* London: GMP Publishers, 1985.

Bioy Casares, Adolfo. *Borges.* Edited by Daniel Martino. Barcelona: Destino, 2006.

Blake, David Haven. *Walt Whitman and the Culture of American Celebrity.* New Haven: Yale University Press, 2006.

Blanco Amor, Eduardo. "Exequias de Federico García Lorca." In Poeta 132–34.

Bloom, Harold. *The Anxiety of Influence: A Theory of Poetry.* New York: Oxford University Press, 1973.

Bogdan, Robert. *Freak Show: Presenting Human Oddities for Amusement and Profit.* Chicago: University of Chicago Press, 1988.

Bonaddio, Federico, ed. *A Companion to Federico García Lorca.* Woodbridge, Suffolk / Rochester, NY: Tamesis, 2007.

———. "Introduction: Biography and Interpretation." In Bonaddio 1–15.

Bones of Contention. Dir. Andrea Weiss. Brooklyn, NY: Icarus Films, 2017.

Bonet, Enrique. *La araña del olvido.* Bilbao: Astiberri Ediciones, 2016.

Bonet Salamanca, Antonio. "El templo de San Francisco el Grande de Madrid." *El culto a los santos: Cofradías, devoción, fiestas y arte.* Edited by Francisco Javier Campos y Fernández de Sevilla. San Lorenzo del Escorial: Ediciones Escurialenses / Instituto Escurialense de Investigaciones Históricas y Artísticas, 2008. 902–22.

Boone, Joseph A., and Nancy J. Vickers. "Introduction: Celebrity Rites." *PMLA* 126.4 (2011): 900–11.

Bordier, Roger. "Whitman et Lorca." *Europe* 47 (1 July 1969): 188–91.

Borges, Jorge Luis. "Kafka y sus precursores." *Otras inquisiciones.* Buenos Aires: Emecé, 1966. 145–48. (Orig. 1951.)

———. "El otro Whitman." *Discusión.* Buenos Aires: Emecé, 1966. 51–54. (Orig. 1929.)

Botrel, Jean–François. "De muertos y huesos ilustres: Los literatos y las honras fúnebres." *"Longtemps j'ai pris ma plume pour une épée." Écriture et combat dans l'Espagne des XVIIIe et XIXe siècles. Hommage à Françoise Étienvre. HispanismeS,* hors–série, No. 1 (2017): 216–36.

Bowra, C. M. *Poetry and Politics, 1900–1960.* Cambridge: Cambridge University Press, 1966.

Boyd, Carolyn. "Un lugar de memoria olvidado: El Panteón de los Hombres Ilustres en Madrid." *Historia y Política* 12 (2004): 15–40.

Boym, Svetlana. *Death in Quotation Marks: Cultural Myths of the Modern Poet.* Cambridge, MA: Harvard University Press, 1991.

Bozal, Valeriano. "Arte de masas y arte popular (1928–1937)." *Cuadernos Hispanoamericanos* Nos. 435–36 (Sept.–Oct. 1986): 745–61.

Braudy, Leo. *The Frenzy of Renown: Fame and Its History.* New York / Oxford: Oxford University Press, 1986.

———. "Knowing the Performer from the Performance: Fame, Celebrity, and Literary Studies." *PMLA* 126.4 (2011): 1070–75.

Breda, Emilio, ed. *García Lorca visto por los poetas*. Buenos Aires: Editorial Plus Ultra, 1986.

Brenan, Gerald. *The Face of Spain*. New York: Farrar, Straus & Cudahy, 1951.

Brereton, Geoffrey. "Two Spanish Writers." *New Statesman and Nation* 44 (18 Oct. 1952): 456.

Breton, André. *Manifestoes of Surrealism*. Translated by Richard Seaver and Helen R. Lane. Ann Arbor: University of Michigan Press, 1969.

Bretón de los Herreros, Manuel. *Obras*. Vol. 5. Madrid: Imprenta de Miguel Ginesta, 1884.

Bringing Up Baby. Dir. Howard Hawks. New York: RKO Radio Pictures, 1938.

Brix, Michel. "Un texte attribué à Baudelaire: 'Biographie des excentriques.'" *Revue d'Histoire Littéraire de la France* 113 (2013): 687–89.

Brown, Rica. "The Bécquer Legend." *Bulletin of Spanish Studies* 18.69 (1941): 4–18.

———. "La fama póstuma de Bécquer: Nuevos datos." *Revista de Filología Española* 52 (1969): 525–35.

Bruquetas Galán, Rocío. "La protección de monumentos y obras de arte en tiempos de guerra: La acción de la Junta del Tesoro Artístico y su repercusión internacional." In Argerich and Ara 201–19.

Bueno, Pepa. "Gibson: 'Es un documento que viene de Granada y oficial. Eso es importantísimo.'" *Cadena Ser* (23 Apr. 2015).

Buñuel, Luis. *My Last Sigh*. Translated by Abigail Israel. New York: Vintage, 1983.

Burgin, Richard. *Conversations with Jorge Luis Borges*. New York: Avon Books, 1970.

Burgos, Carmen de. *Confidencias de artistas*. Prologue by Ramón Gómez de la Serna. Madrid: Sociedad Española de Librería, 193–? (Orig. 1917.)

———. "Olimpia d'Avigny." *Confidencias* 235–38.

———. "Los retratos de Tórtola." *La Esfera* (Madrid) 5, no. 223 (6 Apr. 1918): [14].

———. "Tórtola Valencia." *Confidencias* 185–91.

———. *El veneno del arte. La flor de la playa y otras novelas cortas*. Edited by Concepción Núñez Rey. Madrid: Castalia / Instituto de la Mujer, 1989.

Burgos, Ernesto. "Balada del ausente." In Villén 172–75.

Burguera Nadal, María Luisa. *Edgar Neville entre el humor y la nostalgia*. Valencia: Institució Alfons Magnànim, Diputació de València, Universitat Jaume I, 1999.

Byron, George Gordon, Lord. *The Poems and Dramas*. New York: Thomas Y. Crowell & Company, n.d.

Caballero Pérez, Miguel. *Las trece últimas horas en la vida de García Lorca: El informe que da respuestas a todas las incógnitas sobre la muerte del poeta: ¿quién ordenó su detención? ¿por qué le ejecutaron? ¿dónde está su cuerpo?* Prologue by Emilio Ruiz Barrachina. Madrid: La Esfera de los Libros, 2011.

Caballero Pérez, Miguel, and María Pilar Góngora Ayala. *Historia de una familia: La verdad sobre el asesinato de García Lorca*. Madrid: Ibersaf Industrial, 2006.

Cabañas Bravo, Miguel. "Los viajes misionarios de la poesía y del arte al Caribe en la diplomacia franquista." *El arte y el viaje*. Edited by M. Cabañas Bravo, Amelia López–Yarto Elizalde, and Wifredo Rincón García. Madrid: CSIC, 2011. 699–718.

Las cajas españolas. Dir. Alberto Porlán. Madrid: Drop A Star, 2004.

Calderón de la Barca, Pedro. *El monstruo de los jardines*. Barcelona: Imprenta de Francisco Suriá, 1764.

———. *La vida es sueño. El alcalde de Zalamea*. Edited by Augusto Cortina. Madrid: Espasa-Calpe, 1964.

Calero Carramolino, Elsa. *La copla y el exilio de Miguel de Molina (1942–1960)*. Trabajo fin de grado. Madrid: Universidad Autónoma de Madrid, May 2014.

Camacho, Julia. "La última oportunidad de encontrar a Lorca." *El Periódico* (12 Aug. 2018).

Campbell, Roy. "¡Banderillas de fuego!" *Collected Works* 4: 418–20.

———. *Collected Poems*. 3 vols. Chicago: Henry Regnery Company, 1957.

———. *Collected Works*. 4 vols. Craighall: A. D. Donker, 1985–88.

———. "Federico Garcia Lorca." *Collected Works* 4: 318–19.

———. *Flowering Rifle: A Poem from the Battlefield of Spain*. London: Longmans, Green & Company, 1939.

———. *The Georgiad*. London: Boriswood Limited, 1931.

———. *Light on a Dark Horse: An Autobiography*. Foreword by Laurie Lee. Harmondsworth: Penguin, 1971.

———. *Lorca: An Appreciation of His Poetry*. New Haven: Yale University Press, 1952.

———. *Talking Bronco*. Chicago: Henry Regnery, 1956.

Campoamor, Ramón de. "La originalidad y el plagio." *Revista Europea* (Madrid) 2, No. 95 (19 Dec. 1875): 241–47.

Campoy, Antonio. "Álvaro Retana, el novelista de moda." Retana, *Las vendedo-*

ras de caricias. La Novela de Hoy (Madrid) No. 61 (13 July 1923). In Pérez Sanz and Bru Ripoll, *La erótica* 1682.

—. "Álvaro Retana: Retrato en verso." In Santiago Ibero 3–4.

—. "El novelista ambiguo." In Pérez Sanz and Bru Ripoll, *La erótica* 2040–41.

Canales, Alfonso. "La muerte de Hinojosa." *Jábega* No. 1 (1973): 89–91.

Cañas, Dionisio. "Aquella relación olvidada de Lorca con su novio americano." *El Mundo* (Madrid) (Supplement) (13 Aug. 2011): 1–2.

—. "Epístola a los norteamericanos." *Cuadernos Hispanoamericanos* No. 504 (June 1992): 112–14.

—. "Lorca era muy infantil y muy erótico." *El Mundo* (Madrid) (8 June 2003): 55.

—. *El poeta y la ciudad: Nueva York y los escritores hispanos.* Madrid: Cátedra, 1994.

Cano, Glòria. "La cara oculta de Retana: Una nueva aproximación histórica a su obra." *Illes i Imperis* 10–11 (2008): 273–302.

Cano Ballesta, Juan. *Las estrategias de la imaginación: Utopías literarias y retórica política bajo el franquismo.* Madrid: Siglo XXI, 1994.

Cansinos–Asséns, Rafael. *Ética y estética de los sexos.* Madrid: Júcar, 1973. (Orig. 1921.)

—. *La novela de un literato.* 3 vols. Edited by Rafael M. Cansinos. Madrid: Alianza, 1982–95.

—. *Salomé en la literatura: Flaubert, Wilde, Mallarmé, Eugenio de Castro, Apollinaire.* Madrid: Editorial-América, 1919.

Caparrós Esperante, Luis. "Las fotografías de *Poeta en Nueva York,* de Federico García Lorca: Ensayo de reconstrucción." *Castilla: Estudios de Literatura* 9 (2018): 372–94.

Cappa, G. "Los efectos colaterales del cambio en la Junta: Adiós a la búsqueda de Lorca." *Granada Hoy* (10 Jan. 2019).

Carlyle, Thomas. *On Heroes, Hero–Worship and the Heroic in History.* Philadelphia: Henry Altemus, 1893. (Orig. 1841.)

Carmona, Eugenio. "Epílogo sobre las relaciones entre los nuevos realismos y el arte nuevo en España [1913–1936]." In Inglada, *Ponce de León* 147–63.

Carpenter, Edward. *Days with Walt Whitman, with Some Notes on His Life and Work.* New York/London: Macmillan/George Allen, 1906.

—. *The Intermediate Sex: A Study of Some Transitional Types of Men and Women.* London: George Allen and Unwin, 1908.

Carr, Raymond. *The Spanish Civil War: A History in Pictures.* New York: W. W. Norton, 1986.

Carreras, Luis. *Un casamiento infame: Réplica al duque de la Torre.* Paris: M. Gálvez y Bardaji, 1883.

———. *Los duques de la Torre y el casamiento de su hijo.* 3rd edition. Paris: M. Gálvez y Bardaji, 1883.

Carrete Parrondo, Juan. "Diego Antonio Rejón de Silva y la colección de *Retratos de Españoles Ilustres.*" *Revista de Ideas Estéticas* No. 135 (1976): 211–16.

Carretero, José María (El Caballero Audaz). "Ignacio Sánchez Mejías." *Galería: Más de cien vidas extraordinarias contadas por sus protagonistas y comentadas.* 4th edition. Madrid: Ediciones Caballero Audaz, 1949. 341–44.

———. *La pena de no ser hombre. La Novela de Hoy* (Madrid) 3, No. 86 (4 Jan. 1924).

———. "Tórtola Valencia." *Lo que sé por mí (Confesiones del siglo).* Vol. 3. Madrid: Sanz Calleja, [1916?]. 37–50.

Carrier, Warren. "Some Versions of Lorca." *Poetry* 87.5 (Feb. 1956): 303–07.

Casado Salinas, Juan María. "Cañero, mito de la propaganda bélica." *Diario Córdoba* (12 Feb. 2018).

Casona, Alejandro. "García Lorca, poeta–pueblo." *España Independiente* (Buenos Aires) 2, 22 (1–15 Aug. 1948).

Castillo Cáceres, Fernando. *Noche y niebla en el París ocupado.* Madrid: Fórcola, 2012.

Castro, Adolfo de. *Manual del viajero en Cádiz.* Cádiz: Imprenta de la Revista Médica, 1859.

Castro, Cristóbal de. "El sexo y el vestido." *Nuevo Mundo* (Madrid) 35, No. 1790 (11 May 1928): n. pag.

Castro, Eduardo, ed. *Versos para Federico.* Granada: Editorial Comares, 1998.

Castro Jiménez, Antonio. "Muere Diego Hurtado, colaborador de Benavente y esposo de Mary Carrillo." *Madridiario.es* (19 Sept. 2008).

Castroviejo Blanco Cicerón, José María. *Altura: Poemas de guerra.* Vigo: Editorial Cartel, 1938.

———. *Altura: Poemas de guerra.* 2nd edition. Prologue by Juan Aparicio. Barcelona: Ediciones Jerarquía, 1939.

Caudet, Francisco. "Aproximación a la poesía fascista española: 1936–1939." *Bulletin Hispanique* 88 (1986): 155–89.

———. "Lorca: por una estética popular (1929–1936)." *Cuadernos Hispanoamericanos* Nos. 435–36 (Sept.–Oct. 1986): 763–78.

Causa General: Ministerio de Justicia, 1943; La dominación roja en España. 2nd edition. Prologue by Ricardo de la Cierva. Astorga: Akrón, 2009.

Cavia, Mariano de. "Huesos y cenizas." *Salpicón.* Madrid: Librería de Fernando Fe, 1892. 31–35. (Orig. Mar. 1888.)

———. "Plato del día. Los precedentes." *El Liberal* (Madrid) (25 Jan. 1893): 1–2.

Cejador y Frauca, Julio. "Antonio de Hoyos y Vinent." *Cintarazos (Artículos inéditos)*. Vol. 1. Madrid: Imprenta Radio, 1927. 21–26.

———. "Aspectos literarios." In Retana, *El octavo pecado capital*. Madrid: Ediciones Jasón, 1931. 11–16.

Cernuda, Luis. *Estudios sobre poesía española contemporánea*. Madrid / Bogotá: Ediciones Guadarrama, 1957.

———. "Federico García Lorca (Recuerdo)." *Hora de España* (Barcelona) No. 18 (June 1938): 225–32.

———. "Federico García Lorca: *Romancero gitano*." *Hora de España (Antología)*. Edited by Francisco Caudet. Madrid: Ediciones Turner, 1975. 271–75. (Orig. 1937.)

———. "Historial de un libro (*La Realidad y el Deseo*)." *La Realidad y el Deseo (1924–1962)*. Prologue by José Ángel Valente. Madrid: Alianza, 1998. 481–535.

———. "Líneas sobre los poetas y para los poetas en los días actuales." *Hora de España* (Valencia) No. 6 (June 1937): 64–66.

———. "El Poeta." *Ocnos*. Edited by Francisco Brines. Madrid: Huerga y Fierro Editores, 2002. 55–56.

Cervantes, Miguel de. "Al túmulo del rey Felipe II en Sevilla." *Obras completas*. Vol. 6. *Comedias y entremeses; Poesías sueltas*. Edited by Rodolfo Schevill and Adolfo Bonilla. Madrid: Gráficas Reunidas, 1922. 73–76.

Chabás, Juan. "Vacaciones de La Barraca." In Inglada, *Palabra de Lorca* 329–31.

Chamberlain, Lori. "Ghostwriting the Text: Translation and the Poetics of Jack Spicer." *Contemporary Literature* 26.4 (1985): 426–42.

Chauncey, George. *Gay New York: Gender, Urban Culture, and the Making of the Gay Male World, 1890–1940*. New York: Basic Books, 1994.

Chinchilla Sánchez, Kattia. "La tradición mítica del hermafrodito o andrógino en la Antigüedad y la Edad Media." *Filología y Lingüística* (Puerto Rico) 21.1 (1995): 17–33.

Clariana, Abelardo. "Un absurdo intento de romancero faccioso." *Hora de España* (Barcelona) No. 18 (June 1938): 282–83.

Clayton, Michelle. "Touring History: Tórtola Valencia between Europe and the Americas." *Dance Research Journal* 44.1 (2012): 28–49.

Cleminson, Richard. "'La antorcha extinguida,' la bohemia y la disidencia sexual, en España, principios del siglo XX." *Dossiers Feministes* 10 (2007): 51–60.

———. "El libro *Homosexualidad* del Dr. Martín de Lucenay: Entre el conocimiento científico y la recepción pública de la ciencia sexológica en España a principios del siglo XX." *Hispania* (Madrid) 64.3, No. 218 (2004): 961–86.

Cleminson, Richard, and Francisco Vázquez García. *Hermaphroditism, Medical Science, and Sexual Identity in Spain, 1850–1960.* Cardiff: University of Wales Press, 2009.

———. *"Los Invisibles": A History of Male Homosexuality in Spain, 1850–1939.* Cardiff: University of Wales Press, 2007.

Cleminson, Richard, Pura Fernández, and Francisco Vázquez García. "The Social Significance of Homosexual Scandals in Spain in the Late Nineteenth Century." *Journal of the History of Sexuality* 23.3 (2014): 358–82.

Climent, Juan B. "García Lorca, poeta revolucionario." *Excelsior* (Mexico City) (6 Jan. 1957): 3, 4.

Clúa, Isabel. *Cuerpos de escándalo: Celebridad femenina en el "fin-de-siècle."* Barcelona: Icaria, 2016.

———, ed. *El crimen fue en Granada: Elegías a la muerte de García Lorca.* Barcelona: Lumen, 2006.

Colectivo de Alumnos de la Universidad de Granada. "Acerca del enfrentamiento entre José Antonio Fortes y Luis García Montero. Pensar la literatura." *Rebelión* (15 Nov. 2008).

Coloma, Luis. *Pequeñeces.* Libro tercero. 3rd edition. Bilbao: Administración del "Mensajero del Corazón de Jesús," 1891.

Colvin, Howard. *Architecture and the After-Life.* New Haven: Yale University Press, 1991.

Constán, Sergio. *Wilde en España: La presencia de Óscar Wilde en la literatura española (1882–1936).* Prologue by Luis Antonio de Villena. Astorga: Akrón, 2009.

Conze, Edward. *Spain To-Day: Revolution and Counter-Revolution.* New York: Greenberg, [1936].

Corominas, Joan, with José A. Pascual. *Diccionario crítico etimológico castellano e hispánico.* Vol. 2. Madrid: Gredos, 1980.

Coronado, Carolina. *Un paseo desde el Tajo al Rhin descansando en el Palacio de Cristal. Obra en prosa.* Vol. 3. Edited by Gregorio Torres Nebrera. Mérida: Editora Regional de Extremadura, 1999.

———. *Poesías.* 2nd edition. Madrid, 1852.

Corona poética dedicada a la memoria de la malograda señorita Francisca Madoz y Rojas. Madrid: Imprenta de T. Fortanet, 1850.

Corroto, Paula. "El otro entierro de Federico García Lorca." *Público* (Madrid) (15 Feb. 2012).

Cortés, Valme. "Juicio por injuria al poeta Luis García Montero." *El País* (Madrid) (23 Oct. 2008).

Coste, Grégory. *Érotisme et modernité dans l'oeuvre narrative d'Álvaro Retana (1890–1970): Jeux d'Éros et de miroirs.* Paris: Éditions Publibook, 2012.

Cotarelo y Mori, Emilio. *El conde de Villamediana: Estudio biográfico-crítico.* Madrid: Librería de Victoriano Suárez, 1886.

Cotta, Jesús. *Rosas de plomo: Amistad y muerte en Federico y José Antonio.* Barcelona: Editorial Stella Maris, 2015.

Couffon, Claude. *À Grenade, sur les pas de García Lorca.* Paris: Seghers, 1962.

Covarrubias, Sebastián de. *Emblemas morales.* Madrid: Luis Sánchez, 1610.

———. *Tesoro de la lengua castellana o española.* Edited by Martín de Riquer. Barcelona: Editorial Alta Fulla, 1993.

Crossland, Zoë. "Buried Lives. Forensic Archaeology and the Disappeared in Argentina." *Archaeological Dialogues* 7.2 (2000): 146–59.

Crossman, Richard, ed. *The God That Failed.* New York: Bantam Books, 1959. (Orig. 1949.)

Cruz, Juan. "García Lorca es todos los muertos." *El País* (Madrid) (19 Sept. 2008).

Cruz, Nilo. *Lorca in a Green Dress.* In *Two Sisters and a Piano and Other Plays.* Introduction by Janice Paran. New York: Theatre Communications Group, 2007.

Cruz Casado, Antonio. "Álvaro Retana, 'El novelista más guapo del mundo': Erotismo, frivolidad y moda." *Andalucía y la bohemia literaria.* Edited by Manuel Galeote. Prologue by Lily Litvak. Málaga: Editorial Arguval, 2001. 17–48.

———. "La moda femenina en las novelas eróticas en clave de Álvaro Retana (1890–1970)." *Moda y sociedad: Estudios sobre educación, lenguaje e historia del vestido.* Edited by Emilio J. García Wiedemann and María Isabel Montoya Ramírez. Granada: Centro de Formación Continua de la Universidad de Granada, 1998. 223–34.

———. "Un toque de rosa. Lesbianismo y homosexualidad en algunas novelas de Álvaro Retana." *AnMal Electrónica* 32 (2012): 549–70.

Cunningham, Valentine, ed. *The Penguin Book of Spanish Civil War Verse.* Harmondsworth: Penguin, 1980.

Cunqueiro, Álvaro. "El César escucha cómo cantas." In Villén 130–31; and in Rodríguez Puértolas, *Literatura fascista española* 2: 141–43.

Darío, Rubén. "La joven aristocracia" (1901). *España contemporánea*. Prologue by Antonio Vilanova. Barcelona: Lumen, 1987. 282–89.

————. "Walt Whitman." *Azul*. Buenos Aires: Biblioteca de Cultura, 1888. 119.

Davidson, Michael. *The San Francisco Renaissance: Poetics and Community at Mid-century*. Cambridge: Cambridge University Press, 1989.

Davidson, Robert A. *Jazz Age Barcelona*. Toronto: University of Toronto Press, 2009.

Dead Poets Society. Dir. Peter Weir. Burbank, CA: Touchstone Pictures / Silver Screen Partners IV, 1989.

De Armas, Frederick A. "Embracing Hercules / Enjoying Ganymede: The Homoerotics of Humanism in Góngora's *Soledad Primera*." *Calíope* 8.1 (2002): 125–40.

————. "'The Play's the Thing': Clues to a Murder in Villamediana's *La gloria de Niquea*." *Bulletin of Hispanic Studies* 78.4 (2001): 439–54.

Delgado, María M. *Federico García Lorca*. London: Routledge, 2008.

————. "Memory, Silence, and Democracy in Spain: Federico García Lorca, the Spanish Civil War, and the Law of Historical Memory." *Theatre Journal* 67 (2015): 177–96.

Dennis, Nigel. "Politics." In Bonaddio 170–89.

Dewey, John. "Americanism and Localism." *Dial* 68 (June 1920): 684–88.

Díaz Benjumea, Nicolás. "Revista de la Semana." *El Museo Universal* (Madrid) No. 26 (27 June 1869): 201–2.

Díaz Viana, Luis. *Los guardianes de la tradición: Ensayos sobre la "invención" de la cultura popular*. Oiartzun (Gipuzkoa): Sendoa Editorial, 1999.

Diccionario de la lengua castellana (Diccionario de autoridades). Vol. 3. Madrid: Imprenta de la Real Academia Española por la viuda de Francisco del Hierro, 1732. In *Nuevo Tesoro Lexicográfico del Español* (Real Academia Española).

Diccionario de la lengua castellana. Madrid: Joaquín Ibarra, 1780. In *Nuevo Tesoro Lexicográfico del Español* (Real Academia Española).

Diccionario de la lengua castellana. Madrid: Espasa, 1925, 1927, 1936, 1939, 1950, 1970, 1984, 1992, 2001. In *Nuevo Tesoro Lexicográfico del Español* (Real Academia Española).

Diderot, Denis. *Le Rêve d'Alembert*. In *Le Neveu de Rameau, suivi de six oeuvres philosophiques*. Paris: Le Livre de Poche, 1966.

Diego, Gerardo. "Crónica del Centenario de Góngora (1627–1927)." *Lola* (Sigüenza) época 1, No. 2 (1928): 1–7.

————. *La estela de Góngora*. Edited by Julio Neira. Santander: Servicio de Publicaciones, Universidad de Cantabria, 2003.

———. "D. Narciso Alonso Cortés (1875–1972)." *Boletín de la Real Academia Española* 52 (May–Aug. 1972): 195–209.

Díez de Revenga, Francisco Javier. "Sobre la muerte de García Lorca (La difusión de la noticia en la España republicana)." *Los Cuadernos del 27* 2 (1985): 3–22.

Dinverno, Melissa. "Raising the Dead: García Lorca, Trauma, and the Cultural Mediation of Mourning." *Arizona Journal of Hispanic Cultural Studies* 9 (2005): 29–52.

———. "Wounded Bodies: García Lorca, Memory, and the Ghostly Return of the Past in Miguel Hermoso's *La luz prodigiosa*." *Anales de la Literatura Española Contemporánea* 32.1 (2007): 5–36.

The Disappearance of García Lorca (also known as *Death in Granada*). Dir. Marcos Zurinaga. San Sebastián de los Reyes / Paris: Antena 3 Televisión/ Canal+, 1997.

Dolfi, Laura. *Il caso García Lorca: Dalla Spagna all'Italia*. Rome: Bulzone Editore, 2006.

Dolor y memoria de España en el segundo aniversario de la muerte de José Antonio. Barcelona: Ediciones Jerarquía, 1939.

"Don Luis Hurtado Álvarez" (Esquela). *ABC* (Madrid) (27 Jan. 1989): 95.

Dos Passos, John. *Rosinante to the Road Again*. In *Travel Books and Other Writings, 1916–1941*. New York: The Library of America, 2003. (Orig. 1922.)

Dowling, John. "*Capricho* as Style in Life, Literature, and Art from Zamora to Goya." *Eighteenth-Century Studies* 10.4 (1977): 413–33.

Dudgeon, Patrick Orpen. "From Lorca's Theatre." *Fantasy* No. 27 (1943): 107–12.

Dué, Casey. "Poetry and the Dēmos: State Regulation of a Civic Possession." *Dēmos: Classical Athenian Democracy*. Edited by C. Blackwell. 2003. 1–14.

Duende y misterio del flamenco. Dir. Edgar Neville. Madrid: Edgar Neville Producción / Suevia Films, 1952.

Duque Gimeno, Aquilino. "Hinojosa." *Boletín de la Real Academia Sevillana de Buenas Letras* No. 35 (2007): 189–92.

Durán, Agustín. *Leyenda de las tres toronjas del vergel de amor*. Madrid: Imprenta, Fundición y Librería de D. E. Aguado, 1856.

———. "Prólogo." *Romancero general, o colección de romances castellanos anteriores al siglo XVIII*. Vol. 1. 2nd edition. Madrid: M. Rivadeneyra, 1859. v–xxxvii.

Ecroya, María P. de. "A Children's Home. Somewhere in Spain." *Volunteer for Liberty* (Madrid) 1.11(23 Aug. 1937): 6.

Edwards Bello, Joaquín. *Crónicas*. Santiago de Chile: Talleres "La Nación," 1924.

Eisenberg, Daniel. "Nuevos documentos relativos a la edición de *Poeta en Nueva*

York y otras obras de García Lorca." *Anales de Literatura Española* (Alicante) No. 5 (1986–87): 67–107.

———. "Reaction to the Publication of the *Sonetos del amor oscuro.*" *Bulletin of Hispanic Studies* 65.3 (1988): 261–71.

Eliot, T. S. "Tradition and the Individual Talent." *The Sacred Wood: Essays on Poetry and Criticism.* London: Methuen, 1969. 47–59. (Orig. 1919.)

Ellis, Havelock. *Studies in the Psychology of Sex.* Vol. 2. *Sexual Inversion.* 3rd edition. Philadelphia: F. A. Davis, 1928.

Emerson, Ralph Waldo. "Uses of Great Men." *Representative Men: Seven Lectures.* Boston: Phillips, Sampson, 1856. 9–40. (Orig. 1850.)

E[nde], A[malie] von. "Whitman in Germany." *New York Times Saturday Review* (9 Mar. 1907): 146.

Enders, Victoria Lorée. "Problematic Portraits: The Ambiguous Historical Role of the *Sección Femenina* of the Falange." *Constructing Spanish Womanhood: Female Identity in Modern Spain.* Edited by Victoria Lorée Enders and Pamela Beth Radcliff. Albany: State University of New York Press, 1999. 375–97.

Eneas. "El último español." *El Correo Español* (Madrid) (26 Jan. 1893): 1.

Entrambasaguas, Joaquín de. *Estudios sobre Lope de Vega.* Vol. 2. 2nd edition, revised. Madrid: CSIC, 1967.

Equis. "La historia se repite." *El Siglo Futuro* (Madrid) (22 Oct. 1898): 1.

Erkkila, Betsy. *Walt Whitman among the French: Poet and Myth.* Princeton, NJ: Princeton University Press, 2014.

Erre. "Pasó ayer por Montevideo una de las figuras más representativas de la intelectualidad española." In Inglada, *Palabra de Lorca* 170–74.

Escartín, Jesús. "Una fecha . . . y dos poetas." In Inglada, *Palabra de Lorca* 449–52.

Escobar, Luis. *En cuerpo y alma: Memorias de Luis Escobar, 1908–1991.* Madrid: Temas de Hoy, 2000.

Eshleman, Clayton. "The Lorca Working." *boundary 2* 6.1 (1977): 31–50.

Españoles ilustres, cuyos restos han de ser trasladados al Panteon Nacional en el solemne día de su inauguración, 20 de junio de 1869. Madrid: Imprenta de D. Carlos Frontaura, 1869.

Espín, Manuel. "La biografía inventada de Edgar Neville." *El Siglo* No. 751 (23 July 2007).

Estévez, Manuel Antonio. "*Mar del Sol,* primer libro de Castroviejo: Su celtismo y su deuda con Manoel Antonio." *Madrygal* 9 (2006): 43–51.

Ezpeleta Aguilar, Fermín. "Erotismo y escuela: *Los extravíos de Tony* (1919), de Álvaro Retana." *Hesperia* 9 (2006): 39–55.

Faber, Sebastiaan. *Exile and Cultural Hegemony: Spanish Intellectuals in Mexico, 1939–1975.* Nashville, TN: Vanderbilt University Press, 2002.

A Face in the Crowd. Dir. Elia Kazan. New York: Newtown Productions, 1957.

"Federico García Lorca (Alhambra)." *Dead Poets' Society Memorials* (1 Oct. 2015).

Federico García Lorca / Biblioteca de Andalucía. (Catálogos temáticos de la Biblioteca de Andalucía, 1). Granada: Biblioteca de Andalucía, 1998.

Fernández, Víctor. "Luis Hurtado: la pasión oculta de Lorca." *larazon.es* (24 July 2017).

Fernández Almagro, Melchor. "Genealogía de los rojos." In Gibson, *El hombre que detuvo* 217–21.

———. *Historia política de la España contemporánea 1885–1897.* Vol. 2. 2nd edition. Madrid: Alianza, 1969.

Fernández Cabal, Ricardo, and Francisco Pérez Herrero. "Charla con Federico García Lorca." In Inglada, *Palabra de Lorca* 131–36.

Fernández Cifuentes, Luis. *Teoría y mercado de la novela en España: del 98 a la República.* Madrid: Gredos, 1982.

———. "La verdad de la vida: Gibson versus Lorca." *Boletín de la Fundación Federico García Lorca* 4 (1988): 87–101.

Fernández-Cuesta, Raimundo. "Discurso del secretario general del Movimiento" (20 Nov. 1938). In *Dolor y memoria de España* 55–61.

Fernández Flórez, Wenceslao. "El olor marxista." *ABC* (Madrid) (28 May 1939): 3.

Fernández–Medina, Nicolás. *The Poetics of Otherness in Antonio Machado's "Proverbios y Cantares."* Cardiff: University of Wales Press, 2011.

Fernández de la Mora, Gonzalo. "Maeztu sobre el Rhin." *ABC* (Madrid) (29 Oct. 1961): 3.

Fernández-Morera, Darío, and Michael Hanke. "Roy Campbell: Quixote Redivivus." *Cervantes in the English–Speaking World: New Essays.* Edited by Darío Fernández-Morera and Michael Hanke. Kassel/Barcelona: Edition Reichenberger, 2005. 181–90.

Fernández Muriedas, Pío. "García Lorca y Rafael Alberti, poetas opuestos." In Inglada, *Palabra de Lorca* 315–16.

Fernández Puertas, Víctor. Letter to Luis Rosales (11 Mar. 1989). Archivo Histórico Nacional (Madrid), Diversos—Luis Rosales, 6, N. 35.

Fernández de los Ríos, Ángel. *El futuro Madrid.* Introduction by Antonio Bonet Correa. Barcelona: Los Libros de la Frontera, 1989. (Orig. 1868.)

———. *Guía de Madrid: Manual del madrileño y del forastero.* Madrid: Monterrey Ediciones, 1982. (Orig. 1876.)

Fernández Vieites, Manuel. "Para Álvaro Retana" (1924). In Pérez Sanz and Bru Ripoll, *La erótica* 1710–11.

Ferreiro, Alfredo Mario. "Once horas con Federico García Lorca." In Inglada, *Palabra de Lorca* 250–60.

Fiedler, Leslie. *Freaks: Myths and Images of the Secret Self.* New York: Simon and Schuster, 1978.

———. "Images of Walt Whitman." *An End to Innocence: Essays on Culture and Politics.* Boston: Beacon Press, 1955. 152–73.

Fitts, Dudley. "The Voice of Lorca." *New York Times* (21 Dec. 1952): Section BR, 4.

Flam, Jack D. "With Robert Motherwell." In *Robert Motherwell.* Essays by Dore Ashton and Jack D. Flam. Introduction by Robert T. Buck. New York: Abbeville Press, 1983. 9–27.

Fletcher, John Gould. "Walt Whitman." *North American Review* 219 (Mar. 1924): 355–66.

Flores de la Flor, María Alejandra. "La presencia de los monstruos en la prensa hispánica finidieciochesca." *Trocadero* 24 (2012): 83–104.

Fortes, José Antonio. "Homenaje improcedente y sin fiesta a Federico." In Castro, *Versos* 184–85.

———. *La ideología mata: Cinco intervenciones.* N.p.: Fulminantes / CO.T.A.LI., 2015.

———. *Intelectuales de consumo: Literatura y cultura de Estado en España (1982– 2009).* [Córdoba]: Almuzara, 2010.

———. "Populismo y literatura." *La Jiribilla* (La Habana) 3 (28 Jan. 2005).

Fortuny, Carlos (Álvaro Retana). "Nacimiento, esplendor y ocaso de los imitadores de 'estrellas.'" *ABC* (Madrid) (12 July 1968): 24–25.

———. *La ola verde: Crítica frívola.* Barcelona: Ediciones Jasón, 1931.

Foster, David William. "El gay como modelo cultural: *Eminent Maricones* de Jaime Manrique." *Desde aceras opuestas: Literatura/cultura gay y lesbiana en Latinoamérica.* Edited by Dieter Ingenschay. Madrid/Frankfurt: Iberoamericana/Vervuert, 2006. 119–38.

———. "Jaime Manrique: un novelar queer colombiano." *Revista de Estudios Colombianos* 49 (Jan.–June 2017): 8–16.

Foster, Kevin. "'Your Country Does Not Matter': British and Irish Writers on the Spanish Civil War." *Teaching Representations of the Spanish Civil War.* Edited by Noël Valis. New York: Modern Language Association, 2007. 206–19.

Foucault, Michel. *Abnormal: Lectures at the Collège de France, 1974–1975.* Edited by Valerio Marchetti and Antonella Salomoni. Translated by Graham Burchell. New York: Picador, 2004.

———. *The History of Sexuality.* Vol. 1. *An Introduction.* Translated by Robert Hurley. New York: Vintage, 1980.

———. "Introduction." *Herculine Barbin: Being the Recently Discovered Memoirs of a Nineteenth-Century French Hermaphrodite.* Translated by Richard McDougall. New York: Pantheon Books, 1980. vii–xvii.

Foxá, Agustín de. "Los Homeros Rojos." *ABC* (Madrid) (28 May 1939): 3–4.

———. "José Antonio." In *Dolor y memoria de España* 95–98.

———. *Madrid, de corte a checa.* 3rd edition. Madrid: Prensa Española, 1962.

Fraguas, Rafael. "Cervantes, reenterrado solemnemente." *El País* (Madrid) (11 June 2015).

———. "Plomo y tachuelas para dar con Cervantes." *El País* (Madrid) (27 Jan. 2015).

Franciosini Florentín, Lorenzo. *Vocabolario español-italiano.* Rome: Juan Pablo Profilio, 1620. In *Nuevo Tesoro Lexicográfico del Español* (Real Academia Española).

Franco, Francisco. "Discurso de Unificación" (19 Apr. 1937). *Generalisimofranco.com.*

———. "El mensaje de Franco a todos los españoles en el día de ayer." *ABC* (Sevilla) (2 Oct. 1937): 5.

Franco Martínez-Bordiú, Francisco (with Emilia Landaluce). *La naturaleza de Franco: Cuando mi abuelo era persona.* 2nd edition. Madrid: La Esfera de los Libros, 2011.

Franco Torre, Christian. *Edgar Neville: Duende y misterio de un cineasta español.* Prologue by Vidal de la Madrid Álvarez. Santander (Cantabria): Shangila Textos Aparte, 2015.

Frayer, Lauren. "The Reason Cervantes Asked to be Buried under a Convent." *NPR* (24 June 2015).

Freakish Encounters: Constructions of the Freak in Hispanic Cultures. Edited by Sara Muñoz–Muriana and Analola Santana. *Hispanic Issues On Line* 20 (2018).

Freaks. Dir. Tod Browning. Beverly Hills, CA: Metro-Goldwyn-Mayer, 1932.

Freud, Sigmund. "The Psychogenesis of a Case of Homosexuality in a Woman." *Collected Papers.* Vol. 2. Translated by Barbara Low and R. Gabler. 6th impression. London: Hogarth Press, 1949. 202–31.

Fuentelapeña, Antonio de. *El ente dilucidado: Tratado de monstruos y fantasmas.* Edited by Javier Ruiz. Madrid: Editora Nacional, 1978. (Orig. 1676.)

Fuentes, Víctor. *La marcha al pueblo en las letras españolas, 1917–1936.* Prologue by Manuel Tuñón de Lara. 2nd edition, revised and enlarged. Madrid: Ediciones de la Torre, 2006.

Fussell, Paul. *The Great War and Modern Memory.* Introduction by Jay Winter. Oxford: Oxford University Press, 2013.

Gagen, Derek. "De vivos y de muertos. Alberti, Buero Vallejo and the Ghost of Lorca." *Antípodas: Journal of Hispanic Studies of the University of Auckland* No. 2 (1989): 31–50.

———. "Lorca and 'English' Poetry." *Journal of Iberian and Latin American Studies* 5.2 (1999): 161–72.

García, Manuel, and A. Martínez. "Prólogo." In Romero Murube 9–29.

García Gómez, Emilio. *Poemas arábigoandaluces.* Madrid: Espasa-Calpe, 1943.

García Lorca, Federico. *Así que pasen cinco años. OC* 2: 329–93.

———. *Collected Poems.* Edited by Christopher Maurer. Revised edition. New York: Farrar, Straus and Giroux, 2002.

———. *Doña Rosita la soltera, o El lenguaje de las flores. OC* 2: 527–79.

———. *Epistolario completo.* Edited by Andrew A. Anderson and Christopher Maurer. Madrid: Cátedra, 1997.

———. "Juego y teoría del duende." *OC* 3: 150–62.

———. "Lectura de poemas." *OC* 3: 174–77.

———. *Obras completas (OC).* 4 vols. Edited by Miguel García–Posada. Barcelona: Galaxia Gutenberg / Círculo de Lectores, 1996–97.

———. *Oda a Walt Whitman.* Mexico: Alcancía, 1933.

———. "Paraíso cerrado para muchos, jardines abiertos para pocos: Un poeta gongorino del siglo XVII." *OC* 3: 78–87.

———. *Poesía inédita de juventud.* 4th edition. Edited by Christian de Paepe. Madrid: Cátedra, 2008.

———. ["Un poeta en Nueva York"]. *OC* 3: 163–73.

———. "Poética." *Antología de Gerardo Diego. Poesía española contemporánea.* Edited by Andrés Soria Olmedo. Madrid: Taurus, 1991. 485.

———. *El público. OC* 2: 279–327.

———. *The Selected Poems of Federico García Lorca.* Edited by Francisco García Lorca and Donald M. Allen. 23rd printing. New York: New Directions Books, 1955.

———. *Songs.* Translated by Philip Cummings. Edited by Daniel Eisenberg. Pittsburgh: Duquesne University Press, 1976.

García Lorca, Francisco. "Córdoba, lejana y sola" (1947). In *Federico García Lorca.* 2nd edition. Edited by Ildefonso-Manuel Gil. Madrid: Taurus, 1975. 275–85.

García Lorca, Isabel. *Recuerdos míos*. 2nd edition. Edited by Ana Gurruchaga. Prologue by Claudio Guillén. Barcelona: Tusquets, 2002.

García Montero, Luis. "Lorca era un fascista." *El País* (Madrid) (14 Oct. 2006).

García-Posada, Miguel. *Acelerado sueño: Memoria de los poetas del 27*. Madrid: Espasa, 1999.

García Rodríguez, José Carlos. *El infante maldito: La biografía de Luis Fernando de Orleans, el más depravado príncipe Borbón*. Madrid: Espasa, 2012.

———. *Montpensier: Biografía de una obsesión*. Córdoba: Almuzara, 2015.

García Sánchiz, Federico. "Los pies desnudos donde las cabezas calvas." *La Vanguardia Española* (Barcelona) (16 Mar. 1955): 5.

García Serrano, Rafael. *Diccionario para un macuto*. 4th edition. Barcelona: Planeta, 1979.

Garciasol, Ramón de. "Correo para la muerte (Carta amarga a José Luis Hidalgo)." Edited by Daniel Eisenberg. *Journal of Hispanic Philology* 14 (1990): 129–41.

García de Tuñón Aza, José María. *José Antonio y los poetas*. Prologue by Eduardo López Pascual. Madrid: Plataforma 2003, 2003.

———. "José María Castroviejo, un poeta de *Altura*." *Altar Mayor* (Hermandad del Valle de los Caídos) No. 121 (Apr.–May 2008).

———. "Romero Murube, el poeta que amó a Sevilla." *Altar Mayor* (Hermandad del Valle de los Caídos) No. 119 (Feb. 2008).

García Velasco, Rafael. "Elegía a Federico García Lorca." In Castro, *Versos* 213–15.

Garelick, Rhonda K. *Rising Star: Dandyism, Gender, and Performance in the Fin de Siècle*. Princeton, NJ: Princeton University Press, 1998.

Garfias, Pedro. "A Federico García Lorca." In Castro, *Versos* 216–17.

———. "Héroes." *Hora de España* (Barcelona) No. 14 (Feb. 1938): 321–23.

Garí, Joan. "García Lorca en 2010." *Público* (Madrid) (6 Jan. 2010).

Garosci, Aldo. *Los intelectuales y la guerra de España*. Madrid: Júcar, 1981.

Gasch, Sebastián. "Mi Federico García Lorca." In *Cartas a sus amigos*. By Federico García Lorca. Barcelona: Ediciones Cobalto, 1950. 7–14.

Gautier, Théophile. *Émaux et camées*. Vienna: Manz, Éditeur, n.d.

Gazzaniga, Giuseppe. *Don Giovanni Tenorio o sia Il Convitato di pietra*. Libretto by Giovanni Bertati. Florence: Presso Ant[on] Gius[eppe] Pagani e Comp., 1789.

Géal, Pierre. "L'impossible naissance du panthéon national espagnol." *Hommage à Carlos Serrano*. Vol. 1. Paris: Éditions Hispaniques, 2005. 257–71.

Gedeón (Madrid) (27 Oct. 1898). Cover.

Geist, Anthony L. "Las mariposas en la barba: una lectura de *Poeta en Nueva York.*" *Cuadernos Hispanoamericanos* Nos. 435–36 (1986): 547–66.

———. "Recycling the Popular: Lorca, *Lorquismo,* and the Culture Industry." *Modernism and its Margins: Reinscribing Cultural Modernity from Spain and Latin America.* Edited by Anthony L. Geist and José B. Monleón. New York: Garland, 1999. 151–67.

Gesser, Silvina Schammah. "Legado cultural y administración del pasado: La 'generación del 27' en el Reina Sofía." *Historia Contemporánea* 38 (2009): 113–44.

Gestoso y Pérez, José. *Homenaje rendido por la ciudad de Sevilla a sus ilustres hijos Gustavo Adolfo y Valeriano Bécquer.* Seville: Oficina Tipográfica de Gironés, 1916.

Gibson, Ian. *El asesinato de García Lorca.* Barcelona: Penguin Random House Grupo Editorial, 2018.

———. *The Assassination of Federico García Lorca.* London: Penguin, 1983.

———. *"Caballo azul de mi locura": Lorca y el mundo gay.* Barcelona: Planeta, 2009.

———. *En busca de José Antonio.* Barcelona: Planeta, 1980.

———. "El Estado debe buscar de una vez a Federico García Lorca." *El País* (Madrid) (30 Dec. 2009).

———. *Federico García Lorca.* 2 vols. Barcelona: Crítica, 1998.

———. *Federico García Lorca: A Life.* New York: Pantheon, 1989.

———. "Federico, símbolo de reconciliación." *ABC* (Madrid) (15 Oct. 2009).

———. *La fosa de Lorca: Crónica de un despropósito.* Alcalá la Real: Alcalá Grupo Editorial, 2010.

———. *El hombre que detuvo a García Lorca: Ramón Ruiz Alonso y la muerte del poeta.* Madrid: Aguilar, 2007.

———. *Un irlandés en España: Diario de un año.* Barcelona: Planeta, 1981.

———. *Lorca's Granada: A Practical Guide.* London: Faber & Faber, 1992.

———. *La represión nacionalista de Granada en 1936 y la muerte de Federico García Lorca.* Paris: Ruedo Ibérico, 1971.

———. *Vida, pasión y muerte de Federico García Lorca, 1898–1936.* 4th edition. Barcelona: DeBolsillo, 2010.

Gide, André. *Corydon.* Translated by Richard Howard. New York: Farrar, Straus & Giroux, 1983. (Orig. 1924.)

———. *If It Die . . . An Autobiography.* Translated by Dorothy Bussy. New York: Vintage, 2001. (Orig. 1924.)

Gila, Miguel. *Y entonces nací yo: Memorias para desmemoriados.* Madrid: Temas de Hoy, 1995.

Gil-Albert, Juan. "Dos sonetos a Federico García Lorca." *Hora de España* (Valencia) No. 12 (Dec. 1937): 163.

———. "La poesía en la muerte de Federico García Lorca." *Hora de España* (Barcelona) No. 15 (Mar. 1938): 486–90.

Gillis, John R. "Introduction: Memory and Identity; The History of a Relationship." *Commemorations: The Politics of National Identity*. Edited by John R. Gillis. Princeton, NJ: Princeton University Press, 1994. 3–24.

Gillman, Richard, and Michael Paul Novak, ed. *Poets, Poetics, and Politics: America's Literary Community Viewed from the Letters of Rolfe Humphries, 1910–1969*. Lawrence: University Press of Kansas, 1992.

Giménez Caballero, Ernesto. "Anteprólogo." *Yo, inspector* 3–6.

———. "Aventura con hermafrodita." *Yo, inspector* 135–43.

———. "Conmemoración de García Lorca en el Paraguay." *Federico García Lorca / Guillermo de Torre: Correspondencia y amistad*. Edited by Carlos García. Madrid / Frankfurt am Main: Iberoamericana/Vervuert, 2009. 472–79. (Orig. 1966.)

———. "Decadencia de la poesía española." *La Gaceta Literaria* (Madrid) No. 121 (15 Jan. 1932): 15.

———. "Fama póstuma. Ante el traslado a Madrid de los restos de Pablo Picasso." *La Gaceta Literaria* (Madrid) No. 100 (1 Mar. 1931): 1–2.

———. "Itinerarios jóvenes de España: Federico García Lorca." In Inglada, *Palabra de Lorca* 27–30.

———. "Lorca." *Retratos españoles (Bastante parecidos)*. Prologue by Pere Gimferrer. Barcelona: Planeta, 1985. 165–68.

———. "Nosotros los señoritos y los golfos." *La Conquista del Estado* (Madrid) No. 4 (4 Apr. 1931): 4.

———. "Visitas literarias. Gerardo Diego, poeta fascista." *El Sol* (Madrid) (26 July 1927): 1.

———. *Yo, inspector de alcantarillas (Epiplasmas)*. Prologue by Edward Baker. Madrid: Ediciones Turner, 1975. (Orig. 1928.)

Giner de los Ríos, Francisco. *Estudios de literatura y arte*. 2nd edition. Madrid: Librería de Victoriano Suárez, 1876.

Ginsberg, Allen. *Collected Poems, 1947–1997*. New York: HarperCollins, 2006.

Godwin, William. *Essay on Sepulchres, or, a Proposal for Erecting Some Memorial of the Illustrious Dead in All Ages*. New York: Printed for M. and W. Ward, 1809.

Goebbels, Joseph. "Address for the 150th Anniversary of the Death of Wolfgang Amadeus Mozart at the Vienna State Opera on 4 December 1941." In Levi 257–61.

Goldman, Jonathan. *Modernism Is the Literature of Celebrity.* Austin: University of Texas Press, 2011.

Golijov, Osvaldo. *Ainadamar.* Libretto by David Henry Hwang. Deutsche Grammophon, 2006.

Gómez López-Quiñones, Antonio. "Toward a Pragmatic Version of Memory: What Could the Spanish Civil War Mean to Contemporary Spain?" *Unearthing Franco's Legacy: Mass Graves and the Recovery of Historical Memory in Spain.* Edited by Carlos Jerez–Farrán and Samuel Amago. Notre Dame, IN: University of Notre Dame Press, 2010. 208–20.

Gómez Santos, Marino. *12 hombres de letras.* Madrid: Editora Nacional, 1969.

Gómez de la Serna, Ramón. "Lo cursi." *Lo cursi y otros ensayos.* Buenos Aires: Editorial Sudamericana, [1943]. 7–54.

———. *Mi tía Carolina Coronado.* Buenos Aires: Emecé, [1942].

———. *Pombo.* Madrid: Comunidad de Madrid / Visor Libros, 1999.

———. *La sagrada cripta de Pombo.* Madrid: Trieste, 1986.

González Carbalho, José. *Vida, obra y muerte de Federico García Lorca.* (Escrita para ser leída en un acto recordatorio). Santiago de Chile: Ediciones Ercilla, 1938.

González Domínguez, Federico. "Panteón de los sevillanos ilustres." Universidad de Sevilla, Facultad de Bellas Artes, https://bellasartes.us.es/panteon -de-los-sevillanos-ilustres (accessed 2 May 2021).

González Echevarría, Roberto. "Calderón's *La vida es sueño:* Mixed-(Up) Monsters." *Celestina's Brood: Continuities of the Baroque in Spanish and Latin American Literatures.* Durham, NC: Duke University Press, 1993. 81–113.

González Rendón, Aurelio. *El señorito Pepe.* Monólogo en prosa. Madrid: Sociedad de Autores Españoles, 1905.

González-Ruano, César. "Álvaro Retana." In Villena, *El ángel* 55–56. (Orig. 1923.)

———. "Álvaro Retana visto por César González-Ruano." In Álvaro Retana, *El infierno de la voluptuosidad.* Madrid: Editorial Colombia, 1924. 5–21.

———. "Bajo la sonrisa de *La zapatera prodigiosa.*" In Inglada, *Palabra* 47–51.

———. *Diario íntimo (1951–1965).* Prologue by Francisco Umbral. Madrid: Comunidad de Madrid / Visor Libros, 2004.

———. *Memorias: Mi medio siglo se confiesa a medias.* Madrid: Tebas, 1979. (Orig. 1950.)

Gordon, Robert S. C. "Pasolini's Murder: Interpretation, Event Narratives, and Postmodern *Impegno.*" *Assassinations and Murder in Modern Italy: Transformations in Society and Culture.* Edited by Stephen Gundle and Lucia Rinaldi. New York: Palgrave Macmillan, 2007. 153–65.

———. "'To Speak Oneself and Die': Pasolini and the Poet as Martyr." *Dying

Words: The Last Moments of Writers and Philosophers. Edited by Martin Crowley. Amsterdam/Atlanta: Rodopi, 2000. 56–68.

Gordón Ordás, Félix. "Los intelectuales asesinados." *El Diluvio* (Barcelona) (23 Nov. 1937): 3.

Grande, Félix. *La calumnia: De cómo a Luis Rosales, por defender a Federico García Lorca, le persiguieron hasta la muerte.* Madrid: Mondadori, 1987.

Grass, Roland. "Lorca's 'Canción de jinete.'" *Explicator* 19.3 (1960): 44–47.

Graves, Robert. "A Life Bang-Full of Kicks and Shocks." *New York Times Book Review* (5 Jan. 1958): 6.

Gregory, James. "Eccentric Lives: Character, Characters, and Curiosities in Britain, c. 1760–1900." *Histories of the Normal and the Abnormal.* Edited by Waltraud Ernst. London: Routledge, 2006. 73–100.

Guasp, Ernest. "*Yerma* y su autor en la plaza de Cataluña." In Inglada, *Palabra de Lorca* 399–401.

Guerrero, Fernando. "Responso (Al llorado poeta Federico García Lorca)." In Castro, *Versos* 230–31.

Guillén, Jorge. "Federico en persona" (Prólogo). In *Obras completas.* By Federico García Lorca. 16th edition. Madrid: Aguilar, 1971. xvii–lxxix.

Harkema, Leslie. "'*Felices años veinte?*': *Las chicas del cable* and the Iconicity of 1920s Madrid." *Televising Restoration Spain: History and Fiction in Twenty-First-Century Costume Dramas.* Edited by David R. George, Jr. and Wan Sonya Tang. Cham: Palgrave Macmillan, 2018. 221–39.

———. *Spanish Modernism and the Poetics of Youth: From Miguel de Unamuno to La Joven Literatura.* Toronto: University of Toronto Press, 2017.

Harrison, Robert Pogue. *The Dominion of the Dead.* Chicago: University of Chicago Press, 2003.

Hartzenbusch, Juan Eugenio. *Discursos leídos ante la Real Academia Española en la recepción pública de Don Francisco Cutanda.* Madrid: Imprenta y Estereotipia de M. Rivadeneyra, 1861.

Hatlen, Burton. "Crawling into Bed with Sorrow: Jack Spicer's *After Lorca.*" *Ironwood* 14.2 (1986): 118–35.

Havard, Robert G. "Introduction." *Gypsy Ballads.* By Federico García Lorca. Translated by Robert G. Havard. Oxford: Aris & Phillips, 1990. 1–37.

Herda, John Noel. "Toward an Understanding of Víctor Quintanar: A Comparative Analysis of Clarín's *La Regenta* and *Su único hijo.*" PhD diss., Purdue University, 2012.

Hernández, Carlos, and El Torres (Juan Torres). *La huella de Lorca.* Barcelona: Norma Editorial, 2011.

Hernández, Mario. *Libro de los dibujos de Federico García Lorca*. Granada: Editorial Comares / Fundación Federico García Lorca, 1998.

——. "Prologue: Francisco and Federico García Lorca." *In the Green Morning: Memories of Federico*. By Francisco García Lorca. Translated by Christopher Maurer. New York: New Directions, 1986. vii–xxviii.

Hernández–Catá, Alfonso. *El ángel de Sodoma*. Edited by Maite Zubiaurre. Doral, FL: Stockcero, 2011.

Herrero, Javier. *Lorca, Young and Gay: The Making of an Artist*. Newark, DE: Juan de la Cuesta, 2014.

Herrick, William. *Shadows and Wolves*. New York: New Directions Books, 1980.

Heuer, Jacqueline. "Álvaro Retana recuperado." *Actas. XIII Congreso de la Asociación Internacional de Hispanistas*. Vol. 2. Edited by Florencio Sevilla and Carlos Alvar. Madrid: Castalia, 2000. 643–54.

Hiller, Anna. "Queer Geographies: Federico García Lorca's 'Oda a Walt Whitman' in English Translation." *Spanish and Portuguese across Time, Place, and Borders: Studies in Honor of Milton M. Azevedo*. Edited by Laura Callahan. Basingstoke: Palgrave Macmillan, 2014. 20–36.

Hinojosa, José María. *Black Tulips: The Selected Poems of José María Hinojosa*. Bilingual edition. Translated by Mark Statman. Foreword by Willis Barnstone. New Orleans: University of New Orleans Press, 2012.

Holguín, Sandie. *Creating Spaniards: Culture and National Identity in Republican Spain*. Madison: University of Wisconsin Press, 2002.

Homenaje al poeta Federico García Lorca, contra su muerte. Valencia: Ediciones Españolas, 1937.

Howard, Leslie. "Such is Fame." *New Yorker* (14 Nov. 1925): 16–17.

Hoyos y Vinent, Antonio de. "Hermafrodita." *El pecado y la noche*. Madrid: Renacimiento, 1913. Project Gutenberg Online.

——. "Prólogo." *El secreto de la ruleta*. Madrid: Biblioteca Nueva, 1919. 7–9.

——. "La última encarnación de Hermafrodita." *Las ciudades malditas (Cuentos)*. Madrid: Biblioteca Hispania, [1922]. 55–72.

——. "[Vidas literarias]." *El Día Gráfico* (Barcelona) (9 May 1918). In Pérez Sanz and Bru Ripoll, *La erótica* 2038–39.

Huet, Marie-Hélène. *Monstrous Imagination*. Cambridge, MA: Harvard University Press, 1993.

——. *Mourning Glory: The Will of the French Revolution*. Philadelphia: University of Pennsylvania Press, 1997.

Hughes, Langston. "Spain's Martyred Poet, García Lorca." Radio broadcast

(Madrid, 8 Nov. 1937). 5 pp. Beinecke Rare Book and Manuscript Library, Yale University, JWJ MSS 26, Box 353, Folder 5708.

————. "Spain's Martyred Poet, García Lorca." *Good Morning, Revolution: Uncollected Writings of Social Protest.* Edited by Faith Berry. New York: Citadel Press, 1992. 114–19.

Hurtado Álvarez, Luis. "A la España imperial le han asesinado su mejor poeta." *Falange Auténtica* (18 Oct. 2008). (Orig. 1937.)

————. Letters to FGL (undated). COA–477 and –478, Fundación Federico García Lorca (Madrid).

Hyeronimus. "José María Hinojosa Lasarte." *Hispanismo.org* (17 Dec. 2010).

Iarocci, Michael. "War and the Work of Poetry: Issues in Teaching Spanish Poetry of the Civil War." *Teaching Representations of the Spanish Civil War.* Edited by Noël Valis. New York: Modern Language Association, 2007. 184–95.

Ibarbourou, Juana de. "(Federico en Montevideo)." In Castro, *Versos* 251–54.

Iglesias Caballero, P. "Las cruces de los cordeles." *Blanco y Negro* (Madrid) (5 Apr. 1936): 75.

Ilie, Paul. "*Capricho/Caprichoso:* A Glossary of Eighteenth-Century Usages." *Hispanic Review* 44.3 (1976): 239–55.

Inglada, Rafael. *Alfonso Ponce de León [1906–1936].* Presentation by Juan Manuel Bonet. Epilogue by Eugenio Carmona. Madrid: Museo Nacional Centro de Arte Reina Sofía, 2001.

————, ed. *Palabra de Lorca: Declaraciones y entrevistas completas.* With the collaboration of Víctor Fernández. Prologue by Christopher Maurer. Barcelona: Malpaso, 2017.

Inglis, Fred. *A Short History of Celebrity.* Princeton, NJ: Princeton University Press, 2010.

Insúa, Alberto. *El negro que tenía el alma blanca.* Edited by Santiago Fortuño Llorens. Madrid: Castalia, 1998.

Intellectuals and the Spanish Military Rebellion. London: Press Department of the Spanish Embassy, [1937?].

Iriarte, Tomás de. *El señorito mimado; La señorita malcriada.* Edited by Russell P. Sebold. Madrid: Castalia, 1978.

Iribarren, Manuel. "Letras." In Rodríguez Puértolas, *Literatura fascista española* 2: 402–5.

J.J. "Margarida Xirgu i García Lorca donaren diumenge, a les onze del mati, al teatre Barcelona, un recital de poesies organitzat per l'Ateneu Enciclopèdic Popular." *L'Humanitat* (Barcelona) (8 Oct. 1935): 2.

J.P. "Glosas del día: El poeta y la multitud." In Laffranque, "Federico García Lorca" 339–40.

Jackson Veyán, José. *Los trabajadores.* Pasillo cómico-lírico en un acto. Music by El Maestro [Ruperto] Chapí. 2nd edition. Madrid: R. Velasco, 1891.

Jerez–Farrán, Carlos. "García Lorca, el espectáculo de la inversión sexual y la reconstitución del yo." *Bulletin of Spanish Studies* 83.5 (2006): 669–93.

———. "Transvestism and Sexual Transgression in García Lorca's *The Public*." *Modern Drama* 44.2 (2001): 188–213.

Johnston, David. *Federico García Lorca.* Bath, Somerset: Absolute Press, 1998.

Jordana Fuentes, Jorge. "Epílogo" (to *La rebelión de los estudiantes*, by David Jato, Feb. 1953). In Alcocer 239–42.

Jou, Jordi. "La poesía vista por un poeta: Hablando con Federico García Lorca." In Inglada, *Palabra de Lorca* 423–28.

Juliá, Santos. "Federico García Lorca, muerte y memoria." *Claves de Razón Práctica* 200 (Mar. 2010): 56–60.

Junquera, Natalia. "'Está ahí, hay que seguir buscando.'" *El País* (Madrid) (16 Dec. 2009).

Juvenal. *Juvenal and Persius.* Bilingual edition. Translated by G. G. Ramsay. London / New York: William Heinemann / G. P. Putnam's Sons, 1928.

Kan, Elianna. "My Lost Poet." *Paris Review* (23 Feb. 2015). Blog.

Katz, Daniel. "Jack Spicer's *After Lorca:* Translation as Decomposition." *Textual Practice* 18.1 (2004): 83–103.

Keenaghan, Eric. "Jack Spicer's Pricks and Cocksuckers. Translating Homosexuality into Visibility." *Translator* 4.2 (1998): 273–94.

Kendall, James. *Eccentricity, or a Check to Censoriousness: with Chapters on Other Subjects.* London: Simpkin, Marshall, 1859.

Kennedy, William Sloane. *The Fight of a Book for the World: A Companion Volume to "Leaves of Grass."* West Yarmouth, MA: Stonecraft Press, 1926.

Kierkegaard, Søren. *Repetition: An Essay in Experimental Psychology.* Translated by Walter Lowrie. New York: Harper and Row, 1964.

Kolbert, Elizabeth. "Looking for Lorca." *New Yorker* (22 and 29 Dec. 2003): 64–75.

Koppenfels, Martin von. *Introducción a la muerte: La poesía neoyorquina de Lorca y el duelo de la lírica moderna.* Translated by José Luis Reina Palazón; revised by Rosa Ribas. Kassel: Edition Reichenberger, 2007.

Krafft–Ebing, Richard von. *Psychopathia Sexualis.* Translated by F. J. Rebman. Revised edition. New York: Medical Art Agency, 1922.

Kris, Ernst, and Otto Kurz. *Legend, Myth, and Magic in the Image of the Artist: A*

Historical Experiment. Preface by E. H. Gombrich. New Haven: Yale University Press, 1979.

L. "Carta de Madrid." *Bulletin of Spanish Studies* 3.12 (1926): 175–77.

Labra, Rafael M. de (hijo). "El Panteón de los doceañistas." *ABC* (Madrid) (11 Aug. 1911): 14.

———. *El Panteón Doceañista*. Madrid: Est. Tipográfico de Fortanet, 1913.

Labrador Ben, Julia María, et al. *La Novela de Hoy, La Novela de Noche y El Folletín Divertido: La labor editorial de Artemio Precioso*. Edited by Julia María Labrador Ben. Madrid: CSIC, 2005.

Labrador Méndez, Germán. "Poets of the Dead Society: The Cultural History of Francoist Mass Graves in the Pre-Democratic Poetic Archive." *Legacies of Violence in Contemporary Spain: Exhuming the Past, Understanding the Present*. Edited by Ofelia Ferrán and Lisa Hilbink. New York / London: Routledge, 2017. 223–46.

Laffranque, Marie. "Federico García Lorca. Déclarations et interviews retrouvés." *Bulletin Hispanique* 58.3 (1956): 301–43.

———. *Les idées esthétiques de Federico García Lorca*. Paris: Centre de Recherches Hispaniques, 1967.

Laguardia, Gari. "The Butterflies in Walt Whitman's Beard: Lorca's Naming of Whitman." *Neophilologus* 62.4 (1978): 540–54.

Laín Entralgo, Pedro. "Lecciones de José Antonio: A los obreros españoles." In *Dolor y memoria de España* 20–23.

Larra, Mariano José de. "El álbum." *Artículos* 326–32.

———. *Artículos*. 22nd edition. Edited by Enrique Rubio. Madrid: Cátedra, 2006.

———. "Los calaveras. Artículo segundo y conclusión." *Artículos* 340–49.

———. "El día de Difuntos de 1836." *Artículos* 392–99.

Larrea, Pedro. "Imagen y repercusión de Federico García Lorca en el campo intelectual argentino tras su muerte y durante 1936." *Letral* No. 10 (2013): 29–46.

Lassell, Michael, and Elena Georgiou, ed. *The World in Us: Lesbian and Gay Poetry of the Next Wave. An Anthology*. New York: St. Martin's Press, 2000.

Le Bon, Gustave. *The Crowd: A Study of the Popular Mind*. 5th printing. Introduction by Robert K. Merton. New York: Viking Press, 1966. (Orig. 1895.)

Lecointre, Melissa. "Federico García Lorca: Le crime introuvable, entre droit de la guerre et fait divers." *Lire et écrire le crime en Espagne (XVIIIe–XXe)*. Edited by Marie Franco. Paris: CREC / Université de la Sorbonne Nouvelle-Paris 3, 2015. 229–51.

Leopold, Stephan. "*El mejor Narciso de nuestro bosque*—homosexualidad como táctica en el petrarquismo del Conde de Villamediana." *Memoria de la palabra: Actas del VI Congreso de la Asociación Internacional Siglo de Oro*. Burgos-La Rioja 15–19 de julio 2002. Vol. 2. Edited by Francisco Domínguez Matito and María Luisa Lobato López. Madrid/Frankfurt: Iberoamericana/Vervuert, 2004. 1141–54.

Lerner, Ben. *The Hatred of Poetry*. New York: Farrar, Straus & Giroux, 2016.

———. *Leaving the Atocha Station*. Minneapolis: Coffeehouse Press, 2011.

Letamendi, José de. *Curso de clínica general ó canon perpetuo de la práctica médica*. Vol. 2. Madrid: Imprenta de los Sucesores de Cuesta, 1894.

Levi, Erik. *Mozart and the Nazis: How the Third Reich Abused a Cultural Icon*. New Haven: Yale University Press, 2010.

Levine, Philip. "The Poet in New York in Detroit." *New England Review* 14.1 (1991): 17–21.

———. "The Search for Lorca's Shadow." In *The Mercy*. New York: Alfred A. Knopf, 1999. 31–32.

Ley, Charles David. *La Costanilla de los diablos (Memorias literarias 1943–1952)*. Madrid: José Esteban, Editor, 1981.

Little Ashes. Dir. Paul Morrison. London: APT Films / Aria Films, 2008.

Llera, José Antonio. *Lorca en Nueva York: Una poética del grito*. Kassel: Edition Reichenberger, 2013.

Lloyd, A. L. "Lorca: Poet of Spain." *Left Review* (London) 3.2 (Mar. 1937): 71–72.

———. "Preface." *Lament for the Death of a Bullfighter and Other Poems*. Bilingual edition. By Federico García Lorca. Translated by A. L. Lloyd. London/Toronto: William Heinemann, 1937. ix–xv.

———. "Preface." *Lament for the Death of a Bullfighter and Other Poems*. By Federico García Lorca. Translated by A. L. Lloyd. Melbourne/London/Toronto: William Heinemann, 1953. xii–xvi.

———. "Spain's Poet Whom Fascism Killed." *Daily Worker* (London) (16 Sept. 1936): 4.

Lluch Fabado Valls, Francisco. *Mi diario entre los mártires: Cárcel de Málaga, año 1937*. Alameda: Editorial Dardo, 1937.

Longaker, Daniel. "The Last Sickness and the Death of Walt Whitman." In Traubel, Bucke, and Harned 393–411.

López, Rafa, and Quico Chirino. "La Diputación movió huesos en la zona donde fue fusilado Lorca al hacer el parque en 1986." *Ideal* (Granada) (20 Oct. 2008).

López-Parra, Ernesto. "Los innovadores." *El Liberal* (Madrid) (31 July 1927): 5.

————. "Traición y muerte del señorito Cañero." *El Mono Azul* (Madrid) 1.7 (8 Oct. 1936): 5.

López Pinillos, J[osé] (Pármeno). *Los favoritos de la multitud: Cómo se conquista la notoriedad.* Madrid: Editorial Pueyo, 1920.

————. *El luchador.* 2nd edition. Madrid: Editorial Pueyo, 1916.

López Soler, Ramón. *Los bandos de Castilla.* 3 vols. Valencia: Imprenta de Cabrerizo, 1830.

López de Toro, José. "Carta del Conde de Villamediana a Don Luis Rosales." Archivo Histórico Nacional (Madrid), Diversos-Luis Rosales, 10, N. 75.

Lorca, muerte de un poeta. Dir. Juan Antonio Bardem. Madrid: Acción Films for Televisión Española (TVE), 1987.

Loureiro, Ángel G. "Pathetic Arguments." *Journal of Spanish Cultural Studies* 9.2 (2008): 225–37.

————. "La vida con los muertos." *Revista Canadiense de Estudios Hispánicos* 30.1 (2005): 145–58.

Luna, José R. "La vida de García Lorca, poeta." In Inglada, *Palabra de Lorca* 298–305.

La luz prodigiosa. Dir. Miguel Hermoso. Madrid/Valencia: Azalea Producciones Cinematográficas / Canal 9 Televisió Valenciana, 2003.

M.M. "Popular Culture." *Volunteer for Liberty* (Madrid) 1.14 (13 Sept. 1937): 12.

MacCabe, Colin. "Keyword: Celebrity." Keywords Project, University of Pittsburgh, www.keywords.pitt.edu (accessed 3 May 2021).

Macciocchi, Maria-Antonietta. "Pasolini: Murder of a Dissident." Translated by Thomas Repensek. *October* 13 (1980): 11–21.

MacDiarmid, Hugh. *The Battle Continues.* Edinburgh: Castle Wynd Printers, 1957.

Machado, Antonio. "El crimen fue en Granada." *Antología comentada.* Vol. 1. Edited by Francisco Caudet. Madrid: Ediciones de la Torre, 1999. 331–33.

————. *La guerra: Escritos, 1936–1939.* Edited by Julio Rodríguez Puértolas and Gerardo Pérez Herrero. Madrid: Emiliano Escolar Editor, 1983.

————. "El quinto detenido y las fuerzas vivas." *Poesías completas.* Prologue by Manuel Alvar. 12th edition. Madrid: Espasa-Calpe, 1987. 389–91.

————. *Selected Poems.* Bilingual edition. Translated by Alan S. Trueblood. Cambridge, MA: Harvard University Press, 1982.

Machado y Álvarez, Antonio (Demófilo). "Prólogo." *Cantes flamencos.* 3rd edition. Madrid: Espasa-Calpe, 1975. 13–20.

————. *Estudios sobre literatura popular.* Biblioteca de las Tradiciones Populares Españolas, vol. 5. Seville: Alejando Guichot y Compañía, 1884.

Madariaga de la Campa, Benito. *Aventuras y desventuras de un trotamundos de la poesía: Recuerdo y homenaje a Pío Fernández Muriedas.* Santander: Consejería de Cultura, Turismo y Deporte del Gobierno de Cantabria, 2009.

Madrid, Francisco. *Sangre en Atarazanas.* Edited by Julià Guillamon. Preface by Sergio Vila-Sanjuán. Barcelona: La Vanguardia Ediciones, 2020. (Orig. 1926.)

Mallan, Lloyd. "Death of a Spanish Poet: A True Story." *Daily Clarion* (Toronto) (24 Apr. 1939): 6.

———. "Granada, Oh! Granada." *Fantasy.* Sixth Year. No. 3 = 23 (1939): 50–52.

———. "Granada, Oh! Granada." *Esquire* (Dec. 1940): 68–69.

Mallarmé, Stéphane. *Collected Poems.* Bilingual edition. Translated by Henry Weinfield. Berkeley: University of California Press, 1994.

Mandrell, James. *Don Juan and the Point of Honor: Seduction, Patriarchal Society, and Literary Tradition.* University Park: Pennsylvania State University Press, 1992.

Manrique, Jaime. *Eminent Maricones: Arenas, Lorca, Puig, and Me.* Madison: University of Wisconsin Press, 1999.

———. *My Night with Federico García Lorca / Mi noche con Federico García Lorca.* Translated by Edith Grossman and Eugene Richie. New edition. New York: Painted Leaf Press, 1997. (Orig. 1995.)

Mansilla, Mirtha, and Alfonso López Alfonso. "Introducción." *España levanta el puño.* By Pablo Suero. Edited by Mirtha Mansilla and Alfonso López Alfonso. Seville: Espuela de Plata, 2015. 9–70.

Marañón, Gregorio. "Un caso de intersexualidad de tipo hermafrodítico." *Anales del Servicio de Patología Médica del Hospital General de Madrid* 4 (1928–29): 3–4.

———. *Don Juan: Ensayos sobre el origen de su leyenda.* 4th edition. Buenos Aires: Espasa-Calpe, 1947. (Orig. 1940.)

———. *Ensayos sobre la vida sexual.* Prologue by Ramón Pérez de Ayala. Madrid: Espasa-Calpe, 1951.

———. "Notas para la biología de Don Juan." *Obras completas.* Vol. 4. Edited by Alfredo Juderías. Madrid: Espasa-Calpe, 1968. 75–93. (Orig. 1924.)

———. "Psicopatología del donjuanismo." *Obras completas.* Vol. 3. Edited by Alfredo Juderías. Madrid: Espasa-Calpe, 1967. 75–93. (Orig. 1924.)

———. *Raíz y decoro de España.* 2nd edition. Madrid: Espasa-Calpe, 1941. (Orig. 1933.)

———. *Tres ensayos sobre la vida sexual.* 6th edition. Prologue by Ramón Pérez de Ayala. Mexico City: Editorial Diana, 1962. (Orig. 1926.)

March, Enric H. "Museus anatòmics: quan el cos i les malalties eren un espectacle." *Barcelona Metròpolis* No. 91 (2014): 32–38.

Marí, Jorge. "Objetivo: García Lorca; Nuevas inquisiciones cinematográficas y televisivas sobre la vida, obra y muerte del poeta." *Arbor* 187.748 (Mar.–Apr. 2011): 211–22.

Marías, Fernando. *La luz prodigiosa*. Barcelona: Destino, 1998. (Orig. 1990.)

Marías, Javier. "El folklore de los huesos insignes." *El País* (Madrid) (22 Nov. 2009).

———. "Lorca, Untamed." Translated by Margaret Jull Costa. *Threepenny Review* No. 132 (Winter 2013): 31.

Marín Abeytua, Diego, and Rubén Marín Abeytua. "Tragedia, frustración y bohemia de Armando Buscarini, un poeta maldito." *Letras Peninsulares* 18.1 (Spring 2005): 19–47.

Marlowe, Christopher. *The Plays of Christopher Marlowe*. Edited by Edward Thomas. London / New York: J. M. Dent / E. P. Dutton, n.d.

Márquez Villanueva, Francisco. *Orígenes y elaboración de "El burlador de Sevilla."* Salamanca: Ediciones Universidad de Salamanca, 1996.

Marshall, P. David, ed. *The Celebrity Culture Reader*. New York: Routledge, 2006.

Martín, Adrienne L. "Góngora: 'Poeta de bujarrones.'" *Calíope* 8.1 (2002): 141–60.

Martín, Eutimio. "Antonio Machado y la Generación del 27. Una carta inédita a Federico García Lorca." *Antonio Machado hoy (1939–1989)*. Edited by Paul Aubert. Madrid: Casa de Velázquez, 1994. 237–43.

———. *Federico García Lorca, heterodoxo y mártir: Análisis y proyección de la obra juvenil inédita*. Mexico City: Siglo XXI, 1986.

———. "La 'vis comica' de la poesía falangista." *Cahiers d'Études Romanes* (Aix–en–Provence) No. 6 (1980): 125–44.

Martín de Lucenay, Á[ngel]. *Homosexualidad: Raíces biológicas de la homosexualidad*. Madrid: Fénix, 1933. In *A Virtual Wunderkammer*.

———. *Invertidos célebres*. Madrid: Editorial Fénix, 1933.

Martínez Arnaldos, Manuel, ed. *Artemio Precioso y la novela corta*. Albacete: Diputación de Albacete, 1997.

Martínez Nadal, Rafael. *Federico García Lorca: Mi penúltimo libro sobre el hombre y el poeta*. Madrid: Casariego, 1992.

———. "Introduction." *Poems*. By Federico García Lorca. Translated by Stephen Spender and J. L. Gili. London: Dolphin, 1939. vii–xxviii.

Martínez Olmedilla, Augusto. "Descentralización." *La Vanguardia Española* (Barcelona) (17 June 1958): 7.

Martínez de la Rosa, Francisco. *La conjuración de Venecia*. Edited by José Paulino. Madrid: Taurus, 1988.

Martínez Sierra, Gregorio. "La estatua de Bécquer." *Nuevo Mundo* (Madrid) No. 936 (14 Dec. 1911): [7].

Mata, Pedro. *Tratado de medicina y cirugía legal teórica y práctica*. 2 vols. 4th edition. Madrid: Carlos Bailly-Baillière, 1866.

Matthews, Samantha. *Poetical Remains: Poets' Graves, Bodies, and Books in the Nineteenth Century*. Oxford: Oxford University Press, 2004.

Maurer, Christopher. "García Lorca et le succès: noces de sang." *Magazine Littéraire* No. 249 (Jan. 1988): 28–30.

———. "Lorca, de viva voz." In Inglada, *Palabra de Lorca* vii–xx.

———. "Lorca, from Country to City: Three Versions of *Poet in New York*." *Avenues of Translation: The City in Iberian and Latin American Writing*. Edited by Regina Galasso and Evelyn Scaramella. Lewisburg, PA: Bucknell University Press, 2019. 32–51.

———. "Sobre 'joven literatura' y política: cartas de Pedro Salinas y de Federico García Lorca (1930–1935)." *Estelas, laberintos, nuevas sendas. Unamuno. Valle-Inclán. García Lorca. La guerra civil*. Edited by Ángel G. Loureiro. Barcelona: Anthropos, 1988. 297–319.

———, and Andrew A. Anderson. *Federico García Lorca en Nueva York y La Habana: Cartas y recuerdos*. Barcelona: Galaxia Gutenberg / Círculo de Lectores, 2013.

Max-Bembo (José Ruiz Rodríguez). *La mala vida en Barcelona: Anormalidad, miseria y vicio*. Barcelona: Casa Editorial Maucci, 1912.

Mayhew, Jonathan. *Apocryphal Lorca: Translation, Parody, Kitsch*. Chicago: University of Chicago Press, 2009.

———. *Lorca's Legacy: Essays in Interpretation*. New York/London: Routledge, 2018.

Mayordomo, Joaquín. "Goytisolo aboga por 'dejar en paz' a Cervantes y sus huesos." *El País* (Madrid) (31 Mar. 2015).

McDermid, Paul. *Love, Desire, and Identity in the Theatre of Federico García Lorca*. Woodbridge, Suffolk: Tamesis, 2007.

Medina, Pablo. *Lorca, un andaluz en Buenos Aires, 1933–1934*. Buenos Aires: Manrique Zago y León Goldstein Editores, 1999.

Mello Breyner Andresen, Sophia de. "Túmulo de Lorca." *Geografia*. Lisbon: Edições Ática, 1967. 28.

Mendelssohn, Michèle. *Henry James, Oscar Wilde, and Aesthetic Culture*. Edinburgh: Edinburgh University Press, 2007.

Menéndez y Pelayo, Marcelino. "D. Gaspar Núñez de Arce." *Estudios de crítica literaria*. Madrid: Imprenta de A. Pérez Dubrull, 1884. 273–329.

Merino, Pilar. "Operación Quevedo: La ruta de los huesos." *Clarín: Revista de Nueva Literatura* (25 Sept. 2008).

Merrill, Stuart. "Une lettre de M. Stuart Merrill à propos de Walt Whitman." *Mercure de France* (Paris) No. 380 (16 Apr. 1913): 890–92.

———. "La question Walt Whitman." *Mercure de France* (Paris) No. 394 (16 Nov. 1913): 329–36.

Merry del Val, Marquis de. "Spain: 'Six of One and Half a Dozen of the Other.'" *Nineteenth Century and After* 121 (Jan.–June 1937): 355–71.

Mesonero Romanos, Manuel. *Goya, Moratín, Meléndez Valdés y Donoso Cortés: Reseña histórica de los anteriores enterramientos y traslaciones de sus restos mortales hasta su inhumación en el mausoleo del cementerio de San Justo el día 11 de mayo de 1900*. Madrid: Imprenta de los Hijos de M. G. Hernández, 1900.

———. *Las sepulturas de los hombres ilustres en los cementerios de Madrid*. Madrid: Imprenta de Hernando y Compañía, 1898.

Mesonero Romanos, Ramón de. "Contrastes. Tipos perdidos, tipos hallados." *Escenas y tipos matritenses*. Edited by Enrique Rubio Cremades. Madrid: Cátedra, 1993. 476–511.

———. *Memorias de un setentón*. 2 vols. Madrid: Oficinas de la Ilustración Española y Americana, 1881.

———. "El Panteón Nacional Francés." *Semanario Pintoresco Español* (Madrid) 2.41 (8 Jan. 1837): 9–10.

———. *Recuerdos de viaje por Francia y Bélgica en 1840–1841. Obras*. Vol. 5. Edited by Carlos Seco Serrano. Madrid: Atlas, 1967.

Meyer-Minnemann, Klaus, Ana Luengo, and Daniela Pérez y Effinger. "La Ponencia colectiva (1937) de Arturo Serrano Plaja: Una toma de posición literaria y política en la guerra civil." *Revista de Literatura* 65 (2003): 447–70.

Mill, John Stuart. *On Liberty. Representative Government. The Subjection of Women. Three Essays*. Introduction by Millicent Garrett Fawcett. 1912; London: Geoffrey Cumberlege/ Oxford University Press, 1954.

Mira, Alberto. "After Wilde: Camp Discourse in Hoyos and Retana, or the Dawn of Spanish Gay Culture." *Journal of Spanish Cultural Studies* 5.1 (2004): 25–39.

———. *De Sodoma a Chueca*. Barcelona: Editorial Egales, 2004.

———. "Modernistas, dandis y pederastas: Articulaciones de la homosexualidad en 'la edad de plata.'" *Journal of Iberian and Latin American Studies* 7.1 (2001): 63–75.

————. *Para entendernos: Diccionario de cultura homosexual, gay y lésbica.* 2nd edition, revised and enlarged. Barcelona: Ediciones La Tempestad, 2002.

Moga, Eduardo. "Sobre la poesía y la vida de César González–Ruano." *Cuadernos Hispanoamericanos* No. 764 (Feb. 2014): 2–29.

Molina, Miguel de. *Botín de guerra: Autobiografía.* Edited by Salvador Valverde. With the assistance of Alejandro Salade. Barcelona: Planeta, 1998.

Molina Fajardo, Eduardo. *Los últimos días de García Lorca.* Córdoba: Almuzara, 2011. (Orig. 1983.)

Monegal, Antonio. "Releer a García Lorca en el fin de siglo." *Federico García Lorca (1898–1936).* Madrid: TF Editores, [1998]. 77–81.

————. "La 'verdad de las sepulturas' y la incertidumbre de la escritura." *Federico García Lorca, clásico moderno (1898–1998).* Edited by Andrés Soria Olmedo, María José Sánchez Montes, and Juan Varo Zafra. Granada: Diputación de Granada, 2000. 61–76.

Monlau, Pedro Felipe. *Higiene del matrimonio ó el libro de los casados.* 13th edition, revised. Paris: Garnier Hermanos, [1865]. (Orig. 1853.)

Montero Alonso, José. "La vida literaria: Una charla con Álvaro Retana." *Alma Ibérica* No. 4 (10 Jan. 1924). In Pérez Sanz and Bru Ripoll, *La erótica* 2044–46.

Montes Rojas, Rocío. "Un equipo internacional de peritos asegura que Pablo Neruda no murió de cáncer." *El País* (Madrid) (21 Oct. 2017).

————. "Los exámenes concluyen que Neruda murió de cáncer y no envenenado." *El País* (Madrid) (8 Nov. 2013).

————. "¿Fue Neruda asesinado?" *El País* (Madrid) (4 Dec. 2011).

————. "El poeta de los cuatro funerales." *El País* (Madrid) (27 Apr. 2016).

Montetes-Mairal y Laburta, Noemí. "Luis Rosales, 'mortal antipolítico' (Poesía y política en Luis Rosales)." *Páginas que no callan: Historia, memoria e identidad en la literatura hispánica.* Edited by A. García-Reidy, L. M. Romeu, et al. Valencia: PUV, 2014. 125–38.

Montoliú, Pedro. "San Francisco el Grande: Un museo bajo la mayor cúpula de España." *Madridiario* (12 Nov. 2013).

Moore, John C. "Purity and Commercialization: The View from Two Working Artists, Pericón de Cádiz and Chato de la Isla." *Flamenco on the Global Stage: Historical, Critical, and Theoretical Perspectives.* Edited by K. Meira Goldberg et al. Jefferson, NC: McFarland, 2015. 166–77.

Morales, Felipe. "Conversaciones literarias: Al habla con Federico García Lorca." In Inglada, *Palabra de Lorca* 455–61.

Moreno Mengíbar, Andrés, and Francisco Vázquez García. "Hermafroditas y cambios de sexo en la España moderna." In *Monstruos y seres imaginarios en la Biblioteca Nacional.* Madrid: Biblioteca Nacional, 2000. 91–103.

Moreno Villa, José. *Locos, enanos, negros y niños palaciegos: Siglos XVI y XVII.* Mexico City: Casa de España en México, Editorial Presencia, 1939.

————. *Memoria.* Edited by Juan Pérez de Ayala. Mexico City: El Colegio de México/ Publicaciones de la Residencia de Estudiantes, 2011.

Morla Lynch, Carlos. *En España con Federico García Lorca (Páginas de un diario íntimo, 1928–1936).* 2nd edition, revised. Prologue by Sergio Macías Brevis. Seville: Renacimiento, 2008.

————. *España sufre. Diarios de guerra en el Madrid republicano.* Prologue by Andrés Trapiello. Seville: Renacimiento, 2008.

Morris, C. Brian. "Brief Encounter: Federico García Lorca and Edouard Roditi in Paris (June 1929)." *Bulletin of Spanish Studies* 86.3 (2009): 331–43.

————. "Fat Body, Thin Soul: Lorca's Landscape of Coney Island." *Lorca, Poet and Playwright: Essays in Honour of J. M. Aguirre.* Edited by Robert Havard. Cardiff / New York: University of Wales Press / St. Martin's Press, 1992. 49–70.

————. *Lorca entre la muchedumbre de Nueva York.* Santander: Sociedad Menéndez Pelayo, Conferencias y Discursos, 2000.

————. *Son of Andalusia: The Lyrical Landscapes of Federico García Lorca.* Nashville, TN: Vanderbilt University Press, 1997.

Mozo de Rosales, Emilio. *El señorito de pueblo.* Acto único. Madrid: Imprenta de J. Rodríguez, 1869.

Muñoz, Luis. "Daría algo por leértelo." *Jardín deshecho: Lorca y el amor.* Edited by Christopher Maurer. Granada: Centro Federico García Lorca, 2019. 62–85.

Muñoz Molina, Antonio. "Burocracia del crimen." *El País* (Madrid) (2 July 2011).

Murray, Martin G. "'Pete the Great': A Biography of Peter Doyle." *Walt Whitman Quarterly Review* 12.1 (1994): 1–51.

Namorado, Joaquim. "Romance de Federico." In Castro, *Versos* 486–93.

Nancy, Jean–Luc. "Afterword: Three Questions about *Tombeau of Ibn Arabi.*" *Tombeau of Ibn Arabi and White Traverses.* By Abdelwahab Meddeb. Translated by Charlotte Mandell. New York: Fordham University Press, 2010. 109–15.

Nandorfy, Martha J. *The Poetics of Apocalypse: Federico García Lorca's "Poet in New York."* Lewisburg, PA: Bucknell University Press, 2003.

Navarro, Mary Anderson de. "Tennyson's Funeral." *Tennyson: Interviews and Recollections.* Edited by Norman Page. London: Macmillan, 1983. 196–97. (Orig. 1936.)

Neira Jiménez, Julio. "Construcción crítica y realidad histórica de la Generación del 27." *Epos: Revista de Filología* 34 (2018): 191–209.

Nelken, Margarita. "La casa maravillosa de Tórtola Valencia." *Blanco y Negro* (Madrid) (10 July 1927): 97–101.

Nelson, Cary. "Literature as Cultural Studies: 'American' Poetry of the Spanish Civil War." *Disciplinarity and Dissent in Cultural Studies.* Edited by Cary Nelson and Dilip Parameshwar Gaonkar. New York: Routledge, 1996. 63–102.

———, ed. *The Wound and the Dream: Sixty Years of American Poems about the Spanish Civil War.* Urbana: University of Illinois Press, 2002.

Nemoianu, Virgil. "'National Poets' in the Romantic Age: Emergence and Importance." *Romantic Poetry.* Edited by Angela Esterhammer. Philadelphia: John Benjamins Publishing, 2002. 249–55.

Neruda, Pablo. "El desenterrado (Homenaje al Conde de Villamediana)." *Residencia en la tierra.* 3rd edition. Buenos Aires: Losada, 1969. 126–28.

———. "Federico García Lorca." *Hora de España* (Valencia) No. 3 (Mar. 1937): 227–38.

———. *Viajes al corazón de Quevedo y por las costas del mundo.* [Santiago]: Ediciones de la Sociedad de Escritores de Chile, 1947.

Neville, Edgar. "Una especie de ángel." *Obras selectas* 808–10.

———. "García Lorca." *Obras selectas* 815–17.

———. Letter to FGL (22 Aug.1928). COA–728, Fundación Federico García Lorca (Madrid).

———. "La obra de Federico, bien nacional." *ABC* (Madrid) (6 Nov. 1966): 4.

———. *Obras selectas.* Edited by Miguel Ruiz–Castillo. Madrid: Biblioteca Nueva, 1969.

———. "Otra vez Lorca." In Trapiello, *Las armas y las letras* 569.

———. "Sobre la nostalgia." *Las terceras de "ABC."* Edited by Rafael Flórez. Madrid: Editorial Prensa Española, 1976. 122–25.

———. *Su último paisaje.* Cuadernos de María José, 3. Málaga: Publicaciones de la Librería Anticuaria el Guadalhorce, 1966.

———. "Su último paisaje." *Poemas.* Madrid: Revista de Occidente, 1967. 37–40.

Nicholl, Charles. *The Reckoning: The Murder of Christopher Marlowe.* Revised edition. New York: Vintage, 2002.

Nin Frías, Alberto. *Alexis o el significado del temperamento urano.* Madrid: Javier Morata, 1932.

———. *Ensayo sobre tres expresiones del espíritu andaluz.* Buenos Aires: Edición del autor, 1935.

———. *Homosexualismo creador.* Madrid: Javier Morata, 1933.

———. Letter to FGL (1 Nov.1933). COA–732, Fundación Federico García Lorca (Madrid).

Noel, Eugenio. *Señoritos, chulos, fenómenos, gitanos y flamencos.* Madrid: Renacimiento, 1916.

Nora, Pierre. "Between Memory and History: *Les Lieux de Mémoire.*" *Representations* 26 (1989): 7–24.

Norse, Harold. "We Bumped Off Your Friend the Poet." *Hotel Nirvana: Selected Poems, 1953–1973.* San Francisco: City Lights Books, 1974. 14–15.

Ocaña, retrat intermitent. Dir. Ventura Pons. [Madrid?]: Prozesa/Teide, 1978.

Olmedilla, Juan G. "Ayer se celebró brillantemente el tricentenario de la muerte de Lope, gloria dramática de España." *El Heraldo de Madrid* (28 Aug. 1935): 8.

———. "Rutas mediterráneas: Barcelona; García Lorca y su romancero del pueblo." *El Heraldo de Madrid* (8 Oct. 1935): 16.

Olmedo, Ildefonso. "El segundo fusilamiento de Federico García Lorca." *El Mundo* (Madrid) (24 Apr. 2015).

Onions, C. T., ed. *The Oxford Dictionary of English Etymology.* New York: Oxford University Press, 1966.

Online Etymology Dictionary, www.etymonline.com (accessed 3 May 2021).

Ontañón, Santiago, and José María Moreiro. *Unos pocos amigos verdaderos.* Prologue by Rafael Alberti. Madrid: Fundación Banco Exterior, 1988.

Ortega y Gasset, José. *La deshumanización del arte y otros ensayos estéticos.* 9th edition. Madrid: Revista de Occidente, 1967. (Orig. 1925.)

———. "La moral del automóvil en España." *El Sol* (Madrid) (24 Aug. 1930): 3.

———. "Los problemas concretos." *El Sol* (Madrid) (14 Mar. 1931): 1.

———. *La rebelión de las masas.* 36th edition. Madrid: Revista de Occidente, 1962. (Orig. 1929.)

Ortiz, Gloria. *The Dandy and the Señorito: Eros and Social Class in the Nineteenth-Century Novel.* New York: Garland, 1991.

Ortiz Lozano, Francisco. "Federico García Lorca y los falangistas." *Falange Auténtica* (26 Sept. 2005).

Ortiz de Pinedo, José. "El pecado de celebridad." *La Esfera* (Madrid) (23 Aug. 1924): 23.

Orwell, George. *Homage to Catalonia.* Introduction by Lionel Trilling. Boston: Beacon, 1966. (Orig. 1938.)

———. *The Road to Wigan Pier.* London: Penguin, 1937.

Otero Seco, Antonio. *Écrits sur García Lorca dont sa dernière Interview.* Édition bilingue. Rennes: La Part Commune, 2013.

Ovid. *The Metamorphoses.* Translated by Horace Gregory. New York: New American Library, 1958.

Ozouf, Mona. "The Pantheon: The École Normale of the Dead." *Realms of Memory: The Construction of the French Past.* Vol. 3. *Symbols.* Edited by Lawrence D. Kritzman. Directed by Pierre Nora. Translated by Arthur Goldhammer. New York: Columbia University Press, 1998. 325–46.

Paepe, Christian de. "F. García Lorca entre amnesia y memoria." *La memoria histórica en las letras hispánicas contemporáneas.* Edited by Patrick Collard. Geneva: Librairie Droz, 1997. 73–85.

———, ed. *Catálogo de la correspondencia a Federico García Lorca. 6. Catálogo general de los fondos documentales de la Fundación Federico García Lorca.* Madrid: Consejería de Cultura de la Junta de Andalucía / Fundación Federico García Lorca, 2003.

Paepe, Christian de, and Manuel Fernández-Montesinos García, ed. *La Biblioteca de Federico García Lorca. 8. Catálogo general de los fondos documentales de la Fundación Federico García Lorca.* Madrid: Fundación Federico García Lorca, 2008.

Pala, Mauro. "Facets of the *Risorgimento:* The Debate on the Classical Heritage from Byron's *Childe Harold* to Leopardi's *Canzone ad Angelo Mai.*" *British Romanticism and Italian Literature: Translating, Reviewing, Rewriting.* Edited by Laura Bandiera and Diego Saglia. Amsterdam: Rodopi, 2005. 193–207.

Palacio Valdés, Armando. *El señorito Octavio. Obras.* Vol. 2. Madrid: Aguilar, 1965.

Palenque, Marta. *La construcción del mito Bécquer: El poeta en su ciudad, Sevilla, 1871–1936.* Seville: ICAS, 2011.

———. *El poeta y el burgués (Poesía y público, 1850–1900).* Seville: Alfar, 1990.

Pardo Bazán, Emilia. *Un viaje de novios. Obras completas.* Vol. 30. 6th edition. Madrid: Editorial Pueyo, 1919.

Paré, Ambroise. *On Monsters and Marvels.* Translated by Janis L. Pallister. Chicago: University of Chicago Press, 1982.

Parrot, Louis. *Federico García Lorca.* With the collaboration of Marcelle Schveitzer and Armand Guibert. Paris: Pierre Seghers Éditeur, 1947.

Pascua, Virgilio de la. "Los libros: *El octavo pecado capital;* Álvaro Retana." *El Día* (Madrid) (11 May 1921). In Pérez Sanz and Bru Ripoll, *La erótica* 1642.

Pasolini, Pier Paolo. *Heretical Empiricism.* Edited by Louise K. Barnett. Translated by Ben Lawton and Louise K. Barnett. Bloomington: Indiana University Press, 1988.

————. *The Selected Poetry of Pier Paolo Pasolini*. Bilingual edition. Edited and translated by Stephen Sartarelli. Foreword by James Ivory. Chicago: University of Chicago Press, 2014.

Pastor Díaz, Nicomedes. Prologue to *Obras completas*. By José Zorrilla. Edited by Narciso Alonso Cortés. Valladolid: Librería Santarén, 1943. 13–24.

Pastor Mateos, Enrique. *El Panteón de Hombres Ilustres*. Madrid: Instituto de Estudios Madrileños, 1970.

Payne, Stanley G. *España: Una historia única*. Translated by Jesús Cuéllar. Madrid: Temas de Hoy, 2008.

————. *Fascism in Spain, 1923–1977*. Madison: University of Wisconsin Press, 1999.

Pearce, Joseph. *Unafraid of Virginia Woolf: The Friends and Enemies of Roy Campbell*. Wilmington, DE: ISI Books, 2004.

Pekron, Rebecca. "'En vue de plus tard ou de jamais': Poetic Community in Stéphane Mallarmé's *Tombeaux*." *French Studies* 68.3 (2014): 328–43.

Peláez Martín, Andrés, ed. *Vestir el género frívolo: Álvaro de Retana (1890–1970)*. Madrid: Museo Nacional del Teatro, 2006.

Pemán, José María. "García Lorca." *ABC* (Madrid) (5 Dec. 1948): 3.

————. *Poema de la Bestia y el Ángel. Poesía. Obras completas*. Vol. 1. Edited by Jorge Villén. Madrid: Escelicer, 1947.

Penón, Agustín. *Miedo, olvido y fantasía: Crónica de la investigación de Agustín Penón sobre Federico García Lorca Granada-Madrid (1955–56)*. 2nd edition. Edited by Marta Osorio. Granada: Comares, 2009.

Peral Vega, Emilio. *Pierrot/Lorca: White Carnival of Black Desire*. Woodbridge, Suffolk: Tamesis, 2015.

Percy, Walker. *Love in the Ruins: The Adventures of a Bad Catholic at a Time near the End of the World*. New York: Avon Books, 1981. (Orig. 1971.)

Pereda Valdés, Ildefonso, ed. *Cancionero de la guerra civil española*. Publicación del Comité Pro-Defensa de la República Española. Montevideo: Claudio García y Compañía, 1937.

Pereiro Otero, José Manuel. "De metrópolis a necrópolis: La escritura del cementerio en Mariano José de Larra." *Siglo Diecinueve* No. 20 (2014): 9–26.

Pérez Ferrero, Miguel. "Los españoles fuera de España." In Inglada, *Palabra de Lorca* 309–14.

————. "Voces de desembarque: Veinte minutos de paseo con Federico García Lorca." In Inglada, *Palabra de Lorca* 37–42.

Pérez Firmat, Gustavo. *Literature and Liminality: Festive Readings in the Hispanic Tradition*. Durham, NC: Duke University Press, 1986.

Pérez Galdós, Benito. *Ensayos de crítica literaria*. Edited by Laureano Bonet. Barcelona: Ediciones Península, 1972.

———. "Observaciones sobre la novela contemporánea en España." In *Ensayos* 115–32. (Orig. 1870.)

———. "La sociedad presente como materia novelable." In *Ensayos* 173–82. (Orig. 1897.)

———. *El terror de 1824*. Episodios nacionales, segunda serie. Madrid: Obras de Pérez Galdós, 1904.

———. *Tristana*. Madrid: Imprenta de "La Guirnalda," 1892.

Pérez Sanz, Pilar, and Carmen Bru Ripoll. *La erótica en la España del 1900–1936*. Vol. 4. Madrid: Instituto de Ciencias Sexológicas, n.d. In *A Virtual Wunderkammer*.

———. *La sexología en la España de los años 30. Tomo IV: Álvaro Retana, "El sumo pontífice de las variedades." Revista de Sexología* Nos. 40–41 (1989).

Perloff, Marjorie. *The Poetics of Indeterminacy: Rimbaud to Cage*. Princeton, NJ: Princeton University Press, 1981.

Perriam, Chris. "Gender and Sexuality." In Bonaddio 149–69.

Picón, Jacinto Octavio. "El sepulcro de Sagasta." *El Imparcial* (Madrid) (27 June 1904): [1].

Pineda Novo, Daniel. "En la noche sensual de su Granada . . . " In Castro, *Versos* 339.

Pinto, Ernesto. "Federico García Lorca: gitano auténtico y poeta de verdad." In Inglada, *Palabra de Lorca* 264–75.

Plenn, Abel. *Wind in the Olive Trees: Spain from the Inside*. New York: Boni & Gaer, 1946.

Pliny. *Natural History*. Vol. 9. Translated by H. Rackham. Cambridge/London: Harvard University Press / William Heinemann, 1961.

Poeta, Salvatore J. *La elegía funeral en memoria de Federico García Lorca (Introducción al género y antología)*. Madrid: Playor, 1990.

Pollin, Alice. "Walt Whitman y García Lorca: Corrientes literarias y traducciones." *Boletín de la Fundación Federico García Lorca* Nos. 10–11 (1992): 181–90.

Porpetta, Antonio. *Escritores y artistas españoles (Historia de una Asociación centenaria)*. Madrid: Asociación de Escritores y Artistas Españoles, 1986.

Pozo Felguera, Gabriel. *Lorca, el último paseo: Claves para entender el asesinato del poeta*. Granada: Ultramarina, 2009.

Prado, Benjamín. "Desentierren a Lorca, por favor." *El País* (Madrid) (25 June 2004): 14.

Prados, Emilio. "Llegada." *El Mono Azul* (Madrid) 1.4 (17 Sept. 1936): 4.

Precioso, Artemio. "A manera de prólogo." In Retana, *El encanto de la cama redonda* 5–11.

———. "A manera de prólogo." In Retana, *Flor del mal* 3–9.

Predmore, Richard L. *Lorca's New York Poetry: Social Injustice, Dark Love, Lost Faith.* Durham, NC: Duke University Press, 1980.

Prieto Pérez, Santiago. "El Panteón de Hombres Ilustres de Madrid." *Dendra Médica: Revista de Humanidades* 11.1 (2012): 26–42.

Prieto y Prieto, M[anuel]. *Panteón Nacional: Descripción de San Francisco, Decreto de las Cortes Constituyentes de 1869 con los apuntes biográficos de los grandes hombres cuyos restos quedan depositados al inaugurarse el Panteón.* Madrid: Imprenta de T. Fortanet, 1869.

Primo de Rivera, José Antonio. "Discurso de la fundación de Falange Española" (29 Oct. 1933). *Obras completas* (online), www.rumbos.net/ocja (accessed 3 May 2021).

———. "Discurso sobre la revolución española" (19 May 1935). *Obras completas* (online), www.rumbos.net/ocja (accessed 3 May 2021).

———. "Señoritismo" (25 Jan. 1934). *Obras completas* (online), www.rumbos .net/ocja (accessed 3 May 2021).

Pujals, Esteban. *España y la guerra de 1936 en la poesía de Roy Campbell.* Madrid: Ateneo, 1959.

Queralt, María Pilar. *Tórtola Valencia.* Barcelona: Lumen, 2005.

Quevedo, Francisco de. *Grandes anales de quince días: Obras serias.* Paris: Casa Editorial Garnier Hermanos, [1881?]. 167–222.

———. *Obras completas I. Poesía original.* 2nd edition. Edited by José Manuel Blecua. Barcelona: Planeta, 1968.

Quinet, Edgar. "Le Panthéon." *Paris Guide.* Première Partie. Paris/Brussels: Librairie Internationale / A. Lacroix, Verboeckhoven et Cie, Éditeurs, 1867. 658–70.

Rachilde (Marguerite Vallette-Eymery). *Monsieur Vénus.* Prologue by Maurice Barrès. Paris: Félix Brossier, Éditeur, 1889.

Ramos Carrión, Miguel. *Los señoritos.* Comedia en dos actos, y en prosa. Madrid: Imprenta de José Rodríguez, 1874.

Ramos Espejo, Antonio. *García Lorca en Fuente Vaqueros.* 2nd edition. Granada: Diputación Provincial de Granada / Patronato Cultural Federico García Lorca, 1998.

Ramos Otero, Manuel. "Lorca." *El libro de la muerte*. Río Piedras, PR/Maplewood, NJ: Editorial Cultural / Waterfront Press, 1985. 45–46.

Ravenscroft, Janet. "Invisible Friends: Questioning the Representation of the Court Dwarf in Hapsburg Spain." In *Histories of the Normal and the Abnormal*. Edited by Waltraud Ernst. London: Routledge, 2006. 26–52.

Redondo, Tomás H. "José Antonio, poeta del imperio." In *Dolor y memoria de España* 151–53.

Reina, Manuel Francisco. *Los amores oscuros*. Madrid: Temas de Hoy, 2012.

Rejano, Juan. "García Lorca: Raíces de su personalidad." *Nivel* (Mexico City) 46 (1966): 3.

———. "García Lorca: Su obra poética." Conferencia impartida por el poeta Juan Rejano en la Escuela Normal Superior (6 Oct. 1970). Fundación Juan Rejano.

———. "Para un aniversario: García Lorca y España." *Romance* (Mexico City) 1.15 (1 Sept. 1940): 20.

———. *El poeta y su pueblo: Un símbolo andaluz; Federico García Lorca*. Mexico City: Ediciones del Centro Andaluz, 1944.

Requeni, Antonio. *González Carbalho*. Buenos Aires: Ediciones Culturales Argentinas, 1961.

Retana, Álvaro. *Al borde del pecado*. Barcelona: Sopena, 1916.

———. "A manera de prólogo: Confidencias indiscretas." *El veneno de la aventura* 5–19.

———. *La carne de tablado (Escenas pintorescas de Madrid de noche)*. Madrid: Imprenta V. H. de Sanz Calleja, n.d. [1918].

———. *Egmont de Bries. Su vida. Sus amores. Su arte. Sus canciones*. (Los favoritos de la fama) Madrid: Imprenta de R[afael] Caro Raggio, 1921.

———. *El encanto de la cama redonda*. *La Novela de Hoy* (Madrid) 1, No. 29 (1 Dec. 1922).

———. *Estrellas del cuplé (su vida y sus canciones)*. Madrid: Editorial Tesoro, 1963.

———. *Flor del mal*. *La Novela de Hoy* (Madrid) 3, No. 106 (23 May 1924).

———. *Historia del arte frívolo*. Madrid: Editorial Tesoro, 1964.

———. *La hora del pecado*. *La Novela de Hoy* (Madrid) 2, No. 42 (2 Mar. 1923). In *A Virtual Wunderkammer*.

———. *Las "locas" de postín. A Sodoma en tren botijo*. Introduction by Luis Antonio de Villena. Madrid: Odisea Editorial, 2004.

———. *Las "locas" de postín. Los ambiguos. Lolita buscadora de emociones. El tonto*. Edited by Maite Zubiaurre, Audrey Harris, and Wendy Kurtz. Doral, FL: Stockcero, 2013.

————. *La mala fama*. Madrid: Biblioteca Hispania, 1922.

————. *Mi alma desnuda*. Madrid: Biblioteca Hispania, 1923.

————. *Las mujeres de Retana*. *La Novela Corta* (Madrid) 7, No. 319 (21 Jan. 1922).

————. *Una niña "demasiado moderna": Delirantes extravíos de una ingenua libertina*. (Novela libertina). Madrid: Biblioteca Hispania, 1919.

————. *Ninfas y sátiros (Escenas pintorescas de Madrid de noche)*. Madrid: Biblioteca Hispania, 1918.

————. *El octavo pecado capital*. Madrid: Biblioteca Hispania, n.d. [1921].

————. *El veneno de la aventura*. *La Novela de Noche* (Madrid) 1, No. 4 (15 May 1924).

————. *El vicio color de rosa*. Madrid: Biblioteca Hispania, [1920].

Reynolds, David S. *Walt Whitman's America: A Cultural Biography*. New York: Alfred A. Knopf, 1995.

Rich, Nathaniel. "The Passion of Pasolini." *New York Review of Books* 54.14 (27 Sept. 2007): 77–80.

Riesenfeld, Janet. *Dancer in Madrid*. New York: Funk & Wagnalls, 1938.

————. Intermission Guest: Lux Radio Theatre, "The Gilded Lily" (11 Jan. 1937). At Oldtimeradiodownloads.com.

Riggs, David. *The World of Christopher Marlowe*. New York: Henry Holt, 2004.

Río, Ángel del. "Introduction." *Poet in New York*. By Federico García Lorca. Translated by Ben Belitt. New York: Grove Press, 1955. ix–xxxix.

Ríos, Blanca de los. "El viaje de Tirso a Santo Domingo: La génesis de *El rey don Pedro en Madrid* y la creación del *Don Juan*." In *Obras dramáticas completas*. By Tirso de Molina. Vol. 2. Madrid: Aguilar, 1962. 513–85.

Ríos Carratalá, Juan Antonio. *Una arrolladora simpatía: Edgar Neville; de Hollywood al Madrid de la posguerra*. Barcelona: Ariel, 2007.

————. *El tiempo de la desmesura: Historias insólitas del cine y la guerra civil española*. Barcelona: Barril & Barral, 2010.

Rioyo, Javier. *La vida golfa: Historia de las casas de lenocinio, holganza y malvivir*. Madrid: Santillana Ediciones Generales, 2003.

Rivalan Guégo, Christine. *Fruición-ficción: Novelas y novelas cortas en España (1894–1936)*. Translated by María Concepción Castroviejo Bolíbar and Christine Rivalan Guégo. Gijón: Ediciones Trea, 2008.

————. *Lecturas gratas o ¿la fábrica de los lectores?* Madrid: Calambur Editorial, 2007.

Rivas, Alberto F. "Rossini fue cocinero y músico con mucho de eso que llaman 'duende.'" In Inglada, *Palabra de Lorca* 186–89.

Rivas-Cherif, C[ipriano]. "La muerte y la pasión de García Lorca." *Excelsior* (Mexico City) 41, 1 (6 Jan. 1957): 1, 4; (13 Jan. 1957): 1, 4; (27 Jan. 1957): 3.

Rivers, W. C. *Walt Whitman's Anomaly.* London: G. Allen, 1913.

Roa, Raúl. "Federico García Lorca, poeta y soldado de la libertad." *Revista de las Indias* (Bogotá) 1.5 (Mar. 1937): 42–45.

Robledal, Narciso. "El duende se hizo carne . . ." In Inglada, *Palabra de Lorca* 207–13.

Rocca, Pablo, and Eduardo Roland. *Lorca y Uruguay: Pasajes, homenajes, polémicas.* Alcalá la Real (Jaén): Alcalá Grupo Editorial, 2010.

Roditi, Edouard. *Poems, 1928–1948.* Norfolk, CT: New Directions Books, 1949.

Rodríguez, Pablo. "Búsqueda de los restos de Lorca: 'El informe de la UGR es un despropósito.'" *Ideal* (Granada) (7 May 2019).

———. "El informe de Justicia tumba la tesis de que Lorca fue enterrado en Alfacar." *Ideal* (Granada) (22 Jan. 2019).

Rodríguez Alcayna, Javier. "En busca de Garcilaso." *Diariocrítico* (10 Dec. 2012).

Rodríguez Gutiérrez, Borja. "'Eco solemne de la multitud': José Zorrilla, poeta popular." *Tradición e interculturalidad: Las relaciones entre lo culto y lo popular, siglos XIX–XX.* Edited by Dolores Thion Soriano-Mollá, Luis Beltrán Almería, Solange Hibbs-Lissorgues, and Marisa Sotelo. Zaragoza: Institución "Fernando el Católico," 2013. 183–89.

Rodríguez Lence, José. "Un rato de charla con García Lorca." In Inglada, *Palabra de Lorca* 190–94.

Rodríguez Marcos, Javier. "Las deudas pendientes de la memoria." *El País* (Madrid) (21 Oct. 2009).

Rodríguez Navas y Carrasco, Manuel. *Diccionario general y técnico hispanoamericano.* Madrid: Cultura Hispanoamericana, 1918. In *Nuevo Tesoro Lexicográfico del Español* (Real Academia Española).

Rodríguez Puértolas, Julio. "Fascismo y poesía en España." *Actas del Séptimo Congreso de la Asociación Internacional de Hispanistas.* Vol. 2. Edited by Giuseppe Bellini. Rome: Bulzone Editore, 1982. 883–91.

———. *Literatura fascista española.* 2 vols. Madrid: Akal, 1986.

Roffé, Reina. *El otro amor de Federico: Lorca en Buenos Aires.* Buenos Aires: Plaza & Janés, 2009.

Rogers, Gayle. *Modernism and the New Spain: Britain, Cosmopolitan Europe, and Literary History.* Oxford: Oxford University Press, 2012.

Rojas, Carlos. *El ingenioso hidalgo y poeta Federico García Lorca asciende a los infiernos.* Barcelona: Círculo de Lectores, 1980.

———. *The Ingenious Gentleman and Poet Federico García Lorca Ascends to Hell.* Translated by Edith Grossman. New Haven: Yale University Press, 2013.

Rojas, Pablo. "Un intelectual en la Talavera de la II República: Ernesto López–Parra (1895–1941). Más allá del ultraísmo." *Cuaderna: Revista de Estudios Humanísticos de Talavera* 9–10 (2001–2): 139–65.

———. "El poeta Ernesto López-Parra excomulgado del ultraísmo." *Revista de Literatura* 71.141 (2009): 111–36.

Rojek, Chris. "Celebrity and Religion." In Marshall 389–417.

Rojo León, Armando. "Llanto por Federico García Lorca." In Poeta 101–03.

Rolfe, Edwin. "A Federico García Lorca." In Nelson, *The Wound and the Dream* 192.

Romacho, Francisco. "Gibson y la extraña familia." *La Opinión de Granada* (27 Sept. 2009).

"El *Romancero gitano* de Lorca cobra vida con el crowdfunding y las ilustraciones de 250 artistas." *Historias de Luz.* Video (23 Apr. 2017). YouTube, www.youtube.com/watch?v=_pM3DC7Ua4I (accessed 3 May 2021).

Romera, Edgardo. "Cantes por la muerte de Federico García Lorca." In Poeta 232–41.

Romero Murube, Joaquín. "No te olvides . . ." In Villén 65–66.

———. *Siete romances.* Edited by Manuel García and A. Martínez. Huelva: Editorial Point de Lunettes, 2004.

———. *Verso y prosa.* Edited by Francisco López Estrada. Seville: Ayuntamiento, 1971.

Roncagliolo, Santiago. *El amante uruguayo: Una historia real.* Alcalá la Real: Alcalá Grupo Editorial, 2012.

Rosales, Luis. Borrador de *Pasión y muerte del Conde de Villamediana* (1969). Archivo Histórico Nacional (Madrid), Diversos—Luis Rosales, 34, N. 4.

———. Borradores mecanografiados de la *Pasión y muerte del Conde de Villamediana* (1969). Archivo Histórico Nacional (Madrid), Diversos—Luis Rosales, 32, N. 2.

———. "Carta de Luis Rosales." *ABC* (Madrid) (29 Mar. 1972): 14.

———. Letter to Pablo Neruda. Undated. Archivo Histórico Nacional (Madrid), Diversos—Luis Rosales, 15, N. 56.

———. *Pasión y muerte del conde de Villamediana.* Madrid: Gredos, 1969.

———. *Pasión y muerte del conde de Villamediana. Discurso leído el día 19 de abril de 1964 en su recepción pública.* Contestación de D. Dámaso Alonso. Madrid: Real Academia Española, 1964.

————. Passports (1949–50). Archivo Histórico Nacional (Madrid), Diversos —Luis Rosales, 97, N. 6.

Rosenbaum, Sidonia C. "Federico García Lorca: Bibliografía." *Revista Hispánica Moderna* 6.3–4 (1940): 263–79.

Rothenberg, Jerome. *The Lorca Variations: I–XXXIII.* New York: New Directions, 1993.

Rozas, Juan Manuel. "Introducción biográfica y crítica." *Obras.* By the Conde de Villamediana. 3rd edition. Madrid: Castalia, 1991. 7–59.

Rubio Jiménez, Jesús. *La fama póstuma de Gustavo Adolfo Bécquer y Valeriano Bécquer.* Zaragoza: Prensas Universitarias de Zaragoza, 2009.

————. "Un marco para el retrato literario modernista. Ensayo de aproximación." *Literatura hispánica y prensa periódica (1875–1931).* Actas del Congreso Internacional, Lugo 25–28 de noviembre de 2008. Coordinated by Javier Serrano Alonso and Amparo de Juan Bolufer. Edited by Claudio Rodríguez Fer, Cristina Patiño Eirín, Luis Miguel Fernández, and Ana Chouciño Fernández. Santiago de Compostela: Universidad de Santiago de Compostela, 2009. 323–55.

Rubio Jiménez, Jesús, and Antonio Deaño Gamallo. *Vivir de la pluma: 24 cartas inéditas de Salvador Rueda y Rubén Darío a Leopoldo Alas, "Clarín."* Alicante: Biblioteca Virtual Miguel de Cervantes, 2014. www.cervantesvirtual .com/obra/vivir-de-la-pluma-24-cartas-ineditas-de-salvador-rueda-y -ruben-dario-a-leopoldo-alas-clarin (accessed 4 May 2021).

Ruiz Aguilera, Ventura. "Apoteósis. El 20 de junio de 1869." In *Españoles ilustres* 57–61.

Ruiz Amezcua, Manuel. " . . . En Granada, ¡en su Granada!" *Las reliquias de un sueño.* Madrid: Huerga y Fierro Editores, 2019. 79–81.

Ruiz Gisbert, Rosa. "José María Hinojosa, el gran olvidado." *Isla de Arriarán* (Málaga) 29 (June 2007): 181–99.

Ruiz Mantilla, Jesús. "Abrir las fosas cura." *El País* (Madrid) (3 Oct. 2009).

————. "García Lorca: ¿a la tercera va la vencida?" *El País* (Madrid) (27 Oct. 2015).

Russo, Vito. *The Celluloid Closet: Homosexuality in the Movies.* New York: Harper & Row, 1981.

Sabugo Gallego, Nemesio. *Benavides: Episodio español transcendente.* Prologue by Emilio Sáez. León: Ediciones Leonesas, 1989.

Sáenz, Vicente. "Consideraciones sobre civilización occidental a propósito de Federico García Lorca." *Repertorio Americano* (San José, Costa Rica) 34.23 (18 Dec. 1937): 353–57.

Sáenz de la Calzada, Luis. *"La Barraca": Teatro universitario.* Prologue by Rafael Martínez Nadal. Madrid: Revista de Occidente, 1976.

Sahuquillo, Ángel. *Federico García Lorca and the Culture of Male Homosexuality.* Translated by Erica Frouman-Smith. Foreword by Alberto Mira. Jefferson, NC / London: McFarland, 2007.

Salado, José Luis. "En el ensayo general de *Yerma.*" In Inglada, *Palabra de Lorca* 345–48.

Sala Rose, Rosa, and Plàcid Garcia-Planas. *El marqués y la esvástica: César González-Ruano y los judíos en el París ocupado.* Barcelona: Anagrama, 2014.

Salazar, Theresa. "Wounded Reporter Penned Letter on Back of Civil War Poster." *Volunteer* 34.1 (Mar. 2017): 12–14.

Salinas, Pedro. "Federico García Lorca." *Modern Language Notes* 87.2 (1972): 169–77. (Orig. 1942.)

———. "Federico García Lorca." In Castro, *Versos* 383–85. (Orig. 1945.)

Salinas, Pedro, and Jorge Guillén. *Correspondencia (1923–1951).* Edited by Andrés Soria Olmedo. Barcelona: Tusquets, 1992.

Sánchez Álvarez-Insúa, Alberto. "Prólogo." In Álvaro Retana, *"Los extravíos de Tony (Confesiones amorales de un colegial ingenuo)" y "Mi novia y mi novio."* Madrid: Odisea Editorial, 2009. 5–12.

Sánchez Barbudo, Antonio [S.B.]. "La muerte de García Lorca comentada por sus asesinos." *Hora de España* (Valencia) No. 5 (May 1937): 391–92.

———. *Los poemas de Antonio Machado: Los temas; El sentimiento y la expresión.* Madison: University of Wisconsin Press, 1969.

Sánchez Estevan, Ismael. *Jacinto Benavente y su teatro: Estudio biográfico crítico.* Barcelona: Ediciones Ariel, 1954.

Sánchez Gómez, Luis Ángel. "Las exhibiciones etnológicas y coloniales decimonónicas y la Exposición de Filipinas de 1887." *Revista de Dialectología y Tradiciones Populares* 57.2 (2002): 79–104.

Sánchez Pastor, Emilio. *El señorito Arturo.* Drama en tres actos y en prosa. Madrid: R. Velasco, 1900.

Sánchez Rodríguez, Alfonso. "El 'caso' Hinojosa y su repercusión en los manuales de historia literaria." *Analecta Malacitana* 11.2 (1988): 363–69.

———. *Este film inacabado: Diez entrevistas con familiares, amigos y contemporáneos de José María Hinojosa (1993–1998).* Málaga: Centro Cultural de la Generación del 27, 2002.

San de Velilla, Antonio. *Sodoma y Lesbos modernas: Pederastas y safistas, estudiados en la clínica, en los libros y en la historia.* Barcelona: Ameller, 1932.

Sanín Cano, Baldomero. "El coronel Teodoro Roosevelt." *El oficio de lector.* Edited by J. G. Cobo Borda. Caracas: Biblioteca Ayacucho, 1978. 172–75.

San Rafael. "Cintarazos." *El Correo Militar* (Madrid) (22 Oct. 1898): 1.

Santa Cruz, Abel. "A Federico García Lorca, muerto." In Castro, *Versos* 390–94.

Santiago Ibero (José Sánchez Moreno). *Álvaro Retana: "El Petronio del siglo XX." Celebridades de Varietés* (Barcelona) 2, No. 30 (1926).

Santonja, Gonzalo, ed. *Todo en el aire. Versos sin enemigo: Antología insólita de la poesía durante la guerra incivil española.* Barcelona: Galaxia Gutenberg / Círculo de Lectores, 1997.

Santos, Antonio. *Cirujía elemental veterinaria.* Madrid: Establecimiento Tipográfico Militar de los Señores Mateo y Torrubia, 1852.

Sassone, Felipe. *Cambio . . . (Aventura de amor). Los Novelistas* (Madrid) 1, No. 6 (19 Apr. 1928).

Saunders, Henry S., ed. *A Whitman Controversy, Being Letters Published in "Mercure de France," 1913–1914.* Introduction by Henry S. Saunders. Toronto: Henry S. Saunders, 1921.

Saz, Agustín del. "Garcilaso de la Vega (1536–1936)." *Gente Conocida* (Cádiz) 1.1 (1 Feb. 1937): 2.

Schehr, Lawrence R. "Translator's Introduction." In Willy vii–xii.

Schickel, Richard. *Intimate Strangers: The Culture of Celebrity.* Garden City, NY: Doubleday, 1985.

Schneider, Franz. "Lorca's 'Canción de jinete.'" *Explicator* 20.9 (1962): 140–43.

Schonberg, Jean-Louis (Baron Louis Stinglhamber). *Federico García Lorca. L'homme-L'oeuvre.* Preface by Jean Cassou. Paris: Plon, 1956.

Schreck, Bettina. "Eccentricity and Deterritorialization in Natalie Barney's *The One Who is Legion.*" *Gender Forum* No. 27 (2009): 34–51.

Schreckenberg, Stefan. "La conmemoración del centenario de Federico García Lorca como contribución a la memoria cultural de España: Dos documentales de TVE y Canal +." *Lugares de memoria de la guerra civil y el franquismo: Representaciones literarias y visuales.* Edited by Ulrich Winter. Madrid / Frankfurt am Main: Iberoamericana/Vervuert, 2006. 223–37.

Schulberg, Budd. "Your Arkansas Traveler." *Some Faces in the Crowd.* New York: Random House, 1953. 3–44.

Schwartz, Barth David. *Pasolini Requiem.* New York: Pantheon Books, 1992.

Schwartz, Kessel. "Culture and the Spanish Civil War: A Fascist View, 1936–1939." *Journal of Inter-American Studies* 7.4 (1965): 557–77.

Schwenk, Bernhart, and Michael Semff. "Introduction." *Pier Paolo Pasolini and*

Death. Edited by Bernhart Schwenk and Michael Semff. Ostfildern / New York: Hatje Cantz / D.A.P., 2005. 18–22.

Sender, Ramón J. *Réquiem por un campesino español*. 19th edition. Barcelona: Destino, 1991. (Orig. 1953.)

Sepúlveda, Enrique. *La vida en Madrid en 1886*. Madrid/Seville: Librería de Fernando Fe / Librería de Hijos de Fe, 1887.

Serna, Vicente. "El Ausente." In Villén 177–78.

Serra, Francisco. "La 'restaurada' nación española y el culto a la muerte." *Cuartopoder* (12 Apr. 2012).

Serrano y Domínguez, Francisco (Conde de San Antonio), and Juan Chinchilla. *Defensa de los Duques de la Torre*. Madrid: Tipografía de Manuel G. Hernández, 1883.

Serrano Plaja, Arturo. "En la muerte de Federico García Lorca." In Castro, *Versos* 395–98.

———. "Ponencia colectiva." *Hora de España* (Valencia) No. 8 (Aug. 1937): 83–95.

Sharpe, Emily Robins. *Mosaic Fictions: Writing Identity in the Spanish Civil War*. Toronto: University of Toronto Press, 2020.

Shelley, Mary. *Frankenstein, or The Modern Prometheus*. New York: Books, Inc., n.d. [1940].

Shipman, Andrew J. "Recent Impressions of Spain." *A Memorial of Andrew J. Shipman: His Life and Writings*. Edited by Condé B. Pallen. New York: Encyclopedia Press, 1916. 17–31. (Orig. 1910.)

Sibbald, K. M. "'Cómo canta la zumaya': An Ornithological Excursus on Lorca's 'Romance de la luna, luna.'" *Hispanic Studies in Honour of Geoffrey Ribbans*. Edited by Ann L. Mackenzie and Dorothy S. Severin. Liverpool: Liverpool University Press, 1992. 265–74.

Sieburth, Stephanie. *Inventing High and Low: Literature, Mass Culture, and Uneven Modernity in Spain*. Durham, NC: Duke University Press, 1994.

Sinclair, Alison. "Elitism and the Cult of the Popular in Spain." *Visions and Blueprints: Avant-garde Culture and Radical Politics in Early Twentieth-Century Europe*. Edited by Edward Timms and Peter Collier. Introduction by Raymond Williams. Manchester: Manchester University Press, 1988. 221–34.

64 Questions on Spain: The Spanish Controversy. With acknowledgements to José A. Sobrino and Aurelio Valls. Madrid: Editorial Oficina de Información Diplomática, 1953.

Smith, Lillian. *Strange Fruit*. New York: Reynal and Hitchcock, 1944.

Smith, Paul Julian. "A Long Way from Andalusia." *TLS* (7 Aug. 1998): 10–11.

———. "The Lorca Cult: Theatre, Cinema, and Print Media in 1980s Spain." *Contemporary Theatre Review* 7, Part 4 (1998): 65–80.

———. "Lorca's Legacy: Writing in the Institution." *Fire, Blood, and the Alphabet: One Hundred Years of Lorca.* Edited by Sebastian Doggart and Michael Thompson. Durham, County Durham: University of Durham, 1999. 31–42.

———. *The Theatre of García Lorca: Text, Performance, Psychoanalysis.* Cambridge: Cambridge University Press, 1998.

Smith, Richard Candida. "Inventions and Imitations: Tradition and the Advanced Guard in the Work of Edouard Roditi." [Interview with Edouard Roditi Transcript.] University of California, Los Angeles Oral History Program, 1986.

Soria Olmedo, Andrés. "Introducción." *Treinta y una entrevistas a Federico García Lorca.* Revised edition. Edited by Andrés Soria Olmedo. Atarfe: Entornográfico Ediciones, 2017. 13–24.

———. "Lorca en Víznar: Memoria pública, memoria privada." *El País* (Madrid) (17 Sept. 2004).

———. "Lugares intelectuales." *Granada Hoy* (2 May 2009).

Soto, Antonio ("Boy"). "Ronda gitana: Persecución, captura y secuestro del poeta Federico García Lorca." In Inglada, *Palabra de Lorca* 276–81.

Southworth, Herbert Rutledge. *El mito de la cruzada de Franco: Crítica bibliográfica.* Paris: Ruedo Ibérico, 1963.

Spender, Stephen. "Speaking for Spain." *New Republic* 128 (2 Feb. 1953): 18–19.

———. "The Talking Bronco." In Cunningham 440–43.

———. *World within World.* New York: St. Martin's Press, 1994.

Spender, Stephen, and John Lehmann, eds. *Poems for Spain.* London: Hogarth Press, 1939.

Spicer, Jack. *After Lorca.* N.p.: n.p., 1974. (Orig. 1957.)

The Spirit of Lorca. Dir. Mike Dibb. London/Munich: British Broadcasting Corporation (BBC) / RM Arts, 1986.

Stainton, Leslie. *Lorca: A Dream of Life.* New York: Farrar, Straus & Giroux, 1999.

Stoller, Robert J. "Facts and Fancies: An Examination of Freud's Concept of Bisexuality." *Women and Analysis: Dialogues on Psychoanalytic Views of Femininity.* Edited by Jean Strouse. Boston: G. K. Hall, 1985. 343–64.

Stradling, Robert. "The Death of Don Juan: Murder, Myth, and Mayhem in Madrid." *History Today* 43.5 (May 1993): 11–17.

————. "Inspired Neglect? Three Fascist Artists of the Spanish Civil War." *The Spanish Civil War: Exhuming a Buried Past.* Edited by Anindya Raychaudhuri. Cardiff: University of Wales Press, 2013. 188–207.

Strand, Mark. *The Story of Our Lives, with The Monument and The Late Hour.* New York: Alfred A. Knopf, 2002.

Suero, Pablo. "Crónica de un día de barco con el autor de *Bodas de sangre.*" In Inglada, *Palabra de Lorca* 161–69.

————. "Los últimos días con Federico García Lorca." In Inglada, *Palabra de Lorca* 475–85.

Synge, J. M. *Riders to the Sea.* In *Three Irish Plays.* Introduction by Harrison Hale Schaff. Boston: International Pocket Library, 1936. (Orig. 1904.)

Tambling, Jeremy. *Becoming Posthumous: Life and Death in Literary and Cultural Studies.* Edinburgh: Edinburgh University Press, 2001.

Thomson, César. "Música y teatros." *La Vanguardia* (Barcelona) (28 Aug. 1931): 2.

Thornton, Lawrence. *Under the Gypsy Moon.* New York: Doubleday, 1990.

Tierno Galván, Enrique. "Aparición y desarrollo de nuevas perspectivas de valoración social en el siglo XIX: Lo cursi." *Desde el espectáculo a la trivialización.* Madrid: Taurus, 1961. 79–106. (Orig. 1952.)

Tisa, John, ed. *The Palette and the Flame: Posters of the Spanish Civil War.* New York: International Publishers, 1979.

Toledano Molina, Juana. "Erotismo y censura en Álvaro Retana." *El cortejo de Afrodita: Ensayos sobre literatura hispánica y erotismo.* Edited by Antonio Cruz Casado. Málaga: Universidad de Málaga, 1997. 259–66.

Toll, Gil. *Heraldo de Madrid: Tinta catalana para la II República española.* Prologue by Miguel Ángel Aguilar. Seville: Renacimiento, 2013.

Tomaševskij, Boris. "Literature and Biography." *Readings in Russian Poetics: Formalist and Structuralist Views.* Edited by Ladislav Matejka and Krystyna Pomorska. Introduction by Gerald L. Bruns. Cambridge: MIT Press, 1971. 47–55. (Orig. 1923.)

Toro Ballesteros, Sara. "El escritor que se pintó a sí mismo: Los figurines de Álvaro Retana." *Creneida* 3 (2015): 184–208.

Torre, Guillermo de. "Federico García Lorca." *Tríptico del sacrificio.* Buenos Aires: Losada, 1948. 55–85.

Torrecilla, Jesús. "Estereotipos que se resisten a morir: El andalucismo de *Bodas de sangre.*" *Anales de Literatura Española Contemporánea* 33.2 (2008): 229–49.

Tovar, Antonio. "Lecciones de José Antonio: José Antonio y el campo." In *Dolor y memoria de España* 23–29.

Trapiello, Andrés. *Las armas y las letras: Literatura y guerra civil (1936–1939)*. 3rd edition. Barcelona: Destino, 2010.

———. "Causa general II." *El País* (Madrid) (25 Apr. 2010).

Traubel, Horace L. "At the Graveside of Walt Whitman." In Traubel, Bucke, and Harned 437–52.

Traubel, Horace L., Richard Maurice Bucke, and Thomas B. Harned, eds. *In Re Walt Whitman*. Philadelphia: David McKay, 1893.

Trevor, D. "Poets of the Spanish War." *Left Review* (London) 3.8 (Sept. 1937): 455–60.

Ulacia Altolaguirre, Paloma. *Concha Méndez: Memorias habladas, memorias armadas*. Presentation by María Zambrano. Madrid: Mondadori, 1990.

Umbral, Francisco. *Lorca, poeta maldito*. Madrid: Biblioteca Nueva, 1968.

Unamuno, Miguel de. *En torno al casticismo*. 7th edition. Madrid: Espasa-Calpe, 1968.

El Universo de Lorca. Granada, Parque de las Ciencias, 1998, www.parquedeciencias .com/parquedeciencias/historico/otrasactividades/el–universo–de–lorca .html (accessed 3 May 2021).

El Universo de Lorca. Guión literario y banda sonora original del programa del planetario. Granada: Parque de las Ciencias, 1999.

Universo Lorca. Website, www.universolorca.com (accessed 3 May 2021).

Usó, Juan Carlos. *Orgullo travestido: Egmont de Bries y la repercusión social del transformismo en la España del primer tercio del siglo XX*. Santander: El Desvelo Ediciones, 2017.

Vaill, Amanda. *Hotel Florida: Truth, Love, and Death in the Spanish Civil War*. New York: Farrar, Straus & Giroux, 2014.

Valis, Noël. "*Ángel Guerra*, o la novela monstruo." *Revista Hispánica Moderna* 41.1 (1988): 31–43.

———. "Celebrity, Sex, and Mass Readership: The Case of Álvaro Retana." *Kiosk Literature of Silver Age Spain: Modernity and Mass Culture*. Edited by Jeffrey Zamostny and Susan Larson. Bristol/Chicago: Intellect Books, 2017. 127–51.

———. *The Culture of Cursilería: Bad Taste, Kitsch, and Class in Modern Spain*. Durham, NC: Duke University Press, 2002.

———. "Homosexuality on Display in 1920s Spain: The Hermaphrodite, Eccentricity, and Álvaro Retana." *Freakish Encounters: Constructions of the Freak in Hispanic Cultures*. Edited by Sara Muñoz-Muriana and Analola Santana. *Hispanic Issues On Line* 20 (2018): 190–216.

———. "Introducción." In Badanelli 7–68.

————. "Introducción." *Poesías*. By Carolina Coronado. Madrid: Castalia / Instituto de la Mujer, 1991. 7–41.

————. "Lloyd Mallan: Lincoln Brigade Volunteer and Early Lorca Translator." *Anales de la Literatura Española Contemporánea* 47.1 (2022) (in press).

————. "Lorca's *Agonía republicana* and its Aftermath." *Bulletin of Spanish Studies* 91.1–2 (2014): 267–94.

————. "Lorca's Grave." *Yale Review* 104.3 (2016): 40–56.

————. "An Ordinary Life." *First Things* No. 301 (Mar. 2020): 29–34.

————. "Palacio Valdés' First Novel." *Romance Notes* 20.3 (1980): 317–21.

————. "Prólogo/Prologue." *Hasta que la boda nos separe / Until the Wedding Does Us Part*. By Roberto Lumbreras. Bilingual edition. Translated by Herlinda Charpentier and Robert L. Saitz. Madrid: Albert Editor, 2013. 7–17.

————. *Sacred Realism: Religion and the Imagination in Modern Spanish Narrative*. New Haven: Yale University Press, 2010.

————. "The Society Reporter, Status, and Writer Impotence in Felipe Trigo's *El Semental*." *Bulletin of Spanish Studies* 90.3 (2013): 357–74.

————. "When the Dead Are Always with Us: Ayala's *Diálogo de los muertos*." *Hispania* 89.4 (2006): 710–17.

Valle–Inclán, Ramón del. "Breve noticia acerca de mi estética cuando escribí este libro." *Corte de amor: Florilegio de honestas y nobles damas*. Madrid: Imprenta de Balgañón y Moreno, 1908. 13–30.

————. *La corte de los milagros*. Madrid: Espasa-Calpe, 1961.

————. "Modernismo." *El modernismo*. Edited by Lily Litvak. Madrid: Taurus, 1991. 17–19. (Orig. 1902.)

Valverde, Salvador. "El Dibujante de las elegancias escénicas: Cómo Álvaro Retana, nuevo ave fénix, vuelve a surgir de sus cenizas con otro nombre." *¡Tararí!* No. 6 (22 Nov. 1930). In Pérez Sanz and Bru Ripoll, *La erótica* 961–64.

Vázquez García, Francisco. "Los orígenes de una leyenda: Cádiz como ciudad de 'invertidos' (1898)." *Hispania Nova: Revista de Historia Contemporánea* No. 15 (2017): 1–23.

Vázquez García, Francisco, and Richard Cleminson. "El destierro de lo maravilloso: Hermafroditas y mutantes sexuales en la España de la Ilustración." *Asclepio* 63.1 (2011): 7–38.

Vázquez Ocaña, Fernando. *García Lorca: Vida, cántico y muerte*. Mexico City: Biografías Gandesa, 1957.

Vega, Lope de. *La Dorotea*. Edited by Edwin S. Morby. Madrid: Castalia, 1958.

Velasco Maillo, Honorio M. "El folklore y sus paradojas." *Reis: Revista Española de Investigaciones Sociológicas* No. 49 (1990): 123–44.

Vélez de Guevara, Luis. *El diablo cojuelo.* Edited by Ángel Raimundo Fernández González. Madrid: Castalia, 1980.

Vernet Pons, Vicenç. "La estrategia ficcional en la novela de Álvaro Retana." PhD diss., Universitat Rovira i Virgili, 2008.

Vico, Giambattista. *The New Science.* Translated by Thomas Goddard Bergin and Max Harold Fisch. Ithaca, NY: Cornell University Press, 1994.

Vidal Corella, Vicente. "El crimen fue en su Granada: 'Yo he visto asesinar a García Lorca.'" In Gibson, *La represión* 142–43.

———. "The Crime Was in Granada, His Granada: 'I Saw García Lorca Being Assassinated.'" In Gibson, *Assassination* 219–21.

Vilallonga, José Luis de. *Furia.* Translated by Robert Speaight. London: Weidenfeld and Nicolson, 1976.

Vila-San-Juan, José. *García Lorca, asesinado: Toda la verdad.* Barcelona: Planeta, 1975.

Villa, Antonio de la. "Un evadido de Granada cuenta el fusilamiento de García Lorca." In Dolfi 142–44.

Villén, Jorge, ed. *Antología poética del Alzamiento, 1936–1939.* Cádiz: Establecimientos Cerón y Librería Cervantes, 1939.

Villena, Francisco. "De una historia que vio la Alhambra." In García de Tuñón Aza, *José Antonio* 67–69. (Orig. 1937.)

Villena, Luis Antonio de. "Álvaro Retana, en el abanico de la 'novela galante-decadente.'" *Epos: Revista de Filología* No. 8 (1992): 317–25.

———. *El ángel de la frivolidad y su máscara oscura (Vida, literatura y tiempo de Álvaro Retana).* Valencia: Pre-textos, 1999.

———. "Prólogo." *"Princesas de aquelarre" y otros relatos eróticos.* By José de Zamora. Seville: Renacimiento, 2012. 9–16.

———. "Una tribu dorada y suprema (El orbe de Pepito Zamora)." *Una aproximación al arte frívolo: Tórtola Valencia y José de Zamora.* Edited by Andrés Peláez and Fernanda Andura. Madrid: Comunidad de Madrid, 1988. 27–40.

Viola, Manuel Simón, and José Luis Bernal. "Introducción." *Ocho estampas extremeñas con su marco.* By Francisco Valdés. Badajoz: Diputación Provincial de Badajoz, 1998. 7–33.

A Virtual Wunderkammer: Early Twentieth-Century Erotica in Spain. Website, http://sicalipsis.humnet.ucla.edu (accessed 12 Mar. 2021).

Wahnón, Sultana. "La recepción de García Lorca en la España de la posguerra." *Nueva Revista de Filología Hispánica* 43.2 (1995): 409–31.

Walsh, Andrew Samuel. *Lorca in English: A History of Manipulation through Translation.* New York / London: Routledge, 2020.

Wardropper, Bruce W. "The Modern Spanish Elegy: Antonio Machado's Lament for Federico García Lorca." *Symposium* 19.2 (1965): 162–70.

Webb, Jessica. "*Herculine Barbin:* Human Error, Criminality, and the Case of the Monstrous Hermaphrodite." *Hosting the Monster.* Edited by Holly Lynn Baumgartner and Roger Davis. Amsterdam: Rodopi, 2008. 153–62.

Weber, Max. "The Sociology of Charismatic Authority." In Marshall 55–71.

Weich, Horst. "El silencio en la poesía amorosa del Conde de Villamediana." *Memoria de la palabra: Actas del VI Congreso de la Asociación Internacional Siglo de Oro.* Burgos-La Rioja 15–19 de julio 2002. Vol. 2. Edited by Francisco Domínguez Matito and María Luisa Lobato López. Madrid/Frankfurt: Iberoamericana/Vervuert, 2004. 1841–49.

Weston, Rowland. "History, Memory, and Moral Knowledge: William Godwin's *Essay on Sepulchres* (1809)." *European Legacy* 14.6 (2009): 651–65.

Westover, Paul. "William Godwin, Literary Tourism, and the Work of Necromanticism." *Studies in Romanticism* 48.2 (2009): 299–319.

Wharton, Edith. *The House of Mirth.* Introduction by Mary Gordon. New York: Library of America, 2009.

Wheelwright, John. "The Poetry of Lorca." *Poetry* 51.3 (Dec. 1937): 167–70.

Whiston, James. *Antonio Machado's Writings and the Spanish Civil War.* Liverpool: Liverpool University Press, 1996.

Whitman, Walt. *The Complete Poems.* Edited by Francis Murphy. London: Penguin, 2004.

————. *Leaves of Grass.* Brooklyn, NY, 1855.

Wilde, Oscar. *The Picture of Dorian Gray.* New York: Boni and Liveright, n.d. [1918].

Williams, M. E. "Roy Campbell, Lorca, and the Civil War." *Leeds Papers on Lorca and on Civil War Verse.* Edited by Margaret A. Rees. Leeds: Trinity & All Saints' College, 1988. 93–107.

Williams, William Carlos. "Introduction to Charles Sheeler—Paintings—Drawings—Photographs (1939)." *Selected Essays.* New York: Random House, 1954. 231–34.

Willy (Henri Gauthier-Villars). *The Third Sex.* Translated by Lawrence R. Schehr. Urbana: University of Illinois Press, 2007.

Wilson, Edward M. Review of Luis Rosales, *Pasión y muerte del Conde de Villamediana* and of Juan Manuel Rozas, ed., *Obras,* by the Conde de Villamediana. *Bulletin of Hispanic Studies* 47 (1970): 166–70.

Wolfe, Roger. "Federico García Lorca: Un fósil en busca de acomodo." *Hélice: Revista de Poesía* No. 10 (1997): 25–26.

Woods, Gregory. *Homintern: How Gay Culture Liberated the Modern World*. New Haven: Yale University Press, 2016.

Wordsworth, William. "The Preface to *Lyrical Ballads*." *Prose Works* 1: 45–74.

———. *Prose Works of William Wordsworth*. 2 vols. Edited by William Knight. London / New York: MacMillan, 1896.

———. "Upon Epitaphs (I)" and "Upon Epitaphs (III)." *Prose Works* 2: 125–42; 171–89.

Wright, David. *Roy Campbell*. London: Longmans, Green, 1961.

Wright, Sarah. "Gregorio Marañón and 'The Cult of Sex': Effeminacy and Intersexuality in 'The Psychopathology of Don Juan' (1924)." *Bulletin of Spanish Studies* 81.6 (2004): 717–38.

Ximénez de Sandoval, Felipe. *Camisa azul (Retrato de un falangista)*. Valladolid: Librería Santarén, 1939.

———. *José Antonio (Biografía apasionada)*. 3rd edition, revised. Madrid: Editorial Bullón, 1963. (Orig. 1941.)

Yagüe Bosch, Javier. "Huir de Nueva York: Whitman y Lorca en un dibujo." *Boletín de la Fundación Federico García Lorca* 6, Nos. 10–11 (1992): 213–33.

Yahni, Roberto. "*Poeta en Nueva York:* Descubrimiento de la multitud." *Filología* (Buenos Aires) 26.1–2 (1993): 325–30.

Yardley, Michael. *T. E. Lawrence: A Biography*. New York: Cooper Square Press, 2000.

Yzurdiaga Lorca, Fermín. *Discurso al silencio y voz de la Falange*. Pamplona: Jerarquía, 1937.

Zahorí (Eduardo de Ory). "Pedro Badanelli." *Gente Conocida* (Cádiz), 2, No. 49 (12 June 1938): 3.

Zambrano, María, and Rosa Chacel. *Two Confessions*. Translated by Noël Valis and Carol Maier. Albany: SUNY Press, 2015.

Zamostny, Jeffrey. "Faustian Figures: Modernity and Male (Homo)Sexualities in Spanish Commercial Literature, 1900–1936." PhD diss., University of Kentucky, 2012.

———. "¡Todos a bordo!: Viajes al tercer sexo madrileño en *A Sodoma en tren botijo* de Álvaro Retana." *Divergencias* 7.1 (2009): 55–60.

———. "Tórtola Valencia and Antonio de Hoyos y Vinent: Celebrity and Self–Plagiarism." *Modern Language Notes* 133.2 (2018): 297–317.

———. "Virtual Álvaro Retana: Recovery and Fandom in the Digital Age." *Kiosk Literature of Silver Age Spain: Modernity and Mass Culture*. Edited by

Jeffrey Zamostny and Susan Larson. Bristol/Chicago: Intellect Books, 2017. 153–74.

Zárraga, Miguel de. "*ABC* en Nueva York: Tórtola y su muela del juicio." *ABC* (Madrid) (6 Mar. 1925): 27–28.

Zavales, Viki. "The Taming of the Duende: The Construction of Federico García Lorca as Cultural Icon." PhD diss., Johns Hopkins University, 2001.

Zerolo, Elías. *Diccionario enciclopédico de la lengua castellana.* Paris: Garnier Hermanos, 1895. In *Nuevo Tesoro Lexicográfico del Español* (Real Academia Española).

Zigaina, Giuseppe. "Pasolini and Death: A Purely Intellectual Thriller." *Pier Paolo Pasolini and Death.* Edited by Bernhart Schwenk and Michael Semff. Ostfilden / New York: Hatje Cantz / D.A.P., 2005. 25–37.

Zorrilla, José. *Don Juan Tenorio.* Edited by Luis Fernández Cifuentes. Madrid: Real Academia Española, 2012.

———. "Introducción." *La leyenda del Cid.* Barcelona: Montaner y Simón, Editores, 1882. i–xvi.

Zorrilla de San Martín, Juan. "Lo que dicen de Zorrilla." *El Liberal* (Madrid) (25 Jan. 1893): 1.

Zozaya, Antonio. "El espíritu del tablado." In Retana, *El octavo pecado capital* [1921], appended, n.pag.

Zubiaurre, Maite. *Cultures of the Erotic in Spain, 1898–1939.* Nashville, TN: Vanderbilt University Press, 2012.

Index

427

García Lorca, Federico, works of (*continued*)
amor oscuro, 159, 177; "Sueño" (*Libro de poemas*), 44; *Suites*, 8; *Yerma*, 102, 104, 158–59, 227, 249; *La zapatera prodigiosa*, 226
García Lorca, Francisco, 70, 125, 320n57
García Lorca, Isabel, 3, 102, 118, 320n55
García-Lorca de los Ríos, Laura, 92
García Márquez, Gabriel, 9
García Montero, Luis, 92, 132, 321–22n70
García Serrano, Rafael, 107
Garciasol, Ramón de, 181
García Valdecasas, Alfonso, 317n31
García Velasco, Rafael, 148
Garelick, Rhonda, 184
Garfias, Pedro, 41, 146, 298–99n26
Garosci, Aldo, 297n17
Gasch, Sebastián, 249–50
Gautier, Théophile, 209, 272
gay icon. *See* fame; García Lorca, Federico; Retana, Álvaro; Whitman, Walt; Wilde, Oscar
Gazzaniga, Giuseppe, 55
Géal, Pierre, 302n59
Gedeón, 261
Geist, Anthony, 159, 351n23
Gestoso y Pérez, José, 46
Gibson, Ian, 77, 89, 92, 95, 115, 178, 306n21, 314n17; *La fosa de Lorca* and, 3, 90–91, 94; *Lorca's Granada* and, 11; Lorca's homosexuality and, 159, 160, 164, 177, 179; passion for Lorca, 5, 7, 72, 90; Rafael Alberti and, 294n15; Víctor Fernández Puertas and, 288
Gide, André, 127, 162, 171, 176, 202, 216, 280
Gila, Miguel, 318n41
Gil-Albert, Juan, 39–40, 41, 67, 99
Gillis, John R., 300n44
Giménez Caballero, Ernesto, 105, 109, 120, 316n29, 317–18n37, 340–41n59; avant-garde and, 106, 112, 136–37, 226, 235; hermaphrodite and, 210–11; *pueblo* and, 349n7
Giner de los Ríos, Francisco, 12, 142
Ginsberg, Allen, 33, 161–62, 196, 252, 276, 280, 281, 329n9; Walt Whitman and, 161–62, 196, 254, 290
Godwin, William, 36–37, 65
Goebbels, Joseph, 18

Goethe, Johann Wolfgang von, 202
Goldman, Jonathan, 189, 295n32
Golijov, Osvaldo, 43
goloso, 221, 259
Gómez de la Serna, Ramón, 57, 118, 164, 201, 224, 226
Gómez del Valle, Manuel, 165
Gómez Santos, Marino, 118
Góngora, Luis de, 135, 136, 152, 176–77
Góngora Ayala, María Pilar, 311n63
González Aurioles, Eduardo, 96
González Carbalho, José, 87–88, 99, 131, 309n46
González de Velasco, Pedro de, 205
González Echevarría, Roberto, 209
González Fernández, Baltasar, 324n86
González-Ruano, César, 21, 164, 223, 224, 226, 250; Antonio de Hoyos y Vinent and, 226–27; Lorca and, 226–27; Pedro Salinas and, 347n100; Tórtola Valencia and, 351–52n27
Gordon, Robert S. C., 330n23
Gordón Ordás, Félix, 328n110
Goya, Francisco de, 62, 67, 215
Goytisolo, Juan, 74
Gracia y Justicia, 158
Gramsci, Antonio, 169, 171
Grande, Félix, 178
Grant, Cary, 199
Grass, Roland, 70
Graves, Robert, 122
Grenfell, Julian, 32
Griffith, Andy, 235
Guerrero, Fernando, 148
Guillén, Jorge, 177, 224, 232–33
Guillén, Nicolás, 182

Harris, Frank, 176
Harrison, Robert Pogue, 30, 65, 306–7n25
Hartzenbusch, Juan Eugenio, 175
Havard, Robert, 305n5
Hawking, Stephen, 9
Hearst, William Randolph, 191, 247, 251
Hemingway, Ernest, 6, 122
Heraldo de Madrid, El, 159
hermaphrodite, 160, 202–14, 216, 217–19, 222, 338n38, 339nn47–49, 340n51, 341–42n64; Herculine Barbin and, 340n57; homosexu-